New Keywords

Mary Ann Gresdow

New Keywords

A Revised Vocabulary of Culture and Society

Edited by

Tony Bennett
Lawrence Grossberg
Meaghan Morris

Blackwell
Publishing

BLACKWELL PUBLISHING
350 Main Street, Malden, MA 02148-5020, USA
9600 Garsington Road, Oxford OX4 2DQ, UK
550 Swanston Street, Carlton, Victoria 3053, Australia

First published 2005 by Blackwell Publishing Ltd

3   2006

Library of Congress Cataloging-in-Publication Data

New keywords: a revised vocabulary of culture and society / edited by Tony Bennett, Lawrence Grossberg, Meaghan Morris.
    p. cm.
  Includes bibliographical references.
  ISBN-13: 978-0-631-22568-3 (hardcover : alk. paper)
  ISBN-10: 0-631-22568-4 (hardcover : alk. paper)
  ISBN-13: 978-0-631-22569-0 (pbk. : alk. paper)
  ISBN-10: 0-631-22569-2 (pbk. : alk. paper)
  1. English language—Etymology. 2. English language—Glossaries, vocabularies, etc. 3. Social structure—Terminology. 4. Culture—Terminology. 5. Sociolinguistics. 6. Vocabulary. I. Bennett, Tony. II. Grossberg, Lawrence. III. Morris, Meaghan. IV. Williams, Raymond. Keywords.

  PE1580.N49 2005
  422—dc22

                                                              2004029949

A catalogue record for this title is available from the British Library.

Set in 10.5pt/13pt Bell Gothic
by Kolam Information Services Pvt. Ltd, Pondicherry, India
Printed and bound in the United Kingdom
by TJ International Ltd, Padstow, Cornwall

For further information on
Blackwell Publishing, visit our website:
www.blackwellpublishing.com

Contents

Contents

Contents

Contents

x

Acknowledgments

It's fair to say that this project proved a somewhat larger, if also more interesting and challenging, undertaking than we had anticipated when starting it. This also meant that it took a little longer to finish than we had estimated. We are, then, particularly grateful to Jayne Fargnoli at Blackwell Publishing for, first, her positive vision and enthusiasm in commissioning the project and, just as important, her rock-solid support throughout all phases of its development, and her readiness to wait until we had finished the work in the way we wanted to.

We should also like to thank all of the contributors, first, for agreeing to contribute to this book and, second, for the spirit in which they did so — taking our often detailed editorial comments in good part, and striving to make clear, while also doing justice to, the nuanced histories and uses of the keywords they contributed. We are particularly grateful to those contributors who met all of their due dates on time, especially those who worked to short deadlines to ensure the project's completion, and have long since forgiven those who approached their due dates like a distant mirage on the horizon even when they had in fact passed them.

The project is also one that has been well served by outstanding research assistance — initially from Sophie Taysom, who gathered and distributed to contributors the research materials they needed, and from James Bennett, who collated the editors' comments, ensured consistency across entries, and compiled the references. We owe a real debt, too, to Fiona Sewell, whose expert assistance, and unfailing patience, at the copy-editing stage added immeasurably to the quality of the final product.

And the project could not have been completed without the expert secretarial assistance of, first, Molly Freeman and, later, Margaret Marchant of the sociology discipline at the Open University.

Acknowledgments

Our greatest debt, however, is to Raymond Williams, whose original *Keywords* was, for us, along with most of our contemporaries, a text that was as inspirational as it was indispensable. For us as for many of our fellow contributors, the challenge of writing entries for this volume is one that has both renewed and greatly deepened our appreciation of both the extraordinary range of Williams's knowledge and the depth and durability of his accomplishments. We know, because they told us so, that many contributors were attracted to this project as an opportunity to pay tribute to Williams and his legacy. It is, then, on their behalf, as well as our own, that we dedicate this book to his memory.

Editors and Contributors

Ien Ang

Zygmunt Bauman

Tony Bennett

Jody Berland

Michael Bérubé

Roland Boer

Craig Calhoun

John Clarke

Jennifer Craik

Jonathan Crary

Ann Curthoys

Mitchell Dean

Nicholas Dirks

James Donald

Paul du Gay

Joanne Finkelstein

André Frankovits

Anne Freadman

Simon Frith

John Frow

J. K. Gibson-Graham

Avery F. Gordon

Lawrence Grossberg

Gay Hawkins

Gail Hershatter

Barry Hindess

Ian Hunter

Richard Johnson

Steve Jones

Genevieve Lloyd

Gregor McLennan

Maureen McNeil

W. J. T. Mitchell

David Morley

Meaghan Morris

Stephen Muecke

Karim Murji

Theo Nichols

Bhikhu Parekh

Cindy Patton

Elspeth Probyn

Kevin Robins

Jacqueline Rose

Nikolas Rose

Steven Rose

Andrew Ross

Naoki Sakai

Bill Schwarz

Steven Shapin

Michael J. Shapiro

Editors and Contributors

Jennifer Daryl Slack
John Storey
Terry Threadgold
Anna Tsing
Bryan Turner
Graeme Turner

Valerie Walkerdine
Alan Warde
Frank Webster
Jeffrey Weeks
George Yúdice

Further details can be found on pp. 417–27.

xiv

Abbreviations

The following abbreviations are used in the text:

BCE   Before Common Era (before the period dating from the birth of Christ)

C   Followed by numeral, century (C16: sixteenth century)

CE   Common Era (the period dating from the birth of Christ)

Ch   Chinese

eC   First period (third) of a century (eC16: early sixteenth century)

F   French

fw   Immediate forerunner of a word, in the same or another language

G   German

Gk   Classical Greek

It   Italian

L   Latin

lC   Last period (third) of a century (lC16: late sixteenth century)

lL   Late Latin

mC   Middle period (third) of a century (mC16: mid-sixteenth century)

mE   Middle English (c.1100–1500)

mF   Medieval French

mL   Medieval Latin

oE   Old English (to c.1100)

OED   *Oxford English dictionary: New dictionary on historical principles,* 2nd edn. Eds. J. A. Simpson and E. S. C. Weiner. Oxford: Oxford University Press.

oF   Old French

rw   Ultimate traceable word, from which ''root'' meanings are derived

Sp   Spanish

Abbreviations

Definitions of usage are from the OED unless otherwise indicated. Quotations followed by a name and date only, or a date only, are from examples cited in the OED or in website collections of usage. Other quotations are followed by specific sources.

Dates in square brackets are those of original publication. These have been given for works published before World War I where these are by major figures who have had an important influence on subsequent debates.

We have, for each entry, bolded the first use of the keyword in question and subsequent uses of related words or phrases in which the keyword also occurs. Our purpose in doing so has been to highlight examples of the keywords in use. In the entry for "Culture," for example, **culture** is bolded when it is first used, as is its use in such phrases as **high culture**, **folk culture**, **mass culture**, and **popular culture**.

Introduction

Tony Bennett, Lawrence Grossberg, and Meaghan Morris

Raymond Williams's *Keywords: A vocabulary of culture and society* is justly renowned for providing a whole generation of readers with an effective, reliable distillation of the variety of meanings – past and present – attached to a range of terms that played a pivotal role in discussions of culture and society, and of the relations between them. First published in 1976, however, it is now showing signs of its age in ways that Williams regarded as inevitable in a project that was always more concerned with exploring the complex uses of problem-laden words than it was with fixing their definition (striking though Williams's definitions were for their succinctness, learning, and clarity). For Williams the point was not merely that the meanings of words change over time but that they change in relationship to changing political, social, and economic situations and needs. While rejecting the idea that you could describe that relationship in any simple or universal way, he was convinced that it did exist – and that people do struggle in their *use* of language to give expression to new experiences of reality.

Revising *Keywords* himself for a second edition which included a further 21 words, Williams (1983: 27) reaffirmed his "sense of the work as necessarily unfinished and incomplete." It is in the spirit of his project, then, to observe that its entries for many words cannot take account of what have often been, over the past 30 years, crucial shifts in meaning associated with both their general and more specialist uses (consider **ideology**, **liberalism**, or **media**), and that some words of interest to Williams in 1976 (**career**, for example) or indeed in 1983 (**folk**, **genius**) have lost the special quality of "significance and difficulty" that attracted his attention. Equally, there is no mention in *Keywords* of other words (such as **citizenship**, **gender**, or **sign**) which, today, play a major role in both public discourse and a broad spectrum of academic disciplines. Accordingly, in conceiving of this volume we set out to update Williams's *Keywords* in three basic ways: first, by providing a revised vocabulary of culture and society that includes many terms from Williams's list but offers new discussions of their history and use, taking account of developments over the last 30 years; second, by adding discussions of "new keywords" that have emerged as the vocabulary of culture and society has responded to new social movements, changing political concerns, and new horizons of public debate; third, by deleting those of Williams's keywords that we feel have not sustained their importance in terms of the ways people represent their experiences and give meaning to their perceptions of a changing world.

Given the many encyclopedias, dictionaries, and "bluffer's guides" to academic topics crowding bookshops today, it is important to stress another sense in which this volume was undertaken in the distinctive spirit of Williams's initial inquiry: *New Keywords* is *not* a glossary of contemporary cultural and social **theory** (one of Williams's keywords re-examined in this volume), although many entries draw on theoretical resources to varying degrees. Despite the perhaps overly academic reception of *Keywords* in recent years, its intention was always to provide a useful, intellectually and historically grounded guide to *public* questions and struggles for meaning shared by many people in the field of culture and society. Williams (1976: 13) was careful to define his project in terms that would distinguish it clearly from conventional scholarly dictionaries:

> It is not a dictionary or glossary of a particular academic subject. It is not a series of footnotes to dictionary histories or definitions of a number of words. It is, rather, the record of an inquiry into a *vocabulary*: a shared body of words and meanings in our most general discussions, in English, of the practices and institutions which we group as *culture* and *society*.

The general discussions that interested Williams were not located in specific academic disciplines, but neither did they exclude the fields of scholarly and intellectual debate; instead, the sense of "general" significance that marked a keyword took shape in an encounter or an overlap between two or more social domains of usage. For Williams (1976: 12), a word in general usage was a word with variable uses. Some were "strong, difficult and persuasive words" already in everyday use (**work**, for example), while others might spread from a specialized context to wider discussions; **deconstruction** and **commodity**, both philosophical terms now used in fashion magazines, are examples of this today. Whatever the origins of a word and however erratic the paths it took to enter common usage, it was the fact that it mattered in "two areas ... often thought of as separate" that drew Williams to trace its travels. **Culture**, he pointed out, was the "original difficult word" in this respect, posing new questions and suggesting new connections as it gained importance in the area of **art** on the one hand, and **society** on the other. The sharing of a word across differing domains of thought and experience was often imperfect, he noted, but this very roughness and partiality indicated that the word brought something significant to discussions of "the central processes of our common life."

The "wish," as Williams put it, to recognize and understand these processes across habitually separated areas of activity could suddenly invest ordinary words such as "culture" with a strangeness that unsettled their seemingly transparent meaning, and it could also endow apparently technical, forbidding words with a new and mysterious popularity (**alienation** 30 years ago, **postmodernism** today). In both cases, however, it was a shared desire to articulate something of general importance that forged what Williams called a ''vocabulary'' of culture and society. From this followed his interest in exploring not only the meanings of words but also the ways people group or ''bond'' them together, making explicit or often implicit connections that help to initiate new ways of seeing their world. *Keywords* was organized to highlight ''clusters'' of words, indicated in bold in the text, so that readers might follow and reflect on the interactions, discontinuities, and uncertainties of association that shaped what Williams (1976: 13) called ''particular formations of meaning.'' These formations, too, change over time, dissolving in some cases and reforming in a different way in others as the links we make between words, the importance they have, and the contexts in which they matter are subject to alteration.

Necessarily, then, a revised vocabulary of culture and society should not only update the selection and discussion of individual words but also respond to the changed contexts of ''general'' discussion which people inhabit today. While we have insisted on retaining Williams's emphasis on the public intellectual uses of the terms selected for inclusion, *New Keywords* must achieve this focus in a different manner which takes account of the ways in which both our sense of ''common life'' and our understanding of history have changed since 1976. First, there has been a marked change in the conduct and circulation of intellectual work over the past 30 years: the expansion of higher education, the growth of a research culture linking universities more closely to a wide range of industries and to other public and private institutions, and the proliferation of new media-based modes of pedagogy and discussion have all combined to disperse and multiply the ''areas'' of thought and experience in and across which people wish to make common sense and formations of meaning take shape. These changes have also opened universities and the kinds of knowledge they foster to increased scrutiny and criticism (''culture wars'' in one expression), widening the social field of debate about such issues as the growth of interdisciplinarity and the social role of intellectuals. In accordance with these developments, the inquiry recorded by *New Keywords* is a collective rather than an individual one. This expansion of resources, and the plurality of perspectives it introduces to the project, are necessary today if proper account is to be taken of the now much greater diversity of the fields of both public and academic debate in which a vocabulary of culture and society is implicated and across which it is no less imperfectly shared.

Second, where Williams largely equated the ''English'' language with British usage, our inquiry is an international one – again, necessarily so to take account of the extent to which discussions of culture and society now increasingly flow across national boundaries, with English holding an often oppressively privileged status in limiting as well as enabling much of that flow. However, for practical reasons we focus mainly on usage in Western Anglophone countries, although in some entries (**civilization** and **modern**, for example) the contributors explain that recognizing the complexities occasioned by the entry of particular keywords into the vocabularies of culture and society in other countries is essential to grasping their import. This recognition was also a feature of Williams's *Keywords*: pointing out that many of his most important terms had developed key meanings in languages other than English or "went through a complicated and interactive development in a number of major languages" (1976: 17), he noted that he found it indispensable to trace some of this interaction in such cases as "alienation," and "culture" itself. We, too, would have liked to do more translinguistic as well as transnational tracing – the changing formations of meaning linking such concepts as "liberalism," **market**, **consumption**, "ideology," and **socialism** in China today is a consequential case in point – and we would have liked to follow the often radically divergent uses of English keywords in parts of the world where English is at most a lingua franca or a second language that may be nobody's mother tongue. An "extraordinary international collaborative enterprise" on the scale that Williams thought essential for an adequate comparative study quickly proved to be beyond us, too, for all the enlarged resources and technical means at our disposal.

Collaborating with writers in Australia, Britain, Canada, and the United States was extraordinary labor enough; this volume was five years in the making and could not have been produced at all without the Internet. Yet to explain our project's insufficiencies wholly in terms of the limits of time and technology – real as these are – would be to dodge the "deliberately social and historical" emphasis on *problems* of meaning that Williams (1983: 21) clarified as his own in the revised introduction to his book. The most active problems of meaning are always, he stressed, primarily embedded in actual relationships, and the difficulty of producing a widely usable volume that could offer anything like a genuinely global study of keywords in English is no exception to this; the desire to do so is active, but the relationships needed to achieve it and the level of "generality" in discussion that its realization would presuppose may not yet be sufficiently actual (at least for the editors of this volume) for the project to be feasible in practice: the entries on **globalization** and **the West** included here may help to suggest some reasons why.

Once again, though, this sense of an "unfinished and incomplete" labor that others will need to take up is a vital part of Williams's legacy. He traced the genesis of *Keywords* (1976: 9) to the end of World War II and the sense of entering a "new and strange world" that he shared with other soldiers returning to a transformed Britain in 1945. Recalling an occasion when he and another man just out of the army simultaneously said of their countrymen, "they just don't speak the same language," he goes on with customary deftness to link this spontaneous expression with the vocabulary of inter-generational incomprehension and conflict within families, and with what we might now call the "culture shocks" of class and ethnicity as he experienced them coming from a working-class family in Wales to Cambridge in the late 1930s. Today, in a world increasingly polarized by "culture wars" that are violently real as well as symbolic, there is no doubt that the same expression is still widely used to express "strong feelings" and important differences about ideas that not only create strangeness and unease between speakers of different varieties of English – whether around the world, across the same city, or in a shared workplace or classroom – but also between adjacent departments of knowledge, and practitioners of the same profession or discipline. It was from such "critical encounters," however, that Williams drew inspiration, seeing in them the workings of a central and often very slow process of social and historical as well as linguistic change.

Other modifications we have made to the *Keywords* model are minor compared with the shift to a collective and more international mode of production. While varying in size, Williams's entries in *Keywords* are reasonably consistent in their format, and ours are rather less so. Williams usually begins with a history of the usage of the word in question – and of various subordinate terms – derived mainly from the OED and classic sources in historical semantics. This is then followed by a discussion of contemporary public and scholarly uses of both the keyword and selected subordinate terms, with cross-references throughout to related keywords. This format is broadly followed in this volume with the exception that the explanations of etymological roots are often less detailed and lengthy than in Williams, putting more emphasis on how particular terms are lodged today in crucial sites of debate or mark new kinds of experience: how, for example, does one discuss the etymology of **virtual**? Within any collective work a standardized "format" would be difficult to enforce and, given a general editorial brief requiring emphasis on public intellectual usage, authors have largely followed their own inclinations in deciding what that means, and how to handle both sources and subordinate terms.

xxi

Another issue facing a collective work is posed by the balance Williams achieved between, on the one hand, a reliable scholarly account of a keyword's meanings that could be of use to a general reader to whom some or all of the material might be new, and, on the other, his distinctive interpretation of the word's significance and value. We asked contributors to address the concepts in ways that would reflect their own perspectives rather than aiming to write a "correct," wholly standardized, dictionary-style entry. Yet we did not want to go to the other extreme and have a collection of entirely individualized or partisan approaches to the concepts involved. Looking again at what Williams does it is clear, first, that his entries are all described and (usually) function as essays and, second, that they are generally organized to review some aspects of the history of the concept in question with a view to then commenting on the range of contemporary meanings and the public/political issues these involve – without at all moving on to a prescriptive definition, a glossary-type summary, or a concluding "correct line." Following Williams, then, this volume consists of signed essays (rather than anonymous entries) of varied lengths, all written by engaged intellectuals who are alert to the political issues at stake in the *translation* of key terms across different fields of use – public, everyday, literary, technical, and scholarly – and therefore willing to give a scrupulous account of those differences.

Williams wrote some of his most eloquent critical pages about the uses of dictionaries, in particular of the "extraordinary collaborative enterprise" (1976: 16) of the Oxford

Dictionary. He noted that the OED offered an incomparably rich source of historical information, and it remains unrivalled in this respect today; we supplied all contributors to *New Keywords* with copies of the OED entries relevant to the essays they had agreed to write, and encouraged them (not always successfully) to explore that material. However, Williams observed that the OED had serious limitations in documenting twentieth-century usage and was far less free of active social and political values than its "massive impersonality" might suggest. Today, the cultural biases of the OED are perhaps even more apparent: its extensive entries on "modern," for example, are remarkable for the tone of patronizing mockery or disapproval that accumulates over dozens of citations, muffling any sense that there might be worlds of English in which the word could speak directly of revolutionary passion, of torment, violent displacement, utopian desire, and joy. At the same time, Williams also pointed out that the OED excels more at showing the "range and variation" of meanings than it does in suggesting "connection and interaction." As *Keywords* developed out of notes taken over more than 20 years, Williams was able to supplement the OED's resources from his own extensive reading. We could not ask our contributors to do this, given the ruthless time constraints imposed on academics today, and so along with the OED material we tried to supply, where possible, related entries from other national dictionaries of English as well as from specialized social science, humanities, or cultural studies dictionaries. We also provided copies of appropriate web searches and, where relevant, Williams's entry or entries relating to the same keyword.

In many cases, it proved difficult to go around those entries or to find examples of usage that Williams had not already addressed, and numerous essays included here discuss his interpretations. His accounts of such complex terms as, for example, **empirical**, **experience** (1983), **nature**, and, of course, the famous entry on "culture" itself posed particular difficulties for authors trying to catch the new shadings of significance and value these terms had acquired in public usage by the early years of the twenty-first century. In other cases, the effort to "update" Williams's 1976 entry proved redundant. In the case of **realism**, for example, the currency of the term in the rhetoric of the neo-liberal governments that swept to power in developed countries from the late 1970s is dealt with in his account of the word's corporate and political use to discredit **idealism** by substituting an appeal to "limits" ("*limits* meaning *hard facts*, often of power or money in their existing and established forms") for the orientation toward "truth" that guides those philosophical uses which he also explains with remarkable concision. In this and other instances where Williams's entry remains as pertinent as it was 30 years ago, we have chosen not to revise it merely for the sake of doing so: *Keywords* is and should long remain available as a primary text.

It follows that by no means all of Williams's terms omitted here have lost (in our judgment) their social force as keywords. Among those that we did exclude on those grounds, some still invoke difficult social and political as well as intellectual issues, but *as words* no longer seem to have that edge of energy and uncertainty that marks a keyword in public usage – **sociology** and **anthropology**, for example, are no longer especially contentious as the names of academic disciplines. At the same time, some of Williams's words that we may seem to have ignored are in fact taken up by entries on other terms that may have a broader scope or a sharper significance today: thus we chose **therapy** as more pointed now than **psychological**, substituted **political correctness** for **doctrinaire** and (more debatably) **jargon**, settled on **space** and **place** as more encompassing than **regional**, and on **everyday** as having a wider currency than Williams's **ordinary**. **Underprivilege** is subsumed here by **poverty** (which Williams does not feature) and the issues it raises are also dealt with – along with those of **exploitation** – across a cluster of entries such as **capitalism**, **class**, **development**, and **economy**.

In any collective project, however, many decisions are forced by practical necessity rather than adopted as a matter of principle. Chief among the constraints we faced were those of space in an already substantial book, and time to meet our publisher's deadline, both of which led eventually to the dropping of some proposed terms (**exhibition**, **terrorism**, **waste**) that would have enhanced the book. Other "omissions" were beyond our control as life intervened and authors encountering unexpected difficulties, whether of their own or with our editorial brief, could not be replaced in time, or we did not know how to replace them: entries on **boundaries**, **criticism**, **leisure**, **pleasure**, **pluralism**, **romantic**, and **violence** fell out of the book in this haphazard and mundane way.

This is to say that our exclusions and our additions are, of course, at once as selective and as "arbitrary" as Williams's lists avowedly were in relation to a much wider range of terms that could have been included, but for various reasons were not. To call a selection arbitrary does not mean that it is unmotivated, and our own strong biases in editing this volume will be as evident as – but are, we hope, more explicit than – those that shaped the OED. However, the very nature of the project means that while our choices are contestable they were not capriciously made. Working from different disciplinary backgrounds, political temperaments, and national-linguistic locations, the three editors had long discussions and lively disagreements – sometimes resolved only by the brute force of two to one – about both the individual words to be included and the clusters we would use, following Williams, to shape the volume's social and historical emphases. We ended up with 12 groupings or lines of connection which we felt "bonded" particular keywords into the kind of wish-driven general discussion across different areas that Williams identified: roughly defined, our initial clusters were "art," "communication and the popular," "political economics," "politics and community," "race, ethnicity, colonialism," "sexuality and gender," "politics and the state," "borders of the human," "science," "space and time," "intellectual politics," and "modes of power and society."

Overlapping and entirely subject to criticism, these clusters at least proved their working value in culture and society today by attracting to the project a large number of distinguished contributors who proceeded to blur, ignore, write over, or recast the groupings we had devised. Nevertheless there is no doubt that our way of initially putting the volume together had a more than casual coherence, arising not only from a common debt to the work of Raymond Williams and a meeting-ground in the new discipline of cultural studies which so largely derives from that work, but also from a more impersonal but no less shared historical experience as part of a broad generation of scholars and critics directly formed by the engagements between the academy, the media, popular culture, and social movements that we principally wished to explore. Our approach in this volume is marked, too, by the rise to prominence in universities and the scandalization in the media of new conversations about "theory" (very much a keyword now as it was in Williams's day) that have crossed over occupational as well as faculty and disciplinary lines. Having taught "theory" ourselves to generations of students who went on to take an interest in contemporary scholarly debates into many different non-academic occupations, we have no doubt about the public import of the diverse theoretical reflections on culture and society sustaining those debates.

At the same time, our determination to keep making explicit connections between theoretical and everyday public usage provoked some of the most intense and interesting debates within our project, both between the editors and with contributors, over the five-year period of its planning and preparation. We had some ground rules: no entry could offer an unrelieved commentary on "key thinkers," whether (say) Derrida, Foucault, or Marx; all entries should offer concrete examples of usage; and as far as possible each entry should socially diversify its linguistic sources of evidence. At the same time, we had to recognize that some words with highly technical frames of reference as well as in popular circulation – **evolution**, **gene/genetic**, **representation**, and **text**, for example – might need a different treatment from other, no less complex words (**body**, **celebrity**, **mobility**, **self**) whose apparent simplicity and easy availability could initiate discussion. The most difficult issue, however, turned out to be not avoiding jargon but rather finding an appropriate way of addressing readers across a collectively written volume that is not designed for the exclusive use of a specialist academic audience. A uniform style was impossible to achieve and, having asked authors to clarify their personal take on the questions at issue in their chosen keywords, we did not seek to impose one.

Style, however, was less important than the ways in which authors defined the world they expected to share with readers and the likely interests and priorities that people might bring to this text. We asked authors not to assume in their very first paragraph that the reader's first concern was to know where the writer stood on controversies currently racking research schools in universities, but to begin, where possible, with the keyword itself, its history, and its everyday meanings. We asked that authors avoid giving summaries of the work of beloved thinkers that must be, in the limited space available, either so dense or so minimal that only someone familiar with the work in question could follow the explanation; and we often asked, too, that where relevant (as in most cases it was), priority be given to the treatment of public rather than specialized usage in case of problems in the balance between them caused by lack of space. These demands were not always easy or congenial to work with for scholars whose learning in and passion about their fields of expertise were our basis for inviting them to collaborate with us in the first place. Some contributors pulled out when they realized what we wanted, and we thank them for releasing us early to invite someone else. Others patiently worked through two or three revisions of their texts and we are deeply grateful for their care and labor, which have done so much to enhance the accessibility of this book.

Keywords from the outset was all about usefulness as well as language use, and Williams ended his introduction with a discussion of his problems of presentation – the advantages and disadvantages of an alphabetical, a thematic, or a conceptually structured ordering of terms – and of the ways to make use of a book whose purpose was to foreground the connections and interactions between ostensibly separate words. Suffice it to say here that we have followed his solutions: *New Keywords* is arranged in alphabetical order, but the best way to read it is not from beginning to end but by following the trails of cross-references that take the reader's fancy. Because of its collective authorship this volume is indeed full of concerns or topics that recur and lines of argument that overlap, converge, and diverge in sometimes surprising ways, and by following different orders of reading the reader will find new connections and no doubt make discoveries that have eluded the editors entirely. To enhance this use of the book, we have departed from Williams's model by incorporating references to sources in the entries; these result in networks of further reading to help those who wish to know more about particular keywords to follow their noses at leisure.

There is no doubt that by including an extensive list of references in *New Keywords* we have rendered more explicit the "weight," as it were, of the extensive learning that not only underpins this volume but inspired and sustained the project of *Keywords* itself: academics (and it is often they) who prefer to think of Williams as a "public" intellectual, for whom the constraints and niceties of scholarship were unimportant, may have forgotten the sheer intensity not only of the erudition displayed in his pages but also of the demands that Williams's prose could make of his readers – confident as he was of the intellectual desires and agency of ordinary people. We prefer to think of the extra references given here not as "proof" of the credentials of our authors but rather as a practical response to the increasing engagement and overlap today between academic and other kinds of public writing, including those active in that vast public bibliographic reservoir called the Internet. Above all, we think of references now as simply providing, in the greatly diversified conditions of transnational general discussion it is our purpose to address, just another resource for furthering the aim of *social* usefulness that Williams (1976: 21–2) so memorably defined for his book:

> This is not a neutral review of meanings. It is an exploration of the vocabulary of a crucial area of social and cultural discussion, which has been inherited within precise historical and social conditions and which has to be made at once conscious and critical – subject to change

as well as to continuity – if the millions of people in whom it is active are to see it as active: not a *tradition* to be learned, nor a *consensus* to be accepted, nor a set of meanings which, because it is "our language," has a natural authority; but as a shaping and reshaping, in real circumstances and from profoundly different and important points of view: a vocabulary to use, to find our own ways in, to change as we find it necessary to change it, as we go on making our own language and history.

Aesthetics

Aesthetics is generally defined as the branch of philosophy that concerns itself with the arts, and especially with the sensory, perceptual reception of art. It also deals more generally with sensuous perception in nature and everyday life. It is thus linked with notions such as **synesthesia** (the confusion of one sensory channel with another, as in "hearing colors" or "seeing sounds"), **anesthesia** (the numbing of the senses), and the various media of art and communication insofar as they are addressed to distinct senses (the distinctions between audition and vision, the verbal and visual arts, tactile and oral sensation, etc.). Aesthetics also concerns itself with taste, that is, with the evaluation of art and of various kinds of perceptual experience. It thus invariably addresses questions about the difference between good and bad art, about different kinds of experiences associated with the arts (beauty, sublimity, wonder, disgust, horror), and with specific features of these experiences such as the problem of form and content, the relation of pleasure to moral or political virtue, and the arousal of the emotions.

The coinage of the terms **aesthetic** and "aesthetics" (from Gk *aisthesis*) by Alexander Baumgarten in the C18 marks a historic shift in discussions of art, one that emphasizes the subjective activity of the perceiver or beholder over the objective properties of the material thing that occasions the sensation. Although Baumgarten is universally credited with introducing the term, he is usually nothing more than a footnote to the real discussion of **the aesthetic** in Immanuel Kant (1987 [1764]), Georg Wilhelm Friedrich Hegel (1975 [1835]), and the German idealist tradition. Kant's *Critique of judgment* is arguably the most influential treatise ever devoted solely to aesthetics. Benedetto Croce, Martin

*A*BCDEFGHIJKLMNOPQRSTUVWXYZ

Heidegger, Theodor Adorno (1997), and Nelson Goodman (1976) are among the most prominent C20 philosophers who have developed the concept further.

Although the term has its historical origin in the C18, its application has spread to cover the entire field of reflection on the arts and perception. Thus, Plato and Aristotle are discovered in retrospect to have been "doing aesthetics." Karl Marx's writing (which has relatively little to say about the arts) has been analyzed for its implicit aesthetic theories, and most discussions of the "aestheticization of politics" (Walter Benjamin, 1968) or the "ideology of the aesthetic" (Terry Eagleton, 1990) stem directly from Marx. Indeed, it is hard to think of any major thinker from the ancient religious authorities such as Pseudo-Dionysius to Sigmund Freud who has not engaged in aesthetic inquiry (Turner, 1996), and every culture that has engaged in reflection on this topic may easily be shown to have its own version of aesthetics. It is perhaps best, then, to qualify any historicist marking of the C18 emergence of the term by noting that it has a universal application as well.

Aesthetics in the modern era has been the site of numerous debates, over the objectivity or subjectivity of **aesthetic judgment**, and the relation of **aesthetic experience** to the **non-aesthetic** (variously defined as the practical or utilitarian, the moral and political, or simply as the non-artistic) (Fried, 1998). Raymond Williams (1976: 28) sees this as a symptom of "the divided consciousness of *art* and *society*," and some historians see classical Greek aesthetics as the last time that aesthetics was truly integrated with social and political issues. The aesthetic is itself often qualified by the modifier "merely" or "purely" to indicate, on the one hand, a despised sphere of social irrelevance, the fussiness of the often-denigrated **aesthete**, or, on the other hand, the purity and autonomy of a realm of freedom and disinterestedness (as envisaged by Kant, for example), where pleasure and a liberated imagination can roam. The aesthete, in particular, is often presented as a figure of decadent hedonism, or of an amoral "art-for-art's-sake" attitude. The *art pour l'art* movement, and figures such as Walter Pater and Oscar Wilde, have helped to consolidate a picture of the aesthete as a feminized figure, the projection of a thinly veiled homophobia, and a suspicion that there is something slightly unmanly about a taste for the fine arts. The most vigorous attack on **philosophical aesthetics** as such has been mounted by Pierre Bourdieu, who argues that the whole "purist" tendency of aesthetics is an "expression of the sublimated interests of the bourgeois intellectual" (Bourdieu, 1984: 492).

Aesthetics today is in considerable ferment as the result of two developments: "the de-definition of art" associated with the rise of postmodernism, and the decline of the cult of modernist "aesthetic purity" principally associated with abstract painting and sculpture (Greenberg, 1986). Politically committed art, conceptual art, performance, installations, process art, and other experimental movements have eroded the dominance of a "purist" aesthetics that equated the highest value with a compelling formal, virtuosic achievement within a traditional medium such as painting or sculpture (Fried, 1998). The other development is the rise of the media, beginning with photography in the C19, but accelerating in the C20 with the invention of cinema, radio, television, video, the computer, and the new media, most notably the Internet (Kittler, 1999; McLuhan, 1964; Manovich, 2001). Art exhibitions these days are more likely to consist of television monitors and black-box theaters or constructions of ''fun-house''-style installations than traditional arrays of still images and objects. Media art has required the development of a **media aesthetics**, one which examines the new perceptual universes opened up by virtual reality, the world-wide web, and immersive art environments.

Some theorists have argued that the human sensorium is being restructured by the new media, and that a transformed human consciousness could usher in a new social order – Walter Benjamin's (1968) proletarian revolution or Marshall McLuhan's global village. Others would contend that the **new aesthetics** is merely an acceleration of mass culture and the logic of late capitalism, producing a massive collective hallucination (films like *The Matrix*), ideological mystification at its purest (Adorno, 1997; Baudrillard, 1994; Kittler, 1999). Along with the new aesthetics, a new academic formation known as visual culture or visual studies has emerged, in which the long-standing fascination of aesthetics with visual arts and media has found a disciplinary foothold (Holly and Moxey, 2002). If contemporary aesthetics is indeed undergoing a ''pictorial turn'' (W. J. T. Mitchell, 1994b), it may be time to reopen the equally long-standing association of aesthetics with taste, the channel of orality. If the visual or scopic drive (Lacan, 1981) is what allows us to sample objects and sensations at a safe distance, the oral aspect of aesthetics reminds us that seeing (and hearing) may also be a form of ingestion and incorporation. It may be that we are being forcibly reminded by contemporary media that aesthetics (*pace* Kant) can never insulate itself in the pure, disinterested realm of visual pleasure-at-a-distance, but that we inhabit today a sensory environment of accelerating consumption. Bourdieu's insistence that the Kantian criteria of ''good taste'' are grounded in bourgeois disgust and horror at ''vulgar'' pleasures of the senses may have a new role to play in an age when both art and mass culture are exploring these sensations under the name of aesthetics.

W. J. T. Mitchell

See: *ART, CANON, CULTURE, MODERN, POSTMODERNISM, VALUE.*

Alternative

Alternative is a deceptively straightforward word, surprisingly complex when applied to culture and politics. Contemporary uses are prefigured by an eC19 sense of ''alternative'' (adjective) as ''the other (of two) which may be chosen instead,'' but political meanings derive from the mC20, perhaps the 1960s, when ''alternative'' comes to be defined against the socially mainstream, established, or conventional. Since then, ''alternative'' (adjective) or **alternatives** (noun) have had three rather different locations in political-cultural discourses.

Alternative

In the first, alternatives are placed in opposition to protest or criticism, which are seen as inadequately practical or transforming: it is not enough, it is argued, to criticize or to protest; we must develop alternatives. From a social-reforming liberal or social-demo-cratic point of view, the failure to do so is the characteristic flaw of the "impossible" left and its intellectuals. A similar usage distinguishes a hegemonic move, often conducted, in recent times, from a neo-liberal position: there is **no alternative** (to the market etc.). In these contexts, "alternative(s)" usually refer to state policies and mark an enlargement of political strategy.

"Alternative" signifies differently in relation to "oppositional" or "revolutionary." Raymond Williams, discussing Antonio Gramsci's political ideas, distinguishes between alternative and oppositional meanings and values (1980: 40). Though the difference narrows in the regulated societies of late modernity, forms of life may simply differ from the dominant ways or explicitly challenge them. Williams is emphatic that "even some alternative senses of the world . . . can be accommodated and tolerated within a particular effective and dominant culture" (1980: 32). Alternatives may be emergent, as in the coming to consciousness of a new class, or they may be residual, connected with religion or ruralism. Williams's discussion, though subtle, recapitulates recurrent dichotomies in left-wing thinking. Collective self-defense and corporate identity (for example, orthodox trade unionism) are unfavorably compared with political, critical, or revolutionary con-sciousness or counter-hegemony, a universal or expansive opposition by which subordinated majorities transform the social order (Gramsci, 1971). Similar distinctions, with varying evaluations, have figured in women's movements, in lesbian and gay and queer politics, and in struggles around racism, nationalism, and ethnicity. Here minoritizing strategies, separ-atism, or self-development within communities have been opposed to strategies that univer-salize, transgress boundaries, or deconstruct key binaries of race and nation or gender and sex (Gilroy, 1993b: 63–73; Sedgwick, 1994: 82–90). Here "alternative," like "resist-ance," can mark a political limit or diminution.

These dichotomies, however, have often been challenged. "Living differently" – more co-operatively and less competitively or hierarchically, for example – expresses hope for the future, but is also a kind of direct action. The language has different nuances to describe these challenges: "dissenting," "non-conformist," "subversive," "underground," "fringe," "counter-cultural," as well as "alternative." The history of such aspirations is harder to track than those of more formal agencies. **Alternative ways of living** have fused with anti-industrialism, ruralism, and preference for "the natural," with avant-garde literary and artistic movements (including blues, jazz, folk, or rock music), and with "bohemia" or transgressive practices and spaces like free love, drug-taking, or gay scenes. These manifestations have differed politically and in their social appeal, but living differ-ently has been an element in democratic and egalitarian movements from their beginnings, from utopian communities in the New World and Europe, and ex-slave "maroon" or runaway settlements in the Caribbean and South and Central America, to modern self-education movements and co-operative practices (Robinson, 1983: 173–241; B. Taylor, 1983). From the later 1950s, alternative ways of living were prominent themes in Gandhian anti-colonialism, the civil rights and Black Power movements, the Campaign for Nuclear Disarmament, and, in a more diffused way, the youthful counter-cultures of the 1960s and 1970s, in communes and in hippie lifestyles, and, often in criticism of these "liberations," in the early Women's and Gay Liberation Movements (Cant and Hemmings, 1988; Roszack, 1971; Rowbotham, 1983). Agitations on world peace, internationalism, non-violence, and civil rights have often forged close connections between popular politics, heterodox religious beliefs, and ethical concerns. There are also interesting connections with imaginative fiction, from the tradition of social utopias to contemporary feminist science fiction (Morris, 1970 [1891]; Piercy, 1979).

Today's "alternatives" are bewildering in their range, diversity, and degrees of incorporation, politically and in terms of capitalist consumption. They are rarely articulated as a concerted politics, yet insistence on "alternative" rather than "anti-" retains significance. There are echoes from the counter-culture – **alternative press**, **alternative media**, **alternative theater**, **alternative bookshops**, **alternative comedy**, **alternative education**, **alternative prospectus** (for universities or schools) and the culture of "raves." There are emergent environmental and economic strategies – **alternative energy**, **alternative technology**, **alternative (or ethical) investments**, **alternative consumption** (for example, buying fair-traded goods or boycotting brands with high levels of labor exploitation). There is an array of lifestyle choices with or without wider objectives: **alternative medicine and therapy**, for example, or food reform (from vegetarianism and organic agriculture to "real meat" and "real ale"), or **alternative forms of leisure, sociability, and religion** (such as dance camps, circle dance, and many forms of spirituality).

"Alternative" is gaining new nuances, "pre-emergent" perhaps, from globalization and multiculturalism. Alterity is not only to be performed by dissident minorities, but is found, disconcertingly, in social others, in experiences of difference that can also be transforming. There are signs in the "developed" world today that **alternative politics**, often despised as bourgeois and itself sometimes anti-political, is becoming a pressing necessity, as citizens recognize their complicity in global inequalities, in new forms of empire and warfare, and in environmental fragility. On the activist edge of emergent global politics, the coming together of protest, counter-hegemonic movements, and alternatives can be seen in the slogan of the World and European Social Forums: "Another world is possible" (W. Fisher and Ponniah, 2003).

Richard Johnson

See: *COMMUNITY, MOVEMENTS, REFORM AND REVOLUTION, RESISTANCE, UTOPIA.*

5

Art

Art is one of those terms that seems to live mainly by negation. "But is it art?" is the question that reflects the questioner's suspicion that something is probably not art, but is something else – "mere" craft, technique, kitsch, artisanal labor, or raw material, unredeemed by skillful handling. "Art does not exist" is the opening shocker of E. H. Gombrich's *The story of art* (1978), and "the death of art" is routinely announced at the same moment as a new artistic movement is heralded. Clearly these two statements cannot both be true: if art did not exist, it could hardly die; and if it dies (or is reborn, revived, resurrected), then it must surely exist from time to time. So the questions about art are not only "what is art?" but also "when and where is art?" and what are the conditions that have made it a term worth fighting over. For it seems clear that art is a fighting word – not usually, it must be admitted, in a military or violent sense, but in the intellectual and cultural battles that define taste, canons of value, and social hierarchies.

The history of "art" as a term is generally divided between an early usage, when the word applies quite broadly to all skilled craftsmanship, work, expert techniques, technologies, and professions (**"art" with a lower-case "a"**), and a more modern usage, when the term is endowed with rather more elevated and inflated connotations (**"Art" with a capital "A"**). This modern conception is associated with the emergence of **the artist** as a distinct social or professional role, the cult of **artistic genius** and inspiration, the elevation of the work of art to quasi-sacred status as a fetish object, and the rise of aesthetics and aesthetic judgment as distinct faculties designed for the perception of works of art. The dividing line between the early general usage (which still survives when we talk about the art of cooking, shoemaking, baseball, diving, marketing, or engineering) and the modern aesthetic sense of **Fine Art** is very difficult to locate. Gray areas such as fashion, popular music, dance, and film abound, whose status as Art or art is still contested. These social distinctions are complicated by a plethora of narratives of the rise of Art as a distinctly elevated concept. Some authorities place the rise of Art in the Renaissance, when the emergence of humanism, the rediscovery of classical antiquity, and concentrations of wealth in aristocratic dynasties (the Medici, the royal families of Europe, the papacy) produced a flowering of Fine Art that seemed more intellectually ambitious than the anonymous works of medieval artisans. This argument could also be applied to the courtly arts of several Chinese dynasties, which achieved heights of sophistication and refinement long before Europe; there is a notable Eurocentric bias built in to most discussions of Art, as if it were a Western or modern invention.

Within the Eurocentric narrative of Art, the rise of "Art" with a capital "A" is usually located in the C18 with the emergence of aesthetics as a distinct branch of philosophy. Others place it in the C19 and the Romantic movement, the rise of bourgeois individualism, and the cult of the bohemian genius and the avant-garde. In the C20, numerous deaths of art have been announced, from the destruction of traditional museums and art collections by the Bolsheviks, to the deaths of specific artistic media (painting, the novel, and theater, for example) as a result of technical innovations such as photography, cinema, and television. Insofar as "Art" becomes an honorific term, automatically conferring value on whatever it designates, the denial of the "Art" label to any would-be work of art is best understood as a rhetorical gesture, a claim that something is "bad art," not that it is non-art. Art in the C20 and eC21 has become a thoroughly nominalist concept; art is whatever an artist says it is. The ready-mades of Duchamp, the found objects of Arte Povera, and the emergence of such postmodern artistic movements as minimalism, conceptualism, **performance art**, **land art**, **appropriation art**, scatter pieces, and the Informe have made it necessary to think of art as something like an institutional category (Danto, 1981; Dickie, 1974). The question "is it art?" cannot be answered by an appeal to empirical attributes or a widely accepted definition or canonical precedents, but must be thought of as an invitation to participate in a specific game for which the rules are being constantly revised and improvised. So the question becomes, "what happens if we see this as art?"

This question begs a prior question about what it means to see something *as* art, which threatens to make the whole enterprise thoroughly circular. Small wonder that a number of scholars have declared an end to both **art theory** and **art history** (Belting, 1997; Burgin, 1986), and that aesthetics has been declared an intellectually bankrupt endeavor, only slightly less despicable than the figure known as the aesthete. One common tactic is to change the whole subject and to declare that the very concept of art has been "liquidated" (Buck-Morss, 1996) by new forms of visual culture, material culture, mass culture, or just plain culture. The culture industry is thus seen as the replacement for art, a defeat of refined, polite tastes by vulgar, commercial values (Adorno and Horkheimer, 1972), a defeat of seriousness and high ambition by kitsch (Greenberg, 1986), or (in a more positive key) the triumph of proletarian culture over bourgeois sentimentalism and elite snobbery (W. Benjamin, 1968). Art, and aesthetics along with it, is reduced to an ideology that thinly veils class interests, and the history of art is reduced to a symptom of capitalist culture, either by way of direct complicity with social stratification (Bourdieu, 1984) or as a desperate act of resistance and alienation in the face of the triumphant advance of the culture industry. Even the avant-garde, in Tom Crow's (1995) mordant phrasing, may be little more than the "research and development arm" of the culture industry.

Undeterred by these countervailing tendencies, artists continue to produce art, critics assess it, collectors collect it, and museums and galleries display it to ever-larger audiences. Art historians continue to expand their field into areas (visual culture, new media, pre-modern and non-Western cultures) that go well beyond the canonical notion of Art as a distinctly Western or modern invention. The invention of new technical media, particularly the computer, video, and the Internet, have challenged artists to create new forms, and to take on new social roles. The Internet, particularly, has spawned a host of **artist's collectives** that produce **web-based art** that seems quite different from (while maintaining certain continuities with) traditional artistic practices. The cult of the individual artist

7

is even further eroded by the anonymous productions of **web artists** who insert themselves into the circuits of globalized cyberspace, producing everything from hot-linked perform- ances to immersive environments to subversive software. If art is obsolete, dead, or never existed at all, it has remarkable resilience as a concept and a practical activity.

W. J. T. Mitchell

See: *AESTHETICS, CANON, CULTURE, VALUE.*

Audience

Audience has had a variety of meanings, ranging from the action of hearing ("to give audience," as early as the C14), through the more formal concept of an official, formal, or judicial "hearing." In the C15, an ecclesiastical court was referred to as a "court of audience." The term could be used to describe any occasion of hearing ("In any sermon or other audience," 1426) or the particular occasion of a formal interview, as when one is "granted an audience," usually by a superior. In the C17 and C18, the word came to be more usually associated with the idea of a group of people who are the consumers of a communicative event of some sort. **The audience**, in this usage, then refers to those who are physically, and collectively, present in the same place, as the addressees of a sermon or speech or theatrical production. This was extended, in the C19, to the readers of a book and eventually, to the consumers of other forms of communication.

Audiences of this type are evidently small, by comparison with the **mass audience** for contemporary forms of broadcasting, which perhaps today supplies us with our primary sense of what an audience is. Nonetheless, large-scale audiences are by no means exclusive to the modern age – the theaters of Dionysius and Ephesus were said to hold between 20,000 and 50,000 people, and the Roman Circus Maximus held perhaps 150,000 spectators. From medieval times, in the West, the Christian churches, with their organized systems of regular sermons, pre-dated contemporary forms of broadcasting in transmitting a co-ordinated message to a very large, if geographically dispersed, constituency.

One of the key transformations in the concept of what an audience is began with the invention of printing. The readership of a printed book is an audience of a different kind from that of a theatrical production or sermon. This type of audience is dispersed not only across space, but also across time. The invention of the daily newspaper represented another key shift in the development of **mediated audiences**. The emergence of a daily national press can perhaps be said to have created a broader sense of community and a sense of a collectively shared, secular historical time. The new forms of electronic broadcasting, such as radio and television, introduced a further new dimension as their audiences now consumed the same messages at exactly the same time. Thus broadcast schedules played a significant part in creating a shared sense of a "life in common" for national audiences in the C20 (Scannell, 1988).

In Great Britain, the BBC's first director general, Lord Reith, had as his declared objective the idea that the BBC should function to bring together all the families of the nation into the symbolic union of the "national family." Clearly, in today's multi-channel environment, featuring many forms of satellite and transnational broadcasting, the traditional audiences of national broadcasting systems have now fragmented. New, cross-border forms of broadcasting often now bring together audiences of people who may be geographically dispersed across great distances, to constitute diasporic communities of various sorts.

For many years one of the key concerns of academic **audience research** has been with the question of the media's effects on their audiences, which have often been figured as passive entities, more or less susceptible to the effects of powerful technologies of communication. From this perspective, the question is simply which sections of the audience are affected, and how much, by which particular communications; and there is a long history of research which has tried to demonstrate the behavioral, cognitive, or ideological "effects" of the media on their audiences

In recent years, this idea that the media are directly responsible for making their audiences buy a particular product, vote for this or that politician, or believe some particular ideology has come under considerable strain. Contemporary audience research tends to figure the audience as active in a range of ways. Thus, in what has come to be known as the "uses and gratifications" approach, the audience is seen to make active choices from the media menu available to them, and to interpret the messages they receive in ways determined by their own psychological characteristics. This has been described as an attempt to get away from the issue of what the media do to people, so as to better address the issue of what people themselves actually do with the media at their disposal (Halloran, 1975). Over the last few decades these insights have been further developed in the "encoding/decoding" model developed by Stuart Hall (1981), which has set the frame for much subsequent audience work. In Hall's model the audience is conceived of as actively decoding the messages they receive from systems of mass communications, and interpreting them in a range of ways, drawing on the particular cultural resources which their social position has made available to them.

More recently there has been a flowering of work, now often described as **active audience theory**, which perhaps takes the stress on "what people do with the media" to its limit point. This perspective has often involved a somewhat naïve and uncritical vision of how devices such as the remote control and the video recorder are supposed to have empowered the audience in new ways. Some part of this romanticization of the freedoms of the active viewer to make whatever they like of the messages they receive has perhaps been influenced by contemporary neo-liberal ideologies of consumer freedom.

Unsurprisingly there is now some evidence of a backlash against some of the more fanciful versions of this active audience theory, by critics who reassert the continuing necessity to address the political economy of the media and the ways in which structures of

9

media power continue to limit and frame the activities of their audiences. To this extent, the history of academic research in this field is perhaps best characterized as a continuing dialog between perspectives which stress the power of the media over their audiences, on the one hand, and perspectives which stress the active dimension of how audiences respond to the messages which they receive, on the other.

David Morley

See: *COMMUNICATION, MASS.*

Behavior

Originally relating to the activities of living beings, specifically humans, **behavior** has since become generalized to describe inanimate processes as well. It derives from *havour*, or *havyoure*, in C15 and C16 usage, with connections to oF *aveir* or *avoir* and to the later English *to have*, and retains the legacy of this earlier usage in the sense of possession it implies: **to behave** as, in the reflexive sense, to have or bear oneself. Hence behavior is the manner of conducting or bearing oneself in the external relations of life, implying a degree of control over one's self-presentation in public: "The behauiour of the yong Gentlemen, giues him out to be of good capacity, and breeding" (Shakespeare, 1601). It is noteworthy that in this form the term assumes the separation of the person acting or **behaving** from how they behave. Behavior is thus an external manifestation of some set of internal processes generally suggesting agency or intentionality, but also sometimes involuntary, as in a reflex, for instance. Consider the common injunctions, especially from adults to children, to "behave yourself," or "be on your best behavior." But the term can also be depersonalized, so as to refer to good or bad behavior in general, or as offering a code of practice as to acceptable manners. Or, similarly generalized, it can refer to specific contexts of activity, as in **consumer behavior**, or **sexual behavior**.

Such depersonalization led as early as the C17 to an extension also to inanimate processes, referring to the manner in which a thing acts under specified circumstances or in relation to other things: "In Chemistry the behavior of different substances towards each other, in respect to combination and affinity" (Argyll, 1866). In this context the term refers to some dynamic of change or action within a system, not merely stasis. Thus

ABCDEFGHIJKLMNOPQRSTUVWXYZ

Behavior

Thomas Huxley refers to ''the behavior of water which drains off a flat coast'' (1878). Another common use describes the behavior of machines or vehicles under particular circumstances. With the emergence of systems theory and mathematical modeling in the C20 comes the science of **systems behavior** and, with metaphorical undertones, the concept of a **well-behaved system**, as one whose properties are predictable and controlled rather than disorderly.

As a science, the study of animal behavior, or ethology, of necessity objectifies the organisms it studies. External behavior is all that can be observed. Intentionality can only be inferred and, within the traditions of the science, is discounted. Such an approach can be traced back to the C17 writings of La Mettrie and René Descartes (1999 [1637]), who offered a machine metaphor for non-human animals; by contrast **human behavior**, albeit sometimes machine-like, was said to be animated by the possession of a soul or mind. Ethology focuses on the study of the behavior of animals in natural or semi-natural conditions. It led to the definition of specific reproducible patterns of behavior, as in courtship, for instance, and to the analysis of small segments of activity (for instance grooming), sometimes called ethograms. The systematic study of animal behavior under controlled or laboratory conditions, as animal psychology, began in the eC20, notably with the work of Ivan Pavlov, whose physiological research transformed into the study of how behavior can be changed by training (or conditioning), seen as the establishment of novel reflexes – classically as when a dog learns to salivate in expectation of food when a bell is rung.

Perhaps inevitably, and in reaction to the lC19 school of introspective psychology, regarding non-human animals as **behaving machines** led to attempts to treat humans similarly. This approach, **behaviorism**, was introduced in the US by John Watson and developed by the school of, primarily Anglo-American, psychologists who followed him, notably B. F. Skinner. Strict behaviorism insisted that the true scientific approach was to limit oneself only to the observable manifestations of behavior, and to deny both the legitimacy or possibility of discussing subjective mental processes or subjectivity. As Watson (1924) put it: ''The time has come when psychology must discard all reference to consciousness . . . its sole task is the prediction and control of behavior.'' For Skinner, behavior was a pattern of responses to external stimuli, a pattern that could change predictably as a result of conditioning or training. Whereas in Pavlovian or classical conditioning the animal learned to respond to an external stimulus outside its control (the ringing of a bell), in Skinnerian or operant conditioning the animal learns the outcome of its own behavior, as when pressing a lever results in the arrival of food. The task of psychology then became that of defining the laws that determined these patterns. It was not merely mentalistic descriptions that were discounted; internal neural or physiological processes were also seen as irrelevant to psychological descriptions; the brain could be treated as a black box, and psychology as a branch of physics. Central to behaviorism, perhaps by contrast to all other psychological sciences, was the emphasis on control, as illustrated by Skinner's social visions in *Beyond freedom and dignity* (1972).

Skinner's attempts to describe the development of linguistic skills in children as patterns of stimuli and responses was devastatingly rebutted by Noam Chomsky (1967), and the pretensions of behaviorism dystopically discussed in Aldous Huxley's *Brave new world*. And despite behaviorism's claims to at least account precisely for the behavior of non-human, if not human, animals, the weight of evidence for what came to be ironically described as the "misbehavior of animals" led, by the 1970s, to the demise of behaviorism as a scientific approach within animal or human psychology. In some senses, however, it is possible to regard cognitive or computational psychology as a successor science, sharing behaviorism's penchant for abstract model building rather than ethologically and neuro-biologically grounded explanation.

The residual influence of behaviorism can be seen in certain psychiatric practices and notably in so-called **behavior therapy**. The term is due to Hans Eysenck (1979), who, in the 1950s, used it in contrast to psychotherapy (especially psychoanalysis) and biological psychiatry. Psychotherapeutic methods of treatment involve discussions between therapist and patient which in various ways attempt to expose and analyze the roots of a present condition; biological psychiatry offers to regulate unwanted emotions or undesirable behavior by pharmacological intervention. By contrast with both, behavior therapy in-volves training a person to change their behavior by contingencies of reinforcement. Thus those dealing with disruptive children, and some prison regimes, offer a "token economy" in which "good behavior" is "reinforced" by reward. Behavior therapy is said to be effective in the treatment of certain types of phobia (fear of snakes or spiders, for example) or obsessive-compulsive disorder. As implied by Watson's original behaviorist agenda, the emphasis is thus above all on control.

13

Steven Rose

See: *BIOLOGY, SCIENCE.*

Biology

Biology derives from the Gk *bios*, meaning life, and *logia*, meaning discourse or study. The term was first used by the naturalist Gottfried Reinhold in 1802, adopted by Jean-Baptiste Lamarck, and appeared in English in 1813, but was only brought into more common use by William Whewell in the mC18 ("The term Biology...has of late become not uncom-mon, among good writers," 1847). It has retained this meaning, the study of life and living processes, ever since. Yet, almost from the start, the word used for the study of life processes also became the accepted term for those processes themselves (as in distinguish-ing between a person's biology and their social circumstances). This elision emphasizes the realist nature of the claims made by biology as a science.

Biology

As biology emerged in the C19 as a distinct ensemble of discourses, the issue of their relationship one to the other and to the other natural sciences became an increasingly important question. Were there specific features of life which distinguished it from non-living processes and therefore rendered it irreducible to physics and chemistry? Jacob Moleschott and other mechanical materialists argued that life was but a special form of chemistry ("we are what we eat"), while others claimed the presence of a specific *élan vital*. From the 1920s and 1930s the Vienna school, committed to the hypothesis of the unity of the sciences, argued for the potential reducibility of biology to physics. However, more so than among other natural sciences, the term "biology" embraces a range of discourses and disciplines, and a variety of methodologies, such that it has recently become more common to refer to the **biological sciences** or the **life sciences** in the plural. As the relationship of these disciplines to each other even within biology is unclear and hence the prospect of a unified science of biology embracing all aspects of life processes remains uncertain, the Vienna school's formally reductive approach has fallen out of favor. More recently, and more plausibly, Edward Wilson (1998) has argued that different forms of **biological explanation** must at least be *consilient* – that is, mutually non-contradictory.

The problem is best addressed by considering the question of causal explanations within biology. Consider a frog, jumping into a pool. A physiologist will explain this in terms of the contraction of the muscles in the frog's legs, themselves *caused* to contract by signals arriving through the nervous system that connects brain to leg muscles. A biochemist or molecular biologist offers the reductive explanation that the muscles are composed of protein filaments that slide past one another, *causing* the contraction; these proteins are composed of simpler sub-units (amino acids) and their properties are determined by chemistry and ultimately physics. An ecologist might point to the presence of a predator (a snake) which, observed by the frog, *causes* it to jump, in order to escape. A developmental biologist is concerned with the *causal* processes by which the fertilized egg divides and ultimately forms muscle cells; an evolutionary biologist would point to the evolutionarily honed *causal* adaptations which ensure that frogs which survive and reproduce can observe and respond rapidly to potential predators. The physiologist and developmental biologist locate cause in an immediate temporal sequence of events, sometimes called *proximal* or *functional* explanations. The ecologist offers a *teleonomic* or goal-directed explanation; the evolutionary biologist's explanation is *distal* – that is, it relates the present to the past – but is sometimes given more rhetorical power by being described as causal or *ultimate*.

Each of these types of explanation characterizes a specific style of experimentation, theory-making, and discourse within biology. Some philosophers of biology regard this as a transient situation characteristic of an immature discipline. Thomas Nagel has argued that "higher level" accounts, such as those of the physiologist, are merely descriptive, whereas "lower level" accounts, such as those of the biochemist, are truly explanatory (Nagel, 1998). Others would insist that the accounts, while consilient, are irreducible, and that for some purposes higher-level and for others lower-level accounts might offer the most explanatory power. Explanations thus depend on the purposes for which explanation is required.

Explanatory fault-lines thus run through the biological sciences, but the fissure is that much greater between the biological on the one hand, and the psychological or social sciences on the other. Many biologists argue that psychology is or should be reducible to biology without invoking any special further forces or properties. The case of the social sciences is more complex. Wilson and, following him, other evolutionary theorists maintain that the social sciences are but a specific form of biology appropriate to the evolved status of humans. **Biological essentialism** has also found favor with some feminists and even theorists of negritude, by contrast with social constructivists. A commoner resolution to the issue is to argue that biology ends at birth, and from that point on the social supervenes. Rejecting all of these positions as unsatisfactory, and operating within a more or less explicitly Marxist or dialectical tradition, efforts are also made to derive a **biosocial framework** (S. Rose, 1997). This approach rejects the possibility of partitioning the human condition between the two competing discourses of biology and the social sciences. Instead humans are seen as simultaneously and irreducibly *both* social and biological beings.

Steven Rose

See: *BEHAVIOR, GENE/GENETIC, SCIENCE.*

15

Body

There is considerable uncertainty about the derivation of the term **body**, which seems to have been "adopted... from some foreign source" into English and German (*botich*) by the C3, although the term disappeared in modern German. The most common use of the word refers to "the material frame" of humans and other animals. Deriving from this is its employment to designate matter, material, substance, or three-dimensional figures (as in **heavenly bodies**). Body may also be a shorthand or euphemistic term for corpse (a **dead body**). However, it is used too as a term of relation indicating the main or principal part (the **body of a text** or **body of a vehicle**). It stands for the individual in collective designations such as **anybody, nobody, everybody**, and **somebody**. In contrast, it may also indicate a collective, most notably in **the body politic**, but also in the **corporate body**, or significant accumulation or bulk (the **body of opinion** or **body of evidence**).

Interest and investment in the **human body** have been widespread in Western societies especially since the IC20, as indicated by the extensive proliferation and circulation of relevant terms, including **body language, body image, body management**, and **body work**. Western societies have fostered the emergence and commercialization of sites dedicated to **body culture** (gyms, health clubs, spas, health farms, magazines, videos, etc.) and of regimes for **body management and enhancement** (diets, exercise and **body-building** programs, etc.). Simultaneously there has been rapid development of scientific expertise and technologies oriented toward the management and alteration of the human body: genetic engineering, plastic surgery, hormonal and pharmacological treatment, nanotechnology, prosthetics, and sports and exercise science. Transsexual surgical and hormonal transformations exemplify such developments. For transsexuals and others, such technologies have extended the repertoire of resources available for the realization of the body as "an individual project" (Benson, 1997).

Against this backdrop, the onset of AIDS (acquired immune deficiency syndrome) and BSE (bovine spongiform encephalopathy) in the lC20 and eC21, and scares about anthrax contamination and SARS (severe acute respiratory syndrome), were powerful reminders of limits to individual control and of the vulnerability of the human body. Thus, since the lC20 there have been recurring references to **bodies at risk**. The prevalence of obesity and addictions (complex phenomena associated with pathological interactions between individual will and the body) indicate diverse patterns in the aspirations toward and achievement of individual **body control** in the West. In fact, some view the increasing prevalence of eating disorders and **bodily self-harm** (through deliberate cutting, etc.) in these societies as evidence of the destructive potential of ambitions for individual control and of excessive investment in the **body as a personal project**.

Western philosophy has long been concerned with **mind–body dualism**: the notion that the human mind and body are entirely distinct. Linked to this is the assumption that the mind (in its attributes, capacities, and activities) dominates the body: the mind is associated with transcendence, the body with immanence. Overcoming this dualism (often referred to as the "mind–body problem") has been a major preoccupation of modern Western philosophy, although some would say that the latter has also been implicated in perpetuating that dualism. Nevertheless, as Susan Bordo (1995: 13) contends, this is "no mere philosophical position," since this key dichotomy has been "deployed and socially embodied in medicine, law, literary and artistic representations."

Indeed, in modern Western societies, social divisions and hierarchies have often been linked to the **mind–body split**. There has been a generalized cultural devaluing of those whose lives are considered to be confined to or by **bodily processes** and activities, including: women (who are associated with and assessed according to physical appearance and reproductive activities including pregnancy, giving birth, breast feeding, etc.); laborers (peasants, slaves, servants, and manual workers), and the disabled. Moreover, some groups tend to be overidentified with and through bodily characteristics. This is exemplified in the persistent use of animalistic visual and linguistic imagery in representations of certain ethnic (particularly black) groups and their stereotypical association with physical strength and prowess rather than intellectual abilities and accomplishments. Those from dominant groups (particularly Western, white, heterosexual, middle-class men), in contrast, tend to be represented through and identified with intellectual achievement. Their physical traits and bodily functioning are often ignored or rendered insignificant: they tend to be viewed as "unmarked, neutral, universal and disembodied" (McDowell, 1999: 48).

Thus, this powerful dichotomy – sometimes labeled Cartesian dualism (referring to the C16 philosopher Réné Descartes, regarded as its founding philosophical formulator) – still casts its shadow over Western culture. However, since the IC20 there has been considerable contestation around the body as a locus of power relations. For example, IC20 Western feminists, engaging in what was labeled **body politics**, conducted campaigns for abortion rights and access to contraception, and tackled pornography and other issues pertaining to the control and representation of women's bodies. In fact, the most widely circulated feminist text ever published is *Our bodies ourselves* (1978), produced originally by the Boston Women's Health Book Collective, appearing in many editions in various languages. From a rather different perspective, the French philosopher Michel Foucault claimed that: "The body is directly involved in a political field; power relations have an immediate hold upon it: they invest it, mark it, train it, torture it, force it to carry out tasks, to perform ceremonies, to emit signs" (Foucault, 1977: 25). Foucault traced historical patterns of **body discipline** (in prisons and other settings), highlighting how social norms and conventions are realized and lived through the body. Others have focused on **unruly, excessive or disruptive bodies** as vehicles for social and political resistance or transgression. Since the last decades of the C20 historical scholarship, cultural analysis, and philosophical reflection centered on the body have flourished, spawning an appropriate conceptual vocabulary, referring to **docile bodies**, **(bodily) regimes, surveillance (of bodies)**, biopower and biosociality, grotesqueness and abjection. This coincided with the evolution of social and political theories which articulate and foreground the significance of living in and through the body and the bodily dimensions of social life, employing terms such as **embodiment**, corporeality, inscription (on the body), performance, and performativity.

Maureen McNeil

See: *HUMAN, GENE/GENETIC, NATURE.*

Bureaucracy

The term **bureaucracy** brings together under one heading a wide variety of concepts and ideas. It often functions as a loose cover for a diverse and frequently paradoxical range of complaints about the inequities of central government, of the inherent dysfunctions of formal organizations applying rules to cases, and the ceaseless instrumental rationalization of all forms of human conduct. However, it also carries a specific, technical meaning referring to a body of officials and the procedures, tasks, and ethical codes regulating their conduct within a particular system of administration. It is often difficult to separate out the popular pejorative and technical meanings of the term. As early as 1764, for instance, the French philosopher Baron de Grimm referred to "an illness in France which bids fair to play havoc with us; this illness is called bureaumania," and John Stuart Mill, writing in 1837, referred to "that vast network of administrative tyranny...that system of bureaucracy."

The word is generally considered to derive from F *bureau*, meaning a "writing desk" (more specifically, the cloth covering such a desk) but also a place where officials worked. The addition of a suffix, derived from the Gk for "rule," resulted in a term with a remarkable capacity for cultural mobility. Greek concepts of government having long been domesticated in the European languages, the new term quite easily underwent the same transliterations as "democracy" and "aristocracy," quickly becoming a central feature of international political discourse. The F *bureaucratie* rapidly translated into G *Bureaukratie*, It *burocrazia*, and the English and North American *bureaucracy*. Furthermore, in keeping with the derivatives of "democracy," accompanying "bureaucracy" were **bureaucrat**, **bureaucratic**, and **bureaucratization** (Albrow, 1970: 17). It is not surprising, therefore, that early dictionary definitions of "bureaucracy" were remarkably consistent. *The dictionary of the French Academy* accepted the word in its 1789 supplement, defining it as "Power, influence of the heads and staff of governmental bureaux." An Italian technical dictionary of 1828 referred to it thus: "Neologism, signifying the power of officials in public administration" (both from Albrow, 1970: 17–18). From its earliest deployment, then, the term "bureaucracy" not only refers to a form of governance (public and private) where an important governing role is in the hands of administrative officials; it also functions as a collective designation for those officials.

Most modern analyses of bureaucracy begin with the classic work of Max Weber (1978), who provided the definitive analysis of both the technical and ethical characteristics of bureaucracy – an analysis that also has the significant explanatory advantage of not sliding into pejorative critique. According to Weber, a bureaucracy, whether in public or private administration, establishes a relation between legally instituted authorities and their subordinate officials which is characterized by the following: defined rights and duties, prescribed in written rules that are preserved in files; authority relations between positions which are organized hierarchically; appointment and promotion based on fixed criteria such as merit or seniority; expertise in a given area, normally certified by examination, as a formal condition of employment; fixed monetary salaries; and a strict separation of incumbent from office, in the sense that officials do not own and cannot appropriate to themselves the position they occupy. **Bureaucratic administration** is thus a full-time job, a career, and **bureaucratic office-holding** is a vocation: it constitutes a particular, non-sectarian comportment of the person. For Weber, it is the honor of bureaucrats not to allow their "personal" commitments – to kith, kin, class, or political belief – to determine the manner in which they perform the administrative duties of their office.

The resulting impersonality has been represented by critics as one of the key pathologies to which all bureaucracies are presumed to be subject. In effect, the bureaucratic form of organization is assumed to require humans to act in ways that are regarded as inherently inhuman. This, though, as Weber pointed out, underplays the ways in which individuals are implicated in bureaucracies *qua* roles rather than *qua* the essence of human units. Furthermore, it is to occlude the ways in which in modern, highly specialized, and complex societies, **bureaucratic impersonality** – precisely because of its procedural imperviousness to overriding moral imperatives – is capable of forming a substantive defense against the arbitrary exercise of power.

Most **state bureaux** indicate a great deal of concern with jurisdiction, fixed rules, and written (including electronic) record-keeping, for instance. This, in turn, has made them susceptible to the sorts of criticisms leveled at Weber's ideal type: red tape, conservatism, and inflexibility. Because public institutions have come to be seen as the "epitome" of Weberian bureaucracy, understood pejoratively as a portmanteau term for the defects of large organizations, it is not that surprising that they have continually been subject to calls for their reform or "modernization." Indeed, not only has the idea that **public bureaucracies** need reforming gained a somewhat axiomatic status, but there has often been extensive, though by no means complete, agreement concerning the nature and direction of the required change. Over the last two to three decades, for instance, tolerably similar problematizations of public bureaux and of the core ingredients for their reform have emerged from a variety of locales, and these have over time come to be known collectively as "new managerialism." Central to this program of reform is an attempt to improve the efficiency, economy, and effectiveness (outcomes) of public bureaux through exposing them to the vicissitudes of a governmentally constituted set of quasi-market relations.

These market-type mechanisms are designed to change the ethical codes governing the conduct of public business, by motivating public organizations to mimic the perceived competitive conduct of private enterprises. Such developments have at their core an antipathy to bureaucracy, and are represented as the means through which the rigidities and inflexibilities of that organizational form are to be overcome via an infusion of market-framed entrepreneurialism. Yet they are generally held to have presided over a vast, expensive, and expanding network of audit regimes that is now regularly (and perhaps mistakenly) referred to as "bureaucratic" (Strathern, 2000), but which arguably lacks the integrality, flexibility, and suppleness of the classic Weberian bureau (du Gay, 2000; Law, 2000).

Paul du Gay

See: *GOVERNMENT, MANAGEMENT, PERSON, STATE.*

19

Canon

The word **canon**, from Gk *kanon* meaning a "rule, law, or decree," has a wide range of applications in religion, the arts, law, and literature. The **canonical books** of the Bible were those that were seen as inspired, or certified by ecclesiastical authority, as the authentic word of God, and were contrasted with the apocryphal books of doubtful authority. **Canonization** of a saint is a quasi-judicial process that involves the sifting of evidence of miracles and the records of a saintly life, prior to official church recognition of sainthood. The meaning that most concerns contemporary culture, however, is the question of **literary canons**, the lists of great writers who are usually included in literary anthologies, discussed in the major books of literary history, and taught in schools and universities as the standard texts that are understood to be the heritage of a common literary culture.

Although the term can be (and has been) extended beyond literature to the other arts, it is important to retain awareness of its origins in specifically textual and scriptural traditions, where it is anything but a static or monolithic notion of power and authority. Even within the canon of biblical writings, for instance, there is an explicit conflict between priestly and prophetic traditions of textual reception (Bruns, 1984: 70–2). The prophet Jeremiah was fully capable of challenging the "vain pen of the scribes" and the authority of the Talmud itself (Jeremiah 8:8–9). Insofar as the canon is associated with established law, the entire Christian narrative is one in which the authority of scribes and priests is overturned by a new dispensation. The very idea of the **canon as law, rule, or authoritative text**, therefore, inevitably entails the moment when the law is violated and transformed, the rules rewritten, and the text's authority challenged or replaced by a new utterance. A canon is not a closed,

ABC**D**EFGHIJKLMNOPQRSTUVWXYZ

absolute system, then, but a dynamic, evolving entity that can be reopened, reinterpreted, and reshaped.

The idea of a **secular literary canon** (like that of the **biblical canon**) may be associated with that other great modern institution, the nation. The great writers of a nation, or (by extension) of a people or culture or even a class, thus constitute the repository of cultural capital (Bourdieu, 1984) in which fundamental shared values are to be located, and precedents for new literary achievements may be based. A canon in this sense is virtually equivalent to a tradition or heritage, insofar as it is grounded in a repertoire of narratives, fables, proverbs, exemplary heroes, legends, and principles, whether written or unwritten. Matthew Arnold's notion of touchstones, texts and other cultural productions that seem to exemplify "the best that has been known and said" is often cited as a prime example of the operation of canons. Arnold's clerisy, a kind of secular priesthood of cultural values, continues the association of canons with religious texts and priestly authority (Arnold, 1873: preface).

The question arises, then: how do canons change over time? What are the processes that can lead to change or even to the overturning of a canon? And (most fundamentally) is it possible for a culture or society to exist without canons? This last question might seem frivolous, were it not for the recent history of critical reflection on canons and **canonicity** that has raised exactly this issue. During most of the C20, questions of canon-formation and the values that underlie them were generally ignored in literary study. In the lC20, the study of canons and values suddenly re-emerged as a self-conscious literary topic. The "exile of evaluation" has been attributed by some to conservative humanism and the vain hope of literary scholars for a scientific, "value-free" formulation of their work (Frye, 1969; B. H. Smith, 1988). An equally compelling story would suggest that the coherence of the American and English literary canon began to come under pressure in the 1960s, precisely at the moment that the United States began its climb to supremacy as the world's leading economic and military power, and to establish the English language as a global lingua franca. Both the UK and the US have, over the last half century, experienced a shift in population distribution associated with the break-up of the British Empire, on the one hand, and the emergence of an American empire on the other.

The rise of cultural studies in England was thus associated with new working-class movements and the immigration of non-white citizens of the empire into the British Isles from India, Africa, and the Caribbean. The post-World War II generation of American students became much more diverse in terms of race, class, and gender than any previous cohort of students. Challenges to the **established canon** of "dead white male European" authors came from women, people of color, and first-generation academics who lacked the automatic reverence for traditional literary culture that sustains the stability of a canon. The rise of new academic formations such as women's and gender studies, African-American studies, studies in film, visual culture, and mass culture were accompanied by skeptical and suspicious critical modes (most famously deconstruction and poststructuralism more generally) imported mainly from France. The English and American literary canons buckled under the stress as new literary and non-literary texts began to invade college classrooms, and new ways of reading sprang up on every side. Shakespeare's *Tempest* and Milton's *Paradise Lost* were reinterpreted in relation to postcolonial themes; a new literary and cultural history emerged, in which previously unheard or silenced voices were put into circulation; new anthologies of writings by women and people of color appeared; and previously marginal or minority authors began to crowd onto center stage.

Conservative reaction to these developments raised alarms about the erosion of standards and the loss of fundamental values. The question of the canon became central, in the US, to what were called "the culture wars," and efforts were mounted to roll back the tide of new writers, and to reinstall the traditional canon (Bloom, 1995). Accusations of political correctness, specters of anarchy, unbridled relativism, skepticism, and nihilism filled the op-ed pages of American newspapers, and "Western civilization" was declared to be in grave danger from tenured radicals and multiculturalism. On the left, an equally vulgar reduction of canons to thinly veiled instruments of ideology and tools of domination by dead white males kept the public debate at a fairly low level. Nevertheless, there were efforts at balanced critical investigation into the nature of canons. Some feminist critics went beyond efforts to enlarge the canon, or construct rival, women-centered canons, by seeking to "disrupt the canonical economy as such" (Froula, 1984: 150) with appeals to antinomian, anti-authoritarian precedents such as gnosticism. Other critics tried to re-assert the independence of literary and cultural values from politics and ideology, arguing that the "possible worlds" provided by great art help to prevent "our suspicious attitudes from becoming sufficient accounts of literary works" (Altieri, 1984: 62).

At the beginning of the C21 it seems clear that the notion of **"the" canon**, as an exclusive body of texts whose members are absolutely fixed, is an authoritarian fantasy that no longer exists. There are now multiple canons, and emergent hybrid formations such as "world literature" that are anything but stable or fixed. The study of **canon-formation** and de-formation (Guillory, 1993), however, is now an established field of critical and historical study in its own right.

W. J. T. Mitchell

See: *HERITAGE, POLITICAL CORRECTNESS, VALUE.*

Capitalism

Capitalism refers to a "system which favors the existence of capitalists." A lC19 term, it draws on earlier references (from the C17) to capital as financial ownership of, or investment in, economic enterprises (in the form of stock, shares, or money invested), denoting a distinctive form of private property. Raymond Williams suggests that "capital" drew on more generalized meanings of "chief" or "head" (from L *caput*) (R. Williams, 1976: 51). Subsequent associations with issues of ownership, control, and power seem to confirm this. Historically, **merchant capitalism** – or "mercantilism" – has been used to describe the international trading systems of European cities and states developed from the C14 (Florence, Venice, the Netherlands). However, "capitalism" has been more precisely associated with the system that combined industrialized or factory production with a "free market" for the exchange of money and commodities that developed in Europe in the C19. As an economic system, capitalism has gained increasing dominance, displacing feudal and peasant economies and outlasting its apparent modern competitor (communism, sometimes known as **state capitalism**). Capitalism has been universalized as the "one best way," or at least as the system to which there is no effective alternative. In the eC21, capitalism has embraced, or been embraced by, most societies, linking them in a world market system (sometimes called globalization).

Because the term was originally coined and used by critics (Marxists and socialists, especially), the friends of capitalism have tended to use other, less pejorative, terms – the free market, free enterprise, the market society, entrepreneurialism, and so on. Increasingly, however, the social and geographical dominance achieved by the **capitalist system** seems to have rendered the term less controversial. The critical meanings of the term are strongly associated with Marx's investigations into the workings of the **capitalist mode of production**, especially in the three volumes of *Capital*, the first of which appeared in 1867. Marx's historical materialist method made the mode of production of material life the center of studies of historical development, social structure, and political conflict.

The capitalist mode of production was distinctive in several ways, not least the role played by capital – a fluid and mobile form of property that drove the process of production. Capital changed its shape – sometimes appearing in the form of money, sometimes as the factors of production: materials, premises, machinery, and particularly labor power. A specific form of labor power was also distinctive to capitalism: workers had to enter the labor market and sell their capacity to labor in order to achieve the means of subsistence. In this respect, capitalism differed from earlier modes of production where workers had access to other means of subsistence (agriculture, or simple commodity production for use and exchange). In capitalism, workers were dependent on the wage. For Marx, this dependency was central to the way in which surplus value was produced and extracted. The workers took part in free market exchange – selling their labor (like any other commodity) for as good a price as they could gain. Once purchased, however, the labor power of the worker became the capitalist's to exploit as intensively as he (or she) could manage.

In one of the most engaging passages from *Capital*, Marx captures the transition between free exchange in the market and exploitation in the workplace ("the hidden abode of production"):

23

> When we leave this sphere of simple circulation or the exchange of commodities, which provides the "free-trader vulgaris" with his views, his concepts and the standard by which he judges the society of capital and wage-labour, a certain change takes place, or so it appears, in the physiognomy of our dramatis personae. He who was previously the money-owner now strides out in front as a capitalist; the possessor of labour-power follows as his worker. The one smirks self-importantly and is intent on business; the other is timid and holds back, like someone who has brought his own hide to market and has nothing else to expect but – a tanning. (Marx, 1976[1867]: 280)

For Marxists, all the expansive, innovative and dynamic qualities of the capitalist mode of production have their basis in this relationship between the **capitalist class** and the proletariat. Different phases or periods of capitalism identify how the control and direction of labor power have been organized – simple manufacture (bringing together workers in one place – the origins of the factory system) being superseded by machinofacture (subjecting labor power to the mechanized production line). Subsequently, other phases have been identified. "Imperialism" referred to the competitive domination of colonized nations by Western capitalist states as a means of securing raw material, labor, and markets. "Fordism" referred to the combination of mass production and mass consumption (most developed in C20 USA), involving a social and political compromise between capital and organized labor (in its predominantly white male character). Fordism's crises – the failures of accumulation and profitability – have led some to talk about a shift to "post-Fordism," marked by "flexible accumulation" strategies of investment and labor process organization developed by increasingly mobile – or transnational – capital.

The constant striving of capitalist innovation – a distinctively Marxist emphasis – reflected the effort needed to extract surplus value from the labor process and to overcome the contradictions and antagonisms inherent in the class relations of the capitalist mode of production. This explains why, from the Marxist perspective, capitalism is essentially a system of class conflict and one where class interest and identities are formed and forged in the social relations of production. Other struggles, divisions, and conflicts are secondary to, or derive from, this primary antagonism. Capital must constantly strive to subjugate labor: labor must constantly strive to resist the powers of capital. Others have identified different elements as the central features of capitalism. For some, it has been the entrepreneurial spirit of risk-taking that distinguishes capitalism from other economic systems, which, in turn, legitimates the rewards (profits) that can accrue from being enterprising (Gilder, 1981). Here a stress is laid on deregulation to enable the fullest flowering of enterprise. For some, it has been the market as a co-ordinating institution that has provided the key dynamic, generating individual enterprise and social openness (Hayek, 1944). In this view, the market underwrites a social and political individualism that forms a basis for resisting collectivist or totalitarian forms of rule. In contrast, Polanyi (2001) argued that to function effectively, markets needed to be socially "embedded," and that "free markets" are an impossible, and socially dangerous, vision.

Not surprisingly, there are long-standing arguments about the relationships between capitalism as an economic system and forms of social and political arrangement. Most commentators have seen capitalism as a liberating force – breaking up "traditional" societies and political systems. Marx emphasized the progressive force of capitalism, and the capitalist class, in challenging the old order of feudalism and promoting universalist conceptions of individual liberty against absolutist and monarchical states. Advocates of capitalism continue to stress this "liberating" potential, seeing the spread of market freedoms (alongside free markets) as contributing to the fall of Eastern European socialism, the "opening up" of the Chinese economy (officially known as "socialism with capitalist characteristics"), the development of the Asian Tiger economies, and so on. It is the promise of globalization that entry into the capitalist system modernizes societies as well as creating wealth. This includes an expectation that capitalism has a strong association, or affinity, with liberal democracy as a political system. Indeed, some Marxists argued that (bourgeois) democracy formed the best possible shell for capitalism as it institutionalized and regulated class conflict in ways that enabled continuing **capital accumulation**.

The evidence is a little more ambiguous. The modernizations effected by capitalism tend to be concentrated in the market realm – turning labor power into a commodity by destroying other means of subsistence; creating an array of market choices in commodities and services; and dismantling "non-productive" or "non-profitable" forms of economic and social activity. Sometimes, such changes are associated with the liberalization or democratization of other social institutions (the family, religion, and so on), but not inevitably. There are arguments that the spread of "liberalizing" capitalism has driven the revival of other "traditions" (particularly of religion and ethnicity). Similarly, there are questions about whether capitalism needs democratic political systems. Capitalism seems to have coexisted, more or less happily, with a variety of political systems: racially structured states (South Africa), totalitarian regimes (Indonesia), military juntas (Chile), fascist states (Germany), systems of slavery (Britain, the USA), as well as liberal democracies. For some, the dynamics of globalization have raised questions about whether capitalism needs nation states at all.

These issues have also been important for arguments about the relationship between capitalism and welfare states. For much of the C20, there appeared to be some connection between levels of **capitalist development** and the provision of welfare by the state. This connection was by no means automatic: welfare was one of the sites of political conflict between organized labor and capital in the context of democratic political systems. Welfare, as the British politician Lloyd George once said, "is the ransom property must pay" for continued security. In the period following World War II, the industrialized capitalist economies of North America and Europe created developed welfare states as part of social and political accommodations with labor (and other social groups), which stabilized the conditions of capital accumulation (part of the Fordist period). However, by

25

the end of the C20, the same countries were "reforming" their welfare systems – reducing costs, making welfare more conditional, and re-emphasizing labor market incentives ("welfare-to-work" or "workfare"). Once again, those who support the idea that capitalism as an economic system is inevitably linked to particular types of social or political arrangement need to consider the very diverse and changeable forms of cohabitation.

Capitalism has continued to be an expansive and dynamic system despite the recurrent hopes of critics that events will sound its "death knell" (or that the proletariat will prove to be its "grave diggers"). It has shown a capacity to create new markets, by creating new products or services that produce new demand (international travel, digital technologies, etc.) or by integrating new societies into existing markets (the shift of tobacco consumption to the south and east, for example, when demand declined in the north and west). It has remained technologically innovatory, for example, in new communication technologies (which served as both new commodities and new means of production, distribution, and exchange); and in the subjection of nature to new biotechnologies. It has proved equally flexible in searching out and subjecting new labor forces to the demands of production, willing to bear the costs of geographical mobility in the quest for labor forces that are inexperienced, un-unionized, and unprotected. Flexibility and cheapness are highly valued characteristics of labor power. In the process, deindustrialization in North American and European economies has accompanied the transfer of production processes to South America and Asia.

Perhaps capitalism is essentially contradictory. It combines a restless geographical expansion with the capacity to make everywhere become more of the same. It produces wealth in a variety of forms, while deepening inequalities within and between societies. It celebrates individualism while exercising autocratic powers over labor forces within the enterprise. It champions freedom for all, but as Anatole France remarked, this is the freedom for rich and poor alike to sleep under the bridges of Paris. It depends upon human creativity and innovation while its markets aim at the lowest common denominator to maximize sales. It promises fulfillment while delivering disappointment and despair. It claims its subjection to the rule of law while treating bribery, corruption, and fraud as everyday business practices. Capitalism may be the "only game in town," but it is a mechanism for producing and reproducing winners and losers. Small wonder, then, that it continues to create critics and opponents even as it is proclaimed as the universal, the necessary, the natural, and the best way of organizing human society.

John Clarke

See: *CLASS, COLONIALISM, COMMODITY, ECONOMY, GLOBALIZATION, MARKET, SOCIALISM, WELFARE.*

Celebrity

Celebrity is today used to describe a particular kind of cultural figure. They will usually have emerged from the sports or entertainment industries; they will be visible through the media; and their private lives will attract greater public interest than their professional lives. The celebrity's fame does not necessarily depend on the position or achievements that gave them their prominence in the first instance. Rather, their fame is likely to have outstripped the claims to prominence developed within that initial location. Indeed, the modern celebrity may claim no special achievements other than the attraction of public attention; they are "famous for being famous" (Boorstin, 1973). Consequently, celebrities in the C21 excite a level of public interest that some regard as disproportionate. While this excessiveness may be an intrinsic element of the celebrity's appeal, it is also why celebrity is so often regarded as the epitome of the inauthenticity of mass-mediated popular culture.

The earliest, C17, meaning of the word "celebrity" refers to the "due observance of rites and ceremonies." The mC19 usage is closer to its current meaning, referring to someone who was "much talked about." The connotations acquired over the C20 emphasized both the excessive cultural prominence of the celebrity and the gradual disconnection of this prominence from a sense of legitimacy (P.D. Marshall, 1997). Where "celebrity" once referred to a solemn process of ritual celebration whose legitimacy was relatively unquestioned, it now refers to the popular representation of a cultural figure whose fame is definitive but of questionable legitimacy.

Celebrity is in one sense a mode of representation. As such, it is the product of the rise of the mass media, particularly the electronic media. As newspapers developed and photography was integrated into the reporting of news in the lC19 and eC20, the conditions for celebrity fell into place. With the development of the cinema and the industrial production of the film star, followed by television and the television personality, the media industries became increasingly dependent upon marketing these individuals as a means of attracting audiences to their products. More recently, with the concentration of media ownership and the diversification of media business interests, as well as the development of convergent new media technologies, celebrities are traded like commodities across media platforms and global markets.

The objects of this process have not always been described as celebrities. For most of the C20, they were more likely to be referred to as stars. That term was to some extent displaced by the sheer scale of the proliferation of fame in the 1980s and 1990s. Prior to this, the movie star and the sports star were the primary object of media and public attention. But there are significant differences between these stars and the celebrity. The movie actor or the athlete became a star through a series of achievements – the accretion of associations built up in an exchange with their audiences over repeated performances. Their prominence was closely related to their work. Furthermore, as Richard Dyer argued (1979, 1986), stars may have operated as signs – as carriers of social myths and meanings. Particular stars reflected dominant definitions of "the type of the individual" within their society, and so their significance was socially grounded. The fame of the star had an appropriateness: their celebrity was deserved, they "spoke of" the society, and they even performed important cultural functions.

The shift from the star to the celebrity involves the shedding of much of that significance. Where the star developed their meanings over time, the celebrity erupts into prominence and may disappear just as quickly. Also, audiences regard the celebrity more ambiguously: their success is as likely to be attributed to good fortune as to ability, and they may be objects of derision as well as of desire. Consequently, whereas the star had a certain authenticity that made it possible to argue they served a social function, it has proved more difficult to make such arguments about celebrities, who seem defined by their constructedness.

Yet this distinction can be qualified. Certainly, the capriciousness of fame has occupied commentators throughout the C20 (Braudy, 1986). Boorstin (1973) saw the media presence of film stars and television personalities as emblematic of the phoniness of contemporary popular culture and the kinds of transcendence it appears to offer. Such criticism sharpens at the end of the C20: new kinds of celebrity begin to appear as the television and music industries set out to manufacture their stars, effectively, from nothing. The Spice Girls and the international franchising of the *Big Brother* TV format are the two most obvious examples of this trend. Earlier examples exist – TV's *The Monkees*, for instance – but in the 1990s TV invested in a range of programming formats, all aimed directly at **the production of celebrity**. Celebrity became a career option; the activity required to produce it was a secondary consideration.

Fame now enjoys an unprecedented visibility. Not only do the electronic media offer a greatly expanded set of opportunities, but the mass magazine market, particularly women's magazines, has reinvented itself as the pre-eminent site for the circulation of **celebrity news** – itself, effectively, a new genre of mainstream (rather than special interest) media content.

The new pervasiveness of celebrity has raised questions about its cultural function. Among the provocations to such questions was the international public reaction to the death of Diana, princess of Wales, in 1997 (Kear and Steinberg, 1999). Some saw this reaction as evidence that the public could be manipulated by the media to exhibit quite irrational behavior. Others argued that we can indeed develop relationships with people we know only through the media, in ways that are similar to our relationships with "real" friends and acquaintances (Rojek, 2001).

Celebrity remains a highly ambiguous concept and its operation is often treated with great skepticism. Individual celebrities may overcome this by convincing their public of their authenticity, but the concept itself is seen by many as representing the triumph of the image over the substance, and of the representation over the real.

Graeme Turner

See: *POPULAR, SIGN.*

Citizenship

Citizenship is associated historically with the rise of the European city, the virtues of civility, the institutions of civil society, and the spread of urban civilization. **Citizen** is derived from *cité* as in the Anglo-F *citeseyn, citezein,* or *sithezein.* From the C13, a citizen was simply a member or denizen (*deinsein*) of a city or borough. Caxton in his *Chronicles of England* referred in 1480 to "The cytezeyns of London" and Shakespeare in *The Taming of the Shrew* (1596) describes Pisa as "renowned for graue Citizens." These early references to "citizenship" indicate its limited meaning as simply the inhabitant of a city. Citizens evolved as civilized members of urban society in contrast to country folk. The contrast survived into the C19, when Ruskin in 1860 in *Modern painting* noted that the "words 'countryman . . . villager' still signify a rude and untaught person, as opposed to the words 'townsman' and 'citizen.' " In many European societies, citizenship came to be associated with a particular class position, namely the bourgeoisie. A citizen was a civilian, not a member of the landed nobility or gentry. Samuel Johnson (1755) described the citizen as a man of trade, and not a gentleman. A citizen was a burgess (bourgeois) or freeman, and citizenship was associated with bourgeois not aristocratic culture. In C19 political and economic theory, citizenship was associated with the rise of civil society. The civility of the citizen was a consequence of the pacification of the military society of the feudal aristocracy described by Norbert Elias (2000 [1939]) as "the civilizing process." Citizens were members of civil society and carriers of bourgeois civility. It is important to note that citizenship is characterized by an ambiguity: it is a conduit of individual rights but also reflects the growth of state power over civil society.

29

Although we can detect its ancestry in Greek and Roman political institutions, there is little evidence of *social* citizenship until the modern period. The growth of citizenship in ancient Greece was restricted by the exclusion of women, the presence of class divisions, and its dependence on slavery. Early Christianity also recognized, for example in St Augustine's *City of God* (1972 [413–26]), the importance of citizenship, but separated membership of secular society from citizenship of heaven. The distinction remained a traditional part of Christian teaching and as late as 1792 Bishop Horne confirmed that "our citizenship, as saith the apostle, is in heaven." We might suitably define these early forms as *political* citizenship, and argue that the revolutionary struggles that produced modernity also created modern or social citizenship. Modern citizenship has two important characteristics: it is universalistic, and it is related to the rise of the nation state. The decisive turning point in the construction of modern secular citizenship was the French Revolution, which, in the words of Rouget de Lisle, established the idea that citizens can have legitimate claims against a tyrannical state – "Aux armes, citoyens!"

Modern citizenship is a product of political revolutions – the English Civil War, the American War of Independence, and the French Revolution. These revolutions produced both modern nationalism and citizenship. The creation of nation states necessarily involved nationalistic ''imaginary communities,'' which assumed, and went a long way to create, homogeneous populations. These national communities were held together, against the divisions of class, culture, and ethnicity, by nationalistic ideologies and citizenship. From the Treaty of Westphalia (1648) onward, state-building required national forms of citizenship. The development of print, literacy, and a reading audience made possible the formation of national communities and the origins of civil society. The growth of printing was a technological change that created a vibrant public space and facilitated religious debates that undermined the conventional norms of secrecy and privilege.

In the C19 national citizenship incorporated the working class into capitalism through welfare institutions. Welfare states achieved the pacification of the working class with relatively little concession to the basic issues of class, wealth, and power. Citizenship did not undermine the class structure, and welfare capitalism avoided the revolutionary conflicts that were predicted by socialism. However, there were significant variations between capitalist regimes. In Germany, Otto von Bismarck and Kaiser Wilhelm were reluctant founders of the modern welfare state, and social citizenship was developed with few concessions to civil and political rights. This authoritarian welfare system remained in place until World War I. In Japan, the Meiji Revolution used the monarchy as a legitimating principle in its strategy of conservative modernization, and the Japanese language has no indigenous word for citizenship. Instead the Emperor Meiji in 1890 used the newly coined compound term *shinmin* to denote loyal, subordinate subjects. Russia was in the long run not successful in developing a strategy to retain power and modernize the regime. It favored repression and exclusion, followed by periods of ineffective reform. These regimes, with the possible exception of Germany's, did not develop social citizenship, and civil citizenship was periodically undercut by arbitrary political interventions.

World War I produced two new strategies: fascism and authoritarian socialism. Both were highly repressive, required powerful legitimating ideologies, and did not offer any development of civil citizenship. Both Nazi Germany and the Soviet Union made rapid steps toward social citizenship through state-driven welfare programs. Eventually fascism was defeated, by superior geopolitical alliances and by Soviet tanks rather than by the superiority of liberal democracy, but the military victories of American armies ensured the dominance of the liberal model of domestic politics, which combines civil and political liberties with some development of social citizenship.

Recent British discussions of citizenship have been dominated by T. H. Marshall's *Citizenship and social class* (1950), in which citizenship was a status position that ameliorated class inequalities resulting from a capitalist market. Marshall's theory has been criticized because it is incomplete, neglecting economic citizenship, the growth of worker's ownership, and industrial democracy. While the theory understandably assumed that British society was ethnically homogeneous, it did not address the problems that have become salient in contemporary citizenship – asylum seekers, ethnic exclusion, the status of refugees, and the politics of identity. It is interesting to contrast Marshall's British model with the American case, where ethnicity rather than class has been the crucial issue. In the United States, citizenship is associated with political membership, migration, and ethnicity rather than with welfare rights and social class. For Alexis de Tocqueville in *Democracy in America* (1968 [1835–40]), the absence of centralized, bureaucratic government had encouraged community initiative. Voluntary associations rather than the state flourished to solve local, community problems. The contemporary experience of American citizenship is expressed through a multitude of local and informal associations.

Both British and American paradigms are distinguished from the traditions of continental Europe. In Germany, citizenship (*Bildungsburgertum*) was historically connected with civility and the civilizing process. The bourgeois citizen was an educated and cultivated private person, who depended on the state to guarantee freedoms and to sustain a moral public order. In France, the radical legacy of the Revolution of 1789 was institutionalized in its educational system, which embraced universalistic and secular norms.

In the C20, the entitlements of citizenship were conditional upon work, war, and reproduction. The Marshallian citizen was a worker, a soldier, and a parent, whose social contributions were rewarded through welfare entitlements. The casualization of employment, the termination of conscription and compulsory military service, and the transformation of family life through divorce, gay and lesbian marriage, and the lone-parent household have eroded these social conditions. The economic foundations of traditional citizenship were produced by the Industrial Revolution, but the globalization of the economy has disrupted the necessary relationships between national citizenship, employment, the nuclear family, and the reproductive rights of the heterosexual couple. The neo-liberal vision of citizenship is based on welfare for work, private insurance for health care, private education, flexible retirement, self-help, and healthy lifestyles.

The neo-liberal financial revolution has severely damaged public institutions, especially schools, universities, and public broadcasting systems, that at one time underpinned social citizenship. However, ethnic division is the principal problem facing citizenship today. In *Nation-building and citizenship* Reinhard Bendix (1964) distinguished between a plebiscitarian principle, in which citizens as individuals relate directly to the state on a universalistic basis, and a functional representation principle, in which the social groups to which the individual belongs mediate the relations between individual and state. As a result, citizenship is contested and unequal. While both principles often coincide within the same state, in many African societies the growth of universalistic citizenship has been hampered by the resilience of tribal membership and local identities. However, the difficulties of universalistic citizenship are also characteristic of many European multicultural societies. In France cultural homogeneity is a precondition of republican political unity, which requires cultural assimilation through state guidance. The legacy of the Revolution is that the nation is reflected in the citizen and is produced by a unified educational system. A common educational experience creates common citizenship, but in 1989 the system was challenged by the dismissal of three Muslim students who wore headscarves to school.

31

The parliamentary bill to ban all overt religious regalia was supported by the French senate on March 3, 2004. Many socialist intellectuals view the headscarf as a symbol of patriarchal oppression and feared that the destruction of secular schools would bring about the destruction of the Republic.

Citizenship has become a contested category in cultural conflicts over identity. In many aspects of law and politics, there is a growing tension between global human rights and the social rights of national citizenship. For example, many first-nation peoples, migrant communities, and gay and lesbian couples struggle to realize their cultural rights under human rights legislation, because their social rights cannot be adequately realized within the framework of citizenship. These social changes represent a major challenge to the traditional framework of citizenship rights.

Bryan Turner

See: *CITY, CIVILIZATION, DEMOCRACY, GOVERNMENT, MULTICULTURALISM, NATION, PUBLIC, SOVEREIGNTY, WELFARE.*

City

One of the difficulties with **the city** is that, however the term is used, it invariably attempts to capture more than can be contained by a single concept. When we talk about specific cities like London, Paris, New York, New Delhi, Beijing, Sao Paolo, or Sydney, for example, we recall less their similarities than the distinctiveness of their layout, landscape, history, and (in this age of tourism and marketing) their "image" or "identity." At the same time, the idea of the city evokes a host of contradictory images and connotations: emblematic buildings or skylines; conspicuous wealth alongside poverty and overcrowding; the enigmatic city of crime novels and film noir; the public city of piazza and coffee shop; the anonymity of suburban sprawl and shopping malls. Given this diversity and elusiveness, does it make sense to suppose that cities, whether actual or imagined, have *anything* in common that warrants the use of that singular noun, the "city"?

Etymologically, "city" derives from L *civis*. Even here, the social connotations of the term preceded the geographical. The Romans designated the independent states of Gaul as *civitates*, later narrowing the term to the chief town in which civil government and episcopal authority were located. *Civitates* thus referred primarily to forms of social organization, secondarily to their bearers – **citizens** – and only then by extension to the location of citizenship. The place was still *urbs*, or in oE *burh* (borough). The use of "city" to denote large-scale urban settlements did not become the norm until as late as the eC19, at the same time as the great new **industrial and colonial cities** were emerging.

In these circumstances, "the city" came to refer, minimally, to a built settlement in a specific location, the forms of social interaction that occur in that place, and the symbolic significance of both place and process. The urban historian Lewis Mumford captures the scope of this usage: "The city is both a collection of architectural forms in space and a tissue of associations, corporate enterprises, and institutions that occupy this collective structure and have interacted with it in the course of time" (Mumford, 1968: 447).

Social scientists and urban planners have tried, forlornly, to narrow this inclusive definition by insisting that cities can be distinguished from non-cities by reference to population size and density, the range and level of economic activity, modes of transportation and communication, or styles of government. What motivates such quibbling is the political concern to identify and codify the possibilities and problems of people living together in cities – a reminder of the etymological roots of politics in Gk *polis* (city).

Cities are important politically, first, because they are centers of economic power. They have always acted as magnets and relays for people, information, goods, and capital, and thus formed networks of trade and travel – which is one reason urban populations have always been to a degree transient and migratory, as well as diverse in occupation and language. The acceleration and increasingly global scale of the flow of goods and people over recent centuries – capitalism, colonialism, imperialism – led first to the establishment of a handful of **metropolitan cities** distinct in terms of their size, economic power, and geopolitical influence, and now, under conditions of globalization and instant communication, to a dominant network of **global cities**. Hence Manuel Castells's controversial claim that the city has morphed from a place to a "space of flows" (Castells, 1989).

Cities are important politically, second, because – at least since the C19 – the city has come to signify the problem of how to manage populations. This new discourse produced new metaphors – the city as diseased body or efficient machine – and also an archive of surveys and statistics chronicling the health, literacy, criminality, and productivity of the urban population. These in turn informed new techniques of social engineering and, given an architectural twist, the town planning of Patrick Geddes, Ebenezer Howard's designs for a **garden city**, and Le Corbusier's modernist vision of a *ville radieuse*. (The hubris of this idea that architecture could build a solution to the problems of cities and society led to the reaction against the modernist movement.)

A third political connotation of cities is that, through their spatial segmentation, they render social divisions concrete: their architecture gives both physical form and symbolic expression to political realities. Especially in **capital cities**, a central core functions as the seat of secular and religious authority, but also manifests that power through the monumental scale and theatricality of its public buildings: palaces, parliaments, cathedrals, and more profane temples such as stock exchanges, museums, and theatres. Since the C19, **metropolitan cities** have typically been divided into a central business district and industrial areas, fashionable city residences and peripheral or inner-city ghettos, shopping and entertainment districts, and, increasingly, **suburbs** made possible by new forms of transportation and communication.

The city is thus an inherently political idea, as well as a political phenomenon. From the architecture as well as the histories of cities, we can decipher the management of resources and populations; the distribution of wealth, power, and life chances; and the conflict of interests and desires. But the idea of the city is also coterminous with philosophy. In his *Image of gouvernment* (1540–1), Sir Thomas Elyot (a member of Thomas More's circle) looks back to the Greek ideal of the *polis*: "Aristotle, in defining, what is a Citee, doeth not call it a place builded with houses, and enuironed with wals, but saieth that it is a companie, whiche hath sufficiencie of liuyng, and is constitute or assembled to the entent to liue well." To talk about the city is not only to talk about *where* we live ("a place builded with houses, and enuironed with wals"), or even just about the politics of *how* we live ("a companie, whiche hath sufficiencie of liuying"). The idea has always also entailed thinking about how we *want* to live, about the good life: "the entent to liue well."

This philosophical edge is evident in the language we use to describe the skills, or virtues, that citizens need if they are to live cheek by jowl with strangers. "Civility" (from *civis*) is obviously one, along with "civilization." More ambiguous is "urbanity" (from L *urbs*), with its double-edged nod to the collective nature of **city life** and the style of the **city slicker.** Even astuteness derives from the L *astutes* (craftsmen), using their wits to earn a crust, as distinct from the rights-bearing and publicly deliberating *polites* (citizens).

The philosophical connotations of the city were highlighted in the C5 when St Augustine imagined a **City of God** in deliberate contrast to earthly cities, and so established an enduring cultural opposition between ideal and actuality. Again and again over the centuries, in novels and paintings as well as in philosophical texts, the scale, venality, and illegibility of the big city are contrasted with the **heavenly city** or some secular equivalent. In the C17, Bunyan writes in *The pilgrim's progress*: "Now the way to the Cœlestial City lyes just thorow this Town [of Vanity], where this lusty Fair is kept." In the C18, when the contrast between rural utopia and corrupt city became a commonplace, Rousseau complains that the anonymity of the big city "engenders only monsters and inspires only crimes." In the eC19, at the same time as the *Bildungsroman* told of young heroes or (occasionally) heroines coming to maturity by negotiating the ethical opportunities and carnal snares of **the big city**, writers like Friedrich Schiller, Johann Gottlieb Fichte, and Freidrich Hölderlin were attempting to marry the universal principles of the Greek *polis* with the cultural particularity of medieval German towns in order to imagine ethical community as a burgher-city. At the end of the century, in the more abstract language of sociology, Ferdinand Tönnies counterposed the authentic communitarianism of *Gemeinschaft* against the mechanical solidarity of *Gesellschaft* – a contrast that re-emerges in the 1970s in Raymond Williams's mixed feelings about the possibility of community in the country and, especially, the city (R. Williams, 1973).

As such usages show, there is no clear dividing line between the physical reality of cities and their cultural representation. Cities enact and transmit culture in their very fabric. They provide an architectural backdrop for public interactions and private lives. But the city also exists in the novels we read, the pictures we look at, and the movies we watch. As a result, in the real–imagined city of the C19 and C20, a distinctively modern type of experience emerged. "The city is a state of mind," observed Robert Park, leader of the Chicago school of urban sociology, in 1915 (Park, 1967: 1). This is the city explored by scholars like Georg Simmel (1997 [1903]), Walter Benjamin (1999), Henri Lefebvre (1991), and Michel de Certeau (1984), as well as by theorists and artists inspired by the Situationist concept of psychogeography. How, they have all asked in their different ways, are social forces and relations crystallized in the fabric, institutions, and encounters of the city? And how is that external reality then translated into the interiority of modern experience? The history of the word suggests that, if anywhere, it is *between* the two that the city exists.

James Donald

See: *CIVILIZATION, COUNTRY, PLACE, SPACE.*

Civilization

The OED is a **civilizational project**, dedicated to improving general use of the English language. Its genealogies of English usage model a key feature of **civilizational thinking**: the creation of legacies that not only set standards but also define a cultural space, in this case, English. Awareness of this frame alerts us to its erasure of the globally collaborative histories through which even words at the center of world power are shaped. The OED offers a **civilizational history** of the term "civilization."

35

According to the OED, "civilization" has been used since the lC18 to refer to "the action or process of civilizing or of being civilized." "Civilization is the humanization of man in society," said Arnold in 1879. The OED also points to the use of the term from the lC18 to denote "a developed or advanced state of human society." Examples stress the intersection between pre-modern empires and the colonial encounter. Buckle's 1857 *Civilization* characterizes Egyptian civilization as one which "forms a striking contrast to the barbarism of the other nations of Africa," while differentiating "the civilization of Europe" for its "capacity of development unknown to those civilizations which were originated by soil."

Raymond Williams's *Keywords* opens scholarly and political potentials within this project, offering a rich history of words that allows users to savor and question their meanings. But this is also a civilizational project, teaching the reader to select an English legacy from all our possible pasts. In *Keywords*, Williams traces the association of civilization with "the general spirit of the Enlightenment, with its emphasis on secular and progressive human self-development," as well as its "associated sense of modernity" (R. Williams, 1976: 58). Civilization comes to stand for a "whole modern social process," including (in the thinking of John Stuart Mill, for instance) an increase in knowledge and physical comfort, the decline of superstition, the rise of forward-moving nations, the growth of freedom, but also "loss of independence, the creation of artificial

wants, monotony, narrow mechanical understanding, inequality and hopeless poverty"
(R. Williams, 1983: 58). Williams notes "a critical moment when civilization was used in
the plural" (1983: 59), beginning in French usage in the eC19. From the C19 until the eC21,
the slippage of the term "civilization" between its singular and plural uses has offered a logic
of universal historical destiny to particular racial, religious, and cultural authorities.

Civilization became essential to discussions in anthropology and history in the lC19.
In anthropology, the concept was associated with evolutionary distinctions contrasting
civilization with savagery and barbarism. In history, the concept laid out world regions
associated with imperial state-building and religious conversion. By the mC20, English
discussion – influenced by criticisms of evolutionism – turned to the ahistorical and
relativizing term "culture." Williams's interest in civilization derived from his project to
democratize the idea of culture. Yet other Western legacies kept civilization alive. In 1939,
Norbert Elias (2000) traced the history of French and German commitments to the
concept of civilization. French reformers used the term "civilization" in the mC18, he
argues, to stress the importance of improving elite culture and politics – from within the
elite world of manners. In contrast, German thinkers saw *zivilisation* as an affectation that
could not substitute for the more genuine morality of *kultur.* Elias uses his Germanic
perspective to offer a critical history of the **civilizing process**, in which increasing self-
restraint in everyday human behavior creates an uncomfortable but regularized modernity.
Meanwhile, C20 French thinkers continued to find civilization a productive tool for reform.

Neither Elias nor Williams takes us to the edges of empire, where much word- and
world-making has occurred. Civilization had an explicit influence in world-making in the
period when Europeans established world hegemony, from the mC19 through the mC20.
European expansion was justified as a project of civilization. It did civilize, in the sense of
bringing non-European elites into European ideas of civilization. Non-European elites
made civilization their own, reshaping the concept to forge anti-colonial and nationalist
struggles. Who would inherit the mantle of civilization? Claimants vied for the term and
the world-making heritage it implied. These contests show civilization coming into its
meanings through a globe-traversing, culture-crossing process of translation and contention. Following the "traveling theory" of civilization requires moving in and out of
particular linguistic environments and modes of cultural politics.

Japan in the lC19 and eC20 was an important site for translations of the civilizational
thinking of European expansionism. During the Meiji period (1868–1912), Western civilization became an explicit goal of the reconfigured, emperor-centered state, supporting the
drive for Japanese national strength and fueling Japanese imperialist expansion. In the
1870s and 1880s, translators relied on Chinese characters to translate foreign words, either
adding new meaning to the characters (as with "civilization") or using existing characters to
coin new words (such as "freedom" or "right"). The English word "civilization" was
rendered into Japanese by the neologism *bunmeikaika*, which was written with Chinese
characters but departed from earlier Japanese identifications with Chinese civilization.

Civilization became an official state project: priests appointed by the national government preached throughout Japan on topics including "civilization and enlightenment." The rural populace did not easily accept this program. Many associated civilization and enlightenment with foreigners and with the fearful figure of the blood-sucking stranger. Civilization was sometimes understood temporally, as a state entered into by different societies at different moments, but it was more frequently rendered spatially, and ambitious nation-builders set out to transform Japan into Westernized space. In 1883, prominent critic and educator Fukuzawa Yukichi argued that an elaborate Tokyo palace for the emperor was necessary as a sign of civilization and progress, so that Japan could confer with other nations on an equal footing. He described civilization as a universal development whose initial location in Europe was incidental; Japan, too, could attain it. Well into the eC20 in Japan, civilization meant world civilization. Japan was qualified to participate because of its growing modernity (Figal, 1999; Fujitani, 1996; Howland, 1996, 2002).

Moving through heterogeneous channels, Japanese versions of civilization shaped a variety of social improvement movements – including anti-colonial movements – across Asia. Between 1894 and 1905, Japan gained "civilized" status in international law; others hoped to follow. Japan's complex identification of civilization with the West disrupted earlier patterns of civilizational thinking in China. Accompanied by a growth in Japanese political strength and military might, it helped to destabilize the loyalties of Chinese elites, many of whom went to Japan in search of thinking and technologies that would help them to reconfigure their own place in the world. In Tokyo, Chinese intellectuals joined others from throughout Asia and its diasporic populations to explore pan-Asianism, anarchism, Marxism, and the reconfiguration of gendered relations (Duara 2001; Karl, 2002). Civilizational debates were actively pursued in Chinese journals well into the 1920s. In China and Korea, Japanese-inspired "pan-Asianism," expressed in intellectual debate as well as religious societies, inspired attention to the "spiritual" qualities of "Asian civilization" – at least until Japan's wartime mobilization, and subsequent defeat, discredited these projects. Most young Chinese intellectuals rejected claims to a unified civilizational order in favor of the language of nation, modernity, and revolution. Yet nation and civilization were tightly linked: nation-building was taken as a sign of a higher form of civilization (Duara, 2001).

37

These developments traveled widely. In Dutch colonial Java, for example, Javanese students were impressed when Japanese were granted "European" status; they formed their own civilizational aspirations, particularly after Chinese nationalists in Java offered them the nation as a model for social and cultural mobilization (Pramoedya, 1991a, 1991b). Nation and civilization moved together conceptually through Europe's colonies.

Gandhi's reported quip about **Western civilization** ("It would be a good idea") sums up these great debates: who would be the proper inheritors of the legacy of human improvement? European powers claimed civilization as the reason for their far-flung conquests. Were not the colonial powers enlightening the natives, who had lived until then as savages?

Civilization

But by the eC20, non-Europeans used this very rhetoric to object: was not colonialism a form of savagery to be resisted for the cause of freedom, justice, and equality, the very dreams of which the Europeans spoke so highly? As European critics were also noting (Adas, 1993), was not "Western civilization" limited, warlike, and materialistic? Might Europe's Others carry civilization toward a brighter future?

Civilization has been a player in diverse and contradictory debates. Consider education. In the 1950s and 1960s, French secondary education became embroiled in a fight over "*civilization*" as understood through the history of Ferdinand Braudel (1994). Braudelians wanted to move beyond a one-thing-after-another narrative of French history to teach global social history: civilization was the concept to open this door. Civilization lost and French political history was reinstated. Meanwhile, in the United States, a very different educational battle had begun to unfold.

The US university took up the cause of Western civilization during World War I. The first course was started at Columbia University in 1919 "as a 'war baby', born of the struggle to make the world safe for democracy" (Allardyce, 1982: 706). Similar courses, which brought US citizens inside the heritage of Europe, spread around the country. Courses in Western civilization were mainstays of US college education through the 1960s, at which point educators began to question the exclusion of non-white authors and non-European legacies of scholarship. In the 1970s and 1980s, new courses were organized to offer a more culturally inclusive education; this current became identified as **multiculturalism**. Multicultural curricula stimulated a virulent backlash particularly from conservative alumni, a key source of university funding. A small war broke out in academe in the 1980s, as multiculturalism and civilization were pitted against each other as opposing educational philosophies (Pratt, 1992).

Samuel Huntington's (1993) "The clash of civilizations?" had a powerful impact on this debate by arguing that the term "civilization" was not just relevant to teaching students about the past; civilization might be the organizing feature of post-Cold War politics. With the decline of the nation state, he argued, religion-based cultural politics would be at the base of world order and disorder. His argument, developed further in Huntington (1996), requires the patriotic consolidation of white Christian Western civilization against its competitors and potential enemies, at home and abroad. Huntington's homogeneous and tightly bounded civilizations resonate nicely with those still taught (despite a generation of historians who have refused such boundaries) in world history textbooks (Segal, 2000). Their familiarity and simplicity – as well as their apparent opening to pluralist appropriations – made them immensely charismatic. In the 1990s, conferences on civilizational clash and dialogue were convened across the world.

When US president George W. Bush championed a war of the worlds in 2001, the revised rhetoric of civilization was ready and waiting for him. Bush first turned to the Crusades as his image of war, but he was quickly criticized for alienating Muslim allies. Civilization was safer: on the one hand, it called to mind "Christian civilization" and the specific cultural mobilization against the infidel that he required for the wars; on the other hand, it evoked global civility, and who could be opposed to that? One project aimed to discipline critical scholars by demanding that universities focus on "defending civilization" (Martin and Neal, 2001).

Meanwhile, civilization has proved a useful rhetoric for distinguishing between legitimate and illegitimate forms of warfare. The civilized must punish the uncivilized by any means necessary. In this use of the term "civilization," the Bush administration reached back to colonial precedent. European colonial rule required the unrestrained punishment of the uncivilized for the good of civilization (Lindqvist, 1996). Through this history of civilized slaughter, indeed, the Bush administration's repetition of the term "civilization" invoked a Western civilizational heritage, although not an admirable one.

Anna Tsing and Gail Hershatter

See: *CULTURE, EDUCATION, MODERN, MULTICULTURALISM, NATION, WEST.*

Class

In its most conventional and persistent sense, **class** refers to "a division or order... or rank or grade of society," common in the phrases "higher (upper), middle, lower classes." However, to aficionados of **class distinction**, such crude divisions are susceptible to infinite refinement. Each component may be subdivided, revealing such locations as upper-middle, middle-lower-middle, and so on. It is commonly observed that C18 and C19 British society was particularly obsessed with the niceties and observances of class in this sense, reflected in the novels of Jane Austen, for example (1996 [1813]). However, to say anything is "common" is to immediately risk its disparagement as belonging to the lower (uncivilized and uncultured) classes.

This sense of class – as a social ordering that articulated privilege and deference – has been at the heart of much British controversy about the **class system** and how to overcome it. It was institutionalized in political systems (the House of Lords and the monarchy persisting in a parliamentary democracy), in education systems (the persistence of private education and its privileged routes in universities and employment), and in a variety of cultural and social forms. Elitism, privilege, hereditary advantage, and snobbery have been constant focal points of social conflict and mobilization – though some would argue without much damage to the underlying unequal structures of material resources. The idea of class distinction persists in a variety of social evaluations of people and things – **being classy**, **having class**, distinctions between different classes of traveler in planes, boats, and trains, and so on. It is this sense of a class system of privilege and deference that is evoked in the claim that the USA is a **classless society**. Other meanings of "class," related to the unequal distribution of wealth, income, and power, may nevertheless be relevant to understanding the USA and other societies.

Of course, there are complicated choices of words in describing such class orders. Upper classes are sometimes the "aristocracy" (in-bred to rule with natural authority). **Middle classes** are sometimes the "bourgeoisie," involved in commerce or professions (who manage their breeding rationally and defer gratification). The **lower classes** are sometimes the **laboring classes**, "lower orders," **working class**, or **dangerous and perishing classes** (who simply breed too much). Such issues of rank and privilege overlap with more sociological approaches to class. These have tended to follow the German sociologist Max Weber (1970a) in treating classes as distinguished by positions of relative advantage and disadvantage in terms of wealth and income (largely determined by labor market position). Here, too, classes are hierarchical arrangements, but potentially dynamic ones. Positions may be changed by collective strategies in the labor market, for example (through professional associations or trade unions). Classes affect life chances for individuals – the probabilities of social and occupational mobility; of educational access and achievement; of illness and mortality. They also shape the experiences of individuals, producing the possibility of (more or less coherent) **class consciousness**. Classes, in this Weberian view, are linked to – but not the same as - political organization ("party") and social position ("status"), both of which may be shaped by "non-economic" processes. Much European sociology of the second half of the C20 explored and debated the dimensions and dynamics of **class inequality** in this sense.

This view of **class as market position** has been continually in conflict with a Marxist view of **class as relational**. Here, classes are founding elements of society, and are themselves created by the mode of production. In Marxist analysis, the means of producing material life involve social relations of production, which (historically) involve divisions between classes. In the capitalist mode of production, society is divided between those who own the means of production (the owners of capital, the **capitalist class,** the bourgeoisie, the **ruling class**) and those who must sell their labor (to capitalists) in order to subsist (the proletariat, the working class). The interests of the capitalist class (the accumulation of profit) require the subordination of the working class – in the labor process; in social arrangements, and in political institutions. The interests of the working class are to resist the power of capital by collective organization and to bring about the overthrow or transcendence of capitalism in the transition to a (classless) socialist society (Marx and Engels, 1973[1848]).

Although this stresses the big two classes of capitalist society, Marxist analyses extend far beyond this. They deal with the class relations of other modes of production (Asiatic, feudal, and socialist, for example), and with the shifting class relations produced within societies where more than one mode of production exists (the persistence of feudal classes – landowners and peasants – within capitalist societies, for example). They address interstitial or **contradictory class positions** between the bourgeoisie and proletariat – the middle classes, who have been a thorny problem for Marxist analysis and politics. They examine the complex **class relations** of imperialism – with local (*comprador*) capital in alliance with international capital against the local proletariat and peasantry. Class is thus the central focus through which Marxists view societies – **class positions** produce class interests and the potential for class consciousness; the antagonistic relationships between classes (the struggle to extract surplus value from labor) produces **class conflict**. Ideologies, juridical and political systems, state apparatuses, and cultural formations are implicated in the processes of class conflict – either as the means of ruling-class capacity to continue ruling, or as the site of conflict and contestation.

Not surprisingly, other social cleavages and conflicts have tended to be subordinated to this central focus. Conflicts around gender and racial formations, for example, have been treated as secondary aspects of class conflict ("functional for capitalism") or as epiphenomenal diversions from the "real business" of class conflict. This led to challenges from a range of perspectives and standpoints usually (and overconveniently) summarized as the "politics of difference." Such arguments questioned the assumed social identity of class (as white, male, able-bodied, workers), proposing instead a more complex set of relations, identities, and forms of agency (Gibson-Graham, Resnick, and Wolff, 2000). By the end of the C20, a number of contradictory tendencies were in play. The collapse of "actually existing socialism" in the Soviet Union and Eastern Europe made a Marxist view of class appear redundant – the working classes of the world would never unite, throw off their chains, and build a truly classless society. At the same time, the global spread of capitalism seemed to demonstrate that Marxist views of the dynamic character and universalizing tendencies of capitalism might have some value. To some, class seemed to run the risk of disappearing as an analytic and political category – at a time when class inequalities deepened in the processes of global economic restructuring. The associated rise of neo-liberalism looked like the beginning of a new **class war**: a politics determined to enhance the power of capital, to disorganize and subordinate labor across the world, and to intensify economic and social inequalities.

Perhaps the most puzzling reappearance of class took place in the 1980s in the USA. Conservative commentators – in that most self-confidently "classless" society – discovered that it contained, not classes, but an **underclass** of work-shy, feckless, undeserving, criminal, uncivil, and semi-detached poor people. The concept took hold in popular, political, and policy discourses, mostly articulating the view that excessively generous welfare had "spawned" these disorganized, dangerous, and usually lone- (black-)mother-headed households. Even if Marxists and their critics could not work out how to conduct a compelling analysis of how class might be articulated with gender and racial formation, the conservatives certainly could (Goode and Maskovsky, 2001).

For all these reasons (and more), class continues to haunt the formations of capitalism. Despite the recurring attempts to shrug class off and to naturalize inequalities, attention returns to it. It articulates something distinctive about the experience of inequality and the potential for collective organization (on the part of both capital and labor). While capitalism's social, economic, and political dynamics produce, reproduce, and legitimate inequalities of wealth, income, life chances, and power, the talk will turn to class. Sometimes it will be used to refer to little more than the gap between rich and poor. Sometimes it will be used to challenge concentrations of power and privilege; and sometimes it will be used to rally the poor/excluded/oppressed against the power of capital (and its owners and representatives). Often it will be used to summon up the imagined and desired "classless society" (in all its different meanings). But capitalism without its classes – and without its talk of classes – is unimaginable.

John Clarke

See: *CAPITALISM, ELITE, EQUALITY.*

Colonialism

Colonialism is a general term signifying domination and hegemony, classically in the form of political rule and economic control on the part of a European state over territories and peoples outside Europe. The earliest forms of colonialism in this sense (not all empires were colonial empires) were exhibited in the New World by Spain and Portugal, although **classical colonialism** only flowered later in conjunction with the rise of global capitalism, manifested in the rule by European states over various polities in Asia and Africa. There were exceptions to these rules, as in the case of Japanese colonial domination over Korea and parts of Southeast Asia in the mC20.

"Imperialism" is sometimes seen as an interchangeable term with "colonialism," even as it has often been used to focus on the economic, and specifically capitalist, character of **colonial rule**. Colonialism itself has sometimes been reserved for cases of **settler colonialism**, like Australia and New Zealand, where segments of the dominant population not only rule over but settle in **colonial territories**. The roots of the term in L *colonia*, meaning farm or settlement, *colonus*, meaning settler, and *colere*, meaning cultivate, lend support to this connection. This history of **colonial settlement** has also left its mark on many aspects of earlier and contemporary usage: **colonial architecture**, for example, or **colonial experience** to describe periods of work and residence in settled territories, just as **colonial frontier** applies to the contested zones between occupying and indigenous populations, and **colonial-born** marks a new distinction within the dominant population.

However, most scholars agree that colonialism was in fact a form of rule that was most often not accompanied by European settlement, and that the term "colonialism" entails sustained control over a local population by states that were interested neither in settlement nor in assimilation. As a term of comparative scholarship, "colonialism" in all cases directs attention toward the colonies themselves, whereas the rubric of "imperialism" typically directs attention to the metropole and the global system, in which political and economic imperatives worked to make empire a constitutive condition of the West's global dominance during modern times (Dirks, 1992).

The tensions within and between these key terms help us identify some of the key conditions of colonialism. First, to think about colonialism is to think about the relationship between Europe and other parts of the world (even, as in the case of Japan, when Europe appears to be absent). Spanish colonialism might have preceded formal capitalism, and it might have been, like early Portuguese colonialism, conducted in the name of the church rather than the crown. However, church and crown appeared indistinguishable in colonial settings for the same reasons as many other metropolitan distinctions blurred in the blinding light of **colonial power**. Europe achieved both a large measure of its unique, and uniform, identity and its seemingly insurmountable world position through its claim to mastery over subject peoples in colonial settings. As Franz Fanon once put it, "Europe is literally the creation of the third world" (1963: 102).

Already we run into conceptual as well as historical difficulties. Many of the categories used by **colonizers** and **colonized** alike to understand colonialism were themselves produced through **colonial encounters**. Although **colonial conquest** was predicated on the power of superior arms, military organization, political obsession, and economic wealth, it also produced the conditions for all of these to take on greater significance than could ever have been imagined before. At the same time, military, economic, and political forms of power were inexorably based on a host of cultural technologies; indeed, colonialism was largely a cultural project of control (Cohn, 1995). **Colonial knowledge** both enabled colonial conquest and was produced by it. Cultural forms in newly classified "traditional" societies were reconstructed and transformed by and through colonial interventions, creating new categories and oppositions between colonizers and colonized, European and other, modern and traditional, West and East, even male and female. If, then, Europe is fundamental to the history of colonialism, Europe is also part of a larger set of opposed terms that were in turn produced by colonialism.

Colonialism is also critically linked to the idea of Enlightenment, the age of discovery and reason. Reason gave discovery a justification and a new meaning, but it also took its expanding global laboratory for granted. Science flourished in the C18 not merely because of the intense curiosity of individuals working in Europe, but because **colonial expansion** both necessitated and facilitated the active exercise of the scientific imagination. It was through discovery – the siting, surveying, mapping, naming, and ultimately possessing – of new regions that science itself could open new territories of conquest, among them cartography, geography, botany, philology, and anthropology. As the world was literally shaped for Europe through cartography – which, writ large, encompassed the narration of ship logs and route maps, the drawing of boundaries, the extermination of savages, the settling of peoples, the appropriation of property, the assessment of revenue, the raising of flags, and the writing of new histories (and anthropologies too) – it was also parceled into clusters of colonized territories to be controlled by increasingly powerful European nations, the Dutch, French, and English/British in particular. Marking land and marking bodies turned out to be two sides of the same coin.

And coin was important too. Bullion procured from the New World made the purchase of Asian commodities, from spices to tea, possible. Even as Asian spices made the European diet palatable, sugar had to be imported to make tea potable. The exploding trade in these and other commodities drove the establishment of the first stock markets in the lC17, in Amsterdam and then London. The most prominent stocks traded on Exchange Alley after the glorious revolution of 1688 were shares of East India Company stock. And if empire and capitalism were born hand in hand, they grew up in the same neighborhoods as well. By the mC18, markets in interior India had been significantly penetrated by a wily alliance of trading activity and merchant political power; by the eC19, the China trade not only began to determine mercantile as well as agricultural decisions in the Indian subcontinent but to recalibrate trade across the entire Indian ocean. In India itself, the nascent **colonial state** began to develop complex institutions of revenue administration and collection in response to the growing recognition that local states had always depended primarily on relations around agrarian production rather than trade.

A now receding vocabulary records these economic aspects of colonialism: the **Home and Colonial Stores** established in 1888; McCulluch's 1846 reference to "coffee, indigo, spices, and other foreign and colonial articles"; and the **colonial editions** exported by metropolitan publishers, for example. However, another set of terms – **Foreign and Colonial Office**, **colonial government**, **colonial policy** – recorded another set of relations focused on political rule. Indeed, by the C19, colonialism was as much about the establishment of new political orders as it was about controlling global economic ones (Prakash, 1995). Early experiments in colonial forms of government were initially dominated by the British in India. The loss of the American colonies in the lC18 taught Britain to be extremely cautious about encouraging, even allowing, European settlement, while the growing reliance on land revenue to fund overseas political and military operations led to a deepening involvement in local political and agrarian affairs. Settlements with large landholders were initially introduced as new modes of private property, but soon led to a variety of customized land settlements with village communities and cultivators. Meanwhile, the East India Company worked inexorably to fold more and more territory under its direct rule, only to be stopped by the aggressive expansionist policies of Lord Dalhousie in 1856. The great mutiny was put down, but the even greater revolt it occasioned led to significant changes in colonial policy. Unconquered territories were now to be ruled indirectly, and increasingly the British crown, which assumed rule from the East India Company in 1858, used a variety of barely disguised indirect means to lessen resistance and justify its own extractive and dominant presence (Dirks, 2001).

New indirect modes of colonial rule became increasingly attractive for European powers as the lC19 witnessed yet another world push for colonial domination. The Dutch vied with the French to control both peninsular and archipelagic Southeast Asia. And then came the scramble for Africa, in which the British and French were the main players, joined now by the Belgians and Germans among others. In most of these new colonial territories,

European powers made clear that they had paid some attention to earlier **colonial history**, fashioning new kinds of indirect rule, using local institutions and personnel to ensure loyalty and at the same time mask the European interests and agendas that pushed for more intense global control over trade, production, and markets (Cooper and Stoler, 1997). More than ever, traditions were produced and the idea of tradition promoted to justify indirect rule. Tribes and tribal authorities were used to control territories and their constituent populations, even when the authorities were clearly colonial puppets and the tribes themselves ossified almost beyond pre-colonial recognition.

Tradition could be used to justify the most draconian forms of colonial rule on the grounds of the civilizing and modernizing mission, and traditions could be used to implement both the mirage of **colonial autonomy** and the rationale for **colonial modernity**. Tradition could also be used to explain why nationalism was as foreign to colonial soil as self-rule would be to colonized politics. Thus the colonial investments in ideas of caste, village, chief-ship, and kin-based communities. And thus the colonial astonishment when it turned out that all of these institutions could play a significant role in the growing demand for independence.

Colonialism often justified itself on the grounds that traditional institutions stood in the way of the development of ideas of nationality and the growth of national unity. In fact, colonialism both introduced European notions of national self-determination and hastened the growth of nationalist sentiment (Chatterjee, 1986). Much of the sentiment behind **colonial nationalism** was based on a massive reaction to the indignity of European rule, and the growing recognition of the racial prejudice and economic interest that predicated the rationalizations of colonial ideology. **Decolonization** was a term that disguised the extent to which **colonial independence** was usually the outcome of militant mobilization and sometimes violent resistance to colonial rule on the part of new nations first in Asia and then in Africa. In fact, colonial nationalism was both the antithesis of colonial rule and the vehicle for the development of the first sustained critiques of colonial modernity, liberalism, and the uses of ideas of culture to disguise economic and political interests (Chatterjee, 1993).

Nicholas Dirks

See: *ORIENTALISM, POSTCOLONIALISM.*

Commodity

The earliest recorded senses of the word **commodity**, dating from the eC15, refer on the one hand to a quality or condition of things which makes them convenient or beneficial, and on the other to things themselves which, having this quality, are produced for use or sale. Commodities are, in the most general sense, goods, merchandise, wares, produce. In contemporary economic discourse the word is used mainly to refer to food or raw materials which are traded. The concept of the commodity retains its interest and its importance almost entirely because of its development within Marxist theory as a key to the understanding of the social relations that organize the capitalist system. Taking over its function in classical economics of designating a particular, historically complex state of exchange, Marx (1976 [1867]) deepens this analysis to indicate how the social relations of production characteristic of capitalism are embedded within relations of **commodity exchange**.

In its simplest sense, the Marxist concept of the commodity refers not to things but to the form taken by things when they are produced for exchange rather than for immediate use; in this broad sense, the commodity is to be found (although only occasionally rather than as a dominant form) in many pre-capitalist societies. Every object that is produced is in some sense useful: it has a use-value. Insofar as it can be exchanged with other objects, either directly or by way of money transactions, it can also be said to have an exchange-value, or more generally to have "value": that is, to be measurable within a unified system which sets up the possibility of the equivalence of very disparate and particular use-values (a system which is ultimately grounded in the common measure of human labor). Money, in its various forms, is a medium for the expression of this systematic equivalence of values. In its more complex definition, then, the concept of the commodity refers to a matrix of conditions of exchange (the capitalist market), conditions of production (capital investment and wage labor, which is itself a commodity at another level), and conditions of consumption (private rather than collective appropriation of goods).

It is from this conceptual core that Marx (1976 [1867]) seeks, in the first volume of *Capital*, to derive his understanding of capitalism as a specific historical system. Capital is value which increases through the processes of **commodity production** and exchange. This increment of value, or surplus value, is the value added by labor in production. To understand capitalism in terms of the system of value which governs both the production of goods for exchange and the extraction of profit from labor power is then to understand the historically specific ways in which surplus value is extracted from workers (and the social systems – labor laws, contracts, fear of unemployment, the pleasures of consumption – which underpin this), and the general relations between capital and labor which generate particular, largely antagonistic relations between social classes. The concept of the commodity thus implicates the whole of Marx's mature understanding of capitalism as a systemic whole. Insofar as the **commodity form** both concentrates real social relations in itself and conceals them beneath its thing-like exterior – giving rise to **commodity fetishism** – the analysis of this form further gives Marx an epistemological vantage point from which to understand a mystified reality.

The capitalist system's inner dynamic (its drive to profit) compels it to expand the commodity form wherever it can. **Commodification** thus extends from material to immaterial property and to many of those possessions and activities which had previously been thought to be inalienable. The commercialization of sport over the last 20 or so years is one example of this process; the patenting of products of nature is another. It is in relation to such processes as these that the concept of commodification has passed from the Marxist tradition into general usage (Gregory, 1997; Radin, 2001). Perhaps the central focus of attention has been on the domain of culture and what Adorno and Horkheimer (1972) called the culture industries. The growth of mass markets in film, radio, television, journalism, and paperback books has on the one hand strengthened the pessimistic sense that the industrialized production of cultural forms leads to banal, stereotyped, aesthetically valueless works, yet on the other has weakened the implicit opposition of commodified, ''mass''-cultural works to works of ''high'' art, since the latter too are now industrially produced and marketed. Not only art but intellectual work of all kinds is to a greater or less extent commodified in a capitalist society. Another area in which the logic of commodification has become highly visible is that of stardom and the celebrity, where the marketability of ''personality'' or physical characteristics works in opposition to traditional conceptions of the human as a privileged domain which is withheld from market transactions. In much of the anti-globalization rhetoric of contemporary left politics, finally, the manifestation of the commodity form as brand name is a key to the understanding of global capitalism (Gereffi and Korzeniewicz, 1994).

Whereas Marx's conception of the commodity form stresses both its negative dimensions (the extension of private property in the common wealth) and its positive aspects (the fact that commodity production massively expands the social output of material goods), some of his later followers, such as Georg Lukács, Theodor Adorno, or Herbert Marcuse, think of it as a general process of loss and human impoverishment. Something of Marx's ambivalence might be retained if we were to adopt the insight developed more recently by anthropologists such as Arjun Appadurai (1986) that things are never only commodities but rather move in and out of the commodity state over their lifetime, becoming constantly embedded and re-embedded in non-economic value systems.

47

John Frow

See: *CAPITALISM, CELEBRITY, CONSUMPTION, FETISH.*

Communication

Communication has a number of senses. The oldest is perhaps the action of imparting ''things material,'' which dates back to the C14. While this sense has become rare, it was extended in the C17 to the broader notion of ''access or means of access between two or more persons or places; the action or faculty of passing from one place to another'' or of ''a line of connexion, connecting passage or opening.'' It is here that we can see the long and close relationship of communication to what we would today call transportation.

In the C15, ''communication'' was extended to the facts or information that were imparted, what we might today call the content of communication. The most common modern sense of "communication," which refers to the activity of imparting, or transmitting messages containing, information, ideas, or knowledge, dates back to the lC17. As early as the C15, a second sense stressed not so much the transmission of messages, or their content, but rather the activity of dialogue, interaction, and intercourse – as in the idea of conversation or **interpersonal communication** (and even of sexual intercourse by the C18).

As early as the C17, communication also had another, more participatory sense. Here it referred to a common participation or a shared quality or affinity, as in the Christian **communion**. This is strongly present in the contemporary American English usage, where a speaker may preface their remarks by saying that they wish to "share something" with their hearer or audience. A further sense focuses on the idea of communication as, potentially, a process of "making common to many" a particular set of ideas or experiences. This sense has some part of its roots in the religious idea of "communion" as a participatory process. Here we also begin to see some of the links between ideas of communication and ideas of community, which I will explore below.

There is another important sense of the word which focuses on the technical medium through which communication is conducted. This usage may refer either to the **media of symbolic communication** (language, signs, images – and the technologies by means of which they are often transmitted) or to the **means of physical communication** (roads, canals, railways, ships, airplanes). The historical changes in the relation of modes of symbolic communication to modes of physical transport are a key issue here. The moment when **symbolic communications** became distinct from modes of transport is perhaps best symbolized by the invention of the telegraph, with its capacity to send electronic messages, immediately, over long distances. This development marks a crucial historical shift in the role and function of these two distinct senses of "communication." This sense of historical transformation is paralleled historically both by the debates which surrounded the rise of the mass media of the lC19 and eC20, and by contemporary debates about the significance of the "new media" of the digital/computer age, which are now held to be transforming human communication in fundamental ways.

The study of communication in the lC20 was to a large extent informed by a rather restricted sense of the term, which focused on the factors determining the efficient transmission of information from sender to receiver. Early models of **mass communication** were concerned with how best to achieve the unimpeded transmission of messages between sender and receiver. This approach limited the definition of communication to the purposive transmission of explicit units of information, and conceived of the process in rather mechanistic terms. In the field of interpersonal communication, the limits of this model were perceived by many working in the field of social psychology, who argued for a broader definition, which would also include non-intentional forms of communication (including factors such as what came to be called body language). Their critique was based on the premise that in fact it is impossible (as a matter of principle) not to communicate, whether or not the person concerned consciously wishes to do so (the minimal communication would be that they were feeling non-communicative).

In the broader field of **communications and cultural studies**, this conventional model also came in for significant criticism and development, under the influence of semiology, with its focus on the linguistic and cultural "codes" underlying all acts of communication, and its guiding principle that there can be "no message without a code." The "encoding/decoding" model of communication has been particularly influential in this respect. That model, developed by Stuart Hall (1981), was also influential in shifting attention beyond the merely denotative (or "manifest") level of information which might be conveyed in a message, to the levels of connotative (implied, associative, or "latent") meaning which are routinely carried "on the back of" the seemingly simple units of explicit information which a message might convey. This approach drew on the structuralist model of linguistics to argue that a broad range of cultural codes (in imagery, dress, fashion, and style) could also usefully be studied on the model of language.

Previous models had tended to treat "successful communication" as the normal state of affairs, and had only been concerned with "misunderstandings" as exceptional disruptions in the flow of communications, which needed to be "ironed out." However, the semiological perspective encouraged the questioning of this assumption of the transparency of "normal" communications. Given that the existence of social and cultural divisions in most societies means that the senders and receivers of messages are unlikely to entirely share communicative codes, this new approach treated the variable interpretation of messages as both "normal" and the key research issue to be addressed

Here the issue of power in the fields of communication and culture also came into focus more clearly. This issue had been earlier highlighted by the shift of attention from interpersonal (two-way/dialogic) modes of communication to mass forms of one-way transmission of messages, from the elite groups who controlled the media to large audiences of receivers. The key question here was the manipulative power of mass media discourses (such as political propaganda or commercial advertising) to shape public opinion. The discussion of **mass communications** thus came to be defined as the study of who says what, in which channel, to whom, with what effect. Clearly this approach is informed by an evaluative perspective which poses two-way dialogue as the egalitarian form of what Jürgen Habermas (1970) calls the "ideal speech situation," and is correspondingly concerned with the extent to which mass forms of communication pervert this norm. Evidently, contemporary forms of interactive media, which are held to re-empower the audience, and thus to restore a more democratic mode of dialogue between the senders and receivers of messages, are important here. The issue at stake then concerns the extent to which, for example, television programs which encourage their viewers to ring in and vote on potential plot developments constitute genuine forms of democratic dialogue, or merely its simulation.

However, this focus on the question of who has power over the transmission of information, and how adequately the system allows feedback, is only one dimension of the issue of communication. In relation to the participatory sense of "communication," it is important to note the connection between the terms "communication" and "community," and the role of the former in the very constitution of the latter. Here we also return to the connection with ideas of communion. The key point here is to recognize that a community is not an entity that exists and then happens to communicate. Rather, communities are best understood as constituted in and through their changing patterns of communication. Indeed, today, as new technologies enable cheap and immediate forms of **long-distance communication**, the nuclear family is often strung out along the phone wires, and community is no longer necessarily founded on geographical contiguity. This approach also highlights Roman Jakobson's (1972) idea of the importance of the phatic dimension of communication in "keeping channels open" and connecting people together, rather than in the transmission of information. More fundamentally, to take this perspective is also to grant communications a primary – and constitutive – role in social affairs, rather than to see it as some merely secondary or subsidiary phenomenon

From another perspective, many have argued that the **communications industries** themselves are increasingly central to our postmodern or late modern era. In so far as the defining characteristic of this era is held to be the compression of time and space, and the "transcendence" of geography enabled by the **new communications technologies**, these industries are central to that transformation. They are also increasingly central to the economies of the advanced societies of the world, which are now primarily based on the production and transfer of knowledge and information, rather than the manufacture of material goods. It is not for nothing that **communication skills** are now an increasingly important qualification for employment in these societies, and the absence of the relevant forms of verbal, literacy, or computer skills is enough to consign many of their poorer members to a position of social exclusion.

One could say that ours is an era which is now obsessed with the idea (or perhaps even the ideology) of communication. Telecommunication's advertising campaigns tell us that it is "good to talk"; "talk shows" featuring "ordinary people" dominate the world of daytime television; and mobile phone companies reassure us that we can "take our network with us, wherever we go," so as never to be "out of touch" with our families and friends. In all of this it is crucial to distinguish between technical improvements in the speed or efficiency of the means of communication and the growth of understanding in human affairs.

David Morley

See: *COMMUNITY, INFORMATION, MASS, MEDIA.*

Community

Community was first used in the C14 to refer to a "body of commons" or a social or political entity, as in "Ther is oon emperour and oon hede in a comunnete" (Wyclif, 1380). Since then, the word has been variously used to convey fellowship (as when Mary Shelley's Frankenstein tells his monstrous creation "There can be no community between you and me; we are enemies"), joint ownership, a state or organized society, a common identity, or interests in common. Accordingly, people speak of **scientific**, **academic**, **legal**, **religious**, or **business communities**.

"Community" is more generally used as a "warmly persuasive word to describe an existing set of relationships" (R. Williams 1976: 76), implying a connection – such as kinship, cultural heritage, shared values and goals – felt to be more "organic" or "natural," and therefore stronger and deeper, than a rational or contractual association of individuals, such as the market or the state. These contrasting senses of unmediated and contractual communities acquired a particular historical significance with republicanism, and the bourgeois and Industrial Revolutions. Indeed, the (often conflicted) marriage of the **imagined community** of the nation and representative government to form the nation state provides the adhesive to prevent the war of all against all that Hobbes (1991 [1651]) had feared would take place when particular interests dominate.

In the C19 the concept of nation expanded beyond Rousseau's premise of the general will of the people as the legitimate location of legislative authority, to an understanding of the nation as an organism with a distinctive heritage and teleology. In contrast, liberalism emphasized the right of individuals to form **political communities** with those with whom they identified and to protect their common culture. Alexis de Tocqueville (1968 [1835–40]) feared that the equality fostered by this liberal protection of individual political and civil rights would orient society toward self-interest rather than the good of all, enabling despotism wherever the general will did not prevail. In contrast, it was believed that the mutual assistance characteristic of communities on a smaller scale, such as religious associations, would serve as an antidote to individualism.

For some social theorists, most notably Max Weber (1978), it was not only individualism but capitalist rationalization that weakened the communal bonds that upheld traditional authority. Hence the appeal to the solidary identification of community as a countervailing force. Solidarity was sometimes imagined, nostalgically, as rooted in a quickly disappearing past, such as Thomas Jefferson's cherished **agrarian communities**, which he saw as a salve for the fraying moral fiber of instrumentally and contractually based commercial and industrial life. For others, community was projected into the future, as in Marx and Engels's "return" to an ethical and aesthetic **communalism** or **communism** that reverses the alienation generated by capitalism.

Rapid industrialization, urbanization, and consumerism in the eC20 seemed to bear out the ascendancy of contractually organized urban associations or *Gesellschaften* over communally organized societies or *Gemeinschaften* (Tönnies, 1887). Solidarity was thought to become "mechanical" when small-scale community life was no longer possible, as in the large agglomerations of modern cities with an ever-increasing division of labor. From the 1920s to the 1960s, **urban communities** and **rural communities** became laboratories for the sociological examination of the break-down of the cohesive values that sustained community and formed the basis of social order. Sociologists turned to notions of culture and communication to provide a basis for integrating diverse social groups and protecting society from the consequences of economic competition, immigration and ethnic diversification, deviancy, etc. through practices of **community organizing** (Park, Burgess, and McKenzie, 1967; Parsons, 1937).

The resulting models of assimilation and consensus-building provided normative images of social development that were soon being exported to the rest of the world, particularly so-called underdeveloped or developing societies. It was through these models, informed by the "mass education" endeavors of the British Colonial Office and the technical assistance models advanced by the United Nations and Truman's Point Four programs, that the notion of **community development** was offered as an alternative to communism in the early years of the Cold War. In this way, social science intervention was to transform the backwardness and passivity of **traditional communities** into democratic citizen participation, with improved standards of living and consumer capacity.

These models returned, especially to the United States, as a major strategy for waging the post-civil-rights War on Poverty to "empower" African-Americans and other minorities, who were presupposed to be suffering from a "pathological" deterioration of community largely due to the "culture of poverty" of urban ghettos (Glazer and Moynihan, 1963; Lewis, 1959, 1966). From the post-civil-rights era to the 1990s heyday of multiculturalism, community development played a dual role as occasion for both **community mobilization** and accommodation to the protocols of government and foundation programs. Racialized groups were understood to draw political force from their communities, enabling them occasionally to resist the interventions of the welfare state and to seek recognition.

In developing countries, such as those of Latin America, such **community resistance** and resilience ranges from struggles for interpretive power among **Christian-based community** organizations to the action of self-help groups during emergencies, and even to insurgent mobilizations. In the first case, **poor communities** gained political consciousness of their situation by discussing gospel narratives, informed by their own experiences of oppression; in the second, communities like those affected by the 1985 earthquake in Mexico City rescued neighbors and generally did what the state could not, or would not, do (Monsiváis, 1987). Finally, **indigenous communities** and **peasant communities** in search of recognition and/or protesting mistreatment have challenged political elites and even toppled governments, as in Bolivia in October 2003. Yet even in these contexts, a capillary network of non-governmental organizations (NGOs) aiding **community empowerment** has assimilated much of the effervescence into third-sector forms of governance.

It comes as no surprise that by the mid-1980s, in a context of market-driven economic and political liberalization, the collapse of communism, and the rise of new forms of global governance and new forms of mobilization on the basis of cultural rights (Niec, 1998), the discourse of community is used to legitimate conservative private assistance and self-help projects and liberal public–private partnerships that "empower" communities to govern and even police themselves. Thus we have witnessed a wide range of administrative initiatives, including **community policing**, **community safety**, **community care**, **community sentencing**, **community centers**, and **community arts**. The arts, for example, are to be "suffused throughout the civic structure, finding a home in a variety of community service and economic development activities – from youth programs and crime prevention to job training and race relations" (Larson, 1997: 127).

At the same time, the debates between liberals and **communitarians** have again taken center stage. Liberals argue that principles like freedom and equality are sufficient to protect all individuals, including those belonging to **minority communities** and cultures, while communitarians insist that the political and ethical visions and values necessary for a just society must be rooted in structures of community and tradition. A more radical perspective drawn from the claims of feminist, racialized, and other minority groups holds that such **communities of difference** have a privileged standpoint that needs to be taken into consideration in any vision of justice. They dismiss both liberalism's claim to universalism and communitarianism's definition of communities on the basis of specific cultural heritages as an expression of top-down hegemony, always contestable from the differences that cross-cut communities (Laclau and Mouffe, 1985; I. M. Young, 1990). These communities, like individuals, can be seen as divided and multiple, leading from more general identifications like **lesbian community** to more particular groupings like **latina lesbian community**, whose position delegitimizes the continuing universalistic pretensions of the more encompassing label.

Also, with a growing interest in civil society since neo-liberalism took root in the 1980s and 1990s, many social critics have voiced concern for the loss of community and face-to-face interaction (Putnam, 2000; Sennett, 1998). This loss results from the "virtualization" of society, as television has become the main cultural activity and "surf-by," "call-in," and "point-of-purchase" politics has replaced physical interaction in public spheres. Moreover, the processes that go by the name of globalization – new communications, new economy, new forms of back-and-forth diasporic migrations and supranational formations (Appadurai, 1990) – have taken "community" beyond the restorative function of its traditional opposition to the market and (neo-)liberal individualism (Calhoun, 1998).

From this vantage point, Richard Hoggart's (1957) call to stem the erosion of **working-class community**, or efforts to locate resistance in **subcultural communities** (Hebdige, 1979), belong to a discourse not unlike that of earlier organic communitarians. It is not clear that "community" will retain much of the "warm persuasiveness" that Williams attributed to it. The **European Community**, an initiative aimed at safeguarding against the ravages of globalization, has not been able to construct the feeling of nationhood that Benedict Anderson (1983) attributed to the imagined community. Moreover, much of the chaos which passes for post-socialist transitions (mafia-style capitalism in Russia), the disruptions and dislocation of globalization (the collapse of Argentina), and the proliferating violence and terror in the wake of the Cold War (September 11) presents a set of circumstances in which the darker side of community edges out the positive. While for Manuel Castells (1996) the network society is the spawning ground of innovation and urban renewal, largely rooted in the local, terrorist networks are also (re)new(ed) forms of imagined community. The local is a resource for new articulations of capital and terror, for NGO social justice networking, and even for the **transnational community** of the so-called anti-globalization movement.

George Yúdice

See: *DEVELOPMENT, GLOBALIZATION, MOVEMENTS, NATION, RESISTANCE.*

Conservatism

In its earliest meanings **conservation** possessed a strongly ecological significance, such as the term has regained in our own times. By the IC14 it could speak more generally about a state of affairs, in the human or social world, remaining unchanged or intact. Not until much later was the idea of conservation in the political field adumbrated, carrying with it an explicit conviction that the polity itself was an organic entity which needed careful husbanding. The idea, commonly heard in our own times, that "the fabric" of society needs to be preserved draws directly from this mode of thinking, regarding as inherently destructive any action which upsets the putatively organic nature of social life.

Conservatism, notwithstanding the protestations of its ideologues, is a historical product of the modern period, inextricably bound to the epistemologies and political practices of modernity. Its discursive codification came into being in the IC18, inventing the temporality of the traditional or national past. Here the life of the nation was represented as a continuum, the people in the present being depicted as the natural inheritors of those whose lives had made the nation in the past. Conservatism in this sense worked as a philosophy of the national past, its conception of historical time ineluctably organic. It preceded what was to become its great historic contender – the Jacobin dream of Year One, inaugurated in the calendar of the French Revolution and signifying the virtue of a historical time subject both to the imperative of the present and to the imperative of active human intervention.

Conservative temperaments can be discerned in politics long before the C18. In the social upheaval of mC17 England, for example, Lord Clarendon – arch-royalist and vitriolic enemy of any whisper of popular sentiment – would seem to the modern eye to be an unambiguous **conservative**. And yet such retrospective readings mislead, for his distaste for social change of any sort was bereft of any larger philosophy in which conservation and advance could be thought together (Clarendon, 1958 [1702–4]). What emerged at the moment of the French Revolution, in the making of the division between left and right, was what on the contrary can properly be called a philosophy of **conservative politics**. Its roots lay in the democratic revolutions of the United States and France and in the rather more muted democratic struggles in Britain and Ireland. Its leading location turned out to be counter-revolutionary England, where its master intellectual, acknowledged by subsequent **conservatives** of nearly every conceivable hue, was the Irish Whig Edmund Burke. In Burke's magisterial *Reflections on the revolution in France* (1978 [1790]) – where **conserve** appears as a verb – "the past" was mobilized as an explicit political resource, from which could be divined the sum of human wisdom. (This *mobilization* of the past for political ends is closely connected, in turn, to later manifestations at the end of the C19 of the invention of tradition [Hobsbawm and Ranger, 1983], in which fabricated artifacts or memories of the past were mass produced in the present, establishing a *fictively* organic relation between past and present.) Wisdom, for Burke, was passed through the generations and, supremely, was embodied in the medium of the family: individual life could only have meaning within this larger collective. True knowledge was thus empirical and experiential, a function of the covenant between past, present, and future. It stood in antithesis to a politics driven by abstraction, by reason, and – above all else – by self-conscious ideological commitment. Burkean wisdom, in its ideal form, expressed simultaneously the truths of the divinity, of human nature, and of history itself.

In 1818 Chateaubriand's *Le Conservateur* described as a conservative "one who is a partisan of the maintenance of the established social and political order." In Britain, shortly after, conservatism as a political institution became associated with the duke of Wellington at the end of the 1820s. The idea of the **Conservative Party** first appeared in 1830 to describe the old landed faction of the Tories. On January 1, 1830, the *Quarterly Review* commented that "what is called the Tory might with more propriety be called the Conservative party." By 1840 Thomas Carlyle was writing of **conservatism** to describe what he believed to be the antidote to progress.

Through the C19, and for much of the C20, "conservatism" signified quite distinct political formations. In the continental European sense, conservatism was most often understood to be strictly reactionary, ready to turn back historical time, especially when confronting the challenge of mass democracy. In mC20 continental Europe these forces of reaction found themselves outflanked by a variety of fascist movements, in which they were absorbed, or by which they were destroyed, or with which they had to enter into uneasy alliance. In the Anglophone world "conservative" represented a more deeply liberal politics than it did in continental Europe. In Britain especially, inherited traditions of statecraft (maintenance of order) combined in Conservative politics to embrace – indeed,

55

to advance – mass democracy (Hogg, 1947). Five years after he introduced an unpreced-ented expansion of the franchise the Conservative prime minister Benjamin Disraeli could declare (in 1872): "Gentlemen, the program of the Conservative party is to maintain the constitution of the country." By the second half of the C19 these strictly political meanings carried broader connotations, describing a psychological disposition as much as a political practice. Thus by 1865 the periodical press could announce: "We find girls naturally timid, prone to dependence, born conservatives."

In Britain the C20 sometimes came to be referred to by political scientists as the **Conservative century**, owing to the prolonged dominance of the Conservative Party in the political life of the nation (Gilmour, 1977). But in the lC20, as a result of the collapse of Bretton Woods and of the financial-industrial arrangements which underpinned the post-war settlements in the advanced nations, there emerged in many different variations parties and governments of the New Right. These were radical programmatically (thus alternatively termed the Radical Right), based upon a genuine determination to outflank the social-democratic advances of welfarization. These movements combined in varying degrees a populist authoritarianism – bringing together incessant "calls to the people" at the same time as the state imposed a deepening authority within civil society – with ever-increasing commitments to the free market, creating in the process a quite new conception of conservative politics.

These shifts could first be noted in the United States during the presidency of Richard Nixon, who evolved a peculiarly effective form of **conservative radicalism**, honing the precedents put in place by a generation of white demagogues in the south. Most of all, this was a conservatism organized by those who believed that they needed to fight on every front – in civil society as well as in the state, on the cultural terrain as well as the economic – in order to save the nation from destruction.

Colloquially, this larger, global political transformation was frequently referred to, in generic form, as Thatcherism, after the leading exponent of the new politics in Britain (S. Hall and Jacques, 1983). This was a politics which aimed to outflank its political opponents by seeking their destruction, rather than looking for a measure of accommo-dation: and in spurning an administrative or managerialist conception of politics, it revived – at least rhetorically – an active conception of "the people." The great paradox of this new radicalism, however, was the degree to which the traditional conservative parties themselves came to be regarded as upholders of the now-discredited anciens régimes, and thus suitable candidates for political destruction.

Certain unintended consequences followed. In 1985 one of Margaret Thatcher's original political footsoldiers, Michael Heseltine, could boast that the British Conservative Party was "the most successful political force in the history of mankind." Less than a decade later, having been identified by the Thatcherite zealots as a haven for the old thinking, and having suffered accordingly, it was dead in the water. Despite this prolonged weakening of the institutions of political conservatism at the start of the C21, the term remains readily associated with those who regard themselves as defenders of the – imagined – past, and whose fears rest upon the radical subversion of existent systems of social authority.

Bill Schwarz

See: *LIBERALISM, SOCIALISM.*

Consumption

The root L *consumere* "designated not only the use of things but also any type of removal and various forms of disposal" (Wyrwa, 1998: 432). In English since the C14, early usage of **consume** had an unfavorable connotation – to destroy, to exhaust, to waste, to completely use up – also present in the popular description of pulmonary phthisis as **consumption**. It begat two nouns in English: consumption and, from the C16, **consumer**, both conveying the same sense of destruction. "Consumer" subsequently acquired a neutral sense, with the emergence of bourgeois political economy in the C18, to describe market relationships, contrasting **the consumer** with the producer and, analogously, consumption with production. Thereafter, in the doctrines of economics, "consumer" and "consumption" denote aspects of acts of purchasing commodities in the market and calculations regarding some of their particular and aggregate financial consequences. Political economy was always mostly concerned with the changing value of items in exchange, rather than the uses to which they might be put. Only in the eC20 was consumption conceptualized by economists explicitly as the satisfaction of human needs through economic means (Wyrwa, 1998: 436), prefiguring a positive rather than neutral sense. The generalization of market exchange and expanded volumes of goods and services, corollaries of economic growth, connect together the two senses of consumption as purchase and as destruction. These two senses have sustained an ambivalence whose tensions have had considerable moral and political significance.

The negative connotations of destruction and waste were incorporated in popular moral and social discussion of ways of using things and spending money in modern societies. Puritan cultures were suspicious of modern consumption not only because it might encourage excessive spending rather than saving, but also lest it encourage a desire for luxurious items over and above those necessary for the satisfaction of basic human needs. Mistrust about underlying motivations for increased expenditure was also made apparent in terms like **conspicuous consumption**, coined by Theodor Veblen (1899) to refer to the tendency to mark social status through the competitive display of possessions. The term **mass consumption** frequently carried intimations of regret about the diffusion of demand for standardized items of poor quality, signifying cultural mediocrity. When combined in the mC20 with critiques of increasing commodification in capitalist society, as in the analyses of the Frankfurt School or the New Left, these negative features were viewed as part of a system of domination which pacified subordinate classes in the population.

57

Consumption

Capitalism was found wanting not only for its relations of production but also for its effect in encouraging wasteful, meaningless, privatizing, and enervating cultural behavior.

The IC20 witnessed a thorough revaluation of the ambience of consumption both from within economics, based on the celebration of the power of the consumer as purchaser in a political climate favoring markets, and from the perspective of cultural studies.

For neo-classical economic theory the consumer is an abstract entity, the source of demand in markets, who decides what to purchase, independently of other actors, on the basis of the price and quality of all available items, in light of preferences which are stable and ranked. This model, useful for certain purposes of theoretical reasoning and calculation within economics, has increasingly been adopted and incorporated into practical and popular political discourses. Practically, producers' concerns to estimate demand in impersonal and unstable markets where **customers** are unknown has led to market research putting flesh on the abstract figure of the consumer through sociodemographic and psychographic portraits. Politically, in the ideology of the New Right, such notions legitimate markets and disparage state intervention. State welfare provision, a significant source of **collective consumption**, has been restructured in many countries to respond to market logic and incentives.

Celebration of the ever-expanding merits of consumption through markets has an extended history in the USA, where an optimistic interpretation of abundance has circulated since the IC19. There the term **consumerism** refers to a doctrine validating abundance and prosperity, whereas in Europe it has connotations of self-interest and vulgar materialism. In both Europe and the USA, consumerism also refers to the spread of institutions and movements for the protection and promotion of the interests of consumers, as with **consumer associations**, **consumer movements**, and **consumer co-operatives**. As these flourish, governments have begun to claim more frequently to speak and act on behalf of "consumers," rather than of, say, classes, the nation, or citizens. This is associated with common-sense conceptions of **consumer sovereignty**, **consumer choice**, and **consumer rights**. Matters which in a flourishing welfare state would have been subject to political decision and determination are abandoned to the vagaries of market forces.

Cultural studies also challenged pessimistic interpretations of increased consumption. Partly in defense of the quality of popular culture against elite condescension, and partly as a result of analyzing empirically what people did with commodities after purchase, positive functions of consumption were stressed. **Consumer culture** provided entertainment and stimulation, people engaged with manufactured cultural artifacts in active and creative fashion, and some groups employed the items of mass consumption to subvert dominant values and norms. Jean Baudrillard's (1998) insistence on seeing consumption as primarily a system of signs, rather than a source of use-value, was a notable contribution to the emergent understanding of postmodern culture as visual, transient, ephemeral, and playful, increasingly a means of the free expression of personal and collective identity. Stressing the symbolic aspects rather than the practical uses of consumption, cultural studies inverted traditional judgments concerning its pleasures and satisfactions, and investigated the working of key institutions of contemporary consumption like the shopping mall and advertising.

Nevertheless, there continue to be substantial reservations about (post)modern consumption. Concepts like **consumer society** and consumer culture are still morally and politically ambivalent. Pertinent ethical and political objections to current consumption norms include: the questionable quality of mass-produced goods; escalating environmental problems; a woefully unequal international distribution of resources for consumption; and the tendency for the interests of consumers to override those of the producers of goods and services, as with sweatshops. The moral debate about the virtues of contemporary patterns and justifications of consumption is far from concluded.

Alan Warde

See: *CAPITALISM, COMMODITY, MARKET.*

Copy

The word **copy** moves in English from an original sense of "abundance" (from L *copia*, abundance, copiousness) to the more recent sense of derivativeness; it passes thereby from a sense of plenty ("Spain...hath grete copie and plente of castell," Trevisa 1387; "the copie and varietie of our sweete-mother-toong," Florio 1598) to an emphasis on the scarcity and rarity of originals. The transition from the former, positive sense to the notion of the copy as something secondary which draws all of its value from its derivative relation to the original ("Never buy a copy of a picture. All copies are bad; because no painter who is worth a straw ever will copy," Ruskin 1857) occurs by way of such L phrases as *dare vel habere copiam legendi*, to give or have the power of reading, which then give rise to mL *copia*, transcript. This second line of semantic development, which by the eC17 completely displaces the sense of "abundance," thus has at its core the imitative relation of one representation to another: the transcription of a manuscript to form a second text which repeats the meaning of the first, the exact reproduction of the features of a painting or other work of art (increasingly with the sense of inauthenticity, although not usually of fraudulence).

The habit of thought which associates **copying** with secondariness and derivativeness rather than with fruitful increase is bound up with some of the central doctrines of Western philosophy, as well as with the development of intellectual property doctrine from the C18 onward (Deleuze, 1994; Derrida, 1988). If the core sense of the modern English word "copy" has to do with the imitation of one representation by another, there is also a sense in which representation itself can be thought of as a process of copying ("When a painter copies from the life," Dryden 1700). Indeed, the notion that verbal or pictorial representation is an act of mimesis or simulation of a prior reality, which is not itself a representation, has been fundamental to Western metaphysics since at least Plato's distinction between the idea or form of the bed, the bed made by the carpenter which imitates that abstract form, and the painting of a bed which is twice removed from its original. Plato writes in the *Parmenides* that the ideas or forms "are as it were patterns fixed in the nature of things," whereas "other things are like them and are copies of them." Within this model, representations are by definition less than real. And when this model is mapped on to that of the reproduction of one representation by another, the structure of value is transferred, in such a way that the "original" representation takes on the force of the real or authentic, and the "copy" is understood as having an inferior ontological status.

A copy is thus either the opposite of the real thing, or else the opposite of an original representation. Copying in the latter sense becomes both an important and a largely negative activity in those historical periods – including most areas of Western aesthetic production since the Renaissance – when originality and authenticity are highly valued. The exemplar of the original work is one in which the material form in which the work is embedded is its singular authentic performance. A painting or a sculpture is unique in this sense, in that the ideational structure of the work is entirely coextensive with its material form, and, as a corollary, even the most faithful copy cannot, in theory, exhaustively reproduce this content. A literary work or a musical score, by contrast, has an ideational content which is relatively independent of any particular material embodiment. A poem remains the "same" whether it is typeset or written out by hand; the musical score or the dramatic work is an ideal form which receives variant interpretations in performance.

These distinctions are taken up and elaborated in Western intellectual property doctrine from the C18 onwards: US **copyright law**, for example, protects (a) expressions of ideas in (b) works of authorship fixed in (c) copies or phonorecords (Jaszi, 1991; M. Rose, 1993). The "copy" thus stands at the end of a double series of Platonic substance–expression relations, moving from most to least abstract, and it may in turn form the starting point for the production of a further chain of materializations of the "work." Thus the performance of a work can in its turn become eligible for copyright protection – that is, it can itself be considered an original work. What the distinction between work and copy equally entails, however, is the existence of distinct sets of property rights, since rights of ownership in the material object which a painter sells to the purchaser of a painting, for example, do not necessarily carry with them the rights to make and sell reproductions of the object. These distinctions are founded, finally, in the principle of authorship, the singular act of will and intention which guarantees the uniqueness of the work and which is expressed, literally or metaphorically, in the signature of the artist (Woodmansee, 1994).

Much contemporary thinking about the relation between originals and copies in aesthetic production goes back to Walter Benjamin's essay on "The work of art in the age of mechanical reproduction" (1968). Benjamin argues that technologies of reproduction, from the medieval woodcut through the printing press, the lithograph, photography, and the cinema (and we would now add the photocopier, the personal computer, the tape and disk recorder, and MP3), have radically undermined the privileged value given to the "auratic" original work. The effect of the mass reproduction of representations is to make them, in John Berger's words, "available, valueless, free" (Berger, 1972: 32). We might question the extent to which this revaluation has in fact happened, as the value of originality has, if anything, been strengthened in the regimes of mass reproduction of art. Yet it is clear that in many areas of practice the dependence of copies upon originals has weakened or even been reversed, and that a more positive notion of copying as increase, generosity, abundance has entered deep into popular consciousness. The widespread downloading of music files from the Internet is perhaps the clearest example of this change. This shift away from the Platonic schema, which so influentially organized Western modes of thinking about the structure of the real, has extended to many of the ways in which we think about representation in general. Popular disrespect for the protected status of originals has come to converge with the poststructuralist argument that it is, in principle, impossible to make any absolute distinction between a singular origin and its secondary repetition.

John Frow

See: *ART, REPRESENTATION, WRITING.*

Country

The word **country** comes into modern English from L (*contrata*), through oF (*contrée*), giving us a root sense of *opposition*: "that which lies opposite or fronting the view, the landscape spread out before one." The idea of country as opposition (to self, to city) is crucial to the formation of the kinds of specular and intrepid attitudes to landscape and unknown countries which were to dominate the centuries of European empire. By way of contrast, indigenous attitudes to country are more ones of nurturing and ancestral connection.

Yet one of the two broad meanings of country ("native land") is congruent with this indigenous sense; the other (the "rural or agricultural parts of it") is more in contrast to the urban (R. Williams, 1976: 71). The first meaning is heavily loaded with affect and ideology: in war, for instance, one "dies for one's country." In this respect there is a strong overlap between "country" and "nation," because "nation" is where the state stockpiles its cultural and historical investments. "Country" is where the heart is, so it is most often with this word in mind that homesickness is felt (one does not miss one's nation), and it is in a **new country** that the migrant strives to recreate a sense of belonging.

The link between affective investment and country is made even more easily with the second meaning of "the rural parts" Williams refers to as everything that is not the city or suburbs (R. Williams, 1973: 9). Fueled by ancient bucolic or pastoral genres, and finally intensified as a huge wave of collective nostalgia in the wake of the upheavals of the

European Industrial Revolutions, the idea of country as a primal paradise is nearing its final days in these times of environmental disaster and mad cow disease. So Stephen Greenblatt is almost *obliged* to ironize the pastoral as he stops to take a picture in a beautiful Tuscan valley of a farmer plowing behind a team of white oxen: "Filled with the beauty of the scene, which seemed to leap directly from a painting by Piero della Francesca, I shouted to the farmer in my primitive but enthusiastic Italian, 'What beautiful countryside!' He looked up and, from his vantage point in the field shouted back, 'It's better in the city!' " (Greenblatt, 1996: 26). Opposition once again, of the type made explicit by Raymond Williams (1973). But this peasant's unromantic view is often shared by the bulk of the world's population, for third world ambitions (less so indigenous ones) have lead to massive demographic movements out of rural poverty into the over-crowded cities.

These erstwhile peasants, now city folk, might well identify generations later with their home countries, provinces, and localities, addressing those with whom they have this affinity with the term equivalent to **countryman**: *compatriotes* (F), *paesano* (It), *paisano* (Sp), *landsmann* (G). This, then, constitutes the base community unit defining a people's relationship to its country, and is the closest to the sense of "native." Only by gathering such communities together can the "imagined" community of a nation be formed (B. Anderson, 1983).

The case of Aboriginal Australia can be used to extend the sense of "native" country to its stronger indigenous sense. Most indigenous Australians identify with country via interpersonal relations, including rights and responsibilities for its upkeep, without any sense of country as alienable possession. When asked about their country, indigenous Australians are more likely to talk about "Finke River" than "Australia," even if they are asked this question in New York. They do not circumscribe country in a bounded cartographic way: "Country, to Aborigines, is designated by a track across the land. It is a series of nameable geographical locations interconnected as the itinerary of ancestral travels. The totem identity – that is, the identity with a plant, animal or natural form – designates a track (a song line) and one's country" (Gill, 1998: 299). Clearly such a conception of highly developed interpersonal connections with country – country as kin – runs counter to the capitalist conception of country as alienable and exploitable for purposes of agriculture or mining. In consequence, some of the more interesting problems posed for international law in recent years have concerned indigenous struggles for land rights and water rights ("country" can include waterways and coastal seas).

The pitching into the public arena of these indigenous ideas about country and its management has been joined by the alternatives of the green movement. But the indigenous–green alliances have not always been clear cut. They can often part ways over such issues as the definition of wilderness and the utility of national parks. "Wilderness" can too easily link up with the romantic conception of a primal paradise, where human presence – including indigenous ancestral occupation – is effaced. National park managers have begun to use the vocabulary of "multiple stakeholders" of country where different users may have contradictory practices in the country; such contradictions might, for instance, allow indigenous people the exclusive right to hunt certain native animals.

Legal struggles over country are accompanied by adjacent cultural representations (W. J. T. Mitchell, 1994a), which are a secondary source of its value (its primary one being the source of raw materials). This secondary valuing is nevertheless the source of all knowledge about country, including its cartography and guidelines for its treatment. This knowledge is objectified as cultural representations of country, which can often be called landscapes. Such representations can appear in any medium: *framed* as a landscape painting or photograph; conceived of as a suitable *site* for building (as in landscape architecture); or captured as a *moving image* in the cinema. The aesthetics of such landscapes are politics carried out by other means, for what one learns to *value* in landscape enables one to "culture" forms of life in any site where a "good" way to live is being sought. In the comfort of our homes a "picture window" thus domesticates the "landscaped" country outside, or in a hotel a clichéd painting on the wall reminds us of the aesthetic function supposedly intensifying our relationships to country, creating feelings of homeliness or, indeed, of alienation.

Stephen Muecke

See: *CITY, HOME, NATION.*

Culture

There is now a good deal of hesitancy over the value of the word **culture**. "I don't know how many times," Raymond Williams once said, "I've wished that I'd never heard the damned word" (R. Williams, 1979: 154), registering his frustration that its complexity defied the tasks of ordinary analysis. Adam Kuper (1999) is of much the same mind. The term is now so overused, he argues, that is better to break it down into its component parts and speak of beliefs, ideas, art, and traditions rather than expect to find a set of shared characteristics which brings these together as part of a wider field of culture. Yet the consensus of opinion probably lies with James Clifford when he says that culture is "a deeply compromised idea," but one he "cannot yet do without" (Clifford, 1988: 10).

For at the same time as difficulties have been expressed regarding the value of the vocabulary of culture, the range of contexts in which that vocabulary now figures has multiplied extraordinarily in recent years. Earlier qualified uses of the term – such as **high culture**, **folk culture**, **mass culture**, and **popular culture** – remain, albeit that the judgments these implied in the context of class divisions have been weakened. References to **national cultures** and to **regional cultures**, whether at the subnational or supranational levels, remain, but with the added complication that the boundary lines between what is to count as national and what as regional have become increasingly contested. However, there is also now an extended range of uses relating to forms of difference that operate both within nations and across the relations between them. **Gay culture**, **lesbian culture**, **black culture**, **ethnic cultures**, **diasporic cultures**, and **transnational cultures** are all cases in point. The strong association that has been established between the concept of culture and the notion of lifestyles has generated another range of extensions – from **subcultures** and **counter-cultures** to **club cultures**, **street cultures**, and **drug cultures**. **Body culture**, **consumer culture**, **prosthetic culture**, **material culture**, **sports culture**, **media culture**, and **visual culture** similarly point to a proliferation of usage, while **culture shock** indicates a distinctively modern condition arising from an overexposure to cultural stimulation.

Use of the adjectival **cultural** has, if anything, grown more rapidly. We now live, we are told, in a **cultural economy**; **cultural policies** are an increasingly important field of government activity, with **cultural diversity**, **cultural pluralism**, and **cultural access and participation** important policy objectives. Inner cities are constantly being revived through **cultural development**, **cultural regeneration**, or **cultural animation** programs. **Cultural rights** are now a significant aspect of contemporary citizenship entitlements, while **cultural heritage**, **cultural property**, and the **cultural landscape** are to be preserved and protected. **Cultural imperialism**, **cultural genocide**, **cultural tourism**, **cultural materialism**, and **cultural capital** all indicate an extended use of the adjectival form in more specialist and academic languages. And whole fields of knowledge are now described as cultural. If **cultural studies** and **cultural critique** led the way here, the fields of **cultural psychology**, **cultural history**, **cultural geography**, and **cultural evolution** have followed in short order as a part of the more general **cultural turn** in the humanities and social sciences.

The unqualified use of culture as a normative standard – still best evoked by Matthew Arnold's description as "the acquainting ourselves with the best that has been known and said in the world" (1876) – has, however, become rarer. Its champions, moreover, now typically write in an embattled and militant tone. Harold Bloom's (1995) defense of "great literature" as an improving force in the context of the US **culture wars** is perhaps the most striking example. By and large, however, the belief that a particular canon of literary, music, or artistic works can claim a monopoly of **cultural value** is no longer widely supported. This partly reflects the increased role of democratic and egalitarian sentiment, which has made it harder for intellectual elites to claim any special value for their preferred cultural activities over those of other social groups. The resentment such claims occasioned is evident in the long tradition of satirizing elite claims to cultural superiority that we see in such terms as **culture vulture**, **culture hound**, and **culchah** (or **kulcha** in Australia).

Equally, the waning use of culture as a normative standard reflects the unraveling of the associations which had earlier sustained the meaning of culture as, in Williams's summary, "a general process of intellectual, spiritual and aesthetic development" and – as the most evident fruits of this process – "the works and practices of intellectual and especially artistic activity"(R. Williams, 1976: 80). With its most immediate roots in L *cultura*, referring to the processes of cultivation, caring, or tending, culture implied growth and improvement. This was evident in early horticultural usage where it could refer to both the process of tending for plants and animals ("Such a...plot of his Eden...gratefully crowns his Culture...with chaplets of Flowers" [Boyle, 1665–9]) and the result of such husbandry ("The erth...by...dylygent labour...ys brought to maruelous culture and fertylite" [Starkey, 1538]). The same is true of later scientific usage to refer to the artificial development of microscopic organisms and the growth of plant and animal cells and tissues, where culture can refer to a particular method of growth – that of **tissue culture**, for example – or the chemical substance in which growth is effected, as in **culture medium** or **culture fluid**. This usage was also later extended to the practices through which individuals might seek to develop or improve themselves. This might refer to physical development through the training of the body, as in Hobbes's observation that among the Lacedaemonians, "especially in the culture of their bodies, the nobility observed the most equality with the commons" (1628). Or it might refer to the cultivation of intellectual or spiritual attributes. "The education of Children," Hobbes claimed, comprised "a Culture of their minds" (1991 [1651]).

It is, however, with the transfer of this set of meanings from the nourishment and growth of individuals to that of society that the most decisive change underlying modern usage occurs. In this history, beginning in the IC18 and eC19 and progressing through to the mC20, culture comes to stand for a general process of social improvement. Functioning, initially, as a term more or less interchangeable with civilization in this regard, its IC19 and eC20 development is conditioned by the emergence of an increasing tension between these two terms. Worked through first in German Romanticism, this history was produced and sustained by a set of antagonisms between, on the one hand, civilization as a standard of material progress best indexed by the development of industrial production and, on the other, culture as the embodiment of a set of higher standards in whose name material civilization might be indicted for its shallowness, coarseness, or incompleteness, when viewed from the higher standards of human wholeness or perfection that the notion of culture increasingly came to represent.

This set of oppositions has proved a productive one. It has sustained a distinctive form of social commentary developed, first, in the German as **Kulturkritik**, and continuing into the present as **cultural criticism** or **cultural critique**, in which works of culture serve as the occasion for the identification of the failings and shortcomings of society. The mixing and mingling of the concepts of culture and aesthetics were important in this regard, especially in the role that aesthetics played in locating in the work of art those higher standards of perfection that the emerging concept of culture proposed as an alternative to the standards of industrial civilization. Friedrich Schiller's *Letters on the aesthetic education of man* (1967 [1795]) proved especially important here. Schiller defined the encounter between the person and the work of art as one in which the former was confronted with their imperfections and inadequacies when judged from the higher standards of the art work.

This meant that the experience of art could be transformed into one of self-improvement, as the person would aim to close the gap between their rough empirical self and the poise and harmony represented by the work of art.

If culture thus supplied a set of standards through which industrial civilization might be called to account before a higher court of appeal, it also supplied a means of overcoming the shortcomings that such a court might pronounce. The material and institutional history of culture is important here. Culture, in this specializing and improving sense, existed not just as a set of ideas: in the mC19 development of public libraries, museums, concert halls, and art galleries, it also informed the practices of a new set of **cultural institutions** which aimed to combat the shortcomings of civilization by diffusing the higher standards of culture throughout society. While these shortcomings included the values of industrialism, they also, and more particularly, included the ways of life of the urban working classes and the need to enfold these classes within the improving force of culture if the threat of anarchy were to be averted.

The whole material layout of the C19 city was radically affected by this conception of culture and its mobilization as a moral force through which individuals might be enabled to improve themselves to achieve the kinds of poise, balance, and self-perfection that Schiller spoke of. Arnold captured this sense when he wrote that "culture indefatigably tries not to make what each raw person may like, the rule by which he fashions himself; but to draw ever nearer to a sense of what is indeed beautiful, graceful, and becoming, and to get the raw person to like that" (Arnold, 1971 [1869]: 39). The C18 had been a "display city" (P. Joyce, 2003: 151) where, in promenades and assembly rooms, the well-to-do exhibited their civility and enlightenment without any regard to either their own moral interiors or those of the subordinate classes. In the C19, the transference of the religiously inspired associations of Gothic architecture to libraries, museums, and galleries incorporated a moral address into the built forms of the urban environment, as they beckoned the urban population with the prospect of spiritual and cultural uplift and improvement.

Such conceptions continued to be influential in the C20, informing the development of public broadcast systems and with an ongoing, albeit diminished, impact on cultural policies. The period from the mC19 to the eC21 has, however, witnessed serious challenges to the singular normative view of culture which underlies the culture–civilization opposition. This reflects the challenges that have come from the varied social movements – old and new – which have refused to accept the negative evaluation of their own cultural pursuits that the Arnoldian usage entailed. The socialist and labor movements, feminism, the struggles of indigenous peoples and of minority ethnic cultures, and the identification of the African-American contributions to the cultures of modernism have all taken issue with the classed, gendered, racial, and Eurocentric biases that undermined the universalism of culture's claim to be the best that has been known and said. The increased commodification of all forms of **cultural production** and **cultural consumption** has also blurred any sense of a single division between "real culture" and "the rest." In what are now highly segmented **cultural markets** with their own internal distinctions of value, high culture looks more and more like one cultural market among others.

The use and interpretation of culture within academic debates have both been affected by and contributed to these developments. Williams's own writing on culture has proved important here. By showing how the supposedly universal standards of perfection associated with the normative view of culture turned out, in practice, to have strong connections with the particular values of ruling groups and classes, he extended our sense of what might count as culture. This made it possible for the symbolic aspects of everyday life to be included as well as the products of high culture – and, just as important, to be included on the same terms without any sense of an essential and embattled distinction between "real culture" and "the rest."

As a result of these developments, the view of culture as a standard of perfection has tended to give way to the third of Williams's senses of culture, referring to the "particular way of life, whether of a people, a period or a group" (R. Williams, 1976: 80). Edward Tylor, a key figure in the development of lC19 social anthropology, has often been credited with the responsibility for this view of culture. Williams sees him as a link between Johann Gottfried von Herder's lC18 critique of the Eurocentric values implicit in "universal" histories of culture and civilization, and eC20 forms of **cultural relativism**. The key text here is the passage where Tylor says that culture "is that complex whole which includes knowledge, belief, art, morals, law, custom, and any other capabilities and habits acquired by man as a member of society" (Tylor, 1874: 1). However, the seeming even-handedness that is implied here is, as George Stocking Jr (1968) notes, belied as Tylor proceeds to arrange different cultures into evolutionary stages, in which each stage represents progress from one state of culture development between the twin extremes of "savage and cultured life" (Tylor, 1874: 26).

Yet it is still with good reason that the view of culture as a way of life is referred to as the ethnographic or anthropological definition of culture. For it owes its most influential contemporary formulation to the work of Franz Boas. Trained in German anthropology in the lC19, Boas translated the non-evolutionary assumptions of German anthropology into the first fully developed statement of the principles of cultural relativism during his later work in America. As different cultures set their own standards of value, Boas argued, only serious misunderstanding and social harm can result from attempts to arrange cultures into evaluative hierarchies or evolutionary sequences. As the first social scientist to speak of **cultures** in the plural (Menand, 2002: 384), Boas's work contributed to the broader criticisms of American society as a melting pot in which differences were to be extinguished that was evident in the writings of pragmatists like John Dewey. Boas's sense of the social and relational nature of cultures, defined in terms of their differences from one another, was also evident in William Du Bois's use of the term "double-consciousness" to describe the identities of African-Americans, caught in the relations between white and black cultures.

67

It is this sense of culture as a set of flows and relations that lies behind some of the misgivings that Arjun Appadurai (1996) expresses regarding the continuing value of the ethnographic concept of culture as a "way of life." For this has often led to a tendency to taxonomize cultures by providing a means of dividing societies into separate groups identified in terms of their distinctive beliefs and behaviors. As such, its history has been closely bound up with the development of modern forms of administration. Theodor Adorno was perhaps the first to notice this when he noted that "the single word 'culture' betrays from the outset the administrative view, the task of which, looking down from on high, is to assemble, distribute, evaluate and organise" (Adorno, 1991: 93). It is, however, the uses to which culture has been put in association with the development of colonial forms of administration that have most exercised more recent criticisms of this administrative logic. Used as a way of dividing colonized populations into separate groups identified in terms of their ways of life, the ethnographic concept of culture was integral to the development of colonial systems of rule which aimed to segregate populations along racial and ethnic lines (Dirks, 2001).

There is accordingly, in current usage, a move away from the view that cultures can be described as fixed and separate entities. The terms **cultural hybridity**, **cultural flows**, **transculturation**, **cross-cultural dialogue**, and **cultural in-betweenness** thus all draw attention to the fluidity and impermanence of cultural distinctions and relationships. The change of emphasis that is involved here is best captured by the shift from speaking of **different cultures** to a stress on **cultures in difference**, with the implication that cultural activities are caught up in processes of differing rather than being simply different from the outset. The emphasis on processes of racializing or ethnicizing culture points in the same direction.

Distinctions between nature and culture now also have a weaker force as a result of the increasing sense that the relations between these are best thought of as porous and permeable. Developments in human genetics, biology, biotechnology, genetic medicine, and biotechnology have been especially important here, leading to a series of technological interventions into the human body and nature – from *in vitro* fertilization to genetically modified (GM) crops – which have called into question their separation from cultural processes. The new vocabulary of **cyberculture**, **nanoculture**, **somatic culture**, and **technoculture** reflect these concerns, which are equally central to contemporary popular culture – the *Terminator* movies, for example.

It is a moot point, however, whether, in spite of all these changes, current ways of thinking about and engaging with culture have entirely escaped the pull of the eC19 to mC20 construction of the relations between culture and civilization. However, this now increasingly appears to be best thought of as a historically specific set of mechanisms for sorting populations into groups and managing the relations between them. There was, William Ray (2001) argues, a clear **logic of culture** at work here in the sense that culture, by posing itself as a challenge to, and opportunity for, individual self-improvement seemed to offer a means for individuals to sort themselves into different groups. Culture thus offered an important means for regulating societies by suggesting that their key divisions resulted from the ways in which individuals seemed naturally to differentiate themselves according to how far they did (the respectable middle classes) and did not (the feckless poor) respond to the cultural imperative of self-improvement. This mechanism did not operate in colonial contexts, where the logic of culture as a "way of life" was annexed to the more coercive forms of management associated with "the ethnographic state" (Dirks, 2001). Nor, in other contact histories, has it proved to be easily transportable. The mixture of incomprehension and opposition that resulted from attempts to mobilize (as newly invented terms) art (*bijitsu*) and culture (*bunka*) in the programs of civilization and enlightenment (*bunmei kaika*) characterizing the Meiji period in Japan (Figal, 1999) testify to just how far this logic of culture has been bound and limited to the West. The spread, more generally, however, of differentiated cultural markets and lifestyles, each with its own distinctive styles of consumption and ways of fashioning behavior, has proved a more adaptable way of reshaping social distinctions by virtue of the groups into which individuals seem naturally to sort themselves through the cultural activities they pursue.

Tony Bennett

See: **AESTHETICS, ART, CANON, CIVILIZATION, COLONIALISM, ETHNICITY, RACE.**

69

Deconstruction

Deconstruction is a strategy of critical analysis associated with the work of the French philosopher Jacques Derrida and with a loose grouping of literary critics in the United States, the most prominent of whom was Paul de Man. It has been widely taken up in journalism and other non-specialized contexts as an almost routine synonym for "criticism" or "critique." While these usages are often hostile toward the perceived difficulty of **deconstructive** thought, they also work to domesticate it as a common-sense operation of the disassembling of philosophical preconceptions. In the hands of its defenders, especially in popularizing manuals and critical expositions, deconstruction is frequently understood as a critical *method* or procedure, involving the reversal and then annulment of hierarchically opposed terms. In the hands of its enemies (usually only superficially acquainted with its texts), it is frequently accused of being a form of skeptical relativism. Both positions are a kind of pastiche, but both reflect the difficulty of doing justice to the complexity of the concept. The difficulty is compounded for an exercise in synopsis such as this by the fact that any attempt to fix and delimit a distinctive philosophical or critical position called "deconstruction" has the effect of undermining precisely the deconstructive questioning of closed systems and fixed limits. Deconstruction is a strategy of complication: its characteristic modes of reading have to do with paying close and faithful attention at once to the heterogeneous logics of a text and to the conditions of possibility and of actualization of those logics in framing systems which are neither finite nor closed nor separable from the reader. To summarize is to close off that movement toward relational complexity.

ABC**D**EFGHIJKLMNOPQRSTUVWXYZ

Yet I take courage both from the inevitability of such a closure, and from the fact that Derrida himself at times found it necessary to simplify his argument. In a 1971 interview, collected in English in *Positions* (1987: 41–3), he speaks of a "kind of general strategy of deconstruction," designed "to avoid both simply *neutralizing* the binary oppositions of metaphysics and simply *residing* within the closed field of these oppositions, thereby confirming it." Deconstruction is thus a way of working through a double movement: on the one hand, a movement of overturning or reversal of the asymmetrical binary hierarchies of metaphysical thought (one/many, same/other, essence/accident, speech/writing, center/periphery...), in such a way as to register the constitutive dependence of the major on the minor term; on the other, a movement beyond the framework delimited by these terms (and still operative when their relationship is dislodged) to an always provisional suspension of their force. This suspension operates by means of new, provisional concepts, or "quasiconcepts" as Rodolphe Gasché (1986) calls them, which are often punning conflations of discrete terms (*différance, pharmakon, hymen, archiécriture*) and which "can no longer be included within philosophical (binary) opposition but which, however, inhabit philosophical opposition, resisting and disorganizing it, *without ever constituting a third term, without ever leaving room for a solution in the form of speculative dialectics*" (Derrida, 1987: 43). The quasiconcepts are one-off, temporary solutions to a local problem, and in principle not adaptable to the formulation of new conceptual frameworks. Deconstruction refuses the possibility of transcendental critique. It can neither stand nor arrive at a point outside the field of metaphysics, a point of truth or recognition from which it could denounce error. Its meta-language is always entwined, always complicit, with the languages it reads.

Thus the great categories of Western thought which Derrida is so often accused of nihilistically discarding – truth, reference, reason, intention, presence, the subject – are not annulled in his writings. Each such category is rather *inscribed* within a system which it no longer dominates (Derrida, 1976). The category is thus understood as having effects within a particular historical field rather than carrying any absolute force. The metaphor of textuality (of writing, trace, genre, spacing) used here and throughout Derrida's work is not a way of talking about representation (and of the implication of presence it carries with it), but a way of trying to conceptualize that structure of "differences without positive terms" posited by Ferdinand de Saussure (1966 [1916]: 120) as the very structure of language. Deconstruction is a reading of and toward systems of differential relations which (unlike those of "classical" structuralism) exist and change in time and are open-ended; of modes of being without self-identity or origin; of a presence which is endlessly deferred.

The centrality of literary texts to Derrida's oeuvre, or rather his constant refusal of clear boundaries between philosophical and literary genres, made his practice of reading a compelling model for literary studies. In the hands of Paul de Man (1983) and his Yale colleagues and students, this practice was developed into a sophisticated form of analysis of the ways in which complex texts always already anticipate the deconstructive work performed upon them. If a certain predictability often attached to this pattern of reading, it was nevertheless often offset by the possibility of extending literary modes of analysis to other domains such as theology, law, and politics. In rather different ways, deconstruction has been widely taken up by feminist and postcolonial critics, and in this context the key influence is perhaps that of Gayatri Spivak (1988, 1999) rather than Derrida.

John Frow

See: *DIFFERENCE, REPRESENTATION, SIGN, TEXT, WRITING.*

Democracy

Democracy stems from ancient Gk *demos* = people, *kratos* = rule. For many centuries, in the minds of European elites at least, particular connotations of both **the demos**/people (the poor, the common herd, the plebs, the multitude, the "fickle and ungrateful populace" [Machiavelli, 1531]) and "rule" (not only government, but also influence and "sway") were fused together. This close association, usually a negative one given its hint of "mob rule," was sometimes consolidated more descriptively into a singular substantive reference – "the commonaltie" (Elyot, 1531), "the democratie," "the democracy" (C18–C19). Thus, while democracy served Western political theorists as a conceptual contrast with oligarchy and monarchy, it was only in the lC19 that intellectuals and politicians began to regard democracy as a positive political value in its own right. Given the supposed volatility of the common people, and their openness to manipulation, Byron's (1821) view of democracy as "an aristocracy of blackguards" summed up the mainstream attitude to that point.

An alternative, affirmative tradition had its early statement in Pericles's famous oration on the fallen of the Peloponnesian War (431 BCE), in which Athenian democracy – which, however, excluded women, slaves, and foreigners – is commended as a model to others because power is in the hands not of a minority but of the whole people, and everyone is equal before the law. Much later on, in the Putney Debates of 1647 that followed the English Civil War, Colonel Rainborough revived for the modern period the basic case for popular sovereignty: "every man born in England cannot, ought not, neither by the Law of God or the Law of Nature, to be exempted from the choice of those who are to make laws for him to live under." Heterodox though such "leveling" thoughts were, they still endorsed **electoral democracy** rather than the stronger proposition that a truly **democratic polity** needed underpinning by a truly **democratic society**, a radical proposition taken up by the Diggers in the same period. In the C20, Marxist thought continued this line, systematically positioning substantive **social(ist) democracy** as intrinsically superior to **bourgeois-liberal democracy**, which according to Lenin (1917) was "democracy for the moneybags," and therefore "hypocritical and false through and through." Communist regimes used this doctrine to legitimate the **"people's democracies"** by reference to their provision of public goods and local participation in official or party arrangements, rather than to political freedom and general elections.

As epochal campaigns for **democratization** unfolded, whether in the name of commercial interests, industrialists, the propertyless, women, people of color, or the colonized, so the meaning of "democracy" altered or broadened. Such proto-democratic expressions as constitutional restrictions on absolute power; "parliamentary" consultation; forms of autonomous council and guild decision-making; schismatic developments within the churches; and the representation of the different "estates" of the realm were established even before the onset of modern **liberal democracy**. But as the latter emerged from the heritage of the IC18 revolutions in America and France, further political reforms were explicitly designated as gains for democracy itself: the abolition of slavery, labor legislation, religious toleration, regular elections, universal suffrage, competitive party politics, secret ballots, and independence for colonial dominions. With these democratic landmarks often spreading across borders in the form of international "waves," no more spectacular surge occurred than in the 1980s and 1990s, when the Soviet bloc disintegrated, and when a significant number of authoritarian states in South America, Africa, and Asia adopted democratic constitutions. By the end of the C20, more people could be said to be "experiencing democracy" in some meaningful sense than at any previous time, the ascendancy of specifically liberal democracy being flagged up by Francis Fukuyama (1992) as representing nothing less than the "end of history" itself.

Notwithstanding the continuing drive of the various narratives of democratization, there is considerable contestation over democracy's content and value. As Raymond Williams (1976: 97–8) remarked, "no questions are more difficult than those of democracy, in any of its central senses." This is partly because each process of democratization serves to highlight (new) issues about what exactly *more* and *better* democracy involves, and (changing) issues about the proper *subject, scope,* and *depth* of political "self-determination."

Who or what is the *subject* of democracy? Any straightforward notion of "the (common) people" as the quintessential democratic protagonist now appears slightly dubious or dated. Modern electoral democracy has developed in tandem with the nation state, such that the workings of the democratic polity are deemed to reflect not only current policy preferences, but also the historic aspirations, character, and culture, of the people-nation. This powerful identification of the people with state, with nation, and sometimes with ethnicity too – in some cases *constitutionally* so – has never gone unchallenged, but it has become even more cautiously regarded following harrowing episodes of "ethnic cleansing" during the 1990s (the Balkans, Rwanda), and efforts to export American norms so as to ensure the "triumph of democracy" in the "war on terror" (President George W. Bush, 2003).

Democracy

Once "the people" is imagined not in terms of some lofty and homogeneous General Will (Rousseau), or even as the settled wishes of the *majority*; but rather as the complex gathering of the opinions and perspectives of those diverse groups and individuals who comprise *all* of the people in a given territory, some of the shine rubs off the original ideal. Elite theorists from Plato to Edmund Burke advocated political "guardianship" as the antidote to the likely tyranny of the majority, while the mC20 economist Joseph Schumpeter (1943) presented democracy as "rule of the politician," and the American pluralist scholar Robert Dahl (1971) argued that "polyarchy," in which power is brokered and circulated between a number of minority sociopolitical interest groups, is the best we can do in modern circumstances. Later perspectives qualifying classical democracy include multiculturalism and cosmopolitanism. Multiculturalists (Parekh, 1993, for example) stress the Eurocentrism of liberal-democratic norms and see (Western) identifications of nation and people as being harmful to the claims of cultural minorities. Cosmopolitanism in its lC20 and eC21 form defends a background universal humanism – partly as a counter to the drift toward multicultural particularism – but emphasizes too that under conditions of globalization, democratic practice will become increasingly complex, differentiated, and demanding, having a truly planetary as well as international, regional, national, and local remit (Held, 1995).

These geographical factors clearly affect considerations of the proper *scope* of democratic organization. More generally, the scope of democracy has typically been limited to the official sphere of public government. But in contemporary society, all sorts of previously "non-political" relations are steadily coming under democratic interrogation. **Industrial democracy**, for example, has long been a socialistic concern, intensified by the growth of transnational corporations, and the extent to which economic and social democratization can be advanced while capitalism reigns remains a pivotal question. However, class matters have been joined by those of gender, sexuality, ethnicity, (dis)ability, and other expressions of "the politics of difference." How, it is frequently demanded, can male domination, racism, or discrimination of any kind be legitimated in a polity/society claiming to be democratic, that is, in which citizens are supposed to be free and equal? In these questions, "democracy's" meaning as a specific principle of organization – rule by and for the people/majority – is being expanded into a broader social ethic relating to the conditions and consequences of "deep" democracy. The narrowly "political" democrat can of course answer that it is simply an exaggeration of the scope of democracy to stretch it to questions of basic social organization. Nonetheless, it is widely conceded that democracy needs to be grounded in effective capacities and rights, and so the sequence of civic, political, and social **democratic rights** described by T. H. Marshall (1950) has been extended by some to include cultural, sexual, reproductive, and various other human rights too.

Meanwhile, our understanding of the sphere of government has developed into a multiform notion of governance, signaling the formation of behavior and morals across the whole range of civil society's institutions. Democratic involvement thus comes to pertain not only to parties and parliaments, but also to schools, health-care trusts, and enterprises; and not only to these but also to professional and voluntary associations, leisure clubs and cultural bodies, the mass media, and onward again on to the "democratization of intimacy" (Giddens, 1992): family life, love, personal and sexual relationships. Also, in the "network society" of the eC21, intriguing questions of **cyber-democracy** arise, just as, in our "risk society," popular democratic control over environmental threats and biotechnological developments has become a pressing yet also formidable issue.

In this context, it remains difficult to determine how *deeply* democratic institutions need to be. The benchmark of **direct democracy**, in which the people rule in a collective and unmediated way, was long thought to be unfeasible (as well as undesirable). Government by representatives of the people, stereotyped until the 1960s as men of sound judgment, became the liberal-democratic norm, and *the vote* the paramount democratic event. With the remarkable spread of information technology, however, the prospect of informed **mass democracy** has come back on to the agenda. Yet there are severe practical as well as principled issues about the right kind of balance to strike between direct, representative, and consultative mechanisms, and between the alternative ways of "counting democracy" (majorities, pluralities, proportionalities).

It can even be asked whether any individual, group, or cause can authentically be represented by others, and whether it is enough for democratic politicians to refer to the state of "public opinion" as an acceptable representation of "the people." It is certainly true that our political understandings are formulated within a dense web of discourse that is pervaded by the workings of the mass media. The proposals and personalities of politicians themselves are also "spun" into this web, such that the traditional reference point of an independent people's "mandate" seems remote. Perhaps therefore the people's views can be adequately gauged through mechanisms such as focus groups, opinion polls, specialist consultancies, or targeted electronic debate? In this way, a "managerialist" refiguring of politics has emerged, in which enthusiasm for proper "leadership" is balanced more in terms of "accountability" and "consultation" than of democracy.

If political managerialism and "spin" constitute one aspect of what has been called **post-democratic culture**, large-scale disaffection on the part of the managed is another. At least in the so-called "advanced" democracies, true majorities for presidents or governments are rare; political careerism and opportunism abound; allegiance and affiliation to conventional parties have declined; and functional and ideological links between conventional parties and social constituencies have weakened. The underlying social rationale for this involves the erosion of the politics of class, neighborhood, and representation by processes of individualization, mobility, and consumerism. In this context, mass democratic politics splits into two main constituencies. One of these is engaged in "lifestyle" and "stakeholding" politics, pursuing material interests and "postmaterial" values through informed and articulate lobbying. But another, substantial, section of people is

75

effectively "excluded" and "apathetic," their active control over their own lives and the world at large appearing to be sheer fantasy.

"Radical" responses to problems of cynicism and exclusion highlight the need for enhanced participation and deliberation. Marginalized groups, it is thought, must be present in the democratic process, not represented at a distance (socially as well as physically). And there must be strenuous and inclusive dialog about their concerns. Such deliberation, moreover, while involving rational debate, should not be so class-coded or Eurocentrically framed as to limit the variety and vitality of popular political communication (welcomes, salutes, narratives of involvement, challenges, apologies). But even this kind of **extended democracy** faces problems. For example, we cannot all be present – or will necessarily want to be involved – in all the forums that affect our lives and perspectives, and in any case face-to-face deliberation is by no means exempt from tactics of agenda-manipulation, status exploitation, bullying, or self-interest.

If democratic thought, then, continues to throw up important new as well as long-standing questions, its utopian element – the idea that democracy furthers the achievement of an ideal society through transparent and harmonious resolution of political differences – has probably retreated. Contemporary libertarians, for example (Graham, 2002), regard democracy as simply legitimating ever-increasing and harmful state power. Some post-modernists for their part uphold, rather vaguely and minimally, the "transgressive" energies of a new nomadic global multitude (Hardt and Negri, 2000), while others insist that even robust democratic arrangements cannot eliminate political conflict. In this context, political motivation perhaps comes less from the pull of democracy *per se*, and more from the appeal of the combinations it forms with various – very different – qualifying terms: liberal, representative, egalitarian, radical pluralist, discursive, cosmo-politan, associational, consociational, electronic, socialist, experimental, participatory, and so on.

Gregor McLennan

See: *CITIZENSHIP, ELITE, GOVERNMENT, LIBERALISM, NATION, PARTICIPATION, RADICAL, UTOPIA.*

Desire

Is it the capacity **to desire** that makes us human? **Desire** is both ineffable and at the heart of how we understand ourselves. "Anything your heart desires": from remodeled bodies to the perfect partner and designer child, the advertising industry promises that every desire can be satisfied. Of course the satiation of desire is not quite that simple. The fulfillment of one set of desires often only brings on more desire. As many have argued (R. Williams, 1980; J. Williamson, 1995), capitalism is premised on a cycle of satisfying desire and creating new desires. Paradoxically, this aspirational economy runs on the implicit knowledge that human desire outstrips the range of commodities on offer. While consumer culture translates human desires (for love, happiness, and a good life) into commodity objects, we know we want (something) more. Desire seems to be haunted by its own impossibility. Summarizing a history of Western philosophical accounts about desire, Elizabeth Grosz writes that "desire is both a shortcoming and a vindication of human endeavor" (Grosz, 1995: 176). This description captures a sense of the epic role that desire has often been given in human history.

Where does desire come from? Why is the capacity to desire seemingly intertwined with the acknowledgment that its fulfillment will be thwarted? If this is increasingly obvious in consumer culture – where advertisers play on our knowledge that desire can only, at best, be momentarily satisfied – the tension between the promise and reality of desire can be found in any number of disparate ideas. For instance, many posit that the impossibility of desire is at the heart of infant development, and consequently haunts our adult lives. The neo-liberal philosopher Martha Nussbaum (2001: 192) emphasizes that it is "the human child's unique combination of cognitive capacity and bodily incapacity" which forms the basis of human desire. In other words, we know that we desire an object yet it is beyond our reach, our physical capacity. For the infant, and many speculate that this structure continues in later life, the physical incapacity to obtain a desired object means that the relationship between desire and desire-fulfilled is fraught. In the howl of "I want, I want," we hear the predicament that desire poses.

The idea that desire is a negative experience (we cannot get what we desire or, worse, we desire that which we cannot have) has been most widely promulgated by Sigmund Freud. Given how informative his thoughts have been in Western culture, it's now hard to say whether he described or prescribed our ways of desiring. In other words, it may be that we are molded by Freudian concepts. He did, however, claim a scientific status for his ideas, and a universal structure for the human psyche. Many of Freud's insights flow from his attention to the infant's struggles: "Let us imagine ourselves in the situation of an almost entirely helpless living organism...which is receiving stimuli in its nervous substance" (Freud, 1957a [1915]: 119). At a certain point of development the child begins to enlist others in the quest to secure a **desired object**. The desire – coupled with the inability – to have an object is a powerful image that guides ideas about human sociality and subjectivity.

Freud's ideas, especially about the role of desire in subjectivity, were taken up and extended by Jacques Lacan, a French psychoanalyst. The negative cast of desire was reinforced by Lacan's insistence that desire equaled lack. "Desire is neither the appetite for satisfaction, nor the demand for love, but the difference that results from the subtraction of the first from the second, the phenomenon of their splitting (*Spaltung*)" (Lacan, 1977: 287). As Robyn Ferrell rephrases this, "(*demand for love*) – (*appetite for satisfaction*) = *desire*" (1996: 86). In this sense, desire is the result of the fact that we cannot have what we desire. As an equation it seems convoluted, but in some ways it rejoins older apprehensions about desire as a human shortcoming.

Development

Freudian theory left a legacy where desire is seemingly inevitably couched in sexual terms. In this, not only is desire about sex but desire is figured in gendered ways. In this formulation, desire is seen in terms of an opposition between active and passive. This mirrors and supports the idea of women as passive, negative objects – the embodiment of lack – and men as the active, questing desirers. As many feminists argued (Doane, 1987; Mulvey, 1998), and often using Freud and Lacan to make the point, Western culture is filled with depictions of women as the objects of desire who are seemingly incapable of actively desiring for themselves. If Woman is the very object of desire, how could she possibly actively desire? The British psychoanalytic film theorist Laura Mulvey famously replied that women have to masquerade as men in order to assume a desiring role. In the images of popular culture, women have long been placed in a double bind when it comes to desire. Their bodies embraced the cars and other consumer products to be coveted, yet they were also thought to be more desirous than men, at least as consumers. Indeed, women's reactions to consumer goods were often figured as sexual desire gone wild. In this, "women's desires are sought, bought, packaged and consumed" (to quote the subtitle of Coward, 1984).

By the IC20, and partially as a result of feminist intervention, new images of desire began to emerge. Certainly, women are now portrayed as active desirers. The emphasis in popular culture on the pleasures of the body and sexuality may have broken down the idea of desire as an impossible condition. This has been matched by alternative ideas about desire as a productive force (Deleuze and Guattari, 1987). Desire has become less epic, and is seen as something which moves people, and brings them together in different ways. Desire is increasingly understood as a "productive, actualizing, liberating force" (S. J. Williams, 2001: 85). While desire remains ineffable, alternative ideas and practices of desiring are reworking the negativity of desire, and perhaps gesture to a more joyful basis of humanity.

Elspeth Probyn

See: *BODY, FEMINISM, FETISH, SEXUALITY, UNCONSCIOUS.*

Development

In a number of contemporary uses, **development** still retains the meaning of unfolding, unwrapping, evolving, and changing that it inherits from the IC16 F *desvoleper*. **Developmental psychology** studies changes in, and the evolution of, thinking and behavior in children, adolescents, adults, and the elderly. This use of "development" as change and progress toward a goal also features in the language of music, photography, and mathematics. Commercial enterprises sink vast amounts of money to design and improve products and services, and "R&D" – **research and development** – features on the agenda of most corporate board meetings. "Development" in this sense has the meaning of a carrying to fruition, an improvement, as it does in the consumerist quest for **personal development**. This notion of improvement is most obvious, however, in **real estate development**, with relation to land and the erection of new and very often large buildings, and, in the case of towns and cities, the notion of **urban development**. Thus, "The former Prime Minister of Australia [Paul Keating] has been at the forefront of the debate about Sydney's architecture and its future as a world class city...his call for a revamped philosophy for the future development of Sydney is a contemporary debate not to be missed" (Sustainable Sydney Conference, 2001).

The word **developers** has become a dirty word among those struggling to prevent the reclamation of land and the erection of commercial or other buildings, on the grounds of environmental soundness, heritage value, or the preservation of local – and usually cheaper – housing. Yet it is not only property developers who stand to benefit from **development booms**. Regulators charged with controlling the nature and impact of real estate development reap the benefit of taxes, fees, and personal inducements for **development approvals**, so that even harassed home-owners planning to build an extra attic or add a bathroom will proudly speak of their hard-won "DA."

Raymond Williams (1983) says that the most interesting modern usage of "development" relates to the nature of economic change. However, ever since World War II, the word has been much qualified and **human development**, **social development**, **sustainable development**, **equitable development**, and **people-centered development** have all been added to the vocabulary of intervention in the affairs of what Williams refers to variously as **underdeveloped**, **least developed**, and "backward" countries. And while each of these qualifying terms still relates to economic change, they have different rhetorical importance in l20C and e21C debates on development.

Development in Willams's sense has been promoted by the multilateral **development banks**. At the 1948 Bretton Woods Conference the US and the UK pushed for the establishment of the International Bank for Reconstruction and Development, better known as the World Bank, designed to facilitate private investment in Europe and non-socialist poor countries. Through its lending, the Bank's first priority was the reconstruction of Europe, but as early as 1948 and 1949 specific project loans were also made to Latin American countries. At the same time the World War II Allies, following the model of the Marshall Plan, established bilateral programs to provide support for the reconstruction of Europe and parts of Asia. The provision of what came to be known as **development assistance** was designed to help establish economic structures and political stability and thus to prevent the spread of communism. (The term "aid" for development assistance was for a time thought patronizing, though the media-driven mania for catchy acronyms has recently resulted in "AusAID," "NZAID," and "USAID.")

The success of the Marshall Plan influenced **development thinking** for decades, and the International Bank for Reconstruction and Development spawned Asian, European, African, and Latin American variants that have steered billions into poor countries and designed projects in the "third world." However, even before the collapse of the communist bloc, the term "third world" came into question. Originally coined to differentiate the non-aligned countries — most, former colonies — from the "West" and the communist "East," it was seen as derogative and colonialist. Ever since the fall of the Soviet Union the politically correct term has been **developing countries**, in opposition to the **developed** (sometimes **overdeveloped**) **world** of Europe and North America. More recently, "fourth world" for indigenous peoples, "fifth" for the poor in developed countries, and "sixth" for migrant workers have slipped into the progressive lexicon.

The traditionalist economic model of development has been attacked by social movements, non-government organizations, and special interest groups. The principal criticism rejects the "trickle-down" model for combating poverty, whereby economic growth is held to inevitably benefit the less well-off, but only in the longer term. The insidious corollary to this argument is the claim by authoritarian governments that **economic development** must and should precede **social and political development**. These governments point to the length of time it took for industrializing countries in the C19 to achieve a level of economic stability, and to the fact that only later did their governments begin to focus on civil liberties and social rights.

The "trickle-down" approach is no longer active in popular parlance but it still infects current development paradigms. The negative impact on the poor of the notorious structural adjustment programs promoted by the International Monetary Fund — export-led growth, low inflation, privatization, financial deregulation — is defended on the grounds that eventually the benefits flow downward. The failure of the structural adjustment approach to development became most apparent following the 1997 Asian financial melt-down. For example, Indonesia had over the previous decade seen a 35 percent fall in the level of poverty as measured by the World Bank; this was virtually wiped out overnight.

Economic globalization has succeeded in putting development in the forefront of ideological battles over democratic principles. The rule of the market is perceived to have weakened the nation state, with increasing pressures for privatization leading to a downgrading of services (especially for those who cannot afford to pay for them), and transnational corporations becoming more powerful than most governments in the developing world. Critics have begun to use the term **maldevelopment** to describe a process which is at once interventionist, riddled with conditions imposed on developing countries, disenfranchising of entire populations, and beneficial in the main only to North America and Europe.

The challenge facing **development practitioners** in the West has always been to ensure popular democratic support for budgetary allocation for development assistance. Whereas most development assistance is motivated in reality by the national economic, political, and strategic interests of the donor governments, and whereas these play well among the better-off bourgeoisie, there has always been a need to provide a rationale for the provision of aid. Coupled with demands from civil society organizations in the developing countries, **development agencies** have come up with a series of approaches designed to garner popular support both in their own and in the recipient countries.

This explains the proliferation of new development approaches, paradigms, and terminology to placate a variety of constituencies and lobbies: thus **women in development**, invented in the 1980s to little subsequent demonstrable effect; sustainable development, emphasizing long-term environmental concerns and the design of specific environment projects; equitable development, suggestive of redistributive policies; the UN Development Program's human development mission; and social development. which focuses on access to work, health, education, and information. Not only does the UN have a division devoted to social development but it convened an international World Summit for Social Development in 1994, at which governments committed themselves to specific targets on health, education, and social welfare.

Not unjustifiably, these targets have contributed to anti-globalization activists' skepticism about development. The target contained in the 2000 Millennium Development Goals was to halve the proportion of people living on less than US$1 a day by 2005. That indicator of poverty has been increased to $2 since 2000, but even that measure does not reflect the true dimensions of poverty, and the growing gap between rich and poor, in countries both developed and developing.

In response to their critics the international financial institutions and the bilateral donors have now made loans, debt relief, and development assistance conditional on governments in the developing countries framing their **national development plans** within poverty reduction strategies. The fact is that these plans will have to meet the same criteria as the old structural adjustment programs, but the very words "poverty reduction" play well in the media and have now come to be promoted as virtually synonymous with "development."

Unease with these trends has prompted some to look back to the Declaration on the Right to Development adopted by the UN General Assembly in 1986. This states among other things that the "subject of development" is the "human person," thus aligning the right to development to the other human rights in the International Bill of Rights. The Declaration has little force in international law but it has given rise to yet another qualifying term, the **human rights approach to development**. This maintains that all governments have the obligation to guarantee that the economic and social rights of their citizens are not violated by development initiatives, whether governmental, intergovernmental, or those of transnational corporations, and that the subjects of development have the right to participate in decisions that affect their well-being.

Development is bound to remain a contested term.

André Frankovits

See: *CIVILIZATION, EVOLUTION, HUMAN RIGHTS.*

Diaspora

Diaspora, literally meaning "the scattering of seeds," is derived from the Gk verb *speiro* (to sow) and the preposition *dia* (over). The most well-known, long-standing, and distinct use of the term occurs with reference to the history of forced dispersion of the Jewish people after the Babylonian conquest of Jerusalem in the C6 BCE and the Roman appropriation of Palestine in 70 CE. The long and complex history of the Jews as a people without a homeland found enduring expression in the image of "the wandering Jew" in Christian mythology.

Two other dramatic episodes in this history were the expulsion of Jews from Spain and Portugal in the C15 and the exodus of Jews from Eastern Europe and Russia caused by the escalating number of pogroms in the IC19. It is in this context that the modern application of the term "Diaspora" to the Jews originated, which has multiple meanings. First, **the Jewish Diaspora** was the name given to the countries (outside Palestine) through which the Jews were dispersed; second, it refers to the Jews living in those countries. Most importantly, however, the term refers to the dispersion itself. The capitalization of "Diaspora" in references to Jewish dispersion is indicative of the archetypical status of the Jews among so-called **diasporic peoples**.

The historical association of diaspora with this archetypical Jewish case points to the deeply emotional and political connotations of the term. The **diasporic experience** is often described negatively in terms of exile, isolation, and loss, of displacement from the ancestral homeland as a traumatic experience, where some catastrophic event – often but not always of a political nature – is collectively remembered as the starting point of the original dispersion. Concomitantly, a longing for a *return* to the homeland is classically assumed to be integral to **diasporic consciousness** (Safran, 1991).

In the Jewish case, this longing for return has been expressed politically in the Zionist struggle for the creation of a new Jewish homeland, the modern nation state of Israel in 1947. This development highlights an important assumption in the modern meaning of "diaspora," namely, that all peoples must have a territorially specific homeland and that living away from it is an unnatural and undesirable condition. This meaning of "diaspora" as deviant is strongly associated with the lingering dominance of the modernist global nation-state system and its ideological assumption of perfect overlap of nation, people, territory, and culture.

Apart from the Jews, other groups who can point to a traumatic historical event as the beginning of a forcible displacement from their homeland include the Armenians (genocide), Africans (the slave trade), Irish (famine and British colonization), and Palestinians (the partitioning of Palestine by the United Nations). Cohen (R. Cohen, 1997) calls such cases **victim diasporas**.

However, from the IC20 the term "diaspora" is increasingly used in a more generalized sense to refer to all kinds of groups who have a history of dispersion, groups variously referred to as immigrants, expatriates, refugees, guest workers, exile communities, overseas communities, ethnic minorities, and so on – that is, potentially to all groups living outside their putative homeland – although its application to, say, English migrants in Australia or Western professional expats in third world countries is still not uncontested, due to such groups' perceived lack of experience as an oppressed or traumatized people.

In general, then, the term is reserved to describe collectivities who feel not fully accepted by, and partly alienated from, the dominant culture of the "host society," where they do not feel (fully) at home. In other words, where the classic definition of "diaspora" emphasized the traumatic past of the dispersed group, in today's usage trauma is located as much in the present, in the contemporary experience of marginalization or discrimination in the nation state of residence.

At the same time, the very proliferation of groups who have adopted the language of diaspora to represent themselves – a quick Internet search brings up a wide range of websites for particular **diasporic groups**, including African, South Asian, Armenian, Irish, Palestinian, Russian, Chinese, Vietnamese, Greek, Filipino, Ukrainian, Iranian, Persian, Romanian, Indian, Basque, Belarusian, and Togolese – signals a weakening of the hold of the modern nation state on the identities and identifications of the populations who have come to live within its borders. Diasporic groups imagine themselves as transnational communities whose primary affiliations and loyalties (with coethnic others living elsewhere, including the homeland) lie beyond the boundaries of the nation state.

Kachig Tölölyan, who in 1991 founded the academic journal *Diaspora: A Journal of Transnational Studies*, stated in his inaugural editorial that "diasporas are the exemplary communities of the transnational moment" (1991: 3). The very timing of the journal's establishment is indicative of the rising significance of transnational flows and migrations of people as a consequence of the heightened process of globalization in the closing decades of the C20. In this context the term "diaspora" has increasingly lost its paradigmatic association with exile from home and the myth of return, and has become much more widely and unspecifically used to describe the condition and experience of dispersion as such, which does not necessarily involve trauma and marginalization but also may entail empowerment, enrichment, and expansion. An important recent example is the rise of a powerful Chinese diasporic network – which Cohen (R. Cohen, 1997) calls a **trade diaspora** – in the transnational capitalist business world of the Asia Pacific region (Ong and Nonini, 1997).

One of the most vocal, dynamic, and influential **diasporic movements** in the past few decades has been the **black African diaspora**, comprising people who are descendants of victims of the African slave trade and now live dispersed across the countries on both sides of the Atlantic including the Americas, the Caribbean, the UK, and Western Europe. Arguably, Alex Haley's hugely popular book and TV series *Roots* in the 1970s, which told his family history from when his ancestor Kunta Kinte arrived as a slave on a ship in Maryland in the C18, played a key role in the formation of a diasporic consciousness among many African-Americans. In the 1990s, an alternative, more postmodern vision of the African diaspora – that of a Black Atlantic – was developed by influential black British cultural theorist Paul Gilroy (1993a). Here, "diaspora" signifies the constant renewal of identity through creative hybridity and transformation under the very conditions of dispersal and difference, rather than the need to return to one's "roots." In other words, in the postmodern meaning of "diaspora," the organic link between peoples and homelands has been severed.

Ien Ang

See: *GLOBALIZATION, HOME, MOVEMENTS.*

Difference

Difference emerged as a keyword in cultural politics in the late 1960s. It became a central principle in the political imagination and thinking of a wide range of so-called new social movements that have proliferated since the IC20. In these contexts the word "difference" – literally, the quality of being unlike or dissimilar – loses its descriptive innocence and becomes a highly charged concept, to the point of being elevated as the proud emblem for a passionate political, often personal-political cause. **The right to be different** is one generic motto of this cause, especially in the areas of sexual, racial, and subcultural politics. Here, difference is capitalized on or mobilized as a positive marker of identity and, consequently, as the expression of dissent or critique of the oppressive social homogeneity imposed by the dominant sections of society (often described as "bourgeois," "male," or "white"). In other words, difference is the basis and the condition of possibility of various oppositional forms of identity politics, whose liberating effects work to expose as well as challenge the hegemonic culture of the developed Western world in the second half of the C20. Examples are the feminist movement ("sisterhood is global") and youth subcultural groups such as punk (Hebdige, 1979), or slogans associated with symbolic affirmations of difference such as "black is beautiful" or "queer with attitude." A romantic and/or militant attitude toward difference – and **being different** – is clearly at work in these usages.

In the academy, thinking about difference has similarly been a major concern. It has been the object of heated theoretical debates in a number of fields, where the term has taken on altogether more specialized, complicated, but no less politicized meanings. Much of the debate started off from an engagement with Ferdinand de Saussure's structural linguistics (1966 [1916]), influential in the 1960s and 1970s, which introduced the idea that difference is central to the production of meaning. Put simply, signs (such as words) acquire meaning through their differential relationships with other signs. These relationships can be described as *a/non-a*. A specific mode of difference is opposition, where the relationship between two signs is *a/not-a*. The most extreme form of opposition is that of the binary opposition or dichotomy, which divides a continuum up in two mutually exclusive opposing terms: white/black; self/other; man/woman. In such dichotomies the same and the different are often placed in a hierarchical relationship, as the different is purely negatively defined as that which is not-same, as deviant from the norm (or the normal). The idea that binary oppositions describe systems of domination has been the focus and the starting point of much further criticism and debate, both in the field of theory, especially poststructuralist critical theory, and in conceptions of political practice which have come to be associated with postmodernism.

In theory, Jacques Derrida criticized the unambiguous fixity of meaning that is implied in the binary opposition by introducing the term *différance*, which signifies that which both precedes and exceeds binary oppositions and hence unsettles (destabilizes and defers) meaning. This notion of unsettling binary oppositions has played a crucial role in enabling the articulation of modes of **politics of difference**, which are critical of essentialist notions of identity as the affirmation of (fixed) difference.

Profound engagement with ideas of difference occurred in various strands of feminist theory (whose celebrity representatives include Luce Irigaray, Hélène Cixous, Elizabeth Grosz, and Rosi Braidotti), which enjoyed intense popularity among feminist university students during the 1970s and 1980s. Succinctly, their theorizations of **sexual difference** are characterized by efforts to develop autonomous definitions of "woman" and "femininity," unhinged from their binary relationship to "man" and "masculinity," in which they are inevitably locked into the position of inferior or subordinate counterpart. In this usage, difference becomes emancipated from its status as other-than, and is promoted as simply other, as pure, irreducible difference (not "*a*/not-*a*," but "*a*/*b*"). In more practical political terms, such theories, sometimes called **difference feminism** or postmodern feminism, tend to be critical of equality as the key objective of the women's movement, arguing that the liberal struggle for equality would mean the assimilation of femininity into the dominant, masculine norm; in other words, submitting difference to the "logic of identity."

This kind of theorizing signals the elevation of difference as a value in itself, and with it a common suspicion of philosophical universalism. Closely associated with the rise of postmodernity from the 1970s onward, Western society has seen an unprecedented proliferation of **differences** as a result of processes variously described as fragmentation, diversification, or pluralization. Within feminism itself, this manifested in the falling apart of the unifying notion of global sisterhood in favor of a recognition of differences *between* women (based on race or sexual orientation, for example) and *within* the category "women." The postmodernist sentiments associated with this emphasis on differences are eloquently articulated by African-American philosopher Cornel West:

> Distinctive features of the new cultural politics of difference are to trash the monolithic and homogenous in the name of multiplicity and heterogeneity; to reject the abstract, general and universal in light of the concrete, specific and particular; and to historicize, contextualize and pluralize by highlighting the contingent, provisional, variable, tentative, shifting and changing. (West, 1990: 19)

Difference

Such statements are made **in the name of difference** – a radicalist trend that is in serious tension with more modernist, universalist versions of left politics such as Marxism and socialism. Cornel West is a representative of an influential cohort of black and postcolonial critics (for example, Stuart Hall, Paul Gilroy, Gayatri Chakravorty Spivak, Homi Bhabha) who have contributed to the fact that race, ethnicity, and culture have become central to the politics of difference. In a more general sense this represents a lC20 tendency to treat culture and difference as synonymous: in the discourse of cultural studies, culture necessarily evokes difference (in the sense of particularity), whereas difference is extemporaneously equated with (and reduced to) **cultural difference**.

In parallel with but relatively distinct from these developments in critical discourse, the social insistence of groups on asserting their difference and of political demands for their recognition has become a ubiquitous and, increasingly, a normalized aspect of life in Western democracies, with serious implications for the conduct of public institutions and governance of the modern state. A key example of the state-led recognition of difference is the policy of multiculturalism, which officially sanctions and enshrines ethnic, linguistic, and cultural differences within the encompassing framework of the state. In this bureaucratic context, **difference** becomes the cornerstone of diversity: diversity is a managerial, bird's-eye view of the field of differences, which needs to be harmonized, controlled, or made to fit into a coherent (often national) whole. The celebration of cultural diversity – popularly expressed in community festivals of ethnic food, song, and dance – is an article of faith in self-declared multicultural societies.

Homi Bhabha (1990b) dismisses this uptake of difference as diversity-to-be-managed, arguing that the "*creation* of cultural diversity" implies "a *containment* of cultural difference": "The difference between cultures cannot be something that can be accommodated within a universalist framework. Different cultures... very often set up among and between themselves an *incommensurability*" (Bhabha, 1990b: 208, 209). Bhabha's perspective, motivated as it is by an instinctive suspicion – common among critical theorists – of the notion of management *per se*, exemplifies the big gap between the poststructuralist/postmodern discourse on difference as it has dominated the academic humanities since the lC20 on the one hand, and its use and meaning in more practical governmental and policy contexts on the other. Even so, in both contexts difference (whether or not conceived as diversity) is ideologically endowed with positive meanings: difference is good, and has to be affirmed.

However, at the close of the C20 and especially into the eC21, there were and are increasing signs of discontent with the untrammeled valorization of difference, in both theory and politics. US author Todd Gitlin expressed this discontent in the title of his 1995 book, *The twilight of common dreams*. In his manifesto on *The idea of culture* (2000), British intellectual Terry Eagleton rails against the "fetishisation of cultural difference," reinvoking Raymond Williams's idea of a common culture (which is emphatically not the same as a uniform culture) as a necessary condition of social life. In a broader context, this resonates with the growing resurgence of a more negative meaning of "difference" in the social world: **difference as division**. Right-wing populists throughout the West base their militancy on a fear and resentment of the internal divisiveness presumably emanating from the emphasis on (cultural) difference. At a global level, the destructiveness of an obsession with difference manifests itself in disturbing phenomena such as ethnic cleansing, fundamentalism, and the image of "a clash of civilizations," a strikingly evocative phrase first coined by Harvard Professor Samuel P. Huntington (1993). Against this tendency, calls for a new, humanist universalism – one that stresses "a common humanity" while recognizing differences which the world has come to respect – are becoming increasingly insistent, if still rather impracticable.

Ien Ang

See: *CIVILIZATION, DECONSTRUCTION, ETHNICITY, FEMINISM, FUNDAMENTALISM, GAY AND LESBIAN, GENDER, MULTICULTURALISM, NORMAL, QUEER, RACE, SEXUALITY.*

Disability

Disability is a recent and therefore somewhat mutable term with regard to political practice and/or theories of identity. In political parlance it replaces earlier cognates such as "handicapped" and "crippled": in the US, for instance, the 1975 Education for All Handicapped Children Act was renamed in 1990 the Individuals with Disabilities Education Act. With the passage of the Americans with Disabilities Act in 1990, "disability" entered the language of daily commerce and employment law, under the following heading: "The term 'disability' means, with respect to an individual – (A) a physical or mental impairment that substantially limits one or more of the major life activities of such an individual; (B) a record of such an impairment; or (C) being regarded as having such an impairment." **Disability law** has developed over the past 30 years in tandem with a broad **disability rights movement** (in the UK, sometimes referred to as the DRM) that seeks to redefine disability as a social and political question rather than as a matter of individual impairments:

> What is called the "social model" in the United Kingdom and the "minority group model" in the United States has been the guiding framework for disability theorists since the 1970s, pushing with increasing strength for disability to be seen as a form of social oppression, and the appropriate response is one of civil rights rather than medical or social care. (G. Williams, 2001: 125)

Its recent uses notwithstanding, "disability" has a much longer history than this, and seems for most of its life to have been closely associated with impairment and incapacity. Some of its earliest appearances, lC16–eC17, are related to law and contract rather than

87

to physical impairment: "his disabilitie to performe his promise" (Lupton, 1580); "how you are by this custome disabled in your goods" (James I, 1604). A broad understanding of disability persists in legal discourse through the C20, combining acknowledgment of physical or mental disadvantage with a more nebulous sense of disadvantage in general: cf. "Bringing on the inconveniences, disabilities, pains and mental disorders spoken of" (Tucker, 1768–74) and "The next legal disability is want of age" (Blackstone, 1765–9).

In industrialized nations over the past two centuries, disability has tended to emerge as a policy issue immediately after wars (because of the need to formulate programs for the care of wounded soldiers) and during periods of panic over population and "national character," the latest of which fueled the rise of eugenics in the eC20. In the eC19, anomalies such as Kaspar Hauser and the Wild Boy of Aveyron sparked great interest in disabilities concerning speech and hearing, and indeed in the relation between speech and species membership; over the course of the C19, as Davis (1995) has shown, French theorists such as Adolphe Quetelet and, later, English theorists such as Francis Galton developed accounts of "normal" human attributes and corresponding accounts of "abnormalities" with regard to intelligence and physical attributes. These theories were then mapped onto the emerging science of genetics and onto theories of race and culture that proposed a developmental hierarchy of races culminating in the Western European. (In 1866, for instance, J. Langdon Down identified trisomy-21, now widely known as Down Syndrome, as "Mongolism" because its physical features were associated with Central Asian faces and held to be indicative of an earlier period in the development of the human species.) The curious corollary of such theories, when taken literally (as they most usually were), was the suggestion that the vast majority of the human race in the C19 was in fact woefully deficient in the species features attributed to Western Europeans, which suggests in turn that the vast majority of the human race in the C19 could be said to be **disabled**.

Only in the late 1960s, with the advent of **disability rights advocacy**, did "disability" come to denote a category of human identity along the lines of (and yet complexly distinguished from) race, class, gender, or sexuality. "Disability" was specifically excluded from the language of the US Civil Rights Act of 1964, leaving physical and mental impairment as a legal and social matter to be addressed by other forms of "identity politics." The standard narrative of the history of disability rights advocacy in the US is that of J. P. Shapiro (1993), who details the movement from its origins in the San Francisco Bay Area in the 1960s and 1970s. That history entails not only the attempt to model disability rights on the civil rights movement of the 1950s and 1960s, but also the related attempt to "demedicalize" disability, to see it less as a matter of abnormal species characteristics requiring treatment or cure than as a fluid combination of social stigmata, living arrangements, and legal remedies. There remains a colloquial sense, as well, in which disability is recognized as a changeable or temporary condition, as when workers **go on disability** or baseball players are placed on the **15-day disabled list**. (In such circumstances the flexibility of disability is explicitly accounted for in the legal apparatus guaranteeing disability compensation or allowing baseball teams to modify their rosters.)

Disability and disability issues made a brief appearance in 1990s debates over political correctness, when attention turned to phrases such as "physically challenged" and "differently abled." By and large, such phrases were met with a kind of derision that suggested a widespread anxiety about what constituted "polite" discourse about people with disabilities. In response, some people with disabilities sought to revive the label "cripple" or "crip," for much the same reason as gay and lesbian theorists in the late 1980s revived and resignified the term "queer."

At the same time, "disabled" has retained many of its more neutral, pre-Enlightenment functions; when used with regard to persons, "disabled" and "disabling" tend to connote disease or stigma, but when used with regard to objects the term is often synonymous with "inoperative," as when one speaks of **disabling a function** on one's computer, or **disabling the smoke alarm** in one's apartment. In such cases the term has a specificity (denoting the inability of an object to perform a task) it almost never carries with regard to persons; for it is far more common to speak of an entire person as disabled rather than to refer to her arm or her immune system as disabled. It may be, then, that in this respect contemporary disability rights advocates would prefer the sense of "disabled" generally employed with regard to objects to the sense that seems to dominate our understanding of persons.

Michael Bérubé

See: *GAY AND LESBIAN, NORMAL, POLITICAL CORRECTNESS, QUEER.*

89

Discipline

Is **discipline** a keyword today? There are two uses of the term that would suggest the **era of discipline** is behind us. In the social sciences and humanities, disciplines (sociology or history, for example) are often perceived as too restrictive and narrow to produce interesting work. The move away from disciplines in this sense is associated with the emergence of **interdisciplinary** fields of study such as those of cultural studies. Since the C14, "discipline" has meant a branch of instruction, although the word now also suggests a body of knowledge within a division of scientific labor and an academic specialization in a university.

"Discipline" has a rather musty, Victorian air about it in other contexts. It appears to belong to a dream of a network of **disciplinary** or carceral **institutions**, such as schools, factories, hospitals, almshouses, asylums, prisons, barracks, and so forth, which are designed to bring different populations under control in a society liable to disorder, pathology, debauchery, illegality, idleness, and delinquency. When advocates of progressive education discuss discipline in relation to schoolchildren today, for example, it is associated with a strict form of correction, emphasizing hierarchy, uniformity, authority, examination, and superintendence at the expense of self-development through learning.

Discipline

Michel Foucault (1977) revealed the extent of **disciplinary practices** in producing docile and useful bodies since the Enlightenment and spoke of a **disciplinary society**. Most of his successors are content to note that forms of control and governance have rather been transformed by this emphasis on the self-activating individual. Discipline, with its focus on the body, the normalization of the individual, and the production of correct moral conduct, often in certain institutional enclosures, appears as a somewhat outmoded, clumsy, and inefficient form of governing.

The idea that "discipline" is associated with teaching and learning is fundamental. It is derived from L *disciplina*, meaning the instruction of pupils or disciples (L *discipulus*, pupil). Until the eC17 "discipline" was used in the sense of learning or schooling, such as "If thou haue in greke had all thy discipline, To dispute in latin what needth thee to seeke" (Barclay, 1510). From the C14 a discipline was a branch of instruction. From the C15 "discipline" is associated with proper conduct and action, mental and moral training, summed up in the claim that the "present life was intended to be a state of discipline for a future one" (Butler, 1736). The use of the term "discipline" as a form of military training or drill is almost as old, such as in the "rules, techyings and dyscyplyne of armes" (Caxton, 1489). So too is the use of "discipline" to refer to the orderly conduct and action that might result from such training. For Gibbon (1781), the "discipline of a soldier is formed by exercise rather than by study." The possibility of opposing discipline to learning would therefore appear to be relatively recent.

Apart from education and the military, the institution most associated with discipline has been religion. **Ecclesiastical discipline** is the method for maintaining order in a church or exercising control over its members. Such discipline is dependent upon the **spiritual discipline** of the members of a church and, in both senses, discipline as a practice is opposed to doctrine, which refers to the system of beliefs of a church. The notion of discipline as a practice builds upon the forms of asceticism found in early Christian monasteries, whose function, while ensuring obedience within a religious order, was to increase mastery of one's self and one's body. Discipline is thus related to practices of **self-discipline**, or the mortification of the flesh in penance, which the devout enact upon themselves, a sense of the term captured in the "corporal austerities which are known as 'the discipline' " (Bernard, 1888). The association of discipline with Puritanism is common in everyday speech.

Religious discipline and modern industrial, educational, military, and penal uses of disciplines all ensure obedience. Whereas monastic kinds of discipline work through the renunciation of temptations of the flesh, modern forms seek to increase the utility and capacity of the active human body and its relation to a productive apparatus. For Foucault, discipline is a part of an art of the human body, which establishes a mechanism that can make the body most useful at the same time as it makes the subject most docile. This is a key point in evaluating the contemporary fate of discipline.

In the lC20, it became less than polite to admit that one needed to discipline the workforce or children rather than facilitate their self-actualization, empower them as a team, or just let them have fun. Even moral and political conservatives rarely cast problems in terms of lack of discipline, preferring terms like "moral virtue," "character," "respect," "politeness," etc. This is no doubt a result of the success of movements against discipline in school or in asylums and, later, of new managerial doctrines. But perhaps it is too soon to suggest that we have moved beyond discipline. Certainly there is a secular, leisure- and consumption-oriented concern with different types of discipline: of diet, of exercise, of health, and so on. This is discipline in everything but the word. In economic language, we hear the need for governments to be subject to **fiscal discipline** or executives to be aware of the **global discipline** of competition. In professional sport, poor perform-ance is often attributed to **ill-discipline** or lack of discipline. There are occasional rumblings of a crisis in **school discipline**.

Given that the object of modern industrial disciplines was always to increase the capacities of the active individual in relation to each other, the change of managerial speak may be just that, a change in how we talk about practices and their goals. It is not surprising that with high unemployment and failing Internet companies, a best-selling German book called *End the fun* is reported to be "championing a return to traditional German values of discipline, hard work and rigid punctuality" (*Sydney Morning Herald*, 2002). One can already glimpse new battle-lines over discipline.

Mitchell Dean

See: *EDUCATION, GOVERNMENT, NORMAL, SELF.*

Discourse

The dictionary meanings of **discourse** move from "thought" to speech in its various forms and thence to a sustained conversation or text, sometimes with a didactic orientation (as in a sermon), or an extended piece of reasoning. The corresponding adjective, **discursive**, keeps something of this tension between the senses of talk and ordered argument: the word can mean either "rambling, digressive" or "proceeding by reasoning or argument; rati-ocinative" (in the latter sense the word is often opposed to "intuitive"). In its contempor-ary usage we need to distinguish between **a discourse**, meaning text which is thematically or situationally unified as a coherent formation of knowledge or truth, and "discourse," meaning something like the fact of organized language as a set of social relations of knowledge (Brown and Yule, 1983; Fairclough, 1972).

The force of the concept in the second half of the C20 lay in its provision of an alternative both to Ferdinand de Saussure's couple *langue–parole* and to Noam Chomsky's distinction between competence (innate knowledge of the language system) and perform-ance (Chomsky, 1965; de Saussure, 1966 [1916]). Saussure's conceptual breakthrough in positing the systemic nature of language (*langue*) at the same time made it difficult to understand actual speech or text (*parole*) as anything other than the contingent result of linguistic codes, its variations a matter merely of individual choice. In Chomsky's Trans-formational Grammar, similarly, scientific interest lies in the structure of rules at the generative level rather than in the surface structures of performance.

The concept of discourse emerged from within structural linguistics, perhaps most influentially in Emile Benveniste's distinction between two modes of storytelling, where *histoire* refers to completed events detached in time from the speaker, and *discours* to events which are temporally related to the act of speaking (Benveniste, 1971). The concept of discourse in Benveniste thus foregrounds the position and the social relations of enunciation (roughly: the positions of speaker and of hearer, and the structuring situation within which speech between them happens). In a slightly different sense, the word refers in linguistics to the analysis of utterances at a level higher than that of the sentence, and by extension to the rhetorical dimensions of language: that is, to the situational constraints on text production. The challenge posed by the concept of discourse, and perhaps not yet fully answered, is to understand the organization of speech or writing as being systemic not only at the level of grammar or word-formation but at the semantic and pragmatic levels (what is being said and how this relates to its context of utterance). Language is thus understood to be structured by rules or by rule-like codes and conventions at each of the levels of language-system (*langue*) and discourse (Halliday, 1978; Pêcheux, 1982).

One way of thinking about how the situational, thematic, and formal dimensions of speech and text form relatively coherent clusters is by way of a concept borrowed from literary theory, that of genre (Todorov, 1990). Here the important work was done in an early critique of Saussurean linguistics, that undertaken in the late 1920s by Mikhail Bakhtin writing as or in collaboration with V. N. Voloshinov (the precise authorship of this work is not entirely clear). Bakhtin/Voloshinov (1973) writes of what he calls **genres of discourse**, by which he means normatively structured clusters of formal, contextual, and thematic features, "ways of speaking" in a particular situation. Each genre is stratified as a social practice through the importance of "language-etiquette, speech-tact, and other forms of adjusting an utterance to the hierarchical organization of society" (Bakhtin, 1986: 21). The production of meaning is thus directly correlated with the semiotic constraints of the speech situation. Thus a genre such as prayer, one of the central components of religious discourse in many cultures, creates a unified cluster of possible and appropriate speech positions, possible and appropriate themes, and possible and appropriate linguistic and stylistic forms. This cluster in turn codes relations of discursive power for a particular speech community. The theory brings into a single dynamic the organized fields of semantic material, layered in depth and in complex relation to other fields; appropriate positions of enunciation, authority, and credibility; appropriate patterns of strategic interaction; and appropriate rhetorical and linguistic options.

The other account of the concept of discourse that has been of particular importance for its current usage is developed in the work of Michel Foucault and is formalized in *The archaeology of knowledge* (1972). In its Foucauldian usage, discourse (or, more precisely, the **discursive formation**) is a mode of organization of knowledge in relation to material institutions, and is thus not primarily a linguistic concept. Rather, it has to do with practices and configurations of power, often rooted in organizations which both control and are structured by distinct disciplinary knowledges. The discourses of medicine or of prison reform, for example, construct the possibility for certain truths to prevail, and for others to be without social effectivity or recognition. In so doing they draw upon and reinforce certain structures of discursive authority (the voice of the doctor or the scientist, the regime of truth of the humane social engineer), and displace others (the voices of the patient or the criminal, but also the voices of the naturopath or the faith healer, or the ''archaic'' codes of vengeance and retribution). In the same movement they bring about certain material effects: hospitals and prisons are built which embody a vision of medical treatment or of the reform of souls; certain regimes of treatment or detention are legitimized and prevail against others. This is to say that for Foucault discursive formations are heterogeneous, made up not only of languages in use (''statements'') but also of the material practices and structures which determine whether and how they will be repeated across different social fields, their effects, the speech positions they will make possible, and the objects and truths which they will designate and endow with a certain reality.

The centrality of the concept of discourse to much contemporary theory has made it a target of critics unhappy with the challenge it poses to traditional ways of understanding representation; it has also become so widely and often so glibly used as to have lost much of its precise meaning (Sawyer, 2002).

93

John Frow

See: *DECONSTRUCTION, DIFFERENCE, KNOWLEDGE, REPRESENTATION, SIGN, TEXT, WRITING.*

Economy

Economy became an everyday term in the lC20, denoting a force to be reckoned with outside of politics and society, located both above as a mystical abstraction, and below as the grounded bottom line. Somewhat more than the sum of its parts, **the economy** includes money, markets, commodities, wealth, industry, labor, enterprise, finance, investment, employment, consumption, production, credit, debt, competition, monopoly, and development. Not included in Raymond Williams's *Keywords* (1976), the word would be impossible to ignore in the eC21. Indeed over the last 30 years (the) "economy" has been gathering a new set of powerful and emotive meanings in popular discourse, sliding in the process from the left, where **economism** was always social(ist)ly acceptable, to the right, where systemic thinking that displaces the primacy of the individual is usually outlawed.

Associated in the original Gk with management of a household (*oikos*), "economy" has continued to connote both management and the complex unity, or system, that requires administration – whether it be the household (eC14), the divinity (lC15), the body (mC15), nature (mC15), the mind (mC16), the nation (mC16), truth (lC18), or the **economic system** (eC20). As representations of systems have become increasingly influenced by biological and mechanical theories of self-regulation, the tension embedded within the term "economy" between management (as a practice of intervention) and system (that which manages itself) has periodically loosened and tightened, drastically changing the meaning of the word.

The notion of an economic system encompassing the institutions and arrangements of a society that behave according to **economic principles** is drawn from mC19 delineations of

ABCD**E**FGHIJKLMNOPQRSTUVWXYZ

capitalism as an historically specific form of economic organization. But the groundwork for thinking of economy as a knowable whole was laid in the IC16 and eC17 with the rise of mercantilism and methods of accounting for flows of wealth. According to J. Mitchell (2002: 5–6), **political economy** as developed by Adam Smith and others in the C17 and C18 referred to the "prudent management or 'government' of the community's affairs" – that is, the economy (management) of the polity (society as a complex system). Smith's theorization of civil society as a "self-regulating and beneficent arrangement" (Botto-more, 1983b: 377) provided later political economists with the template for a less benign system organized by the economic principles of competition, accumulation, exploit-ation, growth, and periodic crisis. In this representation "management" to regulate and harness the economy was virtually impossible. Yet submission to its laws could lead paradoxically to mastery, as when proletarian revolution replaced capitalism with an economic system based on different (even opposite) principles. In the eC20, socialists building **planned economies** placed management by the state at the organizational center of the economic system (for example, in E. Preobrazhensky's New Economic Plan for the USSR). In response to the Great Depression, projects of national economic manage-ment were instituted in **market economies** guided by John Maynard Keynes's brand of **macro-economics**, which promised to tame the excesses of capitalism via adjustments to demand.

It was not until the eC20 that "the economy" was widely adopted in popular discourse and disciplinary practice as a "self-evident totality" (T. Mitchell, 2002: 7). For the IC19 exponents of what became modern-day **economics**, the individual's utility-maximizing actions under conditions of scarcity were the focus of the new discipline, not the operations of an underlying system as such. Eager to establish its credentials as a science, **neo-classical economics** borrowed liberally from the flourishing field of physics and mechan-ics, adopting concepts such as equilibrium, elasticity, friction, inflation, expansion, and stability to represent the lawful operations of prices and markets. What brought a notion of economy as a unified system some respectability, distancing it from the discursive grip of socialist revolutionaries, was the interaction of new technologies of analysis and control. The rise of modern nation states, with administrative bureaucracies and jurisdiction over territorial economies, saw an expanded capacity to collect data on commerce, labor, and industry. A burgeoning data bank supported the establishment of national income and product accounts and the tracking of key indicators of economic performance. Meanwhile, in the business world, management accounting (mC19) and financial reporting (eC20) had developed to ensure the efficient and effective administrative co-ordination of large corporations. Methods of accounting for costs, benefits, stocks, flows, capital, and income within closed systems heightened confidence in rational calculability at all levels of analysis. Along with these new techniques of calculation came a renewed sense of mastery over economic matters. Business and management schools proliferated in the mC20, and international agencies (such as the World Bank and International Monetary Fund [IMF]) were established and charged with regulating the development and dynamics of discrete **national economies**. Still, the economy was something that had yet to take over society – it was a functional backdrop – and the term "economy" was most prevalent in advertising, denoting a cheaper or more efficient alternative – the giant **economy size** box of detergent or the **economy class** air fare.

The almost total naturalization of "the economy" in public discourse in recent decades has curiously coincided with globalization and a growing alarm that the autonomy of national economies, and therefore their manageability, is being undermined. With the shift from an understanding of the economy as something that can be managed (by people, the state, the IMF) to something that governs society, the economic imaginary has seemingly lost its discursive mandate and become an objective reality. In this natural(ized) state, the term "economy" harks back to its mC17 theological meaning, "the method of divine government of the world." According to Donald Horne: "Real people, as manifest in 'society,' have been melted down into an abstraction called 'The Economy' which we all serve, as if it rises above us. No-one any longer seems able to speak a human language of economic change; instead politicians recite the latest figures as if they were magic charms" (Horne, 2002: 5).

This naturalization/deification of the economy must be seen in the light of the continued hold of neo-liberal economic orthodoxy over policy since the heady days of Margaret Thatcher and Ronald Reagan. The rejection of economic intervention of any sort (Keynesian, social-democratic, welfarist, "wet") that might hinder the operations of the "free market" is central to the neo-liberal agenda. And in the intensely ideological realm of national economic "deregulation," "the market" and "the economy" have become one and the same. So when we are told that "our" economy must become more efficient if it and we are to survive, the message is that markets must be further freed from regulatory constraints (that is, freed from those interventions that in previous eras were seen as mechanisms of macro-economic mastery).

Increasingly it is the financial press that has become the voice of the economy in its new slimmed-down guise of the market (whether the housing, futures, commodity, currency, or financial market – it doesn't really matter). Sometime within the last 15 years, daily prime-time TV news programs began to include the "market report" along with the weather report. This, together with the integration of large business news sections into mainstream newspapers, marks the widespread popular submission to the economy as manifest in the numbers/latest figures/magic charms that indicate systemic health or disease.

In the academy, neo-classical economics has flourished and taken on the colonizing and fundamentalist project of viewing all aspects of society, from childrearing and membership in voluntary organizations, to educational attainment or criminal involvement (that is, not just market behavior), in terms of games of rational, individual economic calculation. With strong governmental support academic economists have reduced society to "social capital," "human capital," "information capital," etc. As a system, the economy has been reduced to the market, and as a style of calculation and management, it has taken hold of all manner of human interactions.

At the other end of the academic spectrum, in cultural studies and the humanities, a language of economy has taken hold in a very different way. The waxing of interest in representation, discourse, and poststructuralist thought has seen intense discussion of various **economies of meaning**. Refusing to submit to a closed system, or **restricted economy**, in which meaning is conserved, invested, circulated, reproduced, and thus rendered self-evident, social theorists have become interested in writing within a **general economy of meaning** in which multiple meanings are generated and valued.

A hopeful move that mirrors the purging of certitude surrounding the security of meaning in philosophical and social analysis has been the recent proliferation of **economies** in public discourse. While the **welfare economy** has been summarily banished, we increasingly hear talk of the **social economy**, **community economy**, **sustainable economy**, and **green economy**, in which **economic "value"** endowed by the market is challenged and displaced. The systemic monolith of mainstream representation is being supplanted or supplemented by **diverse economies** (Gibson-Graham, 1996). All these innovations are attempts to expand the boundaries of "economy" to include that which has been prohibited – the household, voluntary and community sectors, non-capitalist enterprises, and ethical judgments related to the future, the environment, and social justice. All are attempts to wrest "economy" back from the reductionism of the market and perhaps assert that an economy is, after all, what we make it.

J. K. Gibson-Graham

See: *BUREAUCRACY, CAPITALISM, GLOBALIZATION, MANAGEMENT, SOCIALISM, SOCIETY.*

Education

Few would deny that **education** is both an individual and a social good. However, the nature and the implications of its undoubted benefits are hotly contested. Are the benefits to be seen as private or as public goods – as individual advantage or as collective social enrichment? Is the primary goal of education to be seen as training in economically important skills, as in **vocational education** and **professional education**, or as a preparation for civilized living and citizenship, as in **liberal education**? Keeping in mind the different but often intertwined etymological strands in education may help us better understand some of the misunderstandings and miscommunications that can beset contemporary debates.

The etymology of "education" leads back into two separate but not dissimilar L roots: *educare*, with connotations of "drawing out" or "bringing up"; and *educere*, with connotations of "leading forth." The two strands do not yield disparate senses; they often converge. But they do represent different perspectives. The idea of education as a drawing out goes back to the very beginnings of Western philosophy. Plato's recurring images of the teacher as midwife offer powerful early models for the drawing out of things already there within the student's mind. If what is "led forth" is construed as the student's own inner resources, the second strand is not clearly separate from the first. But *educere* has other associations – as a leading forth of the students themselves at the completion of a process of formation of skills or abilities.

This second idea of education is enacted in our contemporary context in the ritualized ceremonies of graduation that mark the completion of structured programs of learning and accreditation. Having completed a process of initiation, the student is "led forth" into a professional group. More broadly, education can signify the completion of a process of initiation into the privileges and responsibilities of adult life. Here the idea of completion takes on connotations of the preparation for human life in its wholeness. "A complete and generous education ... fits a man to perform ... all the offices ... of peace and war" (Milton, 1644). "Education is the formation of the whole man – intellect ... character, mind and soul" (H. E. Manning, 1875).

This broader idea of "leading forth" has close connections with political thought. Here the role of education in the formation of the individual converges with its role in the preservation and transmission of civic ideals. Education can lead us forth into tightly defined professional structures and practices. But it can also lead us, in less well-defined ways, into the responsibilities of citizenship. It can lead us forth into the relatively homogeneous cultural values and expectations of a traditional community; or into the complexities of hybrid identities and conflicted values of a culturally diverse society.

Not surprisingly, this second strand especially raises issues about equalities of access and opportunities. Which students are to be "led forth" into which privileges? The image of the procession of the educated can also evoke disaffection with the modeling it provides of the finished product. In 1938 Virginia Woolf, in *Three guineas*, contemplated the image of a few determined women traipsing along at the end of the procession of the educated. On what terms, she asked, should women join that procession? "Above all, where is it leading us, the procession of educated men?" (1986: 72).

Thinking of education as a leading forth may well elicit skepticism about the leaders. But it also evokes an idea of access to a shared intellectual space, which resonates with C18 ideas of enlightenment as the attainment of maturity on the part of a society as a whole – a collective readiness to think for ourselves. Immanuel Kant spoke of enlightenment as "man's emergence from his self-incurred immaturity," from the "inability to use one's own understanding without the guidance of another" (1970a [1784]: 54). Kant sees maturity as involving autonomy – a "freedom to make *public use* of one's reason in all matters" (p. 55). In this context education could be seen as enabling citizens to enter a public space of reason – a space of intellectual inquiry and social critique, where the concern for truth transcends the demands of obedience to authority. It remained a largely unrealized Enlightenment dream. But the idea lingers – especially among educators in the humanities. It is a way of thinking of education which is difficult to reconcile with models of professional training, or of entrepreneurial collaboration with industry, which drive funding and policy mechanisms in contemporary universities. With the demise of robust public spaces of collective intellectual life, the connections between the maturing role of education and ideals of citizenship become tenuous.

The two strands in education are not inconsistent. We can be "led forth" by having our inner qualities or characters "drawn out." Nor can the strands be neatly aligned with any particular positions in contemporary debates. But they underlie those debates; and they can cut across one another in ways that exacerbate conflicted attitudes to, and expectations of, education. Thinking of education as a "drawing out" of what is rightfully our own can encourage us to think of its benefits as ultimately an individual and private matter; while the "leading forth" idea encourages concern with the more collective, social dimensions of the process.

Too literal an understanding of the "leading-forth-on-completion" idea can make us think of education as primarily a preparation for adulthood, rather than as ongoing formative processes through which citizens are included in practices of public reflection and social critique. The old Socratic ideal of education was to draw out individual capacities. But it was equally directed to forming life-long habits of shared intellectual inquiry – a drawing out of the inner life of the mind into public intellectual space. Perhaps that old ideal of autonomous but shared critical inquiry can still serve as a useful counter-model to the image of the self-absorbed but unreflective procession of educated men leading us forth, we know not where.

Genevieve Lloyd

See: *KNOWLEDGE, REASON.*

Elite

In its most common usage, **elite** implies a process of selection – which may be natural, social, or cultural – through which a few are distinguished from the many. The notion of natural selection is evident in horticultural usage ("in every fifth row of trees élite trees were selected," 1936), although this implies both natural variation and artificial selection on the part of the gardener. When the term is applied to the relations between social groups, there is the further connotation that the few are not just distinguished from, but exercise some form of power over, the many. Elites may also be distinguished in cultural or intellectual terms. Robert Hughes's defense of democracy provides a case in point: "Democracy's task in the field of art is to make the world safe for elitism. Not an elitism based on race or money or social position, but on skill and imagination" (Hughes, 1993: 201).

However, these neat separations are harder to maintain in practice. There is a long and complicated history in which, in the wake of Charles Darwin's work, the artificial selection associated with horticultural usage was translated into a process of social selection that was to complement the mechanisms of natural selection by separating the fit from the unfit. When linked to notions of racial hygiene, these eugenic conceptions later gave rise to programs of selective breeding designed to protect the purity of the **elite races** – Caucasian or, in Nazi programs, Aryan. Darwinian ideas also formed part of the intellectual background against which the **social theory of elites** was initially developed in eC20 Italy. Vilfredo Pareto, Gaetona Mosca, and Roberto Michels provided an alternative to Marxist class-based accounts of social divisions, suggesting that divisions between powerful and subordinate groups were universal and unavoidable because they were grounded in divisions arising from inequalities in the distribution of innate talents. "So let us make a class of the people," Pareto wrote, "who have the highest indices in their branch of activity, and to that class give the name of *elite*" (*cit.* Bottomore, 1966: 7). These natural divisions were complemented by social processes, like Michels's "iron law of oligarchy" (Michels, 1949), which specified that, in any organization or social group, power would always gravitate upward to concentrate in the hands of a few.

Italian elite theory was also influential in representing the relationship between elites and the rest of society as an elite–mass dichotomy. For Mosca, this division was grounded in the fact that minorities are usually well organized and, by dint of this consideration alone, are able to exercise power over the unorganized majority of the population. This contrast between **elites** and the masses played an important role in the subsequent development of C20 social thought. It gained great impetus from the experience of communism and fascism, in which liberal democracies seemed to tremble on the brink of totalitarianism owing to the growing concentration of power in **political elites**, **military elites**, and **business elites**, and to the social fragmentation of the isolated, dispersed, and atomized masses. The political inflections of these arguments were enormously varied. But they had in common the belief that, while different elites may often act separately, they are also capable of acting in concert – as in C. Wright Mills's famous conception of the **power elite** as "those political, economic, and military circles which as an intricate set of overlapping cliques share decisions" (Mills, 1956). This capacity for the concentration of **elite power** was paralleled by a conception of the masses as detached from the supportive social relationships of classes and communities, and thence vulnerable to elite manipulation and propaganda.

Elite theory continues to provide an account of social hierarchy that is not based on class. The view that elites "are simply those who, for whatever reason, have been able to gain the resources that lend them substantial power and influence" (Etzioni-Halevy, 2001: 4420–1) is still close to Pareto's original definition. Elite theory also continues to be preoccupied with mechanisms of **elite selection** and **recruitment**, and with the means by which elite power is transmitted across generations. These are important considerations in distinguishing **traditional elites**, based on kinship ties, landownership, or religious status, from **new elites**, based on educational qualifications, management and bureaucratic skills, political assets, or distinctive cultural skills. There are also strong connections between **managerial**, **political**, and **bureaucratic elites** and the notions of technocratic expertise. In more recent usage – **media** and **sporting elites**, for example – elites are affected by the principles of fame and celebrity and the new forms of distinction and power arising from contemporary media.

In the recent literature, elites have also been cast in a more favorable light as aiding democracy rather than threatening its destruction. Such assessments depend on the belief that, contrary to Mills's expectations, the competition between elites militates against their combining to exercise general, society-wide forms of power. A plurality of elites facilitates the circulation of power, preventing it accumulating in one place. Elites are also sometimes credited with assisting disadvantaged groups who depend on political or legal elites to represent their interests. The conduct of postcolonial struggles is also often shaped by challenges to the power of traditional elites on the part of new elites, which frequently owe their standing "to Western education, positions in emergent bureaucracies, and trading opportunities provided by the colonial encounter" (Gusterson, 2001: 4417–18).

In ordinary usage, however, elite and its companions – **elitism** and **elitist** – have few unequivocal champions. Their connotations are almost invariably pejorative, even when used by elite members ("what passes for quality on British television is no more than a reflection of the narrow elite which controls it," Rupert Murdoch, Columbia). The reasons for this are complex: elites sit ill with democratic values in public opinion, and **cultural elitism** always finds a ready put-down as simple snobbery. The term also carries connotations of undeserved reward, power, and influence. The major exception is the notion of meritocracy as "government by persons selected on the basis of merit in a competitive educational system," implying forms of selection and influence that are deserved on the basis of the able use of talents acquired in systems of open competition.

Yet, paradoxically, there are connections here between merit as just reward and the origins of "elite" as "someone elected or formally chosen" (R. Williams, 1976: 112), with its roots in L *eligire*, to choose, and thence, via oF *élire*, to *elit* (Denes, 1461: "He may not of reson do so largely ... because he is elyted, as the Comons myght"). This general usage, Williams notes, was extended in theological usage to refer to the elect as those specially chosen by God. This usage found a C19 echo in Coleridge's concept of the clerisy ("a distinct class of learned or literary persons") as a secularized **spiritual elite** that would stand against the leveling tide of industrialism and mass society. This provided the impetus for the secular program of cultural salvation that was to be provided by elites specially trained in "the best that has been thought and known" (Arnold, 1971 [1869]: 56) – a tradition that was continued in the C20 by T. S. Eliot, by F. R. Leavis, and, more recently, by Alan Bloom's (1987) defense of the civilizing role of literary and artistic elites. The idea of a meritocracy broadens the scope of this conception, providing the basis for more broadly based mechanisms of elite recruitment drawing on a broader range of acquired talents. Its theological roots, however, are perhaps not entirely left behind.

Tony Bennett

See: *CLASS, EQUALITY, TASTE.*

Emotion

Emotion was characterized by the Greeks as in opposition to thought, and as being sourced in the body. This dualism has stayed with accounts of emotion through philosophy and into psychology. Plato, Socrates, Aristotle, and the Stoics all stressed the primacy of reason over emotion, a position adopted from the inception of scientific rationalism in the C17 into the present. The wisdom of reason is situated as superior to the dangerous impulses of emotion, the animal passions, which needed to be suppressed or forced into submission through the steady application of an iron will. In the C17 **emotions** were associated with a "moving, stirring, agitation, perturbation" in the body. This stirring implied the passions, art, poetry, but by the C18 had also come to refer to political and social movement or agitation of the social body. In the West from the Greeks onward, it was the male body which was imbued with reason whereas woman was understood as having a body, especially a womb, which placed her outside the rational.

The emergence of psychology in the C19 built upon earlier distinctions to build a theory of emotions linking physiology with thought, providing the basis for a cognitive theory of emotion. Emotions were understood by Wilhelm Wundt, one of the founders of modern psychology, as being created out of a composite of sensation or feelings in the body linked to representations of objects in perception or memory. Emotion was understood as composed of bodily feelings plus ideas or "ideational processes," the ideas to which the feelings have attached themselves. In this way, Wundt and others were able to pursue a rational or cognitive approach to the **science of emotions**, which became the forerunner of cognitive approaches to emotion within C20 academic psychology. Emotions were understood as a key to disease, that is, an absence of reason, to be corrected by therapy. Emotion was also referred to as "affect": William James (1920) writes of a general seizure of excitement, called by Wundt, Lehmann, and other German writers "an *Affect*," and by James "an emotion."

Sigmund Freud made emotion or affect the basis of his approach to psychology: "psychoanalysis unhesitatingly ascribes the primacy in mental life to affective processes, and it reveals an unexpected amount of affective disturbance and blinding of the intellect in normal no less than sick people" (1953a [1913]: 175). Freud's stress on what Wundt had called the "ideational representatives" (the ideas to which feelings had attached themselves) and their relation to psychopathology led to a central emphasis on *phantasy* (unconscious fantasy) and a theory of unconscious defenses against unbearable sensations through the production of *phantasies*, thoughts, and actions which kept the unbearable at bay, thereby producing neuroses. In this account infantile pleasurable bodily sensations (feeding, the breast, touching genitals) served as the basis for later sexual impulses.

Freud could be understood as demonstrating the harm of the repressive Victorian approach to the domination of emotion by reason and will. However, Michel Foucault (1979) argued that, far from repressing and suppressing sexual feeling and bodily sensation, leading to neurosis, the Victorians spoke incessantly about the sexual in the context of medical practice. He argued that emotion became both medicalized and moralized, becoming the object of psychiatry and psychology, in the IC19. By the C20 the examination, exploration, and rationalization of emotions became one of the central features of the way in which people in the West understood their subjectivities.

By the 1960s, emotions were understood as needing expression, and "let it all hang out" became a catchword of those exploring their emotions in T or therapy groups. On the left, theories of ideology which stressed "false consciousness" also placed emphasis on the emotions as a distorting or blinding force, which prevented workers from seeing their chains. The Parisian students of the uprisings at the Sorbonne in May 1968, who placed a new emphasis on emotions such as pleasure ("under the paving stones the beach"), did so in the context of Louis Althusser's (1970) use of Lacanian psychoanalysis to argue that emotions, and in particular the workings of desire, were central to ideology.

The feminism of the 1970s stressed that "the personal is political" and, given the relation of woman to unreason, placed emotions as a central part of the personal to be explored. Consciousness-raising gave way to unconsciousness-raising and feminist approaches to therapy. Popularized accounts of women's **emotionality** emphasized difference from men: *Men are from Mars, women are from Venus* (J. Gray, 1993). Postmodern and feminist deconstructions of these binaries unsettle and contest their opposition and have understood power, authority, and privilege as central to the discursive division between reason and emotion, masculine and feminine. Later approaches from both the social sciences and cultural theory have turned to explanations which understand emotions as created discursively. Here meanings are understood not as reflections of an inner mental state but as expressions of hierarchies of cultural knowledges. Changing the story and meaning we tell about our emotions can be understood as a form of narrative therapy.

The discussion of the role of emotions in public life took on particular significance in Britain after the death of Diana, princess of Wales, in 1997. Diana was a psychological subject *par excellence* who talked about her emotions on national television. The importance of a public outpouring of grief (mass hysteria or people power?), despair with the state of the world, the corruption of politicians, the loss of livelihoods, have all been understood as having a new role to play in public life. Equally, pleasure became politicized within both queer politics and Rave in such movements as the "Right to Party." Within business, a concern with productivity led to the development of terms such as **emotional intelligence**, defined as the ability to monitor one's own and others' emotions, to discriminate among them, and to use the information to guide one's thinking and actions. "The skills that help people harmonize should become increasingly valued as a workplace asset in the years to come" (Goleman, 1995: 160). By sharing feelings, argued Goleman, both groups and organizations become better and therefore more intelligent and successful. While some would understand this as an important public opening up of the **emotional realm** (Samuels, 2001), others would see it as an aspect of the regulation of subjects under neo-liberalism, bringing unreason into central public scrutiny (N. Rose, 1999).

Valerie Walkerdine

See: *BODY, DESIRE, FEMINISM, GENDER, IDEOLOGY, NARRATIVE, QUEER, REASON, SEXUALITY, THERAPY, UNCONSCIOUS.*

Empirical

Empirical and **empiricism** preserve an echo of what Raymond Williams, in *Keywords*, called "the old association between experience and experiment" (R. Williams, 1983: 116): the terms suggest a method grounded in sense impressions, material practice, and/ or tangible data gathered by blind trial, as opposed to methods that depend primarily on the citation of doctrine or the application of inherited practices and rules. In Western philosophy, empiricism has usually been identified with the belief that humans are "blank slates" who learn by practice and accumulated experience, and counterposed on those grounds to "rationalist" *a priori* theories of perception; more colloquially, empiricism is contrasted with theory and abstraction in general, as when people say that they are more interested in **empirical evidence** or **empirical observation** than in what any received authority – in political, intellectual, or religious matters – has to say about the world.

The terms emerged in the IC16 and C17 as a critical part of the post-Copernican secularization of knowledge in the West, particularly with regard to science and medicine. The celebrated experiments of Galileo, for instance, bear witness to a nascent willingness, among people curious about the natural world, to base beliefs about matter and motion on direct observation rather than whatever the church fathers (with regard to science) or ancient Greek authorities such as Galen (with regard to medicine) had instructed their followers to believe. Indeed, what is now commonly referred to as the "scientific method" is precisely this willingness to conduct observations by experiment, and to develop protocols for gauging the reliability and the repeatability of the observations. Empiricism therefore carries with it connotations of good, no-nonsense realism and the supposed certainties of science and brute fact. However, in the early days of the post-Copernican revolution, "scientific method" itself had not been standardized, and empiricism was thus as readily associated with quackery and charlatanism as with experiment and observation: witness Burton's complaint, in the *Anatomy of Melancholy* (1621) that "there be many mountebanks, quack-salvers, Empiricks, in every street" [II.i.iv.i]). This connection between empiricism and fraudulent incompetence may seem thoroughly archaic today, but it was pervasive as late as the mC19, which renders its current obsolescence all the more remarkable. What we now derisively call "patent medicines" and "snake-oil remedies" were called "empirical drugs" in the mC19 (George James, 1839), and empiricism had earned for itself an especially bad name in politics – as in Coleridge's 1817 denunciation of "political empirics, mischievous in proportion to their effrontery, and ignorant in proportion to their presumption" or Frederick Robertson's 1858 dismissal of "a mere empiric in political legislation."

As "empirical" and "empiricism" have shed their connotations with quackery, they have congealed into what we might call "technical" and "colloquial" usages. The technical usage is straightforward, although the matters with which it deals are exceptionally complex: in Western philosophy, it denotes the epistemological tradition which grounds knowledge-claims in "matters of fact and real existence" (David Hume, 1999 [1748]). Empiricism in this sense is widely identified with the philosophy of Hume and (before him) John Locke, and opposed to (a) "rationalist" theories involving *a priori* ideas and categories, and (b) religious accounts of humans' innate tendencies or divinely ordained characteristics. Although **philosophical empiricism** might seem to benefit from its connection with scientific method, it also gives rise to intractable questions about what kinds of knowledge can plausibly be grounded in direct experience: for example, it is one thing to show by experiment how children learn to be cautious around fire or how animals can be taught to associate mealtime with ringing bells, and empiricism has been crucial to the development of behavioral science and operant conditioning. But it is quite another thing to try to explain, by observation alone, the process by which humans become fluent in higher mathematics or in theories of social justice – matters in which there are no hard "sense data" to appeal to. Quite apart from the philosophical skeptic's question of how we can gain reliable **empirical knowledge** about the "given" world, in other words, there may be some features of that "given" world (like mathematics or justice) that are not amenable to being apprehended empirically.

105

In the C20, empiricism has been central to debates in the philosophy of science. The eC20 adherents of logical positivism, who insisted that knowledge- and truth-claims should be based on empirically verifiable phenomena, have been challenged first by Karl Popper (1986; original publication 1934), who substituted "falsifiability" for "verifiability" as a criterion for the value of such claims, and then more thoroughly by T. S. Kuhn (1970; original publication 1962), who argued that observation is guided and constrained by interpretive paradigms that make some features of the natural world available for observation while obscuring others. Following Kuhn, proponents of the belief that our ways of seeing the world are "socially constructed" – by language, custom, interpretive paradigm, ideology, or, for that matter, the history of Western philosophy – have been deeply skeptical of empiricism on the grounds that it is unable to account for the larger social and historical forces that "produce" our perceptions of the world. **Empiricists**, in return, have been deeply skeptical of all such claims about the "social construction" of knowledge, seeing in them various forms of social determinism that fail to account for how empirical evidence might lead us to change our ideas about the world.

In its everyday sense, **the empirical** is simply a synonym for the world of incontrovertible fact, as opposed to flights of fancy or utopian longings; and in political debate, as in Edmund Burke's (1978 [1790]) invocation of "experience," the appeal to hard facts is often, but not always, made on behalf of political conservatism. However, since the empiricist is committed in principle not only to the supposed sureties of experience but to the uncertainties of experiment by trial and error, it is hard to see how empiricism in human affairs can provide the solid ground its adherents sometimes claim for it: for a rigorous openness to the possibility of learning from new data may in fact reveal the necessity rather than the superfluity of theories about what empirical "data" are and how they might best be understood.

Michael Bérubé

See: *EXPERIENCE, KNOWLEDGE, OBJECTIVITY, PRAGMATISM, REASON.*

Environment/Ecology

106

As the idea and practice of nature and culture as separate phenomena gained ascendency in the West, the concepts of **environment** and **ecology** developed to assert different conceptions of separation and connection. "Environment" emerged linked with nature, implying "natural" (that is, not human, not cultural) surroundings. "Ecology" merged as a scientist effort to connect organisms (such as the human) to their environments.

First used in the 1300s with a variety of meanings that depict that which surrounds the (human) subject, **environ** designated what was physically or naturalistically "round about," "in the neighborhood," or the "surroundings." It also meant to make a circle around, to wrap, to clothe, or to enclose. The first known use of "environment" equates the term with something like "circumstances" and is attributed to Holland in 1603, who wrote "I wot not what circumplexions and environments." Thomas Carlyle, in his 1827 essay "Goethe," translates and quotes Goethe using the phrase "an environment of circumstances"(Carlyle, 1860: 228 [Raymond Williams, in *Keywords,* and the OED wrongly attribute this phrase to Carlyle]), which for Carlyle refers to Goethe's "temper and habit of thought" or "state of mind" (p. 226), which calls forth certain human action. Carlyle used the term in *Sartor resartus* (1908 [1831]: 62) to designate the well-kept conditions of a homey cottage and surrounding forest and gardens that provided the context for human action: "the whole habitation and environment ... looked trim and gay." These uses suggest an already complex reference to that which is separated from and surrounds humans (habitat and nature) as well as that which is separate from and produces or gives shape to human action (habitat, nature, habits of thought, states of mind).

Ecology emerged as a science in the late 1800s to study interactions among abiotic components (such as air, water, and soil) and biotic components (such as plants and animals). Its earliest use, influenced by Charles Darwin, posits organisms evolving by adapting to their environment. German zoologist Ernst Haeckel, considered by some the founder of ecology, referred in 1866 to "All the various relations of animals and plants, to one another and to the outer world, with which the Œkology of organisms has to do" and to which the "Doctrine of Adaptation and Heredity" applies (Haeckel, 1887 [1866]: 114). Practicing a "polymorphic" science that develops slowly (McIntosh, 1985: 7), ecologists have differently separated, categorized, and connected what they consider key components. The term **ecosystem** developed in the 1960s to refer to particular systems of relationships among key components. Sometimes humans are excluded from these components; sometimes biological humans are subsumed by other, abstract components: cultures, societies, populations, or communities. The idea that the **ecological relationship** between humans and their environment is reciprocal gains currency unevenly. Aldo Leopold, in his influential 1949 *A sand country almanac* (1968), calls for developing "the ecological conscience" (p. 207), an awareness that "the individual is a member of a community of interdependent parts" (p. 203) in which the role of *Homo sapiens* changes "from conqueror of the land-community to plain member and citizen of it" (p. 204). For Leopold, the basic concept of ecology is that land – in this expansive sense – is a community (p. viii).

In the 1950s, growing concern about the effects of pollution, environmental degradation, resource depletion, and population growth gives rise to a significant presence of people identifying themselves as **environmentalists** (those who are concerned about and/ or act on behalf of the environment). In the 1960s, ecology responds to the widespread sense that the environment has been seriously compromised by humans, technology, and industry as the science to both explain and repair this condition. The connections between the descriptive claims and the political work performed by these claims are sometimes seen as a weakness, sometimes as a strength. While often used as a synonym for the (natural) environment, ecology is also treated as the "ally" of the environmentalist in providing a blueprint for the good life, a particular version of desirable connections among the components of an ecosystem. When functioning as the exemplar of the "natural," ecology indicates "how we ought to re-orient our lives" (Evernden, 1992: 8).

This combined epistemological claim and political valence is evident in some of the most potent voices in the development of contemporary attention to ecology and environment. Leopold (1968: viii) hoped that "When we see land as a community to which we belong, we may begin to use it with love and respect." Environmental philosopher J. Baird Callicott (1982: 174) explained that "ecology changes our values by changing our concepts of the world and of ourselves in relation to the world. It reveals new relations among objects, which, once revealed, stir our ancient centers of moral feeling." In *Steps to an ecology of mind*, Bateson (2000) argued that an **ecological system** is a "living" system

107

of ''patterns'' that emerges in the relationship among a range of components: the environment, humans, technology, and ideas (thinking, attitudes, and values). When ideas are ''wrong'' or ''false,'' the mind is separated from ''the structure in which it is immanent'' (p. 493). Acting on the misplaced premise of separation, one narrowly and self-centeredly ''chop[s] off consideration of other loops of the loop structure''(p. 492), resulting in an ecosystem that is out of balance. If uncorrected, the environment – including humans – will be destroyed. Félix Guattari expands on Bateson's ecology of the mind and designates three ecological registers: the environment, social relations, and human subjectivity. For Guattari the current ''ecological disequilibrium'' betrays the lack of an ''ethico-political'' articulation among the three registers, which will, unless corrected, ''ultimately threaten the continuation of life on the planet's surface'' (Guattari, 2000: 27–8).

The challenges posed by those such as Leopold, Bateson, and Guattari, and taken up by what is loosely called the **environmental movement**, have been met with a timid response by the discipline of ecology and exponents of community. Both tend to separate out the politics as a specialized matter of **environmental ethics**, or more dismissively as a matter of (mere) aesthetics (Odum, 1997: 312). Both tend to keep humans in their separate and central status by reverting, sometimes only subtly, to the idea that the environment is something ''out there'' within which humans live, to which they respond, and over which they have control. Thus, even though, as a current textbook on ecology states, ecology ''integrates the study of organisms, the physical environment, and human society,'' it does so ''in keeping with the Greek root of the world ecology: oikos, the 'study of the household,' the total environment in which we live'' (Odum, 1997: xiii). Studies of community rarely include ''the land,'' or humans as an integral component of ''the land.''

Attempts to lay claim to the terms ''environment'' and ''ecology'' within scientific, political, and philosophic discourses do not contain the excesses with which these terms have been taken up in popular discourse. Since the 1960s, the popular deployment, proliferation, and promiscuity of uses of ''environment'' and ''ecology'' exceed attempts to assign them identifiable referents. Infused with affect, they allude to ''what matters,'' intimate something ''critical'' demanding attention, imply the importance of certain kinds of (inter)relationships, and invoke the idea of (re)connecting in ways that suggest much at stake. One cannot read a specific epistemology or politics off their use in general, even though their uses tend to carry some residue of their etymology. ''Ecology,'' ''eco-,'' and ''ecologist'' retain the residue of science and convey a patina of it. Thus **personal ecology** lends scientific legitimacy to claims about what constitutes a ''healthy'' personal life. **Eco-friendly product** lends a sense that one is contributing responsibly (even scientifically) to saving the planet when purchasing a product. ''Environment,'' ''environmental,'' and ''environmentalist'' continue to convey – however vaguely – the organization of something ''natural'' out there, separate (from us) but connected in significant ways. Thus the fashionable term **computer environment** asserts a non-biological context separate from but highly significant in relation to the shaping and understanding of who we are. The

108

naturalistic residue of the term subtly lends the status of the "natural" to the machine environment. Apart from these valences, the two terms are widely used interchangeably. For instance, it makes little difference if one claims to be an **environmental activist** or an **eco-activist**; both convey the sense that some component of (inter)connectedness or some conception and practice of (inter)connectedness gives meaning to their acts. Similarly, it makes little difference if one is called an **environmental terrorist** or an **eco-terrorist**; both suggest condemnation of an inordinate valuation of some (typically non-human) component over human endeavors or of an inordinate valuation of (inter)connectedness generally.

So potent is the allusion to "what matters" that everyday language and advertising are filled with eco-this and environmental-that: **eco-friendly** and **environmental-friendly products**, **eco-topia**, **environmental well-being**, **environmentally sensitive planning**, **the ecology of aging**, **organizational environments**, and so on. Because meaning and politics cannot be read in general, we are compelled to pay attention to the particular articulations invoked by their use. What matters? What is the nature of the relationships within which this matters? Upon the back of what work of separation, categorization, and hierarchy does it rest? And finally, what is at stake? For everyone seems to agree, at least, that the stakes are high.

Jennifer Daryl Slack

See: *BIOLOGY, COMMUNITY, GENE/GENETIC, HUMAN, NATURE.*

Equality

Equality figures in Greek, Roman, and early Christian ethics and politics, gains currency in English usage from the C15, and becomes a key "reforming idea" (Rees, 1971: 11) in the revolutions of the C17 and C18. In Western traditions, classic formulations are found in Christian belief (especially in certain heresies), in ideas of **equity** or natural law, and in declarations of human rights at times of optimism about social possibilities. In the C19 and C20, equality became a central point of contest, politically and philosophically – and remains so today. The word evokes meanings which are emotional and ethical. While **egalitarianism** is sometimes interpreted pejoratively as a structure of feeling that handles the anger of oppression or discrimination – and may also assuage the guilty feelings of the privileged – it subjects principles and structures of power, resources, and opportunity to ethical scrutiny, asking how far they breach human solidarity and respect for persons. Equality rests, in R. H. Tawney's phrase, on "common humanity" as a "quality worth cultivating" (1964: 16).

The sharpest equalizing claims have come from socially excluded groups, who have often imagined an alternative social order, with, for example, property held in common. Hegemonic processes, in response, have created an institutional and discursive framework through which the fuller meanings of equality have been limited in relation to other social ideals. Pursuing **social equality**, it is argued, may threaten individual freedom or subvert legitimate hierarchies. It may confound "natural," "normal," or "necessary" differences, like the different roles of men and women in childbearing.

In liberal politics, equality may be limited to political and legal arrangements: to **equality before the law** or "one person, one vote" for example. This excludes claims to **equality of condition**, of access to land or other economic resources for example, which are historically associated with peasant or working-class movements. Similarly equality has narrowed down to **equality of opportunity**, historically a bourgeois claim against aristocratic privilege, but extendable, apparently, to all. C20 social democrats and social liberals have typically favored, in addition, definite measures of **social equalization**: typically taxes on inherited wealth, progressive income tax, state provision for the poor, the old, and the unemployed, and universal, non-selective public education. They have argued that social rights, including freedom from poverty, are conditions for democratic political participation (T. H. Marshall, 1977). In "revolutionary" or communist theory and practice, equality means a state of classlessness, with fundamental changes in economic organization and social relationships. This state has not proved easy to achieve, so far, without creating new inequalities.

In the lC20 and eC21, terms like **equal opportunities** and "social inclusion" have replaced "equality" in political discourse. The more libertarian strands in neo-liberalism provide for equitable, legal freedoms as between, for example, groups defined by sexual orientation, but they also prioritize individual freedom, trusting in markets and capitalist enterprise to spread wealth and well-being (Hayek, 1976). As center-left politics has come to terms with these individualistic premises, it has abandoned concern with equality of condition. Intervention has focused not on wealth, power, or privilege, but on the social exclusion of the underprivileged. Governments seek to empower groups so constructed to "help themselves," usually as individuals and often through strongly regulative policies – enforcing entry to low-paid work, for example, or inciting continuous self-invention and "life-long learning" (N. Rose, 1999). Inequalities, often conflated with diversity of provision, are a reward of "talent" and "hard work," just as injustice is defined as "untapped talent" (Commission on Social Justice, 1994: 1). As critiques of meritocracy argue, this version of equality justifies inequalities of a particularly entrenched kind (M. Young, 1961).

While the decades from the 1920s to the later 1950s saw priority given to the **class politics of equality**, the lC20 saw increasing stress on other social relations, especially those of gender and sexuality, race and ethnicity, and disability. A new dynamic of challenge and incorporation highlighted further causes of inequality and produced fresh meanings and keywords.

First, social movements have drawn attention to the **subjective inequalities**, especially to questions of recognition and the effects of misrecognition or misrepresentation on both subordinated and dominant groups. Following the analysis, especially, of black consciousness by anti-racist and anti-colonial intellectuals (Du Bois, 1989; Fanon, 1986), many studies have explored the psychic or emotional aspects of power relations and of different strategies of equalization (J. Benjamin, 1990; Bhabha, 1994). According to this view, changes in consciousness involve complex cultural and psychic processes which are integral to economic and political change.

Second, the older arguments about **equality and difference** have been revived and recast. Should women, for example, strive to become equal to men or will this mean they only come to resemble them in a predominantly "masculine" social order? Should feminists change society according to the specific needs and character of (all?) women? Or will equality come from recognizing diversity and subverting gender difference? These tensions between assimilative, separatist, and deconstructive strategies have been complicated by the revival of (neo-)conservative justifications for inequality, including the attempt to renaturalize key differences, especially those of "ability," race, gender, and sexuality.

One point of conflict is the politics of **equity and access**, where equality is measured by the proportions of black, ethnic minority, or women candidates entering educational institutions or particular (usually professional) occupations. **Equal access**, an aspect of **equal opportunities**, means reforming admission or appointment procedures, to make them culturally "neutral," or to recognize "promise" among underrepresented groups. This has led to charges of discrimination against the privileged, but also risks narrowing the definition of equality to the proper reward of "talent."

Feminists particularly have puzzled over the contradictions between equality and difference. Some argue that equality involves recognizing differences, but making them "costless": recognizing women's role in childbearing, for instance, but accommodating it within employment practices (Littleton, 1997). Others deconstruct the apparent opposition between equality and difference and argue for **equivalence**. Equivalence involves "deliberate indifference to specified differences," but also the recognition of differences which are relevant and valuable (J. Scott, 1997; Walzer, 1983). An example would be recognizing the value of childbearing, housework, or "caring," and rewarding it accordingly. Debates about "disability" have generated similar combinations of principles and deployments of "equivalence." An example would be identifying and meeting a wide range of different special needs among pupils in a mainstream school.

While such detailed struggles can occur in the richer societies, huge discrepancies in human health and wealth world-wide underline the continued relevance of egalitarian principles in the fullest sense. Contemporary warfare adds further offence to **egalitarian sentiment** when it differentially counts human deaths and values human lives differently depending on nationality, "race," faith, or "innocence."

Richard Johnson

See: *ALTERNATIVE, CITIZENSHIP, CLASS, DISABILITY, ELITE, FREEDOM, GENDER, JUSTICE, LIBERALISM, MOVEMENTS, RACE.*

111

Ethnicity

Ethnic and **ethnicity** are derived from Gk *ethnos* meaning "nation, people." A derivation from L *ethnicus* meaning "heathen," referring to people not Christian or Jewish, has historically been confused with the root of these words. "Ethnicity" was added to the updated edition of Raymond Williams's *Keywords* as one of the words that had "become more important" (R. Williams, 1983: 27). This signals one of the paradoxes of ethnicity. Ethnicity and **ethnic affiliations**, defined as a quasi-primordial collective sense of shared descent and distinct cultural traditions, were expected to decline and even disappear with the homogenization associated with modernization and the French model of civic nationalism. The opposite has proved to be the case.

Ethnicity is a term "that is used in a fairly promiscuous way, without there ever being a consensus about its meaning" (Malik, 1996: 174). Indexing a range of non-biological communal identifications, including nationality, religion, history, language, and culture, it is simultaneously treated as separate from race, and as overlapping with it. The conventional social science distinction maintains that race is a biologically derived, often imposed, identification that assumes individuals and groups possess fixed traits and characteristics. Ethnicity, however, is about cultural distinctiveness. When particular minority groups are defined by external bodily markings and regarded as differentiated from the main population, "race" and "ethnicity" are being used interchangeably, just as in C19 anthropology "ethnicity" was used to denote social groupings on the basis of cultural and physical characteristics. In the 1930s "ethnicity" connoted both racial difference and the status of a minority group within a society or a nation: "Like other ethnic units, the Jews have their own standard racial character" (C. S. Coon, 1939). Census categories also overlap ethnic and racial classifications. A justification for the administrative delineation of particular ethnic/racial groups is that it provides a basis for mapping group inequalities and can also offer a baseline against which to measure change.

Ethnicity is commonly identified as a characteristic of some migrant population, so **an ethno** in Australia in the 1970s referred to an immigrant, just as **an ethnic** in current usage often means someone who is "not indigenous," and perhaps also "not white." Treating ethnicity as a defining feature of such groups is problematic. It exoticizes ethnicity as a quality possessed by non-whites and those of non-European descent. It overlooks the ethnicities within the majority population. It obscures the relationship between majority and minority and questions of power and status; thus whites in South Africa are a numerical minority but not one that is deemed "ethnic." It confuses different bases of common identity through religion, nationality, and language, as well as culture. It has served to homogenize both "white" and "non-white" groups in terms of fixed cultural boundaries and forms of belonging. In the UK the use of **minority ethnic** rather than **ethnic minority** is intended to signal that there is also an **ethnic majority**. The increasing use of the term **black and minority ethnic** in social policy and official discourse reflects the differentiated nature of ethnic and/or racial "minorities."

Ethnicity can also be used to identify "white" minorities such as **ethnic Russians** or **ethnic Germans** spread across several countries. In these cases, and in those of **ethnic Turks** in Germany, or **ethnic Kurds** in Iraq, a sense of cultural belonging is based on descent rather than nationality, although whether this is how groups see themselves, or how they are seen, is open to question. Hyphenated identities such as African-American or Italian-American or Black-British also reflect the porous boundaries of ethnic, racial, national, and cultural affiliations and identifications.

Ethnicity is both chic and dangerous, as a component of fashionable commodities, on the one hand, or as something base and elemental, on the other. **Ethnic cultures** are valued differentially for possessing either "good" or "bad" ethnicity. The cultural values of south and east Asians who are relatively educationally and economically successful mark them out as "model minorities," thus making the retention of ethnicity a desirable feature. Conversely, ethnic connections are regarded as culturally dangerous in the case of **ethnicized crime**, such as drug-trafficking gangs and terrorist networks, and where ethnicity is alleged to provide a code of behavior and affiliation that "mainstream" society finds difficult to penetrate.

Ethnicity has cosmopolitan associations when it is linked with styles of art, crafts, fashion, dance, music, cuisine, and street markets. Indeed, this is mainly what is covered in a tourist guide to **ethnic London**. These associations can overlap with the idea of distinct **ethnic zones**, areas of cities that are defined by ethnicity – like the "Chinatown," "Little India," and "Little Italy" districts to be found in many parts of the world. **Ethnic commerce** and **ethnic businesses** use social and cultural capital to network and develop their common interests in and across such zones. **Ethnic products, objects, and styles** drawing upon African, Asian, Aboriginal, Latino, and other "non-Western" cultural traditions have been glamorized in the spheres of consumption and production. They have been valued in ways that suggest **ethnic roots** are something closer to nature, a primordial essence, albeit one that can be reinvented and transformed through use and practice. In its most commercial manifestations a hint of the exotic in ethnicity has become part of a global corporate multiculture where it lends a certain chic to companies – when both British Airways and Qantas adopted **ethnic designs** on their airplanes, for instance.

113

The mainstreaming of **ethnic pluralism** and cultural diversity has been greeted as a sign that a modern, **multiethnic polity** can recognize and proclaim difference. Instead of homogenizing and negating **ethnic difference** through assimilation and integration, there has been some official acknowledgement of **multiethnic "mosaic" societies**. Multiculturalism in Europe, North America, and Australasia can be seen as the outcome of this process. In public and private sector diversity strategies, an ethnically diverse workforce gives businesses a commercial advantage, according to economists. Equal-opportunity and affirmative-action policies are based upon **ethnic monitoring** to check for fairness.

The stress upon ethnicity as a cultural boundary between groups is not always seen as positive. For critics, it marks a celebratory and superficial approach to cultural differences ("saris, samosas and steel bands," as it is summed up in the UK: Donald and Rattansi, 1992) that ignores underlying social and economic inequalities. A culturalist approach, based on food, fashion, and music, is held to produce static, rigid, and ahistorical views of culture that overstate differences between "ethnic" groups and overlook sameness across them. Instead of seeing ethnicity as a cultural characteristic of groups themselves, some stress that it should be understood as a relational social process that marks the boundaries of identification between ethnic groups, though for others ethnicity has sociobiological roots and boundary maintenance is a reflection of that.

Globalization and transnational networks have highlighted the flaws in Orientalist conceptions of ethnicity. In the C19 and C20, the latter transmuted ethnicity into a minoritarian and exotic framework in seeing it as primarily a feature of bounded groups, differentiated from the main population, defined by a shared ethnic culture with impermeable boundaries, inside a nation state with clear borders. Evidence of diasporic networks across nation states has shown that individuals and groups actively develop and engage in regular and sustained social, economic, cultural, and political relations that stretch across national borders. Global culture and diasporas promote forms of hybrid and syncretic cultural forms, for which Stuart Hall (1992a) coined the term **new ethnicities**. The plural "ethnicities" is itself significant in emphasizing internal group differentiation, and ethnicity as a process of becoming rather than a state of being.

Some of the same processes have led to a resurgence of **white ethnicities**. There has been a "white backlash" against multiculturalism through conservative and neo-nationalist movements in Australia and in many European countries, as well as against affirmative-action measures in the USA. Such **ethnic identification** and **ethnic political struggles** can also produce campaigns for justice by minorities such as African-Americans, as well as majorities such as blacks in South Africa. **Ethnic mobilization** and **ethnicization** are most apparent in nationalist movements that have taken the form of asserting claims for self-governance within the nation state (among Scots and Catalonians) or for statehood based on ethnic/national identification (among the Basques, the Irish, and the Quebecois). **Ethno-nationalisms** have led to genocide or **ethnicide**, and to terrorism. This so-called "dark" side of ethnicity suggests that "tribal" affiliations are capable of being mobilized in new ways, and mark a "return of the repressed." Violent conflicts in the former Yugoslavia and Rwanda have defined the **ethnic cleansing** of "others" through expulsion or extermination in the name of **ethnic purity**. These violent manifestations of ethnicity are one form of **ethnic closure** and boundary maintenance, where ethnicity is mobilized in a defensive or reactive way to mark boundaries between "in" and "out" groups, in ways that are often opposed to social change. Groups may also assert a strong notion of their own boundaries in patterns of residential settlement where ethnicity marks status and consumption cleavages. In all these cases, ethnicity stands in for and combines with other social divisions such as caste, class, and stratification.

Karim Murji

See: *DIASPORA, GLOBALIZATION, MULTICULTURALISM, ORIENTALISM, RACE.*

Everyday

References to **the everyday** always involve an implied contrast with some other term, so that, depending on the context, its meaning varies. Where the sense of **everyday** as a daily occurrence prevails – in accounts of the role of broadcast schedules in organizing the dailiness of everyday life, for example (Scannell, 1996) – it is its juxtaposition with the irregular or unexpected that carries most weight. Where "everyday" means casual or informal – as when Dickens dresses Quilp in his "every-day garments" – the implied contrast is with formality, be it of dress ("formal dress") or occasion ("a formal ball"). The sense of the everyday as familiar or ordinary (everyday household objects) similarly implies a contrast with the strange or unusual, the out of the ordinary. This connects with the now predominant sense of the everyday as mundane, unremarkable, and routine, and the contrast that this implies with the extraordinary or remarkable registers not just a departure from **everyday norms** but a challenge to them.

The everyday is, in all of these uses, a boundary term marking distinctions between different times, places, occasions, and, in some contexts, persons. Where, for example, the sense of "everyday" as familiar or ordinary shades over into notions of the common, commonplace, or vulgar, notions of social inferiority are implied. Here, reference to the everyday often serves to distance intellectual or social elites from the commonplace – as in "Persons of no every-day powers and acquirements" (Coleridge, 1817), the literary character who "shrunk from the every-day people in the parlour of the public house" (1847), or the advice that "People who have a cook . . . ought not to dine like everyday folks" (1871). More recently, this stress has been challenged in a more democratic usage affirming that all classes share the rhythms of everyday life. "Everyone, from the most famous to the most humble, eats, sleeps, yawns, defecates; no-one escapes the reach of the quotidian" (Felski, 1999–2000: 16). The notion of **everyday culture**, now often used interchangeably with "popular culture," has similarly been revalued as worthwhile and important precisely because of its ordinary, taken-for-granted qualities.

The boundaries the term establishes also have marked gendered connotations. The sense of the everyday as the time of routine and repetition has been strongly linked with the role of clock time in the organization of work in industrial societies (Thompson, 1993). These new relations of **everyday time** and work discipline, while not limited to the factory (they were echoed, and rehearsed, in the school), formed part of a division between public and private in which the latter – centered on the home – represented an organization of everyday time that was distinct from that of the public world of work. Men and women were differently situated in relation to these times. While the everyday time of work discipline was repetitive, its repetitions – in being linked to the progressive, linear time of modernity – had a forward-looking trajectory: "the clock on the wall or in the waistcoat pocket is but the metronome for a soul already singing to the music of modernity" (Davison, 1993: 6). The time of the home, and that of women within the home, by contrast, was often characterized as one of cyclical repetition, a quasi-natural time deriving from women's alleged closeness to the rhythms of biological time or from their lingering associations with pre-industrial rhythms, as a drag on modernity or the residual reminder of an alternative to it.

Feminist criticisms of these conceptions, changing relationships between work and home, changing patterns of women's employment, and changes in the organization of everyday time into the new "timeless time" (Castells, 1996: 429) of the information society mean that these dualistic conceptions of men's and women's relationships to everyday time now have less force. There is similarly less force to the contrast between the everyday and the religious values transcending the mundanity of everyday life. This contrast, itself quite recent and evident mainly in Christian thought, reflects the increasing secularization of social life – Max Weber's "disenchantment of the world" (Weber, 1970b: 155). It was present, in a more or less routinized form, in the contrast between **everyday wear** and Sunday clothing characterizing C19 sabbatarianism: "Oh! I keeps they for Sundays, I don't put 'em on 'pon everydays" (Elworthy, 1888). In the C20, however, even this distinction lost force as the increasing commercialization of time eroded the distinction between Sundays and weekdays. The sense of the everyday as a "week-day, as opposed to Sunday" has, consequently, now ceded priority to that of "pertaining alike to Sundays and week-days."

Yet if **everyday life** is now widely seen as "leached of transcendence" (Felski, 1999–2000: 16), the critiques of everyday life developed in the exchanges between C20 European social and aesthetic theory aimed to rediscover new sources of transcendence within the everyday itself. From the work of Dada and the surrealists through to the Situationist International of the 1960s, a succession of radical and aesthetic manifestos and movements aimed to disrupt the taken-for-granted familiarity of the everyday, seeking well-springs of social renewal that would chart a course beyond the one-dimensional horizons of a technocratic and bureaucratic age. These concerns have been echoed in sociological critiques of everyday life which have sought to locate, in the seemingly insignificant aspects of everyday life, the repressed echoes of earlier, more authentic forms of social existence in which transcendent values allegedly imbued the rhythms of daily life (Lefebvre, 1971). Attention thus focuses on "the apparently ordinary gestures of the everyday, the unspoken desires of the body and the 'microscopic' expressions of care and solidarity, where the redemptive promise of everyday life continues to persist, in the interstices of more formalised social relations and organisational structures" (Gardiner, 2000: 16–17).

There is, however, a countervailing tradition in which "the need for everydayness" (MacNeice, 1954) is seen as a positive value, an enabling condition of social life. This "everyday" understanding of the everyday is echoed in the contention that the known and predictable routines of everyday life, the TV news for example, offer a sense of "onto-logical security" (Silverstone, 1994) – a sense of the reliability of the world and of one's place within it – that provides a necessary grounding for our actions within the world. The point at issue between these contrasting evaluations of the everyday has been, and remains, that of the role of habit in social life and the part it plays in the mechanisms through which "the social order inscribes itself in bodies" (Bourdieu, 2000: 141).

Tony Bennett

See: *HOME, POPULAR, TIME.*

Evolution

In its most general sense **evolution** means unrolling, unfolding, or opening out. Its origins are from the L *evolvere*, or roll out, first appearing in English in the C17. From the first, the term was used in multiple contexts, and found its way into social, philosophical, and natural scientific discourse. Least common now is the use of the term to represent the logical or rational development of a thesis or argument. There is an obsolete mathematical sense, in which a curve is said to be unfolded or straightened, but essential to the more common use is a sense of temporality, of process, of change over time. Thus in mathematics "evolution" is now employed to describe the development of dynamic equations. Implicit in the concept is the notion of gradual or steady progression, as opposed to revolution. Thus social democrats used to counterpose the prospect of a gradual, peaceful, **evolutionary transition** of capitalist societies to socialism with the swift and violent revolutionary transition offered by communism.

However, the discourse in which the term "evolution" carries most power today is undoubtedly that of the life sciences, and its current use by social scientists is often intended to imply a direct – almost mechanistic – relationship between **evolutionary processes** as biologists understand them and those applicable to social change. Dialogue between biological and social interpretations of evolution has been commonplace since C19 challenges to earlier understandings of the immutability of species. Such views had deep biblical roots within Western culture. The multiplicity of extant living forms was seen as created independently and simultaneously by God. From the C18 on, however, the concept of progression from "lower" to "higher" organisms became more prevalent. The recognition that fossils formed a record of living forms – species – now extinct, the steady pushing back of the estimated age of the earth, and Charles Lyell's principle of uniformitarianism – of the gradual rather than catastrophic molding of the earth's geological and geographical features – were crucial elements. That species might be transformed was hinted at by Erasmus Darwin, and given a potential mechanism by Jean-Baptiste Lamarck (1984) at the beginning of the C19. Lamarck proposed that characteristics acquired during an individual's lifetime as a result of purposeful striving might be transmitted to its offspring, but the logical and empirical flaws in this hypothesis prevented its being regarded seriously.

Evolution

In 1858, Charles Darwin (1859) and Alfred Russel Wallace (2002) independently proposed the mechanism that Darwin (whose own thoughts were strongly influenced by Malthus) called "natural selection." This is based on three premises:

1 like breeds like, but with minor variations;
2 organisms produce more offspring than can possibly survive into reproductive maturity and reproduce in their turn;
3 therefore those "fittest" or more adapted to their environment are the most likely to survive and reproduce.

From which it logically follows that the characteristics of a breeding population will steadily change – evolve – over time, and indeed that in due course descendents of the original population will differ so markedly from it as to constitute a distinct species. The logic is so inexorable that Daniel Dennett has described it as a "universal acid" that applies over the entire gamut of observed phenomena, living and non-living (Dennett, 1995). For example, Gareth Runciman (1998) and others have argued that the archeological record shows transitions in the forms of human artifacts (such as tools) that can be analogized to the transition between biological species, and that a form of natural selection by competition occurs between such different technologies. Similarly, some computer programs are now generated by creating **evolutionary trees** in which alternative routines and subroutines are allowed to compete and the weaker eliminated, again by an analogue of "natural selection." It should be noted, however, that Darwin himself did not originally use the term – he referred to "descent with modification." It was the social theorist Herbert Spencer who popularized the use of the term "evolution" to describe this, and in doing so drew analogies with **social evolution**.

Four aspects of Darwin's theory, as set out in the *Origin of Species*, have proved important for subsequent debates. First, organisms are seen as more or less well adapted ("fit") to their environment. What drives evolution is then the natural selection of more fit over less fit forms. However, fitness is a relative concept, relevant only to the environment of the moment; as the environment changes, so what constitutes fitness does too. This dramatically changes the notion of evolution, hitherto seen as an inevitably progressive tendency, from "lower" to "higher" organisms, from the less to the more perfect. In **biological evolution**, there is no such progression; natural selection cannot predict future environments, merely respond to the exigencies of the here and now. Organs exquisitely evolved in one environment can become redundant in another – as in the loss of eyes in blind, cave-dwelling fish.

Second, the sources of variation on which natural selection can act are random, and not affected by the "striving" of the organism. In the absence of knowledge of genes, not available for a further half-century, Darwin had no way of knowing how such variations arose, or how they could be preserved. This problem led to an eclipse of natural selection theory during the lC19, and with the rediscovery of Gregor Mendel's original genetic observations in the eC20, Mendelian mutations superseded Darwinian natural selection as an explanation for **evolutionary change**. It was not until the 1930s that J. B. S. Haldane, Ronald Fisher, and Sewall Wright generated what became known as the "modern synthesis" of Darwin and Mendel. The sources of variation are changes, by mutation or other mechanisms, in genes (understood today as composed of DNA); natural selection provides the "scrutiny" by which some variations are favorable and preserved, others lost.

Third is gradualism. Darwin insisted that evolutionary change was slow. "Nature does not make leaps." Species change by steady, incremental, infinitesimal modifications over many generations. Evolution is not revolution. This gradualism disconcerted Darwin's own supporters, who found it difficult to see how small variations would not be "swamped" by random breeding in the absence of major leaps ("saltations"). The problem was solved within the modern synthesis when genetic theory showed that genetic variation could be preserved even though hidden and not apparent in the individual organism (the phenotype, as opposed to the genotype). However, Darwinian gradualism has been challenged more recently when Stephen J. Gould and Niles Eldredge pointed out that the fossil record shows long periods of stasis followed by relatively brief periods of rapid change – so-called "punctuated equilibrium" (Gould, 2002).

Fourth, survival until reproductive age, and hence evolutionary change, depends, in part, on competition for scarce resources. Hence "nature red in tooth and claw," "the struggle for existence," and "the survival of the fittest," and the appropriation of the Darwinian metaphor for social purposes, as in social Darwinism, which saw capitalism, nationalism, imperialism, and racism as expressions of underlying biological inevitability. It was this that led Karl Marx to point out how, as a typical Victorian gentleman, Darwin had looked into the natural world and found reflected there the values of a capitalist society. The alternative view, that co-operative behavior aids survival and hence evolutionary success, was advanced by Prince Peter Kropotkin (1996 [1902]) at the end of the C19, and this debate, within biology and among those drawing on its metaphorical power to make social theory, has persisted ever since.

For biologists, evolution is not a theory but a fact as solidly based as any other within the corpus of science. What remains for discussion is the mechanisms of evolutionary change – that is, the degree to which natural selection, narrowly defined, is the only or even the major motor of such change. The modern synthesis emphasized the genetic mechanisms of evolutionary change, and in its wake, orthodox neo-Darwinians produced a new definition of evolution: a change in gene frequency within a population.

This still left at least one major problem unresolved. If individuals compete for scarce resources in order to propagate their genes, how and why might co-operative behavior, which certainly occurs at least among social species, and of course among humans, evolve? The solution proposed by William Hamilton (2001) in the 1960s was to tailor the concept of fitness to the genic level. Siblings have half their genes in common; cousins one-eighth.

Hence behavior that benefits a sib, or a cousin, increases the chance of an individual's genes being transmitted to the succeeding generation via the sib or the cousin. This is Hamilton's concept of inclusive fitness – it pays, in genetic terms, to help those to whom one is closely genetically related.

The consequence was two books which together brought the evolutionary debate into the wider intellectual arena. Richard Dawkins's account of *The selfish gene* (1976) proposed to distinguish between *replicators* – genes – and *interactors* – the organisms within which those genes are embedded. The real business of evolutionary change is carried by the replicators, whose telos is to replicate themselves within succeeding generations; inter-actors are the necessary vehicles by means of which this replication can occur. Nonetheless it is the fitness of the interactors that helps determine whether or not such replication actually takes place. Edward O. Wilson's *Sociobiology* (1975) brought Hamiltonian inclusive fitness into the observed world of animal – including human – behavior. Humans, like other animals, he claimed, tend to behave so as to maximize their inclusive fitness. The implication was that competition and nepotism are inscribed within our selfish genes. To these the National Front added racism, claiming that sociobiology had "proved" that racism and xenophobia were "in our genes."

However, by the 1990s sociobiology had transmogrified into a full-blown theory of human nature, **evolutionary psychology**. This claims that the fundamentals of human nature were established at the dawn of human evolution, during the Pleistocene, a so-called environment of **evolutionary adaptation**. According to this argument, a combin-ation of natural and sexual selection produced humans with large brains, evolved to achieve maximal reproductive success within a social environment. These alleged univer-sals of human nature include male preference for mating with younger fertile women of optimal hip–waist ratios; female preference for mating with older, more powerful men with ample resources; the ability to detect cheats in social interaction; hostility to unrelated strangers; and many other such features. According to the claims of evolutionary psych-ology, these alleged "universals" of human nature, having been laid down in the Pleisto-cene, some 100,000–600,000 years ago, have remained essentially unchanged since, and therefore shape the range of possible societies that humans can create. However, there are those – Edward Wilson and Francis Fukuyama (2002), for example – who would go further, arguing for an **evolutionary ethics**, a code of ethical behavior based upon evolutionary assumptions about the "nature of human nature."

Critics of these positions question the evolutionary, psychological, historical, and social bases for such claims. Where Darwin was pluralistic in his views on the mechanisms of evolutionary change, today's orthodox neo-Darwinians (sometimes called fundamentalist or ultra-Darwinians) focus only on natural and sexual selection as the motors of change, the gene as the unit of selection, and observed traits as *ipso facto* adaptive. By contrast, Gould's major text *The structure of evolutionary theory* (2002) adds contingency, *exapta-tions* (structures originally evolved for one adaptive function and subsequently pressed into other service, such as feathers, serving a thermoregulatory function in reptilian ancestors of birds, but later used for flying), epiphenomena, or accidental consequences of other features (such as the red color of blood, the human chin), and architectural constraints (humans cannot sprout wings and fly because our body mass is too large).

As for evolutionary psychology's claim for the existence of human universals and the fixity of human nature since the Pleistocene, there has been steady genetic change since that period as the human population grew and flowed from its original African location into the entire habitable globe. But many other so-called "universals" appear, on closer inspection, to be so mediated by culture and economy as to defy biologizing. Indeed, if there is one lesson to be learned from these debates it is that attempts to dichotomize "human nature" into an evolved biology upon which the social is superimposed, rather than accepting that we are simultaneously and inextricably both biological and social organisms, are doomed to failure.

Steven Rose

See: *BIOLOGY, BODY, GENE/GENETIC, HUMAN, NATURE, REFORM AND REVOLUTION.*

Experience

121

Experience is one of the most compelling and elusive words in the language. It was once closely allied to "experiment," as in Spenser's "she caused him to make experience / Vpon wild beasts" (*Faerie Queene* V.i.7) (1596), but that sense, as Raymond Williams pointed out in *Keywords*, has long been obsolete. Today the word is more commonly used in a variety of overlapping and sometimes contradictory ways that involve appeals to lived realities and (sometimes) dead certainties. On the one hand, there is the sense, marked most dramatically in Blake's *Songs of innocence and experience* but also in daily usage, that experience is something bitter and chastening: as we grow from childhood to old age, for instance, we **learn by experience** that the world is not to be redrawn according to our desires. For Romantic poets and all who have been influenced by them since the eC19, the accumulation of experience is the deplorable process by which, as Wordsworth put it, "shades of the prison house begin to close / Upon the growing boy" (1806). On the other hand, there is a sense in which "experience" is something greatly to be desired because it bespeaks a heightened and sensually alert mode of living in the world; to speak of something as "quite an experience" is to say that it was memorably out of the ordinary, for good or ill, and certainly Jimi Hendrix's pointed question, "are you experienced?" (1967), suggested a realm of apprehension and cognition unavailable to ordinary mortals who had not yet encountered the **Jimi Hendrix Experience**. (There is an ancillary sense here, having less to do with psychoactive drugs than with sex, in which "experience" is simply shorthand for **sexual experience**, and desired or feared for that reason alone.)

Experience

More generally, "experience" signifies a realm of rocky solidity and certainty, over against the airy abstractions of philosophy and social theory. It often confers authority when it is associated with the direct **experience of life** as opposed to "book learning," and it often serves as a common-sense, eyewitness guarantee of truth: "I know because I was there." Indeed, at around the same time as Wordsworth and Blake were writing dolorous laments about childhood innocence and wizened experience, Edmund Burke was writing in his *Reflections on the revolution in France* (1978 [1790]), "If I might venture to appeal to what is so much out of fashion in Paris, I mean to experience." In *Keywords*, Williams argues against the Burkean association between "experience" and conservatism, since "it is quite possible from experience to see a need for *experiment* or *innovation*" (R. Williams, 1983: 127). Williams differentiates Burke's appeal to what he (Williams) calls **experience past** from **experience present**, which involves "the fullest, most open, most active kind of consciousness" (p. 127) necessary to learn the lessons of experience past. Experience present might then be said to be a kind of gateway to an unspecified experience future, as when we say that a person is "open to new experiences."

Apart from its contradictory usages in ordinary speech, "experience" has also been a loaded term in intellectual debates since the IC20, particularly in feminism and cultural studies. As Stuart Hall (1980) argued, the concept of **quotidian experience** or **material experience** was central to so-called "culturalist" modes of cultural studies (associated with Richard Hoggart, E. P. Thompson, and the early Williams) as opposed to later "structuralist" modes (associated with French Marxist Louis Althusser), which stressed impersonal social conditions and ideologies rather than individuals' immediate perceptions of their world. In early second-wave feminism, "experience" was often adduced to anti-theoretical but not necessarily politically conservative ends, as in the appeal to **the authority of experience**, which sought to validate women's actual lives and perceptions over against dominant masculinist constructions thereof. Some second-wave feminists took their cue from R. D. Laing's *The politics of experience* (1967) – and some others, perhaps, from salient literary foremothers like Chaucer's Wife of Bath, who, disclaiming any knowledge of worldly or secular authorities, begins her Canterbury Tale (1400) by saying, "Experience, though noon auctoritee / Were in this world, is right ynough for me / To speke of wo that is in marriage."

Such appeals to **individual experience** were then challenged by feminist theorizing in the 1980s and 1990s; Joan Wallach Scott's influential essay "Experience" (1992) sought to mediate the growing debate by insisting that experience is not merely given but *produced*. "Documenting the experience of others," she wrote, "has been at once a highly successful and limiting strategy for historians of difference" (p. 24). Its success, for Scott, lay in its ability to conform to the evidentiary protocols of historiography: the new histories of slavery or working-class communities, for instance, looked recognizably like histories. But its limitations were attributed to the "appeal to experience as uncontestable evidence and as an originary point of explanation," which "weakens the critical thrust of histories of difference'' (p. 24) by foreclosing on ''the possibility of examining those assumptions and practices that excluded considerations of difference in the first place''(pp. 24–5). In other words, revisionist historians may be able to recover the experiences of individuals or cultures overlooked by previous histories, but if they rely on experience as ''an originary point of explanation,'' they fail to investigate the larger social conditions that produced those histories and their exclusions. Williams had made a similar point toward the end of his entry in *Keywords*, writing,

> At one extreme experience (present) is offered as the necessary (immediate and authentic) ground for all (subsequent) reasoning and analysis. At the other extreme, experience . . . is seen as the product of social conditions or of systems of belief or of fundamental systems of perception, and thus not as material for truths but as evidence of conditions of systems which by definition it cannot itself explain. (Williams, 1983: 128)

For writers such as Williams and Scott, working between these extremes, experience is neither associated with simple, brute immediacy, nor opposed to the consideration of the larger systemic and historical fields within which individuals and societies move. Yet if experience is any guide, the term ''experience'' will remain compelling and elusive for as long as people use it.

Michael Bérubé

123

See: *EMPIRICAL, KNOWLEDGE, OBJECTIVITY, PRAGMATISM, REASON.*

Family

Historically, **family** has been both a designation of a kinship group and, like all such identifications of attachment, a way of distinguishing, or even of privileging (in terms of rights and duties), a mode of affiliation. In the case of the **ancient family**, philological ambiguities impede precise identification. For example, the boundaries of the **Israelite family** are difficult to determine because the ancient texts do not clearly distinguish families, clans, and households, and it is unclear when the texts are referring to individuals or tribes (Pederson, 1926). In the case of ancient Greece, the documentary evidence is sparse. As a result, one must rely on fictional genres and abstract political treaties within which history is confounded with regulative ideals (Redfield, 1995).

In the cases of the ancient Greeks and medieval Icelanders, their major texts – tragedies in the case of the former and **family sagas** in that of the latter – treat as their pre-eminent ethicopolitical concern the boundaries of **family versus public life**. In addition to its ethicopolitical implications, because ancient and medieval families were frequently coterminous not only with political units but also with occupational units, the historical designation of the family involves an excursion into the vagaries of political economy as well as into modes of governance. Thereafter, because the word "family" has often served, metaphorically, to refer to and to shape a wide variety of modes of privileged association, its performative status has often confounded its referential status.

Especially during historical periods in which collective coherence has been politically privileged – for example in periods of nation building – the meaning of the word "family"

ABCDE**F**GHIJKLMNOPQRSTUVWXYZ

(or household, which is sometimes the substituted word) has been politicized. There has been contestation over its boundaries as well as its degree of legitimate autonomy and its relationship to public life. Thus, for example, the English novel plays a significant role in reflecting (and likely in determining) the meaning of the word "family" during a period of political ferment in the C18. Written during the period of the "rise of the individual" – that is, of the new citizen subject of the nation state – the works of such writers as Daniel Defoe, Laurence Sterne, Henry Fielding, and Samuel Richardson mark the diminution of the **patriarchal family** and shift the understanding of the family from an authority structure to a social unit defined by exchanges of sentiment.

Yet at the same time as the **sentimental family** was displacing the patriarchal one – "the synchronic family of love had displaced the diachronic family of bloodlines" (Maza, 1997: 208) – governance in European states became increasingly oriented toward managing the relationships between their social orders and their economies (Foucault, 1991). Legislation, reflecting the rise of a commercial society, in which bourgeois merchant culture was displacing the cultural authority of **aristocratic families**, began shaping the meaning and boundaries of the family. The Marriage Act of 1753 in England, which invalidated private covenant marriages and required both public licensing and parental consent, was aimed at making the family an efficient producer of a workforce (as well as preventing promiscuity). And in France a **family–state compact** was created in the C16 and early C17, by those who used family funds to purchase judicial offices (Hanley, 1989: 7). The purchasers were ultimately involved in "remold[ing] the social body by constructing and consolidating family networks and displacing patriarchal control over families with the 'magisterial control of the *Parlement* of Paris' " (p. 8). Moreover, as in the English case, the family was shaped by marriage regulations, aimed at keeping the family unit a publicly witnessed and controlled entity.

Subsequently, throughout the C19 and C20, the **modern family** emerged, shaped increasingly by the intervention of governing agencies. A genealogy of the "policing of families" (Donzelot, 1979) shows that by the C18, the **family–politics** relationship had shifted markedly. The social domain had become the primary target of political authority. As a result, whereas from ancient times the family had been construed primarily as a model of governance, in the C18 it became increasingly part of the social formation and thus a target of governmental manipulation. As nationally regulated economies became the rule, the family became less a locus of employment and more a scrutinized agency of socialization whose task it was to prepare children for work outside the family. Paradoxically, the state increasingly pressured the family to exercise a civically responsible authority while, at the same time, proliferating modes of professional intervention that compromised the authority structure within the household.

Governmental, legal, and social norms continue to contend in the process of shaping the meaning of "family," while modern media produce the symbolic environment within which the contention takes place. Visual media, especially feature films and television, now play a significantly larger role than literature in the creation of the regulative ideals shaping perceptions of the family. And because these media are often more progressive than social, political, and religious agencies, the meaning of the word "family" has become extraordinarily contentious. For example, whereas in the early decades of television, the portrayal of **conventional families** (two-parent, heterosexual, child-rearing, with a "working" father and "homemaking" mother) was the rule, in the last two decades of the C20, the family became "a loose, liberal, contractual affair between a miscellaneous number of big and little adults" (Moore, 1992: 56). Changing usage – **reconstituted families** and **single-parent families** – reflects these developments.

Currently, as television and feature films run well ahead of social mores in normalizing families with alternative modes of intimacy – with MTV's "reality show" *The Osbournes* providing a dramatic challenge to traditional answers to the question "what is a functional family" (Hedegaard, 2002: 1) – the warrant for the use of "family" to include same-sex couples is widely contested in a variety of local and national venues. The rights of same-sex couples to have socially and legally recognized marriages and to adopt children are involved in ongoing administrative, juridical, and legislative actions. As a result, in the early years of the C21, the issues surrounding the migration of formerly proscribed modes of intimacy into recognized **family status** constitute a major instability that afflicts the identification of the family (Goldberg-Hiller, 2002).

Michael J. Shapiro

See: *GENDER, HOME, PRIVATE, PUBLIC.*

Fashion

A C14 meaning of **fashion** (from L *facere*) was to "make," and that included what an object was made from – a human face could be fashioned from poor temper, or a strong physique from noble stock. Fashion revealed the essence and origins of the individual: as in "dressed like a Spaniard" or "draped in **Frensche fasshyon**." "Fashion" also referred to a manner, as in **a warlike facion** or **after a fashion**.

From its earliest mention "fashion" has had multiple meanings; it refers to appearances ("fair in faciun for to sei"), styles of behavior ("for fashyon sake"), and social status ("the facyon of the londe"). In the same way as physical characteristics of race and physiognomy have been used to explain psychological properties, so fashion has been invoked to make visible the invisible, specifically the psychological. Appearances can show how the fashionable feel; "the man of quality must, for fashion-sake, appear in love." In the mC18, Lord Chesterfield famously advised his son, "If you are not in fashion, you are nobody" (*cit.* McKendrick, Brewer, and Plumb, 1982: 39).

Other functions of dress include giving warmth and protection. In cultures where clothes are minimal and the body almost fully exposed, there are still strong rules about appearance, decoration, display, and modesty. The body is always a communication system whether it is through dress, masks, scarification, paint, or tattoos. Dress is always "unspeakably meaningful," declared Thomas Carlyle (1908 [1831]). By this logic, being **fashionable** once meant the opposite of its contemporary use, which is often to indicate frivolity, the ephemeral, and the superfluous, as in the dismissive phrase **fashionable French theories.**

Tailoring and eyed needles have been dated back 40,000 years. Fitted or tailored clothes were then a sign of the active barbarian to both the idle Greeks and Romans, who favored draped, loose dress; likewise to the members of the imperial courts of China and Japan, who wore draped garments but distinguished themselves with color and ornamentation. Between the C5 and the C11, across Europe, loose robes were worn by both sexes. Differences in appearances were determined by wealth; the poor wore rougher, woolen garments, the rich favored silks and more ornamentation. In the C12, women's clothes became tighter and more clinging, and by the C14, with early mercantile capitalism and the increasing circulation of goods, **fashionability** can be seen to have arrived. It was quickly adopted as a visible marker of identity, status, and gender. Shapely, revealing clothes, elaborate headdresses and long, pointed shoes were favored by both sexes. The extremities of the body soon became the focus of attention. Thus the codpiece, originally designed for modesty after the shortened doublet came into style, actually drew attention to the very sexual organs it was supposed to hide. In many portraits, the codpieces are depicted as large and elaborate, studded with the family jewels and jutting out from the body, suggestive of the detachable phallus that would arrive several centuries later.

127

Whenever material goods have been in limited supply, possessions including dress have become symbolic of status boundaries. Between the C14 and the C16, sumptuary laws were enacted across Europe as a means to control what an individual could own and how they could present themselves. Distinctive dress for certain occupations (bakers, clergy, physicians, street vendors, etc.) became visible in the late medieval period. Soon after, fashion begins to be written about, and continues to be into the C21. This indicates its significance as a language conveying cultural tastes and distinctions between social levels or classes. With the expansion of ready-made clothing, the wealthy have sought ways of displaying superiority. A high turnover of **fashion styles** separates them from those unable to emulate their levels of material consumption. Thus **unfashionable dress** comes to signify inferior status. At the same time, uniforms and set styles of clothing (the business suit) become identified with specific occupations, gender, and status (white-, blue-, and pink-collar workers).

In the eC20, definitions of fashion and its sociological importance became increasingly contested (Benstock and Ferriss, 1994). Veblen suggested (1899) that women displayed fashions to draw attention to the stature of their husbands and fathers. Virginia Woolf (1929) put the opposite view: that women's fashionability was a relatively simple social amusement, but for men it was an assertion of complex rewards associated with power, authority, and privilege. Oscar Wilde is said to have declared that "fashion is a form of ugliness so intolerable that we have to alter it every six months." He followed Kant in the separation of fashion from beauty; the latter transcended the human condition, giving a sense of freedom. Georg Simmel alternatively defined fashion as part of social progress. The more advanced the age, the more rapidly its fashions changed (Simmel, 1957 [1904]). From the mC20, fashion has become a cornerstone of economic expansion in an increasingly fragmented postindustrial society.

Appearances are unreliable as social indicators. At one moment, it is fashionable to display women's breasts and at another time a V-neck is daring. In the past, the rich have worn heavy clothing embroidered with jewels; now they wear thin garments of diaphanous viscose, cotton, and pure wool. At another time, it was conventional for men to parade in ringlets, high heels, and rouge (Q. Bell, 1947); now only actors and entertainers might do so. Fashion displays the tensions between conformity and repression: it is at once exuberant and reassuring. Particular garments, such as tight-laced corsets, faux animal skins, floating overlays, stiletto heels, black leather pants, sweat pants, and pumped-up trainers, can transmit a multitude of ambiguous messages. A white bridal gown, symbolic of innocence, is remade by Vivienne Westwood into a brazen display of the bride's breasts and fecund sexuality. Here fashion has been displaced by the visual image: appearances represent subcultural interests in S & M, street style, political resistance, and transvestism.

In the mC20, Roland Barthes made fashion intellectually serious with his analysis of it as a conservative system for maintaining order: "Fashion is never anything but an amnesiac substitution of the present for the past" (1985: 289). Barthes contradicted the assumption that fashion was about the new and radical, and argued it was always about preserving the status quo.

Joanne Finkelstein

See: *BODY, FETISH, SEXUALITY, TASTE.*

Feminism

Feminism is an "advocacy of the rights of women." While the term emerged in the 1890s in the context of a lively women's movement, it is now used to describe pro-women ideas and actions from ancient times to the present (Evans, 2001).

Modern Western feminism's origins are often traced to the Enlightenment of the C17 and C18, with its egalitarian and irreverent tendencies, its more fluid social relationships, and especially its valuing of knowledge and education. Greater access to education was one of the first feminist demands. A broader notion of women's rights soon emerged, culminating in Mary Wollstonecraft's *A vindication of the rights of women* (1975 [1792]), now seen as a major text in the emergence of feminist ideas. C19 liberalism, especially in John Stuart Mill's *The subjection of women* (1988 [1869]), strongly advocated liberty and equality of opportunity for women. Mill's work arose from and stimulated the further development of campaigns for women's rights – legal, economic, political, and social – in Europe, North America, and elsewhere. Socialists also frequently advocated the equality of women, seeing women's subjection as a product of feudalism, then capitalism. Women's suffrage, one of the key feminist demands, was won at the national level first in New Zealand, then Australia, and gradually elsewhere. By the end of World War II, feminism in Western countries had succeeded in removing many of women's legal and political disabilities, though sharp social, cultural, and economic forms of differentiation between men and women remained. Simone de Beauvoir's 1949 *The second sex* (1973) drew international attention to the continuing subordination of women throughout the world.

Some time after Women's Liberation erupted in the late 1960s in the United States and elsewhere, the earlier women's movement was dubbed **first-wave feminism**, and **second-wave feminism** was declared to have begun. This new, more radical version can be attributed to many developments: the pull of women into the workforce, and with demographic changes the declining need for their labor in the home; the rapid growth in women's education; and the stark contrast between women's growing expectations and their still-restricted economic, social, and political opportunities.

Second-wave feminism saw all women as oppressed by all men. While differences of class and race were noted, these were not at first thought sufficient to negate or complicate the general oppression of women, manifest in women's lower pay and status in the workforce, low social status, and experience of the more brutal sides of male domination through domestic violence and sexual assault. One of the new movement's key concerns was with women's sexual rights and enjoyment, evident in the titles of key **feminist texts** such as Kate Millett's *Sexual politics* (1970) and Germaine Greer's *The female eunuch* (1970). Where "feminist" had once called to mind a puritanical, dowdily dressed "bluestocking," from the 1970s it frequently suggested women interested in sexuality, often lesbian, who cared little for conventional forms of respectability.

Feminism has long been attached to other diverse political movements. A common categorization has been into liberal, radical, and socialist wings. **Liberal feminism** has focused on the removal of barriers to the achievement of equality with men, and has operated in legal and political arenas with considerable success. **Radical feminism** has emphasized the foundational character of gender differences, and has been more interested in long-range cultural change leading to more respect and autonomy for women. **Socialist feminism** has emphasized the ways in which capitalism requires and perpetuates women's subordination.

Feminism in many parts of the world has permeated many aspects of public and private life, substantially transforming the relations between men and women. One of the major reasons for feminism's success has been its dual emphasis on individual agency and collective power, so often seen in political discourse as alternative sites of human responsibility. Proclaiming "sisterhood is powerful," feminism called on women to band together to change the structures of power. When it said "the personal is political," feminism suggested that individual and social change were part of the same process. Feminism accordingly became a very successful politics of the personal, so that every aspect of life – health, dress, sexuality, friendships, occupation, cultural and leisure pursuits, philosophy – becomes a part of a political project for change. Alongside this emphasis on the personal there has been also a more conventional politics of protest, lobbying, public speaking, campaigning, and organizing. Moderate forms of feminism have been globally supported by the United Nations, with four huge world conferences: Mexico City in 1975 (leading to the United Nations Decade for Women [1976–85]), Copenhagen in 1980, Nairobi in 1985, and Beijing in 1995 (Pettman, 1996).

Yet if feminism has achieved real successes in legislation and cultural practice, it also faces some serious difficulties. Women of color, in the US and elsewhere, pointed out that most **white feminists** did not recognize the benefits they enjoyed from racist institutions and practices. Whiteness became a problem for analysis, and postcolonial and cross-cultural critiques have deconstructed the category "woman" into a thousand fragments. The idea of women as a group with a common social or structural position in relation to men has given way to the idea that women are profoundly divided from one another. Many speak now of **feminisms**, denoting a greater awareness of the different histories of feminism in Asia, Europe, the Americas, and elsewhere. Furthermore, feminism's very success meant that many came to see it as a mainstream rather than alternative movement, exhibiting some of the desires for power that it once so vigorously abhorred. By the 1990s, a right-wing "backlash" against feminism was evident in the West both in media discourse and in the withdrawal of government support for some feminist programs.

In recent years second-wave feminism in the West has declined somewhat as an active political movement, though it continues as a real and active political force in many non-Western countries. New issues have occupied feminist activists, from information technology to religious difference. Two of feminism's greatest strengths – its internationalism and its non-violence – may yet prove to be its most important contribution to humanity.

Ann Curthoys

See: *ALTERNATIVE, LIBERALISM, MOVEMENTS, RADICAL, SOCIALISM.*

Fetish

Fetish has resonances in two major theoretical traditions: Freudian psychoanalysis and Marxism. Both borrowed the term from early colonial and subsequent anthropological usage. Its origins lie in the name given to the objects or charms used by Africans of the Guinea and neighboring coast that embodied magical or supernatural properties. It came to mean any object that was worshiped in its own right by native peoples on account of its inherent magical qualities. It was a simple step from this to understanding a fetish as something that embodied irrational beliefs. Already by the 1860s worship of the constitutional monarchy in Britain was denounced as a fetish.

It is striking that both psychoanalysis and Marxism found this concept useful at roughly the same time, though the concept of the fetish clearly operates somewhat differently in each tradition. For psychoanalysis, the key relationship is with the Oedipus complex, the central mechanism in the acquisition of gendered identity. For Marxism, the link is with the congealing of labor power and commodification. But what is apparent is that **fetishization** is a key to the understanding of the main objects of concern in both theories: the dynamic unconscious and the dynamics of capitalist accumulation. In both cases the fetish masks the underlying, and painful, reality.

Freud first uses the concept in the "Three essays" (1953c [1905]), building on the perceptions contained in the writings of the pioneers of sexology. There was plentiful evidence in their work that many individuals obtained sexual excitation from ostensibly non-sexual objects, whether inanimate or other parts of the body: feet, hands, fur, shoes, etc. This was **the fetish**, which stood in for the genital organ in Freud's theory. In a later essay, "Fetishism" (1961 [1927]), Freud underlined that this was an exclusively masculine perversion, with the fetish standing in for the absent ("castrated") female organs. The fetish is a compromise between the boy's horrified recognition of castration, and his disavowal of it. It allows him the fantasy of a female phallus, whilst accepting its absence. The fetish, and the process of fetishization, are thus absolutely key to some of the most contested of Freud's theories – the Oedipus complex, female castration, male castration anxiety – and hence to Freud's whole understanding of the ways in which the undifferentiated blobs of humanity that are infants acquire the rules of gender, sexuality, heterosexuality, and homosexuality.

Of course, the idea of the **sexual fetish** does not have to carry this theoretical baggage, and its common usage barely refers to it. Conventionally, the term usually refers to any object which has a sexual significance, that is, simply to the substitution and masking rather than the underlying structures that shape the substitution. You do not have to accept Freudian explanations to find the term useful. Thus people readily talk of a **leather** or **rubber fetish**, implying that these materials have a quality which excites erotic attraction. Freud, as we have seen, saw this as a male phenomenon. Various feminist critics, however, have pointed out the existence of fetishism in female-authored texts, and of **female fetishists** in the bedroom and on the couches of analysts as well (N. Schor, 1992: 113–16). Some feminists have gone further, and theorized the centrality of fetishism to lesbian sexuality. By disavowing their own castration, women can turn their whole body into the phallus – making the lesbian a successful female fetishist (De Lauretis, 1994). It has also been argued that fetishization, by sexualizing the object, is analogous to the common male mode of objectification of women. For this reason, the concept has been widely used in feminist film theory and analysis of pornography (Grosz, 1992: 116–17).

The process of displacing the person, and masking the underlying reality in the object of worship, provides the link with the Marxist use of the concept. Marx argued that fetishism was pervasive in capitalist society. It denoted the process whereby material objects, which had certain characteristics imputed to them by the fact of complex social relations, appeared as products of nature. The elementary form of this was the **fetishism of the commodity**, as the bearer of value. Under capitalism, although all commodities are products of labor power in a society organized around complex divisions of labor, the value of a commodity appears to be intrinsic to the thing itself. Classically, gold, as the measure of exchange in the C19, seems to have an intrinsic value, and is worshiped, fetishized. But the labor power that went into it is obscured, so that instead of seeing the object as the product of social labor, the worker seems subordinated to the product itself. The exploitative relationship is hidden (Geras, 1983).

By extension, everything can be commodified, including sexuality. Indeed, it is often argued that in the conditions of late capitalism sexuality has been drawn as never before into market relations. The lure of the erotic is deployed to sell everything from motor cars to exotic holidays, while sexuality is locked into fetishized images of what is desirable, especially through a globalized fashion industry. We still, it seems, want to worship the thing, the object. And as in the original C19 usage, reason has little to do with it.

Jeffrey Weeks

See: *COMMODITY, DESIRE, FASHION, GAY AND LESBIAN, PORNOGRAPHY, QUEER, SEXUALITY, UNCONSCIOUS.*

Freedom

In its ordinary usage **freedom** means absence of restraints or restrictions. Individuals are free when no one stops them from pursuing their goals or doing what they wish to do. ''In this, then, consists Freedom, (viz.) in our being able to act, or not to act, according as we shall choose, or will'' (Locke, 1690). Slavery, in which an individual is the property of another and does the latter's bidding, represents the opposite of freedom. Prisoners, those held hostages, or those who are chained or subjected to restraints imposed by others are not free.

Individuals may not be able to do what they wish to do because of deep-seated complexes and phobias or because of their indecisiveness, lack of self-discipline, and impulsiveness. These individuals are free in the sense that no one is stopping them doing what they wish to do, but they are unable to take advantage of their freedom. They are said to be **objectively free** but not **subjectively free**; they have **legal and political freedom** but not **moral or psychological freedom**.

Individuals may not be able to engage in their self-chosen activities because of the lack of resources. They may wish to go to China, but lack the money to pay for the flight.

Libertarians and some liberals argue that the absence of resources does not affect their freedom, for no one is stopping them from going to China. The fact that their freedom has no value for them or that they are unable to exercise it does not mean that they do not have it. Socialists and others on the left argue that a purely **formal freedom** that cannot be exercised is not really freedom, and that the individuals in question are no different from those held hostage or otherwise prevented from going to China. Although the debate between these two groups is purely linguistic at one level, it has deeper roots. For libertarians, freedom is a condition or a status; for socialists, a power or an active capacity. The two also differ in the kind of society they prefer. For libertarians, a society is free if its members enjoy an extensive system of rights to do what they wish to do. For socialists, a **free society** must also ensure requisite resources to all its members.

In English we have two words, "freedom," from oE *fréodóm*, and "liberty," from L *libertas* (Berlin, 2002). Although they are mostly interchangeable, there are important differences of nuance between them. The term "freedom" is wider in the sense that while it can be generally substituted for "liberty" without a loss of meaning, the opposite is not the case. "Freedom" is generally used in philosophical and moral, and "liberty" in legal and political contexts. We talk of the **freedom of the will** and not the "liberty of the will," of "moral or psychological freedom" but not "liberty," of **free-thinking persons**, the **freedom of the city**, **freedom fighters**, **freedom rides**, and so on. Unlike English, French has only one word, *liberté*, and German only *freiheit*. This does not mean that French and German speakers are unable to express the ideas and distinctions that come easily to their English-speaking counterparts. They either extend the meaning of the word that is available to them or add an appropriate adjective.

Freedom is valued for a variety of reasons. It is posited as a natural condition of all living beings including, and especially, humans. Freedom therefore needs no justification; only the restrictions on it do. Human beings are sacred, ends in themselves, and freedom is both an emblem of their dignity and a source of their self-respect and pride. Freedom is valued also because human beings can grow to their full stature only by making their own choices, exercising their judgments, and learning from their mistakes. It fosters creativity and individuality, explores unfamiliar areas of knowledge, throws up new ideas and inventions, and is the main source of human progress (Cranston, 1967; R. Gray, 1990).

Since an individual's actions affect others and limit their freedom, freedom can never be absolute. Every society devises a system of restraints and relies on such things as social conventions, moral rules, public opinion, and laws to enforce it. In close-knit traditional societies, the power of public opinion, social customs, and collective pressure is so great that there is little need for formally codified laws. In modern societies, the law plays a far more active role, which is why we define and discuss freedom in relation to it. The state is both valued and feared, and its powers are subjected to constitutional constraints.

How much freedom individuals should enjoy has not proved easy to determine (Raz, 1986). Libertarians argue that freedom should be restricted only when it is likely to harm

Fundamentalism

others. Harm, however, is not easy to define. Besides, most societies rightly ban public nudity, indecent exposure, and so on even though these may cause no obvious harm to others. They also ban the sale of body parts, addictive drugs, self-mutilation, and even assisted suicide, even when these activities only harm the individuals involved.

Freedom is an important value, but so are equality, justice, social harmony, and public morality. These values conflict, and every society needs to strike a workable balance between them in light of its moral traditions, circumstances, and general culture. Although all societies need to show a minimum respect for human freedom as embodied in the universal declarations of human rights, their moral and political structures are bound to vary.

Bhikhu Parekh

See: *HUMAN RIGHTS, INDIVIDUAL, LIBERALISM.*

Fundamentalism

Widely used as a pejorative term to designate one's fanatical opponents – usually religious and/or political – rather than oneself, **fundamentalism** began in Christian Protestant circles in the eC20. Originally restricted to debates within evangelical ("gospel-based") Protestantism, it is now employed to refer to any person or group that is characterized as unbending, rigorous, intolerant, and militant. The term has two usages, the prior one a positive self-description, which then developed into the later derogatory usage that is now widespread. As a phenomenon, fundamentalism is a specific cultural, religious/ideological, and political formation only possible in later capitalism.

Since the bombing of the World Trade Center on September 11, 2001, the term has gained a much wider currency, mostly derogatory. Thus, those believed responsible are **Islamic fundamentalists**, whereas the USA itself has been designated as **politically fundamentalist** (Ali, 2002). Israel's suppression of Palestinians is driven by **fundamentalist Jews**, while the Palestinians themselves are also fundamentalists. Often, fundamentalism is synonymous with terrorism, or at least has become in popular usage the basis for terrorism. Another significant usage is in neo-liberal dismissals of positions deemed non-pragmatic: **feminist fundamentalism** and **environmental fundamentalism** are the most common. In these cases, fundamentalism is interchangeable with "fascist." The assumption is that anything that threatens liberal, Western culture and society is by definition fundamentalist.

The associations of irrational commitment, fanaticism, militancy, and terrorism make fundamentalism a useful term. It allows a dominant Western culture and society, aggressively led by the United States, to demonize its opponents as irretrievably antagonistic to the hegemonic values of "freedom" and "democracy." The term provides a justification for the violent oppression of those who oppose such values. However, the use of "fundamentalism" is itself an imposition of a term that comes from within Western Christian culture. Thus, the way in which opposition is characterized within Christianity

134

becomes a way of dealing with opposition in other situations, whether religious, political, or cultural conflict. Such usage is both an example of an effort to understand opposition and an attempt to deny the viability of that opposition.

The term began as a positive self-description, whose history lies in American Protestantism (Marsden, 1980). It was first used in 1920 by Curtis Lee Laws in the Baptist journal *Watchman-Examiner*: he speaks of those who "do battle royal for the Fundamentals," those who believe and defend what were newly identified as the **fundamentals of the faith**. He was referring to a series of 12 pamphlets, published between 1915 and 1920, that isolated particular Christian doctrines, defending them against the inroads of theological modernism and liberalism: the inerrancy or literal truth of the Bible, the virgin birth of Christ, the substitutionary atonement of Christ, his bodily resurrection, the reality of miracles, Christ's deity, and the second coming of the savior at the end of history.

Christian fundamentalism is unique since it selects certain positions and elevates them to absolutes. This fundamentalism is a subgroup of evangelical Christianity (Harris, 1998), often calling itself "conservative evangelical." Although related to the various revivals in Europe and the United States, it is suspicious of the enthusiastic and emotional nature of these movements, which now include Pentecostalism and the Charismatics.

Christian fundamentalism is also defined by what it opposes: Romanism, socialism, atheism, modern philosophy, Spiritualism, Darwin and evolutionary theory, liberal (Protestant) theology, and the use of critical methods to interpret the Bible. In response, the linchpin for fundamentalists is the inerrancy of the Bible, the belief that "Scripture is without error or fault in all its teaching" (Boone, 1989: 26). Inerrancy marks the dependence on a text, in this case the Bible. It is an effort at a seamless ideology of power, a hegemonic drive that will not allow any deviation. Christian fundamentalism also includes dispensationalism (belief in seven stages or dispensations from creation to Christ's final reign), the Keswick holiness movement (personal victory over sin, witnessing about Christ and support of missions), emphasis on personal conversion, daily Bible reading and prayer, the growth of large churches, and public battles over evolution vs. creationism, abortion, and capital punishment.

How is it, then, that fundamentalism, with its own distinct history in American Protestantism, has become a blanket term that is readily ascribed to Muslims, Hindus, Jews, feminists, environmentalists, and even (in Australia) economists? The features of the term's wider usage began within the conflicts of Christian Protestantism, moving from self-description to describing opponents. The first stage of this shift was to other fanatical religious forms, and then to non-religious forms of political opposition.

The social, cultural, and economic context of Christian fundamentalism was the crisis following World War I. The era of swing jazz, the Russian Revolution, the socialist radicalism of inter-war USA, the revolutionary experimentalism in art, architecture, and music, and the rapidly changing sexual mores all played a role. Christian fundamentalism is one way of dealing with such changes, especially for lower middle and working classes, often rural, outside the mainstream Christian churches whose members were economically secure and could feel some measure of control. For those with less sense of control, the combination of economic insecurity – the monetary crises of the 1920s, 1930s, and later, the abandonment of the Bretton Woods accord in 1973 – with rural isolation produced a situation in which the certainties of fundamentalism provided an ideological resource against capitalism's perpetual change, disruption, and, to paraphrase *The Communist Manifesto*, the melting of all that is solid into air.

Similarly, fundamentalism was ascribed to Shiite sections of Islam and the followers of Rama within Hinduism. Both groups exhibited comparable tendencies: the response of the rural and urban working classes and petit bourgeoisie to the increasing presence of global capitalism and its associated cultures. This response is explicitly anti-American and anti-Western and cast in religious terms, but it would not have taken place without the presence of capitalism. Accustomed to the usage of the term in the West, commentators described these movements as fundamentalist.

Like Christian fundamentalism, these movements are politically militant. On the one hand, fundamentalists expect the end of the world, the immediate transport to "heaven," to be with Christ, or Allah, or even Rama; on the other, they intervene directly in politics. The Taliban in Pakistan and Afghanistan, the now defunct Moral Majority of Jerry Falwell or Pat Buchanan's run for presidential office, and the vast Hindu political movement of the BJP (Bharatiya Janata Party) in India, all are part of the political mobilization that fundamentalism provides. The paradox is that whereas within the United States politicians must ensure the fundamentalist vote (presidential candidates often declare themselves to be "born again" Christians), when the fundamentalists are external they become a threat to Western society. Thus, terrorism against the United States, England, and Australia is the act of so-called fundamentalists, but internal terrorism is not.

The central place of the private individual, working itself out in personal piety and salvation, is also a legacy of the Enlightenment and liberal culture. However, such intense devotion at a private level works itself out in collective action, being seen as a fanaticism at odds with the presumed urbane tolerance of capitalist culture.

Although fundamentalism has associations of irrationalism it is a distinctly rationalistic development, heir to the Enlightenment as much as the spiritual beliefs and practices described as New Age. In Christianity this involves matching up the Bible with scientific positions on geological ages and evolution, and in the underlying assumptions that God's truths are propositional. Muslim and Hindu fundamentalisms are also rationalist, for they too operate with propositional truth, clear statements in their respective Scriptures that cannot be gainsaid.

Not only rationalistic, but also textual, each form of religious fundamentalism cannot exist without a sacred text. This text is understood in a new way, as the inerrant words of Muhammad, and therefore Allah, of God, or of Rama. In doing so, the various leaders can obscure their own claims to authority in terms of the authority of the texts in question.

Then there is pseudo-traditionalism, claiming a mythical, pristine, and organic community that fundamentalists seek to restore before the moral and political depredations of modern society. The deep contradiction here is that fundamentalism happily uses whatever technology is available to spread its pseudo-traditionalism: cable TV, video, Internet, and communications media. Yet such notions – the community of the New Testament, or of Muhammad's Medina, or of Hindu society before Islamic and British invasions – are myths that express an oppositional ideology, although the imagined communities are distinctly dystopian and repressive in terms of gender, race, sexuality, and morality.

The focus on and exacerbation of features of religious fundamentalism – opposition to some elements of capitalism, militancy, irrationalism, and fanaticism – enabled the application of the term to political and cultural movements that are not necessarily religious. Other features were left behind, such as the basis on a sacred text and pseudo-traditionalism, and the term has become one of dismissal. In this way, feminism, environmentalism, anarchism, and gay and lesbian movements could be characterized as fundamentalist. In each case, the use of the term marks recognition of opposition to the dominant forms of capitalism and liberal culture, whether patriarchies, environmental degradation, capitalism itself, or a dominant heterosexual culture.

Roland Boer

See: **GLOBALIZATION, HOLOCAUST, WEST.**

Gay and Lesbian

The widespread use of **gay** and **lesbian** to refer to male and female homosexuality dates back to the late 1960s and early 1970s, and is associated with the emergence of the **gay liberation** movement. Starting in 1969 in the USA, and rapidly spreading to most other Western countries, its defining characteristic was a rejection of the stigma and prejudice associated with homosexuality, and a new willingness on the part of homosexual people to openly affirm their sexual identities (''coming out''). The new movement consciously adopted the self-description of gay as a rejection both of the clinical and medicalized category of homosexual, and of the host of pejorative terms, especially the word ''queer,'' which had been traditionally used to label and stigmatize homosexuality. The subsequent linkage of gay and lesbian was a powerful signal that while the histories of male and female homosexuality were linked by a common institutionalized hostility, lesbians and gay men were not the same (Weeks, 1977).

This concern with language can be seen as but the latest stage of the attempt to put into acceptable words the experience of same-sex eroticism – for long the sin too awful to be named among Christians. The term ''homosexuality'' itself was invented in the 1860s by the Hungarian writer Karoly Maria Benkert, and was an attempt to break with the traditional execration of ''sodomites.'' The invention of the word, alongside others with similar implications, such as ''invert,'' ''urning,'' or ''third-sexer,'' can be seen as a public sign of the articulation of a distinctive identity organized around same-sex desires. Interestingly, the term pre-dated ''heterosexuality'' (originally implying what we today would call ''bisexuality''), and the emergence of these terms can be seen as part of the

*ABCDEF**G**HIJKLMNOPQRSTUVWXYZ*

restructuring of sexual categories and identities which led to a sharper distinction between heterosexuality (the norm) and homosexuality (the sexual other). Although terms such as "homosexuality" developed originally as assertions of the validity of same-sex desires (pioneering writers like Benkert, Ulrichs, and Magnus Hirschfeld were campaigners and propagandists as much as theorists and scientists), it was through the first generation of sexologists that the new language gained currency in the C20. Homosexuality to a large extent became a clinical term, and "the homosexual" became the bearer of a distinctive organization of desire. Although never exclusively referring to men, it was generally the case throughout the eC20 that most studies of homosexuality generally concentrated on its male forms, and female homosexuality was largely subsumed within this.

"Gay" and "lesbian" as terms had older origins than "homosexuality," though the meanings have subtly changed. "Gay" acquired associations of immorality in the C18, and prostitutes were commonly described as **gay women** in the C19. It is through this link that "gay" seems originally to have become associated with male homosexuality, largely because the milieu of casual sexual contacts between men and women and men and men overlapped, and certainly in terms of the criminal law little distinction was made between female prostitution and male homosexuality. "Gay" thus became a covert name for homosexual activity. It seems to have acquired a recognizably contemporary meaning in the USA by the late 1920s (Katz, 2001: 158). By the 1960s, it was widely used in references, for example, to **gay bars**.

"Lesbian" can be traced back to the eC17, referring to inhabitants of the Greek island of Lesbos, home of the poet Sappho, whose verses celebrated love between women. "Sapphism" by the lC19 was used to describe "unnatural" sexual relations between women, and "lesbianism" was becoming a commonly accepted adjective in literary and sexological discourse for same-sex relations between women. By the 1930s "lesbian" had become commonly used as a noun; for example, the "mannish woman" could now be described readily as a lesbian.

The evolution of these terms reflects the emergence of distinctive sexual identities and patterns of life. These patterns were constrained and delimited by widespread prejudice, criminalization (of male homosexuality), and institutionalized exclusion, conditions that to a large extent worsened in the 1950s and early 1960s. The emergence of gay liberation can thus be seen as a collective demand for full equality. But the force of that movement was to propel further shifts in meaning. Whilst the terms "gay" and, and to a lesser extent, "lesbian" were generally used to refer to homosexuality by the lC20, within the **lesbian and gay communities** themselves, new challenges emerged. The declared aim of gay liberation had been to end the distinction between homosexuality and heterosexuality. However, the immediate effect of the new movement was to make sharper the distinction between the lesbian and gay world and the institution of heterosexuality. The term **gay and lesbian** seemed to some to signify an almost ethnic-type identity (Epstein, 1998). A number of **lesbian feminists**, on the other hand, sought to distinguish lesbianism from gay male sexuality. Rich (1993), for example, made a distinction between **lesbian existence** and the **lesbian continuum**, with the latter signifying unity among all women in rejecting male domination. This was sharply contested by others who felt that the **lesbian identity** was being desexualized. A further radical challenge to the dominance of gay and lesbian identities as they had developed by the 1980s came from a younger generation of activists who challenged what they saw as the assimilationist tendencies of their predecessors, and resurrected the term "queer" to signal their transgressive intent (Warner, 1993).

Queer activism set itself up against "heteronormativity," and challenged the rigid categories signaled by the terms "lesbian" and "gay." The queer world embraced bisexuals, ambisexuals, transgendered people, sadomasochists, and all who resisted the sexual order. But despite the queer eruption, by the eC21 there were few signs that the words "gay" and "lesbian" were losing their everyday use. On the contrary, they seemed to be on the road to being global signifiers of same-sex activities – though taking on different meanings in different cultural contexts (Altman, 2001).

Jeffrey Weeks

See: *DESIRE, QUEER, SEXUALITY.*

140 Gender

Gender operates as an analytic concept in a wider field of study denoted by related concepts such as women and men, male and female, masculinity and femininity, sex and sexuality. It usually denotes the social, cultural, and historical distinctions between men and women, and is sometimes described as the study of masculinity and femininity.

The concept of gender is often attributed to second wave feminism. It had an older meaning, of "kind," "sort," or "class," and was most frequently used in discussions of grammar. In the 1960s, its meaning shifted when it was used in sexology and psychoanalysis to describe male and female social roles, as when Alex Comfort (1964) wrote of **gender roles** being learned at an early age. Four years later, Robert Stoller (1968) argued that while sex is determined biologically, **gender identity** is the product of psychological and social influences; indeed, gender identity and biological sex can conflict, as in the case of transsexuals. Following Stoller, sex came to be regarded as the biological foundation of male–female differences, while gender was a social and cultural construction. This separating of biology and culture ran contrary to the common-sense beliefs of the time, which assumed that the social and cultural differences between men and women had a sure and necessary biological foundation.

When Women's Liberation emerged at the end of the 1960s, this distinction between biological sex and socially constituted gender provided an intellectual basis for repudiating biological determinism, and envisioning a future different from the past and the present, where men and women had equal opportunities and cultural value. Where "sex" was inescapable, gender was malleable; sex was destiny, gender was free will. Thus gender took on radical political and intellectual connotations, which it retains today (Connell, 2002).

For feminists gender was not only socially constructed, but also organized in all societies in a systematically unequal way. All societies valued and treated the two sexes differently, creating, in Gayle Rubin's (1975) term, a **sex/gender system**. The task for those studying gender came to be first to describe and explain women, so far largely invisible in the social sciences, and second to explain the origins and universality of **gender inequality**. Following American feminist Kate Millett (1970), the systematic unequal organization of gender was often dubbed patriarchy, and the theoretical problem, especially in British feminist thought, came to be how to reconcile a notion of patriarchy with that of social systems defined in other ways: capitalism, for example. By the early 1980s, the notion of patriarchy was coming under critique, seen as taking unequal power relations between men and women for granted, rather than as something to be investigated. The concept of gender, however, survived this critique, valued as more permeable and open, less tied to particular feminist approaches or political positions.

During the 1980s, several developments transformed understandings of sex and gender. One was the overturning of earlier feminist suspicions of psychoanalytic theory as inherently masculinist, and the development of a specifically feminist psychoanalytic body of theory. Approaches derived from Sigmund Freud and later Jacques Lacan became popular, providing tools for theorizing male–female difference as at once an individual and a cultural phenomenon. Another was an increased concern with race and ethnicity. Gender scholarship came to be increasingly challenged by women identifying as coming from ''outsider'' ethnic and racial groups. The emphasis on race and ethnicity increasingly questioned the importance of gender, an examination performed in the name of class a decade earlier. Furthermore, it was not enough to add together the social and cultural effects of race and gender; the task was to see how each was constituted by the other.

A further source of change was the influence of poststructuralist theory, derived especially from French theorists such as Michel Foucault, Jacques Derrida, Julia Kristeva, Jacques Lacan, and Luce Irigaray, and reworked in the Anglophone world. Poststructuralist emphases on the discursive constructions of the body meant the end, or at least the weakening, of the sex–gender distinction. It is not inevitable, poststructuralist theorists argued, that we think of the male and the female body as separate and opposite entities; this dualism is discursively constructed. We can, that is to say, recognize biological differences without seeing them in a binary fashion. Yet if poststructuralism threatened the sex–gender distinction it also, through the work of Judith Butler (1990), revitalized the concept of gender. Gender, Butler argued, is not a noun but rather is ''performative,'' ''always a doing, though not a doing by a subject who might be said to pre-exist the deed'' (pp. 24–5). **Gendered subjectivity** is produced in a series of competing discourses, rather than by a single patriarchal ideology, and **gender relations** are a process involving strategies and counter-strategies of power. Butler's work led to a growing fashion for speaking of **gendering** and **engendering**, and of **engendered social processes**.

In keeping with this interest in identity and performativity came a growing interest in masculinity (Connell, 1995). Not only were women engendered, but men were too. Both masculinity and femininity are continually constructed and negotiated on an everyday basis, their taken-for-grantedness demonstrating just how successful **gendering processes** have been. Today, ''gender'' remains a widely accepted and popular term in public discourse and academic scholarship alike. As feminism declined as an identifiable social movement in many Western countries, many of the women's studies courses established in the 1970s changed their names in the 1990s to **gender studies** (W. Brown, 1997). This signified both a lesser attachment to feminist politics, and the greater attention being given to men and masculinity. Compared to ''women,'' ''gender'' was seen as less threatening, more inclusive, and more theoretically defensible.

In right-wing discourse, gender has become one of the trio of concepts (along with class and race) that constitute the core of ''political correctness,'' and it remains in some quarters a concept to be ridiculed. Nevertheless, because the differences between male and female still have profound meanings in societies around the world – at work, in family, sexual, and emotional life, and in politics and religion – and because ''gender'' has proved durable and flexible in characterizing and analyzing those differences, it remains a key term in public debate today.

142

Ann Curthoys

See: *BIOLOGY, BODY, FEMINISM, NATURE, POLITICAL CORRECTNESS, SEXUALITY.*

Gene/Genetic

Genetic derives from *genesis*, referring to origin. In this very general sense it can refer to, for instance, the origin of an idea or argument, a usage that dates from the C19. This is implicit in the C20 philosophical use of the term, as in **genetic fallacy**, meaning the fallacy of judging the truth or value of an observation on the basis of its origin. However, the most general use lies in biology, where the term **genetics** was coined by William Bateson (1979) in 1905 to describe the study of heredity.

The biological use implying connectedness or relationship by common origin, whether immediately familial or more distantly ancestral, had, however, been apparent earlier. Bateson's formulation itself reflected the growing interest in analyzing the mechanisms of the hereditary process following the rediscovery of Gregor Mendel's experiments originally described in the 1860s (Henig, 2000). On the basis of his famous study of color, shape, and size in several generations of peas, Mendel had concluded that underlying the observed surface characteristics of an organism (today called its phenotype) there lay ''hidden determinants'' or factors, preserved across generations, the combination of which determined its observed characteristics. One of the rediscoverers of Mendel's work, Wilhelm Johannsen, termed these determinants **genes**. The total content of genes in any organism was termed its **genome**; the specific set of genes carried by one member of a species by comparison with another is its **genotype**, to distinguish it from the observed phenotype. However, in these early uses, genes had no specific material existence; they were abstract accounting units to be used in the calculation of statistical probability of the inheritance of specific features.

Studies by Thomas Hunt Morgan, Herman Muller, and others through the 1910s and 1920s provided genes with a material existence and, indeed, a map reference, locating them within the cell and aligning them sequentially within chromosomes, like beads on a string. As genes appeared to exert their power by affecting chemical reactions within the cell, in the 1930s George Beadle and Edward Tatum proposed their one gene/one enzyme hypothesis; that is, that each gene was responsible for the production of one enzyme (enzymes are themselves protein molecules). Experiments in the 1940s and 1950s proved that the **genetic material** was composed of deoxyribonucleic acid, or DNA, and in 1953 Francis Crick and James Watson, on the basis of crystallographic data from Rosalind Franklin, presented their famous double helical model of DNA (Olby, 1974). This provided a mechanism for how the molecule could be copied during self-division and reproduction, and thus, in principle, for **genetic transmission** across generations.

It thus appeared that the term "gene" could be formally reduced to a "specific length of DNA coding for a specific protein." Each strand of DNA is composed of a string of four different units (nucleotides, known as A, C, G, and T). Proteins consist of strings of amino acids, of which there are 20 commonly naturally occurring variants, and specific sequences, each three nucleotides long (ACT, for example), within the DNA molecule "code for" specific amino acids within the protein. Hence the **genetic code**. Crick (1958) formulated what was described as the "central dogma" of genetics, that there is a one-way flow of **genetic information** from DNA to protein. DNA became known as a master molecule controlling all aspects of life.

If this were so, then determining the sequence of nucleotides within an individual's genome would in principle provide knowledge of that individual's predispositions and potential – hence the **Human Genome Project**, largely completed in 2001 (Davies, 2001). From the 1980s on, techniques became available to isolate and copy individual genes or entire genomes (cloning), and increasingly, to insert, remove, or modify specific genes within the genome, first of plants, then of fruit flies, and later of laboratory mammals such as mice. These techniques of **genetic engineering** have occasioned significant public concern regarding the environmental consequences of **genetically modified** (or GM) crops, and further fears that the manipulation of human behavior through the identification of genes responsible for particular kinds of behavior (the **gay gene**, the **fat gene**) recalls earlier attempts to improve the human stock through eugenic programs of selective breeding (Keller, 2000; S. Rose, 1997; Silver, 1998). These fears have been

143

linked to concerns regarding the ethical consequences of patenting genetic information, transforming it into intellectual property owned and controlled by major private corporations.

Over the same period, however, it has also become increasingly apparent that Crick's central dogma is at best an oversimplification (Coen, 1999). First, only a small fraction of genomic DNA (some 2 percent in humans) actually codes for proteins. Some of the rest is regulatory but much is of unknown function, sometimes referred to as junk DNA, or introns. Second, coding regions are not tidily arrayed like beads on a string but are often scattered in sections across the genome. Third, there is more than one way of "reading" the code. The human genome contains some 25,000 genes on current estimates, while there are perhaps 100,000 different proteins in the body. So genes can be "read" in different ways ("multiple reading frames") and the sequences can be differently "edited" before "translation" into proteins. The use of the languages of literature and information technology in this context is significant, indicating that the control and regulation of these processes lies not within the DNA but within the dynamic organization of the cell itself. Far from being a master molecule, DNA is better seen as one player, albeit an important one, within the cellular orchestra. And strangely, at the dawn of the present century, the concept of *the* gene as a unit with a discrete identity seems to be dissolving into complex biochemical and metabolic processes, at the same time as the power of the new genetic technologies (bioengineering) increases.

144

Steven Rose

See: *BIOLOGY, EVOLUTION.*

Generation

It is plainly true that in any particular society at any particular moment there will be a certain number of people of approximately the same age who may therefore be said to belong to the same **generation**. The question, though, is whether this descriptive term has any analytic significance. Are people of the same age really members of a social group? Do the statistical effects of birth rates have cultural consequences?

In everyday discourse "generation" refers to three kinds of experience. Within the household, "generation" describes the difference between parents and their children. In its earliest use (in the C14) the term thus meant the interval of time between the birth of the parents and that of their children, usually computed at 30 years. Even now families are usually conceived as stretching across three generations – grandparents, parents, children – and what is significant here is less the specific age of family members than the age difference between them and how this relates to domestic power and status. For some C20 sociologists "generation" in this sense was a key term in explaining how culture, status, and property are passed from older to newer members of society, how leaders are replaced, and so forth (Eisenstadt, 1956). And this is probably still how most people place them-selves in a generation, by reference to their parents and children, to the continuous process of negotiating family rights and responsibilities.

The second kind of **generational experience** is an effect of people's treatment as members of age groups by the state. Schooling is organized specifically in age terms: at a certain age children have to go to school; they are taught with pupils of the same year group, and continue to be so throughout the education system. Age status is legally regulated too – you have to be a certain age to be criminally responsible, have sex, marry, vote; until you reach full adult age status there are restrictions on what you can do and where you can go. Youth is the social group most likely to identify itself in age terms. It is sometimes argued that longer lives, compulsory retirement, and increased state provision for the elderly have produced an age identity at the other end of the age scale too: the term "gray power" was coined in the 1970s. But there is not yet much evidence of this power being exercised (and "old people" covers a much broader age range than "young people").

The third meaning of "generation" refers to age groups' shared historical experience. This use of the term has become commonplace in the media – think of the casual references to the **sixties generation**, the **punk generation**, **generation X**, and so on. It is assumed here that events have particular effects on people who experience them at a formative age, that the historical setting for people coming of age influences their subsequent attitudes and values. Indeed, the media now seem to assume not just that each group of young people coming of age *may* be affected uniquely by contemporary events, but that it *must* be: every new generation is given a label. A generation's formative experience may also be institutional. A **political generation** describes leaders who came to power at a particular moment and whose attitudes were developed accordingly.

Karl Mannheim, the sociologist who first used the concept of generation in political analysis, suggested that while young people occupy particular occupations and roles in most societies and therefore develop a sense of themselves as an age group (hence the concept of youth culture), age-consciousness rarely becomes **generation-consciousness** (Mannheim, 1944). Only in periods of profound social change or instability does youth culture become political. This was commonly thought to be the case in the 1960s, when both political and social movements were particularly associated with youth culture. It was then that the term **generation gap** was first used. It is less commonly used today, and now seems to refer to relations between parents and their teenage children rather than to political struggle.

One of the problems of "generation" as an analytic term is that the divisions between one age group and another are arbitrary. People are being born continuously; the division of history into age spans is an imposition of arbitrary beginnings and ends. The general effect of C20 social history was to complicate even the domestic experience of generations. Longer lives and delayed pregnancies; second marriages and families; increased geographical and occupational mobility – the effect of such trends has been to break the simple link between age and status (people may now become parents at an age at which, 100 years ago, they would have been grandparents). And status relations in the household are further complicated by the effects of technological change: children are often thought to know more about modern life than their parents.

If it was the C20 welfare state which institutionalized age cohorts, it was the media which gave them cultural shape as consumer groups. **Generational change** became equated with the turnover of fashion and the release dates of films and television series. As a marketing category, though, "generation" is a vacuous concept. It does not tell us anything about changing social attitudes or alliances. The fact that people of a certain age grew up wearing or despising flared jeans is of little moment; class and gender differences remain far more socially significant than age-based agreements about what sounds old-fashioned or looks up-to-date.

"Generation" remains a useful term, though. Take, for example, the familiar account of migrant families in terms of **first, second, and third generation** (first used this way in the USA in the lC19). Each generation clearly does have a different experience of its old and new worlds, and to explore these differences is to get at important questions about the ways in which material history becomes cultural history and vice versa. To what extent do people understand new circumstance according to established norms and habits? To what extent are norms and habits changed by new possibilities? The concept of generation reminds us that culture is produced from the tension between continuity and change.

Simon Frith

See: *TIME, YOUTH.*

Globalization

The concepts of **the globe** as a spherical object and, metonymically, as the planet earth appeared together in the C16. The adjectival form (**global**) appeared in the C17 referring only to the former. In the late C19 "global" appeared in its more common contemporary sense, combining a geographical ("the whole world; world-wide; universal") and a mathematical or logical meaning ("the totality of a number of items, categories, etc.; comprehensive, all-inclusive, unified, total"). In the C20, the more active and historical form – **globalization** – appears, parallel to other comparable historical markers such as "modernization" and "industrialization" and related to the notions of postmodernity.

Does this mean that globalization began in the C20? Certainly there were earlier empires or translocal social systems which, if not covering the globe, extended their power and influence – economically, culturally, and politically – over large expanses of the globe. Marx suggested that capitalism was a globalizing enterprise:

The need of a constantly expanding market for its products chases the bourgeoisie over the whole surface of the globe. It must nestle everywhere, settle everywhere, establish connections everywhere... In place of the old local and national seclusion and self-sufficiency, we have intercourse in every direction, universal interdependence of nations. And in material, so in intellectual production. The intellectual creations of individual nations become common property. (*cit.* Waters, 1995: 6)

In fact, capitalism has always responded to crises of overaccumulation and overspeculation by expanding its territory.

In the mC20, two influential images of globalization circulated between the academy and broader public discourses. First, Marshall McLuhan's **global village** saw the world becoming a single interconnected society as a result of the new media of electronic communication. Second, Immanuel Wallerstein's world-system theory saw the emergence of a new configuration of global economic and social relations. While McLuhan's ideas, built on a kind of technological determinism, were largely associated with speculative, utopian, and counter-cultural visions, Wallerstein's more economic determinism was linked to a socialist left.

In the lC20, a number of developments made globalization a topic of government policy, public concern, and academic debate. In 1973, then US president Richard Nixon abrogated the post-war Bretton Woods agreement, which had established stable systems of monetary exchange and international trade regulation. Coupled with developments in computer technology and electronic communication, this opened up a hugely speculative international finance market, located in monetary and derivatives markets as well as traditional stock markets. The interests of this highly mobile finance capital were not always well served by the nationally organized systems of industrial capitalism. Newly empowered neo-liberal and neo-conservative regimes in the advanced capitalist world championed a new discourse of free trade, deregulation, marketization, and privatization. These governments, including that of Ronald Reagan in the US and Margaret Thatcher in the UK, pushed to (re)negotiate regional and global trade agreements (for example, the North American Free Trade Area, the General Agreement on Tariffs and Trade, and the European Economic Community), and gave new life and power to international regulatory agencies such as the World Trade Organization, and transnational economic institutions such as the World Bank and the International Monetary Fund.

As a result, the 1980s witnessed the growing internationalization of corporate operations and the growing power of multinational corporations, which were no longer under the rigid control of national governments. One result of these developments was a radical shift in the labor market, with many manufacturing jobs moved to the cheaper and more easily exploited labor markets of the developing world, and replaced with less secure, often minimum-wage, service-sector jobs, partly hidden under an ideology that equated the service economy with the knowledge or information economy. Alongside these changes,

147

the 1980s witnessed a major and significant transformation of the structures and size of international investments, by corporations, governments, and financial institutions, re-inforcing the sense of a single world market for money and credit

Discussions of globalization as policy or in relation to particular governmental decisions generally focus entirely on such developments in the economic and technological infra-structure, not only as the driving forces of globalization but also as the very meaning of globalization. As a result, globalization appears as the new ideology of capitalism, with its predictable claim of inevitability: "Anyone who believes that globalization can be stopped has to tell us how he would envision stopping economic and technological progress; this is tantamount to trying to stop the rotation of the earth" (Renato Ruggiero, ex-director-general of the World Trade Organization, *cit.* ILRIC, 2000). Ironically, despite its sup-posed inevitability, globalization is being pushed strongly by various governments, corpor-ations, interest groups, and transnational institutions.

Globalization, then, is the claim that there already exists or is necessarily coming an integrated **global economic market** encompassing all domains of social life. Local economic growth, the dominant definition of economic progress, depends on the reduction of all barriers to all international trade. Any nation's economic future depends upon its willingness to adopt policies committed to deregulation and free markets, and cutting government spending and taxes. Thus the state must undo its role as the provider of social services, as the protector of environments, markets, and populations.

Not surprisingly, the economic discourses of globalization are closely tied to assumptions of technological determinism, and to a powerful ideology of techno-utopianism, in which technological metaphors of networking are used to demonstrate the inherent democratizing possibilities of the new economy. These new technologies, it is claimed, have not only created the conditions for the possibility of exchange on a world-wide scale, but will also eventually democratize the distribution of knowledge, communication, and even wealth and power. Under the discipline of the discourses of globalization, there have been major transform-ations in the territorial organization of economic activity and political-economic power, resulting in a radical redistribution and reorganization – a new concentration – of economic wealth and power. Moreover, new economic institutions and organizations, new political and legal regimes, allow firms to operate across borders more easily, and force nations to negotiate with and find a place within these transnational processes. Finance capital has gained a new visibility in the everyday calculations of ordinary people, even as it has profoundly challenged the power of industrial capitalist regimes in the West. The result is a new geography of power. These processes have also exacerbated the uneven distribution of wealth across and within nations and regions, and the supposed commitment to free trade and competitive markets has actually reduced competition as a result of mergers, takeovers, stock deals, etc. And despite the claims of transnationalization, most large economies of the world are still overwhelmingly domestic, with little evidence that the levels of international trade are surpassing pre-World War I levels.

Some of the key questions surrounding globalization involve cultural practices, exchanges, and flows. Some of these concerns continue the fears of Americanization that preoccupied many nations following World Wars I and II, as first soldiers and then capitalism and the mass media brought the slick entertainment styles of US popular culture to the rest of the world. These issues were raised within the academy as ones of cultural imperialism – was American capitalist culture replacing and destroying all local and indigenous forms of cultural expression? – and in policy debates in discussions of the New World Information Order, a debate staged largely through the United Nations, about the rights of any nation to control the flow of communication across its borders.

New communication technologies and the new regimes of economic life have significantly intensified questions about the circulations of cultural products, including the increasing multinational corporate control of all media and public culture (hence a major issue in global trade policy involves bringing cultural goods into the regimes of free trade), the global tourist industry, and the growing visibility of Western consumer society as the taken-for-granted normative description of contemporary social life and experience. Of course, the question of the **globalization of culture** cannot be limited to concerns about the flows of popular commercial culture, for it involves as well questions about the effects of a rapidly growing **global tourism** industry and its consequences for indigenous populations and economies. More powerfully, however, than either of these domains, the globalization of culture has raised questions about the global normalization and acceptance of what is increasingly thought to be the essence of US if not all Western capitalist cultures: the extraordinarily rapid circulation of commodities of all sorts and, implicitly, the establishment of a consumer society. Sometimes described as McDonaldization or Nike-ification, discussions of globalization and culture then touch upon the question of the very nature of contemporary lived experience.

Many critics argue that globalization cannot be understood as a simple process of homogenization in which everything becomes the same (whether that means Westernized or Americanized or, perhaps, Japan-ized). Instead, globalization has to be seen as more of a process of negotiation, hybridization, or **glocalization**. The forces and pressures of globalization, however they may be conceived, do not simply impose themselves everywhere in just the same ways, with local practices and identities simply succumbing passively to these new forms. Instead, local societies, cultures, economies, and political formations respond in active and distinct ways to the changes that confront them. The results are unique, composed out of the encounter between **the global** and the local. Even the centers of traditional Western culture and power have had to adjust to the demands and transformations of globalization, becoming hybridized in the process. Globalization also involves the voluntary and necessary migrations of people around the world, often former colonial populations moving to the centers of colonial power. These movements have radically changed the ethnic make-up of Western nations that had previously imagined themselves ethnically homogeneous, and have made questions of immigration and national identity some of the most volatile political issues of the lC20 and eC21. As a result, it has been suggested, globalization challenges the assumed normativity of Western culture and identities.

Finally, as a matter of lived experience, globalization is about the changing power of geography over people's lives. For example, some commentators have talked about the decreasing power of geography, pointing to those people for whom new communication technologies have meant the apparent collapse of distance into copresence. On the other hand, for many others, without access to the media, globalization has meant the growing power of unknowable, distant powers over their lives. Globalization signals the new form in which we experience the geography of social relations. It involves not only the sense of increasing interdependence, but also an intensification of people's consciousness of the world as a whole. This can suggest a McLuhanesque vision of a global society in which geography is no longer a primary determinant of social and cultural life and identity, in which there are no borders or boundaries – not only to the flows of money, commodities, people, and power, but also to the flows of sympathy and fellow-feeling. While the geography of influence and effect has significantly expanded during the past 30 years – as countries are rarely able to shield themselves from the impact of decisions and events in other countries – these new relations are no more symmetrical than previous transnational organizations. And while more people may have an awareness of the world and of other peoples, cultures, and places, there is little evidence that this is producing a more harmonious world-society or a more tolerant environment for differences. Whether one thinks of globalization as the shortening of time and shrinking of space (sometimes called time-space compression) or as the annihilation of space by time (Marx's description of capitalism), the questions remain: if globalization, or at least any particular form of globalization, is not inevitable, what are its possibilities?

And since the last decade of the C20, there is some evidence that this question has been placed on the public's agenda with the appearance of organized and sustained dissent from, resistance to, and protest against the dominant discourses and practices of global-ization, including the implications for the labor, environments, or national democratic autonomy of the new economic regimes, the spread of rationalized capitalist markets into all aspects of social life (McDonaldization and genetically modified food, for example), and the imposition of consumption as the proper measure of freedom and democracy. Such efforts, whether from the **anti-globalization movement**, indigenous peoples' movements, or human rights non-governmental organizations, are often based on transnational alli-ances "from below" which use the tools, the technologies, and even the discourses of globalization in order to construct more effective transnational resistances to the domin-ant discourses, organizations, and forces of knowledge/power/wealth.

Lawrence Grossberg

See: *COLONIALISM, INFORMATION, MODERN, NETWORK, POSTMODERN, RESISTANCE, WEST.*

Government

The term **government** conjures up an image of **the government** – the personnel and organization with responsibility for ruling and directing the affairs of a state. But this identification of government and political elite is misleading: we also speak of the **governing body** of a school, of the Church of England, or of world football – of any body that is accorded the power to rule over a domain, an activity, or a group of persons. A prime minister can **govern** a nation, a captain can govern the crew of a ship, a teacher can govern a classroom, parents can govern their children. And one can govern one's demeanor, one's habits, one's passions, one's tongue, one's temper: ''How did the university applaud Thy government, behaviour, learning, speech'' (Ford, 1633). Indeed, to be civilized one must **govern oneself**.

The government, then, is only one of a number of **governments** each with its own jurisdiction, powers, ambitions, and techniques. These are linked by the fact that they all involve authorities who seek to govern: to educate, to control, to influence, to guide, to regulate, to administer, to reform, to manage. To govern is not to crush the persons or processes governed, or to dominate them, but to mobilize them toward some ends. To govern it is necessary to calculate the relation between one's actions and their consequences. Hence government requires knowledge of that which one governs and those who one governs. Reciprocally, attempts to govern have stimulated the development of knowledge of the entities and processes to be governed: the human sciences have been intrinsically bound up with attempts to govern human beings.

Many political arguments depend on the distinction between government exercised by politicians and the apparatuses of the state and civil service – conventionally funded through taxation – and all those other apparently non-political forms through which conduct is governed. When, from the mC19 onward, political liberals in Britain, Europe, and North America criticized **excessive government** they were not arguing that human conduct should not be governed. Rather, their belief was that most government of conduct should not be a matter for the state or politics, but should be left to other authorities – church, family, the market, tradition.

Soviet and Nazi regimes embodied dystopian attempts at **total government**, in which everything was to be known, managed, and ordered by a single, all-seeing authority and its functionaries. Such attempts at the micro-management of all aspects of existence from public space to domestic arrangements and procreation can also be found in some strategies of **colonial government**, such as those employed by the Japanese in Taiwan. Since the eC19, however, liberal democratic governments in the West have always depended upon other loci of government in order to achieve their objectives of prosperity, tranquility, harmony, efficiency, or competitiveness. They have relied upon – and sought to foster and shape – the activities of those who governed various circumscribed domains: factories, organizations, schools, prisons, asylums, families. They have also relied upon the

self-government of individuals and sought to encourage a range of practices from architectural design to schooling to inculcate civility. The problem for **liberal governments** – which have continually troubled themselves with the danger of governing too much – has always been one of trying to so arrange affairs such that the outcomes of these other governing activities would assist, and not resist, their own ambitions.

However, throughout the C20, many argued that the state could no longer rely on these dispersed sites of government to cope with the problems generated by life in complex industrialized and urbanized societies, but must take more direct control. New political technologies, from town planning to social insurance, increased the capacity of the state to control the local practices in which economic life was managed, human disease was combated, moral habits were reformed, civility was inculcated, and so forth. It was this **governmentalization of the state** that was the target of critiques of "big government" in the closing decades of the C20. Some on the left argued that the state had "colonized the lifeworld" (Habermas, 1984; Keane, 1984). On the right, neo-liberals such as Friedrich von Hayek and Milton Friedman argued that attempts by politicians to plan and govern economic, social, and personal life in the name of efficiency, equity, and justice actually created the opposite – dependency, inefficiency, and injustice (Hayek, 1944; Friedman and Friedman, 1980).

As the powers of the **governmental state** came under attack in the closing decades of the C20, political thought tried to free itself from its domination by the image of the state and to recognize that states are the terminal point, not the point of origin, of a range of networks of power. States can only govern to the extent that they are able to translate their calculations and objectives into the judgments of actors in a multitude of territorially distant sites and practices. Michel Foucault's concept of **governmentality** sought to capture these complexities: governing involved not only a certain rationality – a way of thinking about who should govern what, why, according to what legitimacy, and toward what ends – but also a variety of technologies that were more or less successful in linking up centers of political calculation with the diverse zones and activities to be governed (Foucault, 1991; cf. Burchell, Gordon, and Miller, 1991; N. Rose, 1999). In a related attempt to characterize the relations between political rule and practices of government outside the state, the language of **governance** achieved popularity. Sociologists and political scientists took up this term in a descriptive sense to characterize the pattern or structure that emerges as a result of the interactions of a range of political actors – of which the state is only one (Kooiman, 1993). In such a sociology, governance refers to the *outcome* of all these interactions and interdependencies: the self-organizing networks that arise out of the interactions between a variety of organizations and associations. It is argued that these are of particular significance today because recent political strategies have attempted to govern not through centrally controlled bureaucracies (hierarchies) or through competitive interactions between producers and consumers (markets), but through such networks. This has resulted in what Rhodes (1994) describes as the "hollowing out of the State." Politics is seen as increasingly involving exchanges and relations among a range of public, private, and voluntary organizations, without clear sovereign authority. Terms like "actor networks," "self-regulatory mechanisms," "trust," "habits and conventions," "gift relations," and "informal obligations" are utilized to describe the actual operation of the complex exchanges through which governance occurs.

From the 1980s onward, the idea of governance was bound up with a normative evaluation of government and a program to reinvent it. **Reinventing government** became the slogan for the assault on **big government** in the United States, and the title of a series of publications of hearings of the United States Congress Committee on Governmental Affairs in the 1990s. Good governance means less government, politicians exercising power by steering (setting policy) rather than rowing (delivering services): it requires political strategies to minimize the role of the state, to encourage non-state mechanisms of regulation, to reduce the size of the political apparatus and civil service, to introduce "the new public management," to change the role of politics in the management of social and economic affairs. From the 1980s onward, organizations such as the World Bank urged political regimes seeking aid and loans to correspond to this normative image of governance, by privatizing state corporations, encouraging competition, markets, private enterprise, downsizing the political apparatus, splitting up functions, and allotting as many as possible to non-state organizations. The aim was to disperse power relations among a whole complex of public service and private agencies, with independent auditing of public finances, overseen by an independent legal system, political pluralism, and a free press.

153

In the current period, we see attempts to reshape government beyond the territorial confines of the nation state. On the one hand, there are attempts to shift various powers of government upward to transnational bodies such as the United Nations and the European Union. On the other hand, there are attempts to shift other powers of government downward, to localities and communities. Notable, here, is the rise of communitarian thinking in contemporary politics, with its stress on the duties and responsibilities of the citizen that go along with civil and human rights. This marks the most recent attempt to instrumentalize the **ethical self-government** of individuals and collectivities in the service of political objectives from the provision of welfare, through crime prevention, to economic regeneration. Once more, politicians and other authorities discover that to govern effectively, one must govern through reshaping the ways in which formally autonomous political subjects understand and enact their own freedom.

Nikolas Rose

See: *BUREAUCRACY, CITIZENSHIP, COMMUNITY, LIBERALISM, NATION, PRIVATE, PUBLIC, STATE.*

Heritage

In its earliest usages, from the C13, **heritage** carried both spiritual and profane meanings. Spiritually, it could signify a people chosen by God as his peculiar possession – the "heritage of the Lord." In its more profane associations, as "inheritance" or "heirloom," the term referred especially to property or land passed through the generations, and acquired by sons (usually) on the death of their father. Traces of both these original meanings can be discerned in the characteristically modern renditions of "heritage," describing customs which are passed down by tradition: thus "heritage" took on a more comprehensive meaning, referring to everything acquired by one's circumstances of birth. In this broader sense, "heritage" came to be allied in the modern period with the idea of culture itself, working as a particular subset of the larger domain of the symbolic.

This mobilization of an expansive idea of "heritage" also meant that it came to be closely associated with concepts of tradition, such that the terms often came to be interchangeable or synonymous. In the mC20 critics became more knowing about the properties of the interlinked notions of tradition and heritage. Raymond Williams (1958) devoted much energy to theorizing what was essentially *selective* about traditions, while a similar generation of historians alighted upon the idea that tradition was increasingly subject to invention in the present (Hobsbawm and Ranger, 1983). The impulse common to both observations lay in recognition of the degree to which tradition and heritage represent a means for those in the present to organize the (historical) past – sometimes for overtly ideological ends, sometimes not (Lowenthal, 1985).

ABCDEFG**H**IJKLMNOPQRSTUVWXYZ

The proximate concepts of conservation and preservation first emerged in the C19 to embrace a range of social practices devised to safeguard what was coming to be perceived as the "disappearing" past. By the 1850s in Britain the Society of Antiquarians boasted a Conservation Committee; the first wildlife protection act was passed in 1869; in the 1880s the first by-laws to protect endangered plants were passed; and the Ancient Monuments Bill was agreed by Parliament in the same decade. The most notable civic organization along these lines was William Morris's Society for the Protection of Ancient Buildings, founded in 1876 (to care for buildings not only in the United Kingdom, but throughout Europe as well). This accommodated not only Morris's political allies on the left, but intellectuals (like Thomas Carlyle) to whom on all other issues he was a sworn enemy.

In 1895 the National Trust was founded in Britain – the idea of "trust" itself signifying the social or collective ownership of "the past." This is now, more than a century on, the most important and successful voluntary society in the contemporary period, with a membership of more than two million (Cannadine, 2003).

More specifically, though, the particular conception of "heritage" in its modern meanings, according to Raphael Samuel, seems entirely to be a twentieth-century phenomenon (Samuel, 1994). With barely any mention to be found before then, in the eC20 it took off in spectacular form. Yet only much later did political disputation occur. The notion of heritage became a more intensely contested concept – part of a more explicit intervention in the workings of the discursive constitution of public life – in the lC20, across all sectors of the overdeveloped world. From the 1970s or 1980s, in a curious historical transformation which awaits explanation, there emerged a proliferation of cultural interventions which invested in the notion of heritage. Characteristically, the old ruins of the first Industrial Revolution – mines, mills, docklands – found themselves reconstituted as tourist attractions. Old historic homes, humble as well as grand, increasingly were commodified as spectacle. A genre of movies emerged that was classified as **heritage cinema**, and there were parallel developments in television. No part of the historical past, however gruesome or terrifying, seemed immune from the diktats of what came to be known from this period as the **heritage industry**. Entire city centers fell under its sway. In the major Anglophone nations, **heritage-listed** buildings and sites authenticated the relationship of present to past. Much as a century before there occurred the compulsion to invent mass traditions, on Fordist principles, so in the lC20 a post-Fordist explosion of niche heritage-invention took place – sociologically connected, in some urban zones, to gentrification or the phenomenon of loft-living (Zukin, 1988).

Critics skeptical of this rage for heritage (such as Patrick Wright [1985] and Robert Hewison [1987]) coined the term **politics of heritage**, in a bid to expose the political impulses and consequences associated with these new cultural developments. For them, the omnipresence of heritage – coinciding with a perceptible shift to the political right in North America and Western Europe – made it seem as if it should be seen as the cultural armature of the New Right. Others, in more abstract vein, saw it as a manifestation of the arrival of the postmodern, in which the historical past entered a phase of infinite regression, unreachable through the patina of spectacle and commodity. Perhaps the most sophisticated attempt to locate the complex mix of developments which went under the name of heritage came from the French historian Pierre Nora. In an ambitious project, Nora and a host of historians under his command set out to chart the history of memory in the modern French nation. In coming to his own, contemporary, period Nora found public memory colonized by what he termed *les lieux de memoire* – the realms or places of memory (Nora, 1984–93). Contrary to appearances, these realms of memory, far from allowing access to the historical past, obstructed historical thought: rather like heritage in the Anglophone literature, in the lC20, for Nora, *les lieux de memoire* promised much but delivered little, alluding to a past that could never be grasped, known, or experienced. In a contrary conceptual move, the English historian Raphael Samuel, tired of intellectuals exhibiting a characteristic snobbishness about the popular pleasures organized by the heritage industries, embarked upon an ambitious study in which he determined to demon-strate that heritage, far from being destructive of historical consciousness, worked as a great impetus for the arrival of a new form of historical knowledge. These controversies currently underwrite the entire governance or administration of the-past-in-the-present – be it among museum curators, or in the decisions to designate **world heritage sites**, or in local struggles to preserve a neighborhood artifact.

This politicization of the concept of heritage in the lC20 and eC21 rather confirms that the past is not quite as commodified as pessimists fear. What is clear, though, is that the concept of heritage signifies the organization of a new historical moment in the workings of historical time.

Bill Schwarz

See: *HISTORY, MEMORY, TIME.*

History

In the English-speaking world **history** principally signifies a retelling of past events which is professedly true, based (reputedly) on what really happened. "History" in this sense, together with its older generic correlates, *histoire, hystorye, historye,* and *historie,* came to be uncoupled from the more capacious idea of a **story** only in the lC15, with "story" henceforth signifying fiction or some wholly imaginative construct. Evidence of this conceptual division can be witnessed, for example, in the distinction between those of Shakespeare's plays classified as **histories**, and those others, products only (it seems) of the dramatist's imagination – comedies and tragedies, most of all. Antecedents of history-as-truth can be found in the idea of the chronicle, as well as in genealogy. The genealogical roots of historical thought in the Renaissance were evident in the attention paid to men of standing: history was about kingship, and the men with the capacities to rule states, command armies, and conquer territories. The profound, but protracted, recasting of the idea of history, such that it came to embrace human self-development itself, in its totality, constitutes one dimension of what we call modernity. The clearest anticipation of this shift in meaning can be discerned in the field of philosophy in the C18, most particularly in the work of Giambattista Vico (1968 [1744]).

The idea of history as the enactment of human self-development found its most dramatic expression in the philosophy of Georg Wilhelm Friedrich Hegel (1956 [1831]), from which most contemporary debate still derives. Hegel not only construed the terms in which the idea of **world-history** could take effect. He also endeavored to supply his grandiose abstraction's historical, empirical specification, as in his conviction that world-history, or the world-spirit, was manifest in the Prussian state, as it had been earlier (in Hegel's view) in the person of Bonaparte, designated by Hegel as ''the world-spirit on horseback.'' Karl Marx and Friedrich Engels (1973 [1848]) adopted much of this system of thinking, attempting to turn it on its head and render it in material and secular terms: in so doing they launched a radical renovation of the idea of history itself, which spawned an array of new categorizations. Not the least of these was the notion of **historical materialism**, which came to act as an alternative term for Marxism. The debates within Marxism in the lC19, from before Marx's death and in the years which followed, swung between competing readings of the **historical process** (itself an idea of history popularized within Marxism). On the one hand there existed a deep belief in the **historical inevitability** of social emancipation, an intellectual position which drew much from the contemporaneous vogue for **natural history**, and for Charles Darwin especially. On the other, there emerged a heightened faith in the capacities of men (and women) **to make history** themselves.

This centering of human agency in history can also be discerned in the traditions of historical thought which derived from the French Revolution, and which drew too from the spirit of Romanticism. The greatest inspiration in this respect was Jules Michelet (hugely influenced by Vico), who can claim to be the effective inventor of **people's history** in the mC19. In Michelet (1847–53) too we can see a contemporary sensibility in his determination to honor the anonymous dead, and to rescue their memory from oblivion. In one of the great testaments to what (from this period) was termed the **historical imagination** Michelet claimed that the Père Lachaise cemetery in Paris worked for him as ''the laboratory of historical resurrection.'' The second half of the C19 saw the emergence of **historiography**, in the sense of a **professionalized history**, organized on agreed rational procedures (documented, footnoted), and the earliest indications of the figure of the **historian**, as opposed to the general man of letters, or to the amateur figure of the **antiquarian**.

As these developments to professionalize history were at their earliest stage, Thomas Carlyle was already condemning the **''dry-as-dust'' historian**, while – echoing Michelet's populism – J. R. Green was complaining of a history given exclusively to ''drum and trumpet,'' thereby condemning an entire mode of high-nationalist historical thought. One effect of the professionalization of history through the nineteenth century was the naming of a distinct genre of literary production: the **historical novel** (Lukács, 1962) – first viewed (by professional historians) as "romances," appropriate for the feminine sensibility, but unworthy of serious intellectual attention. Nonetheless, debate raged within the historical profession between the "poetic" and the "scientific" dimensions of historical practice, with the latter (in the academy) winning the upper hand for much of the eC20. Professionalization brought an entire new lexicon to the study of history. History itself was divided first into **ancient history** and **modern history**, and thence subdivided into an increasing plethora of categories: ancient, **medieval**, **early modern**, modern, and, later, **contemporary history**. Archeology came to be defined as a separate specialism.

Alongside these attempts systematically to periodize human history, distinct subspecialisms appeared. Until much of the lC19 history was essentially what a modern reader would understand as **cultural history**, in that it took as its natural object of study the history of civilizations. One of the first to make the project of cultural history explicit was Jacob Burkhardt (1944). Thenceforth, in the eC20, the dominant forms of professional history included **economic**, **political**, and **imperial history**. Through the C20 the concept of history assumed a bewildering accumulation of new meanings and connotations.

Politically, deriving from its Marxisant interpretations, the idea of **historical consciousness** proved powerful (and was given philosophical rendition especially by Georg Lukács), in which men and women were deemed to become ever more conscious of themselves and hence of their **historical tasks**. This merged into more determinist readings, common in the 1930s, in which **History** (upper case) appeared as an unforgiving absolute: in this period, those who could read the runes of History – most often associated with the official communist movement – were wont to issue imperatives in its name. A later manifestation of this same sensibility can be discerned in Fidel Castro's moving assertion, while on trial for his life, that "History will absolve me."

In philosophy, history was centered as a preoccupation for at least some strands of thought for the middle period of the C20 – though not much in the Anglophone world. The term **historicism** became a matter of great philosophical contention, both because of its varied meanings, and because it attracted adherents and opponents in equal measure. Perhaps the predominant meaning of "historicism" lay in the intellectual endeavor to situate all systems of ideas (philosophy included) in their historical context, calling into question the formal properties of abstract thought. The greatest theoretical breakthrough in historiography in the C20 was represented by Fernand Braudel's discovery (as he put it) that the object of historical thought was less "the past" than **historical time** (Braudel, 1972). In part this belief derived from Henri Bergson, in part from the mC20 interest in varieties of structuralism. Braudel came to imagine a history in which **structural history** (histories of the ecological world, economic systems, and state forms) would combine with **conjunctural histories** (the histories of events, as he put it). In this, he believed, lay the promise of a properly **total history**, in which every dimension of historical time could be reproduced in the narrative of the historian.

In contemporary times the proliferation of **academic history** has continued apace, with new species of historical specialisms arriving constantly. This continues a new-found engagement with the history of the oppressed which took off from the 1960s and 1970s (**women's history**, **queer history**, **black history** – many of which first took hold as an offshoot of **oral history**). A theme underlying many of these approaches to historical knowledge was the idea that the oppressed had been **hidden from history**: that, in other words, conventional academic history, focusing on the nation and/or on high politics, simply could not *see* that the oppressed possessed a history. This took many forms, the most influential conceptually falling within the realm, first, of **feminist history** and, second, of the group of historians in the Indian subcontinent who developed the school of **subaltern history** (Guha, 1983). While the promise of total history was never fulfilled, it did bequeath flourishing work in the field of *mentalities*, which connected with later, Foucauldian-inspired **genealogical histories** (in, for example, the history of the emotions, of sexuality, of the body, of medicine, of the symbolic force of single commodities, and so on).

At present, an immensely rich moment in academic history combines with an extraordinary popular appetite for knowledge about the past: in **television history**, for example, or in heritage sites or in other forms of commemorative practice. The idea of television history presents a limit-case for thinking about popular forms of historical consciousness. To what degree can a generation cognitively attuned to television gain a critical sense of the external, historical world? For pessimists, television is the principal means in the postmodern world for scrambling historical time, preventing the postmodern subject from reaching the past. For others, of more optimistic persuasion, television becomes the means by which the contemporary world, in all its aspects including its historical determinations, can be ''worked through'' and known. It may be instructive that this proliferation of knowledges about the past has tended to diminish the long-standing division between history and story, the fictional or imaginative properties of history becoming ever more conspicuous. And it is paradoxical that this profusion of representations of the past coincides with expressions of anxiety that – in the postmodern epoch – the capacity for human beings to reach their historical past is all the time diminishing.

Bill Schwarz

See: *HERITAGE, MEMORY, TIME.*

Holocaust

In the 1940s, when rumors of the mass murder of Jews throughout Nazi-occupied Europe leaked across the front line, the biblical term **holocaust** was recalled and redeployed to name it. That act had no precedent in recorded history and thus no established vocabulary name. A new name had to be coined for the act of categorial murder – the physical annihilation of men, women, and children on the ground of their belonging or having been assigned to a category of people on which the death sentence was summarily passed. By the 1950s, the old/new term **the Holocaust** came to be widely accepted as the proper name of the meant-to-be-total destruction of European Jews perpetrated in the years 1940–5 on the initiative of the Nazi leadership.

In subsequent years, though, the usages of the term have been extended to cover the numerous cases of mass murder aimed against an ethnic, racial, or religious group – also the cases in which a disempowering or expulsion, rather than the total annihilation of the targeted group, was the proclaimed or tacit objective. Due to the enormous emotional load of the term and an almost universal ethical condemnation of the actions it stood for, the range of damages inflicted by one human group on another has been stretched over the years much beyond its original field. It has, accordingly, become an essentially contested concept, used in numerous ethnic and other violent group conflicts as a charge raised against the conduct or intentions of the adversary to justify one's own group's hostility.

In popular speech originally most strongly associated with the notion of **nuclear holocaust**, these days "holocaust" tends to be interchangeable with "genocide" – another linguistic novelty of the C20. In 1993 Helen Fein noted that between 1960 and 1979 "there were probably at least a dozen genocides and genocidal massacres – cases include the Kurds in Iraq, southerners in the Sudan, Tutsi in Rwanda, Hutus in Burundi, Chinese . . . in Indonesia, Hindus and other Bengalis in East Pakistan, the Ache in Paraguay, many peoples in Uganda" (Fein, 1993: 6). Since those words were written, the list has been considerably extended; as these words are being written, the list shows no signs of nearing the end. Genocide, in Frank Chalk's and Kurt Jonassohn's definition, "is a form of one-sided mass killing in which a state or other authority intends to destroy a group, as that group and membership in it are defined by the perpetrators" (Chalk and Jonassohn, 1990: 23). In genocide, the power over life intertwines with the power to define. Before the wholesale extermination of a group comes the classification of the group's members, and the definition of group membership as a capital crime.

In many an orthodox war the number of casualties exceeded many times the numbers of many a genocide's victims. What sets genocide apart from even the most violent and gory conflicts is not, however, the number of its victims, but its monological nature. In genocide, the prospective targets of violence are unilaterally defined and denied a right to response. The victims' conduct or the qualities of the condemned group's individual members are irrelevant to their preordained fate. The sufficient proof of the capital offence, of the charge from which there is no appeal, is the fact of having been accused. "Holocaust" conveys much the same meaning. When used in lieu of "genocide," suggesting the similarity of a particular case of mass murder to the destruction of European Jews as the archetype, it is mostly to express the unilateral and premeditated character of the odious and repulsive atrocity and the thoroughness of intended extermination of the doomed category.

This current meaning of "holocaust" bears only oblique relation to the meaning carried by the term appearing in the Leviticus chapter of the Greek translation of the Old Testament, from which it has been derived. That ancient term was recalled, and invoked as a metaphor of the Nazi extermination of the Jews, probably because of conveying the thoroughness of destruction. The Gk term ὁλόκαυστος was a literal translation of the Hebrew "wholly burned," a requirement that the offerings brought to the Temple must be destroyed by fire in their entirety. But the "burning whole" referred to by the ancient term was full of religious meaning: it was meant to express the completeness of the human surrender to God and the unconditionality of human piety. The objects of sacrifice were to be the faithful's most valuable, proud possessions: chosen young bullocks or male lambs, specimens without blemish, as perfect in every detail as was the human reverence to God and the dedication to divine command. Following this other track of metaphorical extension, "sacrifice" came to mean the "surrender of something valued or desired for the sake of something having a higher or more pressing claim."

If this is what the sacrifice is about, the Holocaust was anything but sacrifice. The victims of genocide are not people sacrificed in the name of a greater value. The object of genocide that follows the pattern introduced by the **Nazi Holocaust** is, in Giorgio Agamben's terms, *homo sacer* – "who may be killed and yet not sacrificed." The death of *homo sacer* is devoid of religious significance. What is annihilated is a "bare life," stripped of any value. "In the case of *homo sacer* a person is simply set outside human jurisdiction without being brought into the realm of divine law." He is an object "of a double exception, both from the *ius humanum* [human right] and from the *ius divinum* [divine right]" (Agamben, 1998: 8).

161

We may say that before they were rounded up, deported to the death camps, shot or suffocated, the Jews of Germany and other countries of Nazi-occupied Europe (alongside Roma and Sinti) had been declared a "collective *homo sacer*" - the category whose life is devoid of all positive value and whose murder has no moral significance and commands no punishment. Theirs was *unwertes Leben* – life unworthy of living – like the lives of Gypsies, homosexuals, or those classified as mentally ill and retarded. What all those categories had in common was their unfitness for the *Neue Ordnung* – the social order purified of all undesirable admixtures, blemishes, and imperfections that the sovereign Nazi rulers of Germany set out to build. The vision of a perfect order supplied the criteria setting apart the "fit" from "unfit," subjects whose life deserved to be preserved and enhanced from those who could render no conceivable service to the strength of the new order but instead impaired its harmony; while the sovereign power (a power exercised over humans reduced to "bare bodies") enabled the builders of the new order to admit their subjects into or to exempt them from that order at will. Claiming the right to include or exclude from the realm of legal rights and ethical obligations was the essence of the modern state's sovereignty – and the Holocaust (like the massive purges of "class aliens" in Stalinist Russia) was the most extreme and radical manifestation of that claim.

Mass murders accompanied human history throughout. But the peculiar variety of categorial mass murder called "the Holocaust" would be inconceivable outside the frame of modern society. A systematic murder, conducted over a long period of time, required an enormous amount of resources and frequent adjustment of procedure. It would be hardly possible without the typically modern inventions of industrial technology and bureaucracy, with its meticulous division of labor, strict hierarchy of command and discipline, neutralization of personal (also ethical) convictions, and the managerial ambition to subordinate social reality to a rationally designed model of order – innovations that happened to be as well the prime causes of the modern era's spectacular successes. As John P. Sabini and Mary Silver observed:

> Consider the numbers. The German state annihilated approximately six million Jews. At the rate of 100 per day [this was the number of victims of the infamous *Kristallnacht*, the Nazi-organized pogrom of German Jews] this would have required nearly 200 years. Mob violence rests on the wrong psychological basis, on violent emotion. People can be manipulated into fury, but fury cannot be maintained for 200 years. Emotions, and their biological basis, have a natural time course; lust, even blood lust, is eventually sated. Further, emotions are notoriously fickle, can be turned. A lynch mob is unreliable, it can sometimes be moved by sympathy – say by a child's suffering. To eradicate a "race" it is essential to kill the children. (Sabini and Silver, 1980: 229–30)

To eradicate a "race," in other words, it is necessary to suppress human emotions and other manifestations of human individuality, and submit human conduct to the uncontested rule of instrumental reason. Modernity made the Holocaust possible. It was totalitarian rule that implemented such a possibility.

It was hoped half a century ago that the gruesome knowledge of the Holocaust would shock humanity out of its ethical somnolence and make genocides impossible. This did not happen. The legacy of the Holocaust proved to be a temptation to try final solutions as much as the repulsion such solutions inspire. The problem of making society immune to genocidal temptation stays wide open.

Zygmunt Bauman

See: *COLONIALISM, FUNDAMENTALISM, MEMORY.*

Home

Home implies both rest and settlement, and movement. Home is the place from which things originate (**hometown, home country**) and to which they return, or – where movement is blocked – a place of imagined return. It is a place of belonging, involving a sense of family, intimacy, or affinity among those who live close to each other, surrounded by movement. It is a place to which others come when we are at home to receive them and a place from which things flow to others: for colonial administrations, instructions, like parcels for migrants, always came from home. Home can also be found at the other end of travel and movement – a **home away from home**, or, in colonial histories, a home planted in another's land, as in **home station**. And home can be a beckoning destination, a place of final rest and return: "Til we end in dust, our final rest and native home" (Milton, 1667).

To take things home is to make them safe, to take them out of circulation – as in the **home base** of a game: **home and dry** – just as to **strike home** is the most brutal of blows in denying an opponent the sanctuary of home. To **come short home** is to fail to reach home, or come to grief: "They very often came short home, for the Germans had the better of them" (Defoe, 1722). Homes for **the homeless**, the afflicted, the destitute, and the infirm are places of rest provided against the insecurity of life on the streets, just as **homeland security** aims to place a protective shield around the nation. And it is **at home** that things are properly themselves, where a person's true identity resides.

These various meanings of home accrued a particular symbolism in the C19 through their association with the middle-class household. Defined increasingly in terms of the nuclear family of cohabiting adults and their children, the home acquired marked gendered characteristics as a private, largely feminized domestic sphere separated off from the male-dominated worlds of work and public life. As a "haven in a heartless world," home was, ideally, a place to which the male head of household could retreat for security from, and renewal for, the lacerating rigors of industry and competition. Home is "the place of peace; the shelter, not only from all injury, but from all terror, doubt and division," but only when there is a "true wife" at its center (Ruskin, 1868).

The relationships between rest and movement, private and public, home and away, give rise, in this formation, to unstable and contradictory evaluations of home. Home is devalued as limiting and confining compared to the challenges of risk and danger, and the opportunities for mobility, that are reserved for men outside the home. And home is sentimentally over-valued as a sequestered zone, a place of stable tranquility, where male movement, in coming to rest, is readied to be once again set in motion. At the same time, in the emergence, from the lC19, of domestic science, campaigns for rational and scientific **home management**, and, into the C20, the explosive growth of domestic technologies, the home – an "invaded haven" – is integrated into the world of industrial production and management to which it imaginarily stands opposed. The related development of **home economics** signals the exclusion of women's work in the home from contemporary definitions of the public economy.

The relations between home, rest, settlement, belonging, and movement have had fatal consequences for peoples whose practices of home are not spatially centered in this way. In early contact histories between the old and new worlds, the nomadism of hunter-gatherer societies was interpreted as an index of their savagery. To wander aimlessly without a fixed point of departure and return indicated a lack of civilization, which legitimated colonization as a process of civilizing the savage, and a failure to permanently settle and so effectively own the land, which justified its expropriation.

163

Human

In later histories, the values invested in the home have been creatively reworked in the process of being translated from their C19 Euro-American white and middle-class origins across a range of class and racial divides. The home, and women's place within it, played an important role in nurturing the development of Indian nationalism as an inner sanctum in which a distinctive culture and identity were preserved from violation by the colonizer. "In the world, imitation of and adaptation to Western norms was a necessity; at home they were tantamount to annihilation of one's very identity" (Chatterjee, 1993: 121). Home often played the same role in histories of slavery and racial oppression: "one's homeplace was the one site where one could freely confront the issues of humanization, where one could resist" (hooks, 1990b: 42).

The ambiguity of the values that are attached to the place of home are evident in the literature that has emerged in the context of feminist, gay, and lesbian critiques. Donna Haraway summarizes how home values are now contested:

> *Home*: Women-headed households, serial monogamy, flight of men, old women alone, technology of domestic work, paid homework, re-emergence of home sweat shops, home-based businesses and telecommuting, electronic cottage, urban homelessness, migration, module architecture, reinforced (simulated) nuclear family, intense domestic violence. (Haraway, 1985: 194)

Yet home can also remain a haven in a heartless world, a place to which the true self can retreat and find expression: "not ever being *your whole self* except obviously *in the home*" (Stacey, English lesbian, *cit*. Johnson and Valentine, 1995: 108).

The relations between home – whether understood as place of domicile, hometown, or home country – rest, settlement, belonging, and movement are also being revised in light of new ways of living associated with increased labor mobility and migration. In place of home as "a fixed point in space, a firm position from which we 'proceed'...and to which we return" (Heller, 1981: 239), new uses (home as "a mobile, symbolic habitat, a performative way of life and of doing things in which one makes one's home while in movement [Morley, 2000: 47]), encompass a broader and more fluid set of relationships between traveling and dwelling.

Tony Bennett

See: *COUNTRY, NATION, PRIVATE, PUBLIC.*

Human

Human evolved in English from *humay* and *humain*, and was distinguished from the later *humane* in the eC18. In common English usage it designates members (**human beings**) of a specific race (the **human race**) or species (collectively referred to as

humanity), or refers to the characteristics of the race. Hence, it marks or distinguishes **the human** from other creatures and things, often "lower" animals, machinery, and objects. Evaluating the significance of this designation has been a complex matter which has spawned considerable controversy, as well as derivative terms.

When "nature" is attached to the adjective "human," the attribution of characteristics may take on further significance. In everyday usage, labeling any activity or trait as a matter of **human nature** may simply be a shorthand way of indicating empathy (implying that it is understandable), but it may also indicate that it is inevitable or unchangeable, and/or beyond reproach. While terms such as "instinctive" and "innate" may indicate essential characteristics, it is not always clear that these are distinctly human. Moreover, there has been considerable philosophical and political debate about whether human traits and capacities are given by nature or evolve in culture (sometimes framed as "nature vs. nurture" or "nature vs. culture"). There has been much controversy in modern Western societies both about whether there are "species-typical characteristics shared by all human beings qua human beings" (Fukuyama, 2002: 101) constituting human nature and, if such characteristics exist, about what they might be.

The invocation of the term "human" in descriptions can be evaluative, alluding to the best characteristics of the human race, often linked to virtues such as decency or to understanding or rationality. The related and original substitute term "humane" denotes benevolence or compassion. Strikingly, in the contemporary context, the label "human" may also be used empathetically to suggest limitation, vulnerability, and weakness, as in **he's *only* human** and **we are all human** in commentaries about failure, weakness, or misbehavior. The prefixes "sub-" and "super-" attached to "human" may be a further way of designating standards and achievement. **Subhuman** pertains to situations or conditions considered unfitting or demeaning for human beings. **Superhuman** refers to some activity which is seen as extraordinary or transcending normal human capacities (as in "superhuman effort"). **Humanitarian** implies an activity, person, or institution contributing to collective **human welfare**. However, its currency has come into some disrepute because of skepticism about the benevolence of some interventions so labeled. **Humanist** may be a synonym for humanitarian, although it may also refer to someone who is a student of human affairs or who pursues the studies of the **humanities.** Moral reprobation, in turn, can be registered through related negative nomenclature – **inhuman** and **inhumanity**. A less judgmental but more specific employment of the term "human" implies personal, subjective or individual appeal, as in **human interest**: this is used to identify a particular style of storytelling or presentation of information, especially in media news coverage.

Humanism (in its various manifestations) constitutes one of the most enduring answers to the question: what is the human position in the world? Its origins can be traced to a philosophical and literary movement which emerged in lC14 Italy, revolving around the recovery and rehabilitation of classical Gk and L texts and the reforming of education accordingly. This movement was the mainspring of the European Renaissance. The coining of the term **humanism** (meaning education based on the Gk and L classics) is attributed to the eC19 German educator F. J. Niethammer (Monfasani, 1998: 533). The related term "humanities" is now used to refer not as originally to this classical program of study, but to a broad range of learning and literature (including languages, history, and literature) and related educational programs. Meanwhile, the predominant contemporary usage of the term "humanism" is more generalized, denoting a focus on human agents as the dominant and central actors in the world. Thus, **Renaissance humanism** was an early phase in a much more long-term prioritization of the place and role of human beings in the world order, which sustained the Enlightenment and continued to be influential from the C19 to the eC21 in the West.

Humanism originally constituted a secular realignment, asserting both the significance of humanity rather than God and the human domination of nature. However, power relations among **humans** became increasingly important within this tradition, and since the lC18 the concept of **human rights** has been crucial in political struggles and negotiations in the Western world. The term registers a set of conditions for social and political life that are regarded as universally applicable. *The rights of man* (Paine, 1969 [1791]) articulated this, but the gender specificity of the referent ("man") and the appearance hot on its heels of Mary Wollstonecraft's *A vindication of the rights of woman* (1975 [1792]) indicated problems around the claims to universalism embedded in the concept of human rights. Various emancipatory struggles – including C19 anti-slavery protest; C19 and C20 suffrage struggles; the campaigns for political, social, and legal rights for women, blacks, homosexuals, and indigenous populations; and campaigns against colonialist regimes in the C19 and C20 – are frequently characterized today as **human rights campaigns**. The United Nations' *Declaration of human rights* (1948) is the key C20 document which attempted to establish a universal legal and political framework for conceptualizing rights, a framework within which professional organizations,such as Amnesty International later characterized their transnational activities as human rights work.

Between the lC18 and the lC20, challenges (in the form of social protests and movements, as well as philosophical critiques) to social injustice were often launched in the name of humanism, to realize human rights for specific groups and individuals. Nevertheless, some critics have been suspicious of the patterns of differentiation and hierarchization associated with humanism. For example, Simone de Beauvoir's 1949 *Second sex* (1973) "pioneered feminist scrutiny of the credentials of humanism" (Elliot, 1996: 249). She and other critics have argued that the human – the autonomous rational actor instantiated by humanism, and often referred to as "the liberal subject" – is highly specific and that humanism is oriented toward the interests of white, bourgeois, European men. In the lC20, generalized unease about humanism was intensified and honed with reference to poststructuralism and postmodernism, feminist and postcolonial theory, the intensification of ecological concerns, and developments in biomedical and information technology. In different ways each of these movements or developments raised questions about the category "human." This included questioning "master narratives about humanity" (Halberstam and Livingston, 1995: 4), asking whether humans could or should dominate the natural world, and wondering about the distinctions between humans and other creatures and entities.

In the IC20 challenges to humanism and to assumptions about the human subject sometimes coalesced around the concept of **posthumanism** and its affiliated terms – **posthumanist**, **posthuman**, and **posthumanity**. These terms may denote stances and orientations against humanism. They may also suggest conditions of existence in a world in which humanism is no longer the dominant worldview. However, they sometimes more specifically designate technological capacities which are seen to transcend human abilities and potential. In these different senses, the posthuman is a substitute figure who operates outside the parameters of human existence.

The term "posthuman" is sometimes used very specifically to designate particular technological developments and their consequences (Fukuyama, 2002). Developments in technology, of which artificial intelligence, cybernetics, neuropharmacology, xenotrans-planation, cloning, nanotechnology, genetic manipulation, robotics, prosthetics, and neural-computer integration are only some instances, have been crucial in this regard. However, **transhuman** and **transhumanism** are more specific labels adopted by re-searchers who use new technology in explicit attempts to transcend human life and form.

Thus, posthumanism involves reassessment and reconceptualization of the significance of the designation "human." The coining of this term in the IC20 signals a break from and, some would claim , even a transcendence of humanist frameworks. Posthumanism indicates a shift in orientation toward human relations with **non-humans**, particularly other animate beings (especially animals) and machines. Associated with this term are questions about the power, autonomy, distinctiveness, and identity of the human and about the desire to "absolutize the difference between the human and the nonhuman" (Halberstam and Livingston, 1995: 10).

It may be too sweeping to claim that "people are not afraid of their joint kinship with animals and machines" (Haraway, 1991: 294), not least because concerted defenses of humanism have been mounted (Fukuyama, 2002). Nevertheless, since the IC20, demarca-tion and differentiation of the human figure have become more difficult with the common use of medical technologies such as pace-makers, personality-transforming drugs, and the transfer of organs and genes across species. Technology, however, has not been the only avenue for the exploration of the "joint kinship" to which Haraway alludes, or the only site associated with posthumanism. In Western film and fiction of the IC20 and eC21 there has been a proliferation of figures (monsters, vampires, chimeras, cyborgs) which transcend or disturb the boundaries between humans and other creatures or machines (Hayles, 1999).

Maureen McNeil

See: *BODY, CULTURE, ENVIRONMENT/ECOLOGY, GENDER, HUMAN RIGHTS, JUSTICE, RACE.*

Human Rights

Human rights dialogues have become all the rage in the foreign relations between developing and developed countries in the eC21. Whereas **human rights diplomacy** used to focus on the exposure and condemnation of **human rights violations**, both sides have come to realize that there are benefits in defusing the antagonisms that were inevitable in debates over human rights. This is resulting in **rights** fast becoming divested of any content, particularly in a climate in which the **right to bear arms**, the **rights of the unborn**, and the **right to *in vitro* fertilization** are put by many on an equal footing with the **right to life, liberty, and the pursuit of happiness**.

The foundational moment for modern human rights thought is located in the C17, beginning with Hobbes's right of nature and contracts (1652), Locke's state of perfect freedom (1690), and the 1689 English Bill of Rights, with which Locke was closely associated and which intended to restrict the powers of the king in favor of those of Parliament. The English Bill of Rights also set limits on the legal process and – foreshadowing the 1776 American Declaration of Independence and the 1789 French Declaration of the Rights of Man and Citizen – emphasized the **right to property**. However, it was the American Declaration of Independence that also asserted the "equality of man," his inalienable right to "life, liberty and the pursuit of happiness" (Ishay, 1997). The progression from Rousseau's social contract and Montesquieu's concept of the separation of powers, through to Locke and other proponents of **the rights of man**, thus had as an outcome the rules that were eventually incorporated into the constituent documents of the newly emerged revolutionary states.

The evolution of communitarian, socialist, and anarchist movements in the C19 and their exposure of the exploitation of workers and slaves refined the concept of rights and the relationship between states and the citizen. The elaboration by John Stuart Mill and others of this relationship, and the anti-colonialist struggles of the eC20, added the principle of self-determination to the vocabulary of rights.

If there was a heyday for serious proponents of human rights it would have been in the lC20 following the codification of the range of rights outlined in the International Bill of Rights – the 1948 Universal Declaration of Human Rights (UDHR) and the International Covenants on Civil and Political Rights and Economic, Social, and Cultural Rights (1966) – and the raft of treaties, conventions, and declarations that was an outcome of World War II and the creation of the United Nations and its various agencies. The principles of the universality, indivisibility, and interdependence of rights in the UDHR were endorsed in the Declaration and Program of Action adopted by over 180 countries at the Second World Conference on Human Rights in Vienna in 1993. Meanwhile, the strategies of the **civil rights** movement in the USA – though not explicit about the *human* rights framework – provided models for **human rights activists** around the world.

The UDHR makes no distinction between civil, cultural, economic, political, and social rights. Drafted by legal experts from many of the anti-Axis conquering powers, it was adopted by country delegates representing all the regions of the world. There are some who claim that human rights principles can be found in all religions and cultures (Ghai, 1997). Others say that the concept of all beings having equal and inalienable rights may not be intrinsic to all cultures in all periods, yet even these people will allow that all of these cultures accept that people are entitled to live with and in dignity. Human rights represent the codification of those factors that provide the basis for the guarantee of this dignity.

One of the legacies of the Cold War is the arbitrary division between **civil and political** rights on the one hand and **economic, social, and cultural rights** on the other. The respective ideological positions of the West versus the communist bloc are reflected in two separate Covenants. This divide grew even wider as the West in general and the United States in particular increasingly described economic, social, and cultural rights as merely *aspirational*. Because the International Covenant on Economic, Social, and Cultural Rights speaks of "progressive realization," they are supposed not to have the same weight as civil and political rights and accordingly not to require any action until conditions become favorable for their realization (Eide, Krause, and Rosas, 2001).

The argument that the realization of civil and political rights is cost-free while economic, social, and cultural rights demand resources from the state has been contested for some time both in international forums and among human rights experts. However, it is only since the last decade of the C20, and congruent with the popularization of debates around globalization, that a singular focus on economic, social, and cultural rights has emerged. Through the advocacy of international non-government organizations and with greater clarity from the UN Committee on Economic, Social, and Cultural Rights on their normative content, these rights are becoming part of the vocabulary of development professionals, human rights advocates, and community based organizations (UNDP, 2000).

Yet the **rights-based approach to development** is another term increasingly void of meaning. Originally applied to the theory that development was neither achievable nor sustainable without the realization of human rights (HRCA, 1995), the rights-based approach is now part of the policy statements of most development agencies as well as non-government development organizations (NORAD, 2001). There is little evidence of implementation at the field level and the approach usually remains at the level of rhetoric.

However, in those countries that have most recently gained their independence or thrown off the shackles of past dictatorships it is common to find human rights, including economic, social, and cultural rights, incorporated in new national constitutions and planning documents. Examples include post-apartheid South Africa, Nepal, and most recently East Timor. Many such countries find themselves designated as Heavily Indebted Poor Countries, in regular negotiation with the International Monetary Fund (IMF) and the World Bank over their debt repayments and their inability to mitigate the results of structural adjustment programs. Indeed, the increasing gap between rich and poor, both within and between nation states, is now generally accepted as one of the results of globalization. In response to this, development rhetoric focuses increasingly on poverty reduction strategies; not surprisingly, therefore, human rights advocates are using the commitments to which governments are bound by virtue of their constitutions, their national plans, or their adherence to the UN Charter to urge new priorities that will address the realization of rights. This advocacy extends to the international financial institutions, and the coming human rights struggle will challenge the IMF, the World Bank, the World Trade Organization, and corporations to integrate human rights into their activities (Skogly, 2001).

The trend to hold non-state actors equally accountable for the violation of rights is mirrored by the proliferation of sectoral interest groups claiming their rights. Eric Hobsbawm (1996, *cit*. Ishay, 1997) argues that identity groups are about themselves, for themselves, and nobody else, but there is no question that these groups have been influential in the creation of new standards applying to their own situations. For example, organizations active on HIV/AIDS insist that the issue is one of rights rather than health, and the protection of refugees, asylum seekers, internally displaced persons, migrant workers, and, of course, women is firmly situated within the realm of human rights.

The language of human rights now pervades foreign relations discourse. Yet the new polarization brought about by the 2003 "war on terror" provides the gravest threat to hard-won gains in the human rights field. Governments of all political hues and locations have begun to install new regimes of surveillance, curtail civil liberties, and excuse human rights violations. Paradoxically, this is accompanied by renewed activism not only against this "war" but for a greater focus on holding governments accountable for the realization of rights. Meaningful "participation" is thus an increasing demand in debates about the role of both international and national financial institutions. To be meaningful, however, participation depends on a knowledge of rights, on the freedom to claim them, and on culturally appropriate action. Culture is all too often left out of the discourse of rights, and standard-setting on cultural rights is still in its infancy. As Chidi Anselm Odinkalu points out, "The increasing tendency to exclude culture from references to human rights reinforces the marginalization of the poor, the underprivileged, rural workers generally, and rural women in particular, all victims of the negative interpretation of culture as the dominant power" (Odinkalu, 2001: 331). In contrast, the African Commission on Human and Peoples' Rights, which monitors the African Charter on Human and Peoples' Rights (1986), is explicit in the Mauritania Case, stating that "language is an integral part of the structure of culture ... Its usage enriches the individual and enables him to take an active part in the community and in its activities" (*cit*. Odinkalu, 2001: 331).

Human rights and development advocates have recognized that participation is the link between civil and political rights on the one hand and economic, social, and cultural rights on the other. Thus the right to education features high on their agendas, including education for and about human rights. The language of human rights is not about to be muted by the various new axes of power.

André Frankovits

See: *CITIZENSHIP, INDIGENOUS, MOVEMENTS, PARTICIPATION, RESISTANCE, TOLERANCE.*

171

Identity

Identity is to do with the imagined sameness of a person or of a social group at all times and in all circumstances; about a person or a group being, and being able to continue to be, itself and not someone or something else. Identity may be regarded as a fiction, intended to put an orderly pattern and narrative on the actual complexity and multitudinous nature of both psychological and social worlds. The question of identity centers on the assertion of principles of unity, as opposed to pluralism and diversity, and of continuity, as opposed to change and transformation.

In one respect, what is at issue is the cultivation and valuation of self-hood and **personal identity**, with a concern for the sameness and continuity of the individual. Interestingly, the OED shows the first uses of the concept of identity with respect to the individual to occur only in the C17. At this time, there came into existence what Stuart Hall calls the "Enlightenment subject," based on "the conception of the human person as a fully centered, unified individual, endowed with the capacities of reason, consciousness and action . . . The essential center of the self was a person's identity" (S. Hall, 1992b: 275).

The principle of rationality, the idea of personal identity as "the Sameness of a rational being" (Locke, 1690), has been attenuated through the C19 and C20, and the autobiographical self has tended to become organized around a range of other more cultural attributes, such as character, personality, experience, social position, or lifestyle. If there have been significant shifts in the criteria of individual distinction, however, the principles of autobiographical unity and coherence, and of consistency (even accumulation) through time, have remained central to the autobiographical project.

ABCDEFGH**I**JKLMNOPQRSTUVWXYZ

In another dimension, the question of identity concerns particular ways of imagining and instituting social groups and group belonging. In the case of **collective identity**, too, we may say that the principles of unity and continuity have been foregrounded. The logic of identity has worked in favor of integrity and coherence with reference to what came to be figured as the collective self. First, the group has been conceived as a unitary and homogeneous entity, a community of shared substance, and its internal complexity and diversity disavowed; the prevailing images were of a national family, a single body, shared blood, a common home(land). And, second, the group has sought to maintain its culture – its heritage, memories, values, character, particularity, and uniqueness – through time, and to deny the reality of historical change and discontinuity; positive value was placed on the continuity between generations and on the moral force of tradition.

The paradigm case for this particular conception of collective culture has been the nation state, and the ideal of what Benedict Anderson (1983) has famously called "imagined community" (again a relatively modern cultural invention). In this framework, the question of identity has been restricted to the dimension of belonging. Belonging to such a community – a culture in common – has been regarded as the fundamental condition for self-expression and self-fulfillment. As David Miller (1995: 175) puts it, such an identity "helps to locate us in the world," "tell[ing] us who we are, where we have come from, what we have done." If this suggests the meaning and appeal of collective identities for those who belong, we should also recognize the rationale for the collective unit with which they identify. For " 'identities' are crucial tags by which state-makers keep track of their political subjects . . . The kind of self-consistent person who 'has' an 'identity' is a product of a specific historical process: the process of modern nation-state formation" (Verdery, 1994: 37).

Dominant and conventional discourses on identity may be characterized as being essentialist. They make the assumption that the identity and distinctiveness of a person or a group is the expression of some inner essence or property. From such a perspective, identity is a "natural" and "eternal" quality emanating from within a self-same and self-contained individual or collective entity. More recent and critical accounts, however, have tended to adopt an anti-essentialist position, and to emphasize the socially constructed status of all identities. Identities are seen to be instituted in particular social and historical contexts, to be strategic fictions, having to react to changing circumstances, and therefore subject to continuous change and reconfiguration. What is also made clear is that identities cannot be self-sufficient: they are in fact instituted through the play of differences, constituted in and through their multiple relations to other identities. An identity, then, has no clear positive meaning, but derives its distinction from what it is not, from what it excludes, from its position in a field of differences. This may occur at a quite mundane and banal level, in terms of the narcissism of small differences (to use Freud's term), where Britain, say, distinguishes its identity from that of Germany, France, Italy, or Spain. But this logic of distinction may also work in more problematical ways, where differentiation becomes polarization, with one identity positioned in radical opposition to another – to what is regarded as the fundamental alterity of its other. This is the case, for example, in the revitalized idea of civilizational difference, with its speculations about the escalating "clash of civilizations." Here we should attend to the dark side of identity, to the manner in which, in its strategies of differentiation, identity depends on the creation of frontiers and borders in order to distance and protect itself from the imagined threat of other cultures. The resonant post-September 11 image of a world polarized between civilization (the West) and barbarism (the rest) spoke directly to such anxieties. We may say, then, that there is often fear in the soul of identity.

The question of identity – both individual and collective – has become increasingly salient over the last decade as a consequence of the social and cultural transformations associated with globalization. In the eyes of certain observers, the proliferation of trans-national cultural flows (of people, of commodities, of media and information) has seemed to work to destabilize settled and established identities. It has been felt that the national frame, in which people have constructed their identities and made sense of their lives, has been significantly challenged. There has been the sense that societies are becoming more culturally fragmented, while at the same time being increasingly exposed to the homogen-izing effects of global markets. It can seem as if older certainties and points of reference are being eroded, to be replaced by a superficial new world of consumer choice and off-the-peg identity options. Globalization is consequently seen as heralding an **identity crisis**. And the response of those who feel that their identities are being thus undermined has often been to hold on to and to reassert their familiar ("traditional") cultures and identities. All around the world, we have seen new mobilizations of **ethnic, cultural, and religious identities**: neo-nationalisms in Eastern Europe, for example, or religious fundamental-isms, from India to the Middle East to the US. What this represents is a defense of the logic of *intégrisme* (to use the F), a militant hanging on to the principle of **identity as self-sameness**.

For other observers, however, global change has seemed to be about something quite different: about the loosening of old identities that had become restrictive and limiting, and about the opening up of new possibilities, involving more complex and variable identifications. From such a perspective, Stuart Hall has argued that we are seeing the emergence of new kinds of postmodern subjects and identities. The situation has become such that "the subject assumes different identities at different times, identities which are not unified around a coherent 'self'. Within us are contradictory identities, pulling in different directions, so that our identifications are continuously being shifted about" (S. Hall, 1992b: 277).

First, there is an emphasis on the multiplicity of possible identifications. Identities may involve national or religious allegiances, but may also be to do with consumer choices, lifestyles, and subcultures, with gender, generation, and sexuality, or with involvement in social movements (environmentalism, anti-globalization activities, hunting or anti-hunting lobbies). Second, and perhaps more important, this more positive reading of the possibilities of global change draws attention to the different way in which we may now be implicated in social and cultural identities. **Ascribed identities** are seen to be giving way to new possibilities of identification involving choice and negotiation, and in which there is the accommodation of pluralism and diversity (in place of unity) and change and transformation (in place of continuity). The constructed nature of identity is acknowledged and accepted – for some, identity comes to be considered a kind of performance – and this disillusioning process is not regarded as at all problematical: it is possible to recognize that identity is a fiction, and then to live and work with this fiction. Globalization has expanded the repertoire of identity, then, but, more significantly, it has been working to change the basis of our relation to identity.

Kevin Robins

See: *CIVILIZATION, DIFFERENCE, OTHER, SELF.*

Ideology

The term **ideology** (F *idéologie*) was invented by a group of French philosophers in the lC18 and eC19. These Enlightenment thinkers wanted to bring the new scientific method to an understanding of the mind by offering psychological answers to philosophical questions. Ideology, the science of the mind, was the study of the origin and development of ideas. In particular, these philosophers, known as **ideologues**, traced ideas back to empirical reality and more particularly, following John Locke, to sensations. "Ideology" first appeared in English in 1796 in a translation of the work of one of these philosophers, Destutt de Tracy.

It was taken over by Napoleon Bonaparte, who turned the term on its head, using it to attack the defenders of Enlightenment values (especially democracy) because they divorced the problem of governance from "a knowledge of the human heart and of the lessons of history" (R. Williams, 1976: 154). Ideology was abstract knowledge, not rooted in the realities of human life and self-interest. This pejorative use continued and expanded throughout the C19, when "ideology" was used, primarily by conservatives, to label any supposedly extreme or revolutionary political theory or platform, especially derived from theory rather than experience.

In a sense, Karl Marx (and Friedrich Engels) turned this Napoleonic use on its head (as well as turning Hegel's philosophy, which privileged the reality of ideas over material life and reality, on its head) in the mC19. They returned to the project of the ideologues, offering a theory of the origin and development of ideas, but they located the answers in history and social life. Marx and Engels argued that ideas were nothing but the expression of the material relationships of social life, material relationships "grasped as ideas." There are two distinct **theories of ideology** in their work. In the first, they linked ideology directly to the uneven relations of power. And in the second, "ideology" described the

175

unconscious system of beliefs belonging to any particular class or social group. Both uses assume the possibility of a better – more scientific – knowledge.

According to the first position, ideology is a misrepresentation of the actual material conditions of life, presenting the world as if seen through a camera obscura (in which the image is always upside down). Ideology is distorted knowledge, producing a state of false consciousness for all those living within its understanding of reality. This illusory representation of reality serves the interests of the ruling economic class, which also has the power to define acceptable knowledge of the world. In *The German ideology*, Marx and Engels wrote: "The ideas of the ruling class are in every epoch the ruling ideas; i.e., the class, which is the ruling material force of society, is at the same time its ruling intellectual force" (1974 [1846]: 61). On this view, not only are people living lives that are alienated (or inauthentic), they cannot even realize or recognize that they are alienated.

The second position, while continuing to assert that ideological forms are the expression of material relations, defines ideology as the forms in which people become conscious of their world. On this view, every social class has its own set of ideas that are a direct expression of its material conditions and interests. All ideologies are necessarily partial, offering an incomplete and abstract picture of the world to the group that lives within the world as described by those ideas. The Hungarian philosopher Georg Lukács (1971) argued that this could only be overcome when the working class became fully conscious of itself as the universal class, making its ideology universally true.

This division within the concept of ideology – between a narrow conception of direct determination by relations of power and a broader conception of socially located knowledge – has continued within Marxist and sociological theory. For example, Karl Mannheim (1976) distinguished between particular, explicit political ideologies and the broad *Weltanschauung* or worldview of a society or social group.

Two thinkers have been particularly influential in the past decades in reshaping academic theories of ideology. Antonio Gramsci (1971) emphasized the complexity of the relationships that define human reality at any particular time and place; and he rejected the assumption that such relationships were the necessary result of transcendental forces – like the economy. Consequently, he opposed the tendency to assume that class and/or economic relations necessarily provided the truth about everything. Instead, he argued that human reality was the product of the work of producing or articulating relationships. His concept of hegemony describes an ongoing struggle to create **ideological consensus** within a society, while his concept of common sense emphasizes the fragmentary and contradictory nature of the unconscious meanings and beliefs with which people make sense of their world.

Building on Gramsci, theorists like Ernesto Laclau and Stuart Hall (1996) emphasize that the ideological significance of a text is never directly available from the text itself. A text does not wear its ideological position on its back for all to see. One cannot know it ahead of time, as if it were based simply on the class position or social location of its producer. Hence, ideology is always a matter of work. It cannot be understood in terms of one **dominant ideology**, for it is always an ongoing **ideological struggle**.

Louis Althusser (1970) once more turned the concept on its head by defining ideology as the systems of representation in which people live their relationship to the real conditions of their lives. Ideology is an indispensable dimension of human life, the means through which experience itself is produced. Experience becomes a political reality rather than a natural "fact" that remains free of political determination. For Althusser, then, ideology is always embedded in the actual material practices of the language use of particular social institutions, which he called **ideological state apparatuses**.

One of the most important results of these theoretical developments was that it enabled the concept of ideology to extend its reach beyond the Marxist focus on class, to encompass other dimensions of social division including race, gender, and sexuality. As a result, ideological theories of racism, patriarchy, and homophobia became important aspects of critical thinking in the lC20.

Outside the academy, "ideology" continued to have multiple meanings. It can refer narrowly to an explicit set of political beliefs, such as liberal, conservative, or socialist ideologies, usually assumed to be in conflict. It was in this sense, for example, that some social commentators claimed **the end of ideology** as a result of the supposed liberal consensus following World War II (D. Bell, 1960).

"Ideology" can also refer to broader systems of beliefs, ideas, and attitudes that have direct implications for political commitments and actions. In this sense, the Cold War was seen as a battle between **communist and capitalist ideologies**. Such uses tend to treat "ideology" as a relatively neutral term, since all sides can be said to have an ideology. Yet even so, there is something implicitly negative about the concept, for it is taken to suggest an unnecessary battle between camps, which should be overcome either by consensus among the sides, or by the victory of one side over the others.

Still, the most common use of "ideology" in the l20C was pejorative: ideology is opposed to "fact," "logic," "reason," "philosophy," and even "truth." It is always the other side – and never one's own – that has an ideology. It was in this sense that conservative politicians have always spoken about communism as an ideology.

In the l20C and e21C, the salience of ideology as a political or critical concept has diminished somewhat, partly as a result of the end of the Cold War. The perceived victory of "democratic capitalism" over communism seems to have produced, especially in the West, a perception that there are no longer any alternatives and hence no opposing ideologies. Instead, the struggle is more likely to be seen as a clash of civilizations (often understood as religions).

Nevertheless, the notion of ideology continues to operate in domestic politics, as part of what has been called the "culture wars." In fact, it has revised two meanings from its past. First, ideology is opposed to practicality rather than truth, so that it becomes a way of contemptuously dismissing any principled opposition to the status quo. Ideology is equated with idealism and opposed to realism. This is how conservatives in the e21C dismiss the demands of the left. Second, ideology is equated with the passion of moral certainty and absolutism, and opposed to a thoughtful engagement with complexity and differences. For example, during the Iraq War, liberals distinguished George Bush's focus on "big picture ideological campaigns" with Tony Blair's more sophisticated "idealism without ideologues" (Kristoff, 2003).

Interestingly, the academic centrality of the concept in theoretical debates and political analyses has declined in the e21C. There are at least two reasons for this: one is the influence of new ways of thinking about the nature and forms of power, and about the relations of power, language, and ideas, embodied, for example, in broader notions of common sense, representation, and discourse. The other is the perception that the growing dominance of neo-liberal globalization as the framework for international relations, and the growing power of various new conservative moments in many (but not all) Western nations, cannot be explained by theories of ideological domination, consensus, or struggle.

Lawrence Grossberg

See: *CLASS, CULTURE, DISCOURSE, REASON, REPRESENTATION.*

178   *Image*

The historical trajectory of **image** can be partially mapped out along the shift from the OED's originary sense of "imitation in solid form, as statue or effigy" to the wide range of ephemeral and dematerialized images which dominate much of contemporary experience. But the long-standing flexibility and semantic heterogeneity of "image" is equally significant, as demonstrated by the OED's primary meanings: "imitation, copy, likeness, statue, thought, idea, similitude, shadow."

This plurality suggests some of the ways in which "image," since the 1500s, has always been marked by a fundamental ambiguity in its parallel designation of visual, graphic, perceptual, psychic, and verbal imagery. These disjunctions obviously persist into the present, but they were problematized further during the second half of the C20 by the word's increasing remoteness from its long-standing relation to problems of representation. Many of the current meanings and effects associated with image have their origins in mC19 modernity. But those origins have much less to do with reproductive techniques (photography, for example) than with the emergence of new institutional requirements and social imperatives through which many kinds of images merged with dominant economic networks and the industrialization of cultural production. Capitalist modernization had several major consequences: one of these was the marginalization of the sense of the image as interior, as the mental product or creation of an individual. The sweeping devaluation and incapacitation of a human ability to generate one's own images (or **imagination**) is inseparable from the ascendancy of already manufactured external images, which increasingly become the impersonal raw material of psychic life and determine the formal conditions of all so-called **mental images**. The hegemony of global **image industries** entails the cancellation of the **visionary image**. Simultaneously, the cultural efficacy of the **verbal image** in literary practices has diminished markedly, alongside a much broader disempowerment of language and its communicative potential. Powerful communication technologies are introducing hybrid forms, in which inseparable visual and verbal units constitute a universal texture of imagery, operating both within and on the edges of such systems. In the context of developing electronic systems, many influential distinctions (from Lessing's to Nelson Goodman's) between the rhetorical structure of language and image, of words and pictures, are rendered erroneous or obsolete.

It is probably misleading to overemphasize the shift from analogic image-making practices to digital ones. For the overwhelming number of **image functions** today, it is less relevant culturally whether an image was generated by computer or a camera; what matters is that it be compatible with dominant systems of manipulation, convertibility, circulation, storage, and retrievability. The model of image as a kind of coinage, allowing infinite repetition of the same, was already inadequate by the end of the C19. The chronophotography of Etienne-Jules Marey and Eadweard Muybridge signaled a new dispersal of the classical integrity or self-sufficiency of the image as mold, and prepared the way for an array of kinematic, filmic, televisual forms which would operate through what André Bazin called "a plastics of the image in time" (1971: 24), supplanting James Joyce's nostalgic evocation of the image as "a luminous silent stasis" (1914: 213).

Perhaps not coincidentally the work of Marey, in particular, initiated a deployment of the image within institutional strategies of human management and control, which continues unabated today. Images maximize knowledge about the functioning of human individuals as subjects of medical or surveillance technologies through operations of classification, identification, and correlation. Reproductive biotechnologies and genetic engineering pose the practical possibilities of a **genetic image**, code-as-image, that is independent of individual identity and mortality, surpassing the terms of Shakespeare's admonition in sonnet 3, "Die single and thine image dies with thee" (IC16).

Though the English infinitive **to image** (with its etymological connection to *imitation*) has been in use since the C14, pervasive IC20 **imaging technologies** imply something radically discontinuous: the image as a field of productivity from which value (in the form of information) can be extracted. Not only does the contemporary image subsist on the now familiar axis of time but it also exists as part of an indefinite virtual sequence of technical possibilities (of enhancement and analysis), in which exclusively non-human "imaging" capabilities extract information from images or generate images out of information and quantitative data. The more ways in which something can be "imaged," the more it is subject to predictability and regulation, the more imagery is synonymous with systems of knowledge production. The image is simultaneously commodity and site of productivity, to be consumed and worked on in a single circuit as raw material and consumable product. In related ways, the prevalent sense of the image's unlimited malleability defines key features of contemporary agency and subjectivity: everything or everyone has an image which both constitutes identity and is the site of ceaseless self-fashioning and remaking. Thus the related terms **public image**, **image consultant**, **to remake one's image** define a milieu in which image is both modulating veneer and essence. A vaguely Platonic skepticism of the image persists, but it persists in a culture for which there is nothing meaningful behind or beyond that insubstantial surface or screen.

The second half of the C20 saw a diversity of deeply skeptical responses to the cultural centrality of images, from William S. Burroughs's (the image as virus and narcotic [1964]) to Jean Baudrillard's (the image as depthless simulacrum [1984]). Against such pessimism and cynicism, some key questions concern to what extent images and image-making can participate in practices of resistance – to what extent there can be a politics and counter-practices of the image distinct from the logic of commodification, of instrumentally coded information. The failure of eC20 attempts to build an affirmative **politics of the image** (the films of Sergei Eisenstein and surrealism, for example) led to different but more compromised strategies of appropriation and a dubious hope that dominant codes could be turned against themselves. More recently there has been the suggestion that creative relations between a global field of images and new social imaginations are emerging, as, for example, in Arjun Appadurai's insistence that images are the basis for the empowerment of "imagination as a social practice" and are raw materials for "constructed landscapes of collective aspirations" (1996: 31).

Jonathan Crary

See: *REPRESENTATION, SIGN, SPECTACLE, VIRTUAL.*

Indigenous

Communities of **indigenous peoples** define themselves through strong identification with place. This contrasts with identities which change through history and identify with their history-making capacity. Thus the word **indigenous** emerged as "history-making" European empires labeled colonially subjugated peoples as Natives, Indians, or Aborigines, with a mixture of some admiration for their erstwhile sovereignty and considerably more disdain for their seeming lack of modernity.

Having drowned under the waves of C19 colonial power, the term "indigenous" re-emerged more positively as a postcolonial identity tag in the 1980s and 1990s after political movements initiated by indigenous peoples spread around the world, reaching a high point when 1993 was declared the Year of Indigenous People. Significant in the **indigenous political lobby** were the Native American peoples of Canada and the US, arctic peoples like the Sami of Finland, the Maori of Aotearoa/New Zealand, and the indigenous peoples of Australia. Indigenous peoples are often in the position of having to petition the nation for prior rights over an internal territory. Their priority may be due to earlier occupation by migration, which was then usurped by some colonial power (as in Aotearoa/New Zealand); or they may identify as indigenous if their occupation is so ancient as to seem autochthonous *and* if their culture and economy is very different from that of the nation or people which surround them. Thus Kalahari Bushmen are a hunter-gatherer economy crossing African state borders, the Dalits in the subcontinent of India have a traditionally restricted role in the economy, and the Ainu of Japan have tended to be excluded from the Japanese economy. But the Basques crossing the western French and Spanish border do not identify as indigenous even though their occupation is primordial and their language unique, because they are economically integrated in France and Spain.

The idea of viable indigenous peoples around the world emerged as part of a decolonizing effort that overturned social Darwinist and colonialist conceptual hierarchies. This social vision tended to see different races as representing stages of human physical and cultural evolution. Australian Aborigines could thus be identified, at the beginning of the C20, as "showing anatomical characters very rare in the white races of mankind, but at the same time normal in ape types" (Duckworth, 1904: 69). They were not seen as viable or modern cultures and they were expected to die out because of physical and cultural handicaps. The new perspective of cultural relativism, emerging from anthropological thought, flattened evolutionist hierarchies and tended to see indigenous peoples as having their own cultures and civilizations without reference to Europe as a higher level of achievement. Indigenous peoples, thus having in principle regained a degree of dignity and justice, then had to struggle to regain a lost economic base, which mainly centered on ownership and rights to exploit their ancestral lands which had most often been subsumed within the nation states of the new world.

In 1972 the UN made an important step when its Subcommission on Prevention of Discrimination and Protection of Minorities commissioned a *Study of the problem of discrimination against Indigenous populations* on a world scale (Cobo, 1986–7). While the report detailed the ways indigenous peoples have been defined and classified by governments around the world (and often in terms of these peoples "not matching up" to standards of development, or even in terms of their appearance), it made a significant move toward self-definition: "the fundamental assertion must be that Indigenous populations must be recognized according to their own perception and conception of themselves in relation to other groups" (Cobo, *cit*. Dodson, 1994: 5). The UN document supplements this right to identity with a link to human rights: "The community has the sovereign right and power to decide who belongs to it, without external influence" (Cobo, *cit*. Dodson 1994: 5). Indigenous Australian leader Mick Dodson notes that the definition provided by this study "remains the major reference point for the international community":

181

Indigenous

> Indigenous communities, peoples and nations are those which, having historical continuity with pre-invasion and pre-colonial societies that developed on their territories, consider themselves distinct from other sectors of the societies now prevailing on those territories, or parts of them. They form at present non-dominant sectors of society and are determined to preserve, develop and transmit to future generations their ancestral territories, and their ethnic identity, as a basis of their continued existence as peoples in accordance with their own cultural patterns, social institutions and legal systems. (Cobo, *cit.* Dodson, 1994: 5)

Clearly this definition tries to set the conditions under which cultural continuity can be assured and economic and social development can proceed. In reality, this development has had to compete with other items on government agendas, and in many cases against the competing interests of mining corporations, industrial fisheries, pastoralists, or power-generation facilities. In many cases activist politics has been and still is the tool for **indigenous groups** in these struggles, as they form alliances with environmentalist groups and non-governmental organizations. In other instances specific deals have been struck with governments or corporations so that indigenous peoples can have some control over activities on their lands and gain excise or royalty income in the process. In recent years the concept of multiple stakeholders has emerged as a way of recognizing the plural interests of different communities over territories such as national parks. These might have nominally been returned to native title, but in practice are used by tourists, miners, scientists, and so on.

Recent genetic research on the creation of genetically modified foods and the Human Genome Project have focused attention on the rights of indigenous peoples to protect their own DNA (and that of their plants) from sometimes unscrupulous bio-prospectors working for government agencies or pharmaceutical corporations. While successful research is very valuable in all senses, the indigenous people involved have had to fight for an adequate return on their biological property, just as they have had to assert intellectual property rights for designs and art works which for many years had been appropriated. In this area a significant amount of cultural criticism has been done to ''correct'' demeaning or stereotypical modes of representation of indigenous peoples in the press or in cultural productions. The concept of **indigenous self-determination** emerged in the 1970s as a tool for indigenous peoples to regain control over their cultural and economic production. **Indigenous political movements** have thus produced something of a global cultural renaissance, even if progress for human rights and economic viability still has a long way to go.

Stephen Muecke

See: *COLONIALISM, COUNTRY, HUMAN RIGHTS, POSTCOLONIALISM.*

Individual

Individual comes from L *individuum*, meaning that which is indivisible or cannot be broken up further. In early English usage, it implied the inseparability of bonded elements, as in references to "the hye and indyuyduall Trynyte" (c.1425) and, later, "*Indiuiduall*, not to bee parted, as man and wife" (Cockeram, 1623). From the C17, however, a new and more atomizing conception of **the individual** emerges as a necessarily singular entity. An **individual item** is one that is separate from others. Every human being, who occupies a distinct and self-enclosed body, is **an individual**: "Every man in his physical nature is one individual single agent" (Butler, 1729). These changes of usage formed part of a profound change in the understanding of the person and their relations to society.

Human beings are born into particular families, castes, clans, religious communities, and the wider society. In tribal societies, their social status exhaustively defined their identity such that they identified themselves and were identified by others as sons and daughters of so and so, members of a particular caste, residents of a particular village, and followers of a particular religion. They rarely saw themselves as unique persons with lives and goals of their own. In the West, classical Athens and especially Rome saw the emergence of the idea of the person. Although their social status mattered much to them and defined part of their identity, individuals also saw themselves as unique persons, enjoying an area of life that was their own and in which they were answerable to none. Roman law embodied this view in its distinction between private and public spheres of life and its system of **individual rights**.

Modernity marked the emergence of a new conception of the person. It destroyed many of the traditional social institutions and radically transformed others, freed men and later women from inherited or ascriptive identities, and defined them as naturally **free and self-determining individuals** who wished to make their own choices, shape their own lives, and form their own relationships with others (Popper, 1962). In the modern view – which, however, has traveled only slowly across racial and colonial boundaries – individuals are naturally equal, sovereign over themselves, bound by no ties or obligations to which they have not freely consented, and authors of their lives (J. S. Mill, 1989 [1859]). Their social identity does matter to them but it is contingent, subject to critical reflection, and revisable.

The modern conception of the person gave rise to two new words in the C19. **Individuality** refers to what distinguishes individuals and marks them out from others. It includes not so much the distinct physical features that all have by birth as their unique intellectual and moral achievements and the kind of person into which they have fashioned themselves. **Individualism** refers to the view that individuals alone are the ultimate social reality and that they are ends in themselves and the sole sources of moral values (Birnbbaum and Leca, 1990; Lukes, 1972; Macpherson, 1973). Society is nothing more than its members and their pattern of relationship, and has only an instrumental value.

Individualism has acquired somewhat different associations in different countries. Its English usage stresses **individual liberty**, minimum state intervention, free thinking, and religious nonconformity – as in John Stuart Mill's notion of the "limit to the legitimate interference of collective opinion with individual independence" (1989 [1859]). In France, where it became popular in the aftermath of the French Revolution, it tends to signify self-centeredness and a spirit of rebellion against social norms. In Germany, where it was closely associated with the rise of Romanticism, it tends to stress creativity and originality.

Individualism is not without its critics. For some it is basically a philosophy of selfishness, placing **individual self-interest** over that of others. This criticism rests on a serious confusion. Individualism asserts that all individuals are ends in themselves, not that only one of them is an end in his or her self. All human beings make claims on each other, and none may pursue his or her interest in disregard of that of others. Individualism therefore implies an ethic of reciprocity and mutual obligations, not of selfishness. Indeed nothing in the philosophy of individualism prevents an individual from sacrificing his or her interests for the sake of others.

Some other criticisms of individualism cut deeper. Hegel in the C19 and his contemporary communitarian followers, socialists, and others argue that human beings are profoundly shaped by their society, that their identity is culturally constituted, and that they are deeply enmeshed in a complex web of attachments and affections. The individualist account of the individual as a self-contained, trans-social, and freely self-determining agent is therefore a dangerous fiction. These critics are generally as committed to the individual and cherish individual liberty and independent thought as much as the individualist, but take a social and richer view of the individual.

Bhikhu Parekh

See: *IDENTITY, MODERN, PERSON, PRIVATE, PUBLIC.*

Industry

In one of its senses **industry** has referred since the C14 to a particular quality of a person. Someone who was **industrious** demonstrated the virtue of persevering to perform a task. In the IC20 the meaning shifted, so that for a person to be described as industrious may now suggest that they are rather boring and lack sparkle – far better, it would seem, to be "smart." Indeed, it is now common to invest non-humans with such a quality – hence "smart machine." By a peculiar twist, this leads us back to the other meaning of "industry," for historically it has often meant **manufacturing industry**, the place where machines were made and put to work. With the spread of capitalist social relations into more and more sectors we now have the **leisure industry**, the **entertainment industry**, and most recently, with the threatened further incursion of commodity relations into human reproduction, the **embryo industry**. Other extensions (though usually disapproving) are the **heritage industry** and, also playing on the idea that something has become a livelihood which should not be so, the **race relations industry**.

This tendency to widen the application of "industry" has not been matched with respect to some of the term's derivative usages. Forms such as **industrial relations** and even **industrialization** have either declined in use or been rivaled by distinctly different concepts. For example, in 1975, a leading student of industrial relations wrote of the subject that most experts would regard it as "virtually self-evident" that they should concentrate their attention on the collective bargaining activities of trade unions (Hyman, 1975: 9). Today, partly in response to the decline in trade unionism, and partly as a consequence of a wider ideological offensive, even the experts themselves are typically no longer to be found in company or university departments of industrial relations. They now inhabit departments of human resource management. Industrial relations has given way to employee relations. In keeping with this, most newspapers no longer have journalists who specialize in industrial relations but only ones who cover employee relations.

"Industrialization" has taken on an extended application with reference to societies that have recently undergone significant economic development. Brazil, South Korea, Taiwan, and Singapore are all commonly referred to as **NICs (newly industrializing countries)**. By contrast, in the advanced capitalist societies, "industrialization" has now been rivaled by another term, **deindustrialization.** This signifies the reversal of the tendency that occurred with the **Industrial Revolution**. In 1978 it was said of the new term "deindustrialization" that it had "gatecrashed the [specialist economics] literature, thereby avoiding the entrance fee of a definition" (Blackaby, 1978: 1). Generally, though, it has come to refer to a decline in employment in manufacturing (rather than in output, which generally continues to grow). As such, it meshes with the idea of a **postindustrial society** – a society which was brought about by a shift of the labor force from agriculture to industry, then from industry to services, followed, in the view of its first modern advocate, Daniel Bell (1974), by the emergence of a new knowledge society.

As Bell himself was aware, the term "postindustrial" had appeared much earlier. It is first found in the work of Arthur J. Penty, a Guild Socialist and follower of John Ruskin and William Morris, who called for a return to a decentralized, small-workshop, artisan society in the eC20 (Penty, 1917, *cit*. D. Bell, 1974: 37). It continued to appear in the lC20, but in its more recent versions it shares little with Bell's own "venture in social forecasting." The more recent versions rest on the assumption that history is in the process of proceeding one step further than Bell had envisaged – from the decline of employment in agriculture, to a decline in manufacturing, and then to a decline in services and – with no new development to make good this supposed loss – to the end of work (Rifkin, 1995). In fact, the idea of an end of work is often advanced with scant regard to the evidence. It gained some plausibility from the unemployment that followed the end of the post-war boom and which challenged the idea of full employment; from the disappearance in particular of many manufacturing jobs in the advanced capitalist societies; and from related fears about the regenerative powers of Western economic systems in the face of the information technology revolution and globalization. In particular, the "re-engineering" of the corporation meant widespread and highly visible job losses, which made it appear, especially to some American commentators, that work truly would come to an end (or would decline in the United States [Greider, 1997], which for many was the same thing).

Over the last 30 years, management consultants and corporations have invented a whole new lexicon of management jargon to camouflage their actions and to stem widespread fear of job loss – the contracting out of work became "outsourcing," the removal of levels of management became "delayering," cutting jobs became "downsizing" (Donkin, 2001: 249). Yet out of the widespread fear of job loss new utopian thinkers have emerged, the so-called **postindustrial utopians** (Frankel, 1987). André Gorz, for example, argues that we should fight not against the destruction of work but against efforts to perpetuate the ideology of work as a source of rights. He looks forward to a guaranteed income for all, and sees a move beyond wage-based society presaging a new freedom (Gorz, 1999). In similar vein, others have argued for a society in which people are no longer allowed to starve to death – or to become increasingly enslaved by addiction to work. In such a society, it is argued, a reduction in work hours for all can make possible a new era of "postwork" in which more time will be devoted to civil labor, and a radical participatory democracy will become a real possibility (Aronowitz and Cutler, 1998; Bowring, 1999). In such a world – remote prospect though it is – there would be plenty of scope for people to be industrious, but they would be much less likely to demonstrate this virtue with reference only to industry.

Theo Nichols

See: *CAPITALISM, COMMODITY, MANAGEMENT, WORK.*

Information

The primary definition is traceable to the C15. Here **information** refers to a record or communication of an event, fact, or subject. This neutral meaning has superseded, but it has not entirely displaced, the notion that information involves the formation of mind or character, as in the novitiate being instructed in information necessary for entry into the clergy, law, or teaching, or even into worthwhile adult life. This secondary sense of information connotes a superior condition, as in someone being an **informed person**. Here an old, now much diminished, conception of information having an uplifting quality remains especially in the adjectival form (**informed**) that has been lost with regard to the noun (information).

The primary meaning of information is characteristically positioned on an ascending scale, above data, but below knowledge and wisdom. Information thus may be a news report of an event ("information from the battlefield is that 20 men were injured"), about a person ("David is 25 years old"), or a place ("Dorset is a county in southwest England"). Precise distinctions between data, information, knowledge, and wisdom are impossible to make, hence the term has fuzzy boundaries. An implied hierarchy of understanding is always evident, with data being the most basic unit ("20 percent of the respondents to the question are graduates"), while knowledge is more generalizable than information ("Boyle's Law states that the pressure and volume of a gas are in inverse proportion to each other at constant temperature"), and wisdom signifies a high level of learning combined with rich experience and capacity to apply both judiciously. It is not difficult to appreciate these distinctions, but their application is fraught with ambiguity (Roszak, 1986). While the words are distinguishable in terms of a move away from the specific toward the general and abstract, they may only be accurately perceived in context.

In common parlance information is conceived semantically – that is, as having meaning, since it is intelligence or instruction about something or someone. Claude Shannon and Warren Weaver (1964), in developing **information theory** in the mC20, defined information in a radically different way. The word "information," in this theory, is used in a special sense that should not be confused with its ordinary usage. Here information must *not* be confused with meaning. In information theory, information is a quantity which is measured in "bits" and defined in terms of the probabilities of occurrence of symbols. It is a definition derived from and useful to the communications engineer whose interest is with the storage and transmission of symbols, the minimum index of which is on/off (yes/no or 0/1). This allows information to be mathematically tractable, but it explicitly ignores information as a semantic phenomenon. Indeed, two messages, one heavily loaded with meaning and another pure nonsense, may be exactly equivalent from the information theorist's point of view. This notion has been enormously influential in mathematics and in the development of computer science, but it is a particular and specialist definition of the word, quite at odds with the everyday conception of information.

It is common to associate information with a reduction in uncertainty, especially in economic and engineering thinking. In these terms, information enables enhanced control, whether over economic affairs or over technological performance. The uncertainty-reducing features of information are central to economic analyses of decision-making, as they are to the identification of errors in the transmission of signals in engineering. However, a countervailing tendency, particularly prominent in current sociology and postmodern thought, associates information with an increase in uncertainty. The argument here is there is so much information now available and unceasingly generated that scarcely anything may be held any longer with surety. Once-firm beliefs are routinely challenged by alternative information nowadays, and there is such an amount of information encountered that people easily come to abandon convictions, whether of morality, religion, or even the "truth" of what is happening in the world. A result is uncertainty, insecurity, and anxiety.

Information

Toward the end of the C20 "information" became a popular prefix to a range of concepts that claimed to identify essential features of an emerging new sort of society. The **information explosion**, **information age**, **information economy**, **information revolution**, and especially **information society** became commonplace descriptions (Castells, 1996–8; Webster, 2002). These covered, and tried to conceive, disparate phenomena, perhaps unwarrantedly. The concepts appeared superficially to capture similar phenomena, yet on closer inspection centered often on quite different things. For example, their concern ranged over a general increase in symbols and signs that accelerated from the 1960s (the information explosion); the development of information and communications technologies, especially the Internet (the **information superhighway**, reputedly coined by US vice-president Al Gore); the increased prominence of information in employment (**information scientists, information labor, information professions**); the growing significance of tradable information (information economy); and concerns for new forms of inequality (the **information divide**, the **information rich/poor**).

There appears to be a broad consensus that the expansion and ubiquity of information, in its many forms, is a distinguishing feature of contemporary societies (Lash, 2002). One may think here of the growth of media technologies (video, cable, television, satellite), of advertising (campaigns, posters, placements), of news and entertainment services (from CNN to Al-Jazeera, from DVD movies to computer games), of fashion, image, and style, of information-intensive occupations (teaching, accountancy, and design, for example), and of the development of education systems around the world. A problem is that the term "information" here may be overextended, having to cover too many areas that, it is suggested, share a common feature. It is questionable whether such activities can be seen legitimately in these homogenous ways. The extraordinary range and differences among things so encompassed – from an increase in the economic salience of information, a remarkable extension of media, and the increased provision of education to technological innovations in computers and communication – may not fit the single category.

Characteristically, conceptions of an information society embrace evolutionary themes, the term suggesting a higher stage of development than hitherto. In this way the information society retains something of the suggestion of a higher-order state evident in the implication of an informed populace. This is especially the case when the synonym "knowledge society" is adopted. When most commentators speak of an information society the implication is that this is a desirable condition. Significantly, the major elements of the information society are the same as those of the postindustrial society as delineated by American sociologist Daniel Bell (1974). It is arguable that the information society is largely a restatement of this somewhat conservative concept (Kumar, 1995).

Where observers recognize problems of inequality in the information age, they may reimagine the areas to argue that the key issue is not maldistribution of material resources (money, food, housing, etc.), but rather a matter of unequal informational access (for example, to education, libraries, Internet facilities). The proposed solutions tend to offer not redistribution of wealth, but instead improved access to information (Norris, 2001).

Frank Webster

See: *KNOWLEDGE, NETWORK.*

Intellectual

Intellectual, denoting a category of people whose social status rests on their claim to **intellectual expertise** (but who are not simply writers, philosophers, or artists), dates from the eC19, and seems to have served at first primarily to mock those who, lacking particular training or skills, aspired to a generalized knowledgeableness and to the authority it brings with it. It is perhaps no accident that the OED's earliest reference in this sense is Byron's put-down of women with pretensions to learning (1819): "But – oh! ye lords of ladies intellectual, Inform us truly, have they not hen-peck'd you all?" The negative connotations, freely extended to men, continue throughout the C19, carrying implications of abstractness, coldness ("cold intellectualism," 1859), and ineffectiveness ("the so-called intellectuals of Constantinople, who were engaged in discussion while the Turks were taking possession of the city," 1898).

Raymond Williams notes in *Keywords* that one of the reasons for this negative valuation is a hostility to rationalistic social theory. Another, he says, is "a crucial kind of opposition to groups engaged in intellectual work, who in the course of social development had acquired some independence from established institutions, in the church and in politics, and who were certainly seeking and asserting such independence through lC18, C19 and C20" (R. Williams, 1976: 141). Williams thus locates the word's field of social tensions in the developing class position of what might be called knowledge workers. Yet it is important to distinguish between this broad sociological way of thinking about intellectuals as a group, and a narrower and more normative conception of intellectuals as a small elite of men and women of letters acting as public spokespersons for the "noble" disciplines of knowledge (philosophy, the arts, the social sciences, the higher natural sciences) and commenting on the full range of public and intellectual affairs. In the latter sense, the intellectual's task of implementing enlightenment and modernity is understood in heroic terms. This image of a "free-floating intelligentsia" (Mannheim, 1976: 155), descended from the *philosophes* of the French Enlightenment and "speaking truth to power" (Said, 1994: 71), is beguiling and sometimes even true, but is best replaced by a more skeptical analysis.

The Italian Marxist Antonio Gramsci argues in *The prison notebooks* that the criterion for distinguishing the activities of intellectuals from those of other social groups must be sought not in the intrinsic nature of those activities but in their social function; all work

189

involves some degree of intellectual creativity, and thus "all men are intellectuals, one could say: but not all men have in society the function of intellectuals" (Gramsci, 1971: 9). What is that function? For Gramsci it is precisely to be the "functionaries" of the superstructures – to administer the state, the legal system, the church, education, and the technical and scientific aspects of production. Intellectuals are managers and professionals, "the dominant group's deputies exercising the subaltern functions of social hegemony and political government" (p. 12). They can be divided between the **organic intellectuals** who arise within every social class except the peasantry, and the **traditional intellectuals**, the priests, administrators, scholars, scientists, and so on, who claim a certain autonomy of the social field, and who thereby betray their lack of it.

If intellectuals are those whose work is socially defined as being based upon the possession and exercise of knowledge, whether that knowledge be prestigious or routine, technical or speculative, then the central question becomes one about the kind of social interests that go along with possessing and exercising knowledge, about whether those interests are strong and coherent enough to give intellectuals some kind of relative independence as a social group, and about how those interests align intellectuals in relation to the power of the state or of a ruling class. Some of the recent answers given to these questions arise out of a dissatisfaction with the ambivalence of the Marxist tradition, at once contemptuous of the complicity of intellectuals with power (a reaction taken to its murderous extreme in the Chinese Cultural Revolution and in the peasant fundamentalism of Pol Pot's Kampuchea), and yet giving them a vanguard role in the revolutionary party. For theorists such as C. Wright Mills (1964), Alvin Gouldner (1979), John and Barbara Ehrenreich (1979), John Goldthorpe (1982), and Erik Olin Wright (1979), intellectuals in the traditional sense must be understood in relation to the larger formation of middle-class knowledge workers who share elements of a common culture and a common class situation.

Alvin Gouldner (1979) uses the concept of a New Class to describe this larger group, taking the term from Milovan Djilas (1957) and others writing about the formation of a "new class" of intellectuals and functionaries in the former communist bloc. Gouldner locates its origins in the Enlightenment processes of secularization and modernization, in the culture of rationality and personal autonomy that emerges from feudalism, and above all in the institutions of public education and of a market in which educational qualifications are exchangeable values. Its importance as a force in developed capitalism is due, however, to structural changes such as the increased importance of technology in production and the specialization of management and co-ordination practices in the design of labor processes and in the market. For the Ehrenreichs (1979), the social function of what they call the professional-managerial class is in the broadest sense the reproduction of the class structure of capitalism, including both the ongoing reorganization of the productive process through scientific and managerial innovation, and the reproduction of social relations through the schooling system and the culture industries. In cultural terms, finally, this stratum or class is given a considerable degree of coherence by a common culture of work (the ethos of professionalism and of service work), a common possession of cultural capital acquired in tertiary institutions, and an orientation to a discursive ethos which relies on justification by argument rather than an appeal to authority or precedent, and which values explicitness, universality of reference, and self-problematization. As enlightened reason, this ethos underlies both technical or instrumental reason and critical or symbolic reason, and is thus at some level common both to intellectuals and to the technical intelligentsia. Whether this makes the knowledge class either a unified or a progressive social force is open to question, but it does explain its commitment to the implementation of modernity in every sense of that word.

John Frow

See: *INFORMATION, KNOWLEDGE, MANAGEMENT, MODERN, REASON, THEORY.*

Justice

In its ordinary usage, **justice** implies treating individuals impartially and giving them their due as determined by general rules or principles. Courts, which apply laws to individual cases, are said to be part of a **system of justice**, and judges are said to dispense or administer justice. Justice is done when the law is applied impartially and without fear or favor. The idea that justice consists in treating similar cases similarly and dissimilar ones differently is beautifully captured by the conventional image of a blindfolded woman holding the **scales of justice** evenly.

Justice, however, is not limited to the application of the law. We often ask if the law itself or the wider social structure is **just** (Barry, 1995; Campbell, 1988). Some writers, usually called positivists, dismiss the question on the ground that since the law is the source of justice, it cannot itself be considered just or **unjust**. It can be a good or a bad, a wise or an ill-conceived law, but not just or unjust. This is an unduly narrow usage of the term that has no sanction either in the ordinary usage or in logic.

The Greeks, who systematically reflected on justice and gave us many of our ideas on the subject, thought that a **just law** or **just society** was one that gave individuals their due or what they were morally entitled to claim. What was due to individuals was determined by what they deserved, and what they deserved depended on their merit or intellectual and moral capacities. Persons of superior capacities deserved greater respect, honor, reward, or higher offices than those with less. The Greek equation of justice with desert, and of the latter with merit, is reflected in our ordinary usage. We say that it is unjust to give to individuals what they do not deserve or merit, and not to give them their **just deserts** for what they do.

ABCDEFGHI**J**KLMNOPQRSTUVWXYZ

Stoics and Christian writers introduced a different conception of justice. While admitting that desert was an important component of justice, they insisted that need was just as important. All human beings were made in the image of God, had equal dignity and worth, and had an equal claim on the earth's resources. Their basic needs had equal claims to satisfaction, and others had a **duty of justice** to meet them. Christian writers, especially Thomas Aquinas, argued that those with superfluous goods had a justice-based duty to share them with the needy, and even that the latter had a right in an emergency to help themselves with these goods. The Christian influence is evident in our ordinary usage. We think it unjust that some people should starve in the midst of plenty or that some should have so little when others have more than enough. The question whether they deserve or merit this is irrelevant.

From the IC18 onward, many writers have pushed the association of justice with need yet further. Human beings have not only basic physical needs, but also many others. They need equal opportunity to develop their talents, and equal access to material and moral resources to lead decent lives. Justice demands that these should be available to them all. This way of thinking is embodied in the term **social justice**, first used in the IC19 (Miller, 1976).

Libertarian writers such as Hayek (1976) and Nozick (1974) question the idea of social justice. In their view it involves a misguided program of redistribution of wealth, an unwise government intervention in the workings of the market, and an unjust interference with individual liberties and right to property. They take a formal and limited view of justice, and contend that a just government should not go beyond maintaining a formal system of rights and liberties.

Justice is concerned not only with the distribution of rights and resources but also with **criminal justice** or the punishment of those who have violated the law. Punishment is generally considered just if it meets the following criteria. First, it should be inflicted only on those who have been convicted of wrongdoing in a fair trial. Second, those guilty of identical wrongdoing should receive the same punishment. Third, punishment should be proportionate to the degree of wrongdoing. Hanging a person for stealing a bar of chocolate is as unjust as imposing a paltry fine for murdering one's spouse. Whether or not we should have capital punishment or the system of imprisonment in the first instance are questions that fall outside the purview of justice.

Like justice, public order, social harmony, freedom, and equality are also great moral and political values (Raphael, 1990; Walzer, 1983). Sometimes they conflict, and then we need to strike a balance. We may suspend the justly deserved punishment of a person when this is in the public interest or as an act of mercy. Affirmative action does injustice to more meritorious candidates, but may be necessary to counter inherited disadvantages or secure social integration. And we may decline to undertake an extensive and otherwise just redistributive program in the interest of liberty or social stability (Rawls, 1999). Since justice itself is part of the conflict, it cannot tell us how to resolve it.

Bhikhu Parekh

See: *EQUALITY, FREEDOM.*

Knowledge

Knowledge is a fiercely contested site in modern societies. Questions of who possesses it – of who is entitled to claim the genuine article – elicit strong emotions. The intensity generated by issues of evidence, of authority, and of expertise reflects a way of thinking of knowledge which has become so familiar that it is difficult to see alternatives.

Although it is an abstraction, knowledge seems a remarkably solid part of our world – a secure end-state, even a product – standing independently of the cumulative struggles of its achievement. It can come as a surprise, then, that its reputed origins emphasize a verbal use – ''to knowledge'' – which has disappeared from the way we now use the term. We cannot now ''knowledge'' our misdeeds (c.1450) or ''knowleche'' ourselves to be traitors (c.1440), as speakers could in the C15. We are unlikely to experience this as a deprivation. But keeping in mind that our familiar noun may be derived from a long-lost verb may alert us to some important but often neglected connotations of knowledge as intellectual activity.

The connotations of end-state and fixity in our current understanding of knowledge come out in the way we now think of knowledge as information or data which can be ''stored'' and ''retrieved.'' The storage metaphor is not new. Samuel Johnson (1753) could observe that ''He is by no means to be accounted useless or idle who has stored his mind with acquired knowledge.'' But such metaphors of well-stocked minds evoke an active exercise of lively intelligence. The same individual mind both stores and puts to use the acquired goods. Contemporary storage metaphors are more likely to evoke virtual repositories of computer systems and data banks. All this no doubt is in many ways a liberation

ABCDEFGHIJ**K**LMNOPQRSTUVWXYZ

for modern knowers. It frees up a great deal of space occupied by unread books on dusty shelves; and it gives us a feeling of security, confident that we – or at any rate someone – can always find again what has been put into storage, should it ever be needed. Ironically, knowledge as solid object seems to have reached its ultimate fixity by being sent into the ether of cyberspace.

The idea of knowledge as standing independent of the processes through which it has been acquired encourages us to think that it also stands above the operations of power – above the passions, the politics, and the institutional contexts of knowers. It is a way of thinking of knowledge that has been challenged by Michel Foucault (1980). Rather than thinking of knowledge as providing a neutral standpoint from which we can evaluate the operations of power, Foucault argues, we should think in terms of changing configurations of **power/knowledge** in specific historical formations.

There is, however, a strong magnetism which draws us to the idea of knowledge as transcendent end-state or product. The idea of a secure – however ethereal – object, which once attained can be stored, accumulated, and cherished, is grounded largely in philosophical ideals of certainty that were refined in C17 rationalism. The conviction that indubitability attaches to any knowledge worthy of the name persists from the philosophy of René Descartes. However, C18 thinkers were more skeptical about the ideal of certainty – more prone to rest **knowledge claims** on experience, common sense, or probability, rather than indubitability. David Hume (1978 [1739]: 274), at the end of book one of *A treatise of human nature*, admonishes himself for his tendency to forget both his skepticism and his modesty in continuing to use such terms as "'tis evident, 'tis certain, 'tis undeniable."

Hume's contemporary Voltaire was also critical of the preoccupation with certainty. Whereas Montaigne's motto was "What do I know?" Voltaire (1971 [1770]: 75) complains in his *Philosophical dictionary* that that of many of his contemporaries is "What do I not know?" Such demands that we admit our lack of knowledge may be taken as a salutary call to humility with regard to overly confident claims to the exalted status of certainty. But there is implicit in Voltaire's sardonic remarks a deeper critique of the ideal of certainty itself. Hume expresses a similar preference for the putting of questions – for the activity of the search, over the fixity of the end-state or products of knowledge. In his famous discussion of curiosity at the end of book two of the *Treatise of human nature*, he compares the love of truth to the activity of hunting: in both the pleasure resides in "the motion, the attention, the difficulty, and the uncertainty" – in the pursuit rather than in having the birds on the table (1978 [1739]: 451).

The celebration of the true wisdom of the philosophers as residing in active seeking and questioning, rather than in the fixity of certainty, runs throughout the history of Western philosophy. Plato identified the philosopher as the lover, the seeker, of wisdom rather than its possessor. True wisdom, as he has Socrates insist in a number of his dialogues, resides not in knowing that one knows but rather in knowing that one does not know. In his own version of the storage metaphor, Plato has Socrates, in the *Theaetetus*, reflect that knowledge cannot be construed on the analogy of birds kept in an aviary; what matters is the attempt to catch and hold them – elusive though that goal may be.

One of our contemporary admirers of Voltaire, the Canadian philosopher and political theorist John Ralston Saul (1995: 313), identifies wisdom, in his *Doubter's companion*, as "life with uncertainty." Such an ideal is bound to be disconcerting to contemporary knowers. We expect certainty and predictability. Our vulnerabilities to fate and fortune are often recast as foreseeable, manageable "risks." Our social practices often presume that when things go badly for us there is always someone who can be held accountable. As the consequences of those assumptions unfold in our legal liabilities, our insurance industries, our health systems, we may well ponder whether knowing that we do not know – but that we must nonetheless continue to think and to judge – may not be a better guide in uncertain times than the illusory security of certainty.

Genevieve Lloyd

See: *INFORMATION, INTELLECTUAL, REASON, SCIENCE, THEORY.*

Liberalism

Although **liberalism** derives from the eC19, the adjective **liberal** has a longer history. The connotations of its early English usage are mainly positive. The **liberal arts** were those judged worthy of free men. When contrasted with the servile or mechanical arts, the term organized a powerful set of social distinctions between those judged to be free from the constraint of occupation and the control of others and those who, lacking such freedom, were denied the capacity for free and autonomous thought required for participation in political and civic affairs. Hence for Edmund Burke the opposition between those of "low rank" and those enjoying "a more liberal condition" (1757).

This equation of "liberal" with "freedom from constraint" is evident in more general usage – to be of **liberal generosity**, or a **liberal host**, for example. Yet the term has also always had pejorative associations in circumstances where freedom from constraint is judged to be carried to excess, resulting in vulgarity or licentiousness – as in Thomas Kyd's reference to stopping "the vulgar liberall of their tongues" (1594).

Aspects of these contrary evaluations characterize the early history of "liberalism" as a key term in the political vocabularies of modern societies (Bramsted and Melhuish, 1978). First used in the early years of the C19 by Spanish writers to describe those of their political leaders who advocated constitutional monarchy and parliamentary government, the term soon traveled to Britain, where the Tories criticized their opponents as "liberal" for advocating "continental" and "un-English" political principles. British Whigs welcomed the term and gave it a laudatory meaning. By the 1840s, "liberalism" had become popular, along with "socialism" and "communism," and came to refer to a more

ABCDEFGHIJK**L**MNOPQRSTUVWXYZ

or less coherent vision of man and society characterized by the wish to free all individuals from arbitrary and unnecessary constraint.

The term subsequently traveled to other European countries and later to the United States, in each of which it acquired somewhat different meanings and represented different policies. In France "liberalism" retains a strong connotation of moral anarchy and rebelliousness; in Britain it stresses individual liberty and limited government; and in the United States, where it did not become current until well into the C20, it conveys a strong and active government, concentration of power in the federal government, and support for affirmative action. Despite these differences between different national traditions, which have persuaded many writers to talk of **liberalisms** in the plural (J. Gray, 1989), certain core ideas remain common to them all.

Those subscribing to the **liberal vision** of human beings and society do not always approve of the policies of political parties calling themselves liberal. In Britain and elsewhere, this has led to a distinction between "liberal" (with a small "l") and **Liberal** (with a capital "L"). The former refers to those sharing the **liberal philosophy**, the latter to **liberal political parties** and their members. Not all liberals are Liberals. And since political parties promiscuously borrow each other's ideas and policies in their competition for power, not all Liberals are always liberal.

Liberalism stresses the supreme value of the individual. Society, state, and nation have no independent existence and value of their own. They are simply the outcomes of individuals related to each other in certain ways, and exist to promote individual well-being. Human beings are endowed with certain common natural desires and capacities, above all rationality, and are all morally equal. As beings who are capable of self-determination and know their interests best, they need and demand the freedom to shape their lives and to make their own choices. For liberals, liberty or freedom is the emblem of human dignity, a major constituent of human well-being, and represents the highest moral and political value (Hayek, 1960).

The state's main task is to maximize individual liberty consistently with that of others. This is best done by establishing a regime of rights, especially to life, liberty, and property, the three fundamental and universally shared human interests. The state cannot protect these rights unless it is strong enough to make its will prevail over all other social agencies. Liberals therefore argue that it should have the monopoly of the right to use force and the capacity to act decisively. Such a state, however, can also pose a threat to individual liberty. Liberals therefore limit it by such means as enshrining basic rights in the constitution, institutionalizing the separation of powers and a system of checks and balances, the independent judiciary, the rule of law, and a strictly regulated use of executive discretion. This complex and much misunderstood idea of a strong but limited government is central to liberal thought.

Historically liberalism grew up in the shadow of and was profoundly influenced by the religious wars of the C17. Liberals remain deeply suspicious of religious passions and seek to tame and keep them out of public life. They advocate a policy of tolerance and view religion as a purely personal matter for individuals. The state neither interferes with it nor allows it to shape the policies of the state, and scrupulously maintains a safe distance from it. The French *laïcité* and the United States doctrine of "the wall of separation" are good examples of this. England, for long envied as the home of liberalism, has an established church, but English liberals have generally been highly critical of it.

The rise of liberalism was closely connected with the emergence of what the C18 writers called the commercial classes and their C19 successors the bourgeoisie. Not surprisingly, it had a strong economic core and advocated laissez-faire or the view that the state should keep out of the economic life of society. In the liberal view the market has its own internal mechanisms to correct its imbalances, and functions best when individuals are left free to decide for themselves what to do with their labor and money. State interference disturbs these mechanisms and is almost invariably misguided. It also tends to combine political and economic power, and poses a grave threat to individual liberty.

When the developing capitalist system began to throw up large pockets of poverty and vast economic inequalities from the middle decades of the C19 onward, liberals were divided (Neal, 1997). Some continued and still continue to advocate the policy of laissez-faire, and bitterly opposed trade unions, minimum wages, laws regulating working conditions, and so on. Initially called **Manchester liberals**, their principles have recently been revived in the free market philosophies characterizing the **neo-liberalism** of the post-Reagan and Thatcher eras. Other liberals saw that at least some form of state regulation of the economy was needed to protect individual liberty and social order. They continued to call themselves liberals and became the historical inheritors of **classical liberalism**. Some of them, such as J. S. Mill (1989 [1859]) and T. H. Green, went even further. They argued that the state had a duty to create conditions in which all its citizens could lead a life of dignity and self-fulfillment. This egalitarian or **social liberalism** – or, in the eC20, **new liberalism** – sometimes brought liberalism closer to socialism and social democracy, and remains a powerful strand in contemporary liberalism.

The rise of the working classes and their demands for the right to vote from the third decade of the C19 onward gave rise to a movement for democracy. Almost all liberals thought that the related ideas of equality and majority rule threatened individual liberty. Some of them continued to oppose democracy. Others, who realized that the democratic movement was unstoppable and had much to be said for it, explored ways of coming to terms with it. **Liberal democracy** as we know it today is a result of this compromise, and all liberals today are strongly committed to it. Its liberal and democratic components regulate each other, and their creative tension explains both the vitality and the conflicts of contemporary liberal democracies.

Bhikhu Parekh

See: *DEMOCRACY, GOVERNMENT, HUMAN RIGHTS, INDIVIDUAL, STATE, TOLERANCE.*

Management

Management derives from the verb "to manage." Williams traces this to It *maneggiare* (to train horses, implying "take in hand"), but notes its intersection with oF *menager,* to use carefully (deriving from *menage,* household) (R. Williams,1976: 189–90). This mixture is visible in the meanings currently in circulation, ranging from a sense of limited achievement (**just managing**, **managing to get by**), through a purposive sense of direct-ing or organizing oneself and/or others, to the more organizationally specific function (managing things and people as a **manager**, emerging in the C18). "Management" usually refers to the practice of directing an enterprise, activity, or organization, or to the group of people who perform such a function – **the management**.

The C20 spread of management is grounded in the rise of the corporate organizational form as the normative model of capitalist enterprise. In the 1940s James Burnham (1941) discussed the **managerial revolution** associated with the separation of ownership and control in corpor-ations, giving effective power of direction and control to a salaried class/cadre of **professional managers**. Although the thesis has been much contested – particularly the view that it marks a shift away from capitalism – the **managerial function** and the **managerial class** have grown consistently. The USA has led the way in the formation of this class as a global phenomenon, exporting both the corporate organizational form and the managerial cadres to staff it.

"Management" has been both a generic term – referring to the practice of co-ordinating organizations – and a dazzling variety of specialized activities and approaches. Reflecting differences in the control processes of organizations, management has been divided into functional subsets (**financial management**, **personnel management**, **marketing**

ABCDEFGHIJKL**M**NOPQRSTUVWXYZ

management, or **image management**) or into organizational hierarchies (**strategic management**, **middle management**, **junior management**, and so on). Attempts in the eC20 to systematize the activity placed a strong emphasis on its rational character, for example, in Taylor's conception of **scientific management** (Braverman, 1974). Such conceptions reveal the imperative to take control of labor processes within the capitalist enterprise. Many of the subsequent innovations in **management style** can be seen as ways to deal with the recalcitrance and intractability of labor forces (though this is usually discussed in terms of motivation and performance). Until the IC20, **management models** evolved quite slowly, but there has been a flowering of innovations, revolutions, and transformations in the market for new managerial tricks, techniques, and tactics. Most of these have had short lives (and a limited evidential base), but have majored in inspiration, excitement, and drama. Searching for "excellence," "transformational leadership," "giants learning to dance," "re-engineering business processes," and "the leadership style of Attila the Hun" have been among the possible routes to success touted in the managerial marketplace.

This development reflects other social trends (particularly in the dynamics of US enterprises). During the period of Fordism, corporate strategy placed great emphasis on horizontal and vertical integration of the enterprise, structured in long chains of general and functionally specific management. This form of management was associated with company identification, the accumulation of experience and seniority, long career ladders, and bureaucratic systems – typified by W. H. Whyte (1960) as the world of the "organization man"(and the gendering of this world was not accidental). The "organization man" was stereotyped as a dull, time-serving, company loyalist – and was viewed as the driving force of the respectable, suburban "mass culture" of white America in the two decades following World War II. The break-up of Fordism, and the Fordist organizational form, was – in part – a crisis of **managerialism** (as well as a crisis of profitability). Many of the innovations of the IC20 – the internationalization of production, downsizing, a more "entrepreneurial" outlook, the gutting of companies by "corporate raiders" – took their toll on managers as well as workers. Loyal company time-servers had no place in this brave new world. Fortunately, the new wave of **management theories** and approaches offered the chance of redemption and reinvention – managers could become "movers and shakers," providing the dynamic force to revitalize enterprises. So the new flowering of management approaches was directed at both reinventing organizations and the psychic drama of reinventing managers.

Management has spread across borders and boundaries in the last three decades. The US model has been spread internationally – challenging models of organizational direction and co-ordination based on other professional disciplines (engineering and production expertise, for example, in Europe and Japan). But it has also crossed boundaries into government and public service organizations which were once dominated by conceptions of administration or bureaucracy. Historically, such conceptions embodied a rather patrician disdain for "business" and its management techniques. But neo-liberal anti-statism exposed the world of administration to managerialist challenges. Installing "management" became the key to controlling public sector costs, to creating flexible organizations that were "customer-centered," and to subordinating intractable public sector workforces (manual and professional). Management was the carrier of "good business practices" from which public organizations needed to learn (Clarke and Newman, 1997). This **new public management** spread internationally (although its most vigorous forms tended to be installed by neo-liberal governments in Anglophone countries).

Management has also become a "technology of the self" within and outside organizational settings. This invocation of the self as a project to be managed is partly shaped by the withdrawal of public provision for collective well-being, such that individuals are told to "take responsibility" for their careers, diets, health, psychic state, and more. It also reflects the desire of employers to secure the loyalty, commitment, and enthusiasm of employees as "enterprising selves" (Du Gay, 1996). The spread of management has been assisted by processes of naturalization. In the broadest sense, the specific formation of management as a social and organizational cadre is aided by the incontrovertible view that "well-managed organizations" are desirable. The blurring of general and specific in the word "management" has enabled the flourishing of a particular form of management (which is cost-conscious, power-hungry, and anti-democratic, and tends toward a messianic view of its own importance). Fortunately, the management have not become popular heroes. "The suits" remains a term of derisory collective identification for managers, while **management speak** is as much despised as academic obscurantism.

John Clarke

See: *BUREAUCRACY, INDUSTRY, MARKET.*

Marginal

The word **marginal** came into use in the IC16 and originally referred to anything "written or printed in the margin of a page...rather than indented." It was not long before its meaning was extended into fields such as botany, zoology, psychology (and in the C19, economics) to refer to anything relating to "an edge, border, boundary or limit." In the eC20, "marginal" was used to refer to an individual or social group "isolated from or not conforming to the dominant society or culture; (perceived as being) on the edge of a society or social unit; belonging to a minority group (freq. with implications of consequent disadvantage)."

The earliest usage, which implied an official or original core of meaning and a personal or added reaction, is still present in the range of contemporary usages. **The marginal** now refers to elements that, from that standpoint of officialdom, are considered unimportant, outside the mainstream, near the lower edge of qualification or function, at the fringe or border.

In the last several decades, politically disenfranchised groups have taken on the metaphor of **the margin** to express their feelings about their place in democracies, or even in the global economy. Some individuals and groups use the idea of **marginality** to describe their generalized sense of being outside the mainstream. Political theorists have developed the idea of margin, and its accompanying concept of "the center," to create new ways to understand language and power (Derrida, 1982; hooks, 1990a). In most contemporary usages, the idea of marginality combines the idea of a dominating force with a spatial metaphor: to be marginal is both to have less power and to be at some distance from the center of power.

Theorists differ in their understanding of what it is that makes a person marginal, and this depends on what is understood to be the "center." If the center is perceived to be economic power, then those without financial resources are marginal. On the other hand, if political power is considered paramount, then those who lack it – even if they have money – are marginal. Most scholars now understand that there are many possible dimensions of marginality – not only economic and political, but also social, cultural, and symbolic. In current usage, almost any difference from "mainstream" or normative values that prevents a person or group from full participation in their society can be said to entail a form of marginality. For example, in societies in which the family is central, single people, especially lesbians or gay men who do not intend to live their lives within families, lack an important form of social network, and thus are marginal to communities that are centered on family relationships. Similarly, cultural forms (music, fashion, etc.) can be marginal in relation to the mainstream culture – at least until the culture industries appropriate such styles as trendy or hip.

The dimensions of marginality are not exclusive, and sociologists have demonstrated the interrelationships among power, class, cultural possession, education, social networks, and money. Thus, one person may be marginal in more than one way, or marginal in some ways, but central in others. For example, in postindustrial democracies, those who live below the poverty line are marginal to social, economic, and political life because they cannot create the forms of identity that are common in consumer-based societies, and they are likely to lack the education and skills to meaningfully advocate for themselves within political and social welfare processes. But because race, money, and education are linked, a wealthy, highly educated African-American may still be marginal to American political life because their racial group is still marginal to the political and social system as a whole.

In postcolonial studies, much consideration has been given to the global relationships between European and American "centers" and the spaces they once occupied as colonizers. This internationalized concept of marginality suggests that not only were the social and political forms of the colonizers – the "center" – imposed, but also the mental patterns. In this **center–margin** relationship, the now-marginal – who indeed may have been the centers of power within their pre-colonized culture or government – are forced to operate within the worldview and values of the colonizer; indeed, they must see themselves as the imposed colonial power sees them (Said, 1978). Indeed, as postcolonial scholars have shown, the elite among the colonized are forced to contest their marginality in the very language of the colonizers, and to engage the categories left behind by the colonial mind (Spivak, 2000).

These theorizations of marginality shed new light on older conceptions of persons who lived between two worlds, but did not or could not fully integrate into either. Focused originally on migrant groups that lived, even for generations, in one location while maintaining familial or even only ideological relations with another place, these older discussions were cast in terms of assimilation. New theories emphasize the multiple perspectives, and hence multiple identities, which the conditions of marginality require. The flexible idea of marginality enables researchers to incorporate the lived experience of migrants – or now transmigrants, that is, those who continually shuttle between centers of power – as they rework their split identities (Manalansan, 2000).

Political organizers and activist scholars are likely to see these multiplicities of identity not as psychically disabling, but rather as resources for creative political transformation. Indeed, many now argue that these kinds of multiple identities and locations are characteristic of the postmodern era, complexities to be celebrated and disentangled from their ''marginalizing'' effects, rather than overcome through incorporation into the ''center.''

Cindy Patton

See: *COLONIALISM, MOVEMENTS, OTHER.*

Market

Market was originally used to denote a place or location where people met to trade goods (from L *mercatus*). Subsequent usages borrow from and expand upon this image, even though a specific location may no longer be implied. The act of exchanging goods, services, or promises for money remains the central and essential activity of **markets**, **market economies**, and **market societies**. These terms define societies in which most economically valorized activity is co-ordinated by **market exchange** (rather than through monopoly control and direction, or by private arrangement). Market societies are distinguished from the ''command economies'' of the former communist bloc. But they are also distinguished from feudal and slave systems, where goods and services, including labor, are controlled through personal or positional obligation. Markets are thus public settings in which private interests meet.

The location element of markets was historically significant, since things and people had to **come to market** in order that they might realize their price. Some places became identified with trade in specific goods and are memorialized in street names (**Haymarket** was where hay was traded, and so on). Markets in this spatialized meaning are the social reference point for the economic meaning of markets as a means of co-ordinating economic activity and interest. This is the view articulated in classical political economy of the C18, notably Adam Smith's view of the "hidden hand of the market" (1977 [1776]) bringing demand and supply together in a productive and profitable dynamic relationship. The demand for a commodity (the capacity and willingness of buyers to purchase at a given price) will, over time, determine the supply of a commodity (the capacity and willingness of producers to provide the commodity at a given price). Although these dynamics of exchange work over time, conventional, or neo-classical, economic theory treats these dynamics as always tending to a point of **market equilibrium**, balancing purchaser and supplier interests. In this way, the "hidden hand" of the market is made up of thousands or millions of micro-transactions, rather than the outcome being directed by any one agent or agency.

Historically, the concept of the **free market** was a political challenge to various forms of monopoly (for example, monopolies in the trade of specific commodities granted by royal warrants). The challenge – articulating the aspirations of a rising capitalist class – aimed to liberate trade from such feudal or traditional constraints. The "free market" has since become a claim to refuse all constraints, interference, and regulation. Governmental controls (of quality, standards, honesty, etc.), national borders (and "protectionist" support of national industries and services), public provision of services (welfare, health, education etc.), and labor organizations (guilds, trade unions, co-operative movements) have all been contested in its name. According to this laissez-faire view, the market requires only the minimal support of the rule of law to function effectively, guaranteeing property rights, and protecting property owners against the propensity of other human beings to take short cuts (theft and cheating) in pursuit of their interests.

At the end of the C20, the "free market" re-emerged as a rallying cry associated with the supposed triumph of capitalism over communism (following the fall of the Soviet Union), and with the process of globalization. The market came to be seen as the only, the necessary, and the preferred mechanism for co-ordinating human activity (Carrier, 1997). It was naturalized as the elementary basis for social life – and its advocates insisted that all social life should be subjected to it (Frank, 2001). Although critics pointed to forms of market failure and social imperfections associated with it (the production and intensification of inequalities, in particular), markets were constantly enlarged. This was so in a geographical sense, as more of the world's economic activities were "opened" up to a global market network. It was also true for a range of services and activities that had stood outside of, if not against, markets in various forms of public ownership or provision (natural resources, welfare services, and so on). The drive toward "free trade" aimed to create markets for all potentially profitable activity. Individuals were invited to understand themselves as consumers, free to choose the commodities and services to meet their needs (or wants) subject only to their financial capacity to buy them (with cash or credit). Credit – or expanded debt – fueled the long consumer boom in the West at the end of the C20.

While **financial markets** led the process of global interconnectedness, the original meanings of "market" persisted in the use of the word to identify places where people went to buy things, albeit with a variable sense of scale. **Supermarkets** (from the 1960s) identified shops where a variety of goods could be purchased, while image and scale inflation led to the creation of **hypermarkets** by the 1990s. These were generally located in out-of-town settings and intensified automobile dependency in Western capitalist societies. In the USA (originally) "market" was often truncated to **mart** in the names of stores and chains of stores (Walmart, K-mart).

Although naturalized as an invisible hand, not susceptible to direct human control, markets are also paradoxically personified. They have states of mind ("the markets are nervous"); they hold views ("the markets will not like the government's plan to . . ."); they are prone to breakdown and failure; and their global interconnectedness makes them vulnerable to epidemic infection (Black Monday, Black Tuesday, etc.). Indeed, so frail are they that they need special care and attention if they are to survive and function happily. As a consequence, a certain ambivalence persists toward markets. Perceived as necessary, they are not to be trusted. Their impersonality seems to conceal biases, rewarding the rich and powerful disproportionately. Their ruthless drive toward economic efficiency drives out other social or human values that cannot be counted. This creates a sense of refusal – the view that not everything can or should be commodified, captured in the regular application to markets of Oscar Wilde's definition of a cynic: a person who "knows the price of everything and the value of nothing."

John Clarke

See: *CAPITALISM, COMMODITY, CONSUMPTION, GLOBALIZATION.*

Mass

In the early Middle Ages, **mass** had only a liturgical sense. But as early as the C14, it took on the sense, in such diverse fields as painting and the military and domestic economy, of forming or gathering individual pieces together. By the C15, it had a certain ambiguity, referring both to "an amorphous quantity of material" and to "a kind of matter capable of being shaped." In the C17, it referred to "the generality of mankind; the main body of a race or nation" and, in the eC18, it was applied to human beings, particularly "a large number . . . collected in a narrow space" or "a multitude of persons mentally viewed as forming an aggregate in which their individuality is lost." It was but a small step to identify the mass, in the eC19, not with the entire population but with "the popular or lower orders."

The term seems initially to be a simply descriptive one, referring to a substantial entity, such as a large mass of material, or to a large number of persons collected together. However, it also has a powerful evaluative dimension. Most usages centrally involve the idea of the way that being part of a mass involves the loss of individuality. This concern has deep historical roots. As early as the 1830s, there is anxiety that as "civilization" advances, power passes increasingly from the individual to the mass – to the point where the individual may get lost in the crowd. To be a member of a **mass society** or a **mass culture** is also to be addressed by powerful systems of communications and **mass media**; the question then is to what extent, in these circumstances, people can still properly exercise their rational faculties.

In such a society it is often argued that **the mass of the people** are corrupted by the blandishments of mass culture and may be governed more by their impulses than by any rational convictions. For elite cultural commentators, the problem posed by the **massification** of society is that it threatens to destroy the very foundation of the Enlightenment tradition of critical thought. This tradition is premised on the notion of the self-conscious individual taking informed and rational decisions. By contrast, **the masses** are seen as irrational, easily swayed, governed by their emotions, and, indeed, as subject to forms of mass hysteria, best analyzed by new disciplines such as that of **mass-psychology**.

To speak of the rise of mass society is also to refer to key processes in the rise of modernity. All the constituent features of what came to be understood as "massification" –, urbanization, industrialization, commercialization, and standardization – are central to the emergence of the mass cultures of modernity. The (un)natural home of all this was the city, now swollen with alienated and anomic crowds of those displaced from the secure communities of the rural past, and vulnerable, in their misery and confusion, to the manipulative power of the new mass media. These **vulnerable masses** are, of course, usually envisaged as Others: the poor, the mob, the crowd, the uneducated – all those who constitute the antithesis of the educated, middle-class, white adult male, who (naturally) encapsulates the tradition of Enlightenment reason. Raymond Williams once observed that no one likes to think of themselves as merely a constituent part of a mass, and that therefore we should extend to others the courtesy of recognizing that there are, in fact no masses, only ways of seeing other people as masses.

For a long tradition of cultural critics in the UK from Matthew Arnold (1971 [1869]) onward, massification meant that the "selective" tradition of elite culture was being overwhelmed by the industrialized and standardized forms of cultural production brought about by commercialization. Commerce was thus seen to be invading the spheres of art and culture, and replacing their individualized, artisanal modes of creativity with the repetitive modes of **mass production** of standardized cultural goods. The essential similarity of these commodities was then merely disguised by clever marketing, which produced the superficial effect of eternal novelty through a process which Theodor Adorno and Max Horkheimer (1972) termed the "pseudo-individualization" of the culture's essentially formulaic products. The commodification of mass culture was thus seen as the corruption of what had been the authentic sphere of artistic creativity, and the consumers were seen as merely passive, and easily manipulated by the forces of commercial marketing.

The European tradition of critical commentary on the development of mass culture found further development during the C20 in the USA, where many scholars developed the central theme of **mass man** as now being open to manipulation by powerful forces beyond his control. This discourse is still very much alive, as can be witnessed by contemporary debates about the supposed "dumbing-down" of mass forms of popular culture. In the mC20, mass culture, especially in the form of **mass consumption**, came to be centrally defined as a feminine sphere – the debased realm of the cheap, the "flighty," and the irrational, devoted to the trivial pleasures of shopping, where the modern woman reigned supreme (Huyssen, 1986). Against all this negativity, there is, however, a more positive view, which is represented by those who follow Williams in seeing popular culture as having an important democratic dimension, in its drive (even if in commercialized forms) toward extension and inclusiveness.

Modernity can be said to have been characterized by mass forms of cultural production and consumption, of which standardization has been the dominant feature. This process perhaps reached its apotheosis in what came to be called the Fordist mode of production, where, as Henry Ford himself said of his early Model T cars, you could have "any color you like as long as it's black," and where, from the consumer's point of view, the key ambition was that of "keeping up with the Joneses." Today, however, the salesperson may be only too happy to let you customize many aspects of your new car's appearance, and consumers may care more about marking their individual tastes by "keeping away from" (rather than up with) the Joneses. All of this indicates a shift (enabled by new computer technologies) toward forms of flexible specialization in modes of production and toward modes of fragmentation and "niche marketing." This is reflected in the move from broadcasting to narrowcasting, in the world of what are perhaps less "mass" media than they used to be. This way (at least in the advanced industrial countries of the world) lies the postmodern era, with its post- Fordist modes of production, in which the process of massification can, in some senses, perhaps be said to be going into reverse. Then again, Adorno and Horkheimer would probably regard all this customization as merely a more sophisticated mode of the process of "pseudo-individualization" through which mass culture disguises its inauthenticity.

David Morley

See: *AUDIENCE, CITY, ELITE, INDIVIDUAL, MEDIA, MODERN, OTHER.*

209

Materialism

As a term in intellectual history and philosophy, **materialism** is most often understood as a name for the belief that the immediate physical world is the most important (or, at an extreme, the only) one that exists. A **materialist**, accordingly, is one who forswears any belief in a spiritual or otherworldly existence, and thus materialism is commonly opposed to various forms of spiritualism. It is also, though less often, opposed to philosophies that give mind priority over (or significant autonomy from) matter; in its insistence that mental states are explicable by physical means, materialism opposes all *a priori* theories of cognition and all suggestions that minds are something qualitatively different from matter. Materialist beliefs have a long and rich history in Western thought, dating back to the pre-Socratic thinkers of the C5 and C6 BCE and attaining, according to most commentators, mature expression in the Latin works of Epicurus and especially Lucretius, whose long poem *De rerum natura* (50 BCE) expounded the theory that the universe is made up of imperceptibly tiny bits of fundamental matter.

It is strange, then, given materialism's position in Western intellectual history, that the most common colloquial use of the word suggests an aggressive indifference to spiritual and intellectual matters alike. From the mC19 onward, "materialist" has been used (usually with a sense of opprobrium) as a rough cognate of "greedy," referring to persons and beliefs whose interests lie in financial gain to the exclusion of all else. And it may be stranger still that some of the best-known uses of the term in recent decades have been associated with rock stars, from George Harrison's rejection of *Living in the Material World* (1973) to Madonna's evocation, via the iconography of Marilyn Monroe in Howard Hawks's *Gentlemen Prefer Blondes* (1953), of the "material girl" whose justification for fortune-hunting is that "we are living in a material world" (1984). Contemporary readers might be forgiven, then, if they understand materialism as something having to do with an unhealthy obsession with money. Likewise, it is quite possible, after hearing appeals for money from ostensibly charitable religious organizations, to imagine that there must be some connection between denouncing and accruing **material wealth**.

The disciplines of the **material sciences**, however, retain a substantive sense of material as "that which pertains to matter," and there is a strong sense in the law that, for example, a **material witness** or a **material misrepresentation** is a singularly important thing – a person or a statement that (so to speak) fundamentally gets to the heart of the matter. Similarly, theorists of **material culture** focus on the physical artifacts and built environments of human societies, as a corrective to scholarly disciplines whose understanding of alien or ancient cultures is based largely on the interpretation of texts. In law as in history as in physics, then, it is worth noting the association of the "material" with the "basic" and the "elemental." In Western intellectual history since the mC19, the association of **materialism** with the basic is most pronounced in Marxism, where the relation between the "superstructure" (which includes, among myriad other things, intellectual histories) and the **material base** of society has provided six generations of thinkers with fertile ground for theorizing. Indeed, Marxism has often been considered synonymous with **historical materialism** and/or **dialectical materialism**, even though historical materialism, properly speaking, simply asserts that historical events have logical and traceable causes that are no less susceptible to analysis than are events in the physical world.

For Karl Marx, by contrast, materialism meant something far more specific, as in this famous passage from the preface to the *Critique of political economy* (1972 [1859]: 4): "The mode of production of material life conditions the social, political and intellectual life-processes in general. It is not the consciousness of men that determines their being, but on the contrary their social being that determines their consciousness." The argument here is not merely that human history can be understood as a series of changes in the tangible infrastructure (from, say, triremes and aqueducts to steam engines and electric lights); more than this, it asserts that the **conditions of material existence** themselves are determinative of the very means by which we understand them and ourselves. Marx's materialism is thus "dialectical" in its insistence that "reality is not an inert collection of material entities to be grasped by detached contemplation, but an interaction between a collective historical human subjectivity and the material world it generates through its material activity or labor" (Habib, 1996: 338). What remains in dispute in the Marxist tradition to date, however, is precisely how that "interaction" takes place, and to what extent it is determined ("in the last instance") by the **means of material production** themselves.

It remains unclear to what extent a materialist approach to history – be it Marxist or non-Marxist – can claim an explanatory power on a par with the disciplines of the physical sciences. Among eC20 philosophical schools, logical positivism claimed the closest allegiance to a scientific sense of materialism, and held on that basis that meaningful statements are only those which can be verified against the world of empirical fact. The degree to which this proposition is accepted today is, appropriately enough, a function of the degree to which philosophy aspires to the condition of material science. For insofar as the physical sciences in the C20 revealed the fundamental particles of matter to be significantly more complex than had previously been thought, **materialist philosophies** such as positivism run the risk of espousing a simpler understanding of both "materialism" and "science" than is found in the actual material sciences.

It seems safe to say, nevertheless, that there is a strong correlation between materialism and secularism: between Lucretius' arguments against the existence of the soul in C1 BCE and the works of Pierre Gassendi and Thomas Hobbes in the mC17, theocratic domination of Western thought effectively forestalled any consideration of materialism, whereas from the C17 onward, most advances in science – from evolutionary theory to atomic theory – that have challenged religious thought have also, and for the same reasons, fostered further debate about the materials of which we are made.

Michael Bérubé

See: *EMPIRICAL, KNOWLEDGE, OBJECTIVITY, PRAGMATISM, REASON, RELATIVISM.*

Media

The notion of a **medium** moved from a broad sense of the middle in the C16 (a middle course, a compromise, moderation, etc.) to a narrower sense of "any intervening substance through which a force acts on objects at a distance or through which impressions are conveyed to the senses" in the C17. Simultaneously in the C17, "medium" was used to describe any intermediate instrument or channel, and finally, in the C18, it was extended to a medium of circulation and exchange such as money. It was thus but a small step to the notion of an environment as a surrounding or enveloping substance, as when the C20 Canadian theorist Marshall McLuhan quipped that whoever discovered the ocean, it was not the fish for whom the water was the medium of their lives. The contemporary idea of a medium (or, in the plural, of **media**) is closely linked to that of the process of dissemination, or circulation, of information by means of some particular channel of communication. Central here is the process of sending signals or signs of some kind, by means of an ordered system, which constitutes the medium for their transmission. The fundamental idea of a medium then refers to an intervening substance through which signals can travel as a means for communication.

Nowadays the term "media" is most commonly used to refer to the institutions of electronic broadcasting, printed magazines, and newspapers which address mass audiences. In this context, by contrast to interpersonal or two-way forms of communication, the emphasis is usually on the sense in which **mass media** constitute powerful one-way systems for communication from the few to the many. In societies with advanced systems of division of labor, people tend to live highly segregated lives, and are thus increasingly dependent on the media for information about events outside their own immediate experience. To this extent, contemporary societies can be claimed to be characterized by the **mediation** of much of our social experience. Indeed, it has become common to refer to the contemporary world as comprised of **mediated** or **mediatized** societies.

The concept of mediation has, as one of its key sources, Walter Benjamin's essay on "The work of art in the age of mechanical reproduction" (Benjamin, 1968). Benjamin's argument is that, in the age of the mass media, rather than the audience having to flock together to the site of the original object, spectacle, or performance, as they did in earlier times, modern techniques of mass reproduction mean that **mediated images** of the object or event can be simultaneously transmitted to widely dispersed mass audiences. Thus, it is argued, nowadays we live in the "Generalized Elsewhere" (Meyrowitz, 1985) of a **media world**, and much of our time is spent consuming **mediated narratives** of one sort or another. Indeed, it has been claimed that, as a result of this increasing mediation of experience, we now live in a "society of the spectacle" (Debord, 1994, originally published 1970) which is characterized by our relation to images, rather than to things, or events in themselves. More recently, the French theorist of postmodernity Jean Baudrillard (1988) has argued that we now live in the age of the "simulacrum." However, in relation to the question of just how new all this is, it is worth recalling that 150 years ago, Ludwig Feuerbach already bemoaned the fact that mC19 Europe was living in an "age of images."

Historically, the academic study of the media has largely focused on questions such as how accurately (or with what degree of "bias") the media reflect reality, and in what ways they shape it. In this connection, the key issues have been concerned with the effects of institutional structures, patterns of ownership, and professional norms on the nature of **media messages**, and with their effects on their audiences. The critical tradition, under the influence of Marxism, has often been concerned with the question of the media's role as an agent of powerful groups (political or commercial, elites or classes), purveying ideologies which may conceal the reality of structures of inequality from those who are most disadvantaged by them.

A further perspective focuses on the ritual role of the media in allowing the simultaneous participation of large numbers of people in widely shared forms of cultural life. In this analysis, a substantial part of our experience is seen to take the form of participation in **media events** of one sort or another (whether special events, such as the mass viewing of an occasion such as the televised moon landing, or the mundane ritual practice of nightly television news viewing). These ersatz forms of participation in forms of mediated sociality can then be seen to be the basis of our membership of "virtual" communities of various sorts.

The other main theoretical perspective on these issues has come to be known as that of **medium theory**. This is an approach which focuses not on the institutional structure of media organizations, or on the content of their messages, but on their form. The issue then is how to distinguish the ways in which different media, or different modes of communication – such as spoken language, writing, print, or electronic visual media – will tend to privilege particular modes of understanding and interaction in human communication. This approach is most commonly associated with the work of McLuhan (1964), who famously argued that **the medium is the message**. His central point is that different media of communication (in all its senses) are best understood as "extensions" of particular human capacities and senses – thus the wheel is an extension of the foot, and the camera an extension of the eye. His argument is that, in the age of **global electronic media**, dominated by television's capacity to engage mass audiences with images of faraway events and people, we are drawn into vastly extended modes of communication and community – hence his claim that, in effect, we increasingly live in a mediated "global village," in which our very sensibilities are transformed by the changed relations with others into which the electronic media now insert us.

213

Recently McLuhan's work has once again come to receive considerable attention, after a period of neglect, insofar as his ideas have been seen to be particularly applicable to the potential effects of the new **digital media** and **computerized media**. Many recent discussions of new technologies of communications, such as the world-wide web and the Internet, have drawn (in more or less acknowledged ways) on McLuhan's ideas, in attempting to understand the specificity of the virtual forms of communication and community which characterize the world of cyberspace. One of the key difficulties here lies in recognizing the very real transformative power of these **media technologies** – and the sense that different media may tend to encourage or facilitate different modalities of communication – without falling into an overly determinist mode of explanation of their effects ("technological determinism"). The other difficulty lies in avoiding an ahistorical perspective, which overemphasizes the novelty of recent technological developments and forgets that all historical eras have had to deal with media technologies and forms of communication which are new to them.

The **computer-based media** which have developed in recent years have now been the subject of extensive debate. Enthusiasts claim that the interactive potential of **web-based media** and the Internet are taking us into a more democratic age of individualized and interactive communication, which transcends the limitations of the previous mass media. Cyberspace has been heralded as a new realm of liberation and exploration available at the touch of a mouse. However, in some discussions of the virtual worlds now brought into being by computer technologies, there has been substantial criticism of the extent to which such mediated forms of communication and community can ever be "authentic," or can supplant their conventional forebears without significant loss. This is clearly an important issue, but it has to be recognized that all meaning is mediated in one way or another, and that there is no such thing as "unmediated" communication. Even the supposedly most "authentic" forms of face-to-face communication and dialogue are themselves necessarily "mediated" – by language and other cultural codes.

Besides the computer, the other most important new medium of communication to emerge in recent years has perhaps been the mobile, cellular telephone. For many people, life would now be quite unthinkable without the capacity that this medium offers them to be in instant touch with their network of contacts wherever and whenever they want. Unlike the mass media of previous eras it is a two-way, interactive medium of exchange. Unlike its "parent" technology, the fixed household telephone, the "mobile" is perhaps the individualizing communications medium *par excellence*, whereby a person's mobile phone number now becomes, in effect, their virtual address. As the relevant technologies con-verge, the handset may well become the key nexus of personal communication of the future. However, many **new media** have surprised their developers, in one way or another, and the mobile phone is no exception. Few people anticipated, when it was first introduced, that one of its key uses would be as a medium for text messaging, which would bring the printed word (if in a new, vowel-less "TXT" language, reminiscent of the early days of the telegraph) back to center stage among contemporary electronic media of communication.

David Morley

See: *AUDIENCE, COMMUNICATION, MASS, NETWORK, TECHNOLOGY, VIRTUAL.*

Memory

Memory is an indispensable condition of effective human life, and – consequently – an essential part of human thought, from the earliest myths to the most advanced forms of contemporary neurological science. Not only does the question of memory span the entire history of human thought: from our own late modern, or postmodern, perspective, troubled by the seeming impossibilities of **remembering**, we seem ever more eager to center the operations of memory. At the very dawn of the modern age, for John Locke at least, memory functioned as the necessary adjunct to reason. Memory, Locke believed, contained "the storehouse of our ideas"; through the workings of memory an idea could "be made actual again," in the sense of coming fully into consciousness. Making an idea "actual again," however, proved not merely to be an act of reason. From the lC18 the subjective vicissitudes in making ideas "actual again" received wonderful literary expression: in Jean-Jacques Rousseau, in Johann von Goethe, in William Wordsworth, among others, and a key idea of our own times was anticipated in Percy Bysshe Shelley's conception of "broken memories" (1817).

Through the C19 the development of a specialized science of history (historiography) tended to accentuate the division between **subjective memory** (concerning the inner life) and the **social memories** of larger social groupings (nations above all). That this separation could never be final, however, was conceded in 1849 by Thomas Macaulay, who realized that his own history of England would encompass not only the distant past but also "a time which is within the memory of men still living." By the lC19 the question of memory moved to the center of modern consciousness – evident most of all in the three great modern philosophers of memory: Marcel Proust (1970 [1913]), Sigmund Freud (1962 [1899]), and Edmund Husserl (1991). The opening chapter of Proust's *Remembrance of things past* provides one of the most beautiful explorations of modern memory. Here Proust distinguishes between "the memory of the intellect," or what he called **voluntary memory**, and **involuntary memory**, which exists "beyond the reach of the intellect," but can enter consciousness as a result of a contingent sensuous association. In the most famous passage of all, the sensation of the lime-blossom tea and the now iconic *petite madeleine* release in his fictional character a "vast structure of recollection" – of homely memories of childhood. These were memories which "rose up like a stage set" in his mind – the pretext for many subsequent theorizations of memory which imagine the mnemonic to work like a "theater" (not least in Walter Benjamin).

If for Proust memories offered access to a homely past, in the literature of psychoanalysis memory more frequently is blocked or displaced, subject to unconscious interference and to repression. **Screen memories**, especially, serve to conceal troubled pasts. To reach memory requires not a chance encounter with a sensuousness experience which summons the past, but protracted and painful delving into the inner life, so that which blocks the deepest memories can be peeled away. In Husserl's phenomenological approach, too, memory was an artifact entirely located within the inner subjective life of an individual, obeying the laws of an individual consciousness but quite separate from the workings of social time. A different tradition, during this same period, endeavored to explore the imperatives of **collective memory**, dissatisfied with the perceived subjectivism of too great a focus on individual memory. Some of these explorations can be tracked in Henri Bergson (1991) and in Carl Jung, though they receive their most complete treatment in Maurice Halbwachs (1992), where the erstwhile follower of Henri Bergson shifted allegiance to Emile Durkheim. For Halbwachs, memory was located in social institutions – **religious collective memory**, the **collective memory of the family**, and so on: the emphasis on location brought together time and space, ensuring that the locations of memory were as significant for Halbwachs as their temporal sequencing.

This IC19 and eC20 fascination with memory coincided with the organization of collective memory in institutions and in the market which we have subsequently come to understand as invented traditions, in which spurious pasts are mobilized in the present in order to provide a sense of continuity, often overlaid with nostalgia. In popular life the C20 saw a vast proliferation of souvenirs and **memorabilia**, associated especially but not exclusively with the growth of mass tourism. (Photography was an important catalyst in this respect.) In the earlier part of the C20 there occurred a vogue for fairground **memory-men** (captured by Alfred Hitchcock in the film of *The Thirty-Nine Steps*), whose apparently phenomenal mnemonic capacities turned what were coming to be called **photographic memories** into popular spectacle. By the 1950s a homely notion of **memory lane** was particularly associated with popular music, in which specific tunes took on the role of Proust's *madeleine*.

By the IC20 there occurred a further explosion of interest in memory. In part, this derived from a perception that postmodernist capitalist forms engendered new structures of **amnesia** – that it was no longer possible for the historical past to be retrieved. Theoretically, part of this argument derived from Theodor Adorno's reading of the commodity form – evident, for example, in Fredric Jameson's proposition that the postmodern represents an epoch in which memory is lost (Jameson, 1991). Such arguments were closely linked to the idea that a commodified and base heritage allowed only an ideological recuperation of the past. A second impetus for renewed interest in memory followed from the popularization of **prosthetic memory** – in the form of the **electronic memories** of computers. (This was represented in the new vernacular concerning the amount of memory a computer possessed.) These themes were carried forward as a result too of the digitalization of written and image archives. A third impetus came from a renewed concern in what became known as **popular memory**. But unlike the (loosely functionalist) interest in collective memory a century earlier, enthusiasm for the imperatives of popular memory took a different tack.

On the one hand, this was linked to various popular political movements which sought to retrieve popular memories of the oppressed, in order to further social emancipation – employing, particularly, the new technologies of oral history (Popular Memory Group, 1982). On the other hand, a darker, more psychoanalytically informed sensibility appeared too, preoccupied with **traumatic memories** of unspeakable collective historical experiences. In this the Holocaust loomed large, spawning an entire new intellectual discipline of **memory studies**, with an emphasis on the requirements of **memory work** (Hodgkin and Radstone, 2003). Memory here becomes capacious: it serves a historical function, endeavoring to recall the historical past; it serves a legal function, seeking to redress the wrongs of the past in courts of law; and it serves a therapeutic function, aiming to ease the pain of those in the present who have suffered in the past. How traumatic instances in the historical past – slavery, genocides and ethnocides, the disappearance and torture of vast populations – can be remembered and lived with in the present has become an issue of major public concern in the lC20 and eC21, evident in the spawning of various Truth and Reconciliation Commissions (notably in South Africa, Guatemala, and Chile).

The very capaciousness of this intellectual and political concern with memory has divided the historical profession. Some have welcomed the dimensions of "memory work" (a term first coined in 1939), regarding it as a deepening of the historical imagination. Others are more fearful, believing that the very essentials of history, as the rational arena where a society's memory of its past can be debated according to collectively agreed procedures, are under threat. Traumatic memories of the past also seem to have their individual or subjective correlates. These constitute what has come to be known as the confessional cultures of the eC21, in which individuals face ever-greater incitements to speak their pain and recover memories of past abuse. With connections back to classical psychoanalysis, this has become prevalent in terms of childhood sexual abuse. Those doubtful of the extent of such childhood abuse have coined the term **false memory syndrome** in order to indicate the degree of fabricated memories recuperated. This remains a highly contentious feature of public life.

Bill Schwarz

See: *HERITAGE, HISTORY, HOLOCAUST, TIME.*

217

Mobility

We think of **mobility** primarily as an attribute of life, especially of people who move (depending on circumstances) from their economic status or place of origin. The word first appeared in the C16 to describe gatherings of people appraised as dangerous. The L term *mobile vulgus* was abbreviated in the lC17 to "mob," a "disorderly crowd" or "fickle multitude" whose anger could be dangerous to the aristocracy of church and state. *Vulgus*, meaning common, changed to "vulgar," and "mobile" emerged to describe the capacity for movement or change. From this came the descriptive "mobile" or "movable," and "mobility," a term that described the opinions of crowds, and then the behavior of individuals, and finally, an attribute of things.

People defined in terms of movement and mobility have been the subject of moral panics in modern times. Tramps and migrants in the US, and Gypsies and Jews in Europe, were by the mC19 seen as threatening to social order and subject to special legal and political administration (Cresswell, 2001). Who and what could move across which borders? Disputes about distinctions between peoples, and between people and things, continue to trouble corporate and government practices today. "Mobility" expresses different, sometimes contradictory meanings underlying our most fundamental beliefs about progress, freedom, individuation, and power.

Law, ideology, and commerce have reinforced a sense of mobility as a universal good, denied only to problematic subjects. Being **mobilized** means military duty, or being catalyzed by inspiration and intent; **immobilized** describes people overwhelmed by fear, poverty, or disability. We speak of **upward mobility** as the attitudes and opportunities that enable an individual to become more wealthy, and **downward mobility** as the process whereby individuals or groups move into impoverishment. The former dominates the narratives of Western culture and shapes the films, biographies, social practices, and personal dreams of an increasing portion of the world's population. Neo-liberal thought views mobility as an individual challenge or attribute, and downward mobility as the "fault" of the individual involved. By emphasizing achievement and failure as individual occurrences, the media often obscure the influence of social and legal systems on the politics of mobility. Individuals and families experiencing downward mobility are thus often surprised by it.

While "upward" and "downward mobility" seem to have clear meanings and values, **geographical mobility** involves more ambivalent associations. Associated with improved status, mobility has become a widely sought individual right, affecting immigration, border policies, and urban density in sought-after destinations. But greater prestige isn't necessarily attained by migrants or refugees in their new location. Many are despised for their association with poor areas, regardless of their individual status. Whether leaving behind poverty, natural disaster, or political oppression, many pay a toll from their social and other assets. Here social and geographical meanings combine in what Doreen Massey has called the "geometry of power" (1994). The lasting power of these "power-geometries" in the recent surge of global migration demonstrates a continuing hierarchy of national and regional cultures.

A third use of "mobility" refers to physical attributes and reminds us of those who are unable to move without prosthetic assistance. Lacking mobility in parts of their body, the "differently abled" have become an increasingly vocal group who argue that better social policies would allow them greater mobility. This is a compelling need when social resources for disabled people are reduced and they are isolated or forced out of their homes to find companionship and care (Butler and Parr, 1999).

Throughout the C20, technological change has intensified what Raymond Williams termed **mobile privatization**, creating tools to enhance the mobility and connectedness of individuals (telephones, cars) rather than the well-being of communities (trains, public space). Economic and moral associations between mobility and improvement were transferred to communication and information technologies, where telecommuting made information mobile rather than people. By the 1970s, advocates argued that faster, more mobile communications technologies would create a more democratic public sphere, and mobility and miniaturization overwhelmed the development of communications media, not necessarily with that effect. Today the cell phone represents a synthesis of connectedness, efficiency, and freedom, a vision celebrated in film, TV, and advertising (where throwing it away signals a daring but temporary freedom from constraint). **Mobile phones** have transformed social and personal interactions and speeded up working conditions in many occupations. The miniaturization and digitalization of media have enhanced rapid capital accumulation, transnational expansion, financial speculation, and massive corporate failures. Digital telecommunications have created new sites for information and communication among alternative and dissident groups, while exacerbating privatization in everyday life and politics (Morley, 2000; Myerson, 2001).

Social mobility, **geographical mobility**, **physical mobility**, and the **mobility of capital**, **information**, and other commodities: each displays conflicting economic and cultural effects. Mobility is widely advocated as a positive attribute in the workforce, but it can diminish the autonomy of the employees, subjecting them to unwanted relocations that can disperse their personal roots. While capital and information are increasingly freed from spatial contexts, many employees remain stuck in poorly paid, hazardous jobs behind assembly lines or screens. The omnipresent mobile telephone allows people to converse from any location. Yet the mobile phone allows governments and corporations to use comprehensive surveillance methods to locate and acquire information about telephone users. In each of these cases the link between mobility and freedom turns back upon its users, or is "reversed," in Marshall McLuhan's terminology (McLuhan and McLuhan, 1988), and exacerbates conflicts as well as links between mobility and autonomy. The commercial mainstream encourages us to embrace the increased mobility of data, objects, and people, but we should subject this idea to continuous critical scrutiny.

Jody Berland

See: *COMMUNICATION, DISABILITY, MEDIA, SPACE.*

Modern

Commonly used to indicate a more or less recent phase of time, **modern** is also one of the most politically charged keywords circulating across languages in the **modern world**. Closely associated since the IC18 with the notions of "progress" and "development" attributed to the West, the attribute "modern" describes a wide range of historical phenomena characterized by continuous growth and change: in particular, science, technology, industry, secular government, bureaucracy, social mobility, city life, and an "experimental" or **modernist** approach in culture and the arts. However, when viewed as a distinctive quality emanating out of "the West," or claimed as a property of particular social groups, **the modern** becomes a standard against which other customs or ways of life are judged **premodern**. A **modernization project** then prescribes a "reform" or a "revolutionary change" in accordance with that standard. So difficult is it now to disentangle the history of the modern from the global impact of Western European colonialism that many people around the world regard their local word for "modern" as a translation of an "original" European word. In this way, the linguistic and social diversity of the world is often still measured against an imaginary norm of **modernity** equated with Western European historical experience.

The beginnings of "modern" were unremarkable. Entering English from IL *modernus* in C6, "modern" derives from the L adverb *modo* meaning "just now." Raymond Williams (1976) points out that the earliest English uses were close to our casual use of "contemporary" to indicate that something exists at the time of speaking or writing: "our maist gracious quene moderne" (1555) is not necessarily a paragon of fashion but simply the queen of the time, and "thy former as well as modern kindness" (1700) means not that you are progressive in your treatment of others but that you have been kind to me lately as you have been in the past. Meanwhile, "contemporary" meant "co-temporary" or "of the same period," and indicated things existing together, whether in the present or at periods in the past. In the usage of communities outside Western Europe, many of the terms used today to connote "modern," such as *jindai* in literary Chinese, once meant something like the L *modo* and carried no special reference to "the West" – which did not exist in "pre-modern" times as a globally central model.

In **modern English**, the chronological sense of a "period" became attached to "modern" through the habit of contrasting **ancient** with **modern times** that emerged just before the Renaissance, becoming common from IC16 ("the writings of the auncient and moderne Geographers and Historiographers," 1585), and in C16 L a "Middle Age" or "medieval period" appeared (*media aetas, medium aevum*). During the C17 and C18 this periodizing use was sharpened, especially in the study of **modern languages**, to distinguish a past regarded as finished from a relatively recent time that could begin a good while ago and engulf the present: "another Book overwritten in a small Modern Greek hand, about 150 years ago" (1699); "our English Tongue ... may be said to equal, if not surpass all other Modern Languages" (1706). As the sense of rivalry in the second example suggests, the consolidation of a comparative attitude within as well as toward the evaluation of historical periods began to endow "the modern" with its modern complications.

One of these is the emergence of a two-sided way of thinking about time. From the C17, "modern" could be used to establish both continuity over an extended present marked off from a long-ago past, and a sharp discontinuity between the present and the past. On the one hand, the expansive sense of a **modern age** long enough to dwarf the significance of "now" was reinforced through the natural sciences: "if such species be termed modern, in comparison to races which preceded them, their remains, nevertheless, enter into submarine deposits many hundred miles in length" (1830). This temporally capacious "modern" entered the vocabulary of English education, with **modern schools** from the mC19 offering subjects other than classical L and Gk; in the discipline of history the **early modern** period in Europe still begins just after medieval times. On the other hand, from the IC16 a more discriminating use of "modern" began to highlight "the novelty of the present as a break or rupture with the past" (P. Osborne, 1996); "Modern warre, is the new order of warre vsed in our age" (1598). This stress on novelty could also organize an evaluative opposition between "now" and "then": "the women of this Modern age had . . . need of amendment" (1656).

A second complication is that this polemical use makes "modern" the keyword of a struggle over values presented as though it were a claim about historical time. An important precedent in lC17 French literary circles was the **Quarrel of the Ancients and Moderns** ("Battle of the Books" in eC18 Britain), when the Renaissance-based doctrine of the superiority of the classics (within which the word "archaic" could be a term of praise) was challenged by a Modern party aspiring, under the growing prestige of **modern science**, to surpass their achievements. This form of polemic persists in academic "canon wars" today, and "Battle of the Books" still works as a rubric to organize cultural disputes in the media. However, as Raymond Williams (1976: 208) points out, most pre-C19 English uses of "modern," "modernity," and "modernist" were, in comparative contexts, disparaging of the new or, in the case of **modernize** (first used with reference to buildings, spelling, and dress), apologetic about it: "I have taken the liberty to modernize the language" (1752); "He scruples not to modernize a little" (1753).

The "Western" modern gathers complexity and force with the sense of a variable future that develops in the mC18 as the Christian vision of an inevitable Judgment Day was challenged by the optimistic, secular spirit of the Enlightenment, with its growing awareness of "New Worlds" thriving beyond Europe. For most C18 thinkers, a real or imaginary encounter with "other" peoples was a pretext for criticizing their own societies and imagining ways to reform them in a future now open to change by human action. However, modeled as it was on the custom of comparing the present unfavorably with the past, this more exploratory approach to comparison marks a third complication in the European history of "modern": cultural differences coexisting with each other in time could be evaluated as though some ways of life were more admirable because more archaic, elemental, and pristine than others. The romantic figure of the "noble savage" (1703, Baron de Lanton) emerges in this context. Initially a vision of what human moral life would be like in light of natural religion, "the savage" came to be contrasted favorably with "civilized man" in ways that rebuked the decadence of the latter at the cost of denying to the former a full participation and belongingness in present historical time (Fabian, 1983).

Rendered militant and self-consciously "historic" in the lC18 by the American and French Revolutions, "modernity" developed an affirmative sense of the times being "other and better than what had gone before" (P. Osborne, 1996: 348). It became a good thing to be modern and then, under the influence of new theories of evolution, a historically necessary thing: in the C19, a doctrine of the inevitability of "progress" was consolidated by the benefits brought to many in the West by the Industrial Revolution and an imperialism armed with a "civilizing mission:" "gunpowder and printing," Thackeray

221

observed, "tended to modernize the world" (1860). By the time this global view of history became possible, "the modern" was opposed to the traditional, the backward, and the primitive everywhere, rather than compared with the ancient, classical, or medieval in Europe. The idea that some cultures existing in the present really belonged to a past stage of human development was, in a fourth complication, projected spatially on to the map of the world; the progression of time from the past to the future was equated with a movement from a geographic location outside **modern Western civilization** to another within it. Conversely, "the rest" of the world could be seen as suffering from time-lag: "Nigeria needs to prove that it is stable, modern-minded and representative," opined the *Guardian* in 1970.

This geopolitical twist was profoundly consequential, especially as a cultural export of global European and, later, American imperialism. Not only did "the modern" and "Western" become indissociable, with the latter imagined as "central" to a process of world historical development believed to be universal, but people in many parts of the world began to map geopolitical directives on to their pasts and futures, ordering their destinies and desires accordingly. The prescriptive view that to modernize was to Westernize political institutions, social customs, and economic practices formed the basis of **modernization theory** in mC20 sociology, and in designated "backward" zones within the West, as well as in communist countries and in postcolonial nations established in the "developing world," poor workers, women, native peoples, "minority" cultures, rural societies, peasant communities, and underclasses were targeted for redemption by the missionary force of the modern (Chakrabarty, 2000; Haebich, 1992).

In a lethal variant of this salvationism, underpinned from the lC19 by social Darwinist theories of racial selection, remnant people were "doomed" to disappear – a myth made into an agenda by C20 racist movements and state administrations (McGregor, 1997) and into a genocidal program by mC20 Nazism. The terror and complacency of progress had costs for its beneficiaries as well as its victims: if the Holocaust was a product of **modern bureaucratic rationality** (Bauman, 1989), fascism had and arguably still has a popular cultural appeal as an ostensibly **anti-modern** movement. As a promise of release not only from the great political and economic disasters of modern times but from both the relentless pace of change and the mundanity of **modern everyday life**, fascism shares a reactionary cultural impulse with nativist movements around the world that idealize whatever "traditions" they can cast as not-modern or non-Western – thereby reaffirming the latter's primacy (Sakai, 1997).

Nativist movements have joined both fascism and communism in condemning **artistic modernism** as "foreign," "decadent," "bourgeois," "elitist," or a combination of these. Narrowly referring to the experimental literature and art produced between the 1880s and 1940s – with phases of intensity in eC20 Europe, Russia, and East Asia and mC20 USA that attracted people from around the world to the modernist "capital cities" of Paris, Berlin, Shanghai, and New York – modernism is widely understood as a commitment to discarding tradition and criticizing all conventions of representation. Yet even within **affirmative modernism**, a sense of loss and dissipation afflicts the modern from its inception: in Baudelaire's famous essay on "The painter of modern life" (1845), the best-known passages dwell on "the ephemeral, the fugitive, the contingent" and dream of an art to distil "the eternal from the transitory" (see P. Osborne, 1996). Arguably, the arts that most closely fulfilled this dream turned out to be those creations of **modern technology**, photography, and cinema – fully modern arts despised by many **modernist critics** for their mass-cultural accessibility and their links to the folk-based popular traditions of magic, the fair, vaudeville, and sensationalist narrative. Yet those links gave cinema in particular a critical force. One of the most enduring images from the late years of **high modernism** is that of the resilient "little man" caught up in the machinery of mass production – played by Charlie Chaplin in *Modern Times* (1936).

Simple, pejorative uses of "modern" to imply deterioration have never lost their force. Complaints about the bad effects of modernity on females, for example, have proved durable, along with praise for the "old-fashioned girl" – "you...are not a modern woman; have neither wings to your shoulders, nor gad-fly in your cap; you love home" (1753). The **modern woman** has recurringly created scandal as a sign of social change: the lC19 suffragette, the eC20 flapper, the mC20 career girl wearing her New Look, and the lC20 liberated woman all aroused anxiety about the future in those predominantly white, Western, middle-class environments in which they first appeared. Another complication with "modern," then, is its capacity to represent what may well be slow, long-term processes of transformation as a series of sudden, sharp shocks – each one novel, yet repetitive of something that has happened before. Rendered banal as **modern fashion** in consumer culture, the modern's significance deflates until it becomes, as Raymond Williams (1976: 208) notes, "equivalent to IMPROVED," and thence a topic of irony: "Peace and Quiet poured down the sink, In exchange for a houseful of '**modern conveniences**'" (1937, Edna St Vincent Millay).

By the lC20, "modern" had largely lost its connotations of future shock and historical rupture, becoming in general usage a period term for an established stylistic tradition with its origins in the past (**modern architecture**, **modern dance**, **modern jazz**). However, "modernity" became a fertile ground for innovation in cultural history and theory (W. Benjamin, 1973; Berman, 1982; Kern, 1983), not least because **modern disciplines** such as anthropology and history were shaped by modernity's imperial adventurism and ideologies of time (Thomas, 1989). The problem of defining the modern was revived by debates about **postmodernism**, and criticism of "Western" historical narratives centered on white male protagonists paved the way for alternative accounts of **modern experience** as lived on the margins of those narratives by women (Felski, 1995) and enslaved and colonized people (Gilroy, 1993a; C. Hall, 2002), and in cities and cultural centers beyond the West (Baykam, 1994; Harootunian, 2002; Lee, 1999) where arguably the "shock" of **capitalist modernity** was and is at its most intense. In the eC21, perhaps the most fruitful

223

experiments in thinking about modernity are emerging in parts of the world where "the modern" retains its ambivalence – and thus something of its promise.

Meaghan Morris and Naoki Sakai

See: *BUREAUCRACY, DEVELOPMENT, EVERYDAY, EVOLUTION, HOLOCAUST, WEST.*

Movements

Like many terms that acquire a special political meaning, **movement** has diverse general meanings: a part of a symphony, a switch, a change over space and time. This last sense, combined with the idea of strategy or intentionality, now means the coalescing of minority or dominated groups. Two world wars had reshaped political borders, democracy was on the rise, but still minority groups in countries in North America and Britain struggled to achieve the same rights and standard of living as the dominant social groups. "Movement" began to refer specifically to groups of people coming together to seek political, economic, cultural, but especially social change (Smelser, 1962). The US **civil rights**, **Black Power**, **anti-war**, **student**, **women's**, **ecology**, and **gay movements** prompted a new label: **social movements**. At the same time, colonized people, especially on the African continent, pursued dramatic political change as **people's revolutionary movements** (Andrews, 1983). Global media enabled both groups to learn of each other's activities and successes; postcolonial groups and minorities within large democracies soon identified with each other and envisioned a world-wide "movement" for the "liberation" of all subjected peoples.

The new "movements" differed from older campaigns aimed at expressing political dissent, using forms of speech that were daring and mediagenic, from profanity and selective violence to bra-burning and adoption of flamboyant forms of attire. The **new social movements** (Touraine, 1985) frequently rejected or offered revision to the political theories that predominated, especially liberalism, Cold War diplomacy, and rigid gender roles. Unlike older campaigns – for example, the quest for women's suffrage, which agreed with democratic ideals and wanted them extended equally to women – the new social movements had more generalized demands: for visibility, to do their own thing, to be freed from the constraints of gender tyranny, to be self-determining in every way. The target of the new social movements was as much prevailing mainstream attitudes as it was swaying the electorate or changing state administrative practices. Indeed, many observers and citizens did not accept the new social movements as appropriately political, either because their demands had more to do with seemingly "private" cultural and social issues (sexuality, ethnic styles, *feelings* of exclusion) or because their modes of address were seen as hostile, intentionally uncommunicative, and self-righteously vague.

It was unclear who movements represented and how such representation worked, and this was both a strength and weakness of the movements (Snow et al., 1986). Claiming to speak on behalf of those who could not speak for themselves, either because they were afraid or because they did not even realize they were oppressed, movements were able to quickly capture public attention, even in the absence of a clear constituency. But on the other hand, sympathizers who disagreed with some actions or demands were easily excluded from movement decision-making – they were tools of the opposition, or exhibiting false consciousness. Because the new social movements based their claims on the essential qualities of the oppressed – their race, sex, sexuality, regional experience, religion, age grouping – they could be continually bogged down in debates about who expressed the most correct version of a labeled social experience ("identity"), and potential supporters from other "identities" would be mystified about how to help **movement groups**.

The idea of movements implies relocation from one place to another. The new social movements generally argued either that their kind of person had been ignored or "marginalized," and needed to be brought into the "center" or "made" visible, as if on a stage; or they argued that their kind of person had been forced to accommodate to an alien and hostile culture, that is, they had been forced into a "mainstream" at the cost of their true, but devalued historical or cultural traits. Here, the solution was to be allowed quasi-separate spaces, as in Afrocentric afternoon school programs, or to be allowed to appear in mainstream spaces, that is, in public in historically or culturally significant garb; for example, Sikhs' and Muslims' battles to wear headgear required by religious mandates, or African diasporal people's quest to be allowed to wear braids or bright *kente* cloth that was at odds with white norms of corporate attire.

225

Social movements emerged in the context of and made use of new concepts of how society functions. Although they inherited the progressive idea that the world is generally improving – "moving forward" – the use of personal identity, the focus on issues of social and cultural self-determination, suggested that the economic arrangements were not the only arena for political dissent. Social movements, focused on community self-determination and the crafting of tolerant and creative human relationships, were nevertheless also indebted to Marxist analysis of class. This led to paradoxical activism that often exacerbated the class lines that movements tried to break down. For example, gay activists believed that homophobia forced lesbians and gay men to concentrate their social life within bars, few of which were community-owned. Community ownership could address the specific characteristics of bars and lead to the cultivation of new values that could help decrease homophobia, but this would at the same time undercut the need for such community institutions. Similarly, the **black civil rights movement** was ambivalent about the role of black people in mainstream society and economy. Activists sought integration at all levels – schools, workplaces, social places – but this came at the cost of the vitality of black-owned businesses. Simultaneously claiming citizenship within and disaffection from their nations and societies, social movements soon disintegrate at the moment they overcome oppression.

Cindy Patton

See: *DIASPORA, FEMINISM, MARGINAL, RADICAL, SOCIALISM.*

Multiculturalism

Multiculturalism, as distinct from the adjective **multicultural** ("of or pertaining to a society consisting of varied cultural groups"), first came into wide circulation in the 1970s in Canada and Australia as the name for a key plank of government policy to assist in the management of ethnic pluralism within the national polity. In this context, the emergence of the term is strongly associated with a growing realization of the unintended social and cultural consequences of large-scale immigration. Coined by a Canadian Royal Commission in 1965, this governmental use of "multiculturalism" is widely supported and endorsed by its proponents as both a progressive political imperative and an official article of faith – a term associated in principle with the values of equality, tolerance, and inclusiveness toward migrants of ethnically different backgrounds. "Canadian multiculturalism is fundamental to our belief that all citizens are equal. Multiculturalism ensures that all citizens can keep their identities, can take pride in their ancestry and have a sense of belonging" (Government of Canada, 2001). Typically, multiculturalism here is a social doctrine that distinguishes itself as a positive alternative for policies of assimilation, connoting a politics of recognition of the citizenship rights and cultural identities of ethnic minority groups (Kymlycka, 1995; C. Taylor, 1992) and, more generally, an affirmation of the value of cultural diversity.

By the IC20, it had become commonplace for Western liberal democracies to describe themselves as multicultural societies, even though only a few had embraced official policies of multiculturalism. Even nation states which had traditionally been known as fiercely homogeneous, such as Germany and Japan, could no longer avoid acknowledging the ethnic and racial diversification of their populations. As a result of intensifying global migrations, "the world becomes increasingly a place of multi-ethnic states, with up to 30% of the population coming from other societies" (Davidson, 1997: 6). "Multicultural" is thus often equated with **multiethnic** in public discourse, which in turn is conflated with **multiracial**, indicating the extent to which debates on multiculturalism are concerned predominantly with the presence of non-white migrant communities in white, Western societies. In this context, multiculturalism is variously evoked as a response to the need to address real or potential ethnic tension and racial conflict.

For example, in Britain a Commission on the Future of Multi-Ethnic Britain, set up in 1998 by the Runnymede Trust, was "devoted to the cause of promoting racial justice" and to proposing ways of "making Britain a confident and vibrant multicultural society at ease with its rich diversity." The Commission's report, *The future of multi-ethnic Britain* (Runnymede Trust Commission on the Future of Multi-Ethnic Britain, 2000), also known as the Parekh Report after the Commission's chairperson, Bhikhu Parekh, stated famously that "Britain is both a community of citizens and a community of communities, both a liberal and a multicultural society, and needs to reconcile their sometimes conflicting requirements" (p. 1). This statement illustrates the unresolved, complex, and ambiguous relationship between multiculturalism and the political philosophy of liberalism, although the phrase **liberal multiculturalism** is also used descriptively by academic analysts to refer precisely to the diversity management policies of governments.

In a more activist context, "multiculturalism" stands for a left-radicalist attempt to overturn dominant, monocultural conceptions of history and society, which were considered ethnocentric or even racist. In the USA, multiculturalism in this sense came into wide public use during the early 1980s in the context of public (state) school curriculum reform. School curricula were criticized for their so-called Eurocentric bias and their failure to acknowledge the achievements of women, people of color, or people from outside the tradition of Western civilization. Most controversial in this regard is the movement known as Afrocentrism, which in various versions has sought to document the centrality of African cultural traditions to the foundation of American and Western history, and to celebrate that African tradition so as to increase the self-esteem and educational success of African-American students.

Overall, the burgeoning language of multiculturalism signals a heightened awareness of and concern with the increasingly problematic and disjunctive relationship between race, ethnicity, and national identity in the lC20 and eC21. This also accounts for why "multiculturalism" has remained a controversial concept despite its now common circulation. While the precise meaning of the word is never clear, it refers generally to the dilemmas and difficulties of the politics of difference.

227

Critics come from both conservative and radical angles. Left-radical critics have found fault in (liberal) multiculturalism because it allegedly depoliticizes or aestheticizes difference by emphasizing the cosmetic celebration of cultural diversity, rather than the socially transformative struggle against racism or white supremacy. For them, multiculturalism stands for a strategy of containment of resistance and revolt rather than for a true desire for the elimination of racial/ethnic oppression. In a more postcolonial vein, the celebrationist notion of diversity – the practical expression of which can be witnessed in the proliferation of **multicultural festivals** organized by local governments in areas with a high presence of migrant populations – is often dismissed by cultural critics because of its exoticizing, folkloristic, and consumerist nature: "Multiculturalism in Australia is acceptable as a celebration of costumes, customs, and cooking" (Stratton, 1998: 97). From the perspective of postcolonial and postmodern theory, multiculturalism is criticized for its implicit assumption that "ethnic groups" are the inherent proprietors of "culture" and that "cultures" are fixed and static realities. These diverse critical strands have in common that they consider multiculturalism, as a state-managed policy and discourse, as not going far enough in transforming the white-dominated dominant culture. Hence, the term **critical multiculturalism** is sometimes coined as a radical alternative to liberal multiculturalism. Unlike the latter, the former sees "diversity itself as a goal, but rather argues that diversity must be affirmed within a politics of cultural criticism and a commitment to social justice" (McLaren, 1994: 53; see also Chicago Cultural Studies Group, 1994).

Conservative critics, on the other hand, accuse proponents of multiculturalism of political correctness and a particularist pursuit of identity politics. These critics generally argue against multiculturalism because they see it as encouraging separatism and as a threat to national unity and social cohesion. Thus, Australian prime minister John Howard said in 1988: "My argument with multiculturalism is not that it respects and tolerates diversity but rather in many ways it emphasizes division" (*cit.* Stratton, 1998: 67). So controversial was the very word "multiculturalism" for a short period after 1996, when Australia was swept by a right-wing populist backlash, that it was routinely referred to as "the M-word." By 2002, however, according to the *Australian* newspaper, reporting on Howard's apparent concession that multiculturalism had "acquired a certain meaning and place in our society," "the M-word is kosher again" (Steketee, 2002: 12). The addition of a national specification to the general term, as in "Australian multiculturalism," is commonly deployed by Howard as a way of imposing the unifying umbrella of national identity on the tapestry of diversity, which he, and others like him, consider as having a dangerous potential for unleashing centrifugal forces within society.

Very similar controversies have raged in other countries as well. In the UK, the Parekh Report, particularly its multiculturalist notion of Britain as a "community of communities," was widely criticized by conservatives as a recipe for the balkanization of society. In the USA, multiculturalism was similarly attacked for promoting national division, as reflected in the title of Arthur J. Schlesinger's best-selling book, *The disuniting of America*. Invoking the US's motto *E pluribus unum*, Schlesinger argues that multiculturalism, especially in its radical version, is based on a "cult of ethnicity" and an "obsession with difference," unsettling "the balance between *unum* and *pluribus*" (Schlesinger, 1992: 133). All these critics stress the need for a "common culture" if a nation is to function peacefully.

One effect of the fallout of the terrorist attacks on the USA on September 11, 2001, has been a heightened concern with the possibility of a global "clash of civilizations" (Huntington, 1993), specifically between Islam and "the West," with grave implications for the place of the millions of Muslims now living in liberal-democratic societies. As they are now in danger of being positioned as "the enemy within," and their culture and religion dismissed as backward or inferior by some extremist right-wing politicians, especially in Western Europe (including the Italian prime minister, Silvio Berlusconi), the multiculturalist credo of valuing and protecting cultural diversity is increasingly countered by a renewed call for assimilation or for a halt on immigration altogether – unrealistic desires in the complex realities of the globalized, postmodern world.

In the eC21, then, as globalization has become generally, if sometimes reluctantly accepted as a fact of life, the issues which were first addressed by multiculturalism – that is, how to deal with the proliferation of ethnic and cultural differences within the nation as national borders become increasingly porous – have become increasingly urgent and complex, even as the term itself is becoming more and more problematic. As the name for a consensual idea it seems to have become unworkable, but it is still necessary as an heuristic concept that points to the uneasy and contested space between exclusionary and homogenizing modes of nationalism, on the one hand, and on the other, the unrealistic utopia of a rootless cosmopolitanism where everyone is supposedly a ''world citizen'' in a borderless world.

Ien Ang

See: *CIVILIZATION, DIASPORA, DIFFERENCE, ETHNICITY, LIBERALISM, NATION, POSTCOLONIALISM, RACE, WEST.*

Narrative

A **narrative** is a story, told by a **narrator** about events which may be factual, fictional, or mythical. These attributes of narrative vary historically. The earliest references to narrative define it as "That part of a deed or document which contains a statement of the relevant or essential facts" (mC16–eC19). This meaning derives from the L rhetorical term *narratio*, which was used to describe "that part of a speech or discourse in which the facts are presented." This implies a distinction between the presentation of "facts" and other parts of a speech or discourse in which the "moral" or "conclusion" is presented (Wales, 2001: 264). This usage is still prevalent in law courts where it is used of parts of a judicial, defense, or prosecution summation. Yet narrative has also been contrasted with the notion of factually based argument in being used to describe someone who is "garrulous or talkative," particularly old men: "the tattling quality of age, which ... is always narrative" (C17 and eC18). The eC17 also sees the term being used to refer to "a consecutively developed story" and, by the mC20, this has become the dominant usage, one applying whether the story is told in words, performance on stage, the gestures of mime, or pictures.

C20 uses of "narrative" have also been affected by its relations to myth. As Raymond Williams notes, this term "came into English as late as eC19" and meant "a fable or story or tale, later contrasted with *logos* and *historia*." Myth was always to do with "fabulous narration" (Williams, 1983: 210–12). As a consequence of being used "negatively as a contrast to fact, history and science," it has come to be associated with "the difficult modern senses of *imagination, creative* and *fiction*" (p. 212). Narrative came to have

ABCDEFGHIJKLM**N**OPQRSTUVWXYZ

similar connotations through its connections with myth (as story or tale) and in the lC20 the difference between apparently timeless narratives of the mythical or fictional kind and the legitimating, time- and history-bound **grand narratives** of history and science became the focus of Jean François Lyotard's work on the condition of knowledge in postmodernism. Whereas science had once been in conflict with narratives, considering them mere fables, modern science had in fact woven a series of narratives about itself. "I will use the term *modern*," Lyotard writes, "to designate any science that legitimates itself with reference to a metadiscourse of this kind making an explicit appeal to some grand narrative, such as . . . the emancipation of the rational or working subject" (Lyotard, 1984: xxiii). If postmodernism has challenged these grand narratives, Lyotard contends that narrative is still essential to science, seeing "the little narrative [*petit recit*]" as "the quintessential form of imaginative invention, most particularly in science" (p. 60).

Lyotard's work recognized the centrality of narrative to all human activity and commu-nication. It also identified the productive aspect of narrative, the fact that narrative is a way of constructing, not just representing, realities and selves. This recognition became central to a **cultural politics of narrative**, initially in debates about history (White, 1973) and subsequently in feminist (Butler, 1990) and postcolonial theory (Bhabha, 1990a), radical educational theory (Freebody, Muspratt, and Dwyer, 2001), and critical discourse analysis (Fairclough, 1995). In these varied contexts, challenging legitimated narratives and offering alternative stories came to be seen as a way of contesting the power of institutions to offer their own versions of the world as the only legitimate versions.

All of this work owes something to the academic study of narrative (**narratology**), which derives from the much earlier traditions of formalism (Propp, 1968) and structur-alism (Barthes, 1979). Vladimir Propp's work on the Russian fairy-tale involved a typical kind of narrative grammar or poetics. He was able to show that the abstract system which made possible the generation of a wide variety of stories was in fact very simple, consisting of a small number of roles (character types), functions (actions or events significant to the plot), and ways of combining these. In later forms of **narrative analysis** (Genette, 1980), distinctions are made between what is being told – the actual chronological sequence of the events being narrated, called *histoire* by Genette – and the plot structure constructed by the teller – the order of events as told, which Genette calls *récit*. The act of storytelling itself is called *énunciation*.

A further important distinction is made between what is integral to the fictional world of the narrative, called the *diegesis,* and what is external to that world – the *extra-* or *non-diegetic*. The principal parts of a narrative – *setting* (or orientation), *complication* (something that sets off the narrative train of events), *climax* (when events come to a head, as when the hero and villain join in direct combat), *denouement* (resolution; for example, the hero wins), and *coda* (or closing act, as in "and they all lived happily ever after") (Toolan, 1988), as well as dialogue, and, in the case of visual or **filmic narrative**, elements such as *mise-en-scène*, or sound – may all be integral to the narrative world and are thus a part of the diegesis. However, as soon as an author steps out of that frame and speaks directly to the reader (or a character directly addresses the camera in a film), for example, what is occurring is non-diegetic, although still a part of the reader/viewer's experience of the narrative as a whole.

The reader/viewer is sometimes called the **narratee**, but there may also be a narratee — in the sense of the person to whom the story is told — within the narrative. Miranda listening to her father's story at the beginning of *The Tempest* is a case in point. It is often difficult to distinguish such a narratee from the *implied reader*, who, as Umberto Eco has argued, is implicit in every text, which he sees as ''a lazy machine asking the reader to do some of its work'' (Eco, 1994: 3). The implied reader is a *model reader*, a ''sort of ideal type whom the text not only foresees as a collaborator but also tries to create'' (p. 9). The actual or *empirical reader* is different and does not necessarily follow the text's or the narrative's instructions. An early example of the role of the reader at work in dialogue with a **narrative text** is offered by Roland Barthes in his account of reading in *S/Z* (1975), a study of Balzac's short story *Sarrasine*.

This critical vocabulary has been incorporated into the analysis of all kinds of spoken and written narratives, visual, film, and media texts in a broad-ranging literature (Hartley, 1982; Heath, 1983; Metz, 1981; Silverstone, 1985) which, by engaging with the analysis of storying in a mass-mediated society, has demonstrated how necessary the continued understanding of the link between narrative and myth — and the deconstruction of the apparent naturalness of both — still are.

Terry Threadgold

See: *SIGN, TEXT, WRITING.*

Nation

''Bonaparte made kings; England makes nations.'' William Bentinck's proclamation (*cit.* Peabody, 1996: 209) on landing with his forces at Palermo in 1811 had the immediate aim of fostering the growth of Italian **nationalism** and enlisting its support in the British campaign against French and Austrian power in the Italian peninsula. But it also appealed to the romantic view of **nations**, as having a life of their own and a right to manage their own affairs, which had been influential in, and actively promoted by, the French Revolution in the years before Napoleon seized power. The abbé Sieyès (1789) defined ''nation'' as ''a union of individuals governed by one law, and represented by the same law-making assembly'' — which implied not only that every nation should have a state of its own (or at least a substantial measure of self-government) but also that it could be seen as a legitimate source of political authority. The suggestion that this earlier French commitment to self-determination for all nations had been betrayed gave added force to

Bentinck's claim that the French suppressed the rights of nations while the British aimed to set them free.

The word itself derives from the L *nasci* (to be born) through *nationem* (a breed or stock), and its early usage referred to a distinct aggregate of people associated with each other by common descent or history, or to a number of persons drawn from such an aggregate. In medieval universities, for example, it referred to a body of students from a particular region, country, or group of countries. By the end of the C18, the more political connotations invoked by Bentinck and Sieyès had come to the fore. In some more recent uses – **the Nation of Islam** or **Queer Nation** – the term has lost much of its earlier association with common descent.

The claim that nations had a right to self-determination was often regarded as a matter of principle. It could also be seen as seeking to undermine the legitimacy of the large **supranational states** which dominated much of continental Europe in the C19 and eC20 or, more simply perhaps, as a pragmatic response to the threat to peace and security posed by the existence of powerful and unsatisfied national aspirations. While not advocating self-determination for all nations, the Covenant of the **League of Nations** nevertheless called for "the prescription of open, just and honorable" relations between them. The Allied powers that founded the League at the end of World War I also recognized that many of the states created by the peace settlements contained significant **national minorities** for whom self-determination would not be practicable. Accordingly, they established a minorities protection regime, consisting of treaties overseen and guaranteed by the League, designed to prevent discontent among these minorities from escalating into a cause of war.

To say that nations have a right to self-determination is to acknowledge that nations and states are distinct. The conflation between them nevertheless persists in various contexts – for example, in the conventional usage of the word "international" or in the name of the **United Nations**, which is an organization of states. There have been many attempts to define nations in terms of the possession of a common language, culture, or descent, a distinct territory, and so on. In an influential lecture, "What is a nation?," delivered in 1882, Ernest Renan argued that definitions based on such objective attributes would never be able to distinguish all the groups we recognize as nations: the examples of Belgium and Switzerland were sufficient to undermine the claim that nations are defined by a common language. What ultimately holds a nation together, Renan insisted, is "the fact of sharing, in the past, a glorious heritage and regrets, and of having, in the future, [a shared] program to put into effect": the very existence of the nation is therefore "a daily plebiscite" (Renan, 1996 [1882]: 53). This image of the nation as "a large-scale solidarity" reflects an aspiration which has played a significant role in many **nationalist movements**, but, since people who belong to the same nation often have radically different views about its past and its future, it is no more successful in defining a nation than the objective attributes which Renan disputes.

Nation

A different version of the idea that nations exist in the minds of their members appears in Benedict Anderson's observation (1983) that nations are "imagined communities": nations, like other large collectivities, must be imagined because they exist on too large a scale to be directly experienced by their members. They differ from imaginary communities of other kinds in being imagined as sovereign communities, each with a well-defined population and territory distinct from those of other nations. Where Renan stresses commitment to a common heritage, Anderson focuses on the mundane experiences of common membership. This focus invites us to examine not just the work of **nation states** and **nationalist movements** in promoting their own preferred vision of the nation and **national heritage**, but also the broad range of conditions which serve to promote a sense of shared **national identity**: the vernacular languages, the fabricated rituals and traditions, the newspapers and journals, shared time-zones, the administrative and tax-gathering apparatuses, border controls, currency, maps, postage stamps, and other artifacts which seduce and cajole the most diverse individuals and groups into imagining that they belong together in the one nation. Nothing in these conditions requires those who experience themselves as members of the one nation to have the same image of the imagined community to which they all claim to belong.

If the nation is an imagined community, then nationalism is a project which aims to adapt the social and political order to the requirements of some preferred **national imaginary** through a process, often contested, of **nation building**. It might, for example, promote the interests of an established nation, foster the growth of a **national consciousness** where it had not existed before, fight to secure an independent state or some lesser measure of self-government, campaign for the expulsion or assimilation of alien elements in the nation's midst or to recover lost **national territories**, defend the nation's language or culture against foreign intrusions, or fashion a **national tradition** by incorporating elements of folksong into musical compositions. Nationalist political movements have taken diverse political forms, some of them being relatively liberal and cosmopolitan in character and others distinctly less so; many of the differences between them reflect contrasting perceptions of the nation or nations concerned. On the one hand, a nation could be seen in the manner of the abbé Sieyès's definition, that is, as one *sovereign* people among a number of others. On the other hand, as Renan's discussion would suggest, it could be seen as a *unique* or *distinctive people* held together by more exclusive ties of blood, language, or religion. The fact that these opposed views may be held by different members of the one nation, leading to correspondingly different views about who belongs to the nation and who does not, suggests that there is no straightforward relationship between a nation and the character of the nationalist movements which claim to act in its name.

Nationalists frequently appeal to the long and distinguished past of their own nation. Thus, when indigenous peoples in North America insist on their status as **First Nations** they are certainly drawing on long-standing linguistic practice – the OED cites references to **Indian Nations** from as early as 1650 – but they are also asserting their right, as nations, to self-determination and laying claim to an historical existence stretching back to a period preceding the European invasions and well before the emergence of most European nations. Nevertheless, historians and social scientists generally agree that, like the states whose legitimacy they sometimes support and sometimes undermine, nations are artifacts of the modern system of states, and that their national traditions are either newly invented or substantially reworked versions of established traditions.

From the time of their first appearance, nations and nationalisms have been subject to the play of geopolitical conflict. Thus, during the Napoleonic Wars, the British deployed the claim that nations had a right to self-determination both in their dealings with the rest of Europe and in their covert attempts – for fear of offending Spain – to wean independence movements in Spanish America away from their alliance with France. This claim also supplied an emancipatory gloss to British imperial maneuvers in India. In all three cases, British policies were represented as promoting conditions in which nations suppressed by alien rule – by the French, the Spanish, or the Marathas – could re-emerge and flourish. The growth of nations has been fostered by established states working to **nationalize** their own populations or to destabilize their geopolitical opponents, by the practices of imperial governments, and by nationalist movements seeking to create or to enlarge states of their own. The successful construction of nations inevitably disrupts other imagined communities which have the misfortune to cut across or to fall within their boundaries, some of which, like the Basques, the Kurds, and the Palestinians, might themselves lay claim to national identity.

235

Barry Hindess

See: *COLONIALISM, GOVERNMENT, HERITAGE, STATE.*

Nature

Raymond Williams (1983: 219) assessed that **nature** is "perhaps the most complex word in the [English] language" and that there is an "extraordinary amount of human history" (1980: 219) embedded in this term. He traced the evolution of the descriptive form (**natural**) into an independent noun, as a shortened version of the L phrase *rerum naturum* (**nature of things**). In its earliest (C13) usage "nature" referred to an inherent or essential quality or character of something. The power in this sense of "nature" and of "natural" as inherent, fundamental, universal, and/or necessary is in the attribution of fixity, with the implication of immutability. In the eC21 this remains the most generalized and possibly the most persistent sense of these terms. Closely linked to it is the contemporary sense of "natural" meaning "appropriate" or "fitting," often contrasted with that which is considered artificial, contrived, and/or inappropriate.

Generalized usage of "nature" developed from the C14 in Europe into a designation of "the inherent force which directs... the world" (sometimes including human beings)

(R. Williams, 1980: 219). This sense of nature or **Nature** as an overarching and guiding agency continues into the eC21. However, there have been significant changes in the metaphors and models associated with it. Since the C14 in the West, Nature has been personified and conceptualized as operating, in turn, as goddess, divine deputy, monarch, constitutional lawyer (in the C18), and breeder (in the late C19) (R. Williams, 1976).

Since the C16 the term "nature" also designates the material world. Traditionally this apparently simple use denotes all matter that exists in the world without the intervention of human agency or activity. In this sense, human operations are distinguished from **natural forces**. "Culture" is the term which commonly refers to human activity, products, and accomplishments. Controversies about the relative power and significance of human agency and the possibility of change and transformation are often posed as **nature vs. culture** or **nature vs. nurture**. Since the C16, human ambition may be expressed in terms of a desire to *transcend* nature. Related to this is the long-standing pattern in the Western world of gendering culture as masculine and nature as feminine (de Beauvoir, 1973). The personification of **Mother Nature** is the most enduring expression of this pattern.

Since the lC19 in the Western world, evolutionary theory, as formulated primarily by Charles Darwin (1859), has provided an influential framework for understanding the operations of nature (although this theory has been rejected by Christian fundamentalists in North America and other groups). The focus of Darwin's attention was on reproduction. He characterized nature's various manifestations under the powerful principle of **natural selection**: the idea of species development, over long periods of time, through the elimination of traits hindering their survival. Through his detailed sketching of evidence of the operation of this principle Darwin conjured a complex picture of nature's distinctive creative powers. Nevertheless, he developed his ideas of natural selection with reference to the activities of breeders and early agricultural capitalists. Moreover, Darwin's vision of nature as an ostensibly autonomous sphere mirrored many of the features of industrial capitalism, particularly its competitiveness (R. M. Young, 1985). Thus, whilst sketching **nature's operations**, Darwin was looking over his shoulder at and was possibly influenced by industrial capitalism. Despite this, his insistence that nature's patterns were distinct and his determination to eschew political connections rendered his picture of an autonomous nature highly credible and influential.

Social Darwinism, which first emerged in Britain and the USA in the 1870s and was revived in the 1970s, adapted evolutionary theory and applied it to analyze social and political life. It contends that human biology results in an inevitable competitive social struggle for existence. Since the 1970s, there have been three other major mobilizations of ideas of nature in overarching **naturalizing theories**, which provide sweeping accounts of human behavior and social life. From the mid-1970s sociobiology was offered as "a new synthesis" (E. O. Wilson, 1975): an all-embracing, naturalizing framework. It claimed that every aspect of human behavior derived from the operation of natural selection, which was linked with a pervasive drive to reproduce. Toward the end of the C20, in what has been described as "a new mutation," social Darwinism flourished yet again, with a more individualistic orientation, in the guise of evolutionary psychology. The latter claims "to explain all aspects of human behavior, and thence culture and society, on the basis of universal features of **human nature** that found their final evolutionary form during the infancy of our species" (H. Rose and Rose, 2000: 1). Finally, in the lC20 and eC21 the ambitions and expectations for the emerging science of genomics have excelled those associated with all previous naturalizing frameworks. Spinning off from genomics are claims that it can explain an extensive range of human conditions, including not only virtually all diseases but also various behavior patterns and predispositions, among them violence and homosexuality.

There are strong theoretical interconnections between social Darwinism, sociobiology, evolutionary psychology, and the recent social extensions of genomics. Moreover, the common reductionist imperative of these influential theories is the contention that complex social, economic, and political phenomena can be rendered comprehensible with reference to the operation of a single **natural force** or **process** (natural selection, for example) or a single **natural structure** (genes, for instance). Critics have protested against the simplifications and fatalism implicit in such **naturalizations** and the conservative social vision which they bolster. Those contesting **genetic naturalization** contend with a further complication: genomics is accompanied with notable ambitions for genetic engineering, which promises not just to identify but also to alter and eliminate problematic genes. Unlike its predecessors, this naturalizing theory of the social world has a transformative, possibly even eugenic potential, which renders it both more powerful and more threatening than its antecedents.

While grand naturalizing theories were emerging in the lC20, there were also new explorations of the generalized use of the terms "nature" and "natural." These included analyzing how particular characteristics came to appear inherent, universal, or necessary. Identifying ideological dimensions of apparently **natural characteristics** (including those associated with "race" and gender) was one phase in this process. These challenges were fueled by civil rights and social movements of the late C20 which tackled inequalities linked to notions of **natural differences** (particularly those associated with "race," ethnicity, gender, and sexuality). In some quarters, this fostered skepticism about the attribution of *any* inherent qualities. From the late 1980s this was expressed through negative evaluations of "essentialism" and "essentializing" (terms often used to designate such naturalizing practices) (Fuss, 1989). Indeed, criticizing the very *process* of characterizing traits as natural (that is, identifying and condemning essentializing) became a critical practice during the 1990s. More recently, there has been some tracing of the *social processes* and *mechanisms* through which certain traits or characteristics **become naturalized**. Some see the identification of these mechanisms and patterns as undermining the claim that there *are* **natural traits** or **natures**, suggesting instead that there are practices and processes which have **naturalizing effects**.

237

Nature

Modern Western sensibilities to and orientations around ideas of nature were forged in the wake of the Industrial Revolution and the spread of industrial capitalism from the lC18 and eC19. As production became more technological and commercially oriented, there was an imaginative investment in the idea of nature as a *distinct sphere* and in **natural persons** (peasants or children, for example) and spaces (nature as the wilderness), which were considered to be untouched by these processes. The Romantic movement (lC18 and eC19) epitomized, articulated, and aestheticized the expansion of interest in nature and **the natural**, but was by no means the only manifestation of this conceptual, emotional, and political response to industrialization.

Since the lC20 there has been a general sense in the Western world of there being few areas and less material in the world which are untouched by human intervention and industry. In the face of wide-scale perceptions that there is, in this sense, less nature and few, if any, processes or forces unmarked by human activity, the designation "natural" may seem rather inappropriate or problematic. In this sense, from the lC20 there has been more self-consciousness and, in some cases, reticence about the use of the terms "nature" or "natural." Indeed, it may not be too contradictory to claim that, in this respect, the term "nature" itself has been denaturalized.

Yet, somewhat ironically, more and more Westerners have turned to the world of industrial production to get their **natural fix**. As Marilyn Strathern (1992: 197) notes, the designation "natural" has been "slapped onto products as a new dimension." Far from seeing industrial manufacture as antithetical to **natural processes and products**, many contemporary consumers are attracted to manufactured products (including food products, cosmetics, etc.) that offer the natural as their "superadded dimension." Hence, despite intellectual interrogation of the term "nature" and of naturalization in the West, the lC20 and eC21 have seen a proliferation of the commercial usage of the term. In the contemporary marketplace the appeal of the natural is palpable and cashable.

Meanwhile, since the lC20, wide-scale concern about contamination of various kinds (bovine spongiform encephalopathy [BSE], foot and mouth disease), depletion of key resources, and risks associated with technoscientific innovations (genetically modified foods) has given an immediacy and concreteness to the imperative to understand human agency in the **natural world**. Ecology movements, environmental sciences, and green politics address and are themselves manifestations of such concern. Some regard explicit invocation of nature and the natural as distinct realms as crucial in tackling the problems that have been foregrounded through these channels. Others remain deeply skeptical about this and other returns to nature (and Nature) in the C21.

Against this background, the recent deployments of the terms "organic" and "environment" as popular surrogates for the terms "natural" and "nature" are striking. During the lC20 "organic" emerged as an attractive *substitute* for the term "natural" to designate processes and products both of manufacture in the conventional sense and of reproduction (eggs, seeds, etc., often also industrialized), identified with limited levels of or "appropriate" forms of human activities (although the specification of this varies and is often vague). Similarly, in this period, the term "environment" increasingly replaced "nature" in reference to "the material world" in popular and scientific parlance. Unlike "natural" and "nature," the terms "organic" and "environment" do not neatly demarcate a sphere distinct from human agency. These linguistic developments seem to address the desire for containment and limitation of industrial production, which has been a recurring impulse powering ideas of nature and the natural since the Industrial Revolution. In this sense, they register, without resolving, the complications deriving from the human place *in* nature.

Modern ideas of nature and the natural were forged in the wake of the Industrial Revolution and the expansion of industrial production in the Western world. Against this background, reproduction was designated (particularly through evolutionary theory) as the pre-eminent sphere and manifestation of nature's operations. This framework seems to have been disturbed, and it is currently being reconfigured in the wake of the technologiza-tion and commercialization of reproduction. The last decades of the C20 brought intense commercialization of all forms of reproduction – vegetation, animal, and human – from seeds, to cloned sheep, to human embryos fertilized *in vitro*. Moreover, the emphasis on the difficulties of and obstacles to human reproduction signaled by the term "assisted repro-duction," which designates a wide range of recent technoscientific practices, makes it more difficult to regard reproduction as the *distinct* sphere of nature or the domain of natural forces. If the sphere of reproduction no longer looms as the quintessential domain of nature for many Westerners, there is considerable apprehension and fear around this disturbance. Since the late 1970s and the birth of the first "test-tube baby," Western popular media have generated and aired stories that revolve around the dangers in tampering with natural processes of reproduction. This is an example of the continuing power of the **idea of nature**: it haunts and animates the contemporary Western world in countless ways.

239

Maureen McNeil

See: *BIOLOGY, BODY, EVOLUTION, GENE/GENETIC, HUMAN, SEXUALITY.*

Network

Network is traceable to the eC16 and indicates a web of connections (often, but not exclusively, technical) which link objects, institutions, and/or people. Commonplace ex-amples are the **railway network**, the **television network**, and the **Oxbridge network**.

During the C20 "network" has been used in the social sciences in various ways. **Social network analysis** developed especially after World War II (J. Scott, 1992). It originated in the UK, chiefly in social anthropology (especially at Manchester University under the tutelage of Max Gluckman), as a means of identifying people's interrelations. A suggestion of this work was that networks changed through time, and with the decline of rural life, from few but strong networks to many but weak networks in a modern urban age. By and large this anthropological tradition uses the word "network" in a metaphorical sense, to capture qualitative features of relationships (co-operative as opposed to independent, for example) such as those between marriage partners in different social classes (Bott, 1971) and between members of a Norwegian fishing village (Barnes, 1954).

However, during the 1950s network analysis grew as a distinctively mathematical dimension of sociology and social psychology in the United States. A theme of this technical and professionalizing subdiscipline was to identify and analyze points connected by lines. By calculating the number of relationships, their frequency, direction, and perceived weight, a sociogram (a diagrammatic representation of social networks) might be produced to depict particular networks. This evolved into the science of sociometry, much used by social psychologists, though network analysis has also produced influential work on, for example, interlocking directorates in American corporations. Network analysis of this kind was much influenced by the work of George Homans (1950) on small group behavior and by his writing on exchange theory, which in turn fed in to the emergence of rational-choice theory in the late 1960s.

In social science thinking about networks, and more broadly, there has long been a close association with technological change. The increased availability of the telephone, and more recently the full range of telecommunications and computer technologies, as well as the spread of means of transport such as road, railroad, and airplane, led many to assume a close, and even direct, relationship between technologies which facilitate connections and changed social patterns. Toward the end of the C20 Manuel Castells (1996) took to characterizing the "information age" as a **network society**. The emergence of the Internet especially has given credibility to this description. The concept suggests that information and communications technologies (ICTs) reduce limits of time and space, and result in relations being conducted on a planetary scale in real time. The consequence is that flows of information – hence networks – are crucial to contemporary existence. Places still matter, especially those such as cities which act as nodes for these information flows, but crucial are the ways in which networks operate. For instance, social movements, to be effective, must be capable of mobilizing support through **ICT networks**, and modern-day economies must maintain around-the-clock **financial networks**.

It is suggested that a certain category of person is key to the network society. Robert Reich (1991) defines this as the symbolic analyst, he or she who is best equipped to prosper in an instantaneous and rapid-changing world. The symbolic analyst is he or she who analyses, assesses, and acts on information flows to maximum effect, and facility on the network is critical to this. A prerequisite is high-level education which provides the necessary communicative, analytical, and strategic skills.

The network society is thought to be one which brings increasing freedom to individuals. The suggestion is that there have developed **networks of choice**. These have supplanted older forms of network, which imposed obligations to family and neighbors, and replaced them with more fragile yet more individually appealing forms. It is noteworthy that the spread of **virtual networks**, which are thought to be central to the development of choices, is imagined to be a means of establishing electronic communities (networks of people sharing beliefs and/or interests at a distance) at a time when long-term communities are said to be disappearing.

Thinking about networks tends toward the favorable. The verb **to network** usually carries a positive connotation, as in **well networked**. Interestingly, this inflection sheds an earlier suspicion of the word. During the mid- to IC20 there was widespread suspicion of the exclusionary and privileged aspects of networks, such as the **Rotary networks**, the **golf club network**, or the **old school tie network**. Though nowadays we are said to inhabit an exciting and satisfying network society, this old-fashioned and negative implication still carries some resonance.

Frank Webster

See: *COMMUNICATION, INFORMATION, MOVEMENTS, VIRTUAL.*

Normal

Few words have more power, actual and symbolic, than **normal** and its associated terms – **norm**, **normality**, **normalize**. **The normal** is the usual, the average, the common. But the normal is also the desirable – for who but the perverse wants to be **abnormal**? And the normal is also the healthy, for what is abnormality but a deviation from health? And the normal is also an expectation, for only the eccentric or rebellious will not wish to conform to the prevailing **norms of conduct**.

These words begin to acquire their contemporary meaning in the C19. By 1855 it was common to understand a norm as a standard, a model, a pattern, or a type which could serve as a guide for others – be it in literature or theology. But Ian Hacking (1990) points to earlier usages. There is the geometrical, in which normal and orthogonal are the equivalent L- and Gk-derived terms for a line at right angles to another – already containing, as Hacking notes, the idea of straightness as opposed to crookedness. Even more significant was the idea of normal within the French sciences of life. In the IC18, as pathology became associated with individual organs, the normal became the inverse of pathology. François Joseph Victor Broussais turns that idea around – the pathological state was not completely distinct from the normal; rather the pathological was simply deviation from the normal. Auguste Comte extended Broussais's principle to collective organisms – in society, too, the pathological was a deviation from the normal. But for Comte normality, like health, was that toward which progress tended and that for which we should strive – normality carries the double meaning of average and perfect.

By the end of the C19, thanks to the work of statisticians, the idea of the norm had become inextricably linked with the distribution of qualities in a population. By the start of that century it was known that a number of phenomena – the variations in astronomic measurement by different observers, the frequency of chance events such as the numbers of heads or tails in a sequence of coin tossing – obeyed "the law of errors": they showed a regularity that could be plotted in a bell-shaped curve that peaked around the average or mean. Adolf Quetelet showed that the same curve applied to biological phenomena such as the chest measurements of Scottish soldiers; he argued that any physical quality in a population would be distributed according to this curve – **the normal curve** – and that the mean point on this curve defined "the average man" (Quetelet, 1835). Francis Galton applied this way of thinking to human intellectual qualities: he argued that the qualities of the intellect in a population were distributed according to the **normal distribution**, and hence, of course, one could identify a norm. This norm could act as a standard against which any individual's intellect could be judged, and its level of deviation calculated. The norm, measured from the perspective of the population, enabled each individual to be "individualized" and allowed some to be judged "abnormal" and "normalized" by instituting corrective procedures to return them to the norm.

In the eC20 the notion of norm acquired a further set of meanings in anthropology and sociology – the standards or conventions of human conduct that are accepted within a specific society or culture. It seemed that every society had its norms, indeed norms were a *sine qua non* of a society. A sociological and anthropological industry grew up to chart these norms, to document the processes (socialization) whereby they were inculcated into members of a society, to analyze the norms' social functions, and to identify the procedures that were used to correct those who would violate them – from social disapproval to punishment. E. M. Forster registered this social pressure toward **normalization**: "Against my will I have become normal. I cannot help it" (1914). For 50 years or so, these ideas were unquestioned. But writers from the 1960s onward asked how certain values came to be accepted as norms and by whom. Some showed that specific norms were historical, others argued that the very idea of the norm only emerged in Western societies in the C18 and C19, as social life came to be overlaid with a grid of authoritative judgments of civility and danger.

In this vein, Georges Canguilhem distinguished between two types of norms that pertain to human life: **vital norms** such as those of temperature or heartbeat, and **social norms** such as those of productive labor or civility (Canguilhem, 1978). The mapping of the one onto the other enables the norms of a particular sociopolitical order to be read as if they arise from the nature of human life itself – a move that legitimates all manner of techniques that turn dissent into deviance, transform difference into deficiency, and reframe control as normalization. The sociology of deviance of the 1960s and 1970s was predicated on such an analysis in its critique of the unquestioned assumptions of criminology and psychiatry, and in its skepticism about the normalizing premises of conceptions of intelligence and heterosexuality.

Most recently, developments in the life sciences have re-posed the issue of norms, normality, and normalization at a molecular level. Many fear that the Human Genome Project will establish the sequence for a normal human genome, allowing for molecular surveillance, discrimination, and/or normalization. But far from a single normal sequence, the very idea of **genomic normality** has been thrown into doubt by the discovery of multiple variations at almost every point in the genome – at the level of the genome the normal is rare. Others fear that molecular neuroscience and neuropharmacology will allow the normalization of human conduct by interventions to control deviations of thought, emotion, or desire at the molecular level. But developments in neuroscience have blurred the boundaries of therapy, correction, normalization, and enhancement. In our culture, who wants to be merely normal? We all aspire to be exceptions, unique, better than well. Perhaps the power of the idea of the norm is reaching exhaustion: we may find new criteria of judgment in the C21.

Nikolas Rose

See: *BIOLOGY, GENE/GENETIC, SOCIETY.*

Objectivity

Objectivity, together with its cognates, **objective**, **objectively**, and **objectivism**, has what might seem to contemporary observers a placid history. There is widespread agreement that the term "objectivity" is synonymous with such things as neutrality, impartiality, and disinterestedness; the **objective observer**, for instance, is able to give a reliable account of events precisely because she or he has no interest in the outcome and is able to make statements and render judgments regardless of their consequences. Apparently, we have managed to agree about what an objective observer is, even though we usually disagree about whether this or that person has in fact served as an objective observer in any given case.

These disagreements are most noticeable in politics – and, to a lesser degree, in journalism – where charges of partisanship and bias are so common as to give the ideal of objectivity something of a quaint air. Indeed, many politicians seem to work with a definition of "politics" in which "politics" itself is antithetical to "objectivity"; thus it is customary to hear that a "political" consideration puts party and partisan interest above all else, rendering **objective assessments** irrelevant or unavailable. In this sense of the "political," one party will oppose something simply because another party has proposed it, without regard for the ("objective") benefits or drawbacks of the proposal itself.

In journalism, by contrast, most parties agree that reporters should be bound by a code of **professional objectivity**. But in the US, with its weak public sector and its private ownership of most media, left-leaning critics of the media have long insisted that journalism is in practice conservative insofar as it is owned and operated by large

*ABCDEFGHIJKLMN**O**PQRSTUVWXYZ*

corporate interests, whereas right-wing critics have insisted in return that journalists themselves are tainted by a liberal bias that prevents them from reporting objectively on such matters as race, sexuality, and religion (Chomsky and Herman, 1988; Goldberg, 2001).

What's curious about the widespread agreement as to the meaning of objectivity in these debates is that the word is one of those rare specimens whose philosophical meaning was once directly opposed to its current meaning. In medieval philosophy the terms "objective" and "subjective" respectively meant what "subjective" and "objective" have denoted in Western philosophy since the C17, and especially since the eC19: the "subjective" denoted those features proper to what we would now call an object and that could be said to exist independently of perception, and the "objective" corresponded to the features of an object as they presented themselves to what we now call the subjective consciousness of an observer. With René Descartes, however, Western philosophy began to associate subject-ivity with a perceiving "I"; and since Immanuel Kant, most Western thinkers have agreed to parcel the world into **objective phenomena** that exist independent of mind, and **subjective phenomena** that are in one way or another mind-dependent (such as injustice) or wholly attributable to mindedness (such as anxiety).

Subjectivity, then, has come to be aligned with the partisan and the partial, and objectivity with all that pertains to objects as in themselves they really are (in Matthew Arnold's phrase). One of the central questions for the philosophy of mind in the C19–C20 has accordingly been how to construe the boundary between objective and subjective phenomena, particularly with regard to matters such as color (which may or may not exist independently of our perception of them). Similarly, one of the central questions for moral philosophy has been how to parse out the potential domain and applicability of moral truth-claims, such that sentences like "it is wrong to torture another human being" might be understood to be grounded differently – that is, more objectively – than sentences like "it is wrong to eat pastrami with mayonnaise." The idea here is that the latter judgment is a mere "subjective" matter of taste, since the eating of pastrami with mayonnaise presumably affects no one but the person eating the sandwich, however much it may offend the sensibilities of everyone else in the delicatessen. The practice of torture, by contrast, is widely felt *not* to be a simple matter of taste, but rather a serious moral issue calling out for intersubjective forms of agreement that will allow us to condemn torture "objectively," without regard to who is being tortured or why.

Since the mC19, but especially in recent decades, social theorists have debated whether the standard of objectivity pertinent to the natural sciences, which pertains to things such as quasars and quarks, is appropriate to the social sciences, which involve things like kinship rituals, torture chambers, and parliamentary procedures. Proponents of objectivity in the social sciences claim that neutral, disinterested scholarship is the only medium by which we can obtain reliable knowledge in such fields as history, economics, anthropology, and sociology. Critics of objectivity counter-argue that no observation of human affairs can

245

escape the inevitably human parameters of the observation itself, and that invocations of objectivity with regard to human affairs are therefore (knowingly or not) veils for partisan agendas that do not recognize their own partisanship. Not all critics of objectivity, however, are wont to accuse their opposite numbers of bad faith; some argue more moderately that "objectivity" is merely the wrong term for complex intersubjective forms of agreement. Richard Rorty, for example, has argued in a string of books beginning with *Philosophy and the mirror of nature* (1979) that utterances designated as "true," whether in the realm of the natural sciences or in the realm of moral philosophy, should be understood not as accurate descriptions of mind-independent objects but as useful claims that have managed over time to "pay their way" (R. Rorty, 1982), thus providing pragmatic grounds for broad agreement among human investigators.

Some moral philosophers claim that Rorty's position on objectivity amounts to a shallow relativism in which all value judgments are of equal standing. Be this as it may, it can be safely – and perhaps objectively – said, at the very least, that while most people agree that objectivity is akin to impartiality, philosophers continue to disagree strenuously as to whether objectivity is merely another name for human agreement.

Michael Bérubé

See: *EMPIRICAL, KNOWLEDGE, MATERIALISM, PRAGMATISM, REASON, RELATIVISM.*

246

Orientalism

The Orient was a figure of speech in Western thought as early as the plays of Aeschylus and Euripides. Originally a place associated not only with the political threat of Persia but with other more general threats of excess and mystery, it was only many centuries later that it congealed into a distinctive field of knowledge conveyed by the term **Orientalism**. The OED, securely situated in the West, assigns the meaning of "the Orient" to "that region of the heavens in which the sun and other heavenly bodies rise, or the corresponding region of the world, or quarter of the compass" – as in Shakespeare: "Lo! in the orient when the gracious light / Lifts up his burning head" (sonnet vii, 1600). The OED then traces the term "Orientalism" to a gradually emerging "character, style, or quality ... that was associated with the modes of thought or expressions and fashions of Eastern nations." In this process, the association of the Orient with the qualities of the sun – as "brilliant, lustrous, shining, glowing, radiant, resplendent" – were transferred to the East as a mixture of the unknown, the exotic, and the fabulous. Yet there has always been a haziness about precisely where the Orient begins and where it ends. By the mC18, it was thought to begin formally as the European crossed into Istanbul, although for many it conjured up the vast space beyond Europe that stretched from the provinces of Ottoman rule in the Balkans all the way across Asia to Tokugawa Japan.

Orientalism came to be commonly recognized as the general field of scholarship and learning pertaining to a global geography dominated by the division between East and West in the C18. The term is first recorded in 1769, and Byron could, by 1811, refer with confidence to "Mr Thornton's frequent hints of profound Orientalism." However, the term continued to carry with it a more general meaning as well. "Orientalism" could refer both to knowledge of "the Orient" and to the constellation of images, essences, sensibilities, and characteristics associated with a generalized "Other." These latter ideas, accumulated over centuries, only became the pretext for scholarly knowledge once European imperialism recruited Orientalism to the colonial project of conquest and control. Formal Orientalist scholarship is impossible to date, but one of its originary moments was the publication in 1697 of Barthelemy d'Herbelot's *Bibliothèque orientale,* a work of great breadth consulted by scholars well into the C19 (Schwab, 1984). The C18 saw a literal explosion of Orientalist knowledge, with important milestones ranging from George Sale's translation and interpretation of the Koran (1734) to William Jones's "discovery" that Sanskrit was an ancient "Indo-European" language (Trautmann, 1997). In 1784 Jones established the Asiatic Society of Bengal, convening regular scholarly gatherings and publishing *Asiatic Researches.* He translated key Persian and Sanskrit texts while presiding over the colonial judicial establishment in Calcutta until his death in 1794. India became the first European laboratory for Orientalist knowledge, as the British struggled to learn and master both classical and vernacular languages and to establish revenue and legal systems that could be justified as consistent with "native" custom (Cohn, 1995).

Orientalism came under attack from utilitarians such as James Mill, who made Jones the principal target of his influential, and voluminous, *History of British India* published in 1817 (J. Mill, 1997). Mill, a life-long servant of the East India Company in London, argued that Jones and **the Orientalists** had portrayed ancient Indian civilization in far too glowing a light, neglecting the woeful inadequacies of government and the urgent need for reform. If Orientalism had been a form of knowledge that was used both to chart and to justify early colonial rule in India, it did not survive as an official ideology of imperialism. For much of the eC19 the "anglicists" argued for the introduction of English education while the "evangelists" advocated the spread of missionary activity and the conversion of souls (Viswanathan, 1989), at least until the great rebellion of 1857 led instead to the implementation of an "ethnographic" state (Dirks, 2001). During the last century of colonial rule in India, the British attempted to disturb "tradition" and "custom" as little as possible, using what they thought to be fixed local institutions to serve as the bulwarks of a permanent imperium. However, it was precisely the colonial administrative interest in understanding tradition that gave new life to an Orientalist mandate, though now with a focus on society and culture rather than civilization and texts. In the lC19 and eC20, as formal British interests expanded from India across the Indian Ocean, spanning much of the region from Malaya to Egypt and reaching far into Africa as well, Orientalism became increasingly contemporary in its interests and social scientific in its methodology. Anthropological concerns with cultural difference and racial determination became critical to both the scholarly study and the popular imagination of an Orient that was to be preserved in its traditional form so that it could be ruled in perpetuity.

Perhaps the greatest challenge to Europe was to understand Eastern traditions in what seemed their most proximate and dangerous form, namely Islam. If, as Edward Said suggested in his *Orientalism* (1978), Islam represented a lasting trauma for Europe, it also provided an endless justification for Orientalist scholarship. Likened to Christianity when dubbed ''Muhammedanism,'' Islam was simultaneously disparaged as an inferior if not barbaric example of monotheism, and analyzed as the source of potential disaffection and violent rebellion. The great Orientalist H. A. R. Gibb, who taught at Harvard during the middle years of the C20, encapsulated years of Orientalist wisdom when he explained that Muslims had simply rejected ''rationalist modes of thought and ... the utilitarian ethic which is inseparable from them'' (1947: 7). Gibb not only made clear the persistence of an Orientalist idea of Islam – resilient despite the enormous social, political, and cultural transformations of the C20 – but also the easy transfer of Orientalist assumptions to the academies and policies of the United States after World War II. That British and French imperial ambitions were thwarted by the rise and finally the triumph of colonial nationalism did not mean an end to Orientalism, or to its resolute political entailments and aspirations. Indeed, as Said pointed out, Orientalism became the guiding normative framework and conceptual basis for the elaboration of US area studies during the unfolding era of decolonization and the independence of myriad postcolonial nations, a time that coincided, of course, with the Cold War and rising American global hegemony.

When Said used the term ''Orientalism,'' he deliberately confounded the general tendency of thought in which the Orient – whether Islamic, Hindu, or Confucian – was rendered as Europe's unitary ''other'' with more technical bodies of scholarship, ranging from philology, archeology, and classical studies to history, geography, anthropology, and area studies. Drawing on the theoretical proposals of Michel Foucault, Said also stressed the productive nature of Orientalist knowledge. Inextricable from colonial and neo-colonial power, Orientalism participated in the creation of an Orient that has been relentlessly conjured as the object of Western action, intention, and desire. Although in the years after the publication of *Orientalism* many scholars have criticized Said for his apparent acceptance of monolithic views of East and West, many more scholars have demonstrated the extent to which the relationship of colonial power and Orientalist knowledge has had extraordinary, and often devastating, consequences for the postcolonial world. In India, Orientalist understandings of religion have propelled nationalist and now nuclear antipathies between Hindus and Muslims, even as the general idea that religion and caste motivate ancient differences has obscured the powerful legacies of colonial modernity. Much of what is held to be ''tradition'' is in fact the product of the colonial encounter, the outcome of the collaboration of Orientalist knowledge and power. Under colonial conditions, the promises of modernity were always tainted by the ways in which modernity was the ideological wedge of colonial domination. Often the colonized would appropriate colonial ideas of tradition as resistance and refuge, thus playing out Said's story of the effective "Orientalization" of the Orient.

Nicholas Dirks

See: *COLONIALISM, POSTCOLONIALISM.*

Other

The question of **the other** is integrally related to that of identity. Identities are constituted out of the play of difference, on the basis, that is to say, of their difference from other identities, assuming their positive meaning through what they exclude. The matter of the other is, then, the shadow theme in contemporary discourses on identity, with respect to both individual identity and the constitution of the self (in psychoanalysis particularly) and collective identities (in sociology, anthropology, cultural studies). The other is what eludes our consciousness and knowing, and it is what resides outside the sphere of "our" culture and community. It is the non-self and the non-us. How to come to terms with the reality of the other of **otherness**, alterity, the alien, the stranger, the unknown? How to deal with the radically disturbing recognition of the significance of the other for who "we" are?

The fact of the other's existence is an inherently ambiguous and disconcerting reality. On the one hand, the other provokes fear and anxiety. "There is nothing that man fears more," says Elias Canetti (1973: 15), "than the touch of the unknown." There is fear about what the other might do to us, about whether we could survive such an encounter with the unknown. On the other hand, however, there is the deep sense that we also need otherness. For would not a world without difference – a world of self-sameness – be insufferable? The other is necessary for change and creativity to exist in the world (both collective transformation and self-alteration). The other is, then, the cause and the object of ambivalent feelings, attitudes, and thoughts.

In recent cultural debates, much attention has been given to the fearful side of our relation to alterity, that which is associated with racist and xenophobic reactions. Cornelius Castoriadis (most radically) draws attention to a painful reality: "[the] apparent incapacity to constitute oneself as oneself without excluding the other, ... coupled with an apparent inability to exclude others without devaluing and, ultimately, hating them" (Castoriadis, 1997: 17). In the process of **othering**, feelings of rage, hostility, and hatred are projected onto what are regarded as dangerously alien persons or cultures. Through a logic of radical polarization "we" then enter into antagonistic confrontation with what has become our loathed and feared other. An issue of particular concern in postcolonial studies has been the way in which "the West" has been constituted in opposition to an imaginary

"East" (a constructed category that includes both the "Middle East" and the "Far East"). And the concern has been with how this polarizing logic of Orientalism has involved a fundamental denigration of the **Eastern other**. "Oriental" culture has been defined as subaltern culture, regarded as backward and irrational, in comparison with Western modernity and Enlightenment – and feared and hated, too, as a consequence of these imagined negative and deficient qualities. The post-2001 crusading stance of the US toward what was imagined as the "axis-of-evil" other has been just the latest episode of a long-running historical saga.

But, if the other may be a source of menace and disquiet, there is also the dimension in which the other is a source – and a necessary source – of possibility. Otherness may also represent the potential for social and cultural replenishment and renewal. Traveling to other places, for example, traveling in order to encounter other kinds of people and other ways of life, has always seemed, from *The Odyssey* onward, to offer possibilities for putting our routine and familiar world in a new perspective, and for enlarging the idea we have of reality. Elias Canetti, on returning from his journey to listen to "the voices of Marrakesh," wrote: "a marvelously luminous, viscid substance is left behind in me, defying words. Is it the language I did not understand there, and that must now gradually finds its translation in me?" (Canetti, 1978: 23). Travel is about encounters with different realities, and about what happens as a consequence of our experiences of encounter. The point is that we make identifications with other places, persons, and cultures – which means that we incorporate them into ourselves, into minds and imaginations, so as to effect some kind of transformation in who we are and how we see the world. Alterity provokes the experience of cultural translation.

But it is not necessary to voyage to distant places to engage with alterity; we can find the other wherever we are. Early in the C20, a number of sociologists (including Georg Simmel and Robert Park) commented on the presence and significance of "the stranger" in the modern metropolis. They argued that the stranger brought new and revitalizing possibilities to urban culture. The stranger contained dangerous qualities that at the same time entailed civilizing possibilities. The presence of strangers makes possible "an enlargement of cultural horizons sufficient to become aware of other cultures and of the possibility that one's own society may in some ways require their presence" (Redfield and Singer, 1954: 69). Otherness is regarded here as fundamental to the cultural, political life of cities. The other is, of course, the prerequisite for cosmopolitanism to exist at all.

The other may, however, be even closer to home. For Julia Kristeva (1991: 1), "the stranger lives within us: he is the hidden face of our identity" (recall Rimbaud's *Je est un autre*). This recognition of otherness in ourselves, of ourselves as other, takes the sociological perspective on "the stranger" to its full and logical conclusion. For "it is not," as Kristeva (1991: 13) says, "simply – humanistically – a matter of our being able to accept the other, but of *being in his place,* and this means being able to imagine and make oneself other for oneself.'' The city – society – becomes a place in which everyone is, in a certain respect, a stranger, and this condition of generalized otherness is the condition of its creative and civilized possibilities.

Kevin Robins

See: *CITY, IDENTITY, ORIENTALISM, POSTCOLONIALISM, WEST.*

251

Participation

Participation derives from L *participatus*, meaning "made to share." Although the sense of force or coercion is no longer present in contemporary uses of **participate**, **participant**, or "participation", a sense of action or demand remains implicit in current meanings. Many contemporary uses echo the medieval and early Protestant Christian meaning of "participant," which described the consubstantial relationship (sharing as a condition of essential sameness) between God and persons. In this usage, a participation meant manifesting this relationship of sameness, for example, through the sacrament of communion. Significantly, this early sense of "participation" also required active involvement in a fellowship of like-minded believers, with whom one expressed the vision and intention of God. The democratic experiments inspired by the Enlightenment were a secular version of this sense of enacting a will larger than the individual (democracy, human rights, revolution) and of sharing this duty (citizenship, coalition-building, identity politics) with others.

In current usage, participation can mean simply recognizing and acting on one's interconnection with a larger society or set of philosophical ideals. People who vote in elections may experience themselves as participating in democratic processes, even if they never join political organizations. Although they may seem distant cousins to the debates among citizens in ancient forums, new media – telegraph, radio, television, and today, Internet – increasingly enable individuals to experience themselves "in communion with" a society.

In a broader sense, participation is understood as positive actions by an individual toward their society (Janoski, 1998). Even without face-to-face interaction, many

ABCDEFGHIJKLMNO**P**QRSTUVWXYZ

individuals experience their efforts to reduce use of fossil fuels, to recycle, or to engage in random acts of kindness as means of participating in civic life. Individuals who do not belong to formal civic organizations can still share in an ideal of good citizenship that reflects a "consubstantial" relationship with others; they see their attempts to "do the right thing" as benefing others, reinforcing solidarity with fellow citizens. This generalized sense of participation readies individuals to act on behalf of the whole. The state relies on this sense of participation when it institutes a military draft, calls upon citizens to accept tax increases or rationing of goods, or embarks upon treaties or internal policies that limit individual freedom in favor of national security. Political action groups capitalize on this diffuse sense of participation when they challenge normative ideas of citizenship; for example, when rights are sought for previously unrecognized groups (gays, disabled, elderly) or when civil disobedience is used to pursue a "higher good" than the law being broken (Tilly, 1995).

Democratic systems depend upon and elaborate these ordinary and specialized ideas of participation (Held, 1996). The modern concept of coalition, derived from parliamentary democracy systems, envisions participants as sharing economic and politic experiences and, consequently, as having common goals. The objective of participation in a parliamentary system was to unite smaller groups in order to create groups large enough to direct the formal economic and political processes. As democracies evolved, the idea of coalition, and thus the idea of participation, also changed to include shared historical and social experience (Laclau and Mouffe, 1985). In the Anglo-European context, but especially in the US because of its two-party system, this expanded basis for participating in coalition made possible party-like groups that could endure and assert a group agenda. For example, the US Rainbow Coalition, which sought both grassroots change and mayoral, legislative, and presidential electoral wins, based participation on appreciating the similarities among oppressed groups, with slogans like "none of us are free, until all of us are free."

This new basis for participation through shared oppression was often seen to conflict with more conventional, nation-based understandings of commonality. Especially in North America, the new form of coalition-building appeared to conservatives as anti-national. In the US, those who participated in the civil rights movement were often accused of being anti-American. The African-American and, later, women's and gay social movements tried to increase their participation in the political process by changing the meaning of citizenship to include respect for cultural and other differences. The conservative backlash to the new social movements came in part as a counter-movement that tried to reassert the feeling of "participating" in America over the feeling of "participating" in a movement for social change.

Participation need not refer only to political commonality and action. In fact, participation has come to mean involvement or engagement in the activities of any organization or social group. Beginning at least with the Industrial Revolution, but increasingly in the C20, consumer capitalism is understood as a site of participation. Both advertising images and the public display of individual styles enable a deep sense of sharing in a world of exchange of goods. Indeed, those who lack the resources to participate in capitalist exchange often feel that they are left out of – not *sharing* in – this now-fundamental aspect of postmodern life. Feelings of social exclusion based on inability to participate in the economy now loom as significant as inability to participate in the democratic process.

Social scientists, journalists, and policy-makers use a related sense of participation. Despite the rise of positivism within the social sciences, in which researchers moved toward computer-based quantification of large bodies of information, many researchers argue that truly understanding social processes requires immersion in the social world. Like the political notions of participation, the social science method of **participant observation** implies that the scientist and their subject share common, basic elements of humanity. Although challenged as overly reliant on the subjective impressions of elite researchers who misunderstand other worlds, participant observation has also been used by minority or disadvantaged scholars to legitimate their research on their "own" group through use of this scientific method.

Cindy Patton

See: *CITIZENSHIP, DEMOCRACY, MOVEMENTS.*

254

Person

Person is one of the European world's most central yet fluid terms. We speak of ourselves as **persons** and of the **personal domain** as if this notion of an inner moral identity were self-evident. Yet this usage represents just one late line of development in a variegated history. In addition to the background meaning of individual human being, from medieval times "person" could also refer to the body or the body clothed and adorned, in which regard one possessed a fine person or, as we would say, **personal appearance**. "Person" could also mean **personage**, or person of social importance, and it was in this sense that Christ was said to be no respecter of persons. Finally there was an important series of "dramaturgical" meanings of person, signified via the original L word for person, *persona*, and clustered around the idea of **acting in the person of**. This series was dominant in late medieval and early modern times where the meaning of "person" was strongly tied to that of "office," or the duty attached to a role. Here liberties and rights were personal in the pre-modern sense of belonging to the office held (Condren, 1997). "Person" in this sense was a role occupied by human individuals, but stretched beyond them to cover corporations, **legal persons** (which might include business enterprises, towns, and universities), and even the state. Thomas Hobbes captures this (to us) unfamiliar spread of meanings in his definitional comment that: " 'A Person,' is he, *whose words or actions are considered, either as his own, or as representing the words or actions of an other man, or of any other thing to whom they are attributed, whether Truly or by Fiction"* (Hobbes, 1991 [1651]: 111).

The dominant modern meaning, in which person is identified with an **inner moral personality** viewed as the source of rights and duties, derives from the history of Christian theology and forms of worship. In his classic essay on the history of the modern concept of the person, Marcel Mauss thus ties the eclipse of the earlier, pluralistic, "dramaturgical" use of "person" to the Christian doctrine of the soul and associated moral practices (Mauss, 1985). Mauss places particular emphasis on the early modern spread of practices of spiritual direction and self-scrutiny, through which individuals were impelled to unify their "offices" around an inner self for which they were morally responsible. The religious drive to unify roles and duties, and to locate judgment and responsibility in an **inner person**, is visible in the central doctrine of **Christ's two natures and one person**. Here the unity of Christ's human and divine natures is the condition of salvation and provides a powerful model for moral generation (Kobusch, 1997: 29–30). By transposing Christ's double nature onto humanity, Enlightenment moral philosophers such as Immanuel Kant could invoke the distinction between a higher self (rational humanity, **personhood**) and a lower one (visible man), thereby channeling into secular philosophy the aspiration to moral unity driven by the religious desire to elevate a lower self. By contrast with Hobbes's dramaturgical way of conceiving the person, in terms of a scattered plurality of offices, Kant thus offers a unified, intellectualist, and inward conception:

> Personhood, or humanity in my person, is conceived as an intelligible substance, the seat of all concepts, that which distinguishes man in his freedom from all objects under whose jurisdiction he stands in his visible nature. It is thought of, therefore, as a subject that is destined to give moral laws to man, and to determine him: as occupant of the body, to whose jurisdiction the control of all man's powers is subordinated. (Kant, 1997: 369)

Amelié Rorty has argued that the variety of moral, legal, political, and intellectual tasks performed by notions of person is simply too great for any single conception to function as a foundation for all the others (A. O. Rorty, 1988). Despite its familiarity to educated moderns, it would thus be inaccurate to regard the religious-philosophical model of a unified moral personality as simply replacing an earlier conception of person as the capacity in which one acts or bears rights and duties. Rather, the two understandings of person continue to exist in a largely unformulated and sometimes uncomfortable juxtaposition.

We can see this, for example, in the question of the fetus's status as a person, which is central to the intractable conflict over the legal availability of abortion. In Western legal systems the fetus has the status of a **legal person**. This means that its rights and entitlements are contingent – on being born alive – and conditional, typically on the health of the mother, so that the life of the fetus may be terminated should the mother's health be endangered. Many anti-abortion advocates, however, adopt the religious-philosophical conception of the person and view the fetus as a **moral person** possessing rights inherent in a soul or conscience. For these people, who identify personhood with an inner moral being, termination is inherently immoral.

A similar dispute, albeit with a different political coloration, is visible in arguments over the **personal rights** of citizens in liberal democracies. Some writers regard civil and political rights as attached to the citizen as a **persona**, hence as contingent and conditional, usually on the overall purpose of the state, understood as providing security and civil peace. For these writers it is permissible for the state to suspend a range of civil and political rights under conditions – for example, terrorist threat – where this purpose is endangered. Other writers, however, locate civil and political rights not in a contingent persona but in an essential **moral personality**, usually identified with the capacities for reason and moral judgment. For these writers, it is never permissible to suspend such rights, as to do so is to injure the moral person whom they regard as the true end of the state. The different understandings of person bequeathed by history thus continue to play a profound and troubling role in modern life and thought.

Ian Hunter

See: *BODY, HUMAN, INDIVIDUAL, SELF.*

Place

The idea that people are defined by **place** saturates our language. We talk about "taking a stand" and "knowing where she stands," or say that someone "comes over to my way of thinking." People who defy social codes have **forgotten their place**, as opposed to those who **know their place**. A winner is given **pride of place** and a muddled person is **all over the place**. Possessing many uses, "place" designates some mediating ground between the human body and the arrangement of social life. The word derives from the more focused *plaza* (mE, F, Sp, C11) indicating an urban open space or **marketplace**. By the C16, "place" in English refers to foreign towns, an aristocrat's town residence, or a miscellaneous neighborhood.

To know one's place echoes an era when class or social difference was secured by spatial segregation. Peasants were not to enter the salons of the wealthy, immigrants or slaves to assert their rights, women to occupy men's roles. As nationalism emerged in the C18 and C19, the "place" of collective identity was simultaneously exaggerated and fragmented. One's being a "German" or a "Spaniard" encompassed not only territory but also language, religion, and ethnicity; as a citizen each had equal rights. In reality, inhabitants often differed in their religion, came from elsewhere, or found themselves disenfranchised by the national imaginary.

For many artists and thinkers, the C20 brought about a loss of the **sense of place**; the connection between self and place became fragile and arbitrary. Films and songs evoked the alienation of what the Beatles called *Nowhere Man* (Lennon, 1965). Movies, television, and travel encouraged a sense of belonging anywhere and **no place**. Communities were **displaced** by changing economies of production. The search for belonging, accompanied by the earlier discourse of rights, helps account for the post-war rise of identity politics and the demand to identify the "place" a person was speaking from (Keith and Pile, 1993). This expression retains the older sense of social status but introduces the expectation that critics will be reflexive about their own place in structures of power. This kind of "place" isn't necessarily locatable in physical space, but concerns the social location of individuals in terms of power, connection and commitment, and social capital (Morley and Robins, 1995).

Place has become one of the most anxiety-ridden concepts today. With the flow of people, cultures, and commodities across borders, and the rapidity of technological change, do people still have a sense of place? If so, how is it maintained? Are there still local customs to distinguish one place from another? If so, do they limit or empower the people in it? For some, increased mobility and globalization have created **non-places** like airports, banks, and malls, where identity and inhabitation are ceded to commerce and solitary individuality (Augé, 1995). Others argue that the global circulation of capital depends upon difference in **local places** (D. Mitchell, 2000). Similarly, some cyberspace observers emphasize the **placelessness** of identities in virtual space, and argue over whether such fluidity erodes power hierarchies in built environments, or enhances possibilities for diverse social groups and identities (Hillis, 1999).

We can no longer understand "place" just as a place on a map, or where one is situated as a physical body. Even if a person stays in one place, the idea of "his" or "her" place seems to be collapsing; each place's dynamics, meanings, and possibilities are affected by regional and global relations. Places aren't just territorial, they are also political; some are more empowered than others to decide who belongs and who doesn't. Places are contested, intersecting, and uncertain, clearly shaped by power relations and human intents.

This discussion has particular cogency for women. Artists and theorists have shown that we become women and men through learning to live in **gendered places** (N. Duncan, 1996; McDowell, 1999; Massey, 1994); the rise of the private sphere was inseparable from the rise of a specific construction of femininity, while public life and mobility have been largely gendered as masculine. Feminist critics have shown that identity is constructed through embodied experience and connection with others, which is tied to locale – or **inhabited place** – and the sense of belonging. Such locales can be inhibiting for marginalized groups like gays and lesbians, people of color, or people without money. Choosing to leave one place behind, they discover whether their new locale can accommodate their presence. Strategies for defending or celebrating the specificity of place range from policing borders (Nicol and Townsend Gault, 2004) through local traditions in architecture and landscape design (W. J. T. Mitchell, 2002) to art (J. Duncan and Ley, 1993), popular music (Leyshon, Matless, and Revill, 1998), advertising icons, and tourism.

257

Policy

The concern for "sense of place" is acquiring renewed popular urgency because of globalization and environmental destruction. Recent struggles for control over land and resources crystallize a range of issues around territory: deforestation, the constitutional rights of indigenous people, corporate ownership, military expansion, destructive urbanization, agribusiness, and the preservation of species, to name a few. While tied to the rights of specific communities, these struggles often mobilize cross-ethnic alliances. "Place" is more and more demonstrably the outcome of social practice; people determine its shape and meanings.

Jody Berland

See: *INDIGENOUS, MARGINAL, MOBILITY, PRIVATE, PUBLIC, SPACE, VIRTUAL.*

Policy

Policy appears an innocuous term with two current and distinct senses. In the first, an **insurance policy** is a document that states the conditions under which premiums will be paid in return for monetary compensation in the event of a loss of property, livelihood, or even life. The other refers to the plans, programs, principles, or more broadly the course of action of some kind of actor, usually a political one such as a government, a party, or a politician. Thus political bodies and politicians can present and implement different types of policy, such as **foreign policy**, concerning international relations, a **social policy**, typically concerning the welfare state, and an **economic policy**. Policy might include a degree of deliberate inaction, as well as action, as in laissez-faire economic policies that argue for a limited effective role of government in the control of economic matters.

Keynesianism is a theory of how to manipulate public expenditure and investment (that is, **fiscal policy**) to affect and flatten out cyclical fluctuations of the level of employment in a national economy. It is often held to have driven **macro-economic policy** in the 30 or so years after World War II. Due to its concern with the question of unemployment and its favorable understanding of the role of demand created by public expenditure on social benefits and services, Keynesianism was closely allied with a focus on social policy. In the early 1980s neo-liberals sought to displace this macro-economic policy with **monetarist policies** concerned with the problem of inflation and money supply. This new supply-side economic policy was given the names of the two leaders who most heralded its virtues: "Thatcherism" and "Reganomics."

The major sense of the contemporary word "policy" thus seems rather technical. One can be for or against specific policies, or the principles that underlie them, but one cannot imagine government without policy. Combinations such as **policy-making**, **policy framework**, **policy document**, **policy statements**, **policy process**, and even **policy science** emphasize this technical sense of the term. The sparseness of the term contrasts sharply with the etymology it shares with **polity** and with **police**. With "polity," it is derived from

L *politia* and Gk *polis*, both of which refer to city, state, and citizenship. The mE and oF *policie* describes civil administration as an organized and established system or form of government. In France and in other parts of Europe, however, the word "police" had exactly the same connotation of civil administration or organized government.

At its broadest, "police" was the regulation, discipline, and good order in a community or other political unit, such as municipality or city. By way of an association with L *politus* (meaning polish), "police" came to mean a state of refinement, order, and even civilization itself. William Blackstone captured this first sense (1769) when he said that "by public police and economy, I mean the due regulation and domestic order of the kingdom"; Edmund Burke (1791) captured the latter when he accused the Turks of a "barbarous neglect of police." The G *polizei* is both a condition of order within a community and the commands or ordinances that seek the regulation and maintenance of that order (Kne-meyer, 1980). By the C18 this had given rise to a **science of police**, G *Polizeiwissenschaft*, which concerned itself with the content and conditions of order and led to an evaluation of the objectives and proper form of state activity.

Intellectuals associated with the C18 Scottish Enlightenment, such as Adam Smith, viewed "police" both as one of the branches of legislation and as a condition best obtained with the free circulation of labor. In Smith (1978 [1752–4]), "police" is pushed to a certain limit. The market is an instrument of police, which is best achieved by the fewest **police regulations**. If this is so, then it is not surprising that there is a kind of collective forgetting of this condition called police. Police would become a branch of government concerned with keeping the peace by a body of specialist officers. Policy would become the general stance and principles that might be taken to governing the state, given that it is necessary to take into account the law-like mechanisms of the market.

Perhaps the C18 marks the high point of the linkages between **public police** and **public policy**. Despite the development and practice of a modern constabulary police force in the early C19, we should not underestimate the continued availability of terms such as **moral police** (Mill, 1989 [1859]) and the use of "police" as a synonym for civilization (Disraeli, 1845) in the C19. Liberal political philosophers and politicians provide a bridge between "police" and "policy," and we might suspect a more appropriate modern equivalent of *Polizeiwissenschaft* would be "policy science." Indeed, there are many ways in which "policy" carries with it the heritage of "police." In social policy, much debate over what is today called "welfare reform" concerns the character and need for regulation and discip-line of certain sections of the poor. In not only foreign policy but all kinds of areas, policy and policy frameworks increasingly find their justification and objective in the idea of security and the limitation of risk. A policy toward refugees, for example, may require increased border police.

The linkage of policy with security and risk suggests that in some way the two senses of the term we started with might gain a new connection. To make or conduct policy can now be taking out a kind of insurance policy. It is to seek the best and most cost-effective way

259

to find security in a turbulent world presumed to be driven by the forces of economic globalization, or to equip individuals with the means to navigate the risks of their own lives. But for all its pretensions to neutrality or to technical or scientific status, and for all its liberal heritage, behind "policy" stands a shadow of an omnipotent state, administration, or bureaucracy issuing detailed regulations of individual and collective life.

Mitchell Dean

See: *BUREAUCRACY, ECONOMY, MANAGEMENT, RISK, WELFARE.*

Political Correctness

One of the more elusive polemical tags of the lC20 and eC21, **political correctness (PC** for short) can be an insult, an accusation, a joke, or the name of an effort to change a society – in particular, its ways of handling power relations of "race," ethnicity, gender, class, and sexuality – by means of wide-ranging but often small-scale cultural reform. "PC" is primarily a negative term for the ideals and actions of others. Designating an attempt to fight social discrimination by changing everyday speech and behavior, and to enforce such change though public pressure on individuals as well as legal or other institutional sanctions to regulate group conduct, it implies that these measures are petty, rigid, humorless, intolerant, even totalitarian in impulse. **Politically correct** is then a judgment disguised as description; deflecting attention from the substance or value of the reforms in question, it expresses a dismissive attitude to those who advocate change. The latter in turn may reclaim the phrase as an ironic *self*-description.

Used adjectivally, "PC" has largely taken over from "doctrinaire," which Raymond Williams (1976: 108) saw "used, in a political context, to indicate a group or a person or an attitude which can be seen as based on a particular set of ideas" with "the implication . . . that political actions or attitudes so based are undesirable or absurd." However, the more recent term assumes a greatly expanded or, some would say, more diffuse sense of politics. Coming in the wake of feminism, anti-racism, and other social movements active since the 1970s, "PC" can cover diverse minute controversies over etiquette, protocol, attitude, and dress as well as ideas, policies, and programs. It also refers to protests against stereotyping or negative representation of disadvantaged groups in books, films, and other media. The noun phrase combines all these to suggest an organized movement, often with sinister implications: "a new McCarthyism" (J. Taylor, 1991), "intellectual fascism" (P. Brown, 1992), "a new form of thought control" (Kimball, 1990), a "victims' revolution" (D'Souza, 1991).

An ancestral term is found in the "scientific" Marxism invoked by communist regimes in the mC20. For the former a **correct analysis** of social forces, achieved through study and discussion, should guide political action. Under the latter, the penalty for incorrect ideas or behavior – meaning, subversive or merely critical of the regime in question – might be prison, exile, or death. However, in liberal democracies the casual use of "politically correct" or "ideologically sound" reversibly to assert or mock a pious conformity to group norms ("party-line" or **correct-line thinking**) emerged among feminist, Black Power, and anti-war activists in the early 1970s. Perry (1992) records a 1971 exchange between writers Toni Cade (Bambara) and Audre Lord over Cade's wish to raise her daughter as a "correct little sister," and she cites such period humor as: "We *could* stop at McDonalds ... but it wouldn't be politically correct."

These uses from the left of politics were almost exclusively adjectival and played on doubts about the difference in C20 historical experience between principle and dogma, liberation and repression. So when the US president, George Bush, Snr, declared from the right in 1991 that "the notion of political correctness has ignited controversy across the land" (Aufderheide, 1992: 227), left activists were puzzled, affirming no such notion or noun. However, adding to the old doubts a new and now typical association between political triviality ("attempts to micromanage casual conversation") and terror ("political extremists roam the land"), Bush's claim that free speech was under attack in liberal societies swept internationally through the media.

As the hot new label spread between different contexts of use, its range expanded to incorporate a host of conflicts arising in advanced capitalist countries from social change, corporate restructuring toward globalization, and the dismantling of welfare states in the lC20. Bush gave his speech at the University of Michigan, and in the USA it prompted furious debate about the effects in higher education of affirmative action policies designed to boost minority participation; of speech codes to protect individuals from expressions of bigotry and hate; of canon revision to diversify a curriculum over-heavy with the works of dead white males; and of the relativism that some feared would follow from multicultural teaching. These debates in turn prompted studies of the funding cuts and declining real participation rates of, especially, black students that also marked this period. One critic saw in charges of PC a "smoke screen" for "downsizing" and restricting access to higher education (Lauter, 1995), and another an "attempt to undermine everything 'public' " (Bérubé, 1995). Still others found in the culture wars the humanities' biggest opportunity in years to reach a wider audience (Newfield and Strickland, 1995).

Elsewhere, the term served different polemical purposes. In Europe academics spoke of PC as an American disease, sometimes a "Protestant" or "puritan" problem. In officially multicultural Australia, bureaucrats were a major target for critics of PC. One wrote scathingly of "government-sponsored diversity," meaning, "conformity enforced" by "the media, academe, the political parties, the thought police" all together (Coleman, 1995). Everywhere, the **political correctness panic** created a folklore of "cases" of victimization based on anecdotes and unsubstantiated rumor. These continued to circulate widely even if refuted; the pleasure they gave seemed more important than the value of their claims to truth. Indeed, as the term began to exhaust itself through extended overuse, the core of its appeal crystallized as a widespread anxiety over the power of language and the inaccessibility of truth in media-saturated societies. Recalling the dystopian regime created by George Orwell in *1984*, opponents and defenders of PC alike accused each other of "Newspeak."

There are signs in recent usage that "political correctness" is reverting to a simple term for orthodoxy. In liberal democracies it still generates ironic spin-offs, such as **economic correctness** (a hostile term for neo-liberalism) or **professional correctness** (Fish, 1995, defending disciplinarity). Its meaning in authoritarian polities is classical. The present writer can attest that in 2000 the expression "the Chinese mainland" was more politically correct than "mainland China" for usage in Hong Kong.

Meaghan Morris

See: *IDEOLOGY, TOLERANCE.*

Popular

Popular is first used in the IC15 as a legal term; an **action popular** is a legal action which can be undertaken by anyone: "Accion populers in divers cases have ben ordeigned by many gode actes and statutes" (1490); "Accion populer... is not geeuen to one man specyally but generally to any of the Queenes people as wyll sue" (1579). Although from the mC16 "popular" is also used as another term for "the people," it is increasingly used to refer only to people of "lowly birth"; as in the phrases "commoun populair" (1552), "any popular or common person" (c.1555), "Patricians and Populars" (1610).

More neutrally, "popular" is used to indicate something that is widespread or generally accepted: "popular sicknesse" (1603), "they keepe him, safe, rich, and populaire" (1608), "popular error" (1616), "Popular, in great fauour with the common people" (1623), "where the diseases are most popular" (1651), "popular language" (1759), "popular diseases" (1803), "popular aphorism" (1875). Beginning in the C19, "popular" is used to designate forms of art and entertainment that appealed to ordinary people: "popular press" (1835), "popular treatese" (1841), "popular songs" (1841), "popular music" (1855), "popular concert" (1859), "popular price" (1885), "popular art" (1898), "popular song industry" (1935). It is this use of "popular" which generates the definition of **popular culture** as culture which is widely favored or well liked by many people. The difficulty with the coming together of "culture" and "popular" in this way is that unless we can agree on a figure over which something becomes popular culture, and below which it is just culture, we might find that "widely favored or well liked by many people" would include so much as to be virtually useless as a conceptual definition of popular culture. On the other hand, if we want a non-evaluative, purely descriptive definition, this may be the only useful one.

The first really sustained and detailed intellectual linking of "popular" and "culture" was developed in the IC18 as a result of a growing interest in the culture of the folk

(Storey, 2003a). It is during the "discovery" of the folk that the term "popular culture" is first coined by Johann Gottfried Herder (Burke, 1981). For the folklorists **the popular** is culture which originates from "the people." This produces in the C20 definitions such as this: "popular culture . . . which is to be sharply distinguished from . . . commercialized 'pop culture' . . . is the style of life of the majority of the members of a community" (1966; Shiach, 1989: 22). "Popular culture," according to this definition, should only be used to indicate an "authentic" culture of the people. One problem with this approach is the question of who qualifies for inclusion in the category "the people." Another problem with it is that it evades any significant discussion of the commercial nature of much of the resources from which popular culture may be made. Nevertheless, according to this usage a clear distinction should always be made between the commodities produced by the culture industries and what people do with these commodities. In some versions of this definition, the popular is almost a pure space of resistance. For example, "popular culture is formed always in reaction to, and never as part of, the forces of domination" (Fiske, 1989: 25).

The study of folklore not only produced a concept of the popular as folk culture, but also helped to establish the intellectual tradition of seeing ordinary people as masses, consuming mass culture. This is because the "discovery" of the rural folk was accompanied (and no doubt driven) by the "discovery" of the urban masses. If the folk represented a disappearing "positive" popular, the new urban masses represented an emerging "negative" popular. Therefore, in the new industrial and urban spaces of Europe and the US, defining the popular as that which is widely favored or well liked by many people increasingly assumed profoundly negative connotations. This way of seeing the popular was able to draw on earlier negative usage, as in "a custome of popular or base men" (1603), "the rascabilitie of the popular" (1633; Shiach, 1989). **Popularity** is also used negatively: "a tumultuous popularity" (1632); "the contagion of the age, the spirit of popularity and republicanisme" (1689), "the depths of popularity" (1701). "Popular" and "popularity" are also used negatively to indicate a desire to win favor with ordinary people: "he was more popular, and desirous of the common peoples good will and fauour" (1595), "Popularity is a courting the favor of the people by undue practices" (1697), "the practices of popular and ambitious men" (1701), "To curry Favour with the vulgar Popularity" (1715).

The popular as an index of lack of quality is supported from early usage by the idea that popular also indicates a large quantity of people: "the most popular part of Scotland" (1817; Shiach, 1989). There is also a sense in which quantity not only reduces quality, it actively supports and encourages corruption: "the Evils that attend this popular World" (1726). The connecting of lack of quality with large quantity is compounded by the use of "popular" to describe things which have undergone a process of simplifying or diluting in order to appeal to the supposed inferior tastes of ordinary people: "popular and plausible theams" (1573), "The popularization of the measure" (1797), "The peculiar 'mission' of this age ... is to popularize among the many, the more immediately practical results of the thought and experience of the few'' (1833), ''in a popular style which boys and women could comprehend'' (1849), ''By popular art we mean creative work that measures its success by the size of its audience and the profit it brings to its maker'' (1947).

The supposed inferiority of the popular becomes very clear when ''popular'' is attached to ''culture'' as a residual category, there to accommodate texts and practices which fail to be ''real'' culture. Those who deploy this definition generally insist that the division between popular and ''real'' culture is absolutely clear; articulated, for example, in such binary oppositions as **popular press/quality press**, **popular cinema/art cinema**, **popular entertainment/art**. According to this definition, popular culture is a commercial culture mass-produced for mass consumption. It is a culture which is supposedly consumed with brain-numbed and brain-numbing passivity. Its audience is a mass of non-discriminating consumers, consuming what is formulaic and manipulative (to the political right or left, depending on who is doing the analysis). Moreover, not only is the division clear, it is transhistorical. This point is usually insisted on, especially if the division is dependent on the supposed essential qualities of things. But even a little knowledge of cultural and social history should make us skeptical of such claims. The work of William Shakespeare, for example, is now seen as the very epitome of ''real'' culture; yet as late as the C19, before the plays became poetry on the page, rather than scripts to be performed, his work was very much a part of **popular theatre** (Levine, 1988). Similarly, opera has been both popular and exclusive since its invention in the IC16 (Storey, 2003b). Therefore, what is important here is not the fact that what is popular and what is ''real'' culture move up and down the ''cultural escalator''; more significant are ''the forces and relations which sustain the distinction, the difference ... [the] institutions and institutional processes ... required to sustain each and to continually mark the difference between them'' (S. Hall, 1998: 448–9).

Ideas about what constitutes the popular have been transformed by recent thinking around debates on postmodernism. Postmodern culture is supposedly a culture in which the distinction between high and popular has been in terminal decline since the 1960s. For some this is a reason to celebrate an end to exclusion and to an elitism constructed on arbitrary distinctions of culture; for others it is a reason to despair at the final victory of commerce (presented as the very embodiment of the popular) over culture.

Although ''the popular'' can be made to carry a range of different meanings, what all these have in common is the idea of L *popularis*, belonging to the people. In particular, the idea of the popular is often a way of constructing, categorizing, and dismissing the cultural and social practices of ''ordinary'' people. In other words, definitions of the popular are never neutral; they are always entangled with questions of culture and power.

John Storey

See: *CANON, CULTURE, MASS, POSTMODERNISM, TASTE.*

Pornography

Etymologically, **pornography** refers to the description of the life and manners of prostitutes and their patrons, and thus by a simple extension the suggestion of "impure," "unchaste," and explicit erotic expression in writing or pictorial form. Hence one possible definition of pornography is illicit activities designed to stimulate sexual desire (with the implicit suggestion of masturbatory activity). It links the term to another word, "obscene," which has an older history, and a more general application, suggesting lewdness, indecency, disgust, and in varying degrees, illegality. Most attempts at controlling pornography are made under anti-obscenity legislation, which in the English and Welsh jurisdiction at least is concerned with controlling representations which have a tendency to "deprave and corrupt"– a notoriously subjective, and culturally shifting rubric.

Explicit erotic representations are as old as human civilization, as sexual imagery scraped on the walls of Stone Age caves suggests. The invention of the term "pornography" in the mC19 (its first recorded use is in the early 1860s) can be seen as part of the zealous Victorian urge to label and categorize sexual behavior which went beyond the norm. But there was more to it than that. The appearance of the word at this time reflects the technological revolution that was making possible the rapid dissemination of photographic images, and a cultural and political climate where the issue of how to regulate illicit sexual behavior, especially female prostitution, was coming to the fore. We may also postulate the creation of a new market (among men) for the explicit circulation of sexual fantasy (usually, though not exclusively, about women); this is also the period when private collectors took pride in collecting the choicer examples of erotic material, creating a mystique around the erotic, and stimulating a demand for a new industry to supply their fantasies.

But the difficulty of distinguishing **the pornographic** and the obscene from the merely erotic or explicit has bedeviled attempts either to control or to tolerate it. The appearance from the 1950s of mass-circulation, sexually titillating magazines, such as *Playboy*, *Penthouse*, and *Mayfair*, and the creation by the 1970s of a multi-billion-dollar international industry suggested both a high demand and a high degree of social acceptance for at least what became known as **soft porn**. Reactions varied. For the moral traditionalist, pornography represented a defilement of sexuality. For the social liberal, pornography might be something to be disliked, even disapproved of, but was generally seen as a matter of personal choice, as long as its manifestations did not sully the public sphere. For some feminists, on the other hand, pornography represented something far more dangerous. In Robin Morgan's famous phrase: "porn is the theory; rape is the practice" (Morgan, 1980: 139).

During the 1970s and 1980s, pornography became redefined as essentially about male violence against women. For some, pornography, by its explicit degrading of women in representations, caused violence toward women. For Andrea Dworkin (1981), however, pornography *was* violence against women: male power over women was exercised through heterosexual penetrative sex, which was violence, and pornography was the main vehicle for male colonization of women. Thus in their attempt to introduce an ordinance outlawing pornography in Minneapolis in the 1980s, Dworkin and her co-campaigner, Catharine MacKinnon, proposed that it be defined as "the graphic, sexually explicit subordination of women whether in picture or in words" (Dworkin and MacKinnon, 1988) – a subtle shift from the original dictionary definition.

A fierce debate subsequently erupted over the meanings and implications of pornography. All feminists could probably agree that pornography tended to objectify the female body, the main focus of **pornographic representations**. They could also agree that the liberal distinction between private and public spheres was inadequate: many crimes against women were committed in the home, and the power relations of men and women were complex, so saying pornography was a matter of personal choice was no answer. But as Dworkin's feminist opponents pointed out, not all pornography was violent, or led to violence. A great deal of pornography did not even relate to heterosexuality: **gay porn** grew exponentially during this period, and that could hardly be described as being about the violent subordination of women. The scapegoating of porn, moreover, obscured the distinction between representations which potentially demeaned the subject, and erotica, designed simply to arouse emotions and bring pleasure. There was a domain of fantasy which needed to be recognized, and which could not be simply identified as "reality." Above all, the **anti-porn campaigners**, in wanting to ban pornography, risked allying themselves with right-wing moral conservatives in narrowing the boundaries of acceptable sexual behavior. Many feminists, in turn, whatever their personal feelings about porn, allied themselves with anti-censorship campaigners (Segal and McIntosh, 1992). Behind this was a strong belief that pornographic representations were a complex product of male-dominated societies, and targeting pornography alone would not touch the roots of continuing inequalities between men and women.

Definitions which play on the illicit nature of pornography, or on its harmful effects, inevitably construct pornography as in itself harmful. This could be said to be both the radical feminist position and that explicitly underlined in the 1986 (conservative) Meese Commission Report in the USA. The Williams Report (B. Williams, 1979) in the UK, on the other hand, explicitly attempted a definition which stressed the function of pornography (sexual arousal) and content (sexually explicit representations). It then set aside questions of morality and of legal restriction to be addressed separately. This was in tune with a liberal strategy of regulation which held that it was not the function of law to lay down what was moral or immoral in relation to sexuality. All society could legitimately do was preserve public decency and prevent harm. This in turn simply reopens the debate in another way. What constitutes harm? What are the limits that could or should be set on public representations of explicit sex? Pornography continues to arouse controversy because it lies on so many fissures in contemporary discourses of sexuality.

Jeffrey Weeks

See: *FEMINISM, FETISH, GAY AND LESBIAN, SEXUALITY.*

Postcolonialism

Postcolonialism has often been interpreted as being more about the "post" than about the "colonial." There are two main reasons for this. The first concerns whether, understood in its more ordinary geopolitical sense, "postcolonialism" refers to a period after **colonialism** or to one still profoundly marked by colonialism's legacies. The second has to do with the relations between postcolonialism and the other "posts" – postmodernity and poststructuralism, for example – which are commonly used to describe contemporary thought and society. These terms are frequently conflated in the Western academy, where **postcolonial theory** and **postcolonial studies** have often been seen as necessarily poststructuralist, and the **postcolonial condition** has been construed as a significant component of the more general condition of postmodernity.

"Postcolonialism" thus reminds us that colonialism remade the modern world and, by shaping the reactions against it, continues to do so. Neither "Europe" nor the "third world," neither colonizers nor colonized, would have come into being without the history of colonialism. Its effects have been more extensive and more disguised – at once all-embracing and yet often intangible – because of the ways in which the cultural categories of the modern world have been reshaped through colonial encounters. Concerns over nationality, ethnicity, the effects of global migration, and the explosive implications of systematic disparities in wealth, health, and political stability between north and south, are all part of the postcolonial condition. Debates over separate schooling, different familial or gender practices, veiling and other religious injunctions, whether in Europe and North America or in formerly colonized countries, all invoke the historical legacies of colonialism (Stoler, 1995).

Despite the ultimate triumph of decolonization, in the face of what was monumental imperial opposition, it is clear that colonialism has not vanished (Mamdani, 1996). It haunts the present not only because the identities and investments that were created to sustain it live on – and, for reasons not unrelated to continued European power, have often gained new life and force – but because the demise of the Cold War has led to new imperial opportunities, obsessions, and dangers. The putative clash of civilizations on which the new American empire rests its political and economic ambition and its cultural justification is just another form of colonialism. Only this time the stakes are even higher, making postcolonial studies a more urgent, and important, priority than ever before.

Postcolonial studies are usually seen as having originated in the critique launched by Edward Said in his *Orientalism* (1978). The general tenets of his argument are by now well known: colonial histories – the historical relations of domination between East and West – produced, and in turn were produced by, a range of discourses in which the colonial "other" was essentialized, inferiorized, feminized, and ultimately naturalized as the always already colonized. The East was constituted as something that could be known, indeed could only be known, through tropes that reproduced relations of domination, even as domination became

267

increasingly seen as the natural condition of the world rather than the result of specific geopolitical forces. Thus students of colonialism have uncovered the complicity of literary, philological, cartographic, historical, and anthropological forms of representation in the project of colonial rule. The ways the categories of knowledge have been shaped by and in the context of colonial relations have done much of the work of colonial domination.

Said drew much of his inspiration from the work of Michel Foucault, whose insistence on the close connections between knowledge and power made it possible for the relationships between systems of thought and power to be examined in ways similar to the forms of cultural analysis developed by earlier Marxist thinkers, such as Georg Lukács, Theodor Adorno, and Antonio Gramsci. Nevertheless, the fact that Said himself was an unrepentant secular humanist, committed to historical and political criticism, has been obscured in much of the work now characterizing the field of postcolonial studies he is said to have inaugurated. Postcolonial studies is thus now strongly influenced by the poststructuralist thought of Jacques Derrida and, in the fields of psychoanalysis, that of Jacques Lacan. This is true of the work of Gayatri Chakravarty Spivak, who draws mainly on Derrida, and of that of Homi Bhabha, who has applied the perspectives of Lacanian psychoanalysis to the study of **postcolonial identities**. Postcolonial studies has also shared in the undifferentiated postmodernist celebration of difference and multiplicity that has characterized some forms of identity politics.

The yield of postcolonial studies has thus been a mixed one. At its best, postcolonial studies has subjected academic practices in Europe and North America to serious scrutiny and devastating critique, disturbing fields such as area studies, anthropology, imperial history, and comparative literature. In turn, postcolonial studies has generated important debate, when it has not been dismissed outright both by traditional disciplinarians and by partisans of an old left that see American multiculturalism and academic poststructuralism as apologists for, if not agents of, global capitalism. However, in becoming too frequently a new subfield in literary (or cultural) studies, postcolonialism has not only become vulnerable to such critique, but has risked losing its original reference to the historical conditions and effects of colonial rule and its global aftermath. Postcolonial studies would gain considerably in strength if it acknowledged the importance of engaging cultural study with economic and political critique, including, among other issues, a careful delineation of the political and economic effects that neo-colonial structures still have on the new world order of autonomous nations.

This would contribute significantly to a more critical understanding of **postcoloniality**. Although postcoloniality is related to current developments in identity politics, multiculturalism, poststructuralism, and postmodernism, it is both far more and far less than these particular terms imply. "Postcoloniality" signifies those places and histories (rather than any particular general theories) that resist (whether actively or by calling attention to histories of exclusion and denigration) the universalization of position and perspective associated with the histories of colonialism (Chakrabarty, 2000). It reminds us of the fact that culture and modernity were always flawed, invariably predicated on violence and domination, the terms of seduction and conquest for colonization itself. Postcoloniality both embodies the promise of the West – the promise that flows from the enlightenment and the birth of nations – and reminds us that the promise is always flawed (Dirks, 1998).

Nicholas Dirks

See: *COLONIALISM, ORIENTALISM.*

Postmodernism

Postmodern was first coined by the English painter John Watkins Chapman in around 1870 to describe what he called "postmodern painting"; a style of painting which was supposedly more avant-garde than French impressionism (Best and Kellner, 1991). The term was then used to describe "postmodern men" (1917), "postmodernism" (1930s; Hassan, 1987), the "post-modern house" (1949), the "post-Modern age" (1946), the "Post-Modern World" (1957; Best and Kellner, 1991), the "postmodern-period" (1959), the "postmodern mind" (1961; Best and Kellner, 1991), "post-Modernist literature" (1965), "post-Modernists" (1966).

Contemporary understandings of "postmodernism" suggest different things depending on context and discourse. The term also signifies differently depending on whether it is used to refer to cultural texts, an historical period, or a mode of cultural theory. Therefore, perhaps the best way to understand the shifting meanings of the term is to distinguish between the overlapping terms which postmodernism embodies: **postmodernity**, **postmodern culture**, and **postmodern theory**.

"Postmodernity" is commonly used as an historical term to indicate the period after modernity, which began with the Enlightenment and ended in the 1960s (Jameson, 1984) or the 1970s (Harvey, 1990). What these accounts have in common is an insistence that the cultural and social changes which have produced postmodernity are inextricably linked to changes in capitalism: from a primary focus on production to consumption (D. Bell, 1976); an historical shift in the West from societies based on the production of things to one based on the production of information and "simulations" (Baudrillard, 1983); from modern "organized" capitalism to postmodern "disorganized" capitalism (Lash and Urry, 1987); from Fordist to post-Fordist modes of production (Harvey, 1990); from national to global, bringing about the advent of "time-space compression," generated by the speeding up of both travel and telecommunications.

Another influential usage of "postmodernism" is to be found in cultural histories which seek to site postmodernism's birth in the cultural changes first noticed in the UK and US in the 1960s. According to this narrative, postmodernism first emerges as an avant-garde rejection of the certainties and social exclusivities of modernism. Susan Sontag (1966) described this rejection as the "new sensibility." Sontag coined the term to describe what she called the abandonment of "the Matthew Arnold notion of culture" as "the best that has been thought and known" (Arnold, 1971 [1869]: 56), claiming that the Arnoldian idea of culture was "historically and humanly obsolescent," and adding that "the distinction between 'high' and 'low' culture seems less and less meaningful" (1966: 302). It is this aspect of postmodernism which is most commonly intended (either positively or negatively) when the term is used in contemporary accounts of cultural production. For example, in architecture "postmodernism" signifies a new vernacular style, which mixes high and low, contemporary and historical – what is often referred to as "double coding" (Jenks, 1991). A similar form of eclecticism is also said to be a feature of postmodern fashions of dress (E. Wilson, 1998). In discussions of pop music culture, "postmodern" is most often used to identify the mixing of popular and art music (classical violinist Nigel Kennedy's album of songs by Jimi Hendrix; Luciano Pavarotti recording with U2; the commercial success of Laurie Anderson's performance piece "O Superman"; the aesthetic seriousness of Bob Dylan and the Beatles).

The academic circulation of the term can be dated to the publication of Jean-François Lyotard's *The postmodern condition* (1984). In this influential account **the postmodern condition** is presented as a crisis in the status of knowledge in Western societies. This finds expression "as incredulity towards metanarratives" (p. xxiv), producing in turn "the obsolescence of the metanarrative apparatus of legitimation," the supposed contemporary collapse or widespread rejection of all overarching and totalizing frameworks ("metanarratives"), which seek to tell universalist stories about the world in which we live.

Again mainly in academic circles, but sometimes more broadly, "postmodernism" is also used to describe a more general condition of contemporary society and its cultural production. Jean Baudrillard (1983), for example, claims that hyperrealism is the characteristic mode of postmodernity. In the realm of the hyperreal, the distinction between simulation and the "real" supposedly implodes; reality and simulation are experienced as without difference. Perhaps it is the case that people no longer mark the distinction between real and imaginary with quite the same degree of rigor as they may have done in the past, but it is difficult to find evidence to support the claim that people can no longer tell the difference. Nevertheless, Baudrillard is probably the best-known theorist of postmodernism, achieving almost cult status in some areas of cultural life.

In similar fashion, and again mostly in academic circles, "postmodernism" is also used to describe the cultural conditions of late capitalism. In this usage, postmodernism is "the cultural dominant of the logic of late capitalism" (Jameson, 1984: 78). Postmodernism, according to this argument, represents "the purest form of capital yet to have emerged, a prodigious expansion of capital into hitherto uncommodified areas" (p. 78). As a result, "aesthetic production . . . has become integrated into commodity production generally" (p. 56). As a consequence, contemporary culture is claimed to be flat and superficial, marked by nostalgia and pastiche. Moreover, culture is no longer ideological, disguising the economic activities of capitalist society; it is itself an economic activity, perhaps now the most important economic activity of all. In many ways this is a position which originates long before postmodernism became an intellectual concept circulating in academia. It is an argument with its roots in C19 accounts of the imposition of so-called mass culture on duped and manipulated masses. More specifically, it is a mode of analysis which is much influenced by (and little developed beyond) the work of the Frankfurt School.

The term "postmodernism" is also used to describe the media saturation of contemporary Western societies. In particular, it is deployed to draw attention to the fact that old cultural production is no longer simply replaced by the new, but is recycled for circulation together with the new (Collins, 1993). There can be little doubt that this is in part a result of the introduction of cable, satellite, and digital media, with their seemingly unrelenting demand for more and more programs to fill what seems like ever-increasing space in, say, television and radio schedules. Moreover, the promiscuous mixing of the old and new has produced in both audiences and producers what Jim Collins (1993: 250) calls a "hyper-conscious intertextuality," which both informs how audiences make sense of cultural texts (reading for intertextuality) and how cultural texts are made (the deployment of conscious intertextuality): for example, television programs such as *Twin Peaks, The Simpsons,* and *The Sopranos*; and films such as *Bladerunner, Blue Velvet,* and *Pulp Fiction*. The same postmodern play of quotations is also a feature of many music videos and television commercials. A similar self-reflexive intertextuality can be detected in the postmodern photography of Cindy Sherman and Barbara Kruger. This aspect of postmodernism was first identified in the 1960s to describe the self-reflexive work of writers such as Samuel Beckett, Jorge Luis Borges, and Thomas Pynchon and is used (for mostly the same reasons) to describe the contemporary fiction of writers such as Kathy Acker and Paul Auster (Hutcheon, 1988).

"Postmodernism" is sometimes used to describe a specific mode of cultural theory, associated, in particular, with the work of Lyotard, Baudrillard, Michel Foucault, Gilles Deleuze and Felix Guattari, and Frederic Jameson (Best and Kellner, 1991). Sometimes this is characterized as a theory about the postmodern and sometimes it is the theory itself which is seen as postmodern (or as poststructuralist).

Like "existentialism" in the 1950s and "structuralism" in the 1960s, "postmodernism" (as both theory and practice) has, since the 1980s, crossed from the academy into discourses and practices of everyday life. But, unlike these other intellectual discourses, postmodernism has not yet become, and, moreover, shows little sign of becoming, a fixed and coherent body of work, with a clearly delimited range of ideas and practices; instead, it continues to mean different things depending on discourse and context of use. It may well have been the term's indeterminacy which both encouraged and facilitated the hoax carried out by New York University professor of physics Alan Sokal, who duped the academic journal *Social Text* into publishing a spoof article on ''postmodern science'' (Sokal and Bricmont, 1998). For some cultural commentators (mostly hostile to post-modernism) this was itself a very **postmodern event**.

John Storey

See: *KNOWLEDGE, MODERN, POPULAR, TASTE, WEST.*

Poverty

Most fundamentally, **poverty** is a condition of want, or scarcity, particularly of subsistence or material possessions, and it is economic development or the social redistribution of wealth that provides its proper solution. But poverty can also simply mean a lack or deficiency of any kind, such as the **poverty of the soul**, the **poverty of the soil**, the ''poverty of your understanding'' (Watts, 1741), or, in the title of a famous book, ''the poverty of theory'' (E. P. Thompson, 1978). Poverty is hence a negative term, opposed to wealth, abundance, fullness, fertility, and productiveness.

The want of the minimal means to survive is what C20 social scientists called **absolute poverty** rather than **relative poverty** or **relative deprivation**. The latter is defined as relative to the usual living standards and lifestyles of the bulk of the population within a country, community, or society (Townsend, 1979: 31). But this distinction would appear to be much older. One of the consequences of a focus on absolute poverty is to reduce the numbers of people thought to be **in poverty** and to suggest, as Thomas Malthus (1798) did, that ''almost all poverty is relative.'' Malthus is famous for his principle of population. Under this principle, the rate of growth of human population would exponentially outstrip the growth of the means for its subsistence, if left unchecked by ''vice and misery'' such as war and famine. Malthus thus proposed that humans were in a fundamental situation of want or scarcity and that poverty was a natural condition of humankind. One of the consequences of such a condition was that assistance to **the poor** should be strongly discouraged, if not abandoned, because such assistance encouraged the poor, as the greater part of humankind, to procreate without regard to their ability to care for their children. This fundamental linkage of poverty with population and with human reproduc-tion was to have a long history that encompasses eugenics and studies of poverty and labor in the C19, and welfare reform and development discourses in the lC20 and eC21. While lC19 eugenicists and social thinkers might seek to curtail the right of various classes of the poor to reproduce (as Charles Booth did of the unemployables), welfare reformers and theorists of development argue that **poverty assistance** (in advanced or in developing countries) should only be provided in a way which increases industriousness, self-sufficiency, and disincentives to reproduction.

The idea of poverty as a natural condition is closely allied with the view that it is this fundamental condition of scarcity that impels humans to labor and to the civilization that labor creates. Patrick Colquhoun (1806: 7) famously argued that poverty is thus functional because it:

> is the lot of man. It is the source of wealth, since without poverty there could be no riches, no refinement, no comfort, and no benefits to those who may be possessed of wealth, in as much as without a large proportion of poverty surplus labour could never be rendered productive in procuring either the conveniences or luxuries of life.

Such ideas led reformers of this period to the conclusion that while poverty itself might be natural for humans and necessary for civilization, many of the forms it took were problematic, and a result of our attempts to interfere with these natural and necessary processes of distribution of wealth that amounted to the "lottery of life." In the lC18 and C19 the demoralized, improvident, and lazy cousin of the poor was the "pauper". In recent years, the paupers' descendents are "welfare queens," or women who deliberately have children to gain social welfare (United States), "scroungers" (Britain), and "dole bludgers" (Australia). More broadly, there are those who would view social assistance as creating a **culture of poverty** that becomes intergenerational, and creates an underclass characterized by their risk of criminality and welfare dependency. While the distribution of populations into the rich and poor is rarely questioned and logically impossible to abolish in a relative sense, and thus still a quasi-natural condition, deliberate attempts to alleviate poverty are often viewed as producing pathological and virulent forms of poverty. One version of this is the **poverty trap**, in which social assistance proves more attractive to the poor than available paid labor.

For the eC19 a distinction was maintained between poverty and the demoralized condition of pauperism or indigence, characterized by a dependence on public charity. Today the underclass or the welfare dependent exhibit not simply lack of access to resources but low self-esteem, risks of ill-health and criminality, exclusion from social networks, and lack of attachment to labor markets. Poverty has thus been linked to a discussion of the character and the morals of the poor for the duration of modern capitalist societies; the space of dissension is between those who view that character as a consequence of social environment and those who view it as innate or inherited. In contemporary jargon, poverty results from social exclusion. While exclusion manifests itself in the character traits of specific populations, the remedy of such exclusion might be found in transforming such traits by compulsory work programs (workfare) or by the provision of training and opportunities to those subpopulations viewed as disadvantaged, that is, as having social barriers to participation in education and paid labor.

A longer discussion of the trajectory of the idea of poverty would link this debate over the moral character of the poor with the history of religious, particularly Christian, moral doctrines, the practice of charity, and what came to be known in the C19 as philanthropy. Almsgiving and caring for the poor, and indeed the project of including the poor, have long been conceived as primary practices of virtue for the church, clergy, and laity alike. Religious orders have prescribed the vow of poverty. However, while both almsgiving and asceticism (the renunciation of worldly possessions/wealth) are viewed as ennobling the soul of the practitioner, the condition of poverty itself has no intrinsic goodness. This, we might say, is as true for contemporary social science as for Christian apologetics.

Mitchell Dean

See: *WELFARE, WORK.*

Power

Power has been a compelling reference point in understanding what motivates people, how they stand with one another, what they are in control of and what controls them, and what the future might hold for human societies. Talk of power and **power-seeking** uniquely bridges the gap between academic and popular opinion concerning the way the world works. Bertrand Russell (1938) summed this up by saying that power is to social science what energy is to physics, because, quite simply, our primary impulse in life is for power. Prior to the modern period in Western thought, this view of power as a self-standing quantum to be deployed in pursuit of self-interest was evident, as in "Poer ynow schal come to me" (Brunne, c.1330), and in Hobbes's (1991 [1651]) stark proposition that the "restless desire for power after power...ceaseth only in death." Descriptions of **power-struggles**, **powers in the land**, **powers behind the throne**, and "the powers that be" (Tyndall, 1526) were thus entirely familiar. Even so, ancient and medieval conceptions of **political power** were much more closely entwined with a more general apprehension of **"the powers"** that direct all human and natural existence, whether couched in Old Testament terms as divine sovereignty ("Power belongeth to God", Psalm 62), or in early modern form as Fate ("that power which erring men call chance" [Milton, 1637]). As forms of rule diversified, and as conceptions of sovereignty became still more secular, power over resources and people came to play a major role, probably the major role, in explaining all social behavior.

In some striking usages, power is almost like a substance with addictive or dangerous properties, as in "intoxicated with power" (Burke, 1791); "power tends to corrupt and absolute power corrupts absolutely" (Lord Acton, 1887); and "power is the great aphrodisiac" (Henry Kissinger, 1971). In a more comprehensive sense, covering both natural and social phenomena, it is not that power itself is a substance but rather that substances (things, people, relations) *possess* powers, that is, qualities and dispositions to act in certain ways, having specific effects on other things or people. To regard the **causal powers** of all things and relations, whether latent or manifest, as that which we most need to grasp is known as a "scientific realist" philosophical outlook (Harré and Madden, 1975).

274

Human individuals are "naturally" able to choose their goals and make things happen, thus realizing their intentions by mobilizing particular aptitudes of mind and body (as in **powers of speech** or **powers of movement**). And some more than others. This individualized sense of power is significant in everyday psychological descriptions of certain people as **powerful personalities**, that is, as gifted, attractive, charismatic, authoritative, leaderly, and to that extent impressively capable of influencing and transforming their situations. The belief that political and social positions of power are largely reflections of the existence of some sort of natural elite of this kind is a typically aristocratic outlook, while the conviction that positions of responsibility and status should be occupied by those who work hard to develop their talents is meritocratic. In a straight cynical view, we all, ultimately, scheme and manipulate to maximize our power. In these views, **social power**, like natural ability itself, is likely to be unequally distributed and rewarded, whether for good or ill. A more sociological approach is to say that, however much individuals may or may not differ in **natural powers**, by and large "most people in most societies adopt behaviors which reflect the relativity of powers amongst *roles* and the *practices* defining them" (Runciman, 1998: 92). Not only behaviors, but attitudes and ideals too – including what we think constitutes "attractive" or "impressive" personalities – are heavily coded by cultural norms and prevailing ideological constructions, as for example in our masculinist notion of what it is to be "dominant," to have a **powerful presence** or **powerful image** (think of **power-breakfasts** and **power-dressing** as ways that aspiring women express their equivalence with executive men).

In the lC20, then, views of history and society featuring the rise and fall of powerful individuals, or alternatively the shifts in the fortunes of the **Great Powers**, or the **balance of power**, were replaced, or at least supplemented, by more firmly social and cultural ways of comprehending the meaning and operation of power, though some fundamental issues remain keenly contested. One important aspect of debate concerns how we are to envisage the **spectrum of power**, given that we include very different relationships and attitudes under this heading. At one end, for example, there is the exercise of sheer physical violence, in which bodies are intentionally brutalized and subjectivities systematically annulled (massacre, rape, slavery, acts of terror). Some mC20 reflections on power (for example, those of the German political thinker Hannah Arendt and the American sociologist Talcott Parsons) in fact exclude unmediated violence from the spectrum of power, because power implies the establishment of some kind of social authority whereby those subject to power still participate in it as a "medium of exchange" around collective goals and means. Between the poles of total physical imposition and (at the other end) freely given consensus, power stretches out in many degrees: repression, oppression, command, compulsion, the rule of law, influence, inducement, status-exploitation, negotiation, seduction, pragmatic acquiescence, and so on. Where some would exclude consensus from the spectrum of power, others point out that consensus is rarely "unconstrained"; instead, it represents a subtle and insidious "hidden face" of power (Lukes, 1974) whereby dominated groups accept the *dominant* groups' conception of their own, and everyone's, interests. Another way of construing the relation between force and consent is through the Italian Marxist Gramsci's (1971) notion of "hegemony". Ruling groups and classes, Gramsci thought, exercise power most effectively through cultural (in the sense of both intellectual and moral) leadership, even if this is ultimately backed up by force, and in doing so recognize and work with the understandings and values of subordinate groups as well as dominant ideologies. Rising or revolutionary forces challenge this existing hegemony by trying to establish a new "national popular" hegemonic settlement of their own.

If power is a limited strategic quantity that one has to possess in order to advance one's interest, then for every **power winner** there is at least one **power loser**. This "zero-sum" notion is reflected in common usages such as **power-seeking**, **power-hungry** (or, in the IC20, "control freakery"), **power-wielding**, and **power-brokering**. On the other hand, especially when related to the virtues of democratic organization, we talk about **power-sharing**, and about groups and individuals being **empowered** by particular initiatives and experiences. If no one else is **disempowered**, this is a "non-zero-sum" version, highlighting our collective **power to do** things rather than wielding **power over** someone else. In a more general way, Foucault (1980) insisted that instead of treating power purely negatively such that it is always portrayed as necessarily repressive and bad, we should appreciate that power is extraordinarily productive. This is not to say that power is "good" as such; rather it is a matter of appreciating how the changing operations and forms of power consistently bring into being new ways of seeing and acting in the world, indeed new subjectivities, on the part of those involved.

As to the principal types or sources of power, the prevailing view is that there are three main forms: **economic**, **political**, and **ideological power**, with **military/coercive power** either an additional one, or a subtype of political power. These power-sources "fundamentally determine the structure of societies" (Mann, 1993: 1). An addendum to this list could be **discursive power**. Foucault (1980) – in a way updating Francis Bacon's slogan "knowledge is power" (1597) – asserted that power was intimately connected to dominant forms of expertise, science, and classification. To "name the world" is thus to define reality and to establish rules about what can validly be known, controlled, and imagined. This kind of **power–knowledge nexus** is not the same as ideological power precisely, because struggles over ways to categorize and measure social phenomena are seldom intentionally political or easily identifiable with specific agents or class interests. Even so, they result in powerful forms of mental and behavioral "discipline," and effective ways of "managing" the populations of modern societies.

Which of the types of power is ultimately primary? Marxists emphasize the imperatives of economic power, while non-Marxists, though not denying that power attaches to economic ownership and control, do deny that this takes priority as such. By the IC20, most Western social thought, including "radical" thought, had become pluralistic in orientation, so that none of the different forms of power is thought to be reducible to any other. Primacy has to be regarded as a contingent matter, liable to change along with its multiple circumstances. This movement away from any "foundationalist" ambition can be witnessed in feminist thinking about power. In the 1970s, the point was to challenge both Marxist and conventional political science nostrums by showing how patriarchy represented a pervasive and systematic **power structure** in its own right – indeed *the* power structure as far as feminists were concerned. This led to certain "theoretical" phrases entering popular discussion: "the personal is political," "male domination," "sexism." However, later on, difficult issues arose among feminists themselves about whether **gender power** was after all the most important form of power, or just one among several; or whether the acquisition, performance, and transformation of gender identities was best grasped at all by reference to something like a **gender power structure** (Squires, 2000).

As to the key **sites of power**, images have oscillated between those of society dominated by one main locus of power (**the power elite**) and those stressing the existence of **multiple powers**, or at least **countervailing powers**. Thus, claims that **sovereign power** lies primarily in the person of the official ruler, or the interests of the ruling class, or the machinations of the power elite have been balanced by a widening of the lens to take in such pluralizing factors as the "parcellization" of power to local lords and worthies under feudalism; the need of the modern liberal-democratic state to respond to numerous societal interest groups and pressure groups; and the impact that social movements in the lC20 had on official politics. A range of familiar phrases encapsulates the influence of social movements and interest groups: **black power, flower power, green power, gray power, pupil power, parent power, peasant power, "power to the people,"** and so on. In our time, the centrality of the nation state is particularly under scrutiny. In conditions of globalization the state is forced to cede much of its sovereignty to supranational bodies, while at the same time Western states face severe challenges to their unity and conceptions of citizenship "at home," in the form of struggles by indigenous peoples, regional movements, stateless nations, and immigrant groups. In addition, power is increasingly viewed as operating in and through all social situations and relations; and is accordingly resisted in innumerable local forms too. This gives us a picture in which power is essentially diverse in nature and outcome, and also spread minutely throughout the social body (Nash, 2000).

Such oscillations in the prevailing understanding of power have effects on our sense of the prospects for power, and for any hopes of "emancipation" from its grip. If we imagine power as all-pervasive, then the very idea of being "liberated," or of heading for some human future "beyond power," seems – at best – fanciful. There thus develops a partial convergence of left and right thinking around the pitfalls of utopian thinking, in which the good society is almost defined in terms of the complete absence of power relations. Salutary though this realism about power may be, it is still worth considering whether our obsession with power – with "the power of power," so to speak – is bound to persist. Perhaps under a different kind of economy and culture, attention might turn again to the centrality of other aspects of human interaction, and other versions of "human nature," based, for example, on creativity, love, nurture, care, or solidarity. Certainly any purportedly radical critique of power and its effects requires some kind of gesture toward what may lie outside it.

Gregor McLennan

See: *GENDER, GOVERNMENT, IDEOLOGY, KNOWLEDGE, RESISTANCE, STATE.*

Pragmatism

Pragmatism is closely related to **practice** and **practicality**, suggesting its association with all that pertains to the immediate, daily workings of the world. To be called a **pragmatist**, in ordinary usage, is to be praised (or blamed) for understanding political realities and/or social constraints. When praised, the pragmatist is credited with hard-headed attention to what it takes to get things done, combined, perhaps, with a necessary indifference to abstract questions concerning the good and the true. When blamed, the pragmatist is contrasted with the "person of principle," who ignores the world's political realities and holds fast precisely to those considerations of the good and the true that must not be slighted or compromised in the interest of achieving some desired end. Thus, in politics, the pragmatist is either the person who smartly and efficiently manages to enact legislation despite the quibbles and cavils of her or his associates, *or* the person who abandons principle in the course of what is usually called (especially by those who are critical of pragmatists) the "horse-trading" and concession-making associated with back-chamber deals and smoke-filled rooms.

Pragmatism's connection to the world of daily business and civil affairs reaches to antiquity, in which the Gk *pragmatikos* was "active, business-like, versed in affairs" or "a man of business or action," and the L *pragmaticus* was "skilled in business, especially law." Along the way, however, "pragmatism" and "pragmatists" picked up some less familiar connotations. From its entry into English in the C16 through the lC19, the term **pragmatic sanction** was in common parlance, denoting a form of state decree issued by the sovereign. The pragmatic sanction literally laid down the law, and doubtless accounts for the secondary connotations of the adjective **pragmatic** from the C16 to the C19, such as "officious," "meddlesome," and "dictatorial" ("it signifies her to be pragmatique, proud, and one that will domineer over her husband": Richard Sanders, 1653). Beginning in the mC19 one finds references to **pragmatic history**, which entails the study of the facts of history with regard to causes, consequences, and the practical lessons to be learned therefrom. It is only in the lC19–eC20, however, that "pragmatism" begins to take on a more specialized philosophical meaning, complexly related to the vernacular sense in which (for example) a **pragmatic solution** is synonymous with a "workable" solution. In philosophy, beginning with the work of C. S. Peirce and William James (the latter of whom quite clearly established pragmatism as a fully formed philosophical position in his book *Pragmatism*, 1979; original publication 1907), "pragmatism" quickly came to denote a school of thought that repudiated most of the Western metaphysical tradition in favor of a seemingly more modest, mundane form of thought in which, as James put it, "'the true'... is only the expedient in the way of our thinking, as 'the right' is only the expedient in our way of behaving" (p. 222).

James's use of the word "expedient" has been controversial, because it suggests that pragmatists can simply believe whatever they want to believe. Yet even though pragmatism is, on these grounds, often aligned with relativism, its deeper philosophical roots secured it a prominent place in the intellectual history of the C20. Most importantly, pragmatism's rejection of Western metaphysics, particularly that philosophical tradition's distinct separation between mind and world, draws strength from the pragmatist view of language, in which language is not a medium for the accurate apprehension of reality as it "really is," but rather a kind of tool humans have developed in order to perform practical tasks that can be accomplished by no other means. For the pragmatist, then, the pursuit of justice should be understood not in the Platonic sense of an attempt to make human affairs correspond to some ideal form of the Good, but instead as a question of how to devise the right linguistic and institutional tools to advance human practices that will serve a specific sense of the good, and then to convince other humans that these are the right tools for the job.

279

Likewise, pragmatists from William James to Richard Rorty (contemporary American philosopher and author of, among many other things, *Consequences of pragmatism*, 1982) tend to be skeptical of the term "truth," since they (rightly) associate it with the metaphysical tradition's insistence that truth is eternal, and external to human interests. In that tradition, truth is conceived as existing in its purest form in the laws of chemistry and physics – which are, of course, impervious to human desires and tool-making skills. The traditional goal of philosophy, accordingly, is to approach that standard of truth, getting gradually closer to an accurate representation of the physical laws of the universe, and to devising laws of human affairs that will have the same transhistorical, immutable status as physical laws. (This is usually referred to as the "correspondence theory of truth," according to which statements are true because they correspond to reality.)

For the pragmatist, however, the physical sciences should be understood not as direct windows onto reality, but as particularly well-honed tools that humans have devised for understanding how things work; and anything that helps those tools do their job, or fit together with other similar tools, is "true" in a pragmatist sense. If a scientific discovery has helped us better understand the motions of stars or the composition of atoms, then it is "true" in the sense that it is a useful belief; and if a moral argument has led us to prefer trial by jury to trial by ordeal, it is a useful belief as well. Moreover, if a scientific or moral argument helps to make better sense of our other scientific or moral arguments, so much the better. (This is usually referred to as the "coherence theory of truth," according to which statements are true because they get things done and cohere with other statements that do the same.) **Philosophical pragmatism** thus shares with ordinary pragmatism the premise that consequences are what really matter in the end, whether these are consequences of belief (as in philosophy) or consequences of action (in ordinary speech).

Michael Bérubé

See: *EMPIRICAL, KNOWLEDGE, MATERIALISM, OBJECTIVITY, REASON, RELATIVISM.*

Private

In general, **private** is the opposite of public. This may signal protection from public gaze and regulation, or it may signal **privation**, and in particular the loss of the rights associated with public statuses, as a deposed king becomes merely a **private citizen**.

Classical Greek and Roman thought regarded freedom, creativity, and political rights as features of the public realm (Arendt, 1998). Women, children, and slaves were all consigned to the **private realm**, meaning that they had little existence beyond that dictated by material desire and necessity. They were accordingly seen as without substantial or important distinctions, a usage that survives in labeling an ordinary soldier who has not attained rank or distinction as **a private**. Development of full personhood was seen as an activity carried out in friendship, political participation, intellectual debate, military service, and other public roles (Weintraub and Kumar, 1997).

Early Christianity gave a greater role to the interior life of individuals, but the link between **privacy** and individual personhood developed most clearly as a core feature of modernity (C. Taylor, 1989). LC18 and eC19 Romanticism symbolizes the trend, but concern for the quality of **private life** was already reflected in early modern art with its multitude of portraits, family groups, and interior rooms. Pioneered especially by bourgeois families, this concern for the virtues and pleasures of domesticity spread widely. Closely related to the new moral emphasis on family life and ordinary affairs was increased awareness of interior experience, emotional life, and personal development. This placed new value on the **private spaces** (both literal and metaphorical) into which one withdrew for spiritual meditation, prayer, and self-examination. Such pursuits focused on self as well as God, and helped to give rise to modern psychology as well as to a more personal orientation to religion (celebrated notably in Protestantism).

This in turn was linked to a new understanding of the body as a properly **private possession**. Increasingly elaborate codes of manners and norms of bodily discipline arose, not least in relation to sexuality, health, and labor (Elias, 2000). A common feature was the treatment of the body as an object of mental control. Movements for hygiene and morality involved the body in new dynamics of shame and eroticism (Foucault, 1986; B. Turner, 1997). Sex organs became **private parts**. An ideology of feminine modesty generally removed women as well as sexuality from public life (though it defined a countertype of immodest ''public women'' – prostitutes – whose properly **private selves** were publicly exchanged). On the other hand, a right to privacy could be construed as an important basis for ascribing to each person control over her or his body.

The logic of possession governed also in defining market exchange as private. **Private persons** enter markets to exchange their **private property**. Their rights to do so were conceptualized in the C17 by extension from the notion of individual labor in the appropriation of the common heritage of Creation or nature (though inheritance raised other questions). Human beings were reconceptualized as possessing individuals (Macpherson, 1962). They were also understood as the self-sufficient primary actors of the market so that privacy was no deprivation to them, but an affirmation of their essential autonomy. This was echoed in a host of secondary forms of privacy: **private homes**, **private offices**, **private clubs**, **private boxes** at sporting events, and even **private washrooms**. Those without private property, by contrast, were commonly without claims to personal privacy. Ironically, officers slept in their own bedrooms and private soldiers in barracks.

A central paradox in thought about private property was the social and often very large-scale character of its production and accumulation (Marx, 1976 [1867]). Money, business corporations, and a range of innovations in financial instruments made relations of property ever more abstract from both individual persons and physical goods produced by their labor. Most corporations are public companies in the sense that their stock is held relatively widely and traded on open markets; many are also created by government charter rather than only **private contract** – as distinct from family businesses. Confusingly, these are still considered part of the **private sector**. This publicness subjects them to levels of regulation not applied to private companies. What is at issue is private (individual) appropriation of the product of public (collective) labor. Understood as tied to the individual, **the private** is opposed to the collective. Understood as rightfully independent of state interference, private is opposed to government. But private property extends beyond the individual. At the same time, **private wealth** could be used for public purposes, as in philanthropic foundations and donations to not-for-profit organizations such as universities or hospitals (Powell and Clemens, 1998).

The liberal tradition combines this economic usage of private with a political meaning. The possessing individuals of market society are also possessors of political rights (and indeed, rights against politics). They hold these as **private persons** – not occupants of public statuses – but the **private rights** empower them to act in public. Indeed, political life is conceptualized in liberal thought as the coming together of **private individuals** to make collective decisions about matters of common interest – that is, the public good. While some features of the public good are essentially shared (for example, clean air is difficult to appropriate in an individually exclusive manner), most are conceptualized as aggregates of (and thus compromises among) **private goods**. This is given one of its most influential formulations in the Benthamite utilitarian slogan, ''the greatest good for the greatest number.''

The boundaries of the public are given, in this tradition, by family and intimate relations and by the market. Each is granted autonomy from intrusions of the public, which is understood primarily as the governmental. Of course, the conditions of family and market life may be highly unequal, not least in the support they give different individuals for action in public. Accordingly, each boundary has been the object of recurrent struggles – from workers' efforts to subject parts of the economy to state regulation through feminist efforts to make the personal political. Ironically, feminists have often treated the non-familial as indiscriminately public, and labor movements have often sought to defend the autonomy of the family from the market.

Also ironically, perhaps, liberal thought has given rise to the very language of rights used increasingly prominently to challenge the autonomy of putatively **private spheres**. Thus people claim rights to education, or jobs, or information about what goes on beyond the closed doors of business corporations. Rights are generally attributes of private individuals, in liberal usage, and conceived significantly as defenses against the intrusion of states. The defense of privacy remains a concern in just this sense, and indeed is renewed with regard to new technologies of surveillance. Yet private rights have become increasingly prominent bases for demands of government action, both domestically and internationally.

By contrast, other traditions emphasize the shared activity involved in creating public institutions. They stress that **private action** by individuals can account for only a fraction of the goods enjoyed by members of modern societies – and also that large corporations are not private in the same sense and often act in ways contrary to the interests of individuals. At the same time, they too would defend the need for individual privacy in relation to governmental surveillance. The idea of "private" remains contested.

Craig Calhoun

See: *BODY, FAMILY, INDIVIDUAL, LIBERALISM, MARKET, PERSON, PUBLIC.*

Public

The concept of **public** derives from Greek and Roman conceptions of the rightful members of polities. Its philological roots lie in the L *poplicus*, of the people, which shifted to *publicus* apparently under the influence of its restriction to *pubes*, adult men. The shift makes clear the tension in the term between a general notion of open access and more specific understandings of who is entitled to membership in **the public**. This persists into modern usage, in which "public" is increasingly opposed to "private," and denotes most prominently, and in varying combinations: (a) the people, interests, or activities which are structured by or pertain to a state; (b) anything which is open or accessible; (c) that which is shared, especially that which must be shared; (d) all that is outside the household; and (e) knowledge or opinion that is formed or circulated in communicative exchange, especially through oratory, texts, or other impersonal media (Calhoun, 2001).

Notions of **public good** and **public administration** both appeared in English by the IC15, reflecting simultaneously the rise of modern states and their concern for the public good (*res publica* or **public things** in L, and often "commonwealth" in English). Securing the public good was initially understood as the responsibility of the king, understood to have "two bodies," one his "private" person and the other his "public" being as sovereign ruler (Kantorowicz, 1957). Kings consulted with other nobles whose **public roles** were ascribed, and often inherited, as specific rights and eventually with a growing number of commoners. Ideals of nobility implied an ability to rise above merely personal concerns, as did the notion of citizenship in a self-ruling **republic**.

Popular rule required **public deliberation**. By the IC18, the notion of a right to **assemble in public**, for example, was increasingly claimed for the citizenry as a whole, by contrast with the specific rights of nobles to assemble and petition the monarch. Instead of inherited position, the capacity to act in public was determined by a combination of character and material possession. The two were linked in the notion of independence, praised for example by Locke (1990), and equally a virtue of mind and a material condition predicated on private property. The capacity to be a **public person** thus reflected in two senses attributes of what would today be considered private persons: their psychology and their wealth.

The idea of public as the whole people or nation was closely related to the notion of public as "open" – like a **public park**. **Public spaces** make possible interaction that is not based on intimacy, but instead connects strangers – like walking down a city street, going to the theater, or participating in a political rally. The public person idealized in this usage is at ease amid the diversity and unfamiliarity typical of cities (Sennett, 1977). The urban analyst Jane Jacobs (1972) famously praised the public character of C19 cities – their sidewalks, cafés, human scale, and mixed-use neighborhoods – and deplored its loss in C20 transformations.

Newspapers and other media support **public discussion** as much as these physical spaces do. Informed **public debate** depends also on **public access** to information. Until the C19, the English Parliament refused to allow its debates to be published. Laws on **public secrets** still vary, as to regulations on how much information private businesses must disclose. The rise of **public-access television** and efforts to defend the openness of the Internet also reflect concern to provide citizens with means to participate in **public communication**.

The political elites that run governments are narrower than the broad publics affected by governments. The same is true of **public discourse**. Even when it is about matters that affect the whole public, only a smaller public is active in it – and this is often a matter of active exclusion, not just apathy. The right of women to speak in public was as much contested until the C20 as their right to vote. There is a distinction, thus, between the public capable of (or entitled to) political speech, and the public that is the object of such speech or its intended political effects.

Democracy centers on trying to give political power to those affected by political action, so democrats have always been committed to expanding political participation. But democracy also depends on the public deliberating effectively about political choices, and enlargement of participation has often seemed to undermine the use of reason in public discourse, substituting techniques of persuasion based on money and mass media. Jürgen Habermas's (1989) famous phrase "structural transformation of the public sphere" refers to the process in which expansion of the **public sphere** achieved democratic enlargement at the expense of the rational quality of discussion (and thus its ability to identify the best policies for the **public interest**). The challenge is to get both at once.

The idea of public debate is not limited to politics. Science itself is often held to depend on its public character, as, for example, findings should be published and theories debated. But while public debate may help to reveal the truth, majority votes may still reflect error (Dewey, 1927). Nor is all public communication rational-critical debate; much is expressive or aesthetic activity, and efforts at persuasion also take other forms (Warner, 2001). And as Arendt (1998) stressed, public communication can include creative "world-making," as, for example, the framers of constitutions help to make countries.

It is always possible for some to try to shape **public opinion** by controlling the availability of information instead of by open discussion. This may involve presenting only positive information, or attempting to restrict public awareness of negative information, or indeed spreading false information. Scientists occasionally fail to report negative results of experiments. Much more often, politicians, business corporations, and others hire **public relations** specialists to manage public opinion.

During the course of the C19 and eC20, the idea of public opinion stopped referring to opinion that had been adequately tested in public debate, and thus deserved the assent of informed citizens, and began to refer to whatever happened to be believed by the mass of people, regardless of the grounds for their beliefs (Habermas, 1989). Beliefs were treated as attributes of individuals, like private property, to be discovered objectively by asking questions separate from actual public discourse. Public opinion research thus focuses not on the forming of opinion through public discourse, but on the use of survey methods to identify the opinions of private persons. These are deemed to be public either because they can be aggregated statistically to represent the whole mass of persons, or because they are on topics of public interest. There is no implication, however, that such opinions have been formed in a public manner, let alone through open sharing of information and rational-critical debate rather than through the management of public relations. A different approach, "deliberative polling," brings representative samples of citizens together for informed discussion, and then asks their opinions. This is designed to simulate some of the benefits of the classical notion of public debate for representative subsets of the large populations of modern states.

The transformation of the notion of public opinion into an aggregate of private opinions was influenced by the rise of liberal individualism and especially of market society and social theories derived from markets (Splichal, 2000). Classical political economy from the C18 on stressed the idea that free trade among a multitude of self-interested individuals would produce **public benefits** (drawing on the older notion that private vices might produce **public goods** and thereby count as **public virtues**). It also suggested that a good market was itself a sort of public, since it worked best when maximally open and unrestricted, and when all participants had equal access to information. Traders thus serve the public; shops are open to the public – as indeed are pubs (**public houses**, which are important not only as businesses but as places for members of the public to meet). Buying, selling, and entering into contracts may be activities of private persons, but they have public effects through the aggregation accomplished by markets. In addition, a marketplace (whether physical or "virtual") is public. Entering into this market–public realm is thus contrasted with remaining in the private realm of non-monetarized exchanges of which the family is the paramount example. This usage would in the lC20 inform feminist theories which analyzed the ways in which women were excluded from public life, including economic activity as well as politics and public communication. How morally laden the distinction of public from private can be is evident in an C18 dictionary of vulgar terminology, which defined "a woman's commodity" as "the private parts of a modest woman and the public parts of a prostitute."

The idea of market is recurrently problematic for the public–private dichotomy. It is based on private property, but it is also public in its openness and its effects. It might be left free from government interference because private, or made the object of government regulation because public. Both terminology and political values are confusing. But it is clear that though prices may be "signals" in markets, the integration of markets is based on objective effects rather than achieved through communicative agreements. Likewise, it is common to speak of **public ownership** or the **public sector** in ways that equate "public" with the state itself. **Public law** is thus the law that regulates the action of the state itself and its relations with citizens, as distinct from the other branches of law that regulate relations among citizens, or the creation of corporations as legal persons. At other times, government is distinguished from the public composed of people who may either resent or support it.

Markets based entirely on the self-interested actions of private actors systematically fail to provide certain sorts of goods, which is a crucial reason why governments intervene in economies on behalf of the public. These public goods are those which must be consumed in shared form (such as security, a clean environment, or indeed a sound money supply). Technical economic usage sometimes restricts the class of public goods to those that in their very nature must be shared, though law can require the sharing of goods which could in principle be privatized, such as public parks, **public schools**, **public television**, and **public beaches** or **public baths**. Governments act not only to provide public goods but to limit public nuisances (like pollution).

Governments are said to act on behalf of the public, but it is a challenge to reconcile the different views of many different groups each of which may engage in its own public communication. Some speak of **publics** and **counter-publics**, in which the latter are

285

simply publics organized in resistance to the **dominant public** or some of its norms – for example, one might speak of a **gay public,** a **radical feminist public**, or a **Christian evangelical public** (Fraser, 1992; Warner, 2001). At the same time, part of the idea of public is precisely that communication furthers integration across lines of difference.

Moreover, publics do not stop at the borders of states. There is growing reference to **international public spheres** – of Islam or Christendom, of human rights activists or global media. Likewise, the international law of states is understood to be a form of public law and a basis for establishing relations among states without merger or violation of sovereignty. Indeed, in the eC19 Europe's major powers (save France) signed a joint declaration proscribing Napoleon as a **public enemy**, with whom neither peace nor truce could be concluded. Similar arguments have been put forward in the eC21 with regard to Saddam Hussein and alleged terrorists.

In short, both the ideas of what the public is and what is in the public interest remain subject to public debate.

Craig Calhoun

See: *FEMINISM, GOVERNMENT, MARKET, PRIVATE, STATE.*

Queer

"We're here. / We're queer. / We're fabulous." "We're queer. / We're here. / Get used to it": some of the most interesting political slogans of the lC20 came from **the queer movement**. From being a term of abuse hurled mainly at gay men, the joyful and in-your-face use of **queer** represents an amazingly successful reworking of an epithet. Eve K. Sedgwick, an American literary critic and **queer studies** expert, remarks that etymologically, "the word 'queer' itself means *across* – it comes from the Indo-European root *-twerkw*, which also yields the G *quer* (traverse), L *torquere* (to twist), English *athwart*" (Sedgwick, 1993: xii). From its roots within activist groups to its established role within cultural theory, "queer" has moved across several domains and is now a widely accepted term to describe and analyze alternative sexual identity.

From the 1980s on, "queer" marked a new strand of activist politics first in the US, and then spreading quickly to the UK and elsewhere. Fed up with government inaction over HIV/AIDS, and disappointed with an assimilationist model of mainstream gay and lesbian politics, groups like **Queer Nation** took to the streets. Rather than assimilate ("we're just like you"), queer confronted. Artist collectives like Gran Fury provided brilliant graphics (Crimp and Rolston, 1990), and **queer groups** plastered the streets with highly imaginative yet simple posters (one featured George Bush Snr's statement about not raising taxes, "read my lips," along with visuals of **queer couples** kissing). Other strategies featured kiss-ins, where large groups of mainly young queers occupied shopping malls and kissed. Queer groups shocked and amused, and instructed people about how HIV/AIDS was devastating **queer communities**. They also made visible to "straight" society the sheer energy of those communities.

*ABCDEFGHIJKLMNOP**Q**RSTUVWXYZ*

Teresa de Lauretis is credited with introducing the term ''queer'' into cultural theory in her 1991 edited special issue of the journal *differences*. De Lauretis saw in queer a way of bringing together gay and lesbian and feminist work, while also reworking the dominant forms of address that privilege ''man'' or ''gay'' over ''woman'' or ''lesbian.'' Instead of reproducing the idea of a binary hetero–homosexual model of identity (Dyer, 1991: 186), ''queer'' was to be an umbrella term for all those outside of heterosexuality, as well as a way of specifying multiple identities. People inhabit many identities simultaneously, and it was argued that queer would provide an alternative to the ''add-on'' model of naming identity categories: black, lesbian, working-class, etc.

In cultural theory, queer has also been greatly enabled by the work of the American feminist philosopher Judith Butler on the performative nature of identity (1990, 1993). Extending J. L. Austin's ideas about *How to do things with words* (1962), Butler argues that speech acts can produce identity. For instance, when we refer to notions about femininity and perform ''being a girl,'' we ''girl ourselves'' and take on normative ideas about what constitutes feminine identity. As a collective performance, categories of masculinity, femininity, and heterosexuality both appear as natural and are unsettled. Butler's argument is that this process is doomed to failure: we can never perfectly perform ideal categories. Most germane to queer, her argument points to an instability at the heart of heterosexual identity. Who can perfectly perform being a heterosexual? As it makes it visible – could heterosexuality be just another choice of identity? – the idea that hetero-sexuality is a performance strips it of its natural status: ''normative uninterrogated 'regular' heterosexuality may not function as a sexuality at all'' (Sedgwick, 1993: 10).

While the emphasis on identity as a performance was perfectly in tune with **queer activism**, one of the more enduring aspects of **queer theory** may have been the destabil-ization of heterosexuality. But if the **queering** of various aspects of supposedly ''straight'' culture (from Shakespeare to soap operas) has been an indication of queer theory's vitality, it has also led to debates and objections. If heterosexuality is to be included under the rubric of queer, and if anything and anyone can be queered, what is the specificity of queer's political objectives or its object of study?

This is an open, and perhaps impossible question that has yet to be definitively answered. As a possible clarification of queer's project, several theorists have argued for ''queer'' to be used in the first personal singular: ''I am queer.'' For Eve K. Sedgwick, ''Queer is transitive – multiply transitive'' (1993: xii). Using ''queer'' in this way allows the speaker and the interlocutor ''to reflect on ways in which language really can be said to produce effects: effects of identity, enforcement, seduction, challenge'' (p. 11). Sedgwick's point is import-ant, although it's not clear that younger generations do self-identify as queer. It may also be true that despite its intentions, queer remains a mainly white phenomenon in the West.

As **queer culture** has been rapidly taken up in advertising and consumer culture, it has lost its marginal status. This would not necessarily be a problem except that for many activists and theorists queer's outsider status was integral to the **queer project**. When previously marginal and **queer "ghettos"** become up-market tourist areas, more notable for their bars and restaurants than for any politics, the oppositional nature of queer becomes questionable (Kirsch, 2000). By the eC21, "queer" began to be seen as a middle-class and maybe even a middle-aged term. This may be because it seems that within urban Western cultures, being queer is less of a problem. While for some being queer is an accepted and even sought-after identity, this ignores the fact that a large percentage of teenage suicides in non-urban areas are committed by **queer youth**.

Interestingly, as "queer" loses something of its vibrancy in the West, it has been taken up outside of Anglo-American culture (Berry, Martin, and Yue, 2002; Patton and San-chez-Eppler, 2000). In several Asian contexts, "queer" is said to be a term more open to cultural specificity and difference than "gay," "lesbian," or "homosexual" (Sullivan and Jackson, 2001). In this way the impetus that Sedgwick identified may be ongoing: that queer describes "the experiential linguistic, epistemological, representational, political adventures" of sexual identities (1993: 8).

Elspeth Probyn

See: *FEMINISM, GAY AND LESBIAN, IDENTITY, SEXUALITY.*

Race

Race is a politically charged and ambivalent word that has evaded precise definition. Derived in English from F *race* and It *razza*, it has meant a tribe or people of common stock, such as **the German race**, and denoted a sensibility, like the notion of the British people as **an island race**. In its most inclusive sense "race" denotes a class of being or a species in the plant or animal kingdoms. Problems arose when it was used to identify supposedly natural divisions within human populations. The idea of "race" in this sense has had wide and damaging consequences due to the view that groups possess fixed traits and particular intellectual and physical characteristics. This led to a belief in **racial purity**, innate **racial difference**, and natural **racial hierarchies**, and informed projects of slavery, apartheid, colonialism, empire, and genocide. Although the idea of race is usually regarded as a "Western" invention, evidence from China indicates the existence of **racial taxonomies** before contact with Europeans, and a faith in the innate superiority of the "**yellow race**." Chinese conceptions of race worked on the semantic similarity of Ch *zu*, meaning both "lineage" and "race," and conflated identity and ancestry with territory and biology (Dikotter, 1992), indicating the sinewy line between **racism**, nationalism, and patriotism.

Ethnology and anthropology in the C18 and C19 saw race as coded in and on the body and believed that science could uncover its patterns. Basic forms of **scientific racism** named three races, Caucasian, Mongoloid, and Negroid, but a bewildering variety of **racial systems** and groupings has been produced over time. These were discredited by C20 science, which provides evidence that there is more genetic variation within so-called **racial groups** than between them. Today sports is one field where the search for "racial"

ABCDEFGHIJKLMNOPQ**R**STUVWXYZ

differences continues – those who assert that such differences are biologically and not socially based claim they are violating a **race taboo**. The **anti-racist** slogan ''there is only one race – the human race'' has been employed as a counter-weight to ideas of **racial divisions** within humankind.

The key question is which human differences are regarded as significant ''racial'' markers. **Race thinking** combines some observable physical differences – skin color, hair texture, facial features, and skull shape – with what lies below the surface – blood, bones, and brain size. Race thinking has gone beyond physical difference to see race as a sensibility, making racial demarcation an aesthetic as well as a physical boundary. For example, in C19 China the **fine races** (the yellows and the whites) were believed to be wise and born to rule, while the **mean races** (blacks, browns, and reds) were thought of as stupid and degenerate (Dikotter, 1992). Social scientists have tried to study **race relations**. Some put ''race'' into quotation marks to highlight its constructed and ideological nature and to underline that it has no real biological referent. It is, however, socially and politically significant and has real effects because inequalities are reproduced through practices of racism. The signification of race through social practices is called **racialization** – various processes by which real or imagined characteristics are used to identify a group as a ''racial'' collectivity, and cultural, political, or ideological situations where race thinking is invoked. This **race-making** is an instance of a **racial essentialism** that treats members of the ''same'' group as if they share some common essence, and overlooks differences within them while understating similarities between ''racial'' groups.

Fears about miscegenation and **race-mixing** have been prominent in the delineation of racial and sexual boundaries. The products of ''mixed'' racial relationships have been called many things, such as mulatto, metisse, coffee-colored, café au lait, and dusky (applied to the actresses Lena Horne and Halle Berry, for example). Hybridity has been viewed as a monstrous form of mongrelization, weakening the stock and the gene pool, but also as a harbinger of a new intercultural, **post-racial** melting pot. In child-adoption policy it has been maintained that ''mixed'' children are really black, because they are regarded as **raced**. Concerns about loss of **racial identity** led to so-called **same-race** adoption policies and a limit on **transracial** or transcultural adoption. This has since fallen out of favor, partly because of confusion about what the ''same race'' means (a similar problem occurs with the **racial matching** of interviewer and interviewee in social research). Mixed race, which replaced terms such as ''half-caste,'' itself became problematic because it implied the existence of pure races in the first place. There is now a preference for ''mixed heritage,'' and one example of a mixed-heritage neologism is ''Caublinasian,'' which the golfer Tiger Woods uses to signal his mixed Caucasian, black, Indian, and Asian origins.

Race is an object of governmental, academic, and everyday knowledge and scrutiny. Official classifications such as censuses both delineate what counts *as* race, and count *by* race. The changing categories of the US Census over time reveal an obsessive concern with demarcating all the ''non white others.'' The latest census indicates 63 different

"ethno-racial" possibilities. According to the 2000 survey one-third of the US population now consists of **minority races**, while some 15 million are "other." In spite of the problematic nature of categorization and counting, census and other data on **racial inequalities** in housing, health, education, employment, and criminal justice can highlight the existence of **racial prejudice and discrimination**, though there is disagreement about the extent to which racism, class, or something else accounts for these inequalities. Spatial residential segregation and differential educational achievement between "races" have prompted debates about a black underclass and the relationship between **race and intelligence**. Census data have been used to promote policies such as affirmative action and contract compliance (though critics claim this is positive discrimination and preferential treatment) and to provide a benchmark against which social change can be measured. For these reasons the terminology of race, racial groups, and belonging has acted as a source of identification and political mobilization for redress against inequalities and unfair practices.

Race matters because it is seen and treated as a key marker of identity, nationhood, and community. Race can determine or influence how people see themselves, how others define them, and the groups they are seen to belong to. Terms such as "black history," "the black experience," or "Asian culture" treat race as a fact of everyday life. Race and racial identity are invoked in guidelines on writing that encourage journalists to consider how issues cut across racial lines. Academic and professional associations also have codes on appropriate language and style to be used when referring to racial minorities. Race does not, however, always have to be explicitly named and can be coded linguistically through certain words – "the ghetto," "immigrant," "street crime," "mugging," "wilding," and "gangsta culture," for example. The use of **racial profiling** by the police in the US is another example of the way in which race and crime are associated. "Ethnicity" is often preferred to "race" because the former is a cultural category, while race has often been an imposed biological categorization. In practice, race and ethnicity have been mixed up with each other and with nationality, citizenship, religion, history, language, culture, and identity. In 1998 the American Anthropological Association (AAA) stated that "race" should immediately be replaced by more correct terms, including "ethnicity" and "ethnic origins." The AAA urged the US Census to drop the use of the word "race."

Race is often related to skin color, especially to colors that are "not white," a fetishism that has been called "epidermalization." Chief among these visual properties has been blackness. The English language is full of words that use "black" to signal menace or threat, or in a derogatory way: blackening, black look, blackleg, black mark, a black lie, black deed, blackmail, etc. The racial significance of the word "black" in such cases is contested by those who maintain that imagined associations have been used to promote political correctness. Thus, in the UK in the 1980s it was suggested that such words, and nursery rhymes like "baa baa black sheep," were being banned because of their "racial" overtones. Blackness and the black experience have been given expression in music such as jazz, blues, soul, gospel, r&b, reggae, rap, and hip hop – the earlier forms were called **race**

music and **race records**, and current usage groups these together as "music of black origin." Concerns about **race and representation** are prominent in the "Blaxploitation" movies, in literature, and in the black aesthetic and black arts movements. Blackness has in some ways been appropriated and commodified in fashion, advertising, and contemporary culture, sometimes in ways that suggest **racial or bodily fetishism**, and prompted concerns about **racial stereotypes**, and representations of "the other," particularly black masculinities. Before that, negrophilia among the Paris avant-garde of the 1920s valued blackness through exoticizing its associations with Africa and with primitivism. Blackness can also be shared imaginatively, where young white people employ the language and "street style" of rap and hip-hop culture, or when a likeness is being drawn between the subordinated position of blacks and particular white groups. For instance, in Roddy Doyle's novel *The Commitments* (1990), and in the film based on it, a young white man says: "The Irish are the niggers of Europe . . . Say it loud, I'm black an' I'm proud."

Blackness has been embraced as a collective identity and a mode of organization and resistance in anti-colonial struggles, by groups such as the Black Panthers, and through the famous slogan "Black is beautiful," which also positively valued African styles and clothing, such as the Afro hairstyle and dreadlocks. In the 1960s **race riots** in the US and a burgeoning civil rights movement went along with Black Power and black consciousness ideologies, through which blackness was no longer considered shameful but reclaimed as a source of pride and communal solidarity. Changes in terminology and self-identification are well illustrated by Henry Louis Gates (1994: 201): "The 'Personal Statement' for my Yale application began: 'My grandfather was colored, my father was Negro, and I am black.' " For a time, "black" also became a shared political term in Britain that encompassed south Asians and sometimes people of Arabic and Chinese origins too, along with African-Caribbeans, when it was argued that being black captured the similar experiences of all of them of both British colonialism and contemporary racism. This inclusivity has fragmented with greater emphasis upon difference and internal class and gender divisions. In the US, hyphenated identities such as African-American and Asian-American (itself the product of a conscious decision to find a better term than the earlier "Oriental") are common. In spite of manifest differences between and within subordinated or subaltern groups, it has been argued that they can employ essentialism strategically to oppose racism.

Afrocentric ideologies seek to restore hidden histories of African civilizations ("Black Athena": Bernal, 1987) and to promote positive images of and role models for black African communities. Race and religion are linked through groups such as the Nation of Islam, which has been attacked for promoting a chauvinist cultural nationalism based on separatism and autonomy. Others take a cosmopolitan approach that aims to develop and affirm different bases of collective identity beyond race, based on transnational, inter-cultural, and diasporic "Black Atlantic" (Gilroy, 1993a) histories of modernity. Proponents of such ideas sometimes also call for deracialization and for ways of imagining "raceless" futures.

"Nigger" (like terms such as "kaffir" in South Africa) is usually considered an offensive and derogatory term used by white supremacists and slave owners. Although its long history as the "nuclear bomb" of racial epithets has kept it out of mainstream culture, its use by some black people and by comedians and film makers was noted some time ago: "Nigger. . . is now frequently employed by the more race-conscious blacks, but only among themselves" (Johnson, 1977). Its wider use and popularization are mainly associated with hip-hop culture (for example, in the full name of the group NWA, "Niggers With Attitude"). Kennedy (2002) argues that its meaning is open to change and varies according to context, though others maintain that "the n-word" has a tainted history that still evokes memories of slavery and **racial segregation**.

Reflecting changes in the use of language, nowadays in the USA "black" and "African-American" are heard alongside, or have been replaced by "people of color" and among feminists, "women of color." These provide umbrella terms uniting people who might be divided by conventional "racial" groupings. It also values color rather than denigrating it. In South Africa "colored" is applied to mixed-race people and not to blacks as such. Color and pigmentation are frequently linked in racial hierarchies that value lightness. In parts of Latin America people are said to be able to distinguish 9 distinct hair colors and 15 textures, along with 13 named shades of skin color from "*lechoso*" (milky white) to "*morado*" (purply black). Terms such as the "color line" (which W. E. B Du Bois regarded as the problem of the twentieth century), "color prejudice and discrimination," the "color problem" ("The time has come to admit there is a color problem in our midst," *The Times*, September 4, 1958), a "color bar," the "color question," and "color consciousness" are some of the ways in which race and color have been associated. So-called "color-blind policies" are in practice often highly racialized and entail reducing race to color.

Though white is itself a color, "people of color" does not include whites. Because whiteness often remains "unseen" in racial terms, whites have been described as "uncolored people." "White" often connotes qualities that are the converse of "blackness," such as purity, cleanliness, virginity, and innocence. Reflecting the hierarchy of lightness, some beauty products offer the promise of lighter complexions, and dangerous skin-bleaching products are sold illegally. Whiteness can also indicate paleness/colorlessness and be associated with pallor, sickliness, and death, as for the Chinese in the C19. In some cases, as in TV police shows, "Caucasian" stands in for "white," even though properly applied "Caucasian" should include Indians too. Most of the time, however, "white" is treated as the norm from which the difference of all "others" is measured. The category "white" has stayed almost unchanged and virtually unqualified in the US Census since 1850. This is notable because whiteness has been an unstable and shifting designation, as when Slavs and Mediterraneans were treated as **a race apart** (Jacobson, 1998); when in the eC20 US courts ruled that the Japanese were not members of any branch of **the white race**; and when the Irish have been inferiorized, denigrated, and simianized in racial terms. In Europe, campaigns against Jewish migration in the C19 claimed that

Jewishness was a hereditary and irremovable quality of blood and that Jews were an **alien race**, associated with crime, disease, and perversion. More recently, ''white'' Eastern Europeans seeking asylum and refugee status have met some similar treatment. As this suggests, whiteness is subject to selective racialization. It is not a simple matter of skin color but one of changing processes of social and political classification. Similarly, membership of the ''yellow race'' has been flexible and expanded to include the Vietnamese at times. South and east Asians have been racialized differentially, sometimes through gendered conceptions of effeminacy. Whites who seek to undermine the privileges of whiteness may be called, and may call themselves, **race traitors**.

Class has been racialized when lower-class whites have been called ''white trash,'' and race associated with a sense of breeding and refinement. Fears about degeneration and **race suicide** in the eC20 were evident in the eugenics movement, which promoted ideas of **racial and sexual hygiene** and the survival of the fittest. A belief in the **master race** (*herrenvolk*) aimed to breed racially pure Aryans, and led to the extermination of millions of Jews and Gypsies in the Holocaust. There are still many active neo-Nazi, anti-Semitic, racist, and fascist white supremacy organizations, such as the Ku Klux Klan.

''Racism'' is a quite recent, C20 word that has been widely applied. In theory and in practice there is more than one form of racism, indicating the adaptability and durability of racial theories. Racisms range from the grossest practices of genocide and slavery, apartheid and separate development (the bantustans) to the denial of citizenship and social rights and to everyday harassment. Immigration laws and citizenship exemplify **institutional racism**, which refers to persistent, systemic, and sometimes covert racism rather than individual prejudices based upon particular psychological traits. In recent times a **new racism** or **cultural racism** has emerged based upon cultural distinctiveness and the defense of ''a way of life,'' rather than hierarchy and the inferiorization of others. This has also been called **postmodern racism** and **racism without races**, and illustrates continual discursive connections between race, culture, and nation. There is a question about whether Zionism is a form of racism (as a 1975 UN resolution decreed), and whether race and racism are what underlies contemporary Islamaphobia and Hindu nationalism.

Anti-racist measures in the UK include a Race Relations Act that seeks to outlaw discrimination, and a Commission for Racial Equality (CRE) to enforce the law. Race in the Act means a group defined by color, nationality, and ethnic or national origins. Other legislation penalizes incitement to **racial hatred**, while in the US and in mainland Europe there are laws against hate speech and hate crimes. Multicultural policies can be a means of redress against **historic racism**, including recognition of the rights of first-nations peoples and the restitution of land rights. Many public and private bodies express a commitment to diversity and equal opportunities and undertake training courses in race or cultural awareness. Critics regard the existence of state-funded anti-racist bodies like the CRE as proof of a professional **race relations lobby/industry**. This is reminiscent of a remark on the mC20 idea of a **race man**: ''A 'Race Man' was somebody who always kept the glory and honor of his race before him... People made whole careers of being 'Race' men and women. They were champions of the race" (Hurston, 1942). "Racially inauthentic" blacks and Asians are variously called "Uncle Toms," or "coconuts" or "choc-ice" (brown or dark on the outside, white on the inside). The idea of race has been tainted, discredited, valorized, reclaimed, and contested. It retains positive and negative features that are both anachronistic and contemporary.

Karim Murji

See: *BODY, DIFFERENCE, ETHNICITY, MULTICULTURALISM.*

Radical

Unlike "socialist," "communist," and even "conservative," **radical** does not primarily refer to politics and culture. Alongside a changing political history, it retains general meanings – "arising from or going to the root," "basic," "fundamental" – and scientific and technical applications. Contemporary usage ranges from the everyday **radical thinking** or **radical flaw** to the root form of a word in linguistics and applications in atomic theory – including the intriguing **free radicals** of medical research (Peterson, 2000).

As Raymond Williams argues in *Keywords* (1983: 251–2), the earliest political associations were with reform: by the lC18 "radical" referred to democracy, popular rights, and sometimes republicanism as opposed to conservatism, aristocracy, and the court. In the eC19, ideals derived from the French Jacobins and the "Atlantic" politics of democrats like Thomas Paine (Paine, 1969 [1791]) coexisted with "socialist," marking the prioritization of politics and the constitution over questions of social relations, though the two were often combined (Claeys, 1989; Thompson, 1963). By the mC19, **radicalism** referred to an ethical and reforming liberalism, but by the lC19 it could apply to right-wing, to centrist, and later to fascist parties, in opposition to liberals, socialists, or communists. **Radical right** or **right-wing radicals** became common appellations.

The second half of the C20 saw similar instabilities. "Radical" was applied pejoratively to the new left and the new social movements of liberation, but was also appropriated by them, usually in contradistinction to "liberal" (Gleeson, 1970; Jacobs and Landau, 1966).This usage seems to have begun in the USA, where, Williams argues, it may have been preferred because of the difficulties of openly avowing socialism or communism, but was soon generalized. "Radical" could designate the movements themselves (**radical feminism**), their media (**the radical press**), and allied trends in academic research and professional praxis (**radical philosophy, radical history, radical education, radical social work**, etc.). In historical research it was used, or revived, to mark certain continuities in a **radical tradition** (Simon, 1972).

"Radical" coexisted interestingly with "alternative" in this period and also with more explicit political designations like "feminist," "socialist," "black," "gay," "anti-racist," etc. Once more, the former conveyed an explicitly political emphasis, but also an engagement with theory and questions of knowledge and power, a connection made through the students' movements of the 1960s and the movement-based informal educational activity of the 1970s. The revival of "Western Marxism" and other critical ideas were key points of articulation (P. Anderson, 1976). "Alternative," on the other hand, usually referred to ways of living and aesthetic and ethical preferences and "feelings," including quite anti-intellectual and certainly anti-academic themes. It is tempting to interpret "radical" as primarily a middle-class political label in this period. Certainly, in many European countries, there were tensions between student-based "68-ist" tendencies and "alternative" politics, on the one hand, and union or party-based working-class militancy, on the other (Widgery, 1976).

The rise of neo-liberal thinking and New Right politics, especially from the mid-1970s, saw another reconfiguration of "radical." Neo-liberals were root-and-branch critics of the post-war political consensus over social welfare, low unemployment, and trade union negotiation. The revival of free market orthodoxies and moral "fundamentals" reasserted "Western" (capitalist and Christian) "basics." New Right movements tended not to adopt the term "radical," but their critics did, in order to describe the movements' assault on post-war orthodoxies and the gains of the 1960s and 1970s (Gamble, 1985; S. Hall and Jacques, 1983;cf. Grossberg, 1992, on the US New Right as "conservatism"). "Radical" became a less comfortable self-identity for egalitarians and socialists, struggling to retain something from their traditions.

As a consequence, "radical" has fallen back to its general meanings and is applied to opposed political positions: by the center-left to their breaks from "old socialism," for example, and by US conservatives to "terrorists." It also functions as an alarm signal that something new, risky, and potentially violent is on the way: possible synonyms here are "drastic" or "uncompromising." It can be applied, disapprovingly, to different fundamentalisms – Christian, Islamicist, neo-liberal – and to both terrorism and state terror: witness the **radical defense strategists** currently so influential within the administration of President George W. Bush. While more oppositional connotations do survive, they often dwindle to personal traits of "awkwardness" or "principle" or to matters of style or stance. **Radical chic**, a 1970s coinage, has resonances with "far out," "right on," and even "politically correct," implying, with some disdain, that radicalism, usually youthful and middle-class, stops at dressing down, verbal manipulation, or a taste for primitive rebels (Wolfe, 1971). More recent commentary, and changes in both style and politics, suggest that it may not be so easy to read off the absence or presence of conviction from anyone's appearance (McRobbie, 1989: 45–8).

Richard Johnson

See: *ALTERNATIVE, FUNDAMENTALISM, REFORM AND REVOLUTION, RESISTANCE, SOCIALISM.*

297

Reason

More than most terms around which the values and aspirations of Western culture have coalesced, **reason** is a construction of the philosophers. The history of the fortunes of reason is the history of Western philosophy. Unresolved tensions in the concept – although they often seem to arise from contemporary disaffection with the philosophical tradition – are largely the residue of past philosophical ideals. Some understanding of the history of philosophy can help us better understand the cacophony of voices – some angry, some exultant – that has come to be the **chorus of reason**.

A reason, in the sense now most familiar, is a circumstance justifying a belief or motivating an action. Our capacity to ground our beliefs and actions in reasons – and to judge the adequacy of those reasons – is readily seen as setting us apart from the limitations of the rest of the world. But the idea of reason as a distinctive human capacity is clearer in its verbal form, **reasoning** – construed as clear, orderly thinking, drawing inferences and reaching conclusions in accordance with logical principles. This use of reason is now associated especially with the refined version of methodical thinking which emerged in C17 philosophy. René Descartes formulated the ideal as the careful assembling of deductive chains of indubitable conceptions of ''a clear and attentive mind which proceeds solely from the light of reason,'' in contrast to the ''fluctuating testimony of the senses or the deceptive judgment of the imagination as it botches things together'' (1985 [1637]: 14).

The **ideal of reason** as a special mode of thought became less restricted in C18 philosophy. But reason remained a way of thinking which was objective rather than subjective, detached rather than emotional, grounded rather than arbitrary. **Enlighten-ment reason** was celebrated as providing a secure foundation for scientific knowledge. But the metaphor of **rational enlightenment** was also extended to political ideals and social practices grounded in the spread of objective knowledge, in contrast to the dark tyrannies bred by superstition.

There is, however, an older, less familiar strand in reason. It once served to ground human beings in the rest of nature just as firmly as post-Enlightenment reason came to separate them from it. This strand comes through the L root *ratio* – associated with ideas of right order, proportion, or harmony. This version of reason does not relate exclusively, or even primarily, to the human mind. Reason, in its philosophical origins, was not merely a human capacity but a feature of the world – a structured order enacted not only in human lives but in the cosmos as a whole. Reason in this sense is continuous with ancient Gk *logos* – the **rational principle** or universal law which is immanent in the world.

Kant and Hegel gave a new twist to this ancient idea of reason as immanent in the world, extending it from the cosmos to human history. History, Kant argued, is not an ''aimless, random process.'' In the apparent chaos of historical events we are to discern not the ''dismal reign of chance'' but the ''guiding principle of reason'' (1970b [1784]: 42).

Reason is for Kant a historical process – the gradual enlightenment through which nature guides us to the goal of a fully rational human nature. Without the stimulus provided by conflict during that process, Kant says, reason would remain an "unfilled void" in the human species. This sanguine view of reason as immanent in the conflicts and vicissitudes of human history finds its boldest expression in Hegel's startling claim, in the preface to *The philosophy of right* (1967 [1821]), that in the long run the irrational cannot prevail – that **what is rational is actual** and **what is actual is rational**. As Gadamer has summed up the Hegelian vision, reason is discernible in the apparently "buzzing confusion of human affairs" no less than in the "calm courses pursued by the stars in heaven" (1981: 35).

Skeptical though we may now be about guarantees of the ultimate rationality of human affairs, "reason" remains an optimistic and reassuring word. We may doubt that reason has delivered on enlightenment hopes. But lingering resonances of ancient ideas of reason carry an assurance that we are basically at home in a world which answers to our own nature; while the idea of reasoning as a distinctively human capacity nonetheless allows us to congratulate ourselves on our superiority to the rest of the world. It can go unnoticed that each of the two strands – of human transcendence and of commonality – is the residue of a different philosophical approach to reason, and that they may be in tension with one another.

Skepticism about the Enlightenment vision of progress is not new. Already in the mC18, Voltaire could express misgivings about contemporary institutions and social practices which were supposed to embody reason. But here there was no distrust of reason itself. God has given us reason, Voltaire says in his *Philosophical dictionary* (1971 [1770]), as he has given feathers to the birds or fur to the bears, and it will persist despite the tyrants or the imposters who want to destroy it through superstition. What has emerged in more recent cultural criticism is, in contrast, a sense of pessimism – even of "crisis" – in relation to reason itself.

After World War II, the Frankfurt School critic Max Horkheimer commented on the apparent **eclipse of reason** in a world which had supposedly achieved the fullness of the Enlightenment dream of progress. On his diagnosis, the modern period has seen a narrowing of the once rich philosophical resources of reason. **Instrumental reason** – exercised in the calculation of means for pre-given ends – has come to eclipse the richer dimensions of **objective reason** that traditionally expressed the ideal of meaningful human life in a rational world (Horkheimer, 1985).

Talk of a **crisis of reason** can seem deeply paradoxical: arguments advanced against reason must, if they are to be convincing, themselves satisfy accepted standards of rational argument. Responding satirically to the suggestion that reason can no longer explain the world in which we live and that we now have to rely on other instruments, Umberto Eco demands to know what alternatives we might imagine: "feeling, delirium, poetry, mystical silence, a sardine can opener, the high jump, sex, intravenous injections of sympathetic ink" (1986: 125). Confronted by a shibboleth like that of the crisis of reason, he suggests, what cries out for definition is not so much reason as the concept of crisis.

Reform and Revolution

Under the influence of the "clear thinking" strand in reason, we may well want to dismiss the contemporary "rage against reason" – as Richard Bernstein (1986) has described it – as anti-intellectual irrationalism. But this would be to ignore both the internal complexity of reason and the ways in which it has been shaped by past philosophical critique. The criticisms of reason offered by contemporary feminists, for example – which are often ridiculed as confirmations of female irrationality – have their precedents in the history of philosophy. Feminists have focused on reason's self-imposed distance from more appealing human traits – capacities for styles of thought imbued with affect and imagination, which have often been associated with women as against the "maleness" of reason.

Such criticism may be best seen not as a repudiation of reason but rather as an attempt to reclaim emotion and imagination as important to intelligent thinking. Similar criticism of prevailing views of reason was offered in the C17 by Pascal, who insisted in his *Pensées* that "we know the truth not only through our reason but also through our heart" (1966 [1670]: 58). Rather than seeing the heart as a source of non-rational insight, Pascal cunningly presented it as having its own "reasons, of which reason knows nothing" (p. 154). In the C18, David Hume also repudiated the idea of a hierarchical dominance of reason over the passions. In his famous ironic inversion of an established hierarchy, Hume observes in his *Treatise of human nature* that "Reason is, and ought only to be, the slave of the passions, and can never pretend to any other office than to serve and obey them" (1978 [1739]: 415).

In our own times, reason's fragile unities and accommodations with other traits seem to have unraveled, leaving us with a sterile, impoverished surrogate for what might have been. But critique of the limitations of prevailing versions of reason has a long philosophical history. What is now most needed is not a search for an alternative, non-rational, "instrument" for dealing with an uncertain world, but an informed critique of our own received versions of reason. Whether or not we then continue to give that name to our preferred ways of thinking is less important than being clear about what they continue to owe to the much celebrated – and much maligned – history of reason.

Genevieve Lloyd

See: *EMOTION, INTELLECTUAL, KNOWLEDGE, SCIENCE, THEORY.*

Reform and Revolution

Reform and **revolution** were regarded as contraries throughout much of the C19 and C20: their supporters saw them as instruments of social change but held radically opposed views about their effectiveness and the risks which they entailed. These disagreements turned in part on different perceptions of the prospects for worthwhile reform within modern constitutional states, but they were also animated by the conflicting views of revolution which emerged in the aftermath of the **French Revolution** of 1789: the belief, on the one hand, that revolution would mark an irreversible forward movement in human affairs, and the fear, on the other, that it would take on a life of its own, moving through an uncontrollable cycle of developments to destroy the hopes, and often the lives, of its original supporters.

The German Social Democratic Party (SPD), the largest and most successful socialist party in the years preceding the **Russian Revolution** of 1917, was strongly influenced by Marxism and accordingly took the view that the socialist transformation of society would be brought about primarily by the political action of the working class. Socialists disagreed about how this transformation should be pursued: one side arguing that it could be achieved through a process of peaceful and **constitutional reform** – essentially by establishing political majorities in elected parliaments and using these to bring about social and political change; the other insisting that more radical political action, a revolution, would also be required. The SPD generally supported the former view, as did the majority Menshevik faction of the much smaller Russian Social Democratic Party. Significant minorities in both parties favored revolution, arguing that the state was an instrument of the ruling class and therefore that serious social change could be brought about only if the state itself were to be overthrown. Otherwise, they insisted, attempts at **social and political reform** would amount to little more than superficial meddling which, by giving the impression that significant changes could be brought about by peaceful means, tended in fact to reinforce the power of the ruling class.

Before the French Revolution the terms ''reform'' and ''revolution'' were not so clearly opposed and, while they carried different meanings, their usages often overlapped. ''Reform'' means literally to **re-form**, to form again, and it can therefore be understood in two rather different senses: to amend, or alter for the better, some faulty state of things and to return something to its original condition. It can thus be seen as either radical or conservative, and sometimes as both at once. These two senses came together, for example, in the Reformation of the eC16: Martin Luther's slogan ''through faith alone'' radically undermined the church's claim to a mediating role between God and the individual believer and it therefore signaled the need for new institutions and practices, but it was also intended to suggest a return to original ways.

''Revolution'' derives from the L *revolutio,* meaning the movement of a thing from one place to another, and the term was used in the early modern period both to indicate an outbreak of political disorder and to signal a change in rulership. Extending the latter meaning, it also came to refer to a great change in the government of a state or, less ambitiously, to significant changes in judicial procedure – that is, to what we might now call **judicial reform**. Since the French Revolution, this meaning has been extended further to cover any substantial change in human affairs, often carrying the additional sense of progress or irreversible forward movement, of a change after which there can be no possibility of return – the **Neolithic, Copernican**, **Industrial**, and

Reform and Revolution

Scientific Revolutions providing particularly clear examples of this more general, non-political usage.

Revolution, in this latter sense, was sometimes associated with political disorder but it could also be an orderly and peaceful process. Reform, too, might be associated with political disorder – as it clearly was, for example, in the Reformation – but such disorder has generally been disowned by the **reformers** themselves. Thus, while there is a degree of overlap in the usage of the two terms, reform normally carries the sense of deliberate intention while revolution, which might well be intended in many cases, can also carry the sense of something that simply happens. Revolution, moreover, is frequently seen as being more substantial or more radical than mere reform: where the latter suggests the senses of deliberation and a return to roots, the former's association with both disorder and movement conveys more the sense of an uprooting.

These various associations of reform and revolution are invoked whenever they are considered as alternatives, but there is a second important sense of revolution which further sharpens the contrast between them. While the term "Copernican Revolution" provides a striking example of the sense of revolution as irreversible forward movement, the publication of Nicolaus Copernicus's *De revolutionibus orbium celestium* in 1543 marked the appearance of the idea of revolution as a circular or orbital movement, as returning to an original point of departure. The belief, still widely held in C16 Europe, that there would be earthly counterparts to significant celestial movements suggested that this usage of the term might also be relevant to social and political developments. The revival of classical political thought, which tended to view all states as moving through a cycle of growth and decay, also favored such a usage. Thomas Hobbes's *Behemoth* (1963 [1679]: 256]) describes the events of the English Civil War and its aftermath as a revolution in precisely this sense: it was "a circular motion of the sovereign power through two usurpers from the late King to his son." Similarly, the **Glorious Revolution** of 1688, which overthrew the Stuart dynasty, was described, at least by its supporters, as "Glorious" because of its outcome and as a "Revolution" because it was seen as bringing about a return to the true constitution of England, and thus as closing a cycle.

The French Revolution of 1789 has evoked all of these different senses, but those of irreversible forward movement and cyclical progression have been particularly important. At first, the Revolution was widely celebrated as liberating the people of France from the oppressions of absolute rule and arbitrary privilege. It was thus seen both as showing the way to the rest of Europe and as marking the beginning of a new era in human affairs; the English radical Charles James Fox described the fall of the Bastille as "the greatest event in the history of the world," while in Germany Friedrich Hegel called it a "magnificent sunrise." The Terror and the subsequent rise to power of Napoleon produced a very different response, suggesting to many observers both that revolution was a destructive force which threatened the property, the livelihood, and even the lives of numerous individuals and that the cyclical movement from absolute monarchy through anarchy, terror, and finally back to absolute rule – this time in the form of military dictatorship – might well be inescapable once the orderly process of constitutional reform had been abandoned. Belief in the existence of such a cycle was widely held, not only by conservative statesmen like Metternich and Bismarck but also by many liberal opponents of absolutism – and even, to some degree, by **revolutionaries** themselves.

Liberals and socialists nevertheless continued to associate the Revolution of 1789 with forward movement. The former, while regretting the violence and disorder with which it had been associated, saw it as demonstrating that absolute rule could not be sustained indefinitely. What was required, in their view, was a system of constitutional government which would enable necessary social and political reforms to proceed in a peaceful and orderly fashion. From this perspective, the choice between reform and revolution as instruments of social change could arise only within less developed political systems: that is, under conditions in which constitutional government had yet to be securely established and movements for peaceful change were likely to be suppressed.

Socialists drew a rather different lesson from the French Revolution, seeing the resort to violence as resulting from the resistance of the ruling class, not simply from the absence of constitutional rule. They therefore tended to view the liberal constitutional state as an instrument of class domination. Nevertheless, while the success of the Revolution provided socialists with a powerful and attractive model, its aftermath also offered a dreadful warning: it was the appeal of revolution, in the sense of forward movement, and the fear that it might move out of control which together drove the socialist debates over reform and revolution. While not denying the class character of the state, many socialists were nevertheless tempted by the liberal view of constitutional rule, believing that it provided conditions in which the working class and its allies could overcome the resistance of the ruling class by peaceful and constitutional means – believing, in other words, that revolution under these conditions was neither necessary nor desirable. The Bolshevik seizure of power in the second Russian Revolution of 1917 radically transformed these debates by forcing supporters of the conflicting views into implacably opposed camps: communists and other revolutionaries on the one side and social democracy as a movement of reform on the other.

Subsequent developments have not been kind to either camp. The history of the French Revolution continued to haunt the supporters of revolution, suggesting that Russia too might have its Thermidor – a condition in which, having destroyed the old order, the revolution devours its own, moving on to impose a leader who will bring about the return of order and stability. Leon Trotsky (1952) described Stalin's rise to power in precisely these terms. The collapse of communism in Europe in the latter part of the C20 and its accommodations with capitalism in other parts of the world suggested to many observers yet another version of the image of revolution as cyclical progression: that of socialist revolution as one of the more destructive routes between capitalism and capitalism. Social democracy, on the other hand, has had many successes, culminating in the Western welfare states of the post-World War II era, but it has abandoned the idea of fundamental social change and much of its earlier internationalism, and its achievements are gradually being wound back under the impact of neo-liberal reforms. It survives as a movement of cautious and progressive reform in Western Europe and a few states elsewhere, but only by adapting its policies to the demands of neo-liberal economic and social agendas.

If the old debate over the relative merits of reform and revolution has largely disappeared from political discourse, both in the West and elsewhere, the desire for fundamental social change persists – not only in what remains of the socialist movement but also in the religious fundamentalisms of Christian North America and parts of the Islamic world, movements for the reform of corrupt and authoritarian states, numerous unsatisfied nationalisms, radical environmentalism, and elements of the anti-globalization movement. However, because the capacities of states to manage their own affairs seem to have been brought into question by globalization and because many of their concerns go beyond the limits of the state, these movements rarely understand their situation in terms of a stark choice between reform and revolution.

Revolution in the limited sense of a change of rulership has not disappeared, but it is now usually called by another name – a coup or a military takeover – and it rarely evokes the earlier contrast with reform. Sometimes it serves as a means of opposing reform but more often, at least for popular and international consumption, it is presented as a temporary break from the normal practices of government, and therefore as providing a space in which much needed reform can take place.

Barry Hindess

See: *CLASS, DEMOCRACY, EVOLUTION, LIBERALISM, RADICAL, SOCIALISM, STATE.*

Relativism

In general usage, **relativism** and its relatives have from the C16 forward involved various senses of being **in relation** to something else, in a grammatical (**relative pronoun**), biological (**distant relative**), or philosophical sense. The notion that relativism requires the understanding of **relations** and **relative positions** is evident in modern scientific senses of **relativity** as well, according to which it has been axiomatic since the IC19 that observations of the physical universe are relative to the motions of the observer and the observed ("Our whole progress up to this point may be described as a gradual development of the doctrine of relativity of all physical phenomena": Maxwell, 1876). A weak form of the scientific and/or philosophical senses of relativity is also at play in many current colloquial uses of the term, as when people say with a shrug, **it's all relative**, as a C20 update of the ancient truism, *de gustibus non disputandum est.*

Philosophical relativism comes in many forms, but it is usually understood to entail some version of the position that there are no absolutes that hold for all times, places, and cultures, and that all moral assertions about the good and the just, together with all epistemological assertions with respect to the true and the knowable, must therefore be judged with respect to the context in which they are made and the goals they seek to achieve. Whenever we argue that one cannot understand the peoples of the ancient world by the standards of the modern, or that the practices of the Maori must be understood from the reference point of the Maori themselves, or that it is not always wrong to lie or to kill, we are employing some kind of **historical**, **cultural**, or **moral relativism**. The term has increasingly generated controversy from the mC20 onward, just as the general awareness of global differences – and global atrocities – has increased during that time. For instance, the discipline of anthropology is founded in part on a methodology in which field researchers are expected to cultivate "the scientific habit of looking at each people's standards and values objectively, seeing them as 'relative' to the particular view of life fostered within the culture concerned" (Keesing, 1958). It is diagnostic of the difficulties attendant upon relativism that what anthropologists consider "objective" in this way, other observers – with, no doubt, relatively different value systems and terminologies– would consider "subjective," insofar as it involves a description of cultural practices that would be comprehensible within those cultural practices themselves, and not with regard to some external standard.

It is commonly charged that **relativists** have no way of adjudicating among truth-claims, and no way of forming judgments on cultural practices ranging from clitoridectomy to genocide. When, for example, the fundamentalist Islamist cleric Ayatollah Khomeini issued a *fatwa* against writer Salman Rushdie in 1989 (allegedly for blaspheming against the Prophet in his novel *The satanic verses* [Rushdie, 1994; original publication 1988]), some Western intellectuals debated whether they could in good conscience condemn the death sentence, or whether doing so would amount to imposing Western notions of secularism and free speech on another culture – whereupon other Western intellectuals condemned them for their flaccid relativism. Conversely, advocates of relativism have countercharged that their critics seek to advance a spurious universalism that really represents the values of one group *as if* they were universal, and that this pseudo-universalism is more accurately described as cultural imperialism. The Western Enlightenment ideal of individual autonomy, founded upon the operation of reason, thus might seem to its proponents to be so self-evident as to be universally applicable across the globe, but in practice may turn out to be fundamentally at odds with the ideals of cultures whose highest values concern the proper fulfillment of duties to religious or worldly authorities.

In one respect relativism is uncontroversial: it asserts that the people of the world, from the beginnings of recorded history through to the present, have devised radically different schemes of value and modes of life. This much is beyond dispute. What *is* controversial is the question of whether some value systems can be said to be "in error" as to the good, the just, and the true – and, if so, "in error" with reference to what. Few contemporary observers would have difficulty disdaining a society whose highest value involved the public torture of slaves, and yet, if all values are to be understood relative to the goals they seek and the societies they sustain, it could be said that in a society in which cruelty and hierarchy were virtues, the public torture of slaves would be understandable. Most relativists would reply that such a society can nevertheless legitimately be condemned by reference to values external to that society. This is the position of prominent "relativists" such as Barbara Herrnstein Smith (1988), who argue that all values must be understood in relation to the goals they seek but that this does not prevent the relativist from discriminating between virtues and vices. The argument is that the relativist does not, in fact, believe that all value systems are "equal" (for at an absurd extreme, this would commit the relativist to an agnostic position on the question of whether relativism itself is wrong), and that the relativist can make value judgments even though these are not grounded in a belief system that could potentially be shared by everyone. The problem in this dispute, however, is that relativists deny the premise of their anti-relativist interlocutors, namely, that moral judgments are meaningless unless they can be so grounded. As a result, the relativist sees the universalist as a potential tyrant, and the universalist sees the relativist as morally unserious. To suggest that the claims of each should be weighed with respect to the goals each seeks to advance would, of course, effectively award the palm to the relativist; to suggest that the claims of each should be weighed "objectively" is to give the game to the universalist. The impasse produced here thus involves a fundamental incommensurability between competing justifications for belief – an appropriate conclusion, perhaps, suggesting that positions on relativism are themselves relative.

Michael Bérubé

See: *EMPIRICAL, KNOWLEDGE, OBJECTIVITY, PRAGMATISM, REASON.*

Representation

Dictionaries of English usually distinguish among three senses of **representation** and its cognates: the symbolic sense, the political sense, and the cognitive sense. The symbolic sense (C15) is partially synonymous with "sign." The OED gives "sleep" as a representation, that is, "likeness" of death (C15), but it is not for that a "sign of" death. The use in which an example serves to represent its class dates from the C19.

In the political sense, representation is the function of **representatives** (C16) who are understood as "speaking for"; the representation of a character by an actor, also dating from C16–C17, may be closer to this sense than to the symbolic one. Lawyers **make representation** for their clients, and in parliamentary democracies representatives make decisions on behalf of the population they represent. **Representative democracy** is contrasted with participatory democracy in this sense.

In the cognitive sense (C14), a representation arises upon the mental formation of a cognition. However, Ian Hacking (1975, 1983) argues that **mental representations** were displaced by **public representations** in C20 philosophy: both "ideas" (C17) and "sentences" (C20) are responsible for the representation of reality in a body of knowledge. If he is right, this sense is no longer distinct from the symbolic one.

The topic of representation is a standard problem in the philosophy of knowledge, and has come to occupy a significant place in media and cultural studies. In both domains, we might expect a representation to be subject to critique, though the methods and point of that critique differ along disciplinary lines. Thus in the former we might investigate the truth conditions of representations, while in the latter we might read the sociocultural determinants of the representation of some class of people or some event in the media, say, or in the discourses of the social sciences. The question that arises in both cases is whether **true representations** are possible, where "true" would include "adequate" as well as "accurate." If they are not, does this indicate the weakness of representation, or its power?

Representations stand for their objects in some sense, but "standing for" is a contested expression. If an object needs a representation, then it is part of that logic that the representation is not its object; but if the representation is different from its object, how can it stand for it truly? The first answer to this is that it substitutes for it under some circumstances. However, such substitution is rare, and very few representations are substitutes. Take as an example national flags, where it is stipulated that a set of colors organized in a certain design should represent the nation. However, there is no sense in saying that it is a case of substitution. Some returned soldiers' (veterans') associations assume the contrary when they protest against suggested changes in the design, as if the country and the flag were indissociable. Debates over this matter resemble the medieval dispute between nominalist and realist accounts of representation. (These revolved around whether, respectively, reality and hence truth were quite independent of language, or whether they depended upon it. The veterans' position is realist in this sense.) The nominalists prevailed, on the grounds that scientific investigation could not get under way if it assumed a realist account of representation.

However, take the example of a word in a language. We cannot have, say, trees in our sentences, we need words to represent them. These are not substitutes, nor could trees reclaim their place in our symbolic interchanges. Moreover, there are many words for "tree," corresponding approximately to the number of languages in the world, and each one of these words may attach to itself a somewhat different range of meanings. For this reason, Fedinand de Saussure (1966) insisted on the term "signify" instead of the term **represent** for what words do: they do not stand for a preformed reality, they make or constitute what counts as reality. However, it is now usual to construe "representation" along Saussurean lines, rather than to banish it from the vocabulary. In contemporary cultural theory, this move provides a premise for contesting nominalism.

The issue is whether there can be said to be any "reality" independent of its representation, and hence, whether any representation could be a neutral record of that reality. This is not to deny that there is something "out there," but to insist that any knowledge of it depends upon the **media and technologies of representation**. The partiality or error of any particular representation is one thing; the centrality of representation in getting it right "in the long run," as Charles Sanders Peirce (Freadman, 2004; Houser and Kloesel, 1998) argued, is another. For this reason, practices of representation are said to interpret the reality they represent, and sometimes (geometrical figures, for example) to construct it. Peirce considered that his position was a form of realism, revised to take account of the fact that representation was a process in time that could, in the best of scientific practice, correct error. Thus the argument for nominalism holds for particular representations only, but the self-critical, interpretive process of representation is consistent with metaphysical realism.

This dispute can be restated as follows: is the governing source and force of knowledge "all in the mind" (Berkeley, 1985 [1710]) or outside it (Locke, 1959) [1690]), leaving imprints upon it through perception? Or are there some hard-wired mental contents that inform the input of the world, as Kant (1982 [1784]) argued? Contemporary cultural theory replaces these philosophical accounts with one based on the workings of language or broader sociocultural and semiotic practices. According to this, all knowledge, including the knowledge of the natural and physical world we call "science," is a function of **practices of representing** that are anything but neutral.

An important issue is the scope and responsibility of any account of representation. Have we done enough if we simply measure the falsity or partiality of some representation, and have we said enough about representation if all we attend to is its correspondence with its object? Take the representation of women as primarily or exclusively childbearers, or the representation of Australia as *terra nullius*. Such beliefs acquired the status of law, and have had far-reaching malefic consequences for their objects and for the societies that adopted them. It is at this point that the critique of representation needs also to attend to the social conditions that give representation its power, and to the consequences of that power.

When representatives represent a client, a constituency, or a principal in some forum, they both "stand for them" and "speak for them." An important debate in political theory concerns the nature and the legitimacy of such speaking for. Is a **political representative** merely a delegate, acting, as does a lawyer in the ideal case, under instruction from her constituents? Or does she have discretion? If so, does she exercise non-mandated power?

Debates also arise concerning the **representativity** of such representatives. It is said that a parliament made up of 99 percent white male members of a single religious persuasion does not "represent" the population, where "represent" means to "be typical of." The complaint relies on the assumption that representation involves exemplification, which is not always the case.

It is important to recognize that **representative government** is not reliably glossed as "government by the people": a government might be said to represent the state *symbolically*, but not to "speak for" the governed population. European monarchies used representations – of the king, the city, etc. – as instruments of practical power. Likewise, post-monarchical governments might use a presidential visit to the site of a disaster for electoral purposes, and perhaps, too, to represent the erased monarchical function itself. In some non-secular societies, representations acquire magical or religious powers: thus the pope both stands for and speaks for Christ as his vicar (that is, representative), whereas an interdiction on representation is common to Judaism and Islam.

With the power *of* representation come struggles for power *over* it. Censorship laws, and media laws more generally, are designed to regulate representation. It is easy to point to the powers of the new **technologies of representation** to circumvent such laws, but these same technologies have provided the means for the theft of representations such as PIN numbers. In such cases, the theft of the representation amounts to the theft of an institutional identity, and hence, power over an individual. How to regulate that power is an urgent question.

Some debates refer directly to the senses distinguished above, and some are concerned with other distinctions. The cultural critic Raymond Williams (1976) focuses on **artistic** and **political representation**, concluding that the degree of possible overlap between them is difficult to estimate. Charles Peirce, who thought of his work as a **philosophy of representation**, finds that it is instructive to think of all representation as "speaking for" its object. The cultural historian Carlo Ginzburg (2001) studies the relationship between substitutive and **mimetic representation** in royal funerary practices of the early Middle Ages. He reminds us that **representational practices** have complex histories.

309

Anne Freadman

See: *DISCOURSE, SIGN.*

Resistance

Across the natural and social worlds, **resistance** is what prevents one force or agency entirely overwhelming another. Where some opposition to invasive force is offered, **the line of least resistance** is likely to be taken. Where there is an almost equal "balance of forces," it is said, light-heartedly, that **"irresistible force"** meets "immovable object." Science, technology, and society intermingle in coinages such as **germ-resistant drugs**, **drug-resistant bugs**, **crease-resistant clothes**, **disease-resistant lifestyles**, and **erosion-resistant conservation practices**. But "resistance" is redolent above all in relation to social conflict and oppression. Indeed, for key theorists like eC20 German sociologist Max Weber and lC20 French philosopher Michel Foucault, the notion of resistance is wholly central to the understanding and exercise of power itself.

Probably the most consistent context for talk of **human resistance** over the centuries has been that of military conflict, sometimes, again, in relation to technological means and consequences – "To putt therewith a great fortificacion aboute the same for resistance of the sayd enimies" (Ellis, 1417). Yet it is the element of subjectivity in "resistance" that gives the term its full resonance, the sense that whatever the material odds may be, the spirit can withstand colonization by others. This can be cast in an individualist way, as in "He intendeth to take possessyon here agaynst my wyll, but he shall be resysted" (Palsgrave, 1530), or in collectivist fashion: "There is yet a spirit of resistance in this country, which will not submit to be oppressed" (Junius, *Letters*, 1769). By the C19 in Europe "civic and national resistance" (Southey, 1827) – that is to say, the people as incorporated in the nation – was imagined to be the principal agent of resistance. In the mC20, such connotations were potently clustered around the **French Resistance**, formed in 1940 by "patriots" committed to repulsing the occupying forces of Nazi Germany. Thereafter, this national-popular image took a different twist, in the rhetoric of anti-colonialist and "third world" struggles aimed against the Western nations themselves. Such shifts in location helped generalize terms like **resistance movement**, **resistance fighters**, **underground resistance**, and **heroes of resistance**.

Not only nations and peoples, but also particular social groups, **resist** the incursions of power: resistance to capitalists and capitalism by the industrial working class; women's resistance to patriarchy; ethnic minority resistance to white "cultural imperialism"; children's resistance to parental power; resistance of the global "South" to the global "North"; and so on. In understanding how resistance operates in the many varieties of these phenomena, distinctions can be made between **active resistance** and passive **resistance**, and between *organized and spontaneous* variants of active resistance. **Organized resistance** itself can be placed along a spectrum of "pressure," "protest," and "revolution" (J. Scott, 2001).

Resistance is also a dimension of individual identity. The societal process of individualization in the eC21 coincides with the weakening of identification with collective social categories like nations, states, classes, genders, and races (Beck and Beck-Gernsheim, 2001). Thus, individual resistance to the dictates of the state or majority cultures is increasingly conducted in the name of the human rights of the person to her or his very own values, behaviors, and routine way of life.

Not only is resistance conducted *by* individuals, it is experienced *within* the self too. In the eC20, psychoanalysis taught that the ego is defended against anxiety through resistance to troubling unconscious impulses and repressed memories. Psychic "health" is then supposed to be achieved by coming to recognize and account for these resistances. By the lC20, a pervasive professional and demotic counseling discourse had emerged around similar precepts: that it is "good to talk" about one's relationships, careers, and sense of self-esteem, because in that way we can "deal with" problematic **inner resistances**. More informally still, personal conflicts of desire, and conflicts between desire and responsibility, are frequently expressed in terms of **resisting temptation**. The Christian and religious core of this sentiment – "be ye thenne strong, to resist and ouercome [temptations]" (Caxton, 1483) – still operates to an extent in both doctrinal and secular mentalities, but is put under increasing pressure by the consumerist, even hedonistic, aspect of modern lifestyle choice. The responsible self battles to resist the seductions of "irresistible" lovers, delicious foods, enhanced experiences, heightened images, and generally the sensuous appeal of everything new or different.

The moral and political connotations of resistance are complex and paradoxical. Initially, there is a definite negative association – resistance is *to* something, before it is *for* anything. Certainly, from the point of view of the dominant, those who resist are seen as merely spoilers, engaging in thoughtless and anarchic "insubordination." However, even couched as pure negativity, the resistance that is embodied in a sullen look, or a desperate act of violence, can be viewed as carrying an affirmative charge. Writers such as the mC20 Canadian sociologist Erving Goffman (1968) and the lC20 postmodernist Jean Baudrillard made the case that resistance is creatively expressed in strategies of hyperconformity to negative stereotypes (the crazy madman or violent prisoner, the "mindless" passivity of "dumbed-down" consumerized masses).

Sociologically, **resistance through rituals** (CCCS, 1978) describes the symbolic richness and inventive solidarity frequently shown by marginalized groups in disruptive social practices that are not conscious movements of protest. In more philosophical terms, resistance has even been positioned as the bastion of human autonomy and dignity in the face of demeaning coercive imposition, whatever its content. Resistance is thus pressed into some grander progressive potential, even if only rather gesturally. German-American mC20 critical theorist Herbert Marcuse, for instance, hoped that all the forms of **resistance to capitalism** would one day add up to a "Great Refusal". Though less holistically and socialistically inclined, commentators in the eC21 also assign to **multiple local resistances** a larger burden, whether as parts of a vast movement against the "growing uniformity of social life" (Mouffe, 1988: 94), or as the harbingers of "new forms of solidarity in which difference will genuinely be respected" (Nash, 2000: 43).

Gregor McLennan

See: *CAPITALISM, MOVEMENTS, POWER, UNCONSCIOUS.*

Risk

Risk, as a synonym for "hazard," "danger," or "peril," is something those living in contemporary liberal-capitalist societies are aware of in many facets of their daily lives. It has become crucially related to the search for security, the provision of welfare, trust in experts and in institutions, and the avoidance or minimization of harm. What has come to distinguish risk from danger or hazard is the attempt to calculate and govern it, both as societies and in individual life. This means that risk is distinguished from mere hazards such as famines, plague, or natural disasters, which might once have been accepted as matters of fate, or as acts of God.

Risk

One possible source of the term "risk" is It *risco*, meaning steep rock or reef. Sailors might well have first used the term, and it is certainly tied to the history of shipping insurance. "Risk" has a broad meaning in commerce as the danger of loss of a ship, goods, or property, and its history is closely linked to the attempt to calculate such risks so that insurers might underwrite them in return for a premium paid. To act with prudence is to act with an attempt to calculate and insure oneself against risk. From the C17, we find examples of people thinking of themselves as **running a risk**. Since the C18, economists have argued that profit is at least partially a return to the **risk-taking** of entrepreneurs. For John Stuart Mill (1965 [1848]) the "difference between the interest and the gross profit remunerates the exertions and risks of the undertaker."

Today, it appears that risk has multiplied. We face risks in our workplaces, our homes, our travel, our investments, our relationships, and as citizens of certain states. Diet, lifestyle, physical and mental health, pregnancy, standard of living, drug use, smoking, alcohol, personal finance, corporate strategies, national security, crime, professional liability, and litigation are just some examples of domains in which we discover ourselves to be **at risk** and act to minimize that risk.

Part of the awareness of risk is related to litigation. Indeed, some parts of the chemical and nuclear industries have become uninsurable due to the difficulties of calculating the costs of a worst-imaginable accident (WIA) in the communities and environments in which they are located. The numerous public health or "health promotion" campaigns found in the mass media are another part of this awareness. Political campaigns, often run around the theme of "law and order," increase the perception of the risk of crime, especially among specific sectors of the population, such as the elderly. The public and mediatized circulation of scientific knowledge and its relation to environmental movements further sensitizes us to the latent, barely visible, but real risks posed by industry and economic development. Our awareness of risk is thus related to public and media discussion, to the publicity accorded to events such as those of 9/11, to all kinds of **risk experts** in counseling and therapy, health care, and financial services, and in the normalization of practices of insurance among large sections of the population. Some have argued that this proliferation of risk has led us to a new, expanded kind of prudentialism (O'Malley, 1996).

While we experience risk as a part of our everyday life, it is something that can be known and calculated by various kinds of experts and is integral to particular social and political practices. Risk can be about the probability of harmful events occurring (for example, accidents at work), and can be a characteristic of certain times and spaces (for example, when and where crime is likely to occur). Above all, it has become a ubiquitous way of dividing populations so that harm might be prevented, reduced, or minimized. Certain individuals, families, communities, and populations are now regarded as at risk or **at high risk** of such things as long-term unemployment, child abuse, breast cancer, or fetal abnormalities. The production of risk as a calculable entity in a variety of ways is thus a fundamental component of policing, biomedicine, and social welfare systems, as well as insurance and investments. The proliferation of our perception of risk is signaled by different forms of calculating risk such as **quantitative risk assessment** and **risk benefit analysis**, and by the **risk profiling** of certain populations likely to commit crime. At the heart of our relationship to risk is the question of trust in experts, in politicians, and in the institutions of contemporary societies.

The proliferation of risk has become a topic for theoretical and academic debate. Sociologists such as Ulrich Beck (1992) have written that contemporary society is **a risk society**. Anthropologists such as Mary Douglas (1995) have examined the cultural understanding of risk in different societies and the gaps between perception and calculation of it. Risk is here related to cultural processes of blame and contamination. Moral philosophers have argued about the role and responsibility of experts in the calculation of risk, the justness of such procedures, obligations to future generations, and the equity of its distributions in time and space.

We might argue that the notion of risk has become a powerful analytical tool as well as a common experience of living in contemporary societies. As such, our societies can be understood as having developed complex mechanisms to navigate and govern risk. The welfare state might be understood as a way of navigating certain risks of living in such societies. Today, this has become at least partially displaced by an individualization of risk through private insurance measures and a focus on another kind of risk, that of the terrorist strike. The new Department of Homeland Security in the United States, the War on Terror, and the doctrine of the pre-emptive strike could all be viewed as a response to the perception of heightened **security risks**. Whether we talk of social welfare or national defense, the perception, calculation, and **government of risk** are thus essential to the ways by which we seek to fulfill the goal of attaining security in our societies.

Mitchell Dean

See: *GOVERNMENT, POVERTY, WELFARE.*

Science

There are words in our culture whose referents are so highly prized that they have scarcely any stable reference at all. Take, for instance, "reality," "reason," and "truth." And take the word which picks out the subculture speaking most authoritatively in the name of reality, reason, and truth: **science**. The instability of reference flows partly from the ways in which "science" folds together description and prescription. It is generally considered good to be **scientific** and to speak in the name of science, and, for that reason, there are many claimants to the title: **domestic science**, **nutrition science**, **management science**. More practices now represent themselves as scientific than ever before.

At the same time, there is a sense in which fewer things are now scientific than ever before. In the early modern period, the L *scientia* just meant knowledge, usually in the sense of a systematically organized body of knowledge, acquired through a course of study. Francis Bacon's *De augmentis scientiarum* (translated in the C17 as *The advancement of learning*) catalogued "the division of the sciences," which were taken to include history, philosophy, the principles of morals, and theology (traditionally, "the queen of the sciences") (Fisher, 1990). When, in 1660, the newly founded Royal Society of London wished to indicate that they were not much concerned with things like civil history, politics, and dogmatic theology, they described their business not as "science" but as "the improvement of natural knowledge." During the course of the C19 and especially the C20, "science" came overwhelmingly to pick out those practices proceeding by observation and experiment, thus jettisoning history and philosophy and leaving the **social sciences** a courtesy title, with limited credibility in the general culture or among **natural**

*ABCDEFGHIJKLMNOPQR*S*TUVWXYZ*

scientists "proper" (Geertz, 2000). Moreover, the global authority of natural scientific method has been increasingly disputed by those human and social "scientists" who reckon that the *Geisteswissenschaften* (or **human sciences**) ought to reject the procedures and goals of the *Naturwissenschaften* (or **natural sciences**).

Linguistically, this more restrictive sense of "science" was an artifact of the way English usage developed and changed in recent centuries. Into the C20, and up to the present, the F plural *les sciences* had a greater tendency to acknowledge procedural and conceptual similarities between, say, geology and sociology, as did the Russian singular *nauka* (with its Slavic cognates) and the G *Wissenschaft* (with its Scandinavian and Dutch cognates). Vernacular English once employed "science" in its original inclusive L sense (as in the skeptically proverbial "Much science, much sorrow"), but by the C19 "science" did not usually need the qualifying "natural" to summon up the idea of organized methodical research into the things, phenomena, and capacities belonging to nature as opposed to culture.

How this shift occurred is still little understood. One of the leading aims of influential C17 English experimentalists was the rigorous separation of bodies of knowledge and epistemic items capable of generating certainty from those which were at best probable or at worst conjectural, arbitrary, or ideologically colored. Insofar as the natural sciences were founded on a basis of legitimate fact, with disciplined means for moving from fact to judiciously framed causal account, they were capable of generating a just degree of certainty. By contrast, those intellectual practices which were founded on speculation or metaphysical dictate, and which were buffeted by human passion and interest, were unlikely to yield consensual certainty. The Royal Society protected the quality of its natural knowledge by policing the boundary between it and the potentially divisive "affairs of church and state" (Shapin, 1996). The condition of certainty in natural knowledge was, thus, a publicly advertised methodical separation between knowledge of things and know-ledge of morals, between "is" and "ought." It was just very hard to keep human passions and interests at bay when the objects of inquiry were things to do with the human condition, and so the prerequisite for scientific certainty was a degree of moral inconse-quentiality. A quality of certainty was, therefore, one means by which the prized designa-tion of "science" might be exclusively attached to methodically proper inquiries into nature. In fact, such an imperative and its boundaries were embraced in C17 England with greater enthusiasm than in France, where René Descartes promised that the outcome of his philosophical method would include a demonstratively certain **science of morals**.

315

Another distinction, increasingly important through the C19, was the ability of intel-lectual practices to predict and control their objects. Bacon's dream was to enlist method-ically reformed natural knowledge in the expansion of man's, and the state's, dominion, but the argument for the material utility of **theoretical science** was not widely credited until the C19, and was not decisively secured until Hiroshima experienced the power which theoretical physicists were capable of unleashing. As the ultimate patron of organized inquiry, the state was to pay for those intellectual practices which could demonstrably enhance its power and increase its wealth. There was much residual skepticism to overcome, but, by the mC19, most Western states had begun to accept their role as paymasters for a range of natural sciences, including certain strands of cartography, geology, astronomy, botany, zoology, physiology, chemistry, and physics.

The emergent human sciences made utilitarian claims as well. Governments were promised the delivery of certain, causal knowledge of the springs of human action: knowledge of which lay knowers themselves were unaware, and knowledge whose possession could be used not just to understand but to manipulate human conduct and belief, exactly as if human beings were molecules (Bauman, 1992). Here the promise of methodically guaranteed certainty – on the model of the natural sciences – might index the capacity of the human sciences to predict and control. Such attempts did *not* fail utterly. Many modern governmental and commercial practices powerfully, if imperfectly, predict and manage human conduct through embedded forms of social-science-in-action. Consider, for example, projections of retail expenditures, traffic engineering, the design of kitchen appliances, and the arrangement of goods on supermarket shelves, though the relations between these embedded practices and academic inquiries is problematic. Moreover, the human sciences have the tremendous capacity, occasionally and uncontrollably, to *realize* their concepts, to see them become vernacularized, and thus a constitutive part of the world that expertise seeks to describe and explain. Consider the careers of such concepts as "charisma," "penis envy," "being in denial," and "the grieving process." But the human sciences have never managed the trick of establishing their unique expertise as sources of such knowledge; these are domains in which the laity do not always defer to academic experts. Accordingly, the flow of cash from government and industry to the different modes of academic inquiry is a vulgar, but surprisingly reliable, index of what is now *officially* accounted a science and what is not.

The *official* reference of "science" promises some definitional stability and coherence. Suppose one just says that science is what is done in the departments of a **science faculty**; that it is what the US National Science Foundation, and the science bits of the Research Councils UK, fund; that it is what's found in the pages of *Science* magazine; and what's taught in science classrooms. This "institutional" or "sociological" sensibility highlights the sense in which one can rightly say that the modern "we" live in a **scientific culture** while acknowledging the fact that a very significant proportion of that culture's inhabitants have little idea of what **scientists** do and know.

But just because the "official" or "sociological" definition of science sets aside its prescriptive aspect, few intellectuals have been content to leave matters there. Efforts to demarcate science from lesser forms of culture, and to make science available as a pattern to be emulated, have traditionally involved the specification of its supposedly unique conceptual content and, especially, its uniquely effective method. Yet, for all the confidence with which various versions of **the scientific method** have been propounded over the past several centuries, there has never been anything approaching consensus about what that method is (Rorty, 1991; Shapin, 2001).

Talk about "the scientific method" is predicated upon some version of the "unity" of science. In the early to mC20 many philosophers embraced a moral mission to formalize the bases of that unity, but, since T. S. Kuhn's (1970) *Structure of scientific revolutions* in 1962, the flourishing of a variety of "disunity" theories indexes the local appearance of a more relaxed and naturalistic mood (Cartwright, 1999; Dupré, 1993; Schaffer, 1997; Shweder, 2001). Disunity theorists doubt that there are any methodical procedures held in common by invertebrate zoology, seismology, microbial genetics, and any of the varieties of particle physics, which are *not* to be found in non-scientific forms of culture. How can the human sciences coherently either embrace or reject "the natural science model" when the natural sciences themselves display such conceptual and methodological heterogeneity? Yet, for all the localized academic fashionability of naturalism and pluralism about the nature of science, the outraged reactions to these tendencies which surfaced in the **science wars** of the 1990s testify to the remaining power of the idea of science as integral, special, even sacred in its integrity (Shapin, 2001). To dispute the coherent and distinct identity of science is to challenge its unique and coherent value as a normative resource, and that is one reason why the idea of a unitary science persists in the absence of any substantial consensus about what such a thing might be.

Steven Shapin

See: *EMPIRICAL, KNOWLEDGE, OBJECTIVITY, THEORY.*

Self

The notion of **self** is one of the most ubiquitous in the lexicon of the modern West. We speak effortlessly of the difference between our **true self** and our **ordinary selves**, in a language where we **confide in ourselves**, experience **self-doubt**, and sometimes take **a good long look at ourselves**. We hear daily discussions of **self-esteem, self-talk**, and **self-empowerment**, coming from psychologists, counselors, talk-show hosts, advice columns, and a multitude of **self-help** books, videos, and on-line guides. Yet, in the opposite direction, a powerful stream of theory insists that **the self** is only the surface effect of impersonal or unconscious forces. The notion of self is now precariously poised between indispensability and non-existence.

Things were not always thus. Not all cultures have posited a self in the sense of a single inner source of conscience and consciousness dedicated to self-reflection. The Homeric Greeks invested the individual with multiple sources of thought and action, some of them being conduits for supra-human forces and gods transmitting the vagaries of fate and fortune directly into human agency and judgment (Dodds, 1973). In medieval English, "self" referred not to an inner personal identity but to the generic idea of sameness, whose echo we can still hear in the idiomatic expression **the self same thing**. When the notion of an **inner self** did emerge in such cultures it was the product of **techniques of the self** – techniques for calling conduct and feeling into question, for relating to oneself as an object of ethical concern – through which an elite could be schooled in the rare and difficult task of cultivating a self (Foucault, 1986; Hadot, 1995).

In Marcel Mauss's classic account, the wider distribution of techniques of the self was driven by the Christian idea of the soul, and in particular by Reformation Protestantism, where techniques of **self-scrutiny** and **self-discipline** were transmitted via print to populations suspicious of the old collective rituals of salvation (Mauss, 1985). Certain of these techniques constituted the true self as an enigma, wrapped in layers of worldliness, hence in need of constant interpretive probing, using special forms of reading and writing (J. P. Hunter, 1966). The spread of print literacy and the growth of a commercial book trade during the C18 permitted these arts of self-concern and self-discovery to migrate from religious culture to the domain of private leisure, where, after surfacing in the aesthetic form of the novel, they would flow into Romantic self-cultivation. The peda-gogical distribution of these techniques via the teaching of literature in C19 mass school systems then gave the capacity for aesthetic **self-questioning** and **self-revelation** an unprecedented dissemination in Western populations (I. Hunter, 1988).

The **religious-aesthetic self** – with its roots deep in the history of Western ethical culture – is not, however, the only pathway to modern subjectivity. Nikolas Rose provides a history of the distinctive **modern psychological self** (N. Rose, 1996). From the lC19, as a result of the interaction between the behavioral requirements of an array of disciplinary institutions (schools, hospitals, asylums, armies, factories) and the behavioral measures and norms of the emergent ''psy-'' disciplines (psychology, psychotherapy, educational psychology, psychological counseling and guidance), a new psychological interior was excavated. Finding its opening at the point where statistical deviation from an institutional norm could be accepted by an individual as a personal failing, this space was at first filled by abnormalities – feeble-mindedness and retardation, shirking and shell-shock – but soon became home to such normal capacities as intelligence and literacy. From here it was a short step to the appearance of personality in all its measurable glory, and an entire psychological lexicon through which individuals could formulate their own aspirations and anxieties in terms of the norms of the institutions they inhabited. It has thus become routine for us to articulate an inner self in such terms as the wish for job satisfaction, the fear of communication failure in our relationships, the concern for a child's low self-esteem, or the desire for self-empowerment. Whether consumed voluntarily in private or administered by human relations ''facilitators'' at work, the discourses and practices of the ''psy-complex'' now permeate public and private lives, allowing the norms governing conduct to be acknowledged as those by which we seek to govern ourselves.

Histories of the religious-aesthetic self and the modern psychological self do not treat the self as illusory. Things stand differently with the broad stream of modernist and postmodernist theory dedicated to the "formation of the subject," which seeks to show that the self is only a surface effect of thoroughly impersonal, non-conscious structures and forces (Foucault, 1971). Today an array of human sciences prefaced by the term "critical" – critical linguistics, sociology, psychoanalysis, Marxism, legal studies, cultural studies – equips those undergoing tertiary education with the capacity to problematize the self by recovering the discourses in which it is spoken, the social relations whose ideological reflection it is, or the unconscious drives it has been vainly called on to master. It remains to be seen whether these acts of deconstruction – carried out on a self rendered enigmatic by those trained in techniques of self-problematization – are something more than a variant of the techniques of the self that have been circulating in our cultures since early modernity.

Ian Hunter

See: *HUMAN, INDIVIDUAL, NORMAL, PERSON.*

Sexuality

Sexuality suggests a host of meanings. On the one hand it appears to refer to one of the most basic features of human life, "our sexuality," the most natural thing about us, the "truth of our being," in Foucault's (1979) phrase. On the other, it is so heavily encrusted with historical myths and entrenched taboos, with culturally specific meanings, that sexuality appears more a product of history and the mind than of the body. Perhaps, as Vance (1984) once suggested, the most important human **sexual organ** is located between the ears. Sexuality as a concept is uneasily poised between the biological, the social, and the psychic. Even Freud confessed to the difficulty of agreeing on "any generally recognized criterion of the sexual nature of a process" (1963 [1917]: 323).

The earliest usage of the term **sex** in the C16 referred to the division of humanity into the male section and the female section; and to the quality of being male or female. The subsequent meaning, however, and one current since the eC19, refers to physical relations between **the sexes – to have sex**. What we know as masculinity and femininity, and what came to be labeled from the lC19 as **heterosexuality**, with **homosexuality** as the aberrant "other," are thus inscribed into the meanings of sex from the start. **Sexual**, a word that can be traced back to the mC17, carries similar connotations: pertaining to sex, or the attributes of being male or female, is one given meaning. **Sexuality** emerged in the eC19 meaning the quality of being sexual, and it is this meaning that is carried forward and developed by the sexual theorists of the lC19.

Sexologists sought to discover the "laws of nature," the true meaning of sexuality, by exploring its various guises and manifestations. They often disagreed with one another; they frequently contradicted themselves. But all concurred that sexuality was in some ways a basic quality or essence which underlay a range of activities and psychic dispensations

319

(Weeks, 1985). Thus Krafft-Ebing became a pioneer in seeing sexuality as something that differentiated different categories of beings – so opening the way to theorizing **sexual identities**. Freud went further. His "Three essays" (1953c [1905]) began with a discussion of homosexuality, thus severing the expected connections between sexuality and heterosexual object choice; and they continued with a discussion of the perversions, so breaking the link between pleasure and genital activity. In the psychoanalytical tradition, sexuality was central to the workings of the unconscious. More broadly, sexuality was becoming a distinct continent of knowledge, with its own specialist explorers. When people spoke of "my sexuality," they meant those desires and behaviors which shaped their sexual (and social) identities, as male or female, heterosexual or homosexual, or whatever.

Against the certainties of this tradition the lC20 saw the emergence of an alternative way of understanding sexuality. "Sexuality" was a social construction, a "fictional unity," that once did not exist, and at some time in the future may not exist again. The sexual theorists John Gagnon and William Simon (1973) have talked of the need to *invent* an importance for sexuality. Michel Foucault queried the very category of "sexuality" itself: "It is the name that can be given to a historical construct" (1979: 105).

Contemporary theorists question the naturalness and inevitability of the sexual categories and assumptions we have inherited. They suggest that the concept of sexuality unifies a host of activities that have no necessary or intrinsic connection: discourses, institutions, laws, regulations, administrative arrangements, scientific theories, medical practices, household organization, subcultural patterns, ethical and moral practices, the arrangements of everyday life. The idea of sex, which seems so foundational to the very notion of sexuality, is itself a product of the discourses. Nothing is sexual, as Plummer (1975) suggests, but naming makes it so. So sexuality can be seen as a narrative, a complexity of the different stories we tell each other about the body (Plummer, 1995), a series of scripts through which we enact erotic life (Gagnon and Simon, 1973), or an intricate set of performances through which the sexual is invented and embodied (Butler, 1990).

This radical redefinition of sexuality has, inevitably, aroused intense controversy. Historical construction seems to deny the whispers and desires of the body itself, as sociobiologists and evolutionary psychologists argue. It appears to question the validity of the sexual identities (homosexual, heterosexual, bisexual, etc.) by which many people have set so much store. This, however, is precisely the point. A historicized approach to sexuality opens the whole field to critical analysis and assessment. It becomes possible to relate sexuality to other social phenomena. New questions then become critically important. How is sexuality shaped, and how is it articulated with economic, social, and political structures? Why do we think sexuality is so important, and to what extent does it now have a global meaning (Altman, 2001)? What is the relationship between sexuality and power? If sexuality is constructed by human agency, to what extent can it be changed?

These theoretical issues have been played out in a historical situation where sexuality as never before has become the focus of cultural and political struggle. The rise of radical sexual social movements such as feminism and gay liberation since the 1960s has been paralleled by the rise of conservative fundamentalist movements equally concerned with the body, gender, and sexuality. Issues such as abortion, homosexuality, and **sex education** have given rise to bitterly contested controversies on a global scale. At the same time, the HIV/AIDS epidemic has dramatized the significance of **sexual health** and its inextricable linkage with issues of identity, diversity, social division, and opposing values. There is a new uncertainty about the meanings of sexuality (Weeks, 1995). In such a situation, we can no longer seek a solution in the definitions of **sexual scientists** or self-styled experts, however well meaning. Only by problematizing the very idea of sexuality as a given of nature does it become possible to rethink the meanings of the erotic.

Jeffrey Weeks

See: *FETISH, GAY AND LESBIAN, PORNOGRAPHY, QUEER, UNCONSCIOUS.*

Sign

Sign refers to a broad class of objects, events, or marks that are used or interpreted to convey some meaning; this can include expressly devised signals, as well as symptoms or natural occurrences, say fossils or weather patterns. In Roman augury, certain arrangements of the entrails of a sacrificial beast counted as a signs, while in mathematics + and (), × and − are **functional signs** serving to articulate the signs around them into meaningful sequences. Badges and logos are signs, as are **shop signs** and the colors of sporting teams. With some of its cognates (**signify**, **significant**, etc.), "sign" is subject to a long-running debate concerning whether it can lend itself to technical usage and hence formal definition. Some attempts make "sign" synonymous with "representation." These rely on the "standing for" criterion: a sign is "anything that stands for something else in some respect or capacity." However, standard usage is broader than this. The alternative, which can be called the "interpretability criterion," is capacious enough to accommodate the standard breadth: if it's interpretable, then it's a sign.

321

The following things might also count as signs in standard usage: vestiges, omens, flags, coins, statues, gestures, apparel and bodily decoration, scars, passports, landmarks, the codified gestures and words used by referees in competitive sports, fingerprints, numbers, diagrams, etc. We **make a sign** with our hands, we distinguish some things for particular uses by putting signs on them, we write names or draw pictures on boards or in lights to give information, and these are all signs. We take (patterns of) events as **signs of the times**. A specialized context for the standard usage is reference to the languages of the deaf as **sign languages**. The earliest attested uses in English of "sign" go back to the C13, with some specialized uses, such as the mathematical ones, dating from the C18–C19; the use of "sign" instead of "symptom" dates from the C19, and "sign" for the trace of someone or something of which one is in pursuit dates from the C17.

Since signs are used or interpreted to convey meaning or information, practices such as painting, photography, radio, television, cinema (Metz, 1974), printing, and the "new media" are commonly known as **sign practices** or "semiotic practices." It is not usual to call them "signs," but it is acceptable to talk of such practices as producing, devising, or making signs. This usage dates approximately from 1970. In the context of these practices, as well as those that rely primarily on language in the strict sense, "conveying meaning or information" is construed as including the full range of genres: telling stories, creating art, expounding and debating academic or legal or political argument, selling consumer goods, performing rituals, etc. Semiotics, the **study of signs**, is the study of anything that can be used to do such things. Umberto Eco (1976) is famous for adding that semiotics is the study of anything that makes it possible to lie.

Of some of these, it would be odd in contemporary English to say that they represent some thing. The test seems to be whether the "standing for" criterion or the "interpretability" criterion is uppermost. Hence, whale-song and punctuation marks are signs, but we do not say that they stand for anything; on the other hand it is usual to think of emblems, national or team colors, badges, coins, and so on as standing for their objects. Such judgments are debatable, as are all judgments concerning standard usage.

Among the proponents of the technical use, further debates concerning definitional models can be discerned, the positions in these debates serving as signs of divergent schools of semiotics. The C20 saw an intensification of these debates, usually revolving around the number of constituents of a sign. The tradition inaugurated by Ferdinand de Saussure (1966) starts from two indissoluble parts; the tradition inaugurated by Charles Sanders Peirce (Houser and Kloesel, 1998) starts from three parts. Further theoretical issues concern how many kinds of signs there are, whether what the sign is a sign of is given in the world (as in trees and tables) or constructed by the sign (the work done in mathematics by 0, for example), and whether these questions should affect the definition. Standard usage has persisted in its wayward ways regardless.

Technical usage is broadly common to a great many languages, whereas the standard usage outlined above is special to English. The impetus for the former came from the Saussurean paradigm as interpreted by the "structuralist school" in the 1960s and 1970s – Roland Barthes (1968) and Julia Kristeva (1989) are the most prominent names – and from Americans such as T. A. Sebeok (1986), who was promoting Peirce at the same time. From the 1950s Roman Jakobson was using elements from both traditions together, and Umberto Eco followed this lead in the 1970s and 1980s with significant theoretical refinements. Most of the current research is conducted in Europe, notably in Denmark, Poland, and Italy, and in Latin America, especially Argentina, Uruguay, Chile, and Brazil. Much of this work has its source in definitions formulated in ancient Greek and Roman sources. The "standing for" criterion derives from the Aristotelian tradition, and the "interpretability" criterion from the Stoic tradition; Saussure's definition (a sign consists of an indissoluble unity of **signifier** and **signified** whose value is constrained by its place in a system) is an attempt to rewrite the "standing for" criterion on anti-nominalist lines. Some theoretical work on signs, for instance that of Peirce, attempts to blend the two.

It has been argued that no technical definition could account for the range of things that count as signs in standard usage and that, furthermore, in order for the term "sign" to do useful work in a theory, certain aspects of standard usage should be set aside with a view to establishing a homogeneous class of signs. The Saussurean reduction, which defined a sign as the smallest signifying unit of a language, was the most drastic. Debates ensued concerning how small a unit might be before counting as non-signifying: for example, diacritical and punctuation marks, though having no representational content, are still interpretable. Following this lead, a musical note would count as a sign, but does not if a sign must "represent"; however, the notation of music does "represent" the sounds. At the other end of the scale, the "smallest signifying unit" also excluded anything that did not count as a "unit of the system," but which was formed by a concatenation of units: sentences, paragraphs, whole texts or even libraries. These may be said to represent something, but under the Saussurean criteria, they are not signs. This idea of the "smallest unit" was quickly extended by analogy to cover the units of any signifying system, and then more broadly again, to those **signifying practices** such as the cinema that were thought to be neither systematic nor based on units.

A different kind of restriction is operated when another Saussurean criterion is brought into consideration. For the purposes of cultural theory, it was thought that **natural signs** and physical symptoms should be excluded; only those signs whose essence was arbitrary in relation to the representation of the world, and conventional and hence relative to other conventional systems, should count as signs. This effectively restricts the class of signs to those that are devised intentionally to convey information etc. (with that intention vested in a collectivity of some sort, not in an individual). Though contemporary cultural theory is inclined to exclude "intention" from its explanations and interpretations, it often relies on a semiotics that assumes it. In any event, it is difficult to maintain this exclusion, given the practices of "science," which can be said to endow bits of nature with the status of signs.

Under the Peircean tradition, anything that counts as a sign in standard usage is matter for semiotics. Seeking a definition to cover this range, Peirce adopted a pragmatic stance: the definition must serve the purposes of philosophy. This is parallel with Saussure, for whom the restrictions detailed above serve the purposes of linguistics. But Peirce never achieved a satisfactory definition (this assessment would be contested by some of his commentators), frequently falling back on lists of examples. The fact that formal definitions are devised for particular disciplinary purposes in both these cases is an important corrective to attempts to establish a **science of signs**, which requires a general definition, but does not impede the study of how they work, and to what effect, under local conditions.

The Saussurean tradition was fashionable during the 1970s, when the term "sign" was sometimes used "in the best cocktail parties" as itself a sign of general allegiance to the

323

view that signs and language are integral to social reality. This is difficult to document, but witness the adoption of the word *Signs* to name the concerns of the feminist journal of that title. As in the parallel case of the journal *Representations*, the title plays to the cross-disciplinary reach of the concept.

Anne Freadman

See: *DISCOURSE, REPRESENTATION.*

Socialism

Socialism has been a contested political sign almost from its eC19 beginnings. In particular, as Raymond Williams argues, there has been tension between socialism as a reforming creed, concerned with the qualification of the capitalist social order, and socialism as a far-reaching alternative way of life, based on co-operation and greater social equality rather than on individualism and competition (R. Williams, 1976: 238–43). Marxism and early communist politics added further layers of meaning, about the means of such a transformation – **utopian socialism** vs. **scientific socialism** or **revolutionary socialism**, for instance – and about the specifications of change itself in terms of political economy, class, and classlessness (Marx and Engels, 1973 [1848]: 62–98; Engels 1962 [1892]: 93–136). In revolutionary or unionist or "workerist" versions, standing politically on the side of workers could be the defining feature, hence designations like "Labor Party" or "Workers' Party." The sharpest period of **intra-socialist** engagements was during the lC19 and eC20 crises of capitalist and imperial hegemony, when different versions of communist, socialist, social-democratic, Labor, or **state socialist**, not to say **national-socialist**, politics were in intense conflict world-wide.

In the last 30 years, socialism has acquired a particularly heavy freight of meanings, many of them burdensome. It is more difficult today, compared even with the early 1980s, to say "We are socialists" without a strong sense of ambiguity (Eve and Musson, 1982). It is hardest, perhaps, in Anglophone countries, in the former Soviet Union, and in Eastern Europe, easier in national formations with recent histories of liberation or strong currents of resistance to globalization – in France, for example, or Spain, or parts of Latin America. Yet the needs and aspirations which socialism has expressed have become clearer and more urgent (Auerbach, 1992; Miliband, 1994), so that the search for a less compromised political vocabulary has forced "new" terms into the language.

The lC20 rise to dominance of neo-liberal and neo-conservative ideas and policies, world-wide, has been decisive here. Neo-liberalism was itself a reaction, in the mC20 heyday of social-democratic reform, to the New Deal and the welfare state. It sought to consign all socialisms to oblivion. Friedrich Hayek, the key neo-liberal philosopher, exposed the difficulties of "planning" or "social engineering" through the state, a critique mounted, somewhat indiscriminately, against national socialism, Soviet communism, liberal collectivism, and state-centered socialism (Hayek, 1944). Knowledge could never match planners' ambitions; we should rely on markets as "spontaneous" institutions, preserving individual freedom and productivity within a framework of law and order. As 30 years of campaigning bore political fruit, government after government and the international (de-)regulatory bodies adopted neo-liberal policies. Neo-liberals had easy explanations for the failures of **actually existing socialism** (Bahro, 1978), the unantici-pated collapse of Eastern-bloc regimes in 1989, and the ending of the Cold War (Fukuyama, 1992).

All aspects of socialism's historical repertoire came under pressure. Trade union and state professional power were challenged and, in Britain especially, **municipal socialism** was stripped of money and discretions. New right politics worked hard to separate "people power" from socialist educational-agitational practices, including adult and working-class education. Socialism was attacked as "power over" not "for" the people (Thatcher, 1989: 205). Its moral initiatives, including anger at injustice, were neutralized by a thorough-going individualism putting individual freedom before social care, while, in a classic contradiction, attacking moral "permissiveness." To be offended now by increasing inequalities was nostalgic or quixotic, veering dangerously toward "extremism" or eccentricity.

The rise of Third Way politics, itself a response to neo-liberal dominance, may leave even deeper marks on the public meanings of socialism, especially in the shape of popular cynicism. In many countries – Aotearoa/New Zealand, Australia, and Portugal, for example – Labor and social-democratic parties have played major parts in privatizing public services and weakening local and labor-movement institutions. In Britain, "New Labour" dropped the commitment to social policies of equalization retained by earlier Fabians and **revisionist socialists**; it seeks to "include" all citizens, but in a preparation for work in a globalized capitalist social order. The coinage **neo-socialism** is sometimes used to describe such adaptations; but while neo-liberalism was a faithful if dogmatic version of classical beliefs, neo-socialism disorganizes the socialist activism and working-class support on which left-of-center parties used to depend.

Not that socialism could have remained unchanged, for post-war social movements had already challenged its fundamental beliefs. Both new right and neo-socialist politics were, in many ways, responses to these movements. While "new left" is sometimes used to describe all of the social movements of the 1950s–1970s, including feminism and the women's movement, gay liberation, different forms of black and anti-racist politics, and movements associated with decolonialization and postcolonial conditions, this disguises key antagonisms. The movements often began with some political connection with social-ism and some theoretical borrowing from Marxist theory (**socialist-feminism**, black Marxism, Euro-communism), but also exposed the social exclusiveness of left traditions.

Critical intellectual work played a major part in this, not only the ferment around "theory," but also the new foci of historical research and "popular memory."

Paradoxically, it was through this critical agenda that a more rounded knowledge of **historical socialisms** emerged. Like other supposedly "universal" movements, all the different (national) socialisms had to undergo their own (international) renovations, still a work in progress, a "true refounding" in Lucio Magri's term (Magri, 1991). One aspect of change alone – the profound rethinking of conceptions of "man" [sic] and "nature," in relation to ecological concerns and environmentalist movements – is a lifetime commitment (Benton, 1989; and compare Grundmann, 1991). Small wonder that many opt to start elsewhere, not within a Marxist framework or a **socialist tradition**.

In one recent linguistic shift, socialism acquires its own hyphen, dividing the word itself – **social-ism**. This formulation matches communitarian versions of the social as "community." In many ways, however, "social-ism" marks a return to what Williams called "the developed sense of the social" which formed socialism's linguistic root in the first place. On its own, "social" is *the* keyword in the discourse of many contemporary opponents of neo-liberalism: "social rights," "social Europe," "social workers," "social capital," "the social sector," "the global (or European) Social Forum," and, generally, "the social" vs. "the market" (Bourdieu, 1998). This "social," and sometimes this "civil society," express thorough-going, transnational resistances to capitalist globalization. On this basis, movements address issues of global poverty and inequality, corporate power, capitalist exploitation, and the destruction of the local environments and the biosphere. Sometimes they take the form of the anti-globalization movement, better termed "globalization from below." Sometimes they issue in activism in and support for non-governmental organizations (NGOs) of many different kinds, in a type of agentful international citizenship. With their "affinity groups" and "coalition politics," these movements seem to bypass or handle differently many of the tangles that beset activists and educators in the IC20. With the help of new communication media, they are capable of concerted action across the globe. "The social" is seen to form the fabric of most people's daily living, just as the earth provides the economic-biological context for life itself. Both have now to be defended as "sustainable."

In this way, perhaps, socialism is coming full circle, as a better, alternative way of life. A key question, perhaps, in this palpable historical "simplification," is how far the puzzling "complexities" of the IC20 can really be left behind.

Richard Johnson

See: *COMMUNITY, CONSERVATISM, LIBERALISM, MOVEMENTS, SOCIETY.*

Society

Recently, **society** became a term of political controversy. Margaret Thatcher notoriously said that "there is no such thing as society. There are individual men and women, and there are families" (1987: 10). Later she was to clarify that her meaning "was that society was not an abstraction, separate from the men and women who composed it, but a living structure of individuals, families, neighbors and voluntary associations ... Society for me was not an excuse, it was a source of obligation" (1993: 626). Despite her antipathy to the term, she uses it in two senses noted by Raymond Williams (1976: 291). The first is a general one of the "body of institutions and relationships within which a relatively large group of people live." But she also recognizes that society can be used as an abstract term for, as Williams put it, "the condition in which such institutions and relationships are formed," as when, for example, we might say that "poverty is caused by society." While Thatcher rejects the possibility of abstraction, she enunciates one version: society as imposing moral obligations.

The images of society as an organism ("living structure") and as a thing can be traced back to the early formalization of **sociology** and **social science** in the C19 and eC20. Society was thought of, by thinkers such as Herbert Spencer and in social Darwinism, as an organism with an evolution replicating that of biological species. Later Emile Durkheim (quoted in Frisby and Sayer, 1986: 38) famously enjoined his readers to "consider social facts as things." As sociology developed, it would nevertheless tend to reject the image of society as a supra-individual entity imposing itself on its members. However, in common speech, it is still possible to oppose "individual" and "society" in phrases such as **conform to society** or **rebel against society**. "Society" tends to survive more in the abstract sense of a quality that inheres in conditions, practices, institutions, and relationships and is indicated by the adjective **social**.

All these uses of the term "society" are relatively recent and tend to overlay what amounts to a much older set of meanings that nevertheless remain in operation. Society is derived from L *societas*, meaning companionship, and L *socius*, meaning companion, friend, or associate, as in "there was such friendship, societies and familiarity between the Religious" (c.1610), or "Mr Woodhouse was fond of society ... He liked very much to have his friends come and see him" (Austen, 1816). Greek political thought, especially that of Aristotle, comes close to a general sense of society when discussing forms of human association or community, particularly that form of association which is the state (Gk *polis*, city-state) and those who comprise it, the citizens. Political community is here drawn in distinction to the private sphere of the family or household, Gk *oikos*, and not to the state, as it might be more recently. Similarly for Thomas Aquinas, a distinction is drawn between worldly political society, L *communitas civilis*, and the divine community, L *communitas divina*, but not between society and community.

In both political and religious uses, however, the notion of society remains connected with ideas of human association and more basically with friendship between free persons (usually men) until the C17 (Frisby and Sayer, 1986: 16). This relationship to friendship, and hence its converse, enmity, means that "society" remains a primary term of inclusion and exclusion, and of alliance and opposition. Its most general sense of a collectivity under a common government, as in a "common wealth is called a society or common doing of a multitude of free men" (Smith, 1577), also presupposes that such a society might be in antagonistic relations with other such multitudes.

One of the more recurrent images of society is an association formed through agreement, consent, or contract. The idea is that society is an active unity of fellowship between human beings, an "assemblie and consent of many in one" (*Mirrour of Policie*, 1599). This is given theoretical form in **social-contract** theory, where the concern remains with a specific form of human association, that of the state, and its relationship with a pre-political (and pre-social) form of existence, the state of nature (Weiner, 1973). The idea here is that the state is a precondition for general human association or friendship. Soon, however, "society," or **civil society**, will come to refer to the activities and relations of individuals, households, and families, which exist independently of, and in some way opposed to, the political structures of the state.

The discovery of a civil society is related to ideas of civilization. Being the domain of the mode of living of free men, the relations (or "conversation") between such men is regulated by more subtle rules of civility (as opposed to the laws of the sovereign), as in Charles I's "Laws of society and civill conversation" (1642). It was becoming possible in England and elsewhere in Europe in the lC17 to think of oneself as living in a civil or **civilized society** within the relative security of the territorial borders provided by the emerging state. It was also possible to expect a certain level of orderly conduct of other members of this society, given the development of practices of personal cultivation such as etiquette and manners. The latter practices give rise to the specific sense of "society" as the leisured, cultured, or upper-class, found until recently in newspapers' **society pages**.

This fact of a territorially unified, relatively stable, civilized nation provides the possibility of thinking, from the mC18, of society as a unity that exists independently of the political order *and* is subject to its own laws of development. Society is thus a "container" for a common way of life of a population marked out by territorial borders and exclusive of other societies, which, as is manifest in war and conflict, can become its enemies. Yet within this container, society is a sphere with its own customs, mores, classes, hierarchies, and stages of development. It can be driven by self-interest, or by bonds of affection and sentiment – and for those such as Adam Smith in the mC18 it was both. Societies thus have values and feelings which unite and conflicts which divide. Juridical and political structures become merely a function of these "naturally" occurring **social relations**.

This discovery of society as a fractured unity independent of political structures has of course immediate implications for the task of governing. All attempts at political rule and law-making have to respect and take into account a knowledge of the dense and somewhat opaque processes of society, particularly the laws of the market and commerce and the principle of population. For those who might be called early liberal thinkers, from Smith to John Stuart Mill, society is framed by law and subject to government, but it occupies real space, although coincident with the territorial boundaries of the national state, which is no longer simply an effect or extension of political arrangements and the state.

By the IC19, contractual association is no longer a founding act but a feature of modern societies based on the individual and individual achievement. Society now can be contrasted with earlier and existing spheres of community, characterized by affective and traditional – or "ascribed" – relationships and statuses.

In the C20, society lost its status as an object of scientific knowledge, as this came to be viewed as a "reification" ("thing-ification") of a condition that obtained within all sorts of relations, institutions, and practices. For Max Weber, the object of sociology was not society but the interpretation of the meaning of **social action**, and from that time sociologists have been more comfortable studying **social class**, social relations, **social interaction**, and so on. In scholarly writings, society has moved from transcendent object to a property of relationships. The adjective "social" begins to describe the dimension of those relationships and practices that are thought to have their source in society. We have institutions such as **social welfare** and **social insurance**. To explain poverty we invoke **social exclusion**, and strive for **social inclusion** as an ethical ideal. "Society" itself tends to be displaced by other abstractions around the word "modernity."

In this sense the claim "there is no such thing as society" merely recapitulates C20 learned opinion. Together with the idea of the decline of the nation state, connected with globalization, we might conclude that the notion of "society" as a unity acting on individuals survives only as a naïveté. Society, however, appears ready to be reinvented as a global phenomenon,; for example, the aspiration in an eC21 university strategic plan to be "a borderless university in a global society." In so far as a **global society** would attempt to fulfill cosmopolitan aspirations of friendship for all humanity, "society" could once again become the word for the highest form of human association. But as the treatment of illegal arrivals in Australia, or the defense of the homeland and a **free society** against terror in the United States, demonstrate, our notions of society are deeply embedded in ideas of a common way of life, secured by the state, within clearly defined borders, and with a sense of those multitudes who are a threat to that life.

Mitchell Dean

See: *CIVILIZATION, COMMUNITY, STATE.*

Sovereignty

Sovereignty is the quality or condition of being **sovereign**, that is, of being supreme or pre-eminent in some particular domain, but the most common modern usage of the term is in the domain of politics, where it refers to the legal and practical capacity of a state to enforce its rule over a specific population and territory. The term is also used to assert a right or to claim a capacity that one does not at present possess – as in China's assertion of sovereignty over Taiwan, and the many indigenous peoples' claims to sovereignty over lands which have been taken from them. To make such a claim is to deny the legitimacy of those who currently rule over the disputed territory.

A closely related idea can be found in the Roman concept of *summum imperium*, which refers to the supreme authority of the Roman people. But the modern view that the state should possess a **sovereign authority** capable of overriding all customary and subordinate authorities developed, along with the state itself, out of attempts to contain the destructive religious warfare of early modern Europe. Sovereignty has since become a central component in a regime of international governance that relies on relations between states and on states' capacities to govern their own populations. In the early stages of this development, Jean Bodin (1576) argued that an ordered commonwealth must have a single determinate authority, a sovereign capable of imposing laws on "subjects in general without their consent" (Bodin, 1992: 23), but he also insisted that a sovereign may not seize a subject's property without good cause and that he should follow the fundamental laws of the constitution. Thomas Hobbes (1991 [1651]) agreed on the necessity of sovereign authority but argued that it made no sense to claim that the sovereign should be subject to such conditions: if the sovereign could be compelled to satisfy them it must be subject to a higher authority, and therefore not in fact sovereign. Hobbes also argued that individuals submit to the **sovereign power** ultimately for their own protection: consequently, sovereignty remains in place only while the sovereign has the power to protect its subjects (Hobbes, 1991 [1651]).

Three issues raised in these early analyses of its character have continued to haunt subsequent discussions of sovereignty: whether it must be indivisible; whether a sovereign could both make law and be subject to law; and whether a sovereign must have the practical capacity to enforce its legal authority. The doctrine of indivisibility appears difficult to reconcile with the fact that most contemporary states are characterized by a constitutional order which explicitly divides the state's powers between a number of distinct centers: between, for example, legislature, executive, and judiciary, an upper and a lower House, or state and federal governments. The constitutional structure of modern states leads some authors (Kelsen, 1945) to argue that sovereignty resides in the constitution itself rather than any one center of authority. This view leaves unresolved the Hobbesian problem of who can impose order under conditions not covered by the constitution: "sovereign," declares Carl Schmitt (1985: 5), "is he who decides on the exception."

The institution of constitutional government appears, if we leave the issue of exceptions to one side, to have resolved the question of whether the supreme law-maker can itself be subject to domestic law. However, the issue remains problematic in the international sphere. If a sovereign is unrestrained by law, then international law has no more authority than **sovereign states** choose to accept. Attempts have nevertheless been made to establish a framework of international law by means of treaties and conventions, such as those on human rights or genocide, some of which may be used by the international community to legitimize military or humanitarian interventions in the internal affairs of states. The 1969 Vienna Convention on the Law of Treaties requires (in Article 18) that signatory nations refrain from taking steps to undermine treaties they sign, even if they subsequently fail to ratify them, while the Treaty to establish an International Criminal Court (now signed by over 60 states) is intended to facilitate the prosecution of individuals for genocide and crimes against humanity. The USA's refusal, after signing, to ratify both this last Treaty and the Vienna Convention, and the ability of lesser powers to flout at least some of the agreements by which they are bound, indicate the limitations of these arrangements.

Finally, the claim that to be truly sovereign a state must have the capacity to enforce its legal authority over its own population and territory brings the sovereignty of many contemporary states into question. During the C19 and eC20 non-Western states were commonly forced into accepting unequal treaties and capitulations that gave extra-territorial status to the civil laws of powerful Western states, both of which seriously undermined their claim to sovereign independence. This suggests that the sovereignty of a state is a function not only of relationships within its own territory and population but also of international conditions: that a state's sovereignty is constructed in its interactions with other states and powerful non-state agencies. Today, the sovereignty of many states appears to be threatened by globalization, by the global influence of the USA, the European Union, and Japan and the regional influence of lesser powers, by the authority of the EU over its member states, by the demands of the International Monetary Fund, the World Bank, the World Trade Organization, and other international agencies, by the power of large supra-national corporations, and by the destructive capacities of international financial markets. **State sovereignty** is sometimes also threatened by powerful internal forces sustained by religious networks, by the illicit trade in armaments, drugs, and diamonds, and by expatriate financial support.

Not all states have been equally affected by these developments: some, in spite of the demands of the EU and WTO, have retained an enviable capacity to manage their own internal affairs, but many others are considerably less fortunate. State sovereignty has not yet had its day, but the state-centered regime has been progressively overlain by forms of international governance in which states are far from being the only significant players.

Barry Hindess

See: *GLOBALIZATION, GOVERNMENT, HUMAN RIGHTS, NATION, POWER, STATE.*

Space

Space and time are simultaneously physical phenomena, social practices, and symbolic ideas. Specifying their diverse meanings tells us much about culture, change, and difference. We think of space and time as interlinked phenomena, but this was not always the case. The earliest recorded uses of the term "space" in English meant what we call time: "Their faith lasted little space" (1300); "For the space of many generations it hath been a shop of Arts and Artists" (Junius, 1638); "After a space, I tired of walking by the Red Sea" (*The Mirror,* 1779). The phrase **a space of time** indicated that space could mean any interval, not specifically extension or distance. These meanings were altered through private appropriation of land ("Yea goo we to than & take owr space," 1460); travel, exploration, and mapping; and measurement techniques in astronomy and typography, which needed a language to describe "spaces" between letters and words (or musical notations) on the printed page ("The Distance between one word and another is called a Space," 1676).

By the C19, space was understood as a distinct physical dimension. Heaven was supplanted by layers of atmosphere comprised of matter. "We are so constituted," wrote Stoddard in 1845, "that we cannot conceive certain objects otherwise than as occupying space." This proposition enabled powerful associations between the body, the self, and private space, together defined and developed by physical boundaries beyond which circulate the lives of others. The assumption of clear borders between self and other, **private space** and **public space**, was foundational to the modern period. It shaped "cognitive maps" in words, mental images, architecture, and urban living, and was reinforced by them. **Personal space**, like physical reality, could be claimed as a straight-forward entity. The body, physical space, and air are parts of an indissoluble whole. Thus the phrase uttered to command restraint to those gathered around someone injured or unconscious: **Give him space!**

In the C20, space and air were redefined as an open-ended dimension above the earth's atmosphere. **Outer space**, the foundation of the science and science fiction of the past century, describes a place waiting to be explored, conquered, and discovered, but also a place that perhaps houses aliens. Just as outer space may comprise unknown dimensions, so it may be inhabited by beings with very different mindsets, perhaps even more aggressive than "we" are. Early science fiction films, like ancient myths, depicted an outer space full of dangerous mysteries. This genre has been part of a number of forces – cultural, technological, military, and political – that together created an atmosphere in which space could be widely reconceived as a territory for military adventure requiring new technologies of conquest. The Cold War was initiated by relative advances of the **space program** in the USSR and the US, for which **space travel** could both represent and advance military preeminence.

Dramatic changes brought by globalizing forces after World War II were mirrored by dramatic changes in how meanings were created in social life, in terms not just of **occupied space** but also of how each society or region understands, constructs, and administers its spaces. Such changes were central to the perceived transformation from modern to postmodern society, characterized by fundamental transformations in space and time (Harvey, 1990; Jameson, 1991; Lefebvre, 1991; Soja, 1989). These terms have been reassembled in science, philosophy, and the academy, and in recurrent fables and games of popular culture, where human and other characters can cross previously impermeable barriers in space or time. New concepts of space and time also play a crucial role in music, literature, cinema, and the visual arts, where perspective is increasingly fragmented and disembodied. Modern approaches to space and time are rhetorically distanced from the newer postmodern perspective in which physical dimensions of space and time are collapsed by new techniques of travel and communication. However, the idea of the transformation of time and space was important to the modern period, which sought to analyze and overcome the physical dimensions of the universe.

During the post-war period, space also began to dominate a rich colloquial slang in English. Someone who wasn't sure who or where they were was **spaced out**; a person so caught up in her imagination that she failed to navigate the physical universe properly was a **space cadet**; someone unsure of a relationship **needs her own space**. Someone who doesn't think like those around him is **in his own space**. If someone is boiling over with anger, just give him space. An overconfident subject **takes up too much space**, doesn't **respect the space you're in**, or even **invades your space**. These phrases represent a vernacular appropriation of terms from one site into another, revealing how much we still associate the personhood of the self with the physical demarcation of private space. They rest on the assumption that a body can or should "belong" to a specific physical space, and vice versa; that one body can trespass on another's; that what one person defines as personal space can be a vehicle for aggression by another. They also recall the influence of post-war gender politics on concepts of politics and the everyday, for aggression is now culturally discernible in the language of the body as well as that of the state.

Struggles over possession of public space emerged with the privatization of agricultural land enacted by the new bourgeoisie in early modern England and Europe. With the enforced transfer of land to private ownership, space previously available for public use was redefined as private property. Struggles over public space emerged from the countering assertion that land was a public good or commons to which public use established a moral claim. Such struggles continue today in indigenous land claims in large portions of the new world and in contests for productive land use in countries with impoverished peasant populations. Indeed, the conflict between property and moral right arises in relation to public spaces of all kinds, including fertile lands in colonial territories; transit routes like rivers and roadways; the open "private" spaces of malls and shopping centers; and the "digital commons" of the Internet. Just as space was important to the architecture of popular thought, so it is central to new movements reacting to the political effects of "globalization."

In the social sciences, critics pose a distinction between space and place to account for altered relationships in a global context. With the rise of large cosmopolitan cities and international travel, as sociologist Georg Simmel observed in the early 1900s, someone may be physically close to you, on a bus or in a shop, yet remote in every other sense: a

333

stranger (*cit.* Allen, 2000: 57). Where closeness had been a matter of spatial proximity, community and belonging became distinct from space and difficult to calculate. The work of C20 artists and writers demonstrated that space and perspective were permeable and subject to vastly different optics and interpretations. The exploration of multiple perspectives advanced the idea that the body need not occupy a single space and that perception need not be tied to the body. New modes of communication promised to "conquer space" through rapidity of movement, enabling subjects to occupy multiple places at once. Thus, space acquired as much relativity in the humanities and social sciences as it had in physics.

Attempts to analyze the effects of globalization have further challenged our understanding of space. Responding to what Anthony Giddens influentially termed "time and space compression" in **global space**, society and space have been reconceived as interdependent entities materially transformed by global mobility and control strategies (Giddens, 1990). Historians attribute the new constitution of space and society to innovations in communications technologies created to "conquer" space. With messages freed from the bodies or media that conveyed them, it became possible to imagine space without society and society without space, giving rise to ambivalent analogies between **cyberspace** and heaven, countered by the critical argument that society and space are embedded in a process of mutual, contradictory production (Lefebvre, 1991; Serres, 1995; N. Smith, 1984; Wertheim, 1999).

"Space" now holds multiple meanings, with strong cultural, physiological, and political associations. Arguably the multiplicity of meanings attached to the term helps to retain its long-standing aura in a culture dedicated to making everything measurable, including the skies, the body, kinship, and belonging. No matter how sophisticated measurement techniques become, there is something in the concept of space that exceeds them. Space has become a generous source for metaphor: one "maps" one's view of the world, or strategies for changing it; one **finds one's space**, and seeks to understand "where" something or someone is "coming from."

Today there is no other word that reaches more readily between our various spheres of action and understanding, from the realm of scientific measurement to the street-wise domain of colloquial invention, from the exploratory language of poetry to empirical studies in behavioral psychology, from social planning to the technically sophisticated projections of military planning. The pervasiveness of the term invites us to ponder why it conveys such powerful affect, and to acknowledge space as a dynamic force in the contemporary struggle for meaning, belonging, and power.

Jody Berland

See: *MOBILITY, PLACE, PRIVATE, PUBLIC, TIME.*

334

Spectacle

That **spectacle**, like the word **specter**, comes directly from the L verb *specere*, "to look at," suggests some of the profound ambivalence which has enduringly associated acts of looking with the questionable reality of appearances. At the same time "spectacle," since Latin antiquity, has designated that which, having a "striking or unusual character," exceeds the normative or habitual character of visual experience. Its sense of "impressive public display" indicates the consistency with which spectacle has been part of non-coercive strategies of power and persuasion, whether in pre-modern despotic or monarchical regimes or within industrial and post-industrial cultural and state formations. Spectacle implies an organization of appearances that are simultaneously enticing, deceptive, distracting, and superficial, and this overlapping of functions supported C20 theories on the analogous functioning of spectacle and ideology.

Overwhelmingly, one now encounters the word as a vague shorthand for a society dominated by effects of electronic media, notably film and television, often compounded with the hegemony of consumer/celebrity culture, and in which individuals are politically neutralized by a reduction to permanent spectator status. Use of the term "spectacle" since the late 1960s has been a direct consequence of the work of Guy Debord, even though its deployment most often has little relation to his work. His analysis of spectacle emerged in the context of a specifically French revision of orthodox Marxism following World War II, when Henri Lefebvre, Edgar Morin, and others developed a critique of post-war consumer society around the status of the commodity in everyday life and of new forms of alienation. By the mid-1960s Debord formulated one of his main theses: "the more the spectator contemplates, the less he [sic] lives; the more readily he recognizes his own needs in the images of need proposed by the dominant system, the less he understands his own existence and desires" (Debord, 1994: 23). The theoretical model of spectacle emerged in the 1960s alongside political analyses and interventions in the terrain of social space, specifically the "psychogeography" of the modern city. Debord and other situationists sought concrete ways of challenging the apparent homogeneity and dominance of the abstract and commodified space of the spectacle. The word came to designate the many ways in which capitalism was inherently incompatible with play and festival, and the ways that it constructed fraudulent simulations of festivity in its celebrations of products and leisure-time consumption.

In *Discipline and punish* (1977) Michel Foucault rejected the model of a **society of spectacle** and claimed that we inhabit a "society of surveillance," implying that spectacle was a constitutive element of pre-modern forms of power, going back to Roman antiquity. Foucault was no doubt aware that the critique of spectacle begins with early Christian theologian Tertullian (1931 [c.197–200]), who insisted that spiritual values were radically incompatible with the lure of the Roman theater and arena. But it can be argued that the modernizing disciplinary processes that Foucault outlines are fully compatible with Debord's account of spectacle as multiple strategies of isolation and social separation, which produce docility and neutralize the body as a political force. Central to Debord's analysis is his insistence that the aim of spectacle is "to restructure society without community."

More recently Antonio Negri and Michael Hardt have affirmed the continuing usefulness of the concept of spectacle in their *Empire*: "In the society of the spectacle, what was once imagined as the public sphere, the open terrain of political exchange and participation, completely evaporates" (Hardt and Negri, 2000: 323). For them the destruction of almost every form of community means that traditional kinds of political struggle become impossible and that new means of resistance must be developed within global technological culture. At the same time Hardt and Negri tilt their model of spectacle away from the desire of commodities and pleasures of consumption to harsher IC20 century realities: "fear is what binds and ensures social order, and still today fear is the primary mechanism of control that fills the society of the spectacle" (p. 323).

Spectacle has also been a crucial part of recent debates in film theory, art history, and cultural studies. Art historian T. J. Clark made it a central part of his influential analysis of visual modernism in France in the 1860s and 1870s, *The painting of modern life*. It is during these decades of the C19 that Clark sees the beginnings of "a massive internal extension of the capitalist market – the invasion and restructuring of whole areas of free time, private life, leisure and personal expression" (T. J. Clark, 1984: 9). He identifies spectacle with this "new phase of commodity production – the marketing-into-commodities of whole areas of social practice which had once been referred to casually as everyday life" (p. 9). This analysis then becomes the basis for evaluating a crisis in the ambiguous status of pictorial representation in the work of Manet, Seurat, and others. In the area of film theory, the work of historian Tom Gunning (1990), for example, employs "spectacle" in a way considerably removed from Debord's work in his insistence that cinema's origins and essential features lie not in earlier forms of narrative, but in a broader range of **spectacles** and attractions that sought to solicit the attention of a spectator through direct stimulation, shock, and surprise.

If spectacle continues to be useful as a critical model, it will be important to determine what it implies for possible local strategies to resist its effects or neutralize its operation. Also, distinctions need to be made about its global diffusion that account for both regional specificity and the market-driven imperatives of multinational homogeneity. Is spectacle now another name for the relentless demolition of singular and autonomous cultural practices everywhere, or is it more significantly a phenomenon of the metropolitan core of a diverse global environment? Finally, the question must be asked whether current configurations of informational, communication, and imaging systems have reconfigured relations of power and subjectivity to such an extent that spectacle may be an inadequate critical tool for their analysis.

Jonathan Crary

See: *COMMODITY, CONSUMPTION, IDEOLOGY, IMAGE.*

State

When Friedrich Nietzsche (1969b [1883–91]: 75) describes the **state** as "the coldest of all cold monsters" he has no existing state in mind: he refers, rather, to a "new idol," an influential modern ideal in which the state appears as an apparatus of government that is impersonal in two fundamental respects. First, the state is expected to be a rational bureaucracy, in which the rights and duties of any office, even the most elevated, are clearly separated from those of the person who occupies that office; the office continues when its holder dies or is replaced, and people are expected to respect the office even if they cannot bring themselves to respect its current occupant. Second, the state is expected to be an entity distinct from the population it governs: unlike the Greek *polis*, which Aristotle describes as a body of citizens, the state is an apparatus which rules over its citizens. The **ideal state** is a cold monster, then, precisely because of its doubly impersonal character; its identification and pursuit of the general interest are intended to be entirely dispassionate.

This ideal presents a normative standard against which the conduct of actual states can be measured. Moreover, if even the most effective of **modern states** fails to live up to its requirements, the ideal itself suggests a ready explanation: namely, that the impersonal workings of the state's machinery have been corrupted, either by the private interests of its officials or by the influence of powerful interests within the broader population. Skeptics, ranging from public-choice theorists on the right to Marxists on the left, have inverted this suggestion, arguing that the state invariably operates in the service of sectional interests and that the image of the state as the disinterested agent of the general interest functions merely to obscure this reality.

The term "state" itself derives from the Latin *status*, meaning "manner of standing" or "condition," and it still carries this sense in such phrases as "state of siege" or "state of mind." More colloquially, "state" may refer to a condition that is particularly disturbing or unusual. Quentin Skinner (1989) has traced the emergence of the more specific, political, usage during the early modern period, showing how the meaning of the term gradually shifted from the condition or the status of something else (of the prince's estate or of the republic) to a substantial apparatus of government clearly separate from the person of the ruler. The appearance of this new concept thus coincided with the emergence of a new field of government, which now referred to the work of regulating the conduct of the **state apparatus** itself, as well as that of the population over which it claims to rule. From this point onward, political discourse placed the state and relations between states at the center of its concerns.

But the establishment of this new concept also required the consolidation of the political and bureaucratic relationships which it invoked, and to understand what this involves we must turn to a different line of development. The 1648 Treaty of Westphalia and other agreements which brought the Thirty Years War to an end are conventionally taken to mark the emergence of a new European order of independent **sovereign states**. While acknowledging the problems posed by the presence of powerful religious differences between Catholics, Lutherans, and Calvinists within territorial units, the Treaty nevertheless granted supreme political authority to territorial rulers within their domains while guaranteeing toleration to the three main confessions no matter what the religion of the ruling house. The principle of non-interference in the internal affairs of a sovereign state served as part of this regime of pacification by restricting the rights of supporters of one religion from intervening in the religious affairs of other participating states. These political arrangements had the novel effect of transforming a condition in which populations were subject to a variety of overlapping and often conflicting sources of authority into one in which rulers were acknowledged as having the primary responsibility for the government of the populations within their territories. Complementing the idea of the state as an impersonal apparatus of rule, we now find that of the state as a sovereign or independent member of the **system of states**.

This last development created an ecological niche in which rudimentary versions of Nietzsche's cold monster were able to establish themselves; the sovereignty which the European system of states secured for its members allowed participating states a degree of freedom from outside interference without which they would not have been able to develop and refine the formidable administrative apparatuses with which Western populations are now familiar. Even so, it was not until the IC19 that the more successful of these monsters were finally able to make the claim – which Max Weber (1978: 54–6) identifies as the most distinctive feature of the modern state – to an effective monopoly of the legitimate use of force within their respective territories.

The formation of a system of states also provided conditions in which international arrangements to regulate the conduct of states themselves could be further refined and developed. This system began as an arrangement of treaties and understandings covering territories and populations in parts of Europe; it therefore imposed few constraints on states' interference in the affairs of those who inhabited territories not covered by these agreements and in which no truly sovereign states were thought to exist. Thus, while states may have found their European activities constrained by the Westphalian system, they were not so restricted in other parts of the world. Indeed, they experienced little difficulty in adapting the doctrine of natural law to provide what they could regard as lawful grounds for territorial expansion elsewhere.

This last feature of the **European states system** allows us to identify two fundamental stages in the spread of that system to other parts of the world. First, the effect of colonial acquisitions outside Europe was to bring new territories and populations into the remit of the Westphalian system. European colonial expansion and the use by **Western states** of a discriminatory "standard of civilization" (Gong, 1984) in their dealings with political unities (among them China, Japan, Russia, the Ottoman Empire, and Thailand) that were not themselves accepted as part of the system of states eventually resulted in the subordination of the greater part of humanity to direct or indirect rule by Western states. This arrangement was formalized through the imposition, on many of those found wanting, of unequal treaties and capitulations granting extra-territorial status to the civil law of Britain and other Western powers. Western colonialism was clearly a matter of subjecting non-European populations to rule by European states, but it was also a matter of incorporating those populations into the European states' system; it was the form in which the European states' system first became global in scope.

Second, the widespread achievement or imposition of political independence dismantled one aspect of colonial rule while leaving the other firmly in place. To be an independent, **postcolonial state** is not to be subject to the rule of another state, but it is still to be a member of the states' system and subject to the regulatory regimes which operate within that system. Thus, independence both expanded the membership of the system of states and set in place a radically new way of bringing non-Western populations under the rule of the states' system. As a result, these populations found themselves governed both by modern states of their own and by the overarching system of states within which their own states had been incorporated. Citizenship, of a kind, was now a universal human condition.

To say that an **independent state** is not ruled directly by another state is not to say that members of the modern system of states engage with each other as equals; on the contrary, the overarching system of states has a clear hierarchical structure, with stronger and weaker states and a number of more or less exclusive inner circles. Few of the recently established states bear much resemblance to the cold monsters of Nietzsche's aphorism, having inherited poorly developed infrastructures and educational systems, and administrative apparatuses designed to serve a system of rule by outsiders. Those that are furthest from its doubly impersonal ideal are for that reason sometimes regarded as **failed states** or **quasi-states** (Jackson, 1990).

Moreover, like many states whose territories were never in fact colonized, they have yet to be admitted to the more exclusive inner circles of the international system of states and they find themselves subject to updated versions of the earlier "standard of civilization." In some respects this condition is reminiscent of the old system of capitulations, since it requires **subordinate states** to conform to legal frameworks already established by Western states if they are to participate in various international arrangements (the Organization for Economic Cooperation and Development [OECD], the General Agreement on Trade and Tariffs [GATT], and its successor, the World Trade Organization [WTO], providing the most obvious examples). It also enables various rogue or failed states to be identified as potential targets of military or humanitarian intervention.

Barry Hindess

See: *BUREAUCRACY, CITIZENSHIP, COLONIALISM, GOVERNMENT, POSTCOLONIALISM.*

339

Taste

Using the word **taste** to describe a particular physical sense is an everyday occurrence: "have a taste of this," "it had the most disgusting taste!" Metaphoric uses of "taste," as in "she has such good taste," are less common. This is because while all of us have a mouth, far fewer of us are considered capable of superior cultural judgments. In the metaphoric transfer from taste as a human sense faculty to taste as an abstract capacity for cultural discrimination, which began in the eC18, something very significant happened. Not only did the body get written out of the story, so too did a wide range of cultural choices and practices. **Good taste** was distanced from the vagaries of the senses and was evident only in relation to a high cultural aesthetic and those who appreciated this. Paradoxically, **bad taste**, evident in condemnations like "how tasteless!" or "it left a nasty taste in my mouth," implies a moral rather than aesthetic offense. It is still most often used to refer to standards of goodness and decency rather than beauty. **Kitsch**, **common**, **ostentatious**, and **lowbrow taste** are more likely to be used when describing an absence of good taste. These terms imply an inability to display distinction and refinement, a preference for the mass, the crass, and the mindless. However, as deference to the supposedly unassailable force of good taste has waned, these terms are often used with pride and defiance, to signal a **counter-taste culture** rather than a lack.

Debates about taste, its origins and operations, emerged during the eC18 as part of the wider development of aesthetics and philosophies of beauty. Taste was identified as the capacity to recognize and evaluate art without being subject to sentiment or reason. For Hume (1965 [1757]), certain qualities inherent in the formal organization of art were

ABCDEFGHIJKLMNOPQRST UVWXYZ

objectively pleasing. Those who failed to recognize this value were suffering from an "apparent defect or imperfection in the organ." For Kant (1987 [1764]), taste was a superior capacity for aesthetic experience that severed art from worldly ends, practical functions, and mere sensory pleasure. These two linked ideas established taste as the preserve of a minority. The aesthetic gaze was disinterested, disembodied, autonomous, and only present in the reception of art, an elite cultural preference. By the IC18 high art was seen as a unified domain defined in opposition to a dangerous and contaminating Other: low culture. Audiences for low culture lacked distance and detachment and this precluded an aesthetic response. In the absence of taste they were trapped in crude and barbaric responses, victims of their own vulgarity.

The naturalization of taste as the product of an autonomous aesthetic logic was thoroughly critiqued by French sociologist Pierre Bourdieu in his landmark study *Distinction* (1984). In seeking to denaturalize taste Bourdieu showed how differences in cultural choices became socially functional. His study of patterns of French cultural consumption and the discourses of value that supported these showed how distinctions of class were transposed onto distinctions of taste (Frow, 1995: 29). The dominant classes' capacity to claim their cultural preferences as the most legitimate, as superior, as the heartland of good taste, was based on the mobilization of cultural capital. Cultural capital involves knowledge of and competency in high cultural codes. It is acquired through the education system and the family and is fundamental to the display of an aesthetic disposition. This disposition involves the use of abstracted and highly formalized cultural valuing systems and an interest and pleasure in cultural forms that is distanced from any sense of practical need.

341

Raymond Williams ends his *Keywords* entry on taste with the suggestion that "taste cannot now be separated from the idea of the consumer" (1976: 266). This astute observation signaled the massive rise in leisure consumption that took off during the 1960s. Consumer capitalism was fueled by post-war growth in disposable income and leisure. It promoted a new ethos of consuming, driven by an economy of desire and dreams, and linking cultural choices to self-expression and identity. The emergence of distinctive markets such as youth was evidence of the powerful role of cultural consumption in fashioning popular tastes and identities. Mass consumption was becoming less the Other to good taste and more a key site where diverse tastes and fashions were promoted through the operations of cultural markets.

Cultural studies has been a key field for studies of this shift. Its focus on popular culture, mass culture, and consumption challenged the authority and legitimacy of **bourgeois taste** by contesting its restricted regimes of value and contempt for mass and popular forms. In opposition to the cerebral and contemplative world of high culture, **popular cultural tastes** were assessed as more direct, sensory, pleasurable, and widespread. Subcultural styles revealed the relationship between cultural choices and oppositional identity. Equally significant was the growth of fashion as a key site for the cultivation of the self and the practice of an everyday aesthetic. The massive proliferation of cultural consumption and markets since the 1980s, sometimes described as the triumph of lifestyle, signals the centrality of symbolic and expressive values in new economic formations. It is now impossible to claim that aesthetic knowledge and judgment are restricted to an elite minority of audiences and forms. In the organization of our selves, rooms, meals, gardens, we make aesthetic decisions with the aid of highly commodified **taste markets**. We also implicitly express our allegiance to various **taste communities** that share the same codes and systems of distinction.

According to Frow (1995) these changes have led to a profound reorganization of **taste and valuing regimes** that has contested any sense of a categorical high–low opposition. **High cultural tastes** have suffered a loss of authority at the same time as the sense of cultural inferiority that characterized lovers of the mass or the popular has largely dissipated. For Frith (1996) the extraordinary diversity and popularity of commercial music are evidence of the fundamental place of aesthetic judgments in everyday cultural consumption and pleasure, and of how **judgments of taste** are inscribed in our bodies; when we find ourselves singing along, swaying, unable to resist the rhythm, the idea of taste as an abstract process of discrimination collapses. The repression of the body and its affective registers has become impossible to sustain in many forms of taste. Popular music, particularly clubbing and raves, reveals this forcibly but so too does food. Witness the convergence of the sensory delights of eating with the rise of diverse taste markets in food. In the gourmet field of wine tasting, for example, the forms of training necessary to acquire good taste involve both heightened awareness of the body's response and accumulated knowledge of systems of classification and discrimination.

Gay Hawkins

See: *AESTHETICS, ART, CANON, CONSUMPTION, CULTURE, FASHION, MASS, POPULAR.*

Technology

Modern shifts in the meaning of **technology** (from fw *tekhnologia*, Gk, and *technologia*, modern L) clearly reflect the rise of industrialization and the onset of economic development tied to science-based innovations. In the eC17, "technology" was used to describe a systematic treatment, for example, a study of the arts, especially the useful or mechanical arts, as suggested by the Greek root, *tekhne* – an art or craft. By the mC19, its chief use pertained directly to industrial crafts. These applied skills and techniques were identified with manufacture and trade, and were distinguished from the more theoretical branches of scientific knowledge. As investment in scientific research increasingly serviced the needs of the state or corporations, the distinction between science and technology eroded – many commentators now refer to **technoscience**. Nevertheless, this distinction is preserved to sustain the belief that science is an objective, value-neutral endeavor, free from the commercial or political taint associated with technology. A related distinction can be found in the difference between **technical**, which describes a specific application or practical detail, and **technological**, which retains the sense of a systematic treatment by describing the logic underlying a collective application of **techniques**.

By the lC19, science-based invention had become the driving force behind capitalist growth, and technology was increasingly used to refer to machinery itself. The **technical crafts** of the artisanal workshop had been subsumed into the factory system, and craft-workers no longer had autonomous control over their tools. Their skills, or technologies, were mechanized, and they had surrendered the psychological, as well as the material, ownership of the product of their labor (Braverman, 1974). In this respect, Marx regarded technology as a weapon of class war, developed and employed to establish control over workers, and to expropriate their labor power with ever-greater efficiency. On the other hand, and like so many subsequent commentators, he placed considerable faith in the revolutionary potential of technology to emancipate workers from excessive toil and physical suffering, and to abolish scarcity and resource-competition forever (Marx, 1973 [1953]).

This contradiction has troubled all advocates of social systems which are propelled by the implicit promise of **technological utopianism**. These include capitalist systems – in which technologically boosted productivity is the source of economic accumulation and consumer abundance – and communist systems – which embraced the machineries of industrialization, along with the division of labor known as Taylorism, in a bid to outpace the capitalist economies. This contest between these political systems gave rise to specialized forms of technological rivalry – the arms race and the space race. This was ultimately concluded in favor of capitalist systems, according to Cold War triumphalists, because centralized communist systems could not accommodate the open, decentralized architecture of **information technology** (IT). This view is typical of **technological determinists**, who believe in a direct causal relationship between technology and its effect in the world at large.

In the US, in the eC20, reform Progressives who called themselves **technocrats** argued for a "revolt of the engineers," whereby government based on the **technical efficiency** of experts would replace the wasteful leadership of capitalist tycoons. This dream of enlightened **technocracy** was revived in the 1970s by proponents of postindustrialism, who saw IT as the key to a knowledge society that would be more humane and rational than the dying industrial order (D. Bell, 1974). Subsequent developments in the fields of microelectronics and biotechnology generated mass production of **high technology** (or **high-tech**), and vernacular usage of the term "technology" is increasingly identified with these material artifacts. High-tech products like software programs often take on an immaterial dimension, and their applications are perceived to operate in a realm that is virtual. Invariably, a cult of enthusiasm accompanies the introduction of these new technologies – **technophilia** – and its boosters employ evangelical rhetoric that belongs to the genre of the **technological sublime**. The tendency to view technology as a transcendental vehicle of

343

non-material yearnings is long-standing. Some historians see a fundamental basis for this cult in Christianity's dream of recovering humankind's fallen divinity (Noble, 1997). As a result, each wave of technical invention in the West has been underpinned by an essentially religious belief in the improvement, redemption, or perfection of the human condition. From the medieval attribution of alchemical properties to metallurgy to the chiliastic age of the Internet, deliverance was proclaimed to be at hand.

The disparity between such exalted promises and the reality of everyday encounters with technologies developed for surveillance, speed-up, deskilling, genetic screening, and state violence has engendered critical responses often characterized as **technophobia**, when they are promiscuous, and **technoskepticism**, when they are informed by risk assessment (Beck, 1992). This sober disposition is bolstered by the experience of women, racial minorities, and indigenous and non-European peoples, whose subjugation, historically, was often administered through applications of technology, and who have learned to be wary of new ones as a result (Adas, 1989; Harding, 1993).

More generally, critics of technology are often disparaged as Luddites, after the eC19 English weavers who resisted the threat to their livelihood posed by automated machinery. Yet it is widely acknowledged that the cult of **technological progress** and productivity has contributed to acute environmental degradation in all parts of the globe. In developing countries, ecological sustainability, along with traditional patterns of life, is often decimated when **technology transfer** is effected without regard for the local context. In response, advocates of **intermediate** or **appropriate technology** champion small-scale technologies that adapt easily to sociocultural lifeways and environmental conditions (Schumacher, 1973). So, too, environmentalists have pushed for the development of **alternative technology** that draws on renewable energy sources and sustainable components. These movements are partly informed by the belief that technologies are not neutral, and that political tendencies, whether authoritarian or democratizing, are internalized as part of their architectural design (Winner, 1986). In some countries, like Denmark, the pressure for more democratic input has been institutionalized in the form of ''consensus conferences,'' convened by panels of citizens to assess the development of new technologies. So, too, the radical democratic potential of networked communication has been upheld by the fierce, anarcho-libertarian allegiance of Internet enthusiasts to the hacker ethic: open standards, free access to information, unregulated speech, the public sharing of code and resources, and the decentralization of authority. Yet the strong, countervailing tendency is in the direction of further privatization and proprietary claims on the part of transnational corporations, as promoted by international legislation on intellectual property.

Andrew Ross

See: *CAPITALISM, INDUSTRY, INFORMATION, RISK, SCIENCE, VIRTUAL.*

Text

The first definitions of **text** in the OED refer to the scriptures: "the very words and sentences of the Holy Scripture; hence the Scriptures themselves" (lC14). It could also mean a short, authoritative passage from Scripture that would be the proper topic for elaboration, as in a sermon. These narrow uses were quickly extended to include the "wording of anything written or printed; the structure formed by the words in their order" (C15). Thus "text" refers to the original, formal, and authoritative body of any linguistic object. Finally, in the C17, "text" is used to refer to "the theme or subject on which one speaks." This history reveals two dimensions along which the referent of text was expanded: first, from the scriptures to a broader range of linguistic objects; and second, from the actual and permanent material words to that which is addressed by the words, what we might call their "subject matter."

For the most part, the common use of "text" has not diverged very much from this etymology. In common use, "text" refers to what the New Critics used to call "the words on the page." The "text of the president's speech" refers to the actual words, order and structure independently of the event of the speech itself. The text is that which fixes some event (such as the speech) and makes it permanent. The text is, in that sense, usually thought of as existing independently of the original **context** in which it was produced, making it into an apparently timeless and placeless object that can be widely shared and scrutinized.

In these ways, text has come to be associated, in the eC21, with all sorts of new information technologies, as in **text processing**, **text editing**, and **text messaging**. And it has even established a presence in the academy, as when the humanities are sometimes described as **text-based disciplines**. In the mC20, **text linguistics** concerned itself with larger units of language than words or sentences as necessary to an understanding of how meaning is produced.

However, text also has a second life, for since the mC20, it has become a highly technical and fertile concept in academic cultural theory. This "linguistic turn" is marked by an increasing concern for **textuality**, which in the eC19 meant something like literary style. Historically, this new technical usage entered the various disciplines and interdisciplines under the influence of structuralism, where the focus of study was the text as a written or spoken artifact. What mattered was to understand in precise linguistic detail those systematic aspects of **textual structure** that facilitated textual coherence and enabled textual communication. This work was based on the theories of language and meaning developed by the eC20 linguist Ferdinand de Saussure, the mC20 anthropologist Claude Lévi-Strauss, and the early work of the literary critic Roland Barthes. These authors argued that language use was enabled by an underlying code or system of rules, which speakers used unconsciously and which could not be changed at will. This use of text sought to displace the author and concepts of individual creativity in favor of understanding the abstract systems which made the production of meaning possible. The reader was freed

345

from the controlling origin of the author and the authored work, and could now negotiate meanings directly with texts. Additionally, Lévi-Strauss and Barthes argued that this perspective could be applied beyond language (in the narrow linguistic sense) to a broad range of semiotic systems. Barthes's *Mythologies* (1973) was a significant text here in demonstrating how it was possible to read cultural forms as widely diverse as wrestling, toys, soap powders, the Eiffel Tower, and motorcars as texts.

This notion of text developed into a pan-disciplinary concept that encompassed any cultural object of investigation, including the full range of media (visual, aural, and corporeal), ritual spectacles and social activities (from presidential inaugurations and wars to sports and shopping), commodities, and spaces (from shopping centers to cities). In literary studies all genres of writing – such as the lyric, the novel, plays and their performances – are now referred to as texts for purposes of analysis. All of these enterprises are seen as aspects of a general **textuality** and as forms of **textual practice**. Moreover, many **cultural texts** are recognized to be multi-media forms in which language is only one dimension.

These notions of text and textuality have redefined some of the most basic assumptions in the academy about the nature of cultural objects, how they work, and the nature of critical activity itself. The first is commonly encapsulated in the notion of **intertextuality**, first introduced in the eC20 to highlight the enabling linguistic features shared by all texts, and extended by Russian Formalist critics to the study of literary systems. The notion was taken up later by Julia Kristeva (1970), Roland Barthes (1971, 1975), and Jacques Derrida (1976) as a radical rethinking of the **contextuality** of texts. Any text is always quite literally a weaving together of other, similarly interconnected, texts. Thus, rather than having a single or stable meaning somehow embodied in its structure or in the "words on the page," the text is engaged in a continuous play of meaning across the field of intertextuality. Consequently, at the very least, meaning is mobile, dispersed, and plural, since any text is always subject to the incessant movement of **recontextualization**. At the same time, both Barthes and Derrida were concerned with demonstrating how the potentially infinite mobility/dispersal of meaning is always constrained and limited in practice by the act of writing and reading.

These concepts of text and textuality have enabled cultural theorists to challenge the assumed separation of an empirically available, non-linguistic material world from its representations in linguistic and non-linguistic (for instance visual) texts. The concepts have provided powerful arguments for an understanding of texts as forms of representation which actively construct and do not just reflect reality. Derrida's often-reported statement that "there is nothing outside the text" is commonly offered as evidence of the idealist denial of material reality. In fact, the statement, more properly translated as "the text has no outside," points to the intertextual and non-referential nature of the production of meaning. But it still remains true that the theory of texts and textuality has led the charge against most forms of realist epistemology and ontology, in the name of a radical theory of linguistic (or discursive) mediation and construction.

The consequences of such a theory for the critic are immense: no longer able to "read" the meaning in "the words on the page," critical activity becomes a creative activity of recontextualization, thus making the critic as much responsible for the production of meaning as is the originary text or author. The line between creative and critical work all but disappears, as both become part of the larger human processes of language and meaning production.

Terry Threadgold

See: *REPRESENTATION, SIGN, WRITING.*

Theory

In its modern sense the word **theory** probably entered English from medieval translations of Aristotle. Etymologically it has the same root (*theoros*, spectator, from rw *thea*, sight) as the word *theatre*: Gk *theoria* is a sight or spectacle, and the literal sense of looking has then been metaphorized to that of contemplating or speculating. In English too there is an early and now obsolete sense of a sight, a spectacle, or a mental view or contemplation. But the major line of development in English deploys theory in contrast to "practice" or "application," to mean "a conception or mental scheme of something to be done, or of the method of doing it; a systematic statement of rules or principles to be followed" ("Your theories are here to practice brought, As in mechanic operations wrought," Dryden, 1674; "A theory that will not admit of application cannot possibly be just," Malthus, 1798). In a more general philosophical and scientific sense, a theory is:

> a scheme or system of ideas or statements held as an explanation or account of a group of facts or phenomena; a hypothesis that has been confirmed or established by observation or experiment, and is propounded or accepted as accounting for the known facts; a statement of what are held to be the general laws, principles, or causes of something known or observed.

Central to this definition is the notion of the systematic relations holding between the components of an explanatory model, and the differentiation of theory from the more tentative conception of a hypothesis. A modification of this sense, however, makes theory mean something like "hypothesis" or even "unfounded speculation," as in the phrase **in theory** (as opposed to "in practice" or "in fact"). Thus Burke (1792): "Whether I am right in the theory or not, ... the fact is as I state it"; and James Mill (1829): "The word theory has been perverted to denote an operation ... which ... consists in supposing and setting down matters supposed as matters observed. Theory in fact has been confounded with hypothesis."

The account of **scientific theorization** in the C20, dominated by the logical positivism of Rudolf Carnap (1969), Karl Popper (1986 [1934]), and others, attempts to reduce the speculative dimension of theorization by requiring the use of rigorous correspondence rules between observation statements and **theoretical meta-languages**. A more positive view of theory, particularly in the social sciences, however, has stressed that observation statements in the natural sciences are always theory-laden and are meaningful only in relation to a particular theoretical framework (Giddens, 1974). The sharp distinction between theory and observation was criticized from the 1960s onward by philosophers such as Hilary Putnam, Imre Lakatos, and Paul Feyerabend, by historians and sociologists of science such as Thomas Kuhn (1970), and by critical theorists such as Theodor Adorno and Jürgen Habermas. In the Hegelian and Marxist traditions theory is understood not in opposition but in dialectical relation to practice (or, more abstractly, praxis): on the one hand, theory is grounded in and shaped by material social institutions, relations, and practices; on the other, the point of **theoretical activity** is not to observe the world but to transform it.

In contemporary usage in the humanities and social sciences, "theory" designates less any particular set of systematic ideas than a politically contested attitude toward the use of abstract explanatory models in humanistic and social inquiry. This usage goes back to the movement from the late 1960s onward to incorporate European thought in a range of fields, including linguistics, anthropology, philosophy, semiotics, psychoanalysis, and Marxism, into Anglo-American disciplines of knowledge, particularly literary studies, sociology, and political philosophy. This movement was not an appropriation of European philosophy as such; rather, it was directed to forms of thinking in the social and human sciences which had been strongly shaped by the model of structural linguistics. These paradigms had at their core some of the following principles: the relationality of elements in a system without positive terms; hence, an emphasis on relations rather than substances; the modeling of non-textual entities on text; the notion that systems are constructs of the analysis, and the building of the observer into the system; and (in the poststructuralist phase) a conception of systems as open-ended and temporal. But these core principles have merged with others drawn from a wider sphere of poststructuralist and "postmodern" thought, including phenomenology and hermeneutics, to form the shifting conglomerate known as theory.

What makes this a recognizable and more or less coherent entity is not, to any significant degree, its content but rather its institutionalization through programs of translation (for example, by New Left Books from the 1960s onward), of popularization (for example, through the Methuen/Routledge New Accents series), and of positions taken in the **theory wars** of the decades from about 1970, which pitted traditionalists against those defined as defenders of "theory" in the university curriculum and in intellectual life more generally. Paul de Man (1986) defined this **resistance to theory** as a resistance to the use of a meta-language concerned not, in the first place, with meaning and reference but rather with the operations that make them possible. But in a broader sense this resistance was a displacement both of political antagonisms and of tensions over the transition from an elite to a mass university system (and the accompanying professional-ization of the academic career).

If theory was, on the whole, victorious in these wars, it has, like all victors, taken on much of the coloring of the conquered population, and has entered into a compromise which guarantees its formal authority at the expense of substantial, but tacit, concessions to its opponents. It is not certain that this victory was not a defeat, and the mood of its erstwhile proponents is perhaps best summed up in book titles such as *What's left of theory?* (Butler, Guillory, and Thomas, 2000).

John Frow

See: *EMPIRICAL, INTELLECTUAL, KNOWLEDGE, OBJECTIVITY, RELATIVISM, SCIENCE.*

Therapy

Therapy implies the treatment of disorders and diseases, both mental and physical, combining a notion of service and attention with that of cure. In the C20 it came to have a particular place in the life of the West. There are hundreds of different kinds of therapy, ranging from forms of **psychotherapy** to **occupational therapy** (rehabilitation through the practicing of work-related tasks like the making of stools, often associated with a stay in a psychiatric hospital in the 1950s–70s) to **art therapy** (the expression of unspeakable emotions through art), **drama therapy**, and **family therapy**, based on a systems approach to family communication and interaction. **Therapeutic communities** are psychiatric institutions offering forms of **group therapy** to inhabitants, who stay there for a prolonged period. More recently, the term "therapy" has been used for New Age practices such as **crystal therapy** or types of massage such as **aromatherapy** (or simply **massage therapy**). It has also been applied to medical treatments such as **chemotherapy**, the use of toxic chemicals to treat cancer, and **hormone replacement therapy**, the use of estrogen and progesterone to treat symptoms of the menopause.

Therapeutic approaches to the possibility of treatment of patients in insane asylums were introduced in the eC20, the best-known of which is **electro-convulsive therapy** (**ECT**), in which electric shocks were administered to patients suffering from psychotic conditions. Though ECT is still widely used, many consider it inhumane and advocate its replacement by **drug therapies** and **psychotherapy**. However, the rapid rise in both the proliferation of kinds of therapy on offer and the use of the term "therapy" has been understood by some as using therapy to replace the confessional (Foucault, 1980), or more generally to be part of the "psy-"sciences (psychology, psychiatry, psychoanalysis, psy-chotherapy [N. Rose, 1985]) through which people are enjoined to work on themselves to become the rational, unitary subject of liberalism through a regime of understanding their interiority, especially their emotions.

Therapy

Many psychoanalysts have argued that psychoanalysis, for example, is not therapy, thereby differentiating it from a notion of the normative judgments of the psy-sciences and cure. For psychoanalysis, "making people better... is a subsidiary exercise, something which may or may not come about" (Frosh, 2002: 10). However, psychoanalysis formed the original and most pervasive basis of **psychotherapy**, and psychoanalytic-based therapies developed different trajectories in Britain, continental Europe, and the USA, for example. During the 1960s, a turn to humanism saw the rise of various types of therapy aimed at uncovering the "true self." In this light many forms of **radical therapy** were understood as aiding a process of liberation. Similarly, feminism also turned to therapy, proposing that the oppression of women resulted in damaging psychic as well as social consequences for women. A continental anti-humanism challenged the very idea of liberation, and certain French psychoanalysts, in particular Jacques Lacan, opposed the therapeutic direction of American psychoanalysis and what was understood as the propping up of the ego in support of liberalism.

In keeping with the classical assumption of emotions as part of the irrational or unreason, various cognitive psychotherapies aim to provide rational bases for behavior, such as **cognitive behavior therapy**. **Narrative therapy** is "founded in the idea that people's lives and relationships are shaped by the performance of meanings that are not reflections of some inner reality but are expressions of hierarchies of cultural knowledges (discourses)" (Byrne-Armstrong, 2002: 22).

Therapy has been extended to any activity which aims to make one feel better, so that consumers in affluent countries can partake of **retail therapy**, indulging in a shopping spree understood as a means of massaging a fragile identity by helping consume it into being. If any activity which makes a person feel good and cared for can be understood as **therapeutic**, therapy can be understood not only in terms of Foucault's confessional but also as an indication of the replacement of practices of caring within families and communities by a set of professional relations purchased in the marketplace. Rose (N. Rose, 1999: 90–1) argues that therapy has become the prime marker of a neo-liberal economy of population management through techniques and practices of self-management:

> Encounters in a diversity of sites that used to be governed by their own codes and values now take a broadly therapeutic form – not just the client's visit to the counsellor, the patient's encounter in the doctor's consulting room or the ward group of the psychiatric hospital, but also the worker's interview with the personnel manager, the parent in debt who visits the Citizens Advice Bureau, the consultation with the lawyer over divorce and child custody.

Everyday life has now been transformed so that everyday circumstances, such as debt, marriage and divorce, changing jobs, giving birth, become the object of clinical reason in which "psychological forces of denial, repression, lack of psychosocial skill are played out, scenarios whose unfolding is dependent upon the level of our self-esteem, affairs whose psychological consequences – neurosis, stress – are as significant as their practical outcomes, occasions for the exercise of interpretation, diagnosis, confession, insight and reformation" (N. Rose, 1999: 90–1).

Chat shows and confessional forms of television can also be understood as blurring the boundary between the public and the private, the confessional and therapeutic. Together with the popular fictional forms which surround us, they provide psychological narratives of our selves and our lives. **Therapeutics** suggest the possibility of the rational overcoming of unhappiness, so that the possibility of a fulfilling and contented life is understood as operating on the basis of a set of norms and practices of self-improvement. In this way, we could be understood as existing within a culture in which therapy forms a central trope through which we are invited to understand ourselves and our everyday relations and practices.

Valerie Walkerdine

See: *EMOTION, SELF, UNCONSCIOUS.*

Time

The English word **time** (like the cognate *tide*; cf. German *Zeit*) derives from Old Teutonic *tî-mon*, from *tî*, to stretch, extend, plus the abstract suffix *-mon* or *-man*; its ultimate root is an inferred Proto-Indo-European word *da(i)*, to cut or divide. The OED defines three broad areas of meaning:

351

> I, "A limited stretch or space of continued existence, as the interval between two successive events or acts, or the period through which an action, condition, or state continues; a finite portion of 'time' (in its infinite sense)" [that is, sense III]; II, "time when: a point of time, a space of time treated without reference to its duration"; III, "indefinite continuous duration regarded as that in which the sequence of events take place."

The fact that each of the key defining terms here either presupposes a concept of temporal duration ("continued," "successive," "period," "duration") or spatializes time ("stretch," "space," "interval," "point") exemplifies the difficulty of apprehending time as a concept in its own right. Ordinary understandings of time may think of it as the flow of events past an immobile observer, or as the background against which events occur, or as a point moving through a stable medium; but these "events" and this "point" disappear as soon as we try to grasp them. A physicist might define time as being made of a linear continuum of instants each of which lasts for zero seconds. The time with which we are most familiar in our daily routines – **clock time** and **calendar time** – is based on spatial measurements (the movement of a hand around a dial, the motions of the earth and sun), and it is arguable that all definitions of time, even the most dynamic, are ultimately reducible to spatial metaphors. One way of thinking about time, then, would be to see it not as an entity or a unitary process but as an ensemble of the measuring systems used to co-ordinate the infinity of state-changes which occur concurrently but with different speeds and durations (where the concepts of a *state* and a *change of state* refer, however, not to real events but to perceived or constructed discontinuities in the flow of the world).

Just as the concept of space is an abstraction from its concrete content, the concept of time is an abstraction from processes of change. Early Greek – and indeed all subsequent – philosophy is dominated by the contrast between a **timeless realm of Being** (which includes the idea of time and for which the model is mathematical number) and a **temporal realm of change**. Where Heraclitus stresses the fluidity of everything and the irreversibility of becoming ("you cannot step twice into the same river"), Zeno's paradoxes (Achilles can never overtake the tortoise, the arrow can never arrive at its destination) posit time as infinitely divisible in the same way that space is. For Aristotle, time is relative to but not identical with motion: it is the numerical aspect of motion with respect to earlier and later. It is in early modern science, however, that the concept of a **transcendental time** is most coherently expressed. Newton writes, in a gloss to *Principia mathematica* (1966 [1687]: 6), that "absolute, true and mathematical time, of itself, and by its own nature, flows uniformly on, without regard to anything external. Relative, apparent and common time is some sensible measure of absolute time (duration), estimated by the motions of bodies, whether accurate or inequable, and is commonly employed in place of true time." Lewis Mumford (1934) has related such notions of an **absolute time** to the appearance around the end of the C13 of the mechanical clock, which "disassociated time from human events and helped to create the belief in an independent world of mathematically measured sequences." By contrast, the phenomenological tradition that perhaps begins with Immanuel Kant's definition (1982 [1784]) of time as one of the *a priori* forms of inner sense, and is continued in Edmund Husserl's (1991) elaboration of a synthetic **time-consciousness**, in Martin Heidegger's grounding (1996) of human being in **temporality**, and in Henri Bergson (1991 [1896]) and Gilles Deleuze's (1994) attempt to theorize a duration which is not reducible to the **spatialization of time** as a succession of discrete instances, seeks to understand time as a matter of lived experience. The belief in a **uniform and homogeneous time** is also undermined by the theory of relativity, which posits that gravitational differences affect time by dilating it; rather than a universally valid order, it posits that every frame of reference has its own particular time.

The human experience of time is grounded in the interplay of two complex natural systems. The first is that of the planetary cycles: the rotation of the earth on its axis, giving rise to the regular alternation of day and night; the rotation of the earth around the sun, giving rise to the year and the seasons; and the rotation of the moon around the earth, giving rise to the lunar month and to the tides. The second is that of the human body, the temporality of which – its rhythms of growth and entropy – give rise to a sense both of irreversibility and of cyclical renewal. The human body is regulated by more than a hundred biological clocks, which in turn are co-ordinated by one or two master clocks monitoring a number of different rhythms: the tenth-of-a-second oscillation of brainwaves, the 1-second cardiac rhythm of systole and diastole, the 6-second respiratory cycle, the 24-hour circadian rhythms of metabolism, digestion, and the sleep–wake cycle, the 28- to 30-day rhythms of the menstrual cycle, the season-by-season circannual rhythms, and the reproductive rhythms of the generation and the lifetime. But these two systems are not separate: circadian rhythms are triggered by signals from the retina about levels of light, which travel by way of the hypothalamus to the pineal gland, which in turn releases hormonal secretions to regulate the body's functions. Calendar times (the day, the month, the year) are all grounded in the relationship between the human body and the planetary cycles.

Beyond these groundings, however, time takes on a fully social existence. We can distinguish between quantitative and qualitative forms of notation. Clock time and calendar time are historically constructed systems which impose a uniform and, in principle, universally applicable measure of duration onto the "natural" cycles (Aveni, 1990; Cipolla, 1977). These systems have, however, always been contested: calendars have characteristically been instruments of imperial rule, and there has been a long and complex politics associated, in the Western world, with the attempt to standardize the calendar and to impose a fit between the lunar months and the solar year. **Greenwich Mean Time** and the division of the world into standard **time-zones** similarly reflect the history of political struggle between nation states. Clock time, the division of the day into 24 hours of equal length, was not used in civil life until the C14 (the Roman "temporal hours" divided the periods of light and darkness into 12 hours each, the length of which varied according to the time of year); and the historical shift from the regulation of work by the rhythms of the day, the season, and the task to **timed labor** and the forms of discipline associated with it were, as Le Goff (1982), Thompson (1993), and others have shown, central to the ways in which industrial capitalism treated time as a scarce resource ("time is money," time can be "wasted") and as a weapon of control of its workforce.

Qualitative modes of notation of time, finally, are those forms of apprehension which distinguish between the different speeds, intensities, and durations of **social time**. Time may be full or empty, repetitive or teleological, cyclical or linear; it is shaped by memory and expectation, by the narrative structures that we give to experience and events, by the distinctions we make between moments of high intensity and moments of "humanly uninteresting successiveness" (Kermode, 1968: 46). Our sense of **historical time** – the time of a world of events larger than our individual lives – depends upon a sense of the shaping of **collective time** in relation to a transcendental order of things, or as a linear progression toward a predestined end, or as a bundle of heterogeneous **time-curves**; it is continuous or discontinuous, expanded or compressed, a smooth flow or a series of disconnected transitions. Time in this sense makes sense of human existence, or fails to; it is a dimension not just of measurement but of our apprehension of the order of the world.

John Frow

See: *HISTORY, MEMORY, NARRATIVE, SPACE.*

353

Tolerance

Ordinarily when we talk of **tolerating** something, be it a practice, a belief, a movement, or behavior, we mean that we should permit or allow it, and not prohibit, persecute, or otherwise interfere with it. **Tolerance** implies that we disapprove of the thing in question and have the power to stop it, but for some reason choose to exercise self-restraint. The L *tolerare*, from which "tolerance" is derived, connotes this idea of forbearance. If we approve of something, we respect and welcome it and the question of tolerating it does not arise. If we disapprove of it but have no power to do anything about it, we acquiesce in or put up with it but cannot be said to tolerate it. We do not tolerate but suffer or put up with bad weather.

Yet this distinction cannot always be so clearly drawn. For in other aspects of its use, "tolerance" implies precisely the ability to withstand what cannot be avoided – as in "the tolerance of Christ's Cross" (1650–3). There are also connections between this usage and the medical sense of tolerance as the ability to absorb drugs and medication in large doses without noticeable effect – an increasing **drug tolerance** thus occasioning the need for larger dosage. A sense of "tolerance" related to the notion of limits is also found in engineering – as a synonym for "margin of error" in manufacturing processes, for example, or, in broadcasting, the **frequency tolerances** of airwave bands. These connotations of limits and edges also inform the political usage of "tolerance." For it is through debates about the forms of belief and behavior that can or should be tolerated that social thresholds of acceptability are marked and organized.

Agents of tolerance can be individuals, organizations, or governments. An individual might strongly disapprove of gays or lesbians, or members of other religions and races, and has the power, if she or he chooses to exercise it, to shun them, ridicule them, deny them jobs, or refuse to work with them. Tolerance consists in not exercising such power. What is true of the individual is also true of organizations. Since the government has the right and the power to ban and suppress beliefs and practices which individuals and organizations do not have, the question of **toleration** is generally raised in relation to it (King, 1976). Unlike "tolerance," which is generally used in relation to individuals, "toleration" is used to refer to government policy. In English as in some other European languages, **tolerationism** (F *tolérantisme*) was sometimes used to refer to a moral or principled commitment to the policy of toleration, but this usage has long disappeared.

The question of tolerance can arise in relation to almost any human activity. We might disapprove of those who talk loudly, dress badly, eat with both hands, walk clumsily, or eat meat. Since such activities are legion, every society generally puts up with most of them. And when it takes note of some, it does not think it wise or prudent to ban them. By and large it seeks to discourage or ban those that in its view affect its survival and identity.

In most societies three sets of activities tend to arouse the greatest concern and have been a subject of heated debates. They are sexuality, religion, and politics. Sexuality affects the most intimate areas of life including the family and gender relations, which is why almost all societies are deeply divided on whether or not to tolerate polygamy, cohabitation, homosexuality, abortion, and sodomy. Religions engage people's deepest beliefs and involve claims of absolute truth, which is why their followers ask why they should tolerate rival religions or alternative interpretations of their basic beliefs. Politics affects the social order and the prevailing structure of power, and societies have debated whether or not to tolerate millenarian, anarchist, communist, and other groups. Historically speaking, religion, which shapes the attitudes to sexuality and politics, has been one of the most intractable and tenacious sources of **intolerance**. Not surprisingly much of the discussion of tolerance since the rise of Christianity in the West has centered on it.

Critics of toleration in the religious and other areas of life argue that it is a form of moral cop-out. Not to prohibit what one disapproves of and has the power to stop is to condone and even to be an accomplice to an unacceptable practice (Wolff, Marcuse, and Moore, 1969). Error or evil has no rights, and hence no claim on our indulgence or self-restraint. Advocates of toleration reject this view.

First, we cannot be absolutely certain that we are right and others wrong. And even if we are in possession of the absolute truth, we have no non-circular way of demonstrating it. This was one of the main arguments advanced by John Locke and Pierre Bayle in favor of **religious tolerance**, in the C17, and it greatly influenced liberalism. Second, even if we disapprove of others' beliefs and practices, we have a duty to respect their right to live by their sincerely held beliefs. Third, even if others are wrong, they should be left free to discover it for themselves. This argument has a particular force in relation to religion, which is a matter of voluntary assent and cannot be coerced. Fourth, tolerance generates the goodwill, gratitude, and loyalty of the tolerated, and leads to a peaceful and stable society. Finally, tolerance tests and intensifies our commitment to our beliefs and practices, for we follow them even when alternatives are available to us.

Writers on the subject have often asked whether tolerance should be extended to the **intolerant**, and have answered in a qualified affirmative (Mendus, 1989). Since tolerance is an important value, it should be extended to all. "The only true spirit of tolerance consists in our conscientious toleration of each other's intolerance" (Coleridge, 1809–10). And since a liberal society must live by its values and not those of its enemies, it owes it to itself to tolerate the intolerant (Waldron, 1993). However, if there were a serious and well-established danger that the intolerant might come to power and put an end to the practice of toleration, we might rightly refuse to tolerate them in the interest of toleration itself.

Bhikhu Parekh

See: *FREEDOM, FUNDAMENTALISM, HUMAN RIGHTS, LIBERALISM, SEXUALITY.*

Tourism

Tourism is often perceived as epitomizing modern sensibilities, a quest for authenticity and otherness, and a sustainable industry. Although the term tourism (cf. F *tourisme, -iste*) dates from the C19 (1811), the phenomenon of **touring** or traveling for recreation accompanied the development of transportation and exploration in the Near East as early as 3000 BCE and earlier in the Far East (Feifer, 1986). Indeed, Plato thought that touring was "rather too common" (Ogilvie, 1937: 661). While early recreational travel was difficult, the desire to travel gained in popularity. From 1500 BCE, "sure signs of tourism, of travel for simple curiosity or pleasure" were evident in Egypt, with travelers bringing back souvenirs and artifacts, turning Egypt into "a veritable museum" (Casson, 1979: 32). The phenomenon escalated in ancient Rome, accompanied by the development of an accompanying infrastructure and generating significant revenue. The popularity of touring grew. Subsequent centuries saw well-to-do travelers joined by pilgrims, clergy, students, and journeymen who combined travel for other purposes (spiritual, educational, employment) with "travel for pleasure" throughout the Middle Ages and the Renaissance (Perrottet, 2002).

The modern definition of tourism appears neutral: namely, the theory and practice of touring; traveling for pleasure; the business of attracting tourists, providing accommodation, entertainment, and tours. However, its usage has pejorative connotations implying superficiality. The **tourist** is often contrasted with the **traveler**. The traveler is an independent, genuine explorer on a quest of discovery, while the tourist is temporarily on holiday, taking time out from everyday routines to sample, but not necessarily engage with, otherness. In fact, there are elements of both motivations in all travel experiences.

Genuine travelers are motivated by the search for authenticity through encounters with other people: questing to experience the exotic delights of other cultures or desiring to visit new sites and attractions. Travelers are depicted as "sensitive" and "enlightened," in contrast to the "vulgar," ignorant, uneducated tourist. Often, in "antiquity no less than in modern times," travel has been blamed for "the decay of manners" (Ogilvie, 1937: 661). As the phenomenon of traveling for pleasure has grown, so too has ambivalence about tourism. Reflecting this, travel writing is preoccupied with distinguishing authentic from inauthentic travel experiences (E. Cohen, 1988). Commentators suggest that the combination of ambivalence, individualism, otherness, pleasure-seeking, and consumerism render tourism the exemplary cultural practice in modern societies (Boorstin, 1973; Turner and Ash, 1975) or the postmodern condition (Urry, 2002).

Cohen identifies different tourist types in terms of their use of industry infrastructure: **drifters**, **explorers**, **individual mass tourists**, and **organized mass tourists** (E. Cohen, 1972). Most tourists venture forth in a **tourist bubble**, protected from too much discomfort and strangeness by varying degrees of home comfort and security. So, contrary to the belief that tourism broadens the mind, many **tourist experiences** paradoxically entrench ethnocentrism and xenophobia, reinforcing existing attitudes and fear of the unknown.

During the C18, the **Grand Tour** – travel around Europe by elites for educative purposes – became a mania. The nature of the travel experience changed accordingly, from an emphasis on the ear and the tongue as the means to learn and record experiences, to an emphasis on the eye and the art of observation. New techniques of witness and hearsay became the essence of travel – captured in the term "sightseeing" (Adler, 1989). As a consequence, tourism became dependent on packaging the spectacle, on making people, places, and things attractive to the eye of the tourist (Rojek and Urry, 1997). The invention of the camera allowed mechanical reproduction of travel highlights (commercial postcards or personal photographs) with a permanent record for nostalgically reliving experiences.

Despite the popularity of the Grand Tour, ambivalence toward the tourists remained palpable, and rose to a fever pitch in the C19 when Thomas Cook initiated his eponymous organized cheap tours for working people in the 1840s (Swinglehurst, 1982). **Cook's tours** (initially to Europe, later to America and the New World) prospered from the outset and Cook commercialized his business by developing new products, destinations, and "contra" deals (reciprocal exchanges of services or products) with suppliers (such as the railways). While some critics hoped that the "characteristic independence of Englishmen" would cause them to eschew such crass pursuits, they were appalled to discover that "the cities of Italy are deluged with droves of these creatures" (*cit*. Fussell, 1979: 32). Entrepreneurs were quick to exploit the demand. The number of ordinary people who traveled for pleasure rapidly increased, aided by new forms of transport, accommodation, guidebook, and destination. Tourism was now a significant **tourist industry**.

As tourism grew internationally, the term **mass tourism** was coined both to capture the size of the phenomenon and to register a certain ambivalence about the trend (Jakle, 1985). Along with the benefits came costs and diverse impacts – some good, some bad. For example, the focus of tourism on privileged travelers visiting less developed sites and less privileged people led to debates about the colonial and postcolonial character of modern tourism, especially the consequences of commodifying third world and indigenous people for the **tourist gaze** (Urry, 2002). Instead of economic riches, tourism produces imbalances between regions and peoples, exacerbated by the repatriation of profits by multinational companies. Related to these impacts, a raft of social, cultural, and environmental issues and impacts still await serious attention. Although internationally tourism has become a key sunrise industry (that is, a new industry to replace declining traditional ones), its boom-and-bust nature and sensitivity to fashion and adverse conditions (natural disasters, war, terrorism) make it a risky industry choice for governments even when they have few industry alternatives (Spain and Fiji, for example).

The continuing popularity of tourism leads commentators to declare that "we are all tourists now," insisting that distinctions between tourists, visitors, recreationists, and consumers are dissolving. As tourists become more sophisticated in their pursuit of new exotic or exciting experiences, some yearn to get behind the packaged fronts of tourism and seek out the backs, beyond the public facades (MacCannell, 1976). In response to the quest for authentic experiences, the tourist industry has developed a range of **alternative tourisms** (**adventure tourism**, **ecotourism**) and **niche tourism** (including **cultural, heritage**, **food and wine**, and **gay tourism**). These offer (apparently) customized experiences off the beaten track, seemingly reviving the romanticism of early touring experiences, yet failing to resolve the contradictions tourism entails.

Jennifer Craik

See: *COLONIALISM, CONSUMPTION, SPECTACLE.*

Unconscious

As early as St Augustine, we can find the idea that part of the mind is unavailable, or **unconscious,** to itself: "I cannot totally grasp all that I am...the mind is not large enough to contain itself: but where can that part of it be which it does not contain?" (Augustine, 1991 [400], *cit.* L. Whyte, 1959: 79). Already here the mind appears as not fully self-aware and, more enigmatically, as existing partly in another realm, which Freud would come to define as "ein anderer Schauplatz" or "another scene."

In *The interpretation of dreams*, Freud insists that "our Unconscious" is not "the same as the Unconscious of the philosophers" (Freud, 1953b [1900]: 614), yet there are numerous precursors for the idea of the mind's limited self-knowledge. From the C18 onward, as well as meaning "lacking the faculty of consciousness," as in "brute unconscious matter," **the unconscious** means "unheeding" (the mind not fully present to itself): "Unconscious we these motions never heed" (Blackmore, 1712). Gradually "the unconscious" comes to mean something demonic (the mind threatened by an unknown part of itself), which Kant refers to as "the dark ideas in Man" (Kant, 1797) or, for the Romantics, something fearful and poetic: "How excellent that the deepest depths of our soul are hidden in the night! Our poor thinking organ would certainly not be able to hear aloud such a soaring ocean of dark waves, without shuddering with anxiety" (Herder, 1778, *cit.* L. Whyte, 1959: 117). As early as 1827, the unconscious was being carried across the globe: "The unconsciousness is really the largest realm in the mind, and just on account of this unconsciousness, the inner Africa, whose unknown boundaries may extend far away" (Richter, 1827, *cit.* L. Whyte, 1959: 133). This link between the unconscious

ABCDEFGHIJKLMNOPQRST*U*VWXYZ

and unknown, threatening worlds will be picked up by Freud when, in order to convey his own limited understanding of female sexuality, he famously refers to it as the "dark continent."

By the C19 the unconscious has become linked to madness. We go mad if our minds reject what we cannot bear to think about – Schopenhauer wrote: "the exposition of the origin of madness... will become more comprehensible if it is remembered how unwillingly we think of things which powerfully injure our interests, wound our pride, or interfere with our wishes; how easily...we unconsciously break away or sneak off from them again" (Schopenhauer, 1969 [1819], *cit*. L. Whyte, 1959: 140). The unconscious also carries a powerful sexual gloss – the German physician C. G. Carus wrote of the unconscious as: "voluptuousness – which is nothing other than the communication of the most intense and vital stimulation of the unconscious sphere of the sexual system to the highest conscious sphere of the nerves" (Carus, 1846, *cit*. L. Whyte, 1959: 149).

Immediately prior to Freud, "the unconscious" becomes part of the language of dynamic psychiatry. The unconscious could be driving mental disturbance, whether as a store of hidden memories; a dissociated part of the personality; or a more "mythopoetic" realm, the site of delusions, possession, and trance. Gradually the unconscious starts to sweep up what is most disturbing or unknowable about mental life. William James wrote of "sleep, fainting, coma, epilepsy and other unconscious conditions" (W. James, 1891). In *The Aspern Papers*, Henry James writes of the "unconscious cerebration of sleep" (H. James, 1983 [1888]: 94).

Despite these precursors, it is Freud who systematically reconfigures the idea of the unconscious as it is most often understood today. "The Unconscious is the true psychical reality," and dreams were the "royal road" through which it could be reached (Freud, 1953b [1900]: 613). For Freud, the unconscious is first of all an assumption. As a principle of explanation, the idea of **unconscious motivation** allows the analyst to make sense of symptoms and dreams which otherwise appear meaningless (Freud, 1957b [1914]). The unconscious has to be "inferred" in exactly the same way as we infer that other people have minds like our own. This adds a ghostly dimension to the unconscious, which is therefore to be imagined not just as another scene, but as another person inside our own minds. Freud offers three accounts of the unconscious: topographically, it refers to something like a place, distinct from the **preconscious** (ideas capable of or on the threshold of consciousness) and from **conscious thought** (what we know we think); dynamically it refers to the activity of repression, which withdraws psychic intensity from ideas so that they lapse into **unconsciousness**; economically it refers to the quality of intensity carried by a particular idea. Thoughts in the unconscious are wholly distinctive in form, under the sway of the "primary processes," notably condensation and displacement, which give to the unconscious its character as "alien" and "incredible" to normal thought ("There are in this system no negation, no doubt, no degrees of certainty," Freud, 1957b [1914]: 186). In the unconscious are drives aiming for discharge ("instinctual representatives which seek to discharge their cathexis," 1957b [1914]: 186); these are usually attached to memory traces of childhood, thoughts which have become shameful or unserviceable in adult life and which therefore fall under the bar of repression.

Arguing against Freud, the French philosopher Jean-Paul Sartre insisted that it was logically inconsistent to posit a part of the mind of which the mind itself was unconscious. People who do not know their own motives are acting out of bad faith by choosing not to see something of which they are at some level aware. In David Archard's terms, "The Sartrean unconscious is that which is comprehended but which escapes knowledge. The Freudian unconscious is radically other to consciousness. For Sartre there can be no such radical heterogeneity in the mind" (Archard, 1984: 50). For Roy Schafer, Freud's unconscious is best translated into action language, as in "she did that unconsciously," instead of being posited as a mental space or entity. This involves a radical redescription, since it dispenses with the idea of an unknowable part to the mind, as well as with the traces of infancy both so central to Freud's theory: "while continuing to emphasize action in the unconscious mode, we shall neither engage in speculation about what is ultimately unutterable in any form nor build elaborate theories on the basis of unfalsifi-able propositions concerning mental activity at the very beginning of infancy" (Schafer, 1976: 10).

For the French psychoanalyst Jacques Lacan, arguably the most influential thinker on these matters since Freud, it is precisely the unknowable aspect of the unconscious which marks the radical nature of Freud's concept. For Lacan, psychoanalysis inverts the Cartesian cogito, "I think therefore I am," into "I am there where I do not think to be," "I am there where I am the very plaything of my thought." Accordingly, Lacan proposes to retranslate Freud's famous definition of the aim of the psychoanalytic cure, "Wo es war soll ich werden" – translated by James Strachey in the Standard Edition of Freud's works as "Where id was there ego shall be" – as "There where it was so shall I come to be" (Lacan, 1977). "Das Es" is the term which replaces the unconscious in Freud's second topography so as to distinguish the dynamic repressed from the merely unconscious. The translation of this term as "the id" has been criticized as a scientific (and Latinate) reduction of Freud's far more elliptical, ungraspable term, "the it." Along this path, and even further away from the Strachey translation, Christopher Bollas describes the analytic process as a kind of shared dreaming, an act of communication between one unconscious and another (Bollas, 1995).

Feminist thought has had a complex relation to the unconscious. For Juliet Mitchell (1973), in her path-breaking *Psychoanalysis and feminism*, the concept of the unconscious is crucial to an understanding of the little girl's internalization of the laws of patriarchy. For French psychoanalytic thinkers such as Julia Kristeva (1980), the unconscious be-comes the site of drives that are resistant to patriarchal symbolic forms. More recently, in an exchange with Lynn Segal over the constitution of female identity, Mitchell reiterates the point that "what makes psychoanalysis psychoanalysis is its contention that the unconscious operates *differently* from the conscious" (J. Mitchell, 2002: 223). The little girl may well be freer than Freud allowed in the way she identifies with caring or parental figures of either sex, but there will always be an intractable, often death-driven, and unknowable part of the mind. Some feminists argue that the unconscious is a politically obstructive concept since it suggests a limit to how far we can control our own minds and destinies; for others the idea of the unconscious acts as a crucial challenge to the coercive norms of social and sexual life.

In more popular political and cultural analysis, the unconscious can suggest invisible but unstoppable forces: "The populace of England were unconsciously on the rapid rise to protestantism" (Froude, 1858); the hidden but central philosophy of an epoch: "art will reflect the fundamental assumptions, the unconscious philosophy of its time" (K. Clark, 1949); and most recently, political motivations – "unconscious identifications" – of which the chief actors, the leaders of the Western world, may be dangerously unaware: "in their analyses and propaganda, they instinctively generate the necessary image of the enemy... it would be unwise to see this as a conscious process" (Lieven, 2002: 19).

Jacqueline Rose

See: *DESIRE, EMOTION, FEMINISM, FETISH, SEXUALITY.*

Utopia

Utopia usually refers to the imagination of a perfect society, based on the inventor's social critique of their own society, and often set in the future or in a world markedly different than the writer's. Coined by Thomas More in 1516 in his *Utopia* (1995 [1516]) and derived from a play on two Gk words, "good place" and "no place," "utopia" and its variants, **utopian** and **utopianism**, are almost always associated, even when the specific vision is considered appealing, with the impractical, the unrealistic, and the impossible.

Utopias and **utopian thought** take many forms, including the hundreds of intentional or separatist communities created in many countries. The best-known form is the genre of European and American literature, conventionally starting with Thomas More and including feminist writers such as Joanna Russ and Ursula K. Le Guin, that creates and peoples a distinct world in which the problems and limitations of the writer's existing world are exposed and overcome (Moylan, 1986). Contemporary scholars tend to distinguish between the commonplace and somewhat restricted definition of utopia as fictional place and the broader meaning of utopia as the wish for, description of, and attempt to create a better and good society. When treated as a general feature of human thought and practice, utopia and the utopian tend to be situated in a much longer history, pre-dating the publication of More's *Utopia* and extending beyond the parameters of Euro-American civilization.

Despite the fact that there is a great deal of "confusion about exactly what makes something utopian, and disagreement about . . . why it is important," "utopia" persists as a term which powerfully conveys the desire for "a better way of being and living" (Levitas, 1990: 2, 7). Utopias and utopian thinking contain a diagnostic and an imaginative component. On the basis of a critical diagnosis of existing political and social arrangements and the values which underlie them, **utopians** always offer alternative ideals and claim these are realizable, often describing new institutional arrangements for doing so. Typically, Western utopians find their contemporary society exploitative, authoritarian, unequal, and alienating, and seek to replace the ruling economic, political, military, social, and knowledge arrangements with ones which promote a harmonious, egalitarian, self-managed well-being. **Utopians** practice a politics of everyday life, placing a premium on inventing and describing social arrangements designed to create an environment in which latent capacities for individual happiness can be fulfilled. Notwithstanding the genealogy of the word, most utopians are distinguished by their willful insistence that the good society is not "no place," but one that we have the human and material resources to build in the present.

In the socialist tradition, the tension between the good place and the no place has been particularly acute. The C19 socialist thinkers Charles Fourier, Henri Saint-Simon, and Robert Owen, nominated as **utopian socialists** despite their rejection of the name "utopian," were notoriously dismissed by Karl Marx and Frederick Engels for being unscientific and naïve (Engels, 1962 [1892]). For Marx and Engels, these utopians failed to understand the primacy of capitalist society and its binary class antagonism and failed to accord the proletariat its appropriate historic role as revolutionary agent. Accused of misunderstanding historical materialism's basic assumptions about human nature, about historical development, and about large-scale social change, the utopian socialists were branded idealists both for their vision of a co-operative, pleasurable, and non-patriarchal society and for their presumption that people possessed the autonomy to imagine and construct small-scale versions of societies free from domination.

Historically, Marx and Engels were the most influential critics of utopianism and established the principal terms by which utopias and utopian thought are criticized (Geoghegan, 1987). The main line of criticism is suspicious of an individual's or group's ability to think and act independently of, and ultimately to transcend, the law-like dictates of the capitalist system.

At the same time, socialists, socialist feminists, and Marxists have been some of the utopians' greatest defenders and theorists. Herbert Marcuse spoke for many when he rejected the oft-heard epithet – that's "merely utopian" – as a management device designed to suppress critical thought and liberatory practice (Marcuse, 1969). Following Ernst Bloch (1995), the utopian is conceived as an active "principle of hope," found in various situations in which individuals and groups "anticipate" in thought or practice their rejection of the totality of the existing society and their dreams for a better one. While oriented toward the future, socialist and Marxist utopians are concerned with how to use everyday "resources of hope" (R. Williams, 1989) to defeat the omnipresent cult of "T.I.N.A. – There Is No Alternative" (Singer, 1999), and to establish an alternative reality principle in which "The dream is real ... The failure to make it work is the unreality" (Bambara, 1980: 126).

A multicultural radical tradition has long been absent from the domain of the utopian. The C17 "many-headed hydra" – commoners, prostitutes, prisoners, indentured servants, slaves, maids, pirates, sailors, runaways, and religious heretics – challenged the making of the modern capitalist world system, but has never been treated as a model of utopian thought and practice (Linebaugh and Rediker, 2000). The legacy of this exclusion has left us with a map of utopia that includes, for example, the English craftsman William Morris, but not the black worker Harry Haywood: numerous white separatist communities, but not one example of maroonage or run-away slave communities in the entire Americas. In 2002, the Second World Social Forum held in Porto Alegre, Brazil, met under the utopian banner, "Another world is possible." The participants, gathered to fight against neo-liberalism and globalization and for democratic globalism, were the contemporary inheritors of the C17 "many-headed hydra."

The other world Porto Alegre conjured, in words and deeds, replaces the fantasy of a common culture realized as a little nation, magically pre-established and founded on good rules given from above, with complex individuals centered in communities negotiating inevitable contradictions and a hostile environment. In this other world, there's a rich living history, filled with legends of people who can fly, end slavery, and also organize meetings and grassroots movements. In this other world, the instinct for freedom is the antithetical core of culture, where the seeds of opposition grow into something much more powerful than skepticism.

Avery F. Gordon

See: **MOVEMENTS, RADICAL, SOCIALISM.**

Value

The notion of **value**, according to some authorities, was once a simple and straightforward economic concept: " 'value' meant the worth of a thing, and 'valuation' meant an estimate of its worth" (Frankena, 1967: 229). But the very same authorities also note that the question of value was already debated in ancient philosophy, that Plato and Aristotle discussed it under the headings of the classical triad of truth, beauty, and goodness, and connected it with questions of justice, morality, virtue, pleasure, utility, and happiness (William, 1998). It seems fruitless, therefore, to be nostalgic for a time when this word had a simple meaning.

Much of the debate over value can be located in the division between the "lumpers" (who dream of an **ultimate value** and a **general theory of value**) and the "splitters" (who want to discriminate many different kinds of value). An equally compelling division is between those who think of value as a mode of judgment (estimation or **evaluation**) versus those who think of it as something like a drive or motivation, a symptom of desire and passionate belief. The most interesting discussions of value (from Plato to Marx to Derrida) pay homage to both sides of these divisions, and thus produce taxonomies of value that grow out of some fundamental postulate about the ultimate value of human life, the purpose of human existence, or the nature of goodness itself. If one starts, as Plato does in the *Republic*, with the assumption that the highest good available to human beings is a life of contemplation, then one will quickly develop a vertical **hierarchy of values** that puts manual work, the pleasure of the senses, or the thrill of athletic competition lower on the ladder. If one begins, as Aristotle does in the *Nicomachean ethics*, with a notion of

ABCDEFGHIJKLMNOPQRSTU**V**WXYZ

value as realized in activity and the development of the faculties, then one will develop a horizontal picture of value as differently realized in different sorts of beings: there will be a "species" goodness differentially associated with the warrior, the poet, and the bricklayer, or (even more fundamentally) with the ox, the cabbage, and the piece of marble. If one starts from Marx's assumption that the ultimate value of human life is productive, creative, liberated work, then a radical division unfolds between the sphere of **use-value** (the practical utility of materials and tools) and **exchange-value** (the fantasmatic realm of money, commodity fetishism, and abstract, alienated labor) (Bottomore, 1983a; Marx, 1976 [1867]). If pleasure is installed as the *summmum bonum* ("the highest good," as it is in hedonism and Epicureanism – see Frankena, 1967), all other forms of goodness (from the delight at a fair judicial decision to a convincing mathematical demonstration to a spectacular orgasm to a job well done) will be traced back to this fundamental source.

A useful way of schematizing **value talk** is to distinguish three varieties based on the classic divisions of philosophy into epistemology, ethics, and aesthetics (W. J. T. Mitchell, 1986). The "true," "good," and "beautiful" correspond to these divisions quite precisely, as do their respective social roles (the scientist, the moralist, and the aesthete). Value talk almost invariably ranks these in order, the most typical hierarchy placing ethics at the top, epistemology second, and aesthetics a distant third. When **aesthetic value** is promoted in this hierarchy, this is generally by means of an appeal to some argument that it improves moral sensibility, or reveals new truths, a strategy that maintains the basic hierarchy of value.

Although some theorists of value have attempted to separate the neutral description of evaluative processes from normative recommendations about what is truly valuable (B. H. Smith, 1988), it seems clear that every discussion of value is more or less explicitly grounded in some beliefs about what is or ought to be truly valuable. Value talk tends to become evaluative talk, and the venerable distinctions between **facts** and **values**, descriptive and normative statements, objective and subjective judgments, **absolute values** and **relative values**, qualitative and quantitative assessments tend to break down in practice. When employing these distinctions (each of which has an enormous literature behind it – see Frankena, 1967) it is best to keep in mind that facts are always mobilized for some purpose, descriptions are never free of bias, objective judgments are widely shared subjective judgments, absolute values are invariably relative to a society and form of life, and quantity becomes quality the moment that language intervenes with categories such as "good," "better," and "best."

This sort of relativism is sometimes attributed to a postmodern consensus that is deeply suspicious of claims to absolute, objective value. At moments of crisis (such as 9/11) absolute values tend to become fashionable, and confident judgments about "evil-doers" circulate unopposed. But skepticism and resistance to claims about absolute value are not unique inventions of postmodernism. Common sense, with its appeal to pragmatic, situational considerations, aligns itself with both sides of the absolutist–relativist struggle.

But there is more to be observed here than a mere pendulum swing between periods of "normalcy," when skepticism and relativism are affordable luxuries, and "states of emergency," when absolute values are asserted on all sides. There is also a venerable tradition of pondering the question of value in a historical, even an evolutionary sense. Value is seen as a human production that is both the goal and motor of human progress. Plato's conception in the *Republic* of the dialectic, Aristotle's notion of the unfolding of faculties, Rousseau's idea of the perfectibility of man, Nietzsche's (1969a [1887]) prophecy of the **transvaluation of values**, and Agamben's (1993) image of the "coming community" are all variations on a historical concept of value as the object of a quest undertaken by the human species as a whole. Images of utopia, of the classless society, of global villages and heavenly cities capture these ideas of **ultimate value** in vivid narratives. To the extent that these utopian visions of **supreme value** have the power to mobilize social movements, value must be placed right alongside geography, scarcity, technology, and genetic predisposition as a causal force in human history. Insofar as "value" becomes reified and deified as a *summum bonum*, hidden god, buried treasure, or El Dorado, it generates a **surplus value** that plays a key role in the dynamics of social history, whether for idealist crusades to repossess a Promised Land, or terrible atrocities in the name of purity, or (most likely) both.

W. J. T. Mitchell

367

See: *AESTHETICS, COMMODITY, NORMAL, OBJECTIVITY, RELATIVISM, TASTE, UTOPIA.*

Virtual

Taken to mean something that exists in effect but not in fact, something perceived as real, the concept of **the virtual** has from the late 1980s largely referred to simulation by technological means. Its most common use is in the term **virtual reality**. "The virtual" has come to denote the perception of the real as created (primarily) by digital, computer-driven means.

Dictionary definitions of "virtual" note it is most frequently used to refer to something that exists in the mind, is imaginary, or is created or simulated by a computer. The OED entry for "virtual" includes among the word's common uses something "That is so in essence or effect, although not formally or actually; admitting of being called by the name so far as the effect or result is concerned." The OED also offers a definition from computing: "Not physically existing as such but made by software to appear to do so from the point of view of the program or the user."

In contemporary usage "virtual" is often used as an adjective to denote something nearly true, as in **virtually certain**, meaning "almost certain." In the realm of technological practice there is reference to "the virtual" as a technological construct meant to convey via the senses and/or the imagination a sensation of reality. It is often used in connection with computer-generated visual media, as in "virtual reality." In the realm of cultural and critical theory "virtual" has served as a judgment about reality and authenticity of experience, characteristically in dualistic relationship with the real. In *Simulacra and Simulation*, for example, Jean Baudrillard (1994) categorizes the virtual as belonging to the category of simulation, of things not real and not reality, of representations that ultimately replace the real.

In either usage "virtual" is inextricably tied to the discourse of authenticity. It is conceptually connected to modernism and to changes in thinking about the original and the real brought about by the advent of recording technologies (beginning with the introduction of the telephone and the phonograph in the IC19, or possibly earlier with the invention of the printing press and mass production). One can find its expression in seminal texts like Walter Benjamin's "The work of art in the age of mechanical reproduction," in which the claim that the illusionary nature of photography and film is "the height of artifice; the sight of immediate reality has become an orchid in the land of technology" (1968: 235) resonates with contemporary experiences of digital technologies.

Increasingly through the 1980s one finds "virtual" used as a word modifying important cultural, social, and theoretical concepts. For example, an anthology edited by David Holmes (1997) includes essays on **virtual identity, virtual bodies, virtual worlds, virtual urban futures**, and the collection itself is titled *Virtual politics*. John Tiffin's and Lalita Rajasingham's book *In search of the virtual class* focuses on distance learning from the perspective that the classroom as a physical space may be replaced by "the effect of a class" (1995: 6), derived from students using networked computers to communicate with one another and an instructor. In his book *War in the age of intelligent machines*, Manuel de Landa (1991) coins the term **virtual war** to examine the mediation of the 1990s Operation Desert Storm by CNN. Such usage of the term "virtual" reflects its application as a means of denoting in shorthand the logic of simulation. Tracing a line from Benjamin's efforts to Baudrillard's writing, one can discern the extent to which development of technologies for the manipulation of sound and image blurred lines between reality, artifice, and perceived experience.

Baudrillard's conception of the virtual connected directly to the experience of the real via media technologies, but had little connection at the time to computer technology. And although one can find much earlier, pre-technological discussions of the virtual, such as the discourse about light and shadow, reality and fantasy, in Plato's "simile of the cave," or in the discourse of stereophonic sound in the 1950s and 1960s, its technological manifestations only became realized in the 1980s with rapid advances in computer and video technology. By the late 1980s one finds the conjunction of virtual and reality. Technologist Jaron Lanier is said to have coined the expression "virtual reality" in the late 1980s (Kelly, Heilbrun, and Stacks, 1989). Virtual reality (often abbreviated as "VR") in this sense is most commonly considered a visual construct, and its perception is experienced along spatial dimensions of width, height, and depth.

VR technology became closely associated with, and popularized by, the writings of cyberpunk authors like William Gibson and Bruce Sterling. In the early 1990s one finds a confluence of discourses in computer technology, science fiction, art, and social and cultural theory merging with popular discourses about technology and the future. The clearest manifestation of this merger occurred in films like *Tron* (1982), *Lawnmower Man* (1992), *Virtuosity* (1995), *eXistenZ* (1999), and *The Matrix* (1999). Howard Rhein-gold's popular book *Virtual reality* (1991) encapsulated the utopian vision of most VR discourse. In it, Rheingold notes the variety of uses to which VR may be put, from art and science to simulating ''sex at a distance ... [and] simulations so powerfully addictive that they replace reality'' (1991: 19). He closes the book with his hope that VR ''will be a new laboratory of the spirit'' (p. 391). Later writers have been more critical of VR, but have still shown a tendency to privilege technology as a means of mediating experience (Biocca and Levy, 1995; M. Shapiro and McDonald, 1992; Steur, 1992).

In the realm of art virtual reality is the site of a shift in perspective, from the artist-centered one developed during the Renaissance to a user-centered one particularly evident in immersive **virtual environments** like the CAVE, a multi-person, room-sized, high-reso-lution, 3D video and audio environment invented at the Electronic Visualization Laboratory at the University of Illinois at Chicago in 1991. As digital technologies have developed one finds the virtual a staple of visual creation. In film-making it has become commonplace since the mid-1990s to find actors inserted into previously filmed footage to provide a historical setting (*Forrest Gump*) or acting with digitally created characters (*Star Wars: Episode I*), and to have actors who died during production digitally added to scenes requiring their character's presence (Oliver Reed in 2000's *Gladiator*). In the military, medicine, and industry virtual reality is regularly employed as a means of providing training and practice. In real estate **virtual walk-throughs** of property are almost as common as ''for sale'' signs in front of homes.

369

Steve Jones

See: *INFORMATION, MEDIA, REPRESENTATION.*

Welfare

The original, and persisting, meanings of **welfare** have to do with the "condition of doing or being well," reflected in the salutation "Fare well." These were dominant until the eC20, when it turned to questions of collective conditions: the well-being "of members of a group or community...esp. as provided for or organised by social effort." Such communities could be nations (**the welfare of the people**) or a specific group within the nation (the laboring poor). In the transition to the C20, political conflicts in industrializing capitalist countries centered on the state's role and responsibilities in securing the **welfare of its citizens**, especially in conditions of "market failure." The creation of collective provision to manage the "social contingencies" of ill-health, unemployment, and old age meant challenging the dominant laissez-faire view of the relationship between state, economy, and individuals. This emphasized a minimal state, a free market, and the responsibility of all individuals to fend for themselves (or face the "workhouse test" if they needed public assistance).

In European, North American, and Antipodean countries, forms of collective provision were established which became identified as "welfare." These centered on the provision of pensions and other cash benefits to assist in periods of economic hardship. Some of these schemes were based on a model of social insurance in which contributions (from employees, employers, and the state) created entitlements. Others, usually described as assistance, relief, or aid, were conditional awards made to people ineligible for insurance benefits (typically the low paid or economically marginalized, or women/mothers). Collective provision of **welfare services** aimed at improving health (individual and public),

ABCDEFGHIJKLMNOPQRSTUV**W**XYZ

education, and housing also emerged. The term "welfare" came to be applied to these forms of collective provision, not least because, as Raymond Williams (1976) noted, the existing terminology of "philanthropy" and "charity" was saturated with associations of patronage, discrimination, and scrutiny of the poor by their "betters."

The motive forces for these developments have been much argued over. For some, they mark the spirit of progress: social concern driving social improvement in response to the evils produced by urbanization and industrialization. In contrast, others identify the new social movements of the IC19 (organized labor and feminism particularly) as forcing new responsibilities upon the state, requiring it to moderate the effects of unregulated capitalism. Still others emphasize the compromises constructed by "reluctant collectivists" who aimed to contain challenges that might otherwise have led to revolution, socialism, or some other fearful outcome. Whatever the combination of forces and interests, industrializing capitalist societies took welfare seriously – as the subject for investigation (through commissions and inquiries, and much of the early social sciences) and action.

The inter-war depression created renewed demands for the regulation of capitalism, and the protection of citizens from its vagaries and failures. The most dramatic response was possibly Roosevelt's New Deal in the USA, creating a program of public works, social insurance, and relief. Elsewhere, demands for a more active and interventionist state multiplied and bore fruit in the 1940s, 1950s, and 1960s in the construction of **welfare states**. This term referred to the perception of purposive, collective intervention in the well-being of the citizens of a country (since welfare states were nation states). It embodied a belief that social improvement could be planned and implemented across a range of conditions: employment, education, health, housing, and income (re)distribution. Welfare states were constructed in compromises that redrew the boundaries between state, market, and family. Policies and practices varied between nations – with the Nordic or "social democratic" model involving the highest levels of state provision, social reform, and redistribution. The "liberal," market-dominated US remained a relative laggard among leading capitalist societies in relation to the public provision of both benefits and services (Huber and Stephens, 2001).

During the 1960s and 1970s, it appeared as though welfare states were an integral feature of advanced capitalism in its Fordist or Keynesian phase. Welfare states helped to secure the social peace and political incorporation necessary to the untroubled pursuit of profit. It was expected that newly industrializing countries would build welfare states as they developed, while struggles in existing welfare capitalism aimed to expand welfare to include excluded groups, attack inequalities, and improve benefits and services. Consequently, the rise of the New Right was a surprise, given its profound anti-welfarism and anti-statism. Neo-liberal inheritors of laissez-faire argued for rolling back the state, setting markets free, enabling consumer choice in welfare services, and creating incentives to work rather than welfare. Neo-conservative inheritors of the Poor Law argued for the need to free people from dependency on the state, remoralize the poor, rebuild the family, and restore social values and authority. Welfare had moved from being a solution to social problems to being the cause of social problems. A work-shy, demoralized, and dangerous underclass was the welfare state's major accomplishment (Murray, 1984).

Welfare was constructed with a specific, and narrower, meaning in the USA (Schram, 1995). Welfare became predominantly associated with public assistance (Aid to Families with Dependent Children) rather than social security or **welfare provision** more generally. **Being on welfare** was identified with households headed by black lone mothers (**welfare queens**) in a particularly vitriolic, racialized, and gendered politics of poverty. The **end of welfare** (in 1996) produced a **workfare** system with punitive conditions about the moral and sexual behaviors of claimants (Mink, 1998).

Welfare remains a contested site. The principle of collective public provision is under threat from privatization, marketization, and globalization, and their articulation in neo-liberal politics (Yeates, 2001). State programs have been cut back or made more conditional while emphasis is placed on corporate, voluntary, and familial sources of pensions, services, and care. Nevertheless, such changes have encountered organized campaigns to defend welfare states, create new rights, and overcome the inequalities of "second-class citizenship." The idea of the welfare state provides a rallying point for political action in countries without such systems, and remains surprisingly popular with people in countries with them. Citizenship – as a basis for **welfare claims** – has emerged as a critical focus for conflicts within, around, and beyond the borders of nation states.

John Clarke

See: *CITIZENSHIP, POVERTY, RISK.*

The West

The West is a fairly recent mythical construct. Older uses of "west" or its equivalent in other languages indicated a direction or an area on a given political map, such as the west–east division of the Roman Empire in the mC3, the division of the Christian church into Western and Eastern from C11 (R. Williams, 1983: 333), the "New World" of the Americas perceived from Europe, or the oceans located furthest west of the Central Kingdom (China). However, the globalizing phrase "*the* West" came into general use only over the past two centuries as the capital originating in Western Europe came to be seen as omnipresent in colonial domination world-wide. "The West" supposedly unifies a group of people called **Westerners** in terms of their residential geographies, traditions, races, pedigrees, and shared civilization; it appears to be a proper name and this is often marked by a capital letter, as it is in this book. However, the term is notoriously slippery, and the unity that it affirms has increasingly been challenged in recent decades.

Used adverbially, "west" suggests a direction and often a movement towards a more or less vaguely indicated place: "There lies your way, due West" wrote Shakespeare in

Twelfth Night (1601). Associated with both the glowing color and growing darkness of sunset, "going west" is an old-fashioned phrase for death or disappearance ("dear old friends now 'gone west,'" 1915; "valuable evidence gone west," 1925), but it more powerfully carries in colonial contexts a utopian promise of space that is all the more alluring for being obscure: Henry Kingsley wrote in Australia of "splendid pastures, which stretch west farther than any man has been yet" (1859), while the famous injunction within the United States to "Go west, young man!" dates from 1851. These uses promote a fiction that "the west" is a definite place as well as a direction or an ever-receding frontier, making it easy to assume that the term can refer to a specific geographic region on the surface of the earth.

However, since the earth is a globe no single, stable location can lay exclusive claim to be west, since any point in the world can be so called from another. A global West can only be delimited within this mundane, universally available "west" if it is distinguished on non-geographical grounds from something *non*-west – the rest of the world, as in **the West and the Rest**. Here, the definition of "the West" is dependent upon how "the Rest" is determined: in 1297 "Engelond" is the far west of the world, but from the C16 and C17 an opposition between Europe and "Asia" or "the Orient" became active, with Orientalism emerging as a field of study and an aesthetic cult from the C18: "Once did she hold the gorgeous east in fee; And was the safeguard of the west" writes Wordsworth of Venice (1802). As these examples suggest, the West can be imagined as an identifiable cartographic referent only when the Rest is also thought of as fixed: "Oh, East is East, and West is West, and never the twain shall meet" sang Kipling erroneously (1892). Yet the **non-West** also moves according to context and political need: defined from the C11 as the Islamic world in contrast to either the Christian or the Greco-Roman West (R. Williams, 1983: 333), it could stretch from the Mediterranean to India and China; shrink to a single enemy ("in the West there seems to be an impression that the fleet of Japan is a mere matter of show," 1902); and, in the C20 and especially after World War II, flow back to Europe as a communism opposed to the non-communist "Western" states.

Even as a cartographic index, "the West" has little coherence. The majority of people living in Western Europe believe themselves to be Westerners, but at the same time many white people in South Africa and Australia insist they too are Westerners. Conversely, people of color in North America are not necessarily recognized as Westerners even if most residents in North America have claimed, especially since the end of World War II, that they too are in the West. So it may appear that the West is primarily a racial index rather than a cartographic one; it is closely associated with racial fantasies of whiteness. But this assessment is at odds with the historical fact that Eastern Europe has been generally excluded from the West, not only during the Cold War but throughout the C20. Moreover, the racial notion of whiteness is loose enough to allow groups who may be excluded from whiteness in some regions of the world – peoples from the Middle East, for example – to be recognized as white in East Asia or North America. As people move from one place to another, their racial identity may well change. Like the concept of race in general, whiteness as a social category is historically so arbitrary that it can hardly be an index of a stable identity.

However, "the West" as a mythical construct achieves powerful effects as it gathers varying and contradicting properties around itself; like the idea of the Orient, "the West" has "a history and a tradition of thought, imagery and vocabulary that have given it reality and presence" (Said, 1978: 5). Yet it is important not to forget that what we believe we apprehend by this myth is ambiguous and incongruous, precisely because "the West" is a reality whose supposed objectivity is globally accepted; as a mythic element it still regulates our hierarchical way of assigning a place to peoples and institutions on the world-historical map. Until a few decades ago, "the West" was unquestioningly used as a historical index to measure how modern a society might be in relation to another, thus mapping geographic location on to a historicist chronology of progress. Beyond as well as within the so-called developed countries, "modernization" *was* **Westernization**, and this formula made it possible to overlook painfully obvious problems with the idea that some societies run ahead of others and that the former are located in the West while the Rest lag behind. In fact every social formation contains things new and ancient just as it includes people young and old, but the fantasy of linear progress represses this complexity. Predictably, "the West" then serves as a norm of modernity against which something specifically local and **non-Western** is frozen in time as non-modern. This does not only lead to the simple denigration of the latter. Typically in ethnic nationalism, a "local" culture is valorized in systematic rivalry with the putative traits of the West.

374

Thus the West plays an ideological role in organizing desires in non-Western societies as much as in so-called Western ones. Until the 1980s many inhabitants of the Rest imagined the West to be the ideal marker of their future and the goal toward which their societies must progress. Recently, however, the power of "the West" as a social imaginary seems to be fading. An increasing number of young people are aware of "non-Western" aspects of societies in Europe and North America as well as of the "Western" aspects of life in many societies in the so-called non-Western parts of the world. It seems that, being neither as threatening nor as alluring as it once was, the figure of "the West" may be to some extent losing its grip on desires in many parts of the world in spite of its militant proponents – and the military might at their disposal.

Naoki Sakai and Meaghan Morris

See: *COLONIALISM, ETHNICITY, ORIENTALISM, RACE, SPACE.*

Work

Work has been part of human activity in all societies. Certainly this was Marx's view in *Capital*, in which work is defined as "purposeful activity aimed at the production of use-values'' and the ''appropriation of what exists in nature for the requirements of man'' (Marx, 1976 [1867]: 290). As such, work was only one aspect of labor. Engels tried to clear the matter up: ''The English language has the advantage of possessing two separate words for these two separate aspects of labor. Labor which creates use values and is qualitatively determined is called 'work' as opposed to 'labor.' Labor which creates value and is only measured quantitatively is called 'labor' as opposed to 'work' '' (Marx, 1976 [1867]: 138n.). Unfortunately, this distinction does not match up with everyday English usage. More common, and not only in England, has been an understanding that ''labor'' is something onerous. Thus Hannah Arendt observes that every European language, ancient and modern, contains two etymologically unrelated words for ''labor'' and ''work'' – Gk *ponein* and *ergazesthai*, L *laborare* and *fabricari*, F *travailler* and *ouvrer*, G *arbeiten* and *werken* – and that, in all these cases, only the equivalents for ''labor'' rather than ''work'' have an unequivocal connotation of pain and trouble (Arendt, 1998: 80n.). Whereas the distinction between work and labor has wide currency, it is not, however, universally observed. For instance, Tilgher tells us in the very first sentence of his classic treatise on the subject ''To the Greeks work was a curse and nothing else'' (Tilgher, 1931: 3).

Much current understanding of work contrasts the present situation to that before the mid-1970s, when people, usually men, had ''proper jobs.'' Proper jobs, also referred to as ''regular jobs,'' were typically full-time, had regular hours and regular pay, and were a product of full employment and a regulated economy. In fact, such jobs have by no means been a constant feature of capitalism. But for a limited period prior to the deregulation of the labor market in the last quarter of the C20, regular work was what work was widely regarded to be, at least in Britain. In retrospect this is evident from the opinion of Raymond Williams, who wrote toward the end of this period: ''Work is the modern English form of the noun *weorc*, oE and the verb *wyrcán*, oE. As our most general word for doing something, and for something done, its range of application has of course been enormous. What is now most interesting is its predominant specialization to regular paid employment'' (R. Williams, 1976: 218–19). Thirty years later, what is most interesting is that ''work'' does not automatically suggest regular, full-time, or even paid employment. Part of the reason for this is that work has itself been a contested concept. The battle to recognize **housework** as work, and therefore deserving of the same respect as waged labor, is one IC20 manifestation of this. Another rather more recent manifestation is the term **sex work**. This has begun to be more widely advanced to privilege the fact that prostitution is a way of earning a living over competing moral bases of assessment. However, the deregulation of the labor market has made for the most change. It has brought to prominence non-standard employment and the **hyphenated worker – part-time workers**, **temporary-workers**, **casual-workers**, and **self-employed workers** (Beynon, 1997: 31).

According to a major recent UK survey (R. Taylor, 2002), 92 percent of workers in 2000 held permanent contracts, and it is easy to exaggerate the extent to which the temporal and other aspects of work have changed (Millward, Bryson, and Forth, 2000). For instance, so-called **portfolio workers** are much discussed but a small minority, as are **tele-workers**. But the public perception is that employees may now find themselves subject to **contract work** (work for a specified period only) or to **agency work** (that is, employed by a party who contracts their labor to the employer for whom they work *de facto* but not *de jure*), or that they may be offered zero-hours contracts (jobs where the employer summons and expels labor at nil notice). Marx himself would no doubt have appreciated a new epithet to describe some of the worse examples of jobs that operate under these conditions – **shit work**. Another relatively recent description for the same type of work, often based in the expanding service sector, is **McJob**.

In the IC20 **deskilled work** came into fashion to refer to the consequences of the process whereby workers were deprived of control over their lives at work (Braverman, 1974). Later the idea of **overwork** gained currency (J. Schor, 1992) – a notion that sits well with the frequent discussion of work and stress, the widespread use of the term **workaholic**, and the introduction of a Japanese term, *karoshi* or death from overwork. This in turn has stimulated the emergence of another hyphenated work concept, **work–life balance,** which has also been partly prompted by the increased entry of married women into the workforce.

Side by side with concern that those who work are working too hard has come concern that no one should be **work-shy**. School-children enter into **work-experience** schemes to socialize them into the world of work. When people have been unemployed for a long time or require help to get into employment for some other reason, they may participate in a scheme that is part of a government **welfare-to-work strategy**.

The decline in the power of organized labor means that a once familiar term, **work stoppage**, is no longer commonly used in the media. Similarly, shifts in the occupational structure have meant a decline in **the works**, typically a factory. **Work-in** (a form of labor dispute typically engaged in by manual workers in the 1970s in an attempt to save their jobs) has given way to **work-out** (the practice whereby typically sedentary workers engage in physical exercise for the sake of their health or appearance). In a further semantic twist, **face work**, which once related to the work performed by miners in the bowels of the earth, now signifies the production of inauthentic smiles by flight attendants at 30,000 feet.

Theo Nichols

See: *CAPITALISM, ECONOMY, INDUSTRY.*

Writing

The OED defines **writing** as "the use of written characters for purposes of record, transmission of ideas etc.," "the art or practice of penmanship or handwriting," "callig-raphy," "literary composition or production," and "wording or lettering scored, engraved or impressed on a surface, inscription," "epitaph." Along the way, different **technologies of writing** are recognized: for example, "traced or formed with a pen" (1582), "typewriting'' (1883), ''writing'' as a process ''causing an item of data to be entered into a store or recorded in or on a storage medium'' (1970), as in **to write to a floppy disk or a CD**. The verb ''writing'' is used not only of the process whereby **written text** is produced to be read but also of that whereby musical notation, for example, is written to be played: ''the composition of music'' (1782). Writing is also used as a noun to mean ''that which is in a written state or form,'' ''something penned or recorded'': for example, **sacred writing** or Scripture, ''the work or works of an author or group of authors,'' ''a written paper or document, having force in law: a deed, bond, agreement or the like'' (in frequent use from the C15). The association of authorship with writing is historically and culturally important because it leads in the C19 to a notion of ownership of writing by authors, which becomes inscribed in copyright law and the new crime of plagiarism, meaning to steal someone's written words (D. Williamson, 1989).

The most common understanding of the significance of writing identifies it as a technique for the visible recording of language which enables the transmission of ideas across time and space and is a characteristic of complex forms of culture and society. The first known writing dates from C6 BCE. Writing is usually seen as a means of transcribing the transience of spoken language into a more permanent recorded form. **Alphabetic writing**, of the kind found in English, is based on the, in practice, unworkable assumption that one letter in the alphabet will represent one sound (phoneme) in the language. Phonetic alphabets of this kind are, however, only one form of writing. Ancient Egyptian hiero-glyphics, Mesopotamian **cuneiform writing** and contemporary Chinese and Japanese **character-based writing scripts** are other examples.

The link made above between speech and writing, in which writing is assumed to represent speech, makes writing a central component of the debates around the relationship between orality and literacy (W. Ong, 1982). The priority of speech in these arguments, the fact that speech always comes first historically, was what made it appear ''natural'' or ''common sense'' to think that cultures which lacked writing, and depended on oral forms of communication, were somehow inferior to, or more ''primitive'' than, so-called ''rational'' societies which had **writing systems**. William Ong's (1982) work, along with that of Jacques Derrida (1976) in a more philosophical context, set out to question these assumptions and the binary sets of values to which they gave rise – **speech/writing**, orality/literacy, primitive/cultured, irrational/rational – where the first item in each pair is always valued negatively in relation to the positive second term. Ong focused on rethinking the complexities of oral societies and oral forms of communication, and on trying to understand how the technology of writing produced new forms of social and cultural life. Derrida's argument was that we needed to develop a **science of writing** (or grammatology) which would stop seeing writing as a failed attempt to represent speech alphabetically, and would understand how the two systems of spoken and **written language** worked independently of each other.

Raymond Williams (1981) addresses these same issues from a cultural materialist perspective when he deals with the impact of writing on societies. For him, writing was an important means of production of culture, but significantly not a human or inherent means, as in the case for example of using language, or singing or dancing. Access to these forms is inherent in being a member of society. Everyone can talk, listen to music, or indeed look at and read visual images, but at the time when Williams was writing "still some forty percent of the world's present inhabitants [could] make no contact at all with a piece of writing" (1981: 93). Writing was related to the development of "complex amplificatory, extending and reproductive technical systems" (p. 90), which make possible new kinds of presentation of writing; television and the disk and cassette in popular music, cinema, sound broadcasting, video cassettes, and tape recorders are all examples of such systems. The development of writing and associated technologies were for Williams productive of "divisive" social relations (p. 92) and for a very long time associated with the equally divisive question of access to literacy, the ability to write and read written texts, which was only available to those with access to certain kinds of specialized training. As Williams (1981: 94–5) points out, it has only been since the IC19 in Western societies that a majority of people "have had even minimal access to this technique," which had, after all, by that time, been transmitting the major part of human culture for more than two millennia.

We could of course now add many more systems to those listed by Williams above: for example, the CD, DVD, mobile phones and tele-texting, e-mail and the Internet, and digital photography, to name just some. He had already realized that such systems as these were producing yet another crucial shift in the relations between a privileged literate culture and a general oral one (1981: 111). Such new forms clearly offer new modes of writing which to some extent seriously challenge the dominance of elite, written and printed public norms. These new forms certainly involve a new multi-modality that enables spoken norms to be written according to new codes of spelling and representation (texting on mobile phones, for example), and utilize the visual (for instance, digital photography) and sound/music as part of their common set of resources for writing with (for example, all mobile phones and computer technologies since the year 2000). For Williams, even the beginnings of these developments in 1981 were offering some kinds of cultural producers "some significant recovery of direct access to their means of production" (1981: 118), and that position is found replicated in much more recent work on new media, which talks of, for example, a "virtual public sphere" in which new kinds of political participation and new kinds of direct access to knowledge, and the power to make knowledge, are now possible (Atton, 2002; Rodriguez, 2001). It is also the case that "literacy," which used to be a term that meant almost exclusively the trained ability to write and read written texts, has been evolving to deal with these new modes of production and social relations. Thus, educational texts now speak of the need to teach multi-literacies which acknowledge these new hybrid forms of writing, communication, and meaning-making (Cope and Kalantzis,

2000). These same technological and social changes are unsettling the meanings of authorship and plagiarism, as evidenced in both the extraordinary legal complexities of attempting to deal with copyright law and the Internet, and the ease with which writers can now write (illegally still) using large chunks of ready-made text from the Internet.

Terry Threadgold

See: *COPY, NARRATIVE, REPRESENTATION, TEXT.*

Youth

Dictionary definitions of **youth** – the time of life between childhood and maturity, a person in that state – are straightforward, but one can make three immediate observations about them. First, youth is a sociological rather than biological category. The physical changes involved in human development have their own descriptive term, "puberty"; the associated psychological changes have been described since the eC20 as "adolescence"; and, in terms of actual age, "teenager", covering people from 13 to 19 (and first used in the USA in the 1940s), is a rather clearer label. Youth is a more flexible concept than any of these. Its meaning is more responsive to social change and more sensitive to political argument.

Second, in its C20 linguistic history, "youth" changed from being primarily a singular to primarily a collective noun. **A youth**, a rather dismissive term for a young man, became "youth," a social category that was as often used adjectivally – **youth culture**, **youth crime**. In its initial meaning, as the transitional stage between childhood and adulthood, "youth" described a state of incompletion. A youth was someone who wasn't yet fully formed, who lacked clear definition. By the end of the C20 "youth" described a way of being, an established social institution.

Third, this shift of meaning involved a rebalancing of youth's positive and negative connotations. The singular meaning – a youth is someone who is gauche, ignorant, and naïve – nowadays tends to be outweighed by the collective meaning – youth as vital, fresh, and free. And one aspect of this redefinition is that being young is no longer age-determined. It's not just that the transition from childhood to adulthood now lasts many

ABCDEFGHIJKLMNOPQRSTUVWXYZ

more years than puberty or even adolescence, but also that grown-ups can now be young too, as a matter of lifestyle.

The historian John Gillis argues that the origins of the contemporary meaning of youth lie in the lC19, when the transition from childhood to adulthood was first seen to be problematic (Gillis, 1974). What matters here is not so much the reasons for this (industrialization, urbanization, and the labor-market need for mass education lengthened the time of youth and disrupted the socializing activities of family and workplace) as the consequences. "Youth" came to describe a social problem, a source of urban crime and nuisance; youth became the object of new sorts of state institution, which themselves gave a new resonance to the term.

Youth clubs and **youth workers**, **youth employment** and **youth opportunities**, can be contrasted to **Young Farmers** and **Young Conservatives**, to football- and cricket-club youth teams, to media celebrations of **young musicians** or **young journalists**. For the state, youth isn't a junior version of something adult but a distinct social problem that can only be tackled by distinct institutions – **youth courts**, **youth prisons**, **youth services**. The policy issue is the failure of some young people to make the transition from childhood to adulthood. The problem of "youth" (who in this context can be distinguished from school and college students) is that they may embrace a permanent state of irresponsibility.

But even its earliest such uses, "youth," while usually describing a male, working-class group, wasn't simply referring to a state of destitution or ignorance. Irresponsibility meant not just crime but hedonism, and it was with reference to hedonism that an alternative account of youth emerged in the eC20, from the market rather than the state. Paula Fass argues that the term "youth culture" originated on US college campuses in the 1920s and 1930s (Fass, 1977). It was here that youth became viscerally associated with pleasure, self-indulgence, and physical qualities (health, vitality, beauty) which were both the object of new consumer goods (cosmetics, sport, dancing, the cinema, cigarettes, jazz, cocktails) and, even more importantly, the model for a new kind of consumer culture.

These two accounts of youth – as a policy problem, as an ideal market – got further confused in the 1950s and 1960s, when **youth hedonism** (particularly sexual hedonism) and **youth consumption** caused intense social anxiety (an anxiety eventually focused on drugs). For a moment in the late 1960s the attempts to regulate youth behavior and the apparent cross-class nature of youth culture gave the term "youth" itself a radical impetus. Youth was read as a challenge to existing norms of sexuality, domesticity, and bureaucracy; such an ideology of youth was articulated in a new cultural form, rock music. By the end of the 1970s, however, "youth" as a description of a market position was clearly more significant than "youth" as a description of a political position.

It sometimes appears nowadays that the meaning of "youth" as a state of transition has gone. The **youth market** has been pushed both up the age scale and down it. The most affluent **youth consumers** these days (labeled **yuppies** – a term based on an acronym for "young urban professionals" – in the 1980s) are, in fact, already established in adult work and relationships, while children in younger and younger age groups – pre-teenagers, pre-pubescents – are equally targeted as a market for fashion clothes, cosmetics, pop groups, computer games, sports merchandise. At the same time, though, youth matters to advertisers and media precisely because people's first market choices – of newspapers, designer labels, beers, cigarettes, banks – are expected to influence their life-long consumer habits.

The C20 contradiction in the meaning of "youth" – a problem of order, a model of consumption – remains obvious in the C21. Take, for example, media descriptions of African-American or Afro-Caribbean youth. They are routinely described as the most problematic social group (in terms of crime, employment, education, sexual responsibility) and the most fashionable youth consumers (in terms of clothes, style, music). Or observe the simultaneous media panics about youth pregnancy, abortion, and promiscuity and use of female youth as the visual ideal of sexual attractiveness and "freedom." "Youth" now describes contradictions rather than transitions, the contradictions of consumer capitalism rather than adolescence. Youth in this sense is more of a symbolic than a material concept. It is a term which expresses a market fantasy – the world of the advertiser and TV scheduler and magazine publisher – rather than accounting for the ways in which in the real world children still become adults.

Simon Frith

See: *FAMILY, GENERATION.*

References

Adas, M. (1989). *Machines as the measure of men: Science, technology, and ideologies of Western dominance*. Ithaca, NY: Cornell University Press.

Adas, M. (1993). The Great War and the decline of the civilizing mission. In L. Sears (ed.). *Autonomous histories, particular truths*. Madison: University of Wisconsin Press.

Adler, J. (1989). Origins of sightseeing. *Annals of Tourism Research*, 16(1), 7–29.

Adorno, T. (1991). *The culture industry: Selected essays on mass culture*. London: Routledge.

Adorno, T. (1997). *Aesthetic theory*. Minneapolis: University of Minnesota Press.

Adorno, T. and Horkheimer, M. (1972). The culture industry. In T. Adorno and M. Horkheimer. *The dialectic of enlightenment*. New York: Seabury Press.

Agamben, A. (1993). *The coming community*. Minneapolis: University of Minnesota Press.

Agamben, G. (1998). *Homo sacer: Sovereign power and bare life*. Stanford, CA: Stanford University Press.

Albrow, M. (1970). *Bureaucracy*. London: Pall Mall Press.

Ali, T. (2002). *The clash of fundamentalisms: Crusades, jihads and modernity*. London: Verso.

Allardyce, G. (1982). The rise and fall of the Western civilization course. *American Historical Review*, 87(1), 695–725.

Allen, J. (2000). On Georg Simmel: Proximity, distance and movement. In M. Crang and N. Thrift (eds.). *Thinking space*. London and New York: Routledge.

Althusser, L. (1970). Ideology and ideological state apparatuses. In L. Althusser. *Lenin and philosophy and other essays*. New York: Monthly Review Press.

Altieri, C. (1984). An idea and ideal of a literary canon. In R. von Hallberg (ed.). *Canons*. Chicago and London: University of Chicago Press.

Altman, D. (2001). *Global sex*. Chicago: University of Chicago Press.

Anderson, B. (1983). *Imagined communities: Reflections on the origin and spread of nationalism*. London: Verso.

Anderson, P. (1976). *Considerations on Western Marxism*. London: New Left Books.

References

Andrews, J. R. (1983). An historical perspective on the study of social movements. *Central States Speech Journal*, 34, 67–9.

Appadurai, A. (ed.) (1986). *The social life of things: Commodities in cultural perspective*. Cambridge: Cambridge University Press.

Appadurai, A. (1990). Disjuncture and difference in the global cultural economy. *Theory, Culture and Society*, 7, 295–310.

Appadurai, A. (1996). *Modernity at large: Cultural dimensions of globalisation*. London: Routledge.

Archard, D. (1984). *Consciousness and the unconscious*. London: Hutchinson.

Arendt, H. (1998). *The human condition*. Chicago: University of Chicago Press.

Arnold, M. (1873). *Literature and dogma*. Boston: J. R. Osgood.

Arnold, M. (1971). *Culture and anarchy: An essay in social and political criticism*. Indianapolis and New York: Bobbs-Merrill. (Original work published 1869.)

Aronowitz, S. and Cutler, J. (eds.) (1998). *Post-work: The wages of cybernation*. New York and London: Routledge.

Atton, C. (2002). *Alternative media*. London: Sage.

Auerbach, P. (1992). On socialist optimism. *New Left Review*, 192, 5–35.

Aufderheide, P. (ed.) (1992). *Beyond PC: Toward a politics of understanding*. St Paul, MN: Graywolf Press.

Augé, M. (1995). *Non-places: Introduction to an anthropology of supermodernity*. London and New York: Verso.

Augustine (1972). *City of God*. London: Penguin. (Original work 413–26.)

Augustine (1991). *The confessions*. Oxford: Oxford University Press. (Original work 400.)

Austen, J. (1996). *Pride and prejudice*. Harmondsworth: Penguin. (Original work published 1813.)

Austin, J. L. (1962). *How to do things with words*. Cambridge, MA: Harvard University Press.

Aveni, A. F. (1990). *Empires of time: Calendars, clocks, and cultures*. London: Tauris.

Bahro, R. (1978). *The alternative in Eastern Europe*. London: New Left Books.

Bakhtin, M. (1986). *Speech genres and other late essays*. Austin, TX: University of Texas Press.

Bakhtin, M. and Voloshinov, V. N. (1973). *Marxism and the philosophy of language*. New York: Seminar Press.

Bambara, T. C. (1980). *The salt eaters*. New York: Random House.

Barnes, J. (1954). Class and committee in a Norwegian island parish. *Human Relations*, 7, 39–58.

Barry, B. (1995). *Theories of justice*. Oxford: Oxford University Press.

Barthes, R. (1968). *Elements of semiology*. New York: Hill and Wang.

Barthes, R. (1971). *Image–music–text*. London: Fontana.

Barthes, R. (1973). *Mythologies*. London: Grenada.

Barthes, R. (1975). *S/Z*. London: Jonathan Cape.

Barthes, R. (1979). Introduction to the structural analysis of narratives. In R. Barthes. *Image–music–text: Essays selected and translated by Stephen Heath*. Glasgow: Fontana/Collins.

Barthes, R. (1985). *The fashion system*. New York: Jonathan Cape.

Bateson, G. (2000). *Steps to an ecology of mind*. Chicago and London: University of Chicago Press.

Bateson, W. (1979). *Problems of genetics*. New Haven, CT: Yale University Press.

Baudrillard, J. (1983). *Simulations*. New York: Semiotext(e).

Baudrillard, J. (1984). The precession of simulacra. In B. Wallis (ed.). *Art after modernism.* Boston: Godine.

Baudrillard, J. (1988). *Selected writings.* Cambridge: Polity.

Baudrillard, J. (1994). *Simulacra and simulation.* Ann Arbor, MI: University of Michigan Press.

Baudrillard, J. (1998). *The consumer society: Myths and structures.* London: Sage.

Bauman, Z. (1989). *Modernity and the Holocaust.* Ithaca, NY: Cornell University Press.

Bauman, Z. (1992). Philosophical affinities of postmodern sociology. In Z. Bauman. *Intimations of postmodernity.* London: Routledge.

Baykam, B. (1994). *Monkeys' right to paint and the post-Duchamp crisis.* Istanbul: Literatür.

Bazin, A. (1971). *What is cinema?* (2 vols.). Berkeley, CA, and London: University of California Press.

Beck, U. (1992). *Risk society: Towards a new modernity.* London: Sage.

Beck, U. and Beck-Gernsheim, E. (2001). *Individualization.* London: Sage.

Bell, D. (1960). *The end of ideology.* Glencoe, IL: Free Press.

Bell, D. (1974). *The coming of post-industrial society: A venture in social forecasting.* New York: Basic Books.

Bell, D. (1976). *The cultural contradictions of capitalism.* New York: Basic Books.

Bell, Q. (1947). *Of human finery.* London: Hogarth Press.

Belting, H. (1997). *The end of the history of art?* Chicago and London: University of Chicago Press.

Bendix, R. (1964). *Nation-building and citizenship.* New York: John Wiley.

Benjamin, J. (1990). *The bonds of love.* London: Virago.

Benjamin, W. (1968). The work of art in the age of mechanical reproduction. In W. Benjamin. *Illuminations.* New York: Harcourt, Brace and World.

Benjamin, W. (1973). *Charles Baudelaire: A lyric poet in the era of high capitalism.* London: New Left Books.

Benjamin, W. (1999). *The arcades project.* Cambridge, MA: Belknap Press of Harvard University Press.

Benson, S. (1997). The body, health and eating disorders. In K. Woodward (ed.). *Identity and difference.* London: Sage in association with the Open University.

Benstock, S. and Ferriss, S. (eds.) (1994). *On fashion.* New Brunswick, NJ: Rutgers University Press.

Benton, T. (1989). Marxism and natural limits: An ecological critique and reconstruction. *New Left Review,* 178, 51–86.

Benveniste, E. (1971). *Problems in general linguistics.* Coral Gables: University of Miami Press.

Berger, J. (1972). *Ways of seeing.* London: BBC and Penguin.

Bergson, H. (1991). *Matter and memory.* New York: Zone Books. (Original work published 1896.)

Berkeley, G. (1985). *The principles of human knowledge.* London: Fontana. (Original work published 1710.)

Berlin, I. (2002). *Liberty.* (H. Hardy, ed.) Oxford: Oxford University Press.

Berman, M. (1982). *All that is solid melts into air: The experience of modernity.* New York: Simon and Schuster.

Bernal, M. (1987). *Black Athena: The Afroasiatic roots of classical civilization.* London: Free Association Books.

References

Bernstein, R. (1986). The rage against reason. *Philosophy and Literature*, 10, 186–210.

Berry, C., Martin, F., and Yue, A. (eds.) (2002). *Mobile cultures: New media in queer Asia*. Durham, NC: Duke University Press.

Bérubé, M. (1995). Truth, justice, and the American way: A response to Joan Wallach Scott. In J. Williams (ed.). *PC wars: Politics and theory in the academy*. New York and London: Routledge.

Best, S. and Kellner, D. (1991). *Postmodern theory*. Basingstoke: Macmillan.

Beynon, H. (1997). The changing practices of work. In R. Brown. (ed.). *The changing shape of work*. Basingstoke: Macmillan.

Bhabha, H. K. (1990a). *Nation and narration*. London: Routledge.

Bhabha, H. K. (1990b). The third space. In J. Rutherford (ed.). *Identity*. London: Lawrence and Wishart.

Bhabha, H. K. (1994). *The location of culture*. New York: Routledge.

Bharatiya Janata Party, www.bjp.org

Biocca, F. and Levy, M. (eds.) (1995). *Communication in the age of virtual reality*. Hillsdale, NJ: Erlbaum.

Birnbbaum, P. and Leca, J. (1990). *Individualism*. Oxford: Clarendon Press.

Blackaby, F. (ed.) (1978). *Deindustrialisation*. London: Heinemann Educational.

Blaug, R. and Schwarzmantel, J. (2001). *Democracy: A reader*. Edinburgh: Edinburgh University Press.

Bloch, E. (1995). *The principle of hope* (3 vols.). Cambridge, MA: MIT Press.

Bloom, A. (1987). *The closing of the American mind*. New York: Simon and Schuster.

Bloom, H. (1995). *The Western canon: The books and schools of the ages*. London: Macmillan.

Bodin, J. (1992). *On sovereignty*. (Julian H. Franklin, ed.) Cambridge: Cambridge University Press.

Bollas, C. (1995). Communications of the unconscious. In C. Bollas. *Cracking up: The work of unconscious experience*. New York: Hill and Wang/Farrar, Straus and Giroux.

Boone, K. C. (1989). *The Bible tells them so: The discourse of Protestant fundamentalism*. Albany, NY: SUNY Press.

Boorstin, D. (1973). *The image: A guide to pseudo-events in America*. New York: Atheneum.

Bordo, S. (1995). *Unbearable weight: Feminism, Western culture and the body*. Berkeley, CA, Los Angeles, and London: University of California Press.

Boston Women's Health Book Collective (1978). *Our bodies ourselves: A health book by and for women* (British edition). (A. Phillips and J. Rakusen, eds.) London: Allen Lane.

Bott, E. (1971). *Family and social network*. London: Tavistock.

Bottomore, T. (1966). *Elites and society*. Harmondsworth: Penguin.

Bottomore, T. (ed.) (1983a). *A dictionary of Marxist thought*. Oxford: Blackwell.

Bottomore, T. (1983b). Political economy. In *A dictionary of Marxist thought*. Oxford: Blackwell.

Bourdieu, P. (1984). *Distinction: A social critique of the judgment of taste*. London: Routledge and Kegan Paul.

Bourdieu, P. (1998). *Acts of resistance: Against the new myths of our time*. Cambridge and Oxford: Polity and Blackwell.

Bourdieu, P. (2000). *Pascalian meditations*. Cambridge: Polity.

Bowring, F. (1999). Job scarcity: The perverted form of a potential blessing. *Sociology*, 33(1), 69–84.

Bramsted, E. K. and Melhuish, K. J. (eds.) (1978). *Western liberalism: A history in documents from Locke to Croce*. London: Longman.

Braudel, F. (1972). *The Mediterranean and the Mediterranean world at the time of Philip II* (2 vols.). London: Collins.

Braudel, F. (1994). *A history of civilizations*. London: Allen Lane.

Braudy, L. (1986). *The frenzy of renown: Fame and its history*. New York and Oxford: Oxford University Press.

Braverman, H. (1974). *Labor and monopoly capitalism: The degradation of work in the twentieth century*. New York: Monthly Review Press.

Breckenridge, C. A. and van der Veer, P. (1993). *Orientalism and the postcolonial predicament: Perspectives on South Asia*. Philadelphia: University of Pennsylvania Press.

Brooker, P. (1999). *A concise glossary of cultural theory*. London: Arnold.

Brown, G. and Yule, G. (1983). *Discourse analysis*. Cambridge: Cambridge University Press.

Brown, P. (1992). Fighting the thought police. *Australian Higher Education Supplement*, April 8.

Brown, W. (1997). The impossibility of women's studies. *differences*, 9, 79–101.

Bruns, G. (1984). Canon and power in the Hebrew scriptures. In R. von Hallberg (ed.). *Canons*. Chicago and London: University of Chicago Press.

Buck-Morss, S. (1996). Response to visual culture questionnaire. *October*, 77, 29.

Burchell, G., Gordon, C., and Miller, P. (eds.) (1991). *The Foucault effect: Studies in governmentality*. Hemel Hempstead: Harvester Wheatsheaf.

Burgin, V. (1986). *The end of art theory: Criticism and post-modernity*. London: Macmillan.

Burke, E. (1978). *Reflections on the revolution in France*. Harmondsworth: Penguin. (Original work published 1790.)

Burke, P. (1981). People's history or total history. In R. Samuel (ed.). *People's history and socialist thought*. London: Routledge and Kegan Paul.

Burkhardt, J. (1944). *The civilization of the renaissance in Italy*. London: Phaidon.

Burnham, J. (1941). *The managerial revolution*. New York: John Day.

Burroughs, W. S. (1964). *Nova express*. New York: Grove Press.

Butler, J. (1990). *Gender trouble: Feminism and the subversion of identity*. New York and London: Routledge.

Butler, J. (1993). *Bodies that matter: On the discursive limits of ''sex''*. London and New York: Routledge.

Butler, J., Guillory, J., and Thomas, K. (eds.) (2000). *What's left of theory? New work on the politics of literary theory*. New York: Routledge.

Butler, R. and Parr, H. (1999). *Mind and body spaces: Geographies of illness, impairment and disability*. London: Routledge.

Byrne-Armstrong, H. (2002). Narrative therapy. *International Journal of Critical Psychology*, 7, 21–2.

Calhoun, C. (1998). Community without propinquity revisited: Communications technology and the transformation of the urban public sphere. *Sociological Inquiry*, 68(3), 373–9.

Calhoun, C. (2001). Civil society/public sphere: History of the concept(s). In *International encyclopedia of the social and behavioral sciences*. Amsterdam: Elsevier.

387

References

Callicott, J. B. (1982). Hume's *is/ought* dichotomy and the relation of ecology to Leopold's land ethic. *Environmental Ethics*, 4(2), 163–74.

Campbell, T. (1988). *Justice*. London: Macmillan.

Canetti, E. (1973). *Crowds and power.* Harmondsworth: Penguin.

Canetti, E. (1978). *The voices of Marrakesh*. London: Marion Boyars.

Canguilhem, G. (1978). *On the normal and the pathological*. Dordrecht: Reidel.

Cannadine, D. (2003). Conservation: The National Trust and the national heritage. In D. Cannadine. *In Churchill's shadow: Confronting the past in modern Britain*. Harmondsworth: Penguin.

Cant, B. and Hemmings, S. (eds.) (1988). *Radical records: Thirty years of lesbian and gay history*. London and New York: Routledge.

Carlyle, T. (1860). *Critical and miscellaneous essays: Collected and republished*. Vol. 1. Boston: Brown and Taggard.

Carlyle, T. (1908). *Sartor resartus and On heroes: Hero-worship and the heroic in history*. London and Toronto: J. M. Dent and Sons; New York: E. P. Dutton. (Original work published 1831.)

Carnap, R. (1969). *The logical structure of the world*. Berkeley, CA: University of California Press.

Carrier, J. (ed.) (1997). *Meanings of the market: The free market in Western culture*. Oxford: Berg.

Cartwright, N. (1999). *The dappled world: A study of the boundaries of science*. Cambridge: Cambridge University Press.

Casson, L. (1979). *Travel in the ancient world*. London, Boston, and Sydney: Allen and Unwin.

Castells, M. (1989). *The informational city.* Oxford: Blackwell.

Castells, M. (1996). *The rise of the network society*. Oxford: Blackwell.

Castells, M. (1996–8). *The information age* (3 vols.). Oxford: Blackwell.

Castoriadis, C. (1997). *World in fragments: Writings on politics, society, psychoanalysis, and the imagination*. Stanford, CA: Stanford University Press.

CCCS (Centre for Contemporary Cultural Studies) (1978). *Resistance through rituals*. London: Hutchinson.

Chakrabarty, D. (2000). *Provincializing Europe: Postcolonial thought and historical difference*. Princeton, NJ: Princeton University Press.

Chalk, F. and Jonassohn, K. (1990). *The history and sociology of genocides*. New Haven, CT: Yale University Press.

Chatterjee, P. (1986). *Nationalist thought and the colonial world: A derivative discourse?* London: Zed Books.

Chatterjee, P. (1993). *The nation and its fragments: Colonial and postcolonial histories*. Princeton, NJ: Princeton University Press.

Chicago Cultural Studies Group (1994). Critical multiculturalism. In D. T. Goldberg (ed.). *Multiculturalism: A critical reader.* Oxford: Blackwell.

Chomsky, N. (1965). *Aspects of the theory of syntax*. Cambridge, MA: MIT Press.

Chomsky, N. (1967). The formal nature of language. In E. H. Lenneberg (ed.). *The biological foundations of language*. Cambridge, MA: MIT Press.

Chomsky, N. and Herman, E. (1988). *Manufacturing consent: The political economy of the mass media*. New York: Pantheon.

Cipolla, C. M. (1977). *Clocks and culture, 1300–1700*. New York: Norton.

Claeys, G. (1989). *Thomas Paine: Social and political thought*. Boston: Unwin Hyman.

Clarendon, earl of (1958). *The history of the civil wars in England begun in the year 1641*. Oxford: Clarendon Press. (Original work published 1702–4.)

Clark, K. (1949). *Landscape into art*. London: John Murray.

Clark, T. J. (1984). *The painting of modern life*. Princeton, NJ: Princeton University Press.

Clarke, J. and Newman, J. (1997). *The managerial state: Power, politics and ideology in the remaking of social welfare*. London: Sage.

Clifford, J. (1988). *The predicament of culture: Twentieth-century ethnography, literature, and art*. Cambridge, MA: Harvard University Press.

Cobo, J. R. M. (1986–7). *Study of the problem of discrimination against Indigenous populations: Report submitted to the United Nations Subcommission on Prevention of Discrimination and Protection of Minorities* (5 vols.). New York: United Nations.

Coen, E. (1999). *The art of genes: How organisms make themselves*. Oxford: Oxford University Press.

Cohen, E. (1972). Towards a sociology of international tourism. *Social Research*, 39(1), 164–89.

Cohen, E. (1988). Authenticity and commoditization in tourism. *Annals of Tourism Research*, 15(3), 371–86.

Cohen, R. (1997). *Global diasporas*. Seattle: University of Washington Press.

Cohn, B. S. (1995). *Colonialism and its forms of knowledge*. Princeton, NJ: Princeton University Press.

Coleman, P. (1995). Cracks appear in PC's shaky edifice. *Australian*, April 4.

Collins, J. (1993). Genericity in the nineties: Eclectic irony and the new sincerity. In J. Collins, H. Radner, and A. Preacher Collins (eds.). *Film theory goes to the movies*. London: Routledge.

Colquhoun, P. (1806). *A treatise on indigence*. London: J. Mawman. *Columbia World of Quotations*, www.bartleby.com/66

Comfort, A. (1964). *Sex in society*. Harmondsworth: Penguin.

Commission on Social Justice (1994). *Social justice: Strategies for national renewal*. London: Vintage.

Condren, C. (1997). Liberty of office and its defence in seventeenth-century political argument. *History of Political Thought*, 18, 460–82.

Connell, R. W. (1995). *Masculinities*. Berkeley, CA: University of California Press.

Connell, R. W. (2002). *Gender*. Cambridge: Polity.

Cooper, F. and Stoler, A. L. (1997). *Tensions of empire: Colonial cultures in a bourgeois world*. Berkeley, CA: University of California Press.

Cope, B. and Kalantzis, M. (eds.) (2000). *Multiliteracies: Literacy learning and the design of social futures*. London and New York: Routledge.

Coward, R. (1984). *Female desire*. London: Paladin.

Cranston, M. (1967). *Freedom: A new analysis*. London: Longman.

Cresswell, T. (2001). The production of mobilities. *New Formations*, 43, 11–25.

Crick, Francis H. C. (1958). On protein synthesis. *Symposium of the Society for Experimental Biology*, 12, 138–63.

Crimp, D. and Rolston, A. (1990). *AIDS demo graphics*. Seattle: Bay Press.

Crow, T. (1995). *Modern art in the common culture*. New Haven, CT, and London: Yale University Press.

389

References

Dahl, R. A. (1971). *Polyarchy: Participation and opposition*. New Haven, CT: Yale University Press.

Danto, A. (1981). *The transfiguration of the commonplace: A philosophy of art*. Cambridge, MA, and London: Harvard University Press.

Darwin, C. (1859). *On the origin of species*. Edinburgh: John Murray.

Davidson, A. (1997). *From subject to citizen*. Cambridge: Cambridge University Press.

Davies, K. (2001). *The sequence: Inside the race for the human genome*. London: Weidenfeld and Nicolson.

Davis, L. (1995). *Enforcing normalcy: Disability, deafness, and the body*. London: Verso.

Davison, G. (1993). *The unforgiving minute: How Australians learned to tell the time*. Melbourne: Oxford University Press.

Dawkins, R. (1976). *The selfish gene*. Oxford: Oxford University Press.

de Beauvoir, S. (1973). *The second sex*. (H. M. Parshley, ed.) Harmondsworth: Penguin.

Debord, G. (1994). *The society of the spectacle*. New York: Zone Books.

de Certeau, M. (1984). *The practice of everyday life*. Berkeley, CA: University of California Press.

De Landa, M. (1991). *War in the age of intelligent machines*. New York: Zone Books.

De Lauretis, T. (1991). Queer theory, lesbian and gay studies: An introduction. *differences*, 3/2 (special issue).

De Lauretis, T. (1994). *The practice of love: lesbian sexuality and perverse desire*. Bloomington, IN, and Indianopolis: Indiana University Press.

Deleuze, G. (1994). *Difference and repetition*. London: Athlone Press.

Deleuze, G. and Guattari, F. (1987). *A thousand plateaus: Capitalism and schizophrenia*. Minneapolis: University of Minnesota Press.

de Man, P. (1983). *Blindness and insight*. Minneapolis: University of Minnesota Press.

de Man, P. (1986). *The resistance to theory*. Minneapolis: University of Minnesota Press.

Dennett, D. (1995). *Darwin's dangerous idea*. Harmondsworth: Penguin.

Derrida, J. (1976). *Of grammatology*. Baltimore, MD: Johns Hopkins University Press.

Derrida, J. (1978). *Writing and difference*. London: Routledge and Kegan Paul.

Derrida, J. (1982). *Margins of philosophy*. Chicago: University of Chicago Press.

Derrida, J. (1987). *Positions*. London: Athlone Press.

Derrida, J. (1988). *Limited Inc*. Evanston, IL: Northwestern University Press.

de Saussure, F. (1966). *Course in general linguistics*. (C. Bally and A. Sechehaye in collaboration with A. Reidlinger, eds.) New York: McGraw-Hill. (Original work published 1916.)

Descartes, R. (1985). Rules for the direction of the mind. In R. Stoothoff and D. Murdoch (eds.). *The philosophical writings of Descartes*. Vol. I. Cambridge: Cambridge University Press. (Original work published 1637.)

Descartes, R. (1999). *Discourse on method, and related writings*. Harmondsworth: Penguin. (Original work published 1637.)

de Tocqueville, A. (1968). *Democracy in America*. Glasgow: Collins. (Original work published 1835–40.)

Dewey, J. (1927). *The public and its problems*. Columbus, OH: Ohio State University Press.

Dickie, G. (1974). *Art and the aesthetic: An institutional analysis*. Ithaca, NY: Cornell University Press.

Dikotter, F. (1992). *The discourse of race in modern China*. London: Hurst.

Dirks, N. B. (ed.) (1992). *Colonialism and culture*. Ann Arbor, MI: University of Michigan Press.

Dirks, N. B. (ed.) (1998). *In near ruins: Cultural theory at the end of the century*. Minneapolis: University of Minnesota Press.

Dirks, N. B. (2001). *Castes of mind: Colonialism and the making of modern India*. Princeton, NJ: Princeton University Press.

Djilas, M. (1957). *The new class: An analysis of the communist system*. New York: Praeger.

Doane, M. A. (1987). *The desire to desire: The woman's film of the 1940s*. Bloomington, IN: Indiana University Press.

Dodson, M. (1994). The end of the beginning: Re(de)finding Aboriginality. *Australian Aboriginal Studies*, 1, 2–13.

Dodds, E. A. (1973). *The Greeks and the irrational*. Berkeley, CA: University of California Press.

Donald, J. and Rattansi, A. (eds.) (1992). ''*Race,*'' *culture and difference*. London: Sage/Open University Press.

Donkin, R. (2001). *Blood, sweat and tears: The evolution of work*. New York: Texere.

Donzelot, J. (1979). *The policing of families*. New York: Pantheon.

Douglas, M. (1995). *Risk and blame: Essays in cultural theory*. London: Routledge.

Doyle, R. (1990). *The Commitments*. London: Vintage.

D'Souza, D. (1991). Illiberal education. *Atlantic Monthly*, March, 51–79.

Duara, P. (2001). The discourse of civilization and Pan-Asianism. *Journal of World History*, 12(1), 99–130.

Du Bois, W. E. B (1989). *The souls of black folk*. New York: Bantam.

Duckworth, W. L. H. (1904). *Studies from the anthropological laboratory: The Anatomy School, Cambridge*. Cambridge: Cambridge University Press.

du Gay, P. (1996). *Consumption and identity at work*. London: Sage.

du Gay, P. (2000). *In praise of bureaucracy*. London: Sage.

Duncan, J. and Ley, D. (1993). *Place/culture/representation*. London and New York: Routledge.

Duncan, N. (ed.) (1996). *BodySpace*. London and New York: Routledge.

Dupré, J. (1993). *The disorder of things: Metaphysical foundations of the disunity of science*. Cambridge, MA: Harvard University Press.

Dworkin, A. (1981). *Pornography: Men possessing women*. London: Women's Press.

Dworkin, A. and MacKinnon, C. (1988). *Pornography and civil rights: A new day for women's equality*. Minneapolis: Organizing against Pornography.

Dyer, R. (1979). *Stars*. London: BFI.

Dyer, R. (1986). *Heavenly bodies: Film stars and society*. London: BFI/Macmillan.

Dyer, R. (1991). Believing in fairies: The author and the homosexual. In D. Fuss (ed.). *Inside/out*. London and New York: Routledge.

Eagleton, T. (1990). *The ideology of the aesthetic*. Cambridge, MA: Blackwell.

Eagleton, T. (2000). *The idea of culture*. London: Verso.

Eco, U. (1976). *A theory of semiotics*. Bloomington, IN: Indiana University Press.

Eco, U. (1986). On the crisis of the crisis of reason. In U. Eco. *Travels in hyper-reality*. London: Picador.

References

Eco, U. (1994). *Six walks in the fictional woods.* Cambridge, MA, and London: Harvard University Press.

Economist (2002). Biology and politics: The great cloning debate. *The Economist,* May 11.

Ehrenreich, B. and Ehrenreich, J. (1979). The professional-managerial class. In P. Walker (ed.). *Between labor and capital.* Boston: South End Press.

Eide, A., Krause, C., and Rosas, A. (eds.) (2001). *Economic, social and cultural rights.* The Hague: Kluwer Law International.

Eisenstadt, S. N. (1956). *From generation to generation.* New York: Free Press.

Elias, N. (2000). *The civilizing process.* Oxford: Blackwell. (Original work published 1939.)

Ellenberger, H. F. (1970). *The discovery of the unconscious: The history and evolution of dynamic psychiatry.* London: Allen Lane.

Elliot, G. (1996). Humanism. In M. Payne (ed.). *A dictionary of cultural and critical theory.* Oxford: Blackwell.

Elman, J. L., Bates, E. A., Johnson, M. H., Karmiloff-Smith, A., Parisi, D., and Plunkett, K. (1996). *Rethinking innateness: A connectionist perspective on development.* Cambridge, MA: MIT Press.

Engels, F. (1962). Socialism: Utopian and scientific. In K. Marx and F. Engels. *Selected works.* Vol. 1. Moscow: Foreign Languages Publishing House II. (Original work published 1892.)

Epstein, S. (1998). Gay politics, ethnic identity: The limits of social constructionism. In P. N. Nardi and B. E. Schneider (eds.). *Social perspectives in lesbian and gay studies.* London and New York: Routledge.

Etzione-Halevy, E. (2001). Elites: sociological aspects. In N. J. Smelser and P. B. Baltes (eds.). *International encyclopedia of the social and behavioral sciences.* Oxford and New York: Elsevier Science.

Evans, M. (ed.) (2001). *Feminism: Critical concepts in literary and cultural studies.* London: Routledge.

Eve, M. and Musson, D. (eds.) (1982). *The Socialist Register.* London: Merlin Press.

Evernden, N. (1992). *The social creation of nature.* Baltimore, MD, and London: Johns Hopkins University Press.

Eysenck, H. (1979). *Uses and abuse of psychology.* Harmondsworth: Penguin.

Fabian, J. (1983). *Time and the other: How anthropology makes its object.* New York: Columbia University Press.

Fairclough, N. (1972). *Discourse and social change.* Cambridge: Polity.

Fairclough, N. (1995). *Media discourse.* London: Arnold.

Fanon, F. (1963). *The wretched of the earth.* New York: Grove Press.

Fanon, F. (1986). *Black skin, white masks.* London: Pluto.

Fass, P. S. (1977). *The damned and the beautiful.* New York: Oxford University Press.

Feifer, M. (1986). *Tourism in history: From imperial Rome to the present.* New York: Stein and Day.

Fein, H. (1993). *Genocide: A sociological perspective.* London: Sage.

Felski, R. (1995). *The gender of modernity.* Cambridge, MA: Harvard University Press.

Felski, R. (1999–2000). The invention of everyday life. *New Formations,* 39, 13–31.

Ferrell, R. (1996). *Passion in theory: Conceptions of Freud and Lacan.* London and New York: Routledge.

Figal, G. (1999). *Civilization and monsters: Spirits of modernity in modern Japan.* Durham, NC, and London: Duke University Press.

Fish, S. (1995). *Professional correctness: Literary studies and political change.* Oxford: Clarendon Press.

Fisher, N. (1990). The classification of the sciences. In R. C. Olby, G. N. Cantor, J. R. R. Christie, and M. J. S. Hodge (eds.). *Companion to the history of modern science.* London: Routledge.

Fisher, W. F. and Ponniah, T. (eds.) (2003). *Another world is possible: Popular alternatives to globalization at the World Social Forum.* London: Zed Books.

Fiske, J. (1989). *Understanding popular culture.* Boston, MA: Unwin Hyman.

Foucault, M. (1971). *The order of things: An archaeology of the human sciences.* New York: Pantheon.

Foucault, M. (1972). *The archaeology of knowledge.* London: Tavistock.

Foucault, M. (1977). *Discipline and punish: The birth of the prison.* London: Allen Lane.

Foucault, M. (1979). *The history of sexuality.* Vol. 1: *An introduction.* London: Allen Lane.

Foucault, M. (1980). *Power/knowledge.* (C. Gordon, ed.) Brighton: Harvester.

Foucault, M. (1986). *The history of sexuality.* Vol. 3: *The care of the self.* New York: Pantheon.

Foucault, M. (1991). Governmentality. In G. Burchell, C. Gordon, and P. Miller (eds.). *The Foucault effect: Studies in governmentality.* Hemel Hempstead: Harvester Wheatsheaf.

Frank, T. (2001). *One market under God: Extreme capitalism, market populism and the end of economic democracy.* New York: Anchor Books.

Frankel, B. (1987). *The post-industrial utopians.* Cambridge: Polity.

Frankena, W. K. (1967). Value. In P. Edwards (ed.). *Encyclopedia of philosophy* (8 vols.). New York: Macmillan.

Fraser, N. (1992). Rethinking the public sphere: A contribution to the critique of actually existing democracy. In C. Calhoun (ed.). *Habermas and the public sphere.* Cambridge, MA: MIT Press.

Freadman, A. (2004). *The machinery of talk: Charles Peirce and the sign hypothesis.* Stanford, CA: Stanford University Press.

Freebody, P., Muspratt, S., and Dwyer, B. (eds.) (2001). *Difference, silence and textual practice: Studies in critical literacy.* Cresskill, NJ: Hampton Press.

Freud, S. (1953a). The claims of psychoanalysis to scientific interest. In J. Strachey (ed.). *The standard edition of the complete psychological works of Sigmund Freud.* Vol. 13. London: Hogarth Press/Institute of Psychoanalysis. (Original work published 1913.)

Freud, S. (1953b). *The interpretation of dreams.* In J. Strachey (ed.). *The standard edition of the complete psychological works of Sigmund Freud.* Vols. 4–5. London: Hogarth Press/Institute of Psychoanalysis. (Original works published 1900.)

Freud, S. (1953c). Three essays on the theory of sexuality. In J. Strachey (ed.). *The standard edition of the complete psychological works of Sigmund Freud.* Vol. 7. London: Hogarth Press/Institute of Psychoanalysis. (Original work published 1905.)

Freud, S. (1957a). Papers on metapsychology. In J. Strachey (ed.). *The standard edition of the complete psychological works of Sigmund Freud.* Vol. 14. London: Hogarth Press/Institute of Psychoanalysis. (Original work published 1915.)

References

Freud, S. (1957b). The Unconscious. In J. Strachey (ed.). *The standard edition of the complete psychological works of Sigmund Freud*. Vol. 14. London: Hogarth Press/Institute of Psychoanalysis. (Original work published 1914.)

Freud, S. (1961). Fetishism. In J. Strachey (ed.). *The standard edition of the complete psychological works of Sigmund Freud*. Vol. 21. London: Hogarth Press/Institute of Psychoanalysis. (Original work published 1927.)

Freud, S. (1962). Screen memories. In J. Strachey (ed.). *The standard edition of the complete psychological works of Sigmund Freud*. Vol. 3. London: Hogarth Press/Institute of Psychoanalysis. (Original work published 1899.)

Freud, S. (1963). Introductory lectures on psychoanalysis (Lecture 21). In J. Strachey (ed.). *The standard edition of the complete psychological works of Sigmund Freud*. Vol. 16. Hogarth Press/Institute of Psychoanalysis. (Original work published 1917.)

Fried, M. (1998). *Art and objecthood: Essays and reviews*. Chicago and London: University of Chicago Press.

Friedman, M. and Friedman, R. (1980). *Free to choose*. New York: Harcourt Brace Jovanovich.

Frisby, D. and Sayer, D. (1986). *Society*. London: Tavistock.

Frith, S. (1996). *Performing rites: On the value of popular music*. Oxford: Oxford University Press.

Frosh, S. (2002). Psychoanalysis and the politics of psychotherapy. *International Journal of Critical Psychology*, 7, 7–10.

Froude, J. (1858). *History of England from the fall of Wolsey to the death of Elizabeth*. London: Parker and Sons.

Froula, C. (1984). When Eve reads Milton: Undoing the canonical economy. In R. von Hallberg (ed.). *Canons*. Chicago and London: University of Chicago Press.

Frow, J. (1995). *Cultural studies and cultural value*. Oxford: Oxford University Press.

Frye, N. (1969). *Anatomy of criticism*. New York: Atheneum.

Fujitani, T. (1996). *Splendid monarchy: Power and pageantry in modern Japan*. Berkeley, CA, Los Angeles, and London: University of California Press.

Fukuyama, F. (1992). *The end of history and the last man*. London: Penguin.

Fukuyama, F. (2002). *Our posthuman future: Consequences of the biotechnology revolution*. London: Profile Books.

Fuss, D. (1989). *Essentially speaking: Feminism, nature and difference*. New York: Routledge.

Fussell, P. (1979). The stationary tourist. *Harper's*, April, 31–8.

Gadamer, H. G. (1981). *Reason in the age of science*. Cambridge, MA: MIT Press.

Gagnon, J. H. and Simon, W. (1973). *Sexual conduct: The social sources of human sexuality*. London: Hutchinson.

Gamble, A. (1985). *Britain in decline* (2nd edition). Basingstoke: Macmillan.

Gardiner, M. E. (2000). *Critiques of everyday life*. London and New York: Routledge.

Gasché, R. (1986). *The tain of the mirror: Derrida and the philosophy of reflection*. Cambridge, MA: Harvard University Press.

Gates, H. L. (1994). *Colored people: A memoir*. New York: Knopf.

Geertz, C. (2000). The strange estrangement: Charles Taylor and the natural sciences. In C. Geertz. (ed.). *Available light: Philosophical reflections on philosophical topics*. Princeton, NJ: Princeton University Press.

Genette, G. (1980). *Narrative discourse*. Oxford: Blackwell.

Geoghegan, V. (1987). *Utopianism and Marxism*. London: Methuen.

Geras, N. (1983). Fetishism. In T. Bottomore (ed.). *A dictionary of Marxist thought*. Oxford: Blackwell.

Gereffi, G. and Korzeniewicz, M. (eds.) (1994). *Commodity chains and global capitalism*. Westport, CT: Praeger.

Ghai, Y. (1997). Rights, duties and responsibilities. *Human Rights Solidarity AHRC Newsletter*, 7(4), 9–17.

Gibb, H. A. R. (1947). *Modern trends in Islam*. Chicago: University of Chicago Press.

Gibson-Graham, J. K. (1996). *The end of capitalism (as we knew it): A feminist critique of political economy*. Oxford and Cambridge, MA: Blackwell.

Gibson-Graham, J. K., Resnick, S., and Wolff, R. (eds.) (2000). *Class and its others*. Minneapolis: University of Minnesota Press.

Giddens, A. (ed.) (1974). *Positivism and sociology*. London: Heinemann.

Giddens, A. (1990). *The consequences of modernity*. Stanford, CA: Stanford University Press.

Giddens, A. (1992). *The transformation of intimacy*. Cambridge: Polity.

Gilder, G. (1981). *Wealth and poverty*. New York: Basic Books.

Gill, S. (1998). Territory. In M. C. Taylor (ed.). *Critical terms for religious studies*. Chicago: University of Chicago Press.

Gillis, J. (1974). *Youth and history*. New York: Academic Press.

Gilmour, I. (1977). *Inside right: A study of Conservatism*. London: Hutchinson.

Gilroy, P. (1993a). *The black Atlantic*. London: Verso.

Gilroy, P. (1993b). *Small acts: Thoughts on the politics of black cultures*. London and New York: Serpent's Tail.

Ginzburg, C. (2001). *Wooden eyes: Nine reflections on distance*. New York: Columbia University Press.

Gitlin, T. (1995). *The twilight of common dreams*. New York: Henry Holt.

Glazer, N. and Moynihan, D. P. (1963). *Beyond the melting pot: The Negroes, Puerto Ricans, Jews, Italians, and Irish of New York City*. Cambridge, MA: MIT Press.

Gleeson, P. (ed.) (1970). *Essays on the student movement*. Columbus, OH: Charles E. Merrill.

Goffman, E. (1968). *Asylums: Essays on the social situation of mental patients and other inmates*. Harmondsworth: Penguin.

Goldberg, B. (2001). *Bias: A CBS insider exposes how the media distort the news*. Washington, DC: Regnery.

Goldberg-Hiller, J. (2002). *The limits to union: Same-sex marriage and the politics of civil rights*. Ann Arbor, MI: University of Michigan Press.

Goldthorpe, J. (1982). On the service class, its formation and future. In A. Giddens and G. Mackenzie (eds.). *Social class and the division of labor: Essays in honour of Ilya Neustadt*. Cambridge: Cambridge University Press.

Goleman, D. (1995). *Emotional intelligence*. London: Bloomsbury Press.

Gombrich, E. H. (1978). *The story of art*. Oxford: Phaidon.

Gong, G. W. (1984). *"The standard of civilization" in international society*. Oxford: Oxford University Press.

References

Goode, J. and Maskovsky, J. (eds.) (2001). *The new poverty studies: The ethnography of power, politics and impoverished people in the United States.* New York: New York University Press.

Goodman, N. (1976). *The languages of art.* Indianapolis: Hackett.

Goodwin, B. (1994). *How the leopard changed its spots.* London: Weidenfeld and Nicolson.

Gorz, A. (1999). *Reclaiming work: Beyond the wage-based society.* Cambridge: Polity.

Gould, S. J. (2002). *The structure of evolutionary theory.* Cambridge, MA: Harvard University Press.

Gouldner, A. W. (1979). *The future of intellectuals and the rise of the new class: A frame of reference, theses, conjectures, arguments and an historical perspective on the role of intellectuals and intelligentsia in the international class contest of the modern era.* New York: Oxford University Press.

Government of Canada (2001). www.pch.gc.ca/multi/what-multi_e.shtml

Graham, G. (2002). *The case against the democratic state.* Exeter: Imprint Academic.

Gramsci, A. (1971). *Selections from the prison notebooks 1929–35.* New York: International Publishers.

Gray, J. (1989). *Liberalisms.* London: Routledge.

Gray, J. (1993). *Men are from Mars, women are from Venus: A practical guide for improving communication and getting what you want in your relationships.* New York: HarperCollins.

Gray, R. (1990). *Freedom.* London: Macmillan.

Greenberg, C. (1986). Avant garde and kitsch. In J. O'Brian (ed.). *Clement Greenberg: The collected essays and criticism.* Chicago: Chicago University Press.

Greenblatt, S. (1996). Expectations and estrangement. *Threepenny Review,* Fall, 25–6.

Greer, G. (1970). *The female eunuch.* London: MacGibbon and Kee.

Gregory, C. (1997). *Savage money: The anthropology and politics of commodity exchange.* Amsterdam: Harwood Academic.

Greider, W. (1997). *One world, ready or not: The manic logic of global capitalism.* New York: Simon and Schuster.

Grossberg, L. (1992). *We gotta get out of this place: popular conservatism and postmodern culture.* London: Routledge.

Grosz, E. (1992). Fetishization. In E. Wright (ed.). *Feminism and psychoanalysis: A critical dictionary.* Oxford: Blackwell.

Grosz, E. (1995). Refiguring lesbian desire. In E. Grosz (ed.). *Space, time and perversion: Essays on the politics of bodies.* London and New York: Routledge.

Grundmann, R. (1991). *Marxism and ecology.* Oxford: Oxford University Press.

Guattari, F. (2000). *The three ecologies.* London and New Brunswick, NJ: Athlone Press.

Guha, R. (1983). *Elementary aspects of peasant insurgency in colonial India.* Delhi: Oxford University Press.

Guillory, J. (1993). *Cultural capital: The problem of literary canon-formation.* Chicago and London: University of Chicago Press.

Gunning, T. (1990). The cinema of attractions. In T. Elsaesser (ed.). *Early cinema: Space, frame, narrative.* London: BFI.

Gusterson, H. (2001). Elites, anthropology of. In N. J. Smelser and P. B. Baltes (eds.). *International encyclopedia of the social and behavioral sciences.* Oxford and New York: Elsevier Science.

Habermas, J. (1970). Toward a theory of communicative competence. In H. P. Drietzel (ed.). *Recent sociology. No. 2: Patterns of communicative behavior.* New York: Macmillan.

Habermas, J. (1984). *The theory of communicative action.* Vol. 1. London: Heinemann.

Habermas, J. (1989). *Structural transformation of the public sphere: An inquiry into a category of bourgeois society.* Cambridge, MA: Harvard University Press.

Habib, M. A. R. (1996). Materialism. In M. Payne, M. Ponnuswami, and J. Payne (eds.). *A dictionary of cultural and critical theory.* Boston: Blackwell.

Hacking, I. (1975). *Why does language matter to philosophy?* Cambridge and New York: Cambridge University Press.

Hacking, I. (1983). *Representing and intervening: Introductory topics in the philosophy of natural science.* Cambridge and New York: Cambridge University Press.

Hacking, I. (1990). *The taming of chance.* Cambridge: Cambridge University Press.

Hadot, P. (1995). *Philosophy as a way of life: Spiritual exercises from Socrates to Foucault.* Oxford: Blackwell.

Haebich, A. (1992). *For their own good: Aborigines and government in the south west of Western Australia 1900–1940.* Nedlands: University of Western Australia Press.

Haeckel, E. (1887). *The evolution of man: A popular exposition of the principal points of human ontogeny and phylogeny.* Vol. I. New York: D. Appleton. (Original work published 1866.)

Halberstam, J. and Livingston, I. (1995). Introduction: Posthuman bodies. In J. Halberstam and I. Livingston (eds.). *Posthuman bodies.* Bloomington, IN, and Indianapolis: Indiana University Press.

Halbwachs, M. (1992). *On collective memory.* Chicago: University of Chicago Press.

Haley, A. (1976). *Roots.* New York: Doubleday.

Hall, C. (2002). *Civilizing subjects: Metropole and colony in the English imagination 1830–1867.* Chicago: University of Chicago Press.

Hall, S. (1980). Cultural studies: Two paradigms. *Media, Culture and Society,* 2, 57–72.

Hall, S. (1981). Encoding/decoding in television discourse. In S. Hall, D. Hobson, A. Lowe, and P. Willis (eds.). *Culture, media, language.* London: Hutchinson.

Hall, S. (1992a). New ethnicities. In J. Donald and A. Rattansi (eds.). "*Race,*" *culture and difference.* London: Sage.

Hall, S. (1992b). The question of cultural identity. In S. Hall, D. Held, and T. McGrew (eds.). *Modernity and its futures.* Cambridge: Polity.

Hall, S. (1996). The problem of ideology: Marxism without guarantees. In D. Morley and K-H. Chen (eds.). *Stuart Hall: Critical dialogues in cultural studies.* New York: Routledge.

Hall, S. (1998). Notes on deconstructing "the popular." In J. Storey (ed.). *Cultural theory and popular culture.* Hemel Hempstead: Prentice Hall.

Hall, S. and Jacques, M. (eds.) (1983). *The politics of Thatcherism.* London: Lawrence and Wishart.

Halliday, M. A. K. (1978). *Language as social semiotic.* London: Edward Arnold.

Halloran, J. (1975). Understanding television. *Screen Education,* 14.

Hamilton, W. (2001). *The narrow roads of gene land.* Oxford: Oxford University Press.

Hanley, S. (1989). Engendering the state: Family formation and state building in early modern France. *French Historical Studies,* 16(1), 4–27.

Haraway, D. (1985). Homes for cyborgs. In E. Weed (ed.). *Coming to terms: Feminism, theory, politics.* New York: Routledge.

References

Haraway, D. (1991). A cyborg manifesto: Science, technology and socialist-feminism in the late twentieth century. In D. Haraway (ed.). *Simians, cyborgs and women: The reinvention of nature*. London: Free Association Books.

Harding, S. (ed.) (1993). *The "racial" economy of science: Toward a democratic future*. Bloomington, IN: Indiana University Press.

Hardt, M. and Negri, A. (2000). *Empire*. Cambridge, MA: Harvard University Press.

Harootunian, H. (2002). *Overcome by modernity: History, culture, and community in interwar Japan*. Princeton, NJ: Princeton University Press.

Harré, R. and Madden, E. H. (1975). *Causal powers*. Oxford: Blackwell.

Harris, H. A. (1998). *Fundamentalism and evangelicals*. New York: Oxford University Press.

Hartley, J. (1982). *Understanding news*. London and New York: Routledge.

Harvey, D. (1990). *The condition of postmodernity*. Oxford: Blackwell.

Hassan, I. (1987). *The postmodern turn*. Columbus, OH: Ohio University Press.

Hayek, F. A. (1944). *The road to serfdom*. London: Routledge and Kegan Paul.

Hayek, F. A. (1960). *The constitution of liberty*. London: Routledge.

Hayek, F. A. (1976). *Law, legislation and liberty*. Vol. 2: *The mirage of social justice*. London and New York: Routledge.

Hayles, K. N. (1999). *How we became posthuman: Virtual bodies in cybernetics, literature and informatics*. Chicago and London: University of Chicago Press.

Heath, S. B. (1983). *Ways with words: Language, life and work in communities and classrooms*. Cambridge: Cambridge University Press.

Hebdige, D. (1979). *Subculture: The meaning of style*. London: Methuen.

Hedegaard, E. (2002). Oh, F***! It's the Osbournes. *Rolling Stone*, 12/28, www.rollingstone.com/features/featuregen.asp?pid=663

Hegel, G. F. W. (1956). *The philosophy of history*. New York: Dover. (Original work published 1831.)

Hegel, G. W. F. (1967). *The philosophy of right*. Oxford: Oxford University Press. (Original work published 1821.)

Hegel, G. F. W. (1975). *Aesthetics: Lectures on fine art*. Oxford: Clarendon Press. (Original work published 1835.)

Heidegger, M. (1996). *Being and time: A translation of Sein und Zeit*. Albany, NY: SUNY Press.

Held, D. (1995). *Democracy and the global order: From modern state to cosmopolitan governance*. Cambridge: Polity.

Held, D. (1996). *Models of democracy* (2nd edition). Stanford, CA: Stanford University Press.

Heller, A. (1981). *Everyday life*. London: Routledge and Kegan Paul.

Henig, R. M. (2000). *A monk and two peas: The story of Gregor Mendel and the discovery of genetics*. London: Weidenfeld and Nicolson.

Hewison, R. (1987). *The heritage industry: Britain in a climate of decline*. London: Methuen.

Hillis, K. (1999). *Digital sensations: Space, identity, and embodiment in virtual reality*. Minneapolis: University of Minnesota Press.

Hobbes, T. (1963). *Behemoth: the history of the causes of the civil wars of England, and of the counsels and artifices by which they were carried on from the year 1640 to the year 1660*. (W. Molesworth, ed.) New York: Burt Franklin. (Original work published 1679.)

Hobbes, T. (1991). *Leviathan*. Cambridge: Cambridge University Press. (Original work published 1651.)

Hobsbawm, E. and Ranger, T. (eds.) (1983). *The invention of tradition*. Cambridge: Cambridge University Press.

Hodgkin, K. and Radstone, S. (eds.) (2003). *Contested pasts: The politics of memory*. London: Routledge.

Hogg, Q. (1947). *The case for conservatism*. West Drayton: Penguin.

Hoggart, R. (1957). *The uses of literacy: Aspects of working-class life with special references to publications and entertainments*. London: Chatto and Windus.

Holly, M. A and Moxey, K. (eds.) (2002). *Art history, aesthetics, and visual studies*. Williamstown, MA: Clark Institute.

Holmes, D. (1997). *Virtual politics: Identity and community in cyberspace*. London: Sage.

Homans, G. (1950). *The human group*. New York: Harcourt.

hooks, b. (1990a). Marginality as a site of resistance. In R. T. Ferguson, M. Gever, T. T. Minh-ha, and C. West (eds.). *Out there: Marginalization and contemporary culture*. Cambridge, MA: MIT Press.

hooks, b. (1990b). *Yearning: Race, gender, and cultural politics*. Boston: South End Press.

Horkheimer, M. (1985). *The eclipse of reason*. New York: Continuum.

Horne, D. (2002). Now there's a thought ... *Sydney Morning Herald, Spectrum*, May 18–19, 4–5.

Houser, N. and Kloesel, C. (eds.) (1998). *The essential Peirce: Selected philosophical writings*. Bloomington, IN: Indiana University Press.

Howland, D. R. (1996). *Borders of Chinese civilization: Geography and history at empire's end*. Durham, NC, and London: Duke University Press.

Howland, D. R. (2002). *Translating the West: Language and political reason in nineteenth-century Japan*. Honolulu: University of Hawaii Press.

HRCA (Human Rights Council of Australia) (1995). *The rights way to development: A human rights approach to development assistance*. Marrickville: HRCA.

Huber, E. and Stephens, J. (2001). *Development and crisis of the welfare state*. Chicago: University of Chicago Press.

Hughes, R. (1993). *Culture of complaint*. Oxford: Oxford University Press.

Hume, D. (1965). *"Of the standard of taste" and other essays*. (J. W. Lenz, ed.). Indianapolis: Bobbs-Merrill. (Original work published 1757.)

Hume, D. (1978). *A treatise of human nature*. (L. A. Selby-Bigge, ed.). Oxford: Clarendon Press. (Original work published 1739.)

Hume, D. (1999). *An enquiry concerning human understanding*. (T. L. Beauchamp, ed.) Oxford: Oxford University Press. (Original work published 1748.)

Hunter, I. (1988). *Culture and government: The emergence of literary education*. Basingstoke: Macmillan.

Hunter, J. P. (1966). *The reluctant pilgrim: Defoe's emblematic method and quest for form in Robinson Crusoe*. Baltimore, MD: Johns Hopkins University Press.

Huntington, S. (1993). The clash of civilizations? *Foreign Affairs*, 72(3), 22–49.

Huntington, S. (1996). *The clash of civilizations and the remaking of world order*. New York: Simon and Schuster.

Husserl, E. (1991). *On the phenomenology of the consciousness of internal time.* Dordrecht: Kluwer Academic.

Hutcheon, L. (1988). *A poetics of postmodernism: History, theory, fiction.* London: Routledge and Kegan Paul.

Huyssen, A. (1986). *After the great divide: Modernism, mass culture and postmodernism.* London: Macmillan.

Hyman, R. (1975). *Industrial relations: A Marxist introduction.* Basingstoke: Macmillan.

ILRIC (International Labour Resource and Information Centre) (2000). *An alternative view of globalization.* www.aidc.org.za/ilric/research/globalisation_1/globalisation_1.html

Ishay, M. R. (ed.) (1997). *The human rights reader.* New York: Routledge.

Jackson, R. H. (1990). *Quasi-states: Sovereignty, international relations and the third world.* Cambridge: Cambridge University Press.

Jacobs, J. (1972). *The death and life of great American cities.* New York: Random House.

Jacobs, P. and Landau, S. (1966). *The new radicals: A report with documents.* Harmondsworth: Penguin.

Jacobson, M. (1998). *Whiteness of a different color: European immigrants and the alchemy of race.* Cambridge, MA: Harvard University Press.

Jakle, J. (1985). *The tourist: Travel in twentieth-century North America.* Lincoln, NE, and London: University of Nebraska Press.

Jakobson, R. (1972). Linguistics and poetics. In R. de George and F. de George (eds.). *The structuralists: From Marx to Lévi-Strauss.* New York: Anchor Books.

Jakobson, R. and Waugh, L. (1979). *The sound shape of language.* Bloomington, IN, and London: Indiana University Press.

James, H. (1983). *The Aspern Papers.* Oxford: Oxford University Press. (Original work published 1888.)

James, W. (1920). *Collected essays and reviews.* New York: Russell and Russell.

James, W. (1952). *Principles of psychology.* Chicago and London: Encyclopaedia Britannica. (Original work published 1891.)

James, W. (1979). *Pragmatism and the meaning of truth.* Cambridge, MA: Harvard University Press. (Original work published 1907.)

Jameson, F. (1984). Postmodernism, or the cultural logic of late capitalism. *New Left Review,* 146, 53–92.

Jameson, F. (1991). *Postmodernism, or the cultural logic of late capitalism.* London: Verso.

Janoski, T. (1998). *Citizenship and civil society.* Cambridge: Cambridge University Press.

Jaszi, P. (1991). Toward a theory of copyright: The metamorphoses of ''authorship.'' *Duke Law Journal,* 455–502.

Jenks, C. (1991). *The language of post-modern architecture.* London: Academy Editions.

Johnson, L. and Valentine, G. (1995). Wherever I lay my girlfriend, that's my home: the performance and surveillance of lesbian identities in domestic environments. In D. Bell and G. Valentine (eds.). *Mapping desire: Geographies of sexualities.* London: Routledge.

Joyce, J. (1914). *Portrait of the artist as a young man.* New York: Viking.

Joyce, P. (2003). *The rule of freedom.* London: Verso.

Kant, I. (1970a). An answer to the question: "What is enlightenment?" In H. Reiss (ed.). *Kant: Political writings*. Cambridge: Cambridge University Press. (Original work published 1784.)

Kant, I. (1970b). Idea for a universal history with a cosmopolitan purpose. In H. Reiss (ed.). *Kant: Political writings*. Cambridge: Cambridge University Press. (Original work published 1784.)

Kant, I. (1974). *Anthropology from a pragmatic point of view*. The Hague: Nijhoff. (Original work published 1797.)

Kant, I. (1982). *Critique of pure reason*. London: Macmillan. (Original work published 1784.)

Kant, I. (1987). *Critique of judgment*. Indianapolis: Hackett. (Original work published 1764.)

Kant, I. (1997). *Lectures on ethics*. Cambridge: Cambridge University Press. (Notes taken by students of Kant's lectures on ethics 1775–80.)

Kantorowicz, E. H. (1957). *The king's two bodies*. Princeton, NJ: Princeton University Press.

Karl, R. (2002). *Staging the world: Chinese nationalism at the turn of the twentieth century*. Durham, NC, and London: Duke University Press.

Katz, J. N. (2001). *Love stories: Sex between men before homosexuality*. Chicago: University of Chicago Press.

Keane, J. (1984). *Public life and late capitalism: Towards a socialist theory of democracy*. Cambridge: Cambridge University Press.

Kear, A. and Steinberg, D. L. (1999). *Mourning Diana: Nation, culture and the performance of grief*. London and New York: Routledge.

Keith, M. and Pile, S. (1993). *Place and the politics of identity*. London and New York: Routledge.

Keller, E. F. (2000). *The century of the gene*. Cambridge, MA: Harvard University Press.

Kelly, K., Heilbrun, A., and Stacks, B. (1989). Virtual reality: An interview with Jaron Lanier. *Whole Earth Review*, 64 (108), 108–12.

Kelsen, H. (1945). *General theory of law and state*. Cambridge, MA: Harvard University Press.

Kennedy, R. (2002). *Nigger: The strange career of a troublesome word*. New York: Pantheon.

Kermode, F. (1968). *The sense of an ending: Studies in the theory of fiction*. Oxford: Oxford University Press.

Kern, S. (1983). *The culture of time and space 1880–1918*. Cambridge, MA: Harvard University Press.

Kimball, R. (1990). *Tenured radicals: How politics has corrupted our higher education*. New York: Harper and Row.

King, P. (1976). *Toleration*. London: Allen and Unwin.

Kirsch, M. H. (2000). *Queer theory and social change*. London and New York: Routledge.

Kittler, F. (1999). *Gramophone, film, typewriter*. Stanford, CA: Stanford University Press.

Knemeyer, F-L. (1980). Polizei. *Economy and Society*, 9, 172–96.

Knight, C. B. (1965). *Basic concepts of ecology*. New York: Macmillan.

Kobusch, T. (1997). *Die Entdeckung der person: Metaphysik der freiheit und modernes menschen-bild*. Darmstadt: Wissenschaftliche Buchgesellschaft.

Kooiman, J. (ed.) (1993). *Modern governance: New government–society interactions*. London: Sage.

Kormondy, E. J. (1976). *Concepts of ecology* (2nd edition). Englewood Cliffs, NJ: Prentice Hall.

Kristeva, J. (1970). *Le texte du roman*. The Hague, Paris, and New York: Mouton.

Kristeva, J. (1980). *Desire in language*. Oxford: Blackwell.

References

Kristeva, J. (1989). *Language, the unknown*. New York: Columbia University Press.

Kristeva, J. (1991). *Strangers to ourselves*. New York: Harvester Wheatsheaf.

Kristoff, N. D. (2003). In Blair we trust. *New York Times*, January 8, A27.

Kropotkin, P. P. (1996). *Mutual aid*. London: Black Rose. (Original work published 1902.)

Kuhn, T. (1970). *The structure of scientific revolutions* (2nd edition). Chicago: University of Chicago Press.

Kumar, K. (1995). *From post-industrial to post-modern society: New theories of the contemporary world*. Oxford: Blackwell.

Kuper, A. (1999). *Culture: The anthropologists' account*. Cambridge, MA: Harvard University Press.

Kymlycka, W. (1995). *Multicultural citizenship: A liberal theory of minority rights*. Oxford: Clarendon Press.

Lacan, J. (1977). The Freudian thing. In J. Lacan. *Écrits: A selection*. London: Tavistock.

Lacan, J. (1981). *The four fundamental concepts of psychoanalysis*. New York: Norton.

Lacan, J. (1997). *Écrits: A selection*. London: Tavistock.

Laclau, E. and Mouffe, C. (1985). *Hegemony and socialist strategy: Toward a radical democratic politics*. London: Verso.

Laing, R. D. (1967). *The politics of experience*. London: Routledge and Kegan Paul.

Lamarck, J-B. (1984). *Zoological philosophy: An exposition with respect to the natural history of animals*. Chicago: University of Chicago Press.

Larson, G. O. (1997). *American canvas*. Washington, DC: National Endowment for the Arts.

Lash, S. (2002). *Critique of information*. London: Sage.

Lash, S. and Urry, J. (1987). *The end of organized capitalism*. Cambridge: Polity.

Lauter, P. (1995). ''Political correctness'' and the attack on American colleges. In M. Bérubé and C. Nelson (eds.). *Higher education under fire: Politics, economics and the crisis of the humanities*. New York and London: Routledge.

Law, J. (2000). *Ladbroke Grove or how to think about failing systems*. www.comp.lancs.ac.uk/sociology/soc055jl.html (version: paddington5.doc)

Lee, L. (1999). *Shanghai modern: The flowering of a new urban culture in China, 1930–1945*. Cambridge, MA: Harvard University Press.

Lefebvre, H. (1971). *Everyday life in the modern world*. London: Allen Lane.

Lefebvre, H. (1991). *The production of space*. Oxford: Blackwell.

Le Goff, J. (1982). *Time, work and culture in the middle ages*. Chicago: University of Chicago Press.

Lennon, J. (1965). Nowhere man. On *Rubber soul*. (Album). Capitol/EMI.

Leopold, A. (1968). *A sand county almanac: And sketches here and there*. London, Oxford, and New York: Oxford University Press.

Levine, L. W. (1988). *Highbrow/lowbrow: The emergence of cultural hierarchy in America*. Cambridge, MA: Harvard University Press.

Levitas, R. (1990). *The concept of utopia*. Syracuse, NY: Syracuse University Press.

Lewis, O. (1959). *Five families: Mexican case studies in the culture of poverty*. New York: Basic Books.

Lewis, O. (1966). *La vida: A Puerto Rican family in the culture of poverty – San Juan and New York*. New York: Random House.

Leyshon, A., Matless, D., and Revill, G. (eds.) (1998). *The place of music*. New York: Guilford Press.

Lieven, A. (2002). The push for war. *London Review of Books*, 24(19), 1–9.

Lindqvist, S. (1996). *Exterminate all the brutes*. New York: New Press.

Linebaugh, P. and Rediker, M. (2000). *The many-headed hydra: Sailors, slaves, commoners, and the hidden history of the revolutionary Atlantic*. Boston: Beacon Press.

Littleton, C. (1997). Reconstructing sexual equality. In D. T. Meyers (ed.). *Feminist social thought: A reader*. New York and London: Routledge.

Locke, J. (1959). *Essay concerning human understanding*. New York: Dover. (Original work published 1690.)

Locke, J. (1990). *Second treatise of government*. Indianapolis: Hackett. (Original work published 1690.)

Lowenthal, D. (1985). *The past is another country*. Cambridge: Cambridge University Press.

Lukács, G. (1962). *The historical novel*. London: Merlin Press.

Lukács, G. (1971). *History and class consciousness: Studies in Marxist dialectics*. Cambridge, MA: MIT Press.

Lukes, S. (1972). *Individualism*. Oxford: Blackwell.

Lukes, S. (1974). *Power: A radical view*. Basingstoke: Macmillan.

Lyotard, J-F. (1984). *The postmodern condition: A report on knowledge*. Manchester: Manchester University Press.

MacCannell, D. (1976). *The tourist: A new theory of the leisure class*. New York: Schocken.

McDowell, L. (1999). *Gender, identity and place: Understanding feminist geographies*. Cambridge: Polity.

McGregor, R. (1997). *Imagined destinies: Aboriginal Australians and the doomed race theory, 1880–1939*. Melbourne: Melbourne University Press.

McIntosh, R. P. (1985). *The background of ecology: Concept and theory*. Cambridge: Cambridge University Press.

McKendrick, N., Brewer, J., and Plumb, J. H. (1982). *The birth of a consumer society: The commercialization of eighteenth century England*. London: Europa.

McLaren, P. (1994). White terror and oppositional agency: Towards a critical multiculturalism. In D. T. Goldberg (ed.). *Multiculturalism: A critical reader*. Oxford: Blackwell.

McLeish, J. (1975). *Soviet psychology: History, theory, content*. London: Methuen.

McLuhan, M. (1964). *Understanding media*. London: Routledge and Kegan Paul.

McLuhan, M. and McLuhan, E. (1988). *The laws of media*. Toronto: University of Toronto Press.

Macpherson, C. B. (1962). *The political theory of possessive individualism*. Oxford: Clarendon Press.

Macpherson, C. B. (1973). *Democratic theory: Essays in retrieval*. Oxford: Clarendon Press.

McRobbie, A. (1989). *Zoot suits and second-hand dresses: An anthology of fashion and music*. Basingstoke: Macmillan.

Magri, L. (1991). The European left between crisis and refoundation. *New Left Review*, 189, 5–18.

Malik, K. (1996). *The meaning of race*. London: Macmillan.

Malthus, T. R. (1798). *An essay on the principle of population as it affects the future improvement of society*. London: Johnson.

403

References

Mamdani, M. (1996). *Citizen and subject: Contemporary Africa and the legacy of late colonialism.* Princeton, NJ: Princeton University Press.

Manalansan, M. (2000). Diasporic deviants/divas: How Filipino gay transmigrants ''play with the world.'' In C. Patton and B. Sanchez-Eppler (eds.). *Queer diasporas.* Durham, NC: Duke University Press.

Mann, M. (1993). *The sources of social power.* Vol. 2. Cambridge: Cambridge University Press.

Mannheim, K. (1944). *Diagnosis of our time.* London: Routledge and Kegan Paul.

Mannheim, K. (1976). *Ideology and utopia: An introduction to the sociology of knowledge.* London: Routledge and Kegan Paul.

Manovich, L. (2001). *The language of new media.* Cambridge, MA: MIT Press.

Marcuse, H. (1969). *An essay on liberation.* Boston: Beacon Press.

Marsden, G. M. (1980). *Fundamentalism and American culture: The shaping of twentieth century evangelicalism.* New York: Oxford University Press.

Marshall, P. D. (1997). *Celebrity and power: Fame in contemporary culture.* Minneapolis and London: University of Minnesota Press.

Marshall, T. H. (1950). *Citizenship and social class and other essays.* Cambridge: Cambridge University Press.

Marshall, T. H. (1977). *Class, citizens and social development.* Chicago: University of Chicago Press.

Martin, J. and Neal, A. (2001). Defending civilization: How our universities are failing America and what can be done about it. www.goacta.org/Reports/defciv.pdf

Marx, K. (1972). Preface to a contribution to the critique of political economy. In R. C. Tucker (ed.). *The Marx–Engels reader.* New York: Norton. (Original work published 1859.)

Marx, K. (1973). *Grundrisse: Foundations of the critique of political economy.* New York: Random House. (Unpublished notes written during the winter of 1857–8 and first published in German in 1953.)

Marx, K. (1976). *Capital.* Vol. 1: *A critique of political economy.* Harmondsworth: Penguin. (Original work published 1867.)

Marx, K. and Engels, F. (1973). The Communist Manifesto. In D. Fernbach (ed.). *Political writings.* Vol. 1: *The revolutions of 1848.* London: Penguin. (Original work published 1848.)

Marx, K. and Engels, F. (1974). *The German ideology.* London: Lawrence and Wishart. (Original work published 1846.)

Massey, D. (1994). *Space, place and gender.* Minneapolis: University of Minnesota Press.

Mauss, M. (1985). A category of the human mind: The notion of person; the notion of self. In M. Carrithers, S. Collins, and S. Lukes (eds.). *The category of the person: Anthropology, philosophy, history.* Cambridge: Cambridge University Press.

Mayr, E. (1988). *Towards a new philosophy of biology.* Cambridge, MA: Harvard University Press.

Maza, S. (1997). Only connect: Family values in the age of sentiment. *Eighteenth Century Studies,* 30(3), 308–19.

Meese, E. (1986). *Attorney General's Commission on Pornography: Final report of the Special Committee on Pornography and Prostitution.* Washington, DC: US Department of Justice.

Menand, L. (2002). *The metaphysical club.* London: Flamingo.

Mendus, S. (1989). *Toleration and the limits of liberalism.* London: Macmillan.

Merchant, C. (1992). *Radical ecology: The search for a livable world.* New York and London: Routledge.

Metz, C. (1974). *Film language: A semiotics of the cinema.* New York: Oxford University Press.

Metz, C. (1981). *The imaginary signifier.* Bloomington, IN: University of Indiana Press.

Meyrowitz, J. (1985). *No sense of place.* Oxford: Oxford University Press.

Michelet, J. (1847–53). *Histoire de la revolution française.* (7 vols.). Paris: Chamerot.

Michels, R. (1949). *Political parties.* Glencoe, IL: Free Press.

Miliband, R. (1994). The plausibility of socialism. *New Left Review,* 200, 3–14.

Mill, J. (1997). *The history of British India.* London: Routledge. (Original work published 1817.)

Mill, J. S. (1965). *Principles of political economy, with some of their applications to social philosophy.* Toronto and London: University of Toronto Press/Routledge and Kegan Paul. (Original work published 1848.)

Mill, J. S. (1988). *The subjection of women.* (S. M. Okin, ed.) Indianapolis: Hackett. (Original work published 1869.)

Mill, J. S. (1989). *On liberty.* (S. Collini, ed.) Cambridge: Cambridge University Press. (Original work published 1859.)

Miller, D. (1976). *Social justice.* Oxford: Clarendon Press.

Miller, D. (1995). *On nationality.* Oxford: Clarendon Press.

Millett, K. (1970). *Sexual politics.* New York: Doubleday.

Mills, C. W. (1956). *The power elite.* New York: Oxford University Press.

Mills, C. W. (1964). *White collar: The American middle classes.* New York: Galaxy.

Millward, N., Bryson, A., and Forth, J. (2000). *All change at work? British employment relations 1980–1998, as portrayed by the workplace industrial relations survey series.* London: Routledge.

Mink, G. (1998). *Welfare's end.* Ithaca, NY: Cornell University Press.

Mitchell, D. (2000). *Cultural geography: A critical introduction.* Oxford: Blackwell.

Mitchell, J. (1973). *Psychoanalysis and feminism.* London: Allen Lane.

Mitchell, J. (2002). Reply to Lynn Segal's commentary. *Studies in Gender and Sexuality,* 3(2), 217–28.

Mitchell, T. (2002). Origins and limits of the modern idea of economy. Unpublished manuscript, Department of Politics, New York University.

Mitchell, W. J. T. (1986). Three theories of value. *Raritan,* 6(2), 63–76.

Mitchell, W. J. T. (ed.) (1994a). *Landscape and power.* Chicago: University of Chicago Press.

Mitchell, W. J. T. (1994b). *Picture theory: Essays on verbal and visual representation.* Chicago: Chicago University Press.

Mitchell, W. J. T. (2002). *Landscape and power.* Chicago and London: University of Chicago Press.

Monfasani, J. (1998). Humanism, Renaissance. In E. Craig (ed.). *Routledge encyclopedia of philosophy.* London and New York: Routledge.

Monsiváis, C. (1987). *Entrada libre: crónicas de la sociedad que se organiza.* Mexico: Ediciones Era.

Moore, M. (1992). The family as portrayed on prime-time television, 1947–1990: Structure and characteristics. *Sex Roles,* 26(1 and 2), 41–61.

More, T. (1995). *Utopia: Latin text and English translation.* (G. M. Logan, R. M. Adams, and C. H. Miller, eds.) Cambridge: Cambridge University Press. (Original work published 1516.)

References

Morgan, R. (1980). Theory and practice: porn and rape. In L. Lederer (ed.). *Take back the night: Women on porn*. New York: Bantam Books.

Morley, D. (2000). *Home territories: Media, mobility and identity*. London and New York: Routledge.

Morley, D. and Robins, K. (1995). *Spaces of identity: Global media, electronic landscapes and cultural boundaries*. London and New York: Routledge.

Morris, W. (1970). *News from nowhere*. London: Routledge. (Original work published 1891.)

Mouffe, C. (1988). Hegemony and new political subjects: Toward a new concept of democracy. In C. Nelson and L. Grossberg (eds.). *Marxism and the interpretation of culture*. Basingstoke: Macmillan.

Moylan, T. (1986). *Demand the impossible: Science fiction and the utopian imagination*. London: Methuen.

Mulvey, L. (1998). Visual pleasure and narrative cinema. In C. Penley (ed.). *Feminism and film criticism*. London and New York: Routledge.

Mumford, L. (1934). *Technics and civilization*. London: Routledge.

Mumford, L. (1968). City. In D. L. Sills (ed.). *International encyclopedia of the social sciences*. New York: Macmillan/Free Press.

Murray, C. (1984). *Losing ground: America's social policy 1950–1980*. New York: Basic Books.

Myerson, G. (2001). *Heidegger, Habermas and the mobile phone*. Cambridge: Icon Books.

Nagel, T. (1998). The limits of reductionism in biology. In *Novartis Foundation symposium*, 213. London: John Wiley.

Nash, K. (2000). *Contemporary political sociology*. Oxford: Blackwell.

Neal, P. (1997). *Liberalism and its discontents*. London: Macmillan.

Newfield, C. and Strickland, R. (eds.) (1995). *After political correctness: The humanities and society in the 1990s*. Boulder, CO, San Francisco, and Oxford: Westview Press.

Newton, Isaac (1966). *Mathematical principles*. Vol. I: *The motion of bodies*. Berkeley, CA: University of California Press. (Original work published 1687.)

Nicol, H. and Townsend Gault, I. (eds.) (2004). *Holding the line: borders in a global world*. Vancouver: UBC Press.

Niec, H. (ed.) (1998). *Cultural rights and wrongs*. Paris: UNESCO.

Nietzsche, F. (1969a). *On the genealogy of morals*. (W. Kauffman, ed.) New York: Random House. (Original work published 1887.)

Nietzsche, F. (1969b). *Thus spoke Zarathustra*. Harmondsworth: Penguin. (Original work published 1883–91.)

Noble, D. (1997). *The religion of technology: The divinity of man and the spirit of invention*. New York: Knopf.

Nora, P. (ed.) (1984–93). *Les lieux de memoire* (7 vols.). Paris: Gallimard.

NORAD (Norwegian Agency for Development Cooperation) (2001). *Handbook in human rights assessment: State obligations awareness and empowerment*. Oslo: NORAD.

Norris, P. (2001). *Digital divide: Civic engagement, information poverty, and the Internet worldwide*. New York: Cambridge University Press.

Nozick, R. (1974). *Anarchy, state, utopia*. New York: Basic Books.

Nussbaum, M. (2001). *Upheavals of thought: The intelligence of emotions*. Cambridge: Cambridge University Press.

Odinkalu, C. A. (2001). Analysis of paralysis or paralysis by analysis? Implementing economic, social and cultural rights under the African Charter on Human and Peoples' Rights. *Human Rights Quarterly*, 23(2), 327–69.

Odum, E. P. (1997). *Ecology: A bridge between science and society.* Sunderland, MA: Sinauer Associates.

Ogilvie, F. W. (1937). Tourist traffic. In E. Seligman (ed.). *Encyclopaedia of the social sciences.* New York: Macmillan.

Olby, R. (1974). *The path to the double helix.* Basingstoke: Macmillan.

O'Malley, P. (1996). Risk and responsibility. In A. Barry, T. Osborne, and N. Rose (eds.). *Foucault and political reason: Liberalism, neo-liberalism and rationalities of government.* Chicago: University of Chicago Press.

Ong, A. and Nonini, D. (eds.) (1997). *Ungrounded empires: The cultural politics of modern Chinese transnationalism.* New York and London: Routledge.

Ong, W. (1982). *Orality and literacy: The technologising of the word.* London and New York: Methuen.

Orwell, G. (1984). *1984.* London: Secker and Warburg.

Osborne, D. and Gaebler, T. (1992). *Reinventing government: How the entrepreneurial spirit is transforming the public sector.* New York: Plume.

Osborne, P. (1996). Modernity. In M. Payne (ed.). *A dictionary of cultural and critical theory.* Oxford: Blackwell.

Paine, T. (1969). *The rights of man.* Harmondsworth: Penguin. (Original work published 1791.)

Parekh, B. (1993). The cultural particularity of liberal democracy. In D. Held (ed.). *Prospects for democracy: North, South, East, West.* Cambridge: Polity.

Park, R. E. (1967). The city: Suggestions for the investigation of human behavior in the urban environment. In R. E. Park, E. W. Burgess, and R. McKenzie. *The city.* Chicago: University of Chicago Press.

Park, R. E., Burgess, E. W., and McKenzie, R. D. (1967). *The city.* Chicago: University of Chicago Press.

Parsons, T. (1937). *The structure of social action: A study in social theory with special reference to a group of recent European writers.* New York: McGraw-Hill.

Pascal, B. (1966). *Pensées.* Harmondsworth: Penguin. (Original work published 1670.)

Patton, C. and Sanchez-Eppler, B. (eds.) (2000). *Queer diasporas.* Durham, NC: Duke University Press.

Peabody, N. (1996). Tod's *Rajast'han* and the boundaries of imperial rule in nineteenth-century India. *Modern Asian Studies*, 30, 185–220.

Pêcheux, M. (1982). *Language, semantics and ideology: Stating the obvious.* London: Macmillan.

Pederson, J. (1926). *Israel: Its life and culture.* London: Oxford University Press.

Perrottet, T. (2002). Tales of ancient roamin'. *Sydney Morning Herald*, Weekend Edition, December 7–8, Travel 3.

Perry, R. (1992). A short history of the term *politically correct*. In P. Aufderheide (ed.). *Beyond PC: Toward a politics of understanding.* St Paul, MN: Graywolf Press.

Peterson, G. (2000). WordNet 1.6 Vocabulary Helper, www.notredame.ac.jp/egi-bin/wn?radical

Pettman, J. J. (1996). *Worlding women: A feminist international politics.* Sydney: Allen and Unwin.

References

Piaget, J. (1979). *Behaviour and evolution*. London: Routledge and Kegan Paul.

Piercy, M. (1979). *Woman on the edge of time*. London: Women's Press.

Pinker, S. (2002). *The blank slate*. Harmondsworth: Penguin.

Plummer, K. (1975). *Sexual stigma: An interactionist account*. London: Routledge and Kegan Paul.

Plummer, K. (1995). *Telling sexual stories*. London and New York: Routledge.

Polanyi, K. (2001). *The great transformation: The political and economic origins of our time*. Boston: Beacon Press.

Popper, K. (1962). *The open society and its enemies*. London: Routledge.

Popper, K. (1986). *The logic of scientific discovery*. New York: Basic Books. (Original work published 1934.)

Popular Memory Group (1982). Popular memory: Theory, politics, method. In R. Johnson, G. McLennan, B. Schwarz, and D. Sutton (eds.). *Making histories: Studies in history writing and politics*. London: Hutchinson.

Powell, W. and Clemens, E. (eds.) (1998). *Private action and the public good*. New Haven, CT: Yale University Press.

Prakash, G. (ed.) (1995). *After colonialism: Imperial histories and postcolonial displacements*. Princeton, NJ: Princeton University Press.

Pramoedya, A. T. (1991a). *Child of all nations*. London: Penguin.

Pramoedya, A. T. (1991b). *This earth of mankind*. New York and London: Penguin.

Pratt, M. L. (1992). Humanities for the future: Reflections on the Western culture debate at Stanford. In D. Gless and B. Herrnstein Smith (eds.). *The politics of liberal education*. Durham, NC: Duke University Press.

Propp, V. (1968). *Morphology of the folktale*. Austin, TX: University of Texas Press.

Proust, M. (1970). *Remembrance of things past*. London: Chatto and Windus. (Original work published 1913.)

Putnam, R. (2000). *Bowling alone: The collapse and revival of American community*. New York: Simon and Schuster.

Radin, M. J. (2001). *Contested commodities*. Cambridge, MA: Harvard University Press.

Radstone, S. and Hodgkin, K. (eds.) (2003). *Regimes of memory*. London: Routledge.

Raphael, D. D. (1990). *Problems of political philosophy*. London: Macmillan.

Rawls, J. (1999). *A theory of justice* (2nd edition). Oxford: Clarendon Press.

Ray, W. (2001). *The logic of culture: Authority and identity in the modern era*. Oxford: Blackwell.

Raz, J. (1986). *The morality of freedom*. Oxford: Clarendon Press.

Redfield, J. (1995). Homo domesticus. In J-P. Vernant (ed.). *The Greeks*. Chicago: University of Chicago Press.

Redfield, R. and Singer, M. (1954). The cultural life of cities. *Economic Development and Cultural Change*, 3, 53–73.

Rees, J. (1971). *Equality: Key concepts in political science*. Basingstoke: Macmillan.

Reich, R. B. (1991). *The work of nations: Preparing ourselves for 21st century capitalism*. New York: Vintage.

Renan, E. (1996). What is a nation?. In G. Eley and R. G. Suny (eds.). *Becoming national: A reader*. Oxford and New York: Oxford University Press. (Original work published 1882.)

Rheingold, H. (1991). *Virtual reality*. New York: Simon and Schuster.

Rhodes, R. A. W. (1994). The hollowing out of the state. *Political Quarterly*, 65, 138–51.

Rich, A. (1993). Compulsory heterosexuality and lesbian existence. In H. Ablelove, M. A. Burall, and D. M. Halperin (eds.). *The lesbian and gay studies reader.* London and New York: Routledge.

Rifkin, J. (1995). *The end of work: The decline of the global labor market and the dawn of the post-market era.* New York: G. P. Putnam's Sons.

Robinson, C. (1983). *Black Marxism: The making of the black radical tradition.* London: Zed Press.

Rodriguez, C. (2001). *Fissures in the mediascape: An international study of citizens' media.* Creskill, NJ: Hampton Press.

Rojek, C. (2001). *Celebrity.* London: Reaktion Books.

Rojek, C. and Urry, J. (eds.) (1997). *Touring cultures.* London and New York: Routledge.

Rorty, A. O. (1988). Persons and personae. In A. O. Rorty (ed.). *Mind in action: Essays in the philosophy of mind.* Boston: Beacon Press.

Rorty, R. (1979). *Philosophy and the mirror of nature.* Princeton, NJ: Princeton University Press.

Rorty, R. (1982). *Consequences of pragmatism: Essays, 1972–1980.* Princeton, NJ: Princeton University Press.

Rorty, R. (1991). Is natural science a natural kind? In R. Rorty (ed.). *Objectivity, relativism, and truth: Philosophical papers.* Vol. 1. Cambridge: Cambridge University Press.

Rose, H. and Rose, S. (eds.) (2000). *Alas, poor Darwin: Arguments against evolutionary psychology.* London: Jonathan Cape.

Rose, M. (1993). *Authors and owners: The invention of copyright.* Cambridge, MA: Harvard University Press.

Rose, N. (1985). *The psychological complex.* London: Routledge.

Rose, N. (1996). *Inventing our selves: Psychology, power and personhood.* New York: Cambridge University Press.

Rose, N. (1999). *Powers of freedom: Reframing political thought.* Cambridge: Cambridge University Press.

Rose, S. (1997). *Lifelines: Biology, freedom, determinism.* London: Penguin.

Rosenberg, A. (1985). *The structure of biological science.* Cambridge: Cambridge University Press.

Roszack, T. (1971). *The making of the counter culture.* London: Faber.

Roszak, T. (1986). *The cult of information: The folklore of computers and the true art of thinking.* Cambridge: Lutterworth.

Rowbotham, S. (1983). *Dreams and dilemmas: Collected writings.* London: Virago.

Rubin, G. (1975). The traffic in women: Notes on the "political economy" of sex. In R. R. Reiter (ed.). *Toward an anthropology of women.* New York: Monthly Review Press.

Runciman, W. G. (1998). *The social animal.* London: HarperCollins.

Runnymede Trust Commission on the Future of Multi-Ethnic Britain (2000). *The future of multi-ethnic Britain: The Parekh report.* London: Profile Books.

Rushdie, S. (1994). *The satanic verses.* London: Vintage.

Russell, B. (1938). *Power: A new social analysis.* London: Allen and Unwin.

Sabini, J. P. and Silver, M. (1980). Survivors. In R. E. Dinsdale (ed.). *Survivors, victims, perpetrators.* London: Hemisphere.

Safran, W. (1991). Diasporas in modern societies: Myths of homeland and return. *Diaspora*, 1(1), 83–99.

References

Said, E. (1978). *Orientalism*. London and New York: Routledge and Kegan Paul.

Said, E. (1994). *Representations of the intellectual*. London: Random House.

Sakai, N. (1997). *Translation and subjectivity: On "Japan" and cultural nationalism*. Minneapolis: University of Minnesota Press.

Samuel, R. (1994). *Theatres of memory*. Vol. 1: *Past and present in contemporary culture*. London: Verso.

Samuels, A. (2001). *Politics on the couch: Citizenship and the internal life*. London: Profile Books.

Sanders, R. (1653). *Physiognomie and chiromancie, metoposcopie, the symmetrical proportions and signal moles of the body*. London: R. White.

Saul, J. R. (1995). *The doubter's companion: A dictionary of aggressive common sense*. Toronto: Penguin.

Sawyer, R. K. (2002). A discourse on discourse: An archaeological history of an intellectual concept. *Cultural Studies*, 16(3), 433–56.

Scannell, P. (1988). Radio times. In P. Drummond and R. Paterson (eds.). *Television and its audience*. London: BFI.

Scannell, P. (1996). *Radio, television and modern life: A phenomenological approach*. Oxford: Blackwell.

Schafer, R. (1976). *A new language for psychoanalysis*. New Haven, CT, and London: Yale University Press.

Schaffer, S. (1997). What is science? In J. Krige and D. Pestre (eds.). *Science in the twentieth century*. Amsterdam: Harwood Academic.

Schiller, F. (1967). *On the aesthetic education of man*. (E. Wilkinson and L. A. Willoughby, eds.) Oxford: Clarendon Press. (Original work published 1795.)

Schlesinger, A. J. (1992). *The disuniting of America: Reflections on multiculturalism*. New York and London: Norton.

Schmitt, C. (1985). *Political theology: Four chapters in the history of sovereignty*. Cambridge, MA: MIT Press.

Schopenhauer, A. (1969). *The world as will and representation*. London: Dover Publications. (Original work published 1819.)

Schor, J. (1992). *The overworked American*. New York: Basic Books.

Schor, N. (1992). Fetishism. In E. Wright (ed.). *Feminism and psychoanalysis: A critical dictionary*. Oxford: Blackwell.

Schram, S. (1995). *Words of welfare: The poverty of social science and the social science of poverty*. Minneapolis: University of Minnesota Press.

Schumacher, E. F. (1973). *Small is beautiful: Economics as if people mattered*. New York: Harper and Row.

Schumpeter, J. A. (1943). *Capitalism, socialism and democracy*. London: Allen and Unwin.

Schwab, R. (1984). *The oriental renaissance: Europe's rediscovery of India and the east, 1680–1880*. New York: Columbia University Press.

Scott, J. (1992). *Social network analysis*. London: Sage.

Scott, J. (1997). Deconstructing equality-versus-difference: Or the uses of post-structuralist theory for feminism. In D. T. Meyers (ed.). *Feminist social thought: A reader*. New York and London: Routledge.

Scott, J. (2001). *Power.* Cambridge: Polity.

Scott, J. W. (1992). Experience. In J. Butler and J. W. Scott (eds.). *Feminists theorize the political.* New York: Routledge.

Sebeok, T. A. (ed.) (1986). *Encyclopedic dictionary of semiotics.* Berlin, New York, and Amsterdam: Mouton.

Sedgwick, E. K. (1993). *Tendencies.* Durham, NC: Duke University Press.

Sedgwick, E. K. (1994). *The epistemology of the closet.* London: Penguin.

Segal, D. (2000). ''Western civ'' and the staging of history in American higher education. *American Historical Review,* 105(3), 770–805.

Segal, L. and McIntosh, M. (eds.) (1992). *Sex exposed: Sexuality and the pornography debate.* London: Virago.

Sennett, R. (1977). *The fall of public man.* New York: Knopf.

Sennett, R. (1998). *The corrosion of character: The personal consequences of work in the new capitalism.* New York: Norton.

Serres, M. (1995). *Angels: A modern myth.* Paris and New York: Flammarion.

Shannon, C. and Weaver, W. (1964). *The mathematical theory of communication.* Urbana, IL: University of Illinois Press.

Shapin, S. (1996). *The scientific revolution.* Chicago: University of Chicago Press.

Shapin, S. (2001). How to be antiscientific. In J. A. Labinger and H. Collins (eds.). *The one culture? A conversation about science.* Chicago: University of Chicago Press.

Shapiro, J. P. (1993). *No pity: People with disabilities forging a new civil rights movement.* London: Times Books.

Shapiro, M. and McDonald, D. (1992). I'm not a real doctor, but I play one in virtual reality: Implications of virtual reality for judgments about reality. *Journal of Communication,* 42(4), 94–114.

Shiach, M. (1989). *Discourse on popular culture.* Cambridge: Polity.

Shweder, R. A. (2001). A polytheistic conception of the sciences and the virtues of deep variety. In A. R. Damasio, A. Harrington, J. Kagan, B. S. McEwen, H. Moss, and R. Shaikh (eds.). *Unity of knowledge: The convergence of natural and human science (Annals of the New York Academy of Sciences),* 935, 217–32. New York: New York Academy of Sciences.

Silver, L. (1998). *Remaking Eden: Cloning and beyond in a brave new world.* London: Weidenfeld and Nicolson.

Silverstone, R. (1985). *Framing science: The making of a BBC documentary.* London: BFI.

Silverstone, R. (1994). *Television and everyday life.* London: Routledge.

Simmel, G. (1957). Fashion. *American Journal of Sociology,* 62, 541–58. (Original work published 1904.)

Simmel, G. (1997). The metropolis and mental life. In D. Frisby and M. Featherstone. (eds.). *Simmel on culture: Selected writings.* London: Sage. (Original work published 1903.)

Simon, B. (1972). *The radical tradition in education in Britain.* London: Lawrence and Wishart.

Singer, D. (1999). *Whose millennium?: Theirs or ours.* New York: Monthly Review Press.

Skinner, B. F. (1972). *Beyond freedom and dignity.* London: Cape.

Skinner, Q. (1989). The state. In T. Ball, J. Farr, and R. L. Hansen (eds.). *Political innovation and conceptual change.* Cambridge: Cambridge University Press.

References

Skogly, S. I. (2001). *The human rights obligation of the World Bank and the International Monetary Fund*. London: Cavendish.

Smelser, N. J. (1962). *Theories of collective behavior.* New York: Free Press.

Smelser, N. J. and Baltes, P. B. (eds.) (2001). *International encyclopedia of the social and behavioral sciences.* Vol. 7. Amsterdam: Elsevier.

Smith, A. (1977). *An inquiry into the nature and causes of the wealth of nations* (2 vols.). Chicago: University of Chicago Press. (Original work published 1776.)

Smith, A. (1978). *Lectures on jurisprudence.* Oxford: Clarendon Press. (Original work published 1752–4.)

Smith, B. H. (1988). *Contingencies of value: Alternative conceptions for interpretive theory.* Cambridge, MA: Harvard University Press.

Smith, N. (1984). *Uneven development: Nature, capital and the production of space.* Oxford: Blackwell.

Snow, D. A., Rochford, E. B., Jr, Worden, S. K., and Benford, R. D. (1986). Frame alignment processes, micromobilization, and movement participation. *American Sociological Review, 51,* 464–81.

Soja, E. (1989). *Postmodern geographies: The reassertion of space in critical social theory.* London and New York: Verso.

Sokal, A. and Bricmont, J. (1998). *Fashionable nonsense: Postmodern intellectuals' abuse of science.* New York: St Martin's Press.

Sontag, S. (1966). *Against interpretation.* New York: Deli.

Spivak, G. C. (1988). *In other worlds: Essays in cultural politics.* New York: Routledge.

Spivak, G. C. (1999). *A critique of postcolonial reason: Toward a history of the vanishing present.* Cambridge, MA: Harvard University Press.

Spivak, G. C. (2000). Explanation and culture: Marginalia. In R. T. Ferguson, M. Gever, T. T. Minh-ha, and C. West (eds.). *Out there: Marginalization and contemporary culture.* Cambridge, MA: MIT Press.

Splichal, S. (2000). Defining public opinion in history. In H. Hardt and S. Splichal (eds.). *Ferdinand Toennies on public opinion.* London: Rowman and Littlefield.

Squires, J. (2000). *Gender in political theory.* Cambridge: Polity.

Steketee, M. (2002). M-word is kosher again, but politics won't let it prosper. *Australian,* May 9, 12.

Steur, J. (1992). Defining virtual reality: Dimensions determining telepresence. *Journal of Communication,* 42(4), 73–93.

Stocking, G. W., Jr (1968). *Race, culture and evolution: Essays in the history of anthropology.* New York: Free Press.

Stoler, A. L. (1995). *Race and the education of desire: Foucault's history of sexuality and the colonial order of things.* Durham, NC: Duke University Press.

Stoller, R. J. (1968). *Sex and gender.* London: Hogarth Press/Institute of Psychoanalysis.

Storey, J. (2003a). *Inventing popular culture.* Oxford: Blackwell.

Storey, J. (2003b). The social life of opera. *European Journal of Cultural Studies,* 6(1), 5–35.

Strathern, M. (1992). *After nature: English kinship in the late twentieth century.* Cambridge: Cambridge University Press.

Strathern, M. (ed.) (2000). *Audit cultures.* London: Routledge.

Stratton, J. (1998). *Race daze: Australia in identity crisis*. Sydney: Pluto Press.

Sullivan, G. and Jackson, P. (eds.) (2001). *Gay and lesbian Asia: Culture, identity, community*. New York: Harrington Park Press.

Sustainable Sydney Conference (2001). *Policies and Practice: Solutions for Sydney's Future* (program).

Swinglehurst, E. (1982). *Cook's tours: The story of popular travel*. Poole: Blandford Press.

Sydney Morning Herald (2002). Don't mention fun. *Sydney Morning Herald*, December 9, http://smh.com.au/articles/2002/12/09/1039379771332.html

Tawney, R. H. (1964). *Equality*. London: Allen and Unwin.

Taylor, B. (1983). *Eve and the New Jerusalem: Socialism and feminism in the nineteenth century*. London: Virago.

Taylor, C. (1989). *Sources of the self*. Cambridge, MA: Harvard University Press.

Taylor, C. (1992). *Multiculturalism and "the politics of recognition."* Princeton, NJ: Princeton University Press.

Taylor, J. (1991). Up against the new McCarthyism. *Sydney Morning Herald*, April 2. (Reprinted from *New York Magazine* and *Literary Review*, London.)

Taylor, R. (2002). *Britain's world of work: Myths and realities*. Swindon: Economic and Social Research Council.

Tertullian (1931). *Apology; De spectaculis*. London and Cambridge, MA: Heinemann/Harvard University Press. (Original works c.197 and c.200.)

Thatcher, M. (1987). Interview. *Woman's Own*, October 31, 8–10.

Thatcher, M. (1989). *The revival of Britain: Speeches on home and economic affairs 1975–1988*. (Alistair B. Cooke, compiler.) London: Aurum Press.

Thatcher, M. (1993). *The Downing Street years*. London: HarperCollins.

Thomas, N. (1989). *Out of time: History and evolution in anthropological discourse*. Ann Arbor, MI: University of Michigan Press.

Thompson, E. P. (1963). *The making of the English working class*. London: Gollancz.

Thompson, E. P. (1978). *The poverty of theory, and other essays*. London: Merlin Press.

Thompson, E. P. (1993). Time, work-discipline and industrial capitalism. In E. P. Thompson. *Customs in common*. Harmondsworth: Penguin.

Tiffin, J. and Rajasingham, L. (1995). *In search of the virtual class*. London: Routledge.

Tilgher, A. (1931). *Work: What it has meant to men throughout the ages*. London: Harrap.

Tilly, C. (ed.) (1995). Citizenship, identity and social history. *International Review of Social History*, 40, Supplement 3, 1–236.

Todorov, T. (1990). *Genres in discourse*. Cambridge: Cambridge University Press.

Tölölyan, K. (1991). The nation-state and its others: In lieu of a preface. *Diaspora*, 1(1), 3–7.

Toolan, M. J. (1988). *Narrative: A critical linguistic introduction*. London and New York: Routledge.

Tönnies, F. (1887). *Gemeinschaft und gesellschaft*. Leipzig: Fues. (English trans. *Fundamental concepts of sociology [Gemeinschaft und Gesellschaft]*. [8th expanded edition.] New York: American Book Company, 1940.)

Touraine, A. (1985). An introduction to the study of new social movements. *Social Research*, 52(4), 749–87.

413

References

Townsend, P. (1979). *Poverty in the United Kingdom: A survey of household resources and standards of living*. Harmondsworth: Penguin.

Trautmann, T. (1997). *Aryans and British India*. Berkeley, CA, and Los Angeles: University of California Press.

Trotsky, L. (1952). *Revolution betrayed*. London: New Park.

Turner, B. (1997). *The body and society*. London: Sage.

Turner, J. (ed.) (1996). *The Grove dictionary of art*. London: Macmillan.

Turner, L. and Ash, J. (1975). *The golden hordes: International tourism and the pleasure periphery*. London: Constable.

Tylor, E. B. (1874). *Primitive culture: Researches into the development of mythology, philosophy, religion, language, art and custom*. Boston: Estes and Lauriat.

UNDP (United Nations Development Program) (2000). *Human development report 2000*. New York: Oxford University Press.

Urry, J. (2002). *The tourist gaze*. London, Thousand Oaks, CA, and New Delhi: Sage.

Vance, C. (ed.) (1984). *Pleasure and danger: Exploring female sexuality*. Boston and London: Routledge and Kegan Paul.

Veblen, T. (1899). *A theory of the leisure class*. New York: American Classics.

Verdery, K. (1994). Ethnicity, nationalism, and state-making. In H. Vermeulen and C. Govers (eds.). *The anthropology of ethnicity: Beyond ''ethnic groups and boundaries.''* Amsterdam: Het Spinhuis.

Vico, G. (1968). *The new science of Giambattista Vico*. Ithaca, NY, and London: Cornell University Press. (Original work published 1744.)

Viswanathan, V. (1989). *Masks of conquest*. New York: Columbia University Press.

Voltaire (1971). *Philosophical dictionary*. Harmondsworth: Penguin. (Original work published 1770.)

von Hallberg, R. (ed.) (1984). *Canons*. Chicago and London: University of Chicago Press.

Waldron, J. (1993). *Liberal rights*. Cambridge: Cambridge University Press.

Wales, K. (2001). *A dictionary of stylistics*. Edinburgh: Pearson Education.

Wallace, A. R. (2002). *Infinite tropica*. (Andrew Berry, ed.) London: Verso.

Walzer, M. (1983). *Spheres of justice: A defence of pluralism and equality*. New York: Basic Books.

Warner, M. (ed.) (1993). *Fear of a queer planet: Queer politics and social theory*. Minneapolis and London: University of Minnesota Press.

Warner, M. (2001). *Publics and counterpublics*. Cambridge, MA: Zone Books.

Waters, M. (1995). *Globalization*. London: Routledge.

Watson, J. B. (1924). *Behaviorism*. New York: Norton.

Weber, M. (1970a). Class, status, party. In H. H. Gerth and C. Wright Mills (eds.). *From Max Weber: Essays in sociology*. London: Routledge and Kegan Paul.

Weber, M. (1970b). Science as a vocation. In H. H. Gerth and C. Wright Mills (eds.). *From Max Weber: Essays in sociology*. London: Routledge and Kegan Paul.

Weber, M. (1978). *Economy and society: An outline of interpretive sociology*. Berkeley, CA: University of California Press.

Webster, F. (2002). *Theories of the information society* (2nd edition). London: Routledge.

Weeks, J. (1977). *Coming out: Homosexual politics in Britain from the nineteenth century to the present*. London: Quartet Books.

Weeks, J. (1985). *Sexuality and its discontents: Meanings, myths and modern sexualities*. London and New York: Routledge.

Weeks, J. (1995). *Invented moralities: Sexual values in an age of uncertainty*. Cambridge: Polity.

Weiner, P. R. (ed.) (1973). *Dictionary of the history of ideas*. Vol. 4. New York: Charles Scribner's Sons.

Weintraub, J. and Kumar, K. (eds.) (1997). *Public and private in thought and practice*. Chicago: University of Chicago Press.

Wertheim, M. (1999). *The pearly gates of cyberspace: A history of space from Dante to the Internet*. New York: Norton.

West, C. (1990). The new cultural politics of difference. In R. T. Ferguson, M. Gever, T. T.Minh-Ha, and C. West (eds.). *Out there: Marginalization and contemporary cultures*. Cambridge, MA: MIT Press.

White, H. (1973). *Metahistory: The historical imagination in nineteenth-century Europe*. Baltimore, MD: Johns Hopkins University Press.

Whyte, L. (1959). *The unconscious before Freud*. London: Tavistock.

Whyte, W. H. (1960). *The organization man*. Harmondsworth: Penguin.

Widgery, D. (1976). *The left in Britain 1956–1968*. Harmondsworth: Penguin.

Wilde, O. (1966). *Complete works*. (V. Holland, ed.) London: Collins.

William, F. (1998). Value. In E. Craig (ed.). *Routledge encyclopedia of philosophy*. London and New York: Routledge.

Williams, B. (1979). *Report of the Committee on Obscenity and Film Censorship*. Cmnd 7772. London: HMSO.

Williams, G. (2001). Theorizing disability. In G. L. Albrecht, K. D. Seelman, and M. Bury (eds.). *Handbook of disability studies*. London: Sage.

Williams, R. (1958). *Culture and society, 1780–1950*. London: Chatto and Windus.

Williams, R. (1965). *The long revolution*. Harmondsworth: Penguin.

Williams, R. (1973). *The country and the city*. London: Chatto and Windus.

Williams, R. (1974). *Television: Technology and cultural form*. Glasgow: Fontana.

Williams, R. (1976). *Keywords: A vocabulary of culture and society*. London: Fontana/Croom Helm.

Williams, R. (1979). *Politics and letters: Interviews with New Left Review*. London: New Left Books.

Williams, R. (1980). *Problems in materialism and culture: Selected essays*. London: Verso.

Williams, R. (1981). *Culture*. London: Fontana.

Williams, R. (1983). *Keywords: A vocabulary of culture and society*. (Revised edition.) New York: Oxford University Press.

Williams, R. (1989). *Resources of hope: Culture, democracy, socialism*. (R. Gale, ed.) London: Verso.

Williams, S. J. (2001). Desire, excess and the transgression of corporeal boundaries. In S. J. Williams (ed.). *Emotion and social theory: Corporeal reflections of the (ir)rational*. London and New York: Sage.

Williamson, D. (1989). *Authorship and criticism*. Sydney: Local Consumption Publications.

Williamson, J. (1995). *Consuming passions: The dynamics of popular culture*. London: Marion Boyars.

References

Wilson, E. (1998). Fashion and postmodernism. In J. Storey (ed.). *Cultural theory and popular culture: A reader*. London: Prentice Hall.

Wilson, E. O. (1975). *Sociobiology: A new synthesis*. Cambridge, MA: Harvard University Press.

Wilson, E. O. (1998). *Consilience*. London: Little, Brown.

Winner, L. (1986). *The whale and the reactor: A search for limits in an age of high technology*. Chicago: University of Chicago Press.

Wolfe, T. (1971). *Radical chic and Mau-Mauing the flak-catchers*. New York: Bantam Books.

Wolff, R. P., Marcuse, H., and Moore, B. (1969). *A critique of pure tolerance*. Boston: Beacon Press.

Wollstonecraft, M. (1975). *A vindication of the rights of woman*. Harmondsworth: Penguin. (Original work published 1792.)

Woodmansee, M. (1994). *The author, art, and the market: Rereading the history of aesthetics*. New York: Columbia University Press.

Woolf, V. (1929). *A room of one's own*. London: Hogarth Press.

Woolf, V. (1986). *Three guineas*. London: Hogarth Press.

Wright, E. O. (1979). Intellectuals and the class structure of capitalist society. In P. Walker (ed.). *Between labor and capital*. Boston: South End Press.

Wright, P. (1985). *On living in an old country: The national past in contemporary Britain*. London: Verso.

Wyrwa, U. (1998). Consumption and consumer society: A contribution to the history of ideas. In S. Strasser, C. McGovern, and M. Judt (eds.). *Getting and spending: European and American consumer societies in the twentieth century*. Cambridge: Cambridge University Press.

Yeates, N. (2001). *Globalization and social policy*. London: Sage.

Young, M. (1961). *The rise of meritocracy 1870–2033*. Harmondsworth: Penguin.

Young, I. M. (1990). *Justice and the politics of difference*. Princeton, NJ: Princeton University Press.

Young, R. M. (1985). *Darwin's metaphor: Nature's place in Victorian culture*. Cambridge: Cambridge University Press.

Zukin, S. (1988). *Loft living: Culture and capital in urban change*. London: Radius.

Notes on Editors and Contributors

Notes on editors

Tony Bennett is professor of sociology at the Open University and a director of the Economic and Social Science Research Centre on Socio-Cultural Change. His publications include *Formalism and Marxism; Outside literature; Bond and beyond: The political career of a popular hero* (with Janet Woollacott); *The birth of the museum: History, theory, politics; Culture: A reformer's science; Accounting for tastes: Australian everyday cultures* (with Michael Emmison and John Frow); *Culture in Australia: Policies, publics, programs* (co-edited with David Carter); *Contemporary culture and everyday life* (edited with Elizabeth Silva); and, most recently, *Pasts beyond memory: Evolution, museums, colonialism.* He was elected to membership of the Australian Academy of the Humanities in 1998.

Lawrence Grossberg is the Morris Davis distinguished professor of communication studies and cultural studies at the University of North Carolina at Chapel Hill. He has written extensively on cultural studies, cultural theory, popular music, and the politics of the New Right. He is co-editor of the journal *Cultural Studies*. His most recent book is entitled *Caught in the crossfire: Kids, politics and America's future.*

Meaghan Morris is chair professor of cultural studies and co-ordinator of the Kwan Fong Cultural Research and Development Programme at Lingnan University, Hong Kong. She has written widely on action cinema, popular historiography, and cultural theory, and her books include *"Race" panic and the memory of migration* (co-edited with Brett de Bary); *Too soon, too late: History in popular culture; Australian cultural studies: A reader* (co-edited with John Frow); and *The pirate's fiancée: Feminism, reading, postmodernism*. She is completing a study of action cinema (supported by the Research Grants Council of Hong Kong) and a biography of Ernestine Hill, for which she held an Australian Research Council Senior Fellowship in 1994–9.

Notes on contributors

Ien Ang is professor of cultural studies and director of the Centre for Cultural Research at the University of Western Sydney. She is the author of several influential essays and books including *Watching Dallas* and *On not speaking Chinese*. Her research covers a broad range of issues including cultural difference and diversity in a globalizing world, the impact of migration and ethnicity, and cultural institutional change. She is an elected fellow of the Australian Academy of the Humanities.

Zygmunt Bauman is emeritus professor of sociology, Universities of Leeds and Warsaw. Recent publications include *Liquid modernity*; *Society under siege*; *Liquid love*; and *Wasted lives*.

Jody Berland is associate professor of humanities, Atkinson College, and director of graduate programs in communication and culture, humanities, music, and social and political thought, York University. She has published widely on cultural studies, Canadian communication theory, music and media, cultural studies of nature, and social space. She is co-editor of *Cultural capital: A reader on modernist legacies, state institutions and the value(s) of art* and editor of *Topia: Canadian Journal of Cultural Studies*. She is completing a book on space and culture in Canada.

Michael Bérubé is the Paterno family professor in literature at Pennsylvania State University. He is the author of four books: *Marginal forces/cultural centers: Tolson, Pynchon, and the politics of the canon*; *Public access: Literary theory and American cultural politics*; *Life as we know it: A father, a family, and an exceptional child*; and *The employment of English: Theory, jobs, and the future of literary studies*. He is also the editor, with Cary Nelson, of *Higher education under fire: Politics, economics, and the crisis of the humanities*.

Roland Boer is senior Logan research fellow in the Centre for Studies in Religion and Theology, Monash University. He has published in biblical studies, Marxist criticism, cultural studies, and postcolonial criticism. His most recent book is *Marxist criticism of the Bible*.

Craig Calhoun is president of the Social Science Research Council and professor of sociology and history at New York University. Among his books are *Critical social theory: Culture, history and the challenge of difference* and *Nationalism*. He is also the editor of the *Dictionary of the social sciences* and *Understanding September 11*.

John Clarke is professor of social policy at the Open University. Having studied management as an undergraduate, he escaped, with great relief, to study at the Centre for Contemporary Cultural Studies at the University of Birmingham. Subsequently he has worked at North East London Polytechnic and the Open University. His work tries to bring cultural analysis to the study of welfare states. He has written extensively on welfare states, managerialism, and the politics of social policy. With Janet Newman, he is the co-author of *The managerial state,* and is currently writing a book on analyzing welfare states and their contemporary transformations.

Jennifer Craik is associate professor of cultural studies and cultural policy at Griffith University, Brisbane. She researches aspects of cultural industries including tourism, fashion, cultural policy, media policy, and popular culture. Publications include *The face of fashion* and *Resorting to tourism*.

Jonathan Crary is professor of art history at Columbia University. A founding editor of Zone Books, he is the author of *Techniques of the observer* and *Suspensions of perception*.

419

Ann Curthoys is Manning Clark professor of history at the Australian National University; in 2003–4 she was G08 visiting professor of Australian studies at Georgetown University, Washington, DC. She is a fellow of the Academy of the Social Sciences in Australia and of the Australian Academy of the Humanities. She has written on many aspects of Australian history; her most recent book is *Freedom ride: A freedom rider remembers*. She is currently working with Susan Magarey on a history of women's liberation in Australia.

Mitchell Dean is professor of sociology and dean of the Division of Society, Culture, Media and Philosophy at Macquarie University, Sydney. He is the author of several books, including *Governmentality: Power and rule in modern society*. He is currently working on questions of sovereignty and international governmentality.

Nicholas Dirks is Franz Boas professor of anthropology and history at Columbia University in the City of New York. He is the author of *The hollow crown: Ethnohistory of an Indian kingdom* and *Castes of mind: Colonialism and the making of modern India,* and editor of *Colonialism and culture* and *In near ruins*. He is currently completing a new book to be entitled *The scandal of empire*.

James Donald is professor of film studies at the University of New South Wales in Sydney. He is author of *Imagining the modern city* and *Sentimental education*, co-author of *The Penguin atlas of media and information*, editor of a dozen books on aspects of the media, culture, and education, and former editor of the journals *Screen Education* and *New Formations*.

Paul du Gay is professor of sociology at the Open University and visiting professor in the Centre for Critical Theory at the University of the West of England. His publications include *Consumption and identity at work: Questions of cultural identity* (edited with Stuart Hall); *In praise of bureaucracy*; and *Cultural economy* (edited with Michael Pryke).

Joanne Finkelstein is in the Sociology Department at the University of Sydney. She has most recently edited a special issue of *Postcolonial Studies* on East–West fashions, and is the author of *The fashioned self* and *After a fashion*.

André Frankovits is the executive director of the Human Rights Council of Australia. He is the co-author of *The rights way to development: Policy and practice* and *Working together*. He is a consultant to the United Nations and has authored numerous articles on human rights in Australian and international publications.

Anne Freadman is professor of French in the University of Melbourne. Her work in cultural analysis investigates the intrication of sign theory and genre. Recent publications include "The visit of the instrument maker," in *The semiotics of writing* (eds. Coppock, Bologna, and Brepols); "Uptake," in *The rhetoric and ideology of genre* (eds. Coe, Lingard, and Teslenko); "The green tarpaulin: Another story of the Ryan hanging," *UTS Review*, 5(2); "The culture peddlers," *Postcolonial Studies*, 4(3); and *The machinery of talk: Charles Peirce and the sign hypothesis*.

Simon Frith is professor of film and media at the University of Stirling. He is author of *Sound effects* and *Performing rites*, and editor (with Will Straw and John Street) of *The Cambridge companion to pop and rock*.

John Frow is professor of English at the University of Melbourne. He is the author of *Marxism and literary history*; *Cultural studies and cultural value*; *Time and commodity culture*; and *Accounting for tastes: Australian everyday cultures* (with Tony Bennett and Michael Emmison). A book on genre is forthcoming.

J. K. Gibson-Graham is the pen name of Julie Graham (professor of geography, University of Massachusetts, Amherst) and Katherine Gibson (professor of human geography, Research School of Pacific and Asian Studies, Australian National University). Gibson-Graham is the author of *The end of capitalism (as we knew it): A feminist critique of political economy* and co-editor with Stephen Resnick and Richard Wolff of *Class and its others* and *Re/Presenting class: Essays in postmodern Marxism.*

Avery F. Gordon is professor of sociology at the University of California, Santa Barbara. She is the author of *Keeping good time*; *Ghostly matters*; and other works. She is currently writing a book on the utopian to be entitled *In the shadow of the bottom line.*

Gay Hawkins is an associate professor in the School of Media and Communications at the University of New South Wales. She has written a book on arts policy, *From Nimbin to Mardi Gras: Constructing community arts*, and co-edited a book on waste, *Culture and waste: The creation and destruction of value*, as well as writing numerous articles on public service broadcasting, new television formats, and media policy.

Gail Hershatter is professor of history and co-director of the Center for Cultural Studies at the University of California, Santa Cruz. She co-directs a seminar on civilizational thinking with Anna Tsing. Her most recent book is *Dangerous pleasures: Prostitution and modernity in twentieth-century Shanghai*, and her current project is entitled "The gender of memory: rural Chinese women and the 1950s."

Barry Hindess is professor of political science in the Research School of Social Sciences at the Australian National University. He has published widely in the areas of social and political theory. His most recent works are *Discourses of power: from Hobbes to Foucault*; *Governing Australia: Studies in contemporary rationalities of government* (with Mitchell Dean); and numerous papers on democracy, liberalism and empire, and neo-liberalism.

Ian Hunter is Australian professorial fellow in the Centre for the History of European Discourses, University of Queensland. He is the author of various papers and books on the history of political, philosophical, and religious thought, most recently *Rival enlightenments: Civil and metaphysical philosophy in early modern Germany.*

Richard Johnson taught at the Centre for Contemporary Cultural Studies at the University of Birmingham (1974–93) and retired from his post as professor of cultural studies at Nottingham Trent University in 2004. He has written, among other topics, on Thatcherism (and education), nationalism and national identity, the anti-terrorist rhetorics of Bush and Blair, and masculinities and politics. He has recently completed *The practice* *of cultural studies* (with Deborah Chambers, Parvati Raghuram, and Estella Tincknell) and edited *Blairism and the war of persuasion: Labour's passive revolution* (with Deborah Steinberg).

Steve Jones is professor of communication and research associate in the Electronic Visualization Lab at the University of Illinois at Chicago. A social historian of communication technology, he serves as senior research fellow for the Pew Internet and American Life Project and is co-founder and president of the Association of Internet Researchers.

Genevieve Lloyd is emeritus professor in philosophy at the University of New South Wales in Sydney and a fellow of the Australian Academy of the Humanities. Her books include *The man of reason: "Male" and "female" in Western philosophy; Being in time: Selves and narrators in philosophy and literature;* and *Spinoza and the Ethics.* She is editor of *Spinoza: Critical assessments* and *Feminism and history of philosophy.*

Gregor McLennan is professor of sociology at the University of Bristol. He taught social sciences at the Open University before moving to New Zealand in the 1990s as professor of sociology at Massey University. He is the author of *Marxism and the methodologies of history; Marxism, pluralism and beyond;* and *Pluralism.* Recent publications include a series of articles in leading journals on questions of explanation and reflexivity in sociology and cultural studies. His current research (empirical and theoretical) is on changes in the modality of ideas and intellectuals in "knowledge society" capitalism.

Maureen McNeil is professor of women's studies and cultural studies and director of the Institute for Women's Studies at Lancaster University, Lancaster. Much of her research, publications, and teaching focuses on the cultural studies of science and technology.

W. J. T. Mitchell teaches literature, art history, and media studies at the University of Chicago, and has served as editor of *Critical Inquiry,* an interdisciplinary quarterly, since 1978. His books include *Blake's composite art; Iconology; Picture theory; The last dinosaur book;* and *What do pictures want?* (forthcoming). For further information, see his website: http://humanities.uchicago.edu/faculty/mitchell

David Morley is professor of communications at Goldsmiths College, University of London. His most recent book is *Home territories: Media, mobility and identity,* and he is currently completing a new volume on questions of culture, media, and technology.

Stephen Muecke holds a personal chair in cultural studies at the University of Technology, Sydney. His most recent book is a volume edited with Gay Hawkins, *Culture and waste: The creation and destruction of value*.

Karim Murji is a senior lecturer in the Faculty of Social Sciences at the Open University. He has published widely on drugs, policing, race and racism, and the media. His latest book is *Racialization: Studies in theory and practice* (edited with John Solomos). He is a member of the editorial board of *Sociology*.

Theo Nichols is distinguished research professor in the School of Social Sciences, Cardiff University. He is author of several books and numerous articles in the general field of economic sociology. A former editor of *Work, Employment and Society*, his current research includes a comparative study of white goods production in China, Taiwan, South Korea, Turkey, and Brazil. His latest book, with Nadir Sugur, is *Global management, local labour: Turkish workers and modern industry*.

Bhikhu Parekh is professor of political philosophy in the University of Westminster and emeritus professor of political theory at the University of Hull. He is the author of seven widely acclaimed books in political philosophy. He was appointed to the House of Lords in 2000, received the BBC's Special Lifetime Achievement Award in 1999, and was awarded the Sir Isaiah Berlin Prize in 2003 for lifetime contribution to political philosophy. He is a fellow of the British Academy.

Cindy Patton is Canada Research chair in community culture and health and Michael Smith senior scholar in population and public health at Simon Fraser University, Vancouver, BC. She is the author of *Inventing AIDS*; *Fatal advice*; *Globalizing AIDS*; and many essays on the discursive aspects of social movements.

Elspeth Probyn is the professor of gender studies at the University of Sydney. Her publications include *Sexing the self*; *Outside belongings*; *Carnal appetites, sexy bodies*; and most recently *Blush: Faces of shame*. She co-edited *Remote control*, a collection of essays and interviews about the media ethics of new forms of television.

Kevin Robins is professor of sociology, City University, London. He is currently involved in an EU-funded research project, "Changing city spaces: new challenges to cultural policy in Europe." He is the author of *Into the image: Culture and politics in the field of vision*.

Jacqueline Rose is professor of English at Queen Mary, University of London. As well as translations and editions of Jacques Lacan's writings on feminine sexuality (with Juliet

Mitchell) and Moustapha Safouan on Lacan and psychoanalytic training, her publications include *The haunting of Sylvia Plath*; *States of fantasy*; *On not being able to sleep: Psychoanalysis in the modern world*; and a novel, *Albertine*.

Nikolas Rose is professor of sociology at the London School of Economics and Political Science and director of the BIOS Centre for the Study of Bioscience, Biomedicine, Biotechnology and Society. He has published widely on the social and political history of the human sciences, on the genealogy of subjectivity, on the history of empirical thought in sociology, and on changing rationalities and techniques of political power. His most recent books are *Governing the soul* and *Powers of freedom: Reframing political thought*. His current research concerns biological and genetic psychiatry and behavioral neuroscience, and its social, ethical, cultural, and legal implications.

Steven Rose is emeritus professor at the Open University, where he directs the Brain and Behaviour Research Group. His research into the cellular and molecular mechanisms of learning and memory has led to the publication of some 300 research papers and various international honors and medal awards, including the Sechenov and Anokhin medals (Russia) and the Ariens Kappers medal (the Netherlands). In 2002 he was awarded the Biochemical Society medal for excellence in public communication of science. As well as his research papers in neuroscience and related fields he has written or edited 15 books. He is a frequent writer and reviewer for general-access magazines such as the *Times Literary Supplement*, *New Scientist*, and national UK dailies. He also has wide experience of radio and television in the context of interviews, discussion, debate, and science programs (he is currently a regular panel member of Radio 4's *The Moral Maze*). BBC 4 transmitted a filmed profile of him in 2003.

Andrew Ross is professor in the graduate program in American studies at New York University. He is the author of several books including *No-collar: The humane workplace and its hidden costs*; *The celebration chronicles: Life, liberty and the pursuit of property value in Disney's new town*; and, most recently, *Low pay, high profile: The global push for fair labor*. He has also edited several books, including *No sweat: Fashion, free trade, and the rights of garment workers*, and, most recently, co-edited *Anti-Americanism: Its history and currency*.

Naoki Sakai is professor of Asian studies and comparative literature at Cornell University, and the inaugural senior editor of *Traces: A multilingual series of cultural theory and translation*, published in four languages, Chinese, Korean, English, and Japanese. He publishes in French and German in addition to the four languages of *Traces*. The fields of his study include comparative thought, early modern visual studies, translation studies, and racism. He is the author of *Voices of the past*; *Translation and subjectivity: On "Japan" and cultural nationalism*; and many other monographs.

Bill Schwarz teaches in the School of English and Drama, Queen Mary, University of London. He is an editor of *History Workshop Journal*.

Steven Shapin is Franklin L. Ford professor of the history of science at Harvard University. His books include *Leviathan and the air-pump: Hobbes, Boyle, and the experimental life* (with Simon Schaffer); *A social history of truth: Civility and science in seventeenth-century England*; and *The scientific revolution*.

Michael J. Shapiro is professor of political science at the University of Hawaii. Among his publications are *For moral ambiguity: National culture and the politics of the family* and *Methods and nations: Cultural governance and the indigenous subject*.

Jennifer Daryl Slack is professor of communication and cultural studies in the Department of Humanities, Michigan Technological University. She has published extensively in the areas of culture and technology, culture and environment, cultural theory, and communication theory. Her recent books include the edited *Animations* (of Deleuze and Guattari) and *Thinking geometrically* (by John T. Waisanen), and the co-authored *Culture and technology: A primer* (with J. Macgregor Wise).

425

John Storey is professor of cultural studies and director of the Centre for Research in Media and Cultural Studies, University of Sunderland. His most recent book is *Inventing popular culture*.

Terry Threadgold is professor of communication and cultural studies, and head, Cardiff School of Journalism, Media and Cultural Studies, Cardiff University. She has published widely in the areas of poststructuralist feminist discourse analysis, performance studies, and feminist legal studies, and on race, identity, and nation in multicultural contexts. Her book *Feminist poetics: Poiesis, performance, histories* remains a key text in the field of feminist poststructuralist discourse analysis. Her most recent research has been on media representation of asylum. She was one of the lead researchers on a 2003 BBC-funded project on the media and the Iraq war.

Anna Tsing is professor of anthropology at the University of California, Santa Cruz. She co-directs a seminar on civilizational thinking with Gail Hershatter. Author of *In the realm of the Diamond Queen: Marginality in an out-of-the-way place*, she is completing a book entitled *A fragile global politics*.

Notes on Editors and Contributors

Bryan Turner is professor of sociology at the University of Cambridge. He is the founding editor of the journal *Citizenship Studies,* and founding co-editor of *Body&Society* (with Mike Featherstone) and the *Journal of Classical Sociology* (with John O'Neill). His early publications on Islam include *Weber and Islam; Marx and the end of Orientalism;* and *Religion and social theory.* His recent publications include *Society and culture* (with Chris Rojek); *Profiles in contemporary social theory* (with Anthony Elliott); *Classical sociology; Generations, culture and society* (with June Edmunds); *Generational consciousness narrative and politics* (edited with June Edmunds); and *Islam: Critical concepts in sociology* (edited). Forthcoming publications are *The New Medical Sociology* and, as editor, the *Cambridge Dictionary of Sociology.* He is a fellow of the Australian Academy of the Social Sciences and a professorial fellow at Fitzwilliam College.

Graeme Turner is professor of cultural studies and director of the Centre for Critical and Cultural Studies at the University of Queensland, Brisbane. His most recent books include *The film cultures reader; Fame fames: The production of celebrity in Australia* (with Frances Bonner and P. David Marshall); *British cultural studies: An introduction;* and *Understanding Celebrity.*

Valerie Walkerdine is professor of psychology in the School of Social Sciences, Cardiff University, and foundation professor of critical psychology in the University of Western Sydney. She has been researching the area of subjectivity across discipline boundaries for many years and is currently researching the transformation of worker subjectivity under neo-liberalism.

Alan Warde is professor of sociology at the University of Manchester. Recent work on consumption includes *Eating out: social differentiation, consumption and pleasure* (with Lydia Martens) and *Ordinary consumption* (edited with Jukka Gronow).

Frank Webster is professor of sociology at City University, and was previously professor of sociology at Oxford Brookes University (1990–8) and at the University of Birmingham (1999–2002). Recent books include *Theories of the information society; Culture and politics in the information age: A new politics;* and *The virtual university? Knowledge, markets and management* (with Kevin Robins).

Jeffrey Weeks is professor of sociology and dean of humanities and social science at London South Bank University. He is the author of numerous books and articles on the history and social organization of sexuality, including *Invented moralities: Sexual values in an age of uncertainty; Making sexual history; Same sex intimacies: Families of choice and other life experiments* (with Brian Heaphy and Catherine Donovan); and *Sexualities and society: A reader* (edited with Janet Holland and Matthew Waites).

George Yúdice is professor of the American studies program and of Spanish and Portuguese at New York University, and director of the Center for Latin American and Caribbean Studies. He also directs the Privatization of Culture Project for Research on Cultural Policy and the Inter-American Cultural Studies Network. His research interests include cultural policy; globalization and transnational processes; the organization of civil society; the role of intellectuals, artists, and activists in national and transnational institutions; and the comparison of diverse national constructions of race and ethnicity. He is the author of *Vicente Huidobro y la motivación del lenguaje poético*; *Cultural policy* (with Toby Miller); and *El recurso de la cultura* (translated as *The expediency of culture*); is co-editor of *On edge: The crisis of contemporary Latin American culture* (with Jean Franco and Juan Flores) and the "Cultural Studies of the Americas" series; and has works in progress on culture and value.

427